The Art of 3D
Computer Animation and Effects

(Top: *Nostalgia*.

The Art of 3D
Computer Animation and Effects

Third Edition

Written and Designed by

Isaac V. Kerlow

WILEY

John Wiley & Sons, Inc.

This book is printed on acid-free paper. ∞

Published by John Wiley & Sons, Inc., Hoboken, New Jersey
Published simultaneously in Canada

ISBN 0-471-43036-6

Printed in the United States of America

10 9 8 7 6 5 4 3 2 1

THIS BOOK IS DEDICATED TO ESTHER AND SERGIO KERLOW

Contents

Preface

The third edition of this book includes many updates and additions that address the new professional realities faced by three-dimensional computer animators and visual effects artists. A lot has changed in this field since this book was first published in 1996. Many of these changes have transformed a field that began as a specialized novelty into a mainstream and mature profession.

Just think about some of the many landmark events that took place during the last half-dozen years. The PC rose in a production world that was previously dominated by high-end (and high-priced) workstations. Computer networks and the Internet, including the development of streaming video on the World Wide Web, came of age during this period. The number of live-action feature films with significant, often stunning, three-dimensional computer animation and visual effects grew significantly. Game consoles with high-power graphics capabilities became popular. The first all-computer-animated feature films were produced, and the use of computers for the production of traditional animated feature films increased. Digital video came of age as a feasible means of movie production, and an all-digital cinema is already a budding reality. The quality of work produced by computer animation students continues to rise worldwide.

Some of the additions to this edition were suggested by colleagues in the computer animation, gaming, and visual effects industries, and a few came at the request of readers of the first and second editions. Some of the new material that you will find in the book includes:

- A **new chapter on visual effects** that presents the most widely used digital techniques.
- An updated chapter on digital production with more detailed information about **production flows** and preparing demo reels.
- Updated animation chapters with additional information on **traditional animation principles**, character development, facial animation, and motion capture.
- An updated historical chapter that includes the first few years of this new millenium, and an **expanded timeline** of computer animation, visual effects, and computer technology.
- **Countless tips** on how to improve the artistic and technical level of your projects.
- **Updated technical information** on model rigging, 2D-3D integration, non-photorealistic rendering, and real-time polygonal models.
- An **updated website** at *www.artof3d.com* contains software and hardware information, a list of selected readings, resources, and links to related websites.
- Over **200 updated or new color images** including work from Canada, China (Hong Kong), Denmark, England, France, Germany, Japan, Korea, New Zealand, Norway, Poland, Spain, Switzerland, and the United States.

Scope of this Book

It would require an encyclopedic work to fully document and present all of the topics and techniques included in this subject. This book does not pretend to be such a work. A significant effort has been made to create a book that is not bound by the particulars of any specific computer program while, at the same time, offers detailed, **practical information** that goes beyond mere theory. The knowledge contained in this book has been distilled from years of working and teaching with a variety of software programs, from reading innumerable software manuals, and from practicing and making mistakes. Hopefully, reading this book will help minimize the number of mistakes you make!

How to Read this Book

MASTERING THE ART AND CRAFT of three-dimensional computer animation and effects can be achieved in different ways. Likewise, this book can be read in **multiple ways**.

For those of you who like the **systematic approach** I recommend that you read the book from front to back in sequential order, and refer to the illustrations and the website listed in the appendix to complement the knowledge presented in the main body of the text.

For those of you who prefer to **learn by doing** or are too impatient to read the whole book from start to end, it might be best to look at the pictures first. But do not forget to **read the captions** as you look at the images. There is a lot of useful information contained in them. You might want to read some of the sections in the book that complement the section you have already read in your software manual. This book contains **information rarely found in manuals** or presented by instructors in lab courses. This information is much more important than it seems at first because it will help you make the transition from being a technician in the software program of your choice to being a creative digital animator or artist.

Using this Book with Software

READ THIS BOOK AS YOU LEARN and experiment with a specific three-dimensional program or by itself without any hands-on work. To those of you who prefer to learn by reading *before* you start the hands-on part of learning, this book offers a **comprehensive introduction** with plenty of theoretical and practical references. Those of you who prefer diving straight into the particulars of a specific computer program—and reading *after* the fact—will find this book complements your experimental approach by offering **clear explanations** in a succinct form. Last but not least, to those of you who learn best by combining the experimental approach with conceptual comprehension, this book offers a **logical progression of topics** that goes beyond the particulars of software manuals.

Book Format

THIS BOOK CONSISTS OF FIVE SECTIONS, each with several chapters. The first section includes a historical background and general design and **production issues**. This section deals with a summary of the major creative and technical trends, a short summary of computer animation and visual effects **milestones**, and lots of advice regarding the **planning** the production of a project. The introductory section makes you think like an *art critic*, and a *producer*. Section II goes right into the details of **modeling** three-dimensional objects and environments. The modeling section makes you think like a *sculptor*. Section III covers many of the most useful **rendering** techniques, both simple and complex. The rendering section makes you think like a *photographer* and a *painter*. The fourth section deals first with many of the issues associated with **telling a story** through moving pictures: basic screenplay writing, storyboarding, and techniques for bringing an animated character to life. The animation section makes you think like an *actor*, a *scriptwriter* and a *cinematographer*. The last section presents many of the issues involved in **recording** and presenting your work, including compositing and visual effects. This section makes you think like a *magician* who pulls off the trick right in front of the audience.

What to Expect from this Book

THIS BOOK SEEKS TO INSPIRE AND TO INFORM. It presents the concepts required to understand the **steps and procedures** that lead to the completion of a fully rendered three-dimensional **computer animation**. Many of the illustrations have been developed to present complex concepts in a way that is clear and **easy to understand**. Considerable effort has also been made so that the book structure and details would be as inclusive as possible: many

software programs and hardware platforms were tested and reviewed so that readers find a consistent treatment and point of view. The main goal of this book is to provide the reader with a solid foundation by presenting an unusual combination of **technique and creativity**.

What Not to Expect from this Book

THIS BOOK IS NOT A COMPUTER SOFTWARE MANUAL. It is not based on a particular software program. Readers who seek information regarding the detailed operation of specific software or the implementation of specific techniques are advised to consult software manuals. Nevertheless, in the interest of linking the concepts presented here with today's available tools, a few **dialog boxes** from a variety of programs are reproduced throughout the book.

This book is not a general introduction to the use of computers. Instead it assumes that the reader is already familiar with the basic use of a computer system, or that the reader is in the process of gaining that knowledge elsewhere. Readers who have used computers and who have a basic understanding of the operation of computer systems are likely to **benefit from this book faster** than readers who have never before used a computer.

About Software Manuals

SOFTWARE MANUALS ARE OFTEN DIFFICULT to understand and they rarely tell the whole story. This is not surprising if we take into account the complexity of the software, the constant upgrades of features, and the short production cycles that individuals and companies have for developing these programs and turning them into **functional and efficient products** within a highly competitive market.

Having been both a user and a writer of user manuals I am familiar with the **frustrations** experienced by both sides. Today's three-dimensional software is so **complex and changing** that we cannot expect any manual to have every single piece of information perfectly digested. My advice is to *take the useful information contained in the software manuals and build on it.* Some of the information required to be a proficient three-dimensional artist and technician is found in manuals and some is acquired through **trial and error**, or from reading books and magazines and consulting with individuals more experienced than oneself. *Learning requires effort.*

General Principles vs. Specific Techniques

MOST OF THE TECHNIQUES described throughout this book are available in most of the three-dimensional software programs **available on the market**. But instead of presenting these modeling, rendering, animation, and output techniques in exactly the same ways they are implemented in a specific computer system, we present them by focusing on their **essential features and capabilities**. Specific implementations of techniques—implementations that differ from system to system—are left untouched. Readers who wish to obtain highly specific information regarding a particular computer program mentioned in this book are advised to consult their specific software **reference manuals**.

Acknowledgments

MANY OF THE IDEAS CONTAINED IN THIS BOOK were developed over the years while practicing and teaching the art and craft of three-dimensional computer animation and effects.

I am grateful to my friends, peers, and students who contributed to the process of completing this book, in particular to every single one of the individuals and companies that allowed me to reproduce images of their amazing visual work or software products. My son Victor for his encouragement. Jennifer for her support. Jason Chayes for capturing dialog boxes. Margaret Cummins and Monique Calello at John Wiley & Sons for their patience and professionalism. Steve Rittler for turning my funny-looking sketches into hilarious illustrations that will hopefully make people laugh while they learn.

I hope that students, independent animators, and members of production companies will find this book useful and relevant to achieving their creative goals. Enjoy!

Hollywood, 2003

SECTION I

Introduction

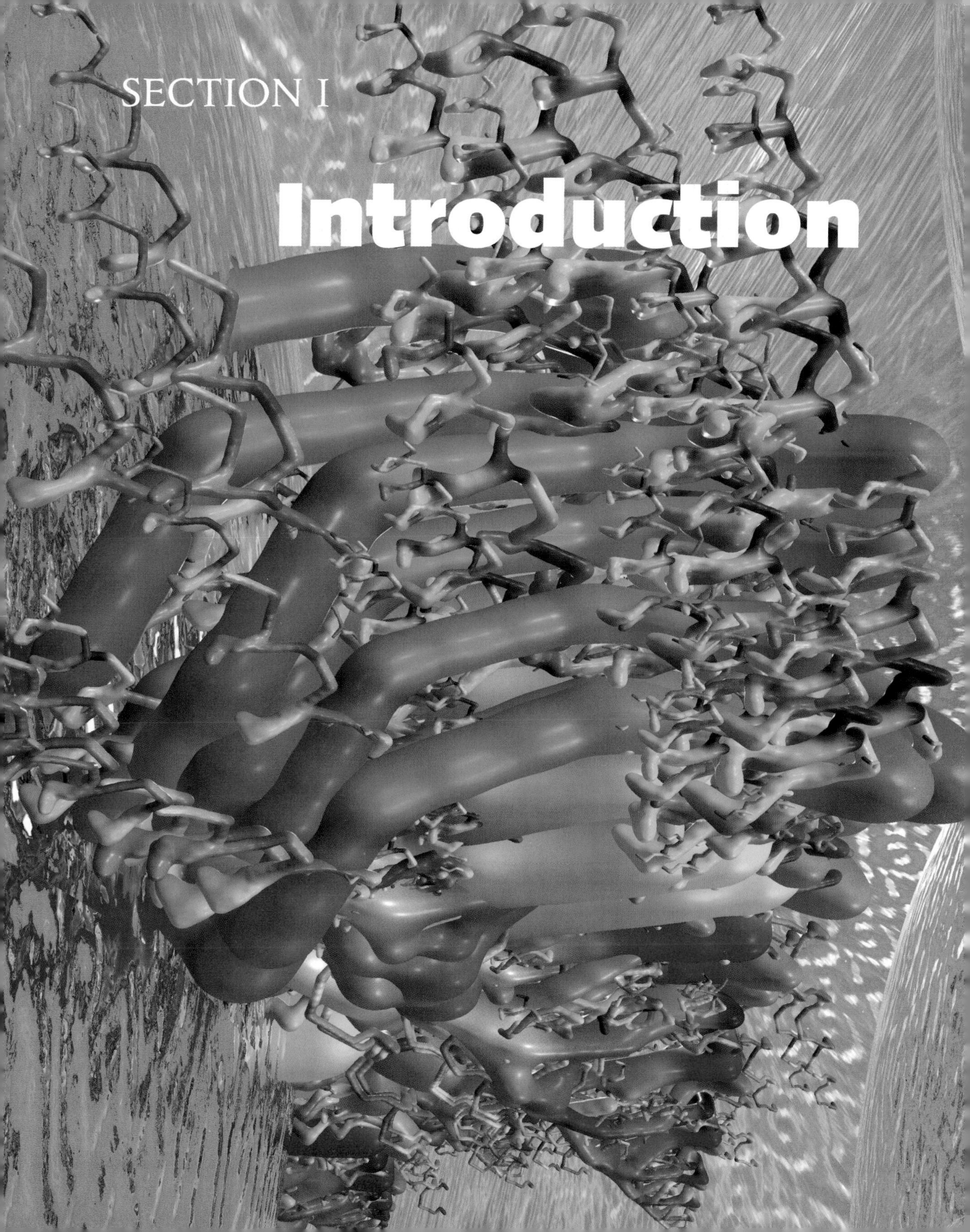

(Previous page) *Brillia* was created with GROWTH, a recursive algorithm that grows complex life forms. The software repeats simple rules that generate fantastic forms inspired by marine life. (© Yoichiro Kawaguchi.)

1.1.1 *Luxo Jr.* presents a charming view of a small curious lamp who seeks bigger challenges. This short, directed by John Lasseter, was a *tour de force* in three-dimensional computer animation because it was one of the first shorts that tried and succeeded in incorporating many of the traditional principles of animation. (© Pixar Animation Studios.)

CHAPTER 1

1

Animation, Visual Effects, and Technology in Context

Summary

A SUMMARY OF EVENTS AND PROJECTS that contributed to the creative and technical development of three-dimensional computer animation and effects techniques is presented in this chapter. The brief historical information presented here provides readers with a simple context in which to frame technical and stylistic discussions related to three-dimensional computer animation and effects.

QUICK INDEX

1.1 A Digital Creative Environment

More than ever before computers have become a part of our life, especially part of our creative, production and professional lives. They can be found everywhere: they coordinate the flow of information in our banking transactions, they digitize our voice and eliminate some of the noise in telephone conversations, they control the fuel injection systems in our cars, and they adjust the settings in photographic and video cameras so that image quality is always optimal. Most of the jobs in the visual professions and trades today require some degree of computer competency. Much of the broadcasting, manufacturing, graphic arts, and entertainment industries have computerized their production. Likewise, many independent artists and design studios develop their work with computers and often deliver it in digital formats.

The transition to increased reliance on computer systems affects many creators and technicians. Large numbers of established visual professionals have retrained to acquire new skills, and young students are eager to learn all the secrets and shortcuts. Expectations range from the sensible to the ridiculous. Those who resist the change altogether, for example, are left behind because the visual world is changing. Those who are overly enthusiastic often have unrealistic expectations. It is now time to find a new balance. It is time to accept the advantages that computer technology has to offer, to continue developing promising possibilities, and to give some time to the options that are in the process of maturing.

www.artof3d.com

Visit this website for a useful collection of links and software resources.

Walt Disney Studios' Animated Feature Movies *

1937 *Snow White and the Seven Dwarfs*
1940 *Pinocchio*
1940 *Fantasia*
1941 *Dumbo*
1942 *Bambi*
1943 *Saludos Amigos*
1945 *The Three Caballeros*
1946 *Make Mine Music*
1947 *Fun and Fancy Free*
1948 *Melody Time*
1949 *The Adventures of Ichabod and Mr. Toad*
1950 *Cinderella*
1951 *Alice in Wonderland*
1953 *Peter Pan*
1955 *Lady and the Tramp*
1959 *Sleeping Beauty*
1961 *101 Dalmatians*
1963 *The Sword in the Stone*
1967 *The Jungle Book*
1970 *The Aristocats*
1973 *Robin Hood*
1977 *The Many Adventures of Winnie the Pooh*
1977 *The Rescuers*
1981 *The Fox and the Hound*
1985 *The Black Cauldron*
1986 *The Great Mouse Detective*
1988 *Oliver & Company*
1989 *The Little Mermaid*

CREATED WITH DIGITAL TECHNOLOGY
1990 *The Rescuers Down Under*
1991 *Beauty and the Beast*
1992 *Aladdin*
1994 *The Lion King*
1995 *Pocahontas*
1996 *The Hunchback of Notre Dame*
1997 *Hercules*
1998 *Mulan*
1999 *Tarzan*
1999 *Fantasia 2000*
2000 *The Emperor's New Groove*, *Dinosaur*, and *The Tigger Movie* *
2001 *Atlantis: The Lost Empire*, *Recess: School's Out* *
2002 *Lilo & Stitch*, *Treasure Planet*, and *Return To Never Land* *
2003 *Jungle Book 2* * and *Piglet's Big Movie* *

Much of today's creation and production of images is indeed performed with the aid of computers. Increasingly, professionals from a wide variety of visual disciplines are working with **digital information**. Some of the traditional visual practices based on drawing, painting, photographic, and video techniques are merging with **digital imaging techniques**. A creative environment that used to exist as a collection of totally separate and unrelated disciplines—each with its own tools, techniques, and media—is turning into an environment where visual people use tools and techniques that cross over different media. As a result some of the traditional barriers between visual disciplines no longer have to exist. There is now, for example, great overlap between the fields of animation, graphic arts, broadcasting, and film. The creative **digital environment** has fostered this overlap because computer technology often provides more creative power to visual people. Decades ago, for example, visual professionals used to purchase tools specialized for their professions. These tools were useful for doing the work in their field, but not in others. A photographer, for example, would use a photographic camera to capture reality on film, and a traditional animator would use a pencil and light table to create animated sequences of drawings on paper. Today's photographers and animators, as well as many other creative professionals, share the computer as the tool—loaded with specialized software—to carry on each of their unique tasks.

Animation and Effects in the Predigital Days

For many of us it is difficult to imagine today that only a few decades ago all animation, effects, and entertainment in general was made, distributed, and consumed without any type of computer or digital technology. But this was the case even a few decades ago. One of the first fully three-dimensional computer animated independent shorts, John Lasseter's ***Luxo Jr.***, was released in 1986 (Fig. 1.1.1), and the first fully three-dimensional computer animated feature film, Pixar's ***Toy Story***, was released in 1995 (page 330).

As we experiment with new modeling, rendering, and animation techniques it is also worthwhile to remember the innovation of many of the animation pionners, both those who developed character cartoon animation and those who pioneered the use of experimental methods such as collage, cutouts, wax, pinhead shadow, object, and abstract painting animation. Among the former we count the New York and Hollywood animators who delivered gag after gag and amused audiences with the likes of Popeye, Woody Woodpecker, Bugs Bunny, Tom and Jerry, and Mickey Mouse. These animators include Max Fleischer, Walt Disney, Walter Lantz, Tex Avery, Friz Freleng, Chuck Jones, and the many talented animators who worked alongside them in their studios. Among the experimental animators we count the French Leopold Survage, and Alexander Alexeieff; the Germans Hans Richter, Oskar Fischinger, and Lotte Reininger; the Canadian Norman McLaren; and the Americans Claire

Parker and John Whitney, Sr. The classic Disney animated movies that popularized the genre were created in the late 1930s and 1940s (Fig. 1.1.2). The well-known twelve principles of animation covered in Chapter 10 were also developed by Disney animators during the same time period (Figs. 1.1.3–1.1.4).

As we seek to invent new digital visual effects it is refreshing to remember that in 1939 Hollywood's Academy of Motion Picture Arts and Sciences (AMPAS) created the Special Effects category in their awards competition. Between 1964 and 1971 the category was renamed Special Visual Effects, and between 1972 and 1976 the category of visual effects was renamed as Special Achievement Award, or one not necessarily given in a particular year. Since then the category has mostly been called Visual Effects. Winners between 1939 and 2003 are listed in the timelines at the end of this chapter.

If we go back a bit further, just to put three-dimensional computer animation in perspective, we find out that the first kinetoscope parlor opened in New York City in 1894. This event was the result of the work of Thomas Alva Edison and his assistant William K. Dickinson to improve the devices for creating images in motion and, above all, the simultaneous recording of sound and motion. Edison and his assistant developed the **kinetoscope**—which means "viewing in motion" in Greek—a closed box in which 50 feet of looped film could be viewed through an opening. The few kinetoscopes equipped with earphones to hear simultaneous music were called **kinetophones**. A few years later on the other side of the Atlantic, during the 1900 Paris Exhibition, a mechanical platform gently rocked by a steam machine presented riders with panoramic views of real and imaginary scenes of the world. In retrospect it is clear that the kinetoscope spawned many other film viewing and projection systems that fueled the growth of the **seventh art**, cinema, and its animation cousin. The panoramic rides so popular at the turn of the nineteenth century are clearly the ancestors of virtual rides and location-based entertainment.

1.1.2 (opposite page) The Walt Disney Studios created the first animated color feature movie in 1937 and dominated animated feature movies for several decades. A line separates movies that were created with and without computer animation technology. (*Movies with an asterisk were produced at the Television Animation division as "straight-to-video" with a theatrical release; all others were produced by the Feature Animation division.)

1.2 The Development of the Technology

Computers, particularly their visual capabilities, are profoundly altering the way in which we create and distribute images. But the powerful computer systems that are so common today—and that everybody takes for granted—have existed for a relatively short period of time.

The ancestors of today's electronic digital computers were mechanical adding machines used to perform repetitive arithmetic calculations. Those early mechanical devices eventually evolved into machines that could be programmed each time they were used to perform different sets of instructions. In the 1940s, electric versions of these computing machines were in operation.

The early computer models were called **mainframes** because all their bulky components were housed in large steel frames. During the 1960s two types of computers were developed. **Minicomputers**,

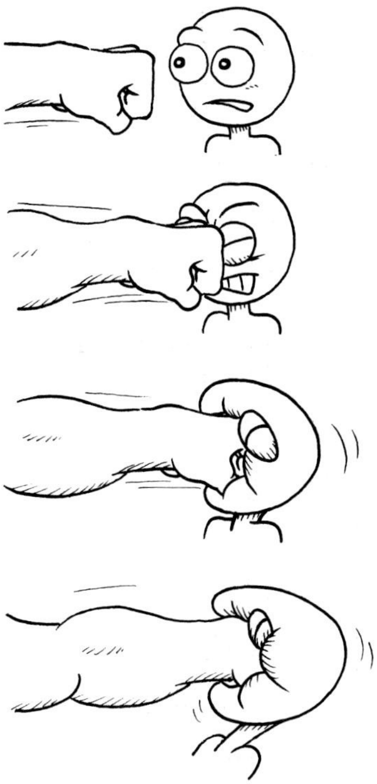

1.1.3 The first of the twelve principles developed by Disney animators in the 1930s, squash and stretch is used here to distort a face after receiving a punch.

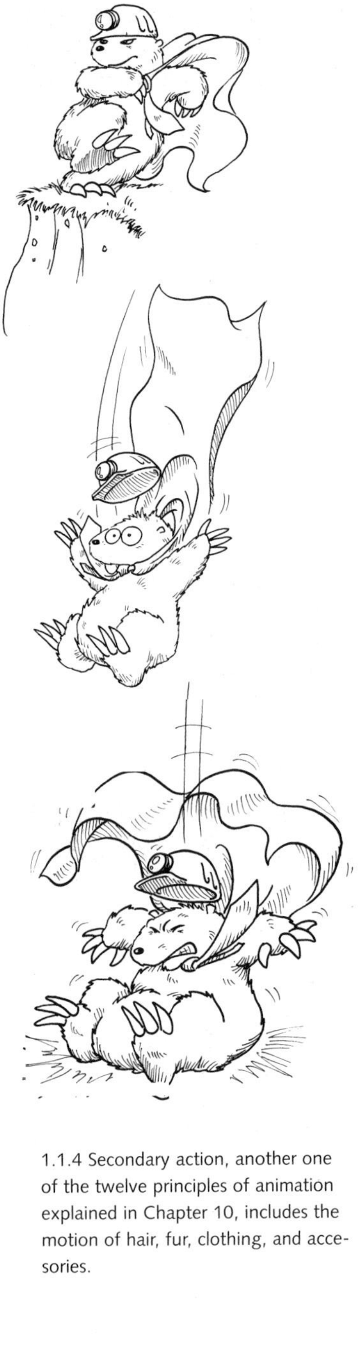

1.1.4 Secondary action, another one of the twelve principles of animation explained in Chapter 10, includes the motion of hair, fur, clothing, and accesories.

smaller and less expensive than mainframes but almost as powerful, were developed in an attempt to bring computers to a wider audience and range of applications. **Supercomputers**, usually bigger and more expensive than mainframe computers, were developed to tackle the most taxing computing projects regardless of the cost and with an emphasis on speed and performance.

Microcomputers were developed in the mid-1970s. Before then the large majority of artists found computers very uninteresting: They were too expensive and cumbersome to operate, and even the simplest tasks required extensive programming. Most models lacked monitors, printers, mice, or graphics tablets. Microcomputers contain millions of microscopic electronic switches on a single **silicon chip**. Some models of microcomputers, such as the Apple Macintosh, the Amiga, and a variety of Intel-based PC computers, were widely embraced by visual professionals during the 1980s (Fig. 1.2.2). Many of today's powerful microcomputers are small enough to be carried in a briefcase. Those that can fit in a pocket still have limited capabilities for professional image creation, but many are quite good at displaying moving images of different degrees of quality. The supermicrocomputer and the parallel computer were developed during the 1980s and have had a great effect on the way visual people use computers. **Supermicrocomputers**—also called **workstations**—are microcomputers built around a powerful CPU that is customized to excel in the performance of a specific task, for example, three-dimensional computer animation. **Massively parallel computers** deal with very complex processing challenges by dividing up the tasks among a large number of smaller microprocessors. Some of these computers may have between a dozen and thousands of processors.

Computer graphics technology was developed in the early 1950s to make visible what was invisible to the human eye. But none of the early computer graphics systems was developed for artistic work. Most of these early applications were related to the military, manufacturing, or the applied sciences and included, for example, flight simulators to train fighter pilots without having to fly a real plane; computer-aided design and manufacturing (CADAM) systems to allow electrical engineers to design and test electronic circuits with millions of components; and computer-aided tomography (CAT) scanners to allow physicians to peek into the human body without having to physically open it.

During the 1950s and 1960s, the early years of computer graphics technology, the computer systems and techniques for creating images were rudimentary and very limited—especially by today's standards. During that period very few artists and designers even knew that computers could be used to create images.

During the 1970s and 1980s computer technology became more practical and useful, and a significant number of visual creators started to get interested in using computers. During the 1990s a significant drop in the prices of computer systems and an increase in their computing power occurred. This situation encouraged many visual professionals to purchase the technology and to integrate it into their daily professional practices. Professionals from all visual disciplines accepted computer technology as it became more powerful, more practical, and less expensive. Figure 1.2.1 lists some of the computer science and engineering pioneers in the field of computer graphics as recognized by their peers through the **SIGGRAPH** awards. Some of the research papers of these pioneers can be found in the proceedings of the SIGGRAPH annual conference. The Association for Computing Machinery's Special Interest Group in Graphics, SIGGRAPH, has been the most influential professional association in the field of computer animation since the 1960s. Many of the major technical innovations in the area of computer animation and related applications have traditionally been presented at this annual international conference. Of special relevance to this book is the selection of international three-dimnsional computer animation presented at SIGGRAPH's Electronic Theatre.

The computer technology necessary for creating three-dimensional imagery and animation has evolved tremendously since the first systems were developed in the 1950s. Within just a few decades the capabilities of hardware and software for creating three-dimensional environments went from simple to highly complex representations that often fool our visual perception.

A complete history of three-dimensional computer graphics technology and creative works remains to be written. However, the information presented in the rest of this chapter summarizes some of the highlights and landmarks. This summary is certainly not exhaustive, and it does not attempt to present a complete and detailed portrait of all the significant events. Instead, it provides a personal account of individual examples and a summary of the major trends.

1950s and 1960s

The decades of the 1950s and 1960s saw the development of the first interactive computer systems, which were further improved during the following decade. The field of computer graphics was so new then that most of the technological innovations from this period are not very spectacular in terms of the visual results they produced. They were, however, fundamental in facilitating the impressive developments that would flourish 20 years later.

The first computer to use CRT displays as output channels was the Whirlwind computer at the Massachusetts Institute of Technology (MIT) in the early 1950s. This system was used to display the solutions to differential equations on oscilloscope monitors. During the mid- to late-1950s the SAGE Air Defense System of the U. S. Air Force used command-and-control CRT displays on which operators could detect aircraft flying over the continental United States. The SAGE operators were also able to obtain information about the aircraft by pointing at their icons on the screen with light pens.

During the 1960s various technology-intensive organizations

ACM SIGGRAPH Computer Graphics Achievement Award	
1983	James F. Blinn
1984	James H. Clark
1985	Loren Carpenter
1986	Turner Whitted
1987	Robert Cook
1988	Alan H. Barr
1989	John Warnock
1990	Richard Shoup and Alvy Ray Smith
1991	James T. Kajiya
1992	Henry Fuchs
1993	Pat Hanrahan
1994	Kenneth E. Torrance
1995	Kurt Akeley
1996	Marc Levoy
1997	Przemyslaw Prusinkiewicz
1998	Michael F. Cohen
1999	Tony DeRose
2000	David H. Salesin
2001	Andrew Witkin
2002	David Kirk
2003	Peter Schroder

ACM SIGGRAPH Steven A. Coons Award	
1983	Ivan E. Sutherland
1985	Pierre Bézier
1987	Donald P. Greenberg
1989	David C. Evans
1991	Andries van Dam
1993	Ed Catmull
1995	Jose Luis Encarnação
1997	James Foley
1999	James F. Blinn
2001	Lance J. Williams
2003	Pat Hanrahan

1.2.1 Recipients of the ACM SIGGRAPH awards for technical research in computer graphics, including the Computer Graphics Achievement Award, and the Steven A. Coons Outstanding Creative Contributions Award.

Timeline of Intel Processors

1971	Intel's first, the 4-bit 4004 with 2,300 transistors, and a 108 KHz clock.
1972	The 8-bit 8008, twice as powerful as the 4004.
1974	The 8080, CPU of the Altair, first personal computer.
1978	The 8086-8088, CPU of the IBM PC.
1982	The 286, first Intel processor that runs software written for its predecessor.
1985	Intel 386, 32-bit chip with 275,000 transistors, 100 times more than the 4004.
1989	The 486, with built-in math co-processor, for graphical interfaces.
1993	First Pentium processor.
1995	Pentium Pro, 5.5 million transistors.
1997	Pentium II, 7.5 million transistors and video processing MMX technology.
1999	Celeron, value-oriented.
1999	Pentium III, 9.5 million transistors.
2000	Pentium 4 debuted with 42 million transistors and 1.5 GHz speed, capable of real-time 3D rendering.
2001	Xeon, for high-performance dual-processor workstations.
2001	Itanium, first in a family of 64-bit processors.

1.2.2 Some of the most popular microprocessors manufactured by Intel since the early days of microcomputers.

developed the first **computer-aided design and manufacturing (CADAM)** systems. The goal of these early CADAM systems was to make the design process more effective by offering users sophisticated design functions and to improve the organization of the manufacturing process by linking the numerical data that represents an image with other types of information, such as inventory and engineering analysis. One of the first CADAM systems was developed by General Motors, and it included various time-sharing graphic stations for designing cars. Other companies, including Boeing Aerospace, IBM, McDonnell Douglas, General Electric, and Lockheed, developed similar systems.

Early attempts to create computer-generated movies took place in several research institutions. Short pieces of animation were produced at Boeing by William Fetter and Walter Bernhart in the early 1960s. Three-dimensional drawings were plotted on paper and filmed one at a time to produce animations of an aircraft carrier landing. Fetter also modeled the human figure for ergonomic studies related to the design of cockpits. At Bell Laboratories, researchers Michael Noll and Bela Julesz produced various stereo computer animations on film to aid in the study of stereo perception. During this period some of the first animation programming languages were developed, but most of them resulted in programs that ran only in a noninteractive mode.

Only a few commercial companies were involved in computer graphics research during these two decades. Most of the technological developments during this period came out of government-funded academic research laboratories such as MIT's Lincoln Labs.

In the early 1960s, computer graphics were developed to visualize objects and situations that were too costly or just impossible to represent otherwise. Flight simulators, CADAM systems, and CAT scanners were among the pioneering computer graphics systems.

The first interactive system, called **Sketchpad**, was developed in the early 1960s by Ivan Sutherland at MIT. This system allowed users to interact with simple wireframe objects via a light pen. This system made use of several new interaction techniques and new data structures for dealing with visual information. It was an interactive design system with capabilities for the manipulation and display of two- and three-dimensional wireframe objects.

By the mid-1960s the first algorithms for removal of hidden surfaces were developed, and the systems for producing full-color surface-shaded animation in real time were improved. General Electric developed a flight simulator that animated and displayed simultaneously as many as 40 solid objects with hidden surfaces removed and in full color. The Mathematical Applications Group, Inc. (MAGI) in Elmsford, New York, was one of the first companies that offered computer-generated animation of fully rendered polygonal objects in the commercial environment. Their process was named **Synthavision**, and its first contracts included simulations for the military and advertising-related projects.

The early three-dimensional computer animation and imaging systems depended on costly mainframe computers that were very slow by today's standards. Most of the programs would run only on a specific type of computer and display device, and were not portable to other systems. The use of computer graphic systems during the 1960s was clearly restricted by the high cost and limitations of the hardware involved.

Virtually all of the graphics software from this period was developed in-house. It was not marketed, and it was minimally documented. Most programs were executed in the batch mode, and very few had any interactive features at all. Users had to input their data almost exclusively through the keyboard; other types of input peripherals that encouraged more artistic freedom were just not available. A few computer systems had graphics screens, but most had monochrome alphanumeric CRT screens or even just teletype or dot matrix printers.

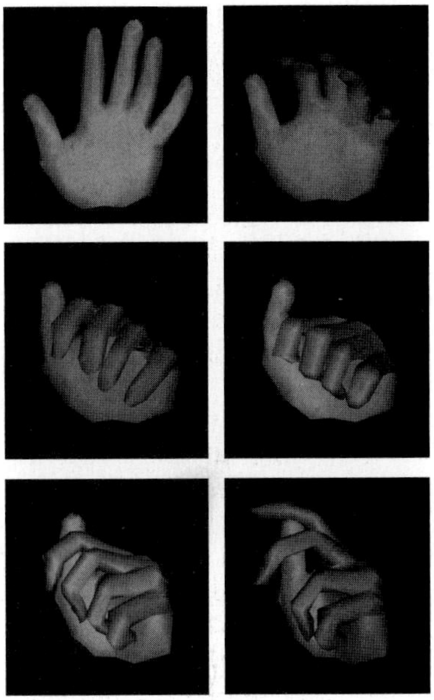

1.2.3a Early example of hand animation. (Courtesy of Ed Catmull.)

1970s

The 1970s was a significant decade for the development of three-dimensional computer animation and imaging technology. Many of the basic rendering techniques still in use today were formulated during the 1970s. Microcomputer technology was also introduced to the consumer markets in the late part of the decade. Compared to mainframe computers, the minicomputers that became quite popular during the 1960s were easier to maintain. During the 1970s these systems also provided significantly more power at a reduced cost.

From the point of view of computer hardware, most of the research and production work done during this decade was based on minicomputers. The new microcomputer systems greatly contributed to the popularization of computer-generated graphics, mainly in the form of videogames. But the microcomputer's 8-bit computing power, memory capabilities, and output solution was insignificant when compared to their high-end counterparts (Fig. 1.2.2). A standard configuration of an early 1970s microcomputer included an 8-bit CPU without any graphics co-processors, less than 100 KB of main memory (RAM), a clock speed of 10 MHz, a low-resolution screen with a maximum palette of 8 colors (or slightly higher if dithering was used), and a limited amount of peripheral storage.

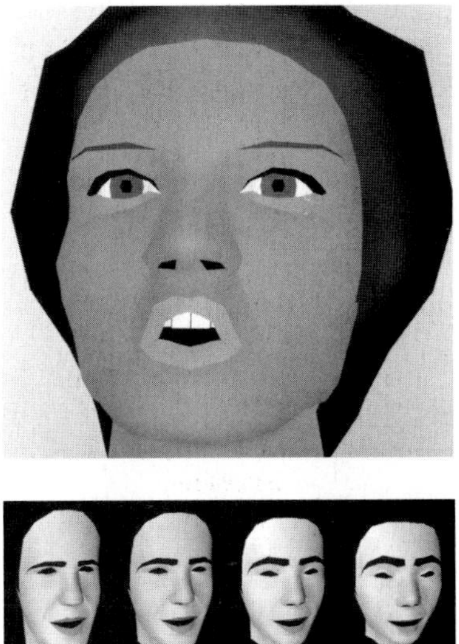

1.2.3b Early examples of face animation. A 1972 model (top) used simple expression interpolation. A later sequence used shape interpolation. (Images courtesy of Frederic Parke.)

During this decade the University of Utah became a primordial force and a center of innovation in three-dimensional computer graphics research. Under the guidance of David Evans, co-founder of Evans & Sutherland, the Department of Computer Science at the University of Utah produced a distinguished roster of Ph.D. students. Many of them developed a large number of the major technical contributions of the decade, such as the original versions of polygonal, Gouraud, and Phong shading; image and bump texture mapping; z-buffering; the subdivision and the painter's algorithms for hidden line removal; antialiasing methods; and hand and facial computer animation (Fig. 1.2.3).

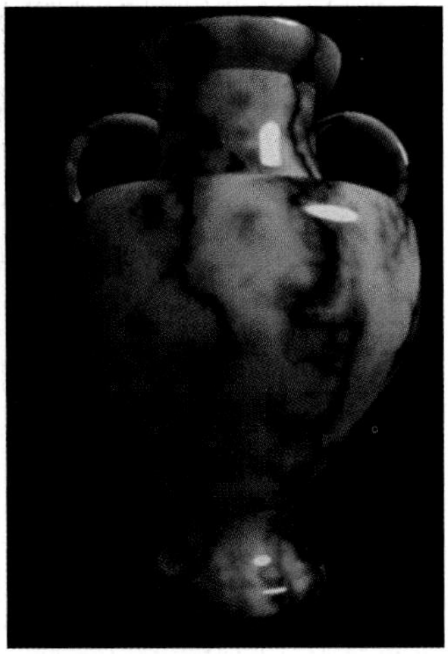

1.2.4 Vase rendered with stochastic textures. (Image courtesy of Ken Perlin.)

1980s

It was during the 1980s when computer graphics technology leaped from being a curiosity into becoming an area of proven artistic and commercial potential. Technologically speaking, this decade started with the uneven coexistence of powerful minicomputer systems with 8-bit microcomputers. But it ended with the combination of powerful 32-bit microcomputers and 64-bit RISC (reduced instruction set computer) graphics workstations at the forefront, and with minicomputers in the back seat. Silicon Graphics Inc., the company that pionnered visual workstations with its **Geometry Engine**, was started by James Clark in 1982. Commercially speaking, this decade started with a handful of companies that pioneered the production of three-dimensional computer animation and imaging. These companies included Digital Effects and MAGI on the East Coast and Information International, Inc. (III) and Robert Abel Associates on the West Coast. These companies operated exclusively with software developed in-house and with much custom-built graphics hardware. The 1980s concluded with the closing of all of the pioneer production houses—or at least of their production divisions—and with the creation of a new group of smaller, leaner, and less research-oriented firms that operated mostly with off-the-shelf hardware and with a mixture of custom and off-the-shelf software.

The bulk of the software research and development during this decade was spent in refining the modeling and shading techniques inherited from the 1970s. Ground was broken with new rendering approaches such as radiosity and procedural textures, and with the development of the first generation of solid user-friendly computer-human interfaces for three-dimensional computer animation and imaging software. The **RenderMan** shading language was released by Pixar in 1988. Some of the software companies that still dominate the high-end tools for three-dimensional computer animation and visual effects production were founded during this period. Wavefront opened in Santa Barbara, California, in 1981. Alias opened in Toronto in 1982, Softimage in Montreal in 1986, and Side Effects Software, also in Toronto, in 1987.

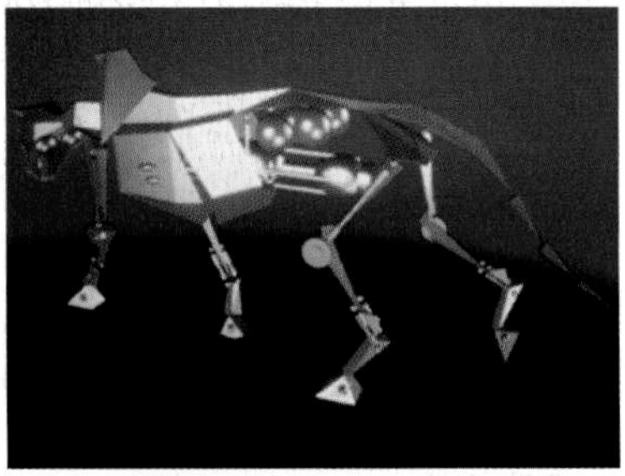

1.2.5 Developed jointly by ToyoLinks and Osaka University, the muscle movement in *Bio-Sensor* was modeled with metaballs and rendered with ray tracing techniques. (Director: Takashi Fukumoto. Technical Director: Hitoshi Nishimura. © ToyoLinks, 1984.)

Some of the leading academic centers in North America involved in three-dimensional graphics research during this period included Cornell University (radiosity rendering techniques), the Jet Propulsion Laboratory at the California Institute of Technology (motion dynamics), the University of California at Berkeley (spline modeling), the Ohio State University (hierarchical character animation, and inverse kinematics), the University of Toronto (procedural techniques), the University of Montreal (character animation and lip syncing), and New York University (procedural textures, Fig. 1.2.4). Significant original research efforts also took place at the University of Tokyo and Osaka University (modeling with blobby surfaces, Fig. 1.2.5), and the University of Hiroshima (radiosity and lighting). A few research centers and private companies invested significant resources in the development and production of shorts that pushed computer graphics technology to its limits (Figs. 1.2.6–1.2.7). Government-sponsored research centers also developed pioneering simulation techniques. Figure 1.2.8 shows a landmark simulation of natural forces. Most of the three-dimensional software products that were commercially available during the first half of this decade lagged behind the exciting work done in research institutions. This was due to the lack of capital investors who fully believed in the commercial potential of the technology. It was also due to the difficulty of implementing computing-intensive techniques with off-the-shelf hardware systems that were not quite as fast as needed and perhaps a bit overpriced.

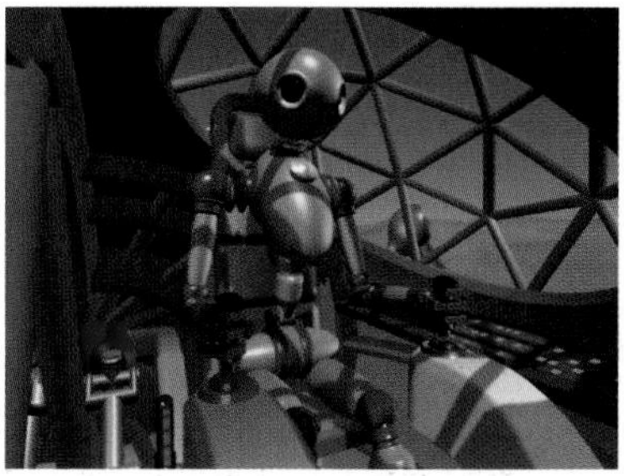

1.2.6 Mechanical ant from the 1984 trailer for *The Works*. (Design, animation, and modeling by Dick Lundin. Robot model by Ned Greene. Images courtesy of Ned Greene and NYIT Computer Graphics Lab.)

Some of the hardware research during the 1980s focused on the development of more powerful general-purpose microprocessors and special-purpose graphics processors, and techniques for the high-speed transfer of visual data. A standard midrange computer system for three-dimensional production during the 1980s, for example, consisted of a 32- or 64-bit microcomputer or supermicrocomputer with one or several graphics processors, clock speeds higher than 50 Mhz, several dozens of megabytes for RAM memory, and extensive peripheral storage.

In terms of output standards, few of the production companies at the beginning of the decade were capable of first-generation output to videotape. Most of the high-end work was output to film first and then transferred to videotape. By the end of the decade, however, video output established itself as the most common output method for computer-generated animation.

Early 1990s

The first half of the 1990s witnessed a major move toward smaller and/or considerably more powerful computer systems. Virtually all of the low-end microcomputers currently in production are based on 32-bit microprocessors, whereas the powerful microcomputer models are centered around 64-bit CISC and RISC processors. A considerable number of models with different features were targeted at different segments of the market, especially systems with multiple processors, and computer systems were sold in a modular form. Supermicrocomputers, or workstations, kept increasing in power while decreasing in price, or remained at the same price level but with additional features.

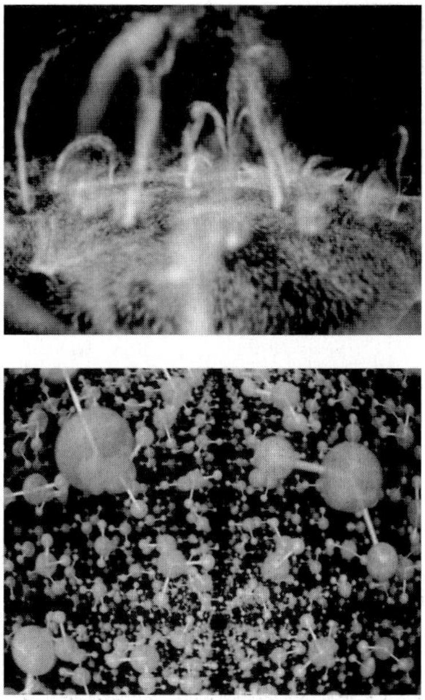

1.2.7 *The Universe* was the world's first stereoscopic (stereo 3D) computer animation rendered and output on 70 mm 15-perf film for projection on an IMAX dome screen. It was created for the Fujitsu Pavillion at Tsukuba Science Expo '85. (© 1985 Fujitsu/Dentsu/ToyoLinks/IMAX.)

Research and development was mostly centered around issues of efficiency, cost, and ease of use. With the midrange hardware systems being powerful enough for most creative needs, a lot of energy and time was spent in optimizing the software techniques. Taking small solid steps took precedence over making large groundbreaking advances. Computer-human interface issues also took precedence in this buyer's market. Users of three-dimensional software became increasingly sophisticated and demanding, and enjoyed new levels of creativity and computing power. Two additional trends of this period

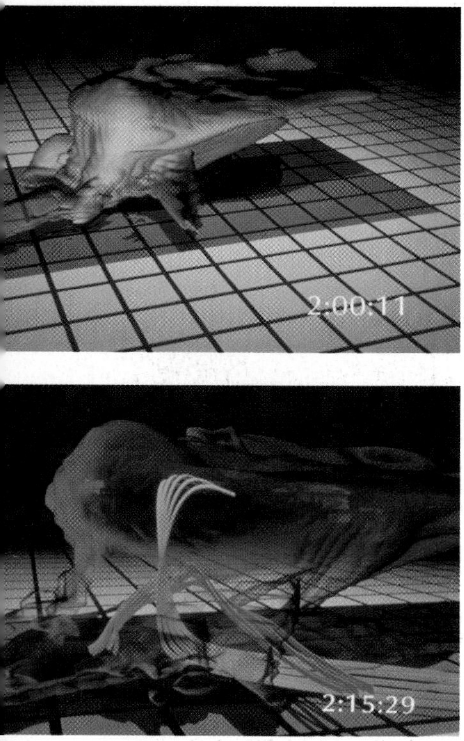

1.2.8 In this simulated snapshot of a severe storm (top) the yellow-gold regions represent small cloud drops and ice particles, and the blue region represents large water drops. The surface grid lines are 10 km apart and the darkened area indicates the horizontal integration domain surface of the storm. The orange-red ribbons (bottom) represent the tracer particles in that rise through the depth of the storm in the updraft, and the blue ribbons represent tracers that eventually fall to the ground in the downdraft. The spatial resolution of the data used in the simulation was 2 km horizontally and .75 km vertically. (Image from "Study of a Numerically Modeled Severe Storm." Courtesy of the National Center for Supercomputing Applications.)

include the rebirth of the electronic game industry (and the growth in jobs, volume, and quality associated with it), as well as the fact that, overall, the computer industry became friendlier and less technical as it tried to mass-market its products to the consumer market.

Late 1990s

During the second half of the 1990s the worlds of computer animation and visual effects production were impacted by the many changes and technological advances that took place in the computer hardware and software industries. Some of the more influential events include the popularization of the **Windows NT** and **Linux** computer operating systems. This trend evolved to a point where even SGI, the computer company formerly known as Silicon Graphics, Inc. and a traditional stalwart of the **UNIX** operating system, began offering NT-based computers in 1999. CPU clock speeds used for production continued to move up, with speeds of 400 and 500 MHz becoming common. Intel and its Pentium line of processors became a significant player in environments where years earlier they had been dismissed as lightweights. Powerful graphics co-processors designed to accelerate the speed of three-dimensional computations also continued to evolve. Some ended up being bundled on the motherboard of PCs, and others continued to be sold as add-on graphics cards. Computer networks became vital to digital production due to the popularization of rendering farms and production in multiple locations. By the end of the decade the use of company **computer intranets** for communications and file transfer and management became the standard practice at most leading centers of digital production.

Major advances in the video industry also had an impact on computer animation and visual effects production. **Digital video** became a reality in the mid-1990s, and by the end of the decade many different types of productions had been realized in the new medium. Late in the decade Sony introduced a **high definition digital video** camera, and in 1999 the company announced that a 24 frame-per-second version (24P HD) was in development. In the same year the filmmaker George Lucas made statements about his plans to shoot live action with such a camera in the ***Star Wars*** second prequel. The success of 1999 alternative films like ***The Blair Witch Project*** and the Danish ***The Celebration*** facilitated the entry of digital video into mainstream production. These two live action films were shot on digital video (the former used only available light) and then were transferred to 35 mm film for theatrical release. The increasingly widespread availablity of 24P HD digital video promises to simplify some production issues in the area of visual effects.

The advent of **digital movie projectors** was another significant development of the late 1990s because it pointed to the fact that one day photographic film might no longer be the dominant medium for motion pictures and animation, not only for home use but also for theatrical releases. Texas Instruments became an early

1.2.9 The short computer animation *Geri's Game* was a technology test-bed for subdivision surfaces modeling techniques and for clothing dynamics. Rendering was done with the RenderMan shading language. (© Pixar Animation Studios.)

leader in the field of digital projectors when it introduced its first DLP model in 1998.

The great popularity and growth experienced by **computer games** and **platform games** translated into many jobs for three-dimensional computer animators, who created hundreds of real-time and prerendered content for personal computers and new game platforms such as Sony's **Playstation**, the **Nintendo 64** and Sega's **Dreamcast**. The arcade version of *Virtua Fighter 3* released by Sega in 1996 brought arcade games to a new level of polygon real-time rendering performance. But the new home console game systems continued to become more sophisticated. The game industry during the 1990s wrapped up with a great demand for computer animators and several exciting games.

In the area of software tools, there were several significant developments during the late 1990s. The modeling technique of subdivision surfaces allows users to build three-dimensional models with different geometry resolutions throughout the model. This technique was developed at the University of Washington and then perfected at Pixar, where the 1997 award-winner *Geri's Game* became the test-bed for this and other new modeling techniques (Fig. 1.2.9). The technique of image-based rendering, refined at The University of California at Berkeley, facilitates the reconstruction of three-dimensional environments based on photographic references taken on location (Figs. 6.8.1–6.8.3). Nonphotorealistic rendering is used to represent three-dimensional geometry with a two-dimensional look. Applications of this approach are of great interest to techni-

Game Platforms General Specifications

Sony Playstation 2
Renders 66 million triangles per second
CPU: 128-bit RISC (Emotion Engine) at 300 MHz
GPU: 147.5 MHz
RAM memory: 40 MB
Media storage: 4.7 GB

Microsoft Xbox
Renders 125 million triangles per second
CPU: 32-bit Pentium III at 733 MHz
GPU: 250 MHz, Nvidia
RAM memory: 64 MB
Media storage: 6.4 GB

Nintendo GameCube
Renders 12 million triangles per second
CPU: 32-bit IBM PowerPC Gekko at 485 MHz
GPU: 162 MHz, ATI/Nintendo "Flipper"
RAM memory: 43 MB
Media storage: 1.5 GB

1.2.10 Specs of three popular game platforms at time of release.

cal illustrators and to those looking for ways to visually integrate traditional animation and three-dimensional computer animation (Figs. 6.9.1–6.9.4). The simulation of water and gas dynamics and brittle matter also gained ground during this period (Figs. 5.5.10, 12.3.3 and 12.3.4).

Early 2000s

Hardware continued its march toward smaller, faster, and cheaper. Graphics boards with powerful GPUs made hardware rendering a reality, both for professional applications and home entertainment. The game industry benefited from this increased computing power for the playback of real-time three-dimensional computer animation. Powerful home game consoles proliferated (Fig. 1.2.10). In 2000, for example, Sony introduced the **Playstation 2**, a system built around a 128-bit processor, that draws 2 million polygons per frame which is about the geometry resolution of an average scene in the 1995 ***Toy Story*** animated feature film. Microsoft introduced the **X-Box** powered by an nVIDIA graphics card capable of drawing up to 125 million polygons per second, and Nintendo introduced the **GameCube**. The game industry continued to overshadow the movie industry in revenues.

Processors for PCs moved to speeds closer to and beyond 2 gigahertz (GHz). Intel's Pentium 4 Processor, for example, debuted in 2000 with an initial speed of 1.5 GHz–compare that to Intel's first microprocessor, the 4004, which ran at 108 KHz! If automobile speed had increased similarly over the same period, you could now drive from San Francisco to New York in about 13 seconds. AMD introduced their 64-bit processor in 2003. 64-bit processors have attracted interest from software developers but at press time Mental Ray is the only 64-bit compatible renderer. In the area of operating systems, relative newcomer Linux became the dominant standard for high-end production, while **Mac OSX** gained a fair amount of attention and use because of its UNIX-like features.

High definition video (HD) continued to develop with the succesful completion of all-digital productions such as *Star Wars: Episode II* and *Spy Kids 2* (Fig. 1.2.11). Different flavors of HD cameras continued to be introduced, most notably Phillips' **Viper** in 2002, prototypes by Olympus and JVC, as well as Sony's **HDC-F950** 4:4:4 full-RGB HD camera system and the improved HDCAM-SR tape format with 4:2:2 10-bit color bandwidth. At the same time the use of digital dailies and the digital intermediate process gained converts in the worlds of movie and TV post-production. File formats for compressing and decompressing files sent via computer networks developed significant. These formats, known as **codecs**, are especially useful for video streaming and resulted in new versions of Apple's Quicktime, Microsoft's Media Player 9, and a few others based on the MPEG-4 video compression standard (read Chapter 15 for more information on compression).

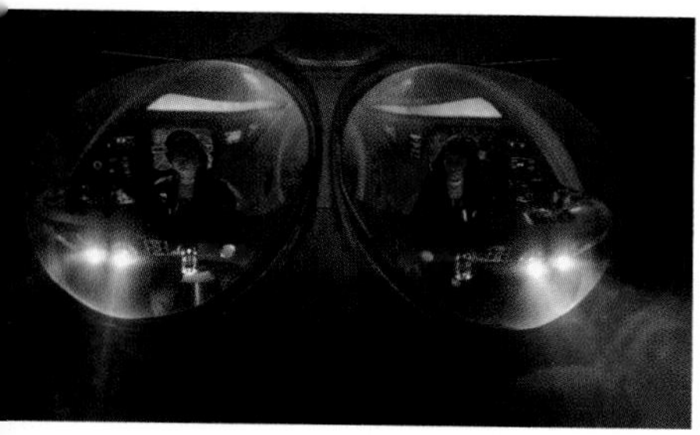

1.2.11 *Spy Kids 2* was one of the first movies to be recorded on High Definition video. (© 2002 Hybride. Images courtesy of Dimension Films.)

The proliferation of DVD players in the home video consumer market during the early 2000s helped fuel a massive distribution of the computer-animated and visual effects "hits" of the period. A *Hollywood Reporter* survey in 2003, for example, indicated a 65 percent increase in DVD purchases between 2001 and in 2002. VHS sales declined an estimated 29 percent during the same period.

1.3 Visual Milestones: 1960–1989

It is both refreshing and illuminating to view, enjoy, and analyze the visual works that became creative milestones in the development of three-dimensional computer animation and imaging. By analyzing these works we can learn about all the computer animation techniques and styles that have evolved into what this field is today.

Some useful sources for learning more about three-dimensional computer animation, as well as other computer animation software resources and links, can be found in the **www.artof3d.com** website (see the appendix). Some of these sources include the **SIGGRAPH Video Review** videotapes, the issues of the **Cinefex** journal of visual effects, and the winners and runner-ups of the American **Academy of Motion Picture Arts and Sciences (AMPAS)** awards in the visual effects category. See the timelines at the end of this chapter for a complete listing of winners and runner-ups in the visual effects and animation categories of the AMPAS awards.

1960s

During most of the 1960s the computer was—in the opinion of most visual artists, critics, and spectators—too cold and technical to be involved in the creation of artistic projects. Similar prejudices about technology arose in the nineteenth century when machines were introduced on a massive scale to the industrial world, eventually becoming commonplace in everyday life. Many turn-of-the-century painters feared the new technology until they learned how to use it and became creative with it. During the 1960s the impact and influence of computers on animation and imaging can be compared to the impact photography had on the visual arts of the late nineteenth century. Miniature painters and engravers feared that the new invention would replace them, and some of them even called it the "invention of the devil."

As mentioned earlier, computers have been used to create images since the 1950s, but the first artistic experiments with computer-based systems did not take place until the early 1960s. Most of the early animations and images produced with computers were not created in art studios but in research laboratories, and most of them used two-dimensional techniques at first. In fact, an unlikely partnership between Bell Labs physicist Billy Klüver and artist Robert Rauschenberg resulted in the 1967 ***Experiments in Art and Technology*** in New York City. But for the most part, the majority of individuals

Rating Systems Across Entertainment Media

Movies, MPAA

G	General Audiences
PG	Parental Guidance
PG-13	Parents Strongly Cautioned
R	Restricted
NC-17	No one 17 and Under

Television, TV Parental Guides

TV-Y	All Children
TV-Y7	Older Children
TV-Y7-FV	Older Children, Fantasy Violence
TV-G	General Audience
TV-PG	Parental Guidance Suggested
TV-14	Parents Strongly Cautioned
TV-MA	Mature Audience Only

Video/Computer Games, ESRB

EC	Early Childhood
K-A	Kids to Adults
E	Everyone (6+)
T	Teen (13+)
M	Mature (17+)
AO	Adults Only
RP	Rating Pending

1.3.1 Ratings across media by the Motion Picture Association of America, the TV Parental Guidelines Monitoring Board, and the Entertainment Software Ratings Board.

who created the early works of computer animation came from the fields of science and engineering, and they lacked formal training in the fine arts. Nevertheless, many of them displayed a strong artistic intention and a significant degree of aesthetic consciousness.

The computer systems that were used by these pioneers were not designed primarily for artistic creation. The IBM model 360 introduced in 1963, for example, was the first family of computers centered around a Fortran-based **time-sharing** system. Compared to today's computers, systems of those years were not very interactive, if they were interactive at all. The computer-human interface of the 1960s was typically opaque, cryptic, and not self-explanatory.

Because using the early computer systems to create animations and images was not easy, many of these early creators had to put more effort into the process of creating the works than into the form and content of the works themselves. Many early computer artists were more concerned with the development of the computer-based imaging tools than with the style of their work. But in spite of all the limitations, the pioneers made effective use of the available technology.

The early computer-generated animations and images are the products of a technology still in the stage of development. The style of these early works was defined in a major way by the limitations of the computer equipment itself, and by the lack of computer programs that were capable of rendering complex images in a variety of ways. Very often complex methods and data structures did not yield correspondingly complex images. Among the American pioneers of computer art we can mention John Whitney, Sr., and Charles Csuri whose early computer-assisted animations date, respectively, from 1961 and 1966. (Csuri's later work can be seen in Figure 6.6.3.)

One of the earliest experiments with computer-generated character animation was ***Mr. Computer Image ABC*** created in 1962 by Lee Harrison III with the **Scanimate** system at Computer Image Corporation (the system won an Emmy Award in 1972).

In 1968 the **Motion Picture Association of America (MPAA)** introduced a new rating system for movies that impacted the work done by filmmakers and animators. This rating system included four categories: G (General Audiences), M (Mature Audiences) R (Restricted) and X (No one under 17). A short time later the M rating was replaced by PG (Parental Guidance). Figure 1.3.1 presents an updated listing of ratings across the major entertainment media.

1.3.2 Landscapes from *Vol Libre* created with fractal techniques. (© 1980 Loren Carpenter.)

1970s

The panorama in computer art changed greatly during the 1970s because of the development of techniques for representing three-dimensional environments and because of the increased involvement of professional artists with computers. Computer-based animation and imaging systems became more interactive than what they were during the 1960s, but they were still not easy to use. Only a few of the artists who got interested in computer technology used it as their

1.3.3 *Tin Toy* presents the story of a good-hearted toy who is willing to risk it all in order to save a baby in danger. (© Pixar Animation Studios.)

primary medium for artistic creation. In addition to their visual work, many of these early artists of three-dimensional computer animation and imaging also contributed to the technical development of their tools by collaborating in the development of software.

During the late 1970s one of the most widely viewed works of three-dimensional computer animation was ***Voyager 2***, created by a team at the Jet Propulsion Laboratory (JPL) led by James Blinn. This work visualized the explorations of the Voyager 2 spaceship, and it is an excellent example of one of the earliest succesful and extensive uses of image mapping techniques. Artist David Em, a visiting artist at JPL, created stills of his own fantastic planets with the same software used by scientists to render the planets of the Solar System.

Other notable examples of computer animation from this period include the 1974 animated film ***Hunger*** created by Peter Foldes under the auspices of the National Film Board of Canada. This work included striking computer-generated interpolations of key poses drawn by hand and painstakingly digitized into the computer software. ***Vol Libre***, a three-dimensional computer animation by Loren Carpenter, shows renderings of fractal mountains with great lyrical force (Fig. 1.3.2). ***The Joggler*** is an early example of a computer-animated human character attempting complex motion created at Information International Inc. (III). In 1974 The New York Institute of Technology (NYIT), in Old Westbury, New York, assembled a computer graphics research group with a notable roster of engineers and programmers. The goal was to develop computer graphics software and hardware to be used for commercial productions. A few years

1.3.4 *Knickknack* presents the hilarious misfortunes of a Casanova toy-snowman who despite the fact that he charms the opposite toy-sex can never seem to get close to them—his bad luck is always one step ahead of him. (© Pixar Animation Studios.)

later Industrial Light & Magic (ILM) was created to develop the visual effects for George Lucas' 1977 ***Star Wars***. This film brought visual effects to the foreground of mainstream culture, but the use of computer technology in this film was mostly limited to the computerized motion control systems used to move cameras and physical miniature models. The blue-screen compositing of the visual effects elements and plates in these films was achieved optically. In 1979 several members of the NYIT research group joined ILM with the goal of integrating computer graphics into visual effects production.

The commercial work done for advertising agencies at Digital Effects, III, MAGI, and Robert Abel and Associates is illustrative of computer animation in the late 1970s. These companies were active until the mid-1980s and then spawned other companies that continued their innovative spirit. Digital Effects was active from 1978 until the mid-1980s, III opened in 1974 and closed in 1982, MAGI was active between 1972 and 1987, and Robert Abel and Associates started in 1971 and closed in 1986.

1980s

In the area of three-dimensional computer animation, the 1980s started with a few exceptional works and ended with a flurry of outstanding projects. This was due to many factors, such as the enhanced technology, the larger market, the maturing of the artists working in the field, and the entry into the workforce of the first art students who attended computer animation and imaging educational programs. The earliest realistic model of the full human figure from this decade is the virtual character Cindy created at III for the 1981 science fiction film *Looker*. The 1982 Disney film ***TRON*** was the first feature film with over 20 minutes of computer animation composited optically with live action; a few of the shots required dozens of passes with filters in front of the optical printer lens. ***TRON*** combined live action with three-dimensional computer animations created by the teams at Robert Abel and Associates, III, MAGI, and Digital Effects. For all of its visual innovation, however, this film was only moderately successful at the box office. The story behind this science-fiction film centered around a videogame designer who somehow ends up inside the virtual world of his creations and has to fight the game challenges that he himself created. The topic of this film also reflected the fact that the popularity of videogames hit a peak in the early 1980s, when Atari was the leading company in this arena. A decade earlier its founder, Nolan Bushnell, had developed the table tennis game *Pong* (1972) that helped launch the videogame industry.

In the area of visual effects for live action film, Industrial Light & Magic continued the excellence in visual effects started just a few years with George Lucas' *The Empire Strikes Back* (1980) and *Return of the Jedi* (1983). *Indiana Jones and the Temple of Doom* became in 1984 their first film to have an all-digital composite shot. *Young Sherlock Holmes* (1985) featured a somewhat convincing jointed character made of flat stained glass-like panels with texture mapping and transparency. In *Flight of the Navigator* (1986) keyframes of the live action footage were scanned and used for spherical reflection mapping to simulate interactive reflections as computer-generated object travelled through the scene, three-dimensional morphing was also used in this movie. *The Abyss* (1989) revolved around the first three-dimensional computer animated character that was realistic enough to blend with the live action background plates. Because of the complex calculations of reflection and refraction, the team had enough time to render the different layers in each frame only once. The different passes (diffuse, specular, refraction, highlights) were composited optically, except for a single shot (when the safety door closes and the water creature is cut in half) that was composited digitally at 8-bits with Photoshop software.

The **Genesis Effect** created in 1982 by Industrial Light & Magic (ILM) for the film *Star Trek II: The Wrath of Kahn* is also of historical interest because it was the first visual effects shot that was created entirely with three-dimensional computer animation techiques, the longest running sequence, and also because it is one of the earliest examples of procedural modeling and particle systems animation. *The Last Starfighter* was the first live action feature film to include a large amount of very realistic computer animation of highly detailed models. The basic production idea at the time was to replace the motion control cameras and the model photography with three-dimensional computer animation. The 28 minutes of computer

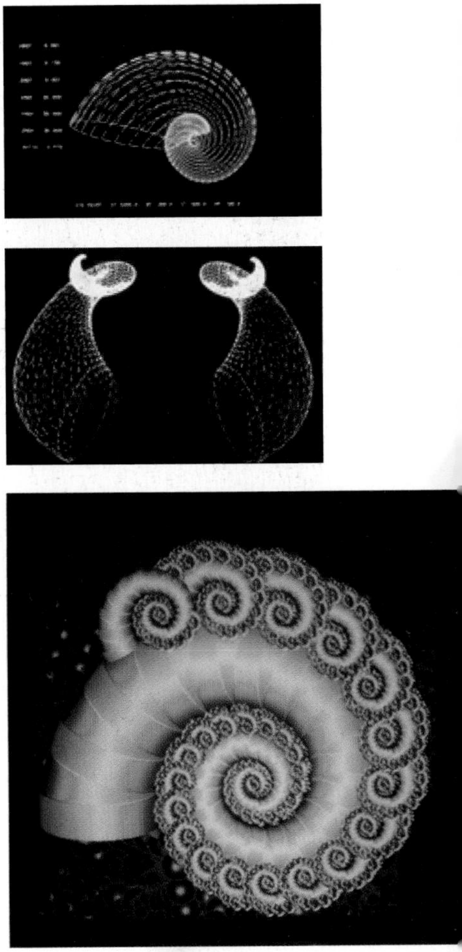

1.3.5 *Shells* (top) and colorful *Tendril* (bottom) are among the first three-dimensional objects created with the recursive GROWTH algorithm. The final complex forms are derived from seed shapes like conch shells, tentacles and coral. (*Shells* © 1976 Yoichiro Kawaguchi, *Tendril* © 1981 Yoichiro Kawaguchi.)

1.3.6 *Dozo* was the first female Synthespian™ performer created by Diana Walczak and Jeff Kleiser. She stars in their 1989 computer generated film *Don't Touch Me*. (© 1989 Kleiser-Walczak Construction Co.)

1.3.7 *Locomotion* was one of the earliest (1988) three-dimensional computer animated shorts to use the technique of squash and stretch. (© PDI/DreamWorks.)

animation for this 1985 film were animated and rendered with a Cray supercomputer at Digital Productions. To avoid aliasing artifacts most of the frames were computed at 20,000 lines of resolution and down-converted to about 1,000 lines.

Other notable works of the early and mid-1980s include ***Bio-Sensor*** created in 1984 at Osaka University and Toyo Links. This work is an impressive example of early figure locomotion and modeling with blobby surfaces (Fig. 1.2.5). The ***Brilliance*** commercial featuring a sexy female robot with convincing realistic motion was created by Abel and Associates, and also the first entirely computer-generated TV ad to be aired during a Super Bowl football game.

Also created during this period were the sublime simulations of light, fog, rain, and skies created at Hiroshima University (Fig. 8.5.2); the intriguing non-edge simulations of clouds and smoke created by Geoffrey Gardner at Grumman Data Systems; and the first ray-traced imaging tests done by Turner Whitted at Bell Labs.

The mid-1980s also saw the rise of leading commercial production houses worldwide. In northern California, Pacific Data Images (PDI) was founded in 1980, Tippet Studios in 1983, and Pixar in 1985. In southern California, Boss Films was active from 1982 to 1997, and Digital Productions was in business from 1981 until the mid-1980s when it evolved into Whitney/Demos Productions for a few years. VIFX opened in 1984 and Rhythm & Hues started in 1987. On the East Coast Cranston-Csuri opened in 1981 in Columbus, Ohio, and closed in 1987, later spawning Metrolight. R/Greenberg Associates opened in New York City in 1981, the Kleiser-Walczak Construction Company was created in 1985, and Blue Sky Studios in 1987. In 1982 Omnibus was started in Canada, and in 1986 it purchased both pioneer Robert Abel & Associates and Digital Productions before filing for bankrupcy a couple of years later. In Paris, Buff opened in 1985, Mac Guff Ligne in 1986, and Sogitec was active from 1986 to 1989 when it merged with TDI to create Ex Machina. CA Scanline opened in Münich in 1989. In Japan Toyo Links opened in 1982, the Japan Computer Graphics Lab (JCGL) was active from 1981 until it was purchased in 1988 by the videogame company NAMCO, and Polygon Pictures opened in 1983.

Throughout the 1980s two constants exemplify the excellence reached by three-dimensional computer animation during the decade. On one hand there was the engaging and amusing character animations by the animation team at Pixar led by John Lasseter, including ***Luxo Jr.*** (1985), ***Red's Dream*** (1987), ***Tin Toy*** (1988), and ***Knickknack*** (1989). These Pixar projects not only pushed the RenderMan shading language to its limits, but also proved that the traditional principles of character animation could be applied to computer-generated works (Figs. 1.1.1 and 1.3.3–1.3.4). On the other hand there was ***Growth***, a series of semi-abstract animations by Japanese artist-programmer Yoichiro Kawaguchi. The series portrays imaginary underwater creatures generated with procedural techniques (Fig. 1.3.5).

The late 1980s witnessed experimentation with a wide variety of techniques ranging from the simulation of natural-looking hair growth to rigid body dynamics and modeling fabric with visible threads. ***Stanley and Stella: Breaking the Ice***, produced by Symbolics Graphics and Whitney Demo Productions in 1987, is a solid and amusing early example of flock animation. ***Don't Touch Me***, created in 1989 by the Kleiser-Walczak Construction Company, represents one of the earliest tours de force in character animation with motion capture techniques (Fig. 1.3.6). The female singer in this piece displayed more body animation and faster motion than any previous attempt; the animation was achieved by applying the motion of a live singer to the virtual character. The demo reels of design and production studios such as Rhythm & Hues and Metrolight in California, Ex Machina in Paris, Digital Pictures in London and Toyo Links in Tokyo (Fig. 1.3.9) are representative of the commercial work of the period.

Independent short computer animations created during the late 1980s have many inspired examples. ***Burning Love*** created by Pacific Data Images in 1988 displayed an emotional quality that had not been seen in too many computer animations of the period, and it also used one of the earliest painterly treatments of three-dimensional computer rendering. ***Locomotion***, also by Pacific Data Images, (1988) illustrated the story of a charming train engine that overcomes a broken bridge and, in the process, displayed great understanding of the traditional animation principles of squash and stretch (Fig. 1.3.7). ***The Little Death*** created by Matt Elson at Symbolics Graphics in 1989 applied the technique of displacement animation onto detailed models of the human figure (Fig. 1.3.8). ***Grinning Evil Death*** (McKenna and Sabiston at MIT's Media Lab) had a sassy, almost sinister sense of humor that was uncommon in computer animations of this period. ***Technological Threat*** created by William Kroyer in 1988 combines hand-drawn animation with three-dimensional computer wireframe animation to present a hilarious view of the automated office (Fig. 1.3.10).

During the second half of this decade Walt Disney Feature Animation, one of the dominant forces in traditional animation, began to experiment with three-dimensional computer animation in its animated feature films. ***The Black Cauldron,*** released in 1985, was the first Disney animated feature film that used computer graphics technology in a small section of the movie to simulate a flying visible light source. ***The Great Mouse Detective*** (1986) contains a one-minute chase sequence almost at the end of the movie where the hero tries to rescue the heroine from the villain in a landscape of menacing gears that threaten to crush them as they try to evade the villain. The gears were modeled and animated with three-dimensional computer animation techniques, and then output as drawings on paper with a pen plotter. This allowed them to be integrated into the traditional production process of the time.

Many of the cityscapes in ***Oliver & Company***, a 1988 Disney release, are populated with animated three-dimensional cars. In addition some of the car interiors are settings for conversations between

1.3.8 The character Lotta Desire from *The Little Death* had a single and continuous skin that covered her entire body, including eyes connected with optical nerves to the back of her eye sockets and animateable irises. This character was also one of the first to use an early version of the surface subdivision technique to raise the polygonal resolution for film output, about 5,000 polygons that were subdivided to 20,000 at rendertime. Lotta Desire also contained internal displacements—not morph targets—to achieve her expressions. (© 1989 Matt Elson.)

1.3.9 Scene based on the designs of French illustrator Jean-Michel Folon, rendered to recreate the softness of pastel colors on paper. (Images courtesy of Toyo Links, from Tokyo Gas Company 1987 campaign.)

hand-drawn cartoon characters, and some close-ups of car exteriors are also backdrops for shots with the canine characters that drive the film. ***The Little Mermaid*** (1989) was the last Disney animated feature film to use traditional ink and paint production techniques. However, the very last scene in the film, where the crowd is waving good-bye, was done digitally with Disney's proprietary **CAPS** software (Computer Animation Production System).

In the area of live action films with computer-generated special visual effects, ***The Abyss*** is a 1989 feature film that crowns the decade with convincing examples of three-dimensional animation, seamless compositing with 70 mm live action footage, and also of a complex production created to a great extent with off-the-shelf systems. One of the most striking moments in this film takes place when the computer-animated water creature emulates the facial expressions of the human actor who also touches the virtual creature with her hand. The MPAA expanded its rating system in 1984 to include a PG-13 category. Few suspected the explosion in popularity, artistic creativity, and significant revenue that computer animation and visual effects were going to play in the following decade (Fig. 1.3.11).

1.3.10 The hilarious *Technological Threat* combined in 1988 three-dimensional wireframe computer animation of the environment and boss with traditional hand-drawn animation of the employees. (© 1999 Kroyer Films, Inc.)

1.3.11 (opposite page) All-time cumulative U.S.-only box office of animated feature movies as of mid-2003.

1.4 Visual Milestones: 1990–Today

The last few years have seen growth in the number of styles and techniques used in three-dimensional computer animation of visual effects. Also significant has been the increasing competitive nature of the field, the continued increase in the power of the tools, and an expansion beyond the traditional centers of production.

Early 1990s

The early 1990s were characterized by refined examples of computer animation as well as a successful revival of special effects for feature films. Three-dimensional computer animation and imaging during this period became quite complex and full of varied styles and attitudes. Many of the projects from this period encompass an exciting body of work and a variety of styles and techniques. By the middle of the decade three-dimensional computer animation and imaging had become a mature and specialized field that finally gained a fair amount of wide recognition. Computer animators and digital artists in general were in great demand due to the increased

1.4.1 Animating flocks of bats in the film *Batman Returns*. The behavior of the bats is based on a flock animation computer model originally developed by Craig Reynolds in 1987. (Additional software written by Andy Kopra. *Batman Returns*™, © 1992 DC Comics. Image courtesy of VIFX.)

production slate of visual effects films, animated films and television series, and computer and platform games.

The early 1990s witnessed a fair amount of company transitions in the field of commercial computer animation and visual effects. The Mill in London and Santa Barbara Studios started in 1990, and Digital Domain opened in 1993. The same year Square opened with the original goal of creating animation for both games and feature film. Sony was the first Hollywood movie studio to consider developing an in-house visual effects and computer animation facility. The result of this idea was Sony Imageworks, which opened in 1992. Later in the decade other Hollywood studios purchased independent computer animation and/or visual effects production houses. Another notable business event of this period was the agreement between Disney and Pixar to codevelop, produce, and distribute several animated feature films.

Several feature films created during the early 1990s used computer-generated visual effects extensively. ***Terminator II***, for example, is a landmark 1991 film by James Cameron with computer animation by Industrial Light & Magic. This film was the first mainstream blockbuster movie to include outstanding three-dimensional morphing effects, the first convincing simulation of natural human motion, global reflections and even a few self-reflections when the digital actor walks through the metal bars. ***The Lawnmower Man***, a 1992 film with computer animation by Angel Studios, was the first feature film of the decade that explored the topic of virtual reality with computer animation. ***Batman Returns*** is a 1992 stylized production with effective examples of flock animation (Fig. 1.4.1). The same year ***Death Becomes Her*** used extensive digital retouching by removing the head of an actress and later tracking a different shot of a talking real

All-Time U.S. Box Office of Animated Feature Movies

Movie	Gross	Year
The Lion King	$312.8	1994
Shrek	$267.6	2001
Monsters, Inc.	$255.8	2001
Toy Story 2	$245.8	1999
Aladdin	$217.3	1992
Beauty and the Beast	$196.6	1991
Toy Story	$191.7	1995
Snow White...	$178.0	1937
Ice Age	$176.3	2002
Tarzan	$171.0	1999
A Bug's Life	$162.7	1998

1.4.2 The first polar bear commercial created by Rhythm and Hues was created in 1993. On the opposite page are frames from the 1996 and 1998 editions (© The Coca-Cola Company. "Coca-Cola," the Coca-Cola Polar Bear design, and the "Coca-Cola" Contour Bottle are trademarks of The Coca-Cola Company.)

head onto the body. *Jurassic Park*, a 1993 film by Steven Spielberg and computer animation by ILM, is an early example of using inverse kinematics skeletons, skin, and local deformation for each muscle. This movie was also a the first example of a computer-generated human stunt double, and a great example of hyperrealistic rendering. A gigantic amount of processing was performed in a relatively short period of time. For the first time in a live action feature film, digital compositing replaced almost entirely photochemical optical compositing for the perfect integration of live action and animatronics (for the close-ups of dinosaur heads) with computer-generated images. *The Flintstones* (1994) is an early example of fur rendering, used for the saber tooth tiger.

Other notable examples of computer animation during the early 1990s include *Primordial Dance* (1991) and *Liquid Selves* (1992), both beautiful examples of computer animations created by Karl Sims with particle systems techniques; the irreverent and amusing *Le Xons Crac-Crac* and *Baston* created in 1991 by Ex-Nihilo and McGuff Ligne; Willam Latham's hypnotic *Mutations* (1991); *Don Quichotte*, an ambitious keyframe animation created in 1991 by Video System; and *Leaf Magic* (1991), a good example of animation with motion dynamics by Alan Norton.

Some of the outstanding work for television commercials includes the 1993 *Coca-Cola Polar Bears* by Rhythm and Hues Studios (Fig. 1.4.2) and the 1994 *Listerine Arrows* by Pixar. Many ambitious and exquisite architectural visualizations were also created in the early 1990s, including ***The Seven Wonders of the World*** (1992) by Electric Images in England, ***The Ancient World Revisited I-III*** (1990-94) by Taisei Corp., and ***De Karnak a Louqsor*** (1992) by Ex Machina. In 1993 ***Myst*** set the standard for prerendered three-dimensional computer animation for computer games (Fig. 1.4.3). The early 1990s also saw great examples of broadcast-quality computer animation created entirely with off-the-shelf microcomputer systems. ***Babylon 5***, for example, is a 1993 TV series and the first mainstream example of high-end three-dimensional computer animation that was initially produced entirely on 32-bit Amiga and Macintosh microcomputers. The now ubiquitous Music Television Channel (MTV) went on air in 1981 and started its Music Video Awards program in 1984, but it wasn't until the 1990s that **music videos** came of age as a viable and original medium for cutting-edge computer animation and visual effects (Figs. 1.4.4 and 9.1.1).

Motion capture systems for character animation experienced an intense development during this period. Some of these efforts included the Facetracker system developed by SimmGraphics to animate the Super Mario character; ***Moxy,*** a virtual TV host animated by Colossal Pictures for the Cartoon Network (Fig. 1.4.5); Acclaim Entertainment's optical system with up to 70 sensors for simultaneous two-person capture (Fig. 12.2.5); and a variety of commercially available motion capture hardware and software.

During the early 1990s computer animation at Walt Disney Feature Animation went from a mere novelty to a significant standard component in the digital production process. Disney's 1990 release ***The Rescuers Down Under*** was the first Disney animated feature film to be produced entirely with the first version of the CAPS software. This landmark event ended 53 years (since 1937) of inking and painting acetate cels. This film also contained a moving vehicle and a few props created with three-dimensional computer animation. ***The Beauty and the Beast*** (1991) includes the memorable ballroom scene where the animated camera follows Beauty and Beast as they dance in a three-dimensional environment that included columns with marble textures and a detailed chandelier. This film was also the first animated feature film to be nominated for an Academy of Motion Picture Arts and Sciences award in the Best Picture category.

In ***Aladdin***'s magic carpet we see the first example of Disney character-driven computer animation. The magic carpet's organic surfaces and detailed texture were animated with cartoony squash and stretch and impeccable timing. The complex textures mapped on the carpet would have surely been a challenge to animate, ink, and paint with traditional production techniques. In addition the three-dimensional computer animation in this 1992 show also included the tiger-cave head rising from the sand dunes, the lava sequence, and countless other animation effects. The computer-generated stampede of wildebeests in ***The Lion King*** (1994) is one of the most striking moments in modern feature animation. It sets up with dramatic force and visual power the terrible events that will take place before the

1.4.3 *Myst* pushed the limits of realistic rendering for what was possible with 8-bit color CD-ROM computer games in the early 1990s. (Screen shot from Myst® CD-ROM computer game. Game and screen shot © 1993 Cyan, Inc®. All rights reserved.)

MTV's Video Music Awards, Best Special Effects

1984 *Rockit*, Herbie Hancock
1985 *Don't Come Around Here No More*, Tom Petty
1986 *Take On Me*, a-Ha
1987 *Sledgehammer*, P. Gabriel
1988 *Hourglass*, Squeeze
1989 *Leave Me Alone*, Michael Jackson
1990 *Sowing the Seeds of Love*, Tears For Fears
1991 *Falling To Pieces*, Faith No More
1992 *Even Better Than the Real Thing*, U2
1993 *Steam*, Peter Gabriel
1994 *Kiss That Frog*, P. Gabriel
1995 *Love Is Strong*, Rolling Stones
1996 *Tonight, Tonight*, Smashing Pumpkins
1997 *Virtual Insanity*, Jamiroquai
1998 *Frozen*, Madonna
1999 *Special*, Garbage
2000 *All Is Full of Love*, Björk
2001 *Rock DJ*, Robbie Williams
2002 *Fell in Love with a Girl*, The White Stripes

1.4.4 List of music videos that have won the Best Special Effects category in MTV's Video Music Awards.

1.4.5 *Moxy*, the virtual host of Cartoon Network's first original animated program, was animated with a live motion capture and motion control system. (© 1993 Cartoon Network, Inc. See Figure 12.2.6 for full credit.)

sequence is over. The wildebeests were animated with a crowd simulation system that predated many of the crowd systems that became popular later in the decade. The wildebeests' shadows and dust was also created with a three-dimensional computer animation system, as was the fire effects animation.

Late 1990s

The second half of the 1990s exploded with productions rich in three-dimensional computer animation in the fields of live action films with special effects, animated feature films, and computer or platform games. In 1995, Pixar's ***Toy Story*** became the first feature animated film to be entirely created with three-dimensional computer animation techniques (Fig. 12.1.1). Three years later two other projects joined the competitive world of three-dimensional computer animation: DreamWorks' ***ANTZ*** (Figs. 2.4.14 and 2.4.16), and Pixar's ***A Bug's Life.*** Three other animated feature films—each from a diferent studio—were released with wide distribution in the United States during 1998: Disney's ***Mulan,*** Nickelodeon's ***Rugrats,*** and DreamWorks' ***Prince of Egypt.*** The animated feature ***Princess Mononoke*** by Hayao Miyazaki was released in Japan during 1997. Not only did this film present a magical view of the world, including a hovering multi-tentacled monster created with 3D computer animation and non-realistic rendering, it also set box-office and TV records. At the time this film was the highest grossing of any film in Japan, and it scored the eighth best TV viewership rating ever.

Not only was the volume of animation production during 1998 impressive, but also the quality and creative diversity was unparalleled in the history of animation. The 1999 animated feature film releases were equally impressive: Disney's ***Tarzan*** and ***Fantasia 2000,*** Pixar's ***Toy Story 2,*** Warner Bros.' ***Iron Giant,*** and Paramount's ***South Park. Fantasia 2000*** became the first animated feature film (over 90 minutes long) to be released exclusively for the IMAX large-screen format for the initial four-month run. ***Toy Story 2*** increased the visual complexity of the computer-generated environments and the human characters in particular; ***Iron Giant*** presented an unlikely hero that was rendered with a non-photorealistic RenderMan shader.

The activity and quality of the craft in the field of visual effects during the later part of the decade was also very high. Just consider some of the many films that featured fully computer-animated main characters with live actors: ***The Lost World: Jurassic Park*** (1993), ***Jumanji*** and ***Species*** (1995), ***Dragonheart*** (1996), ***Titanic, Starship Troopers,*** and ***Mars Attacks!*** (1997), ***Mighty Joe Young, Mouse Hunt,*** and ***Godzilla*** (1998), ***The Mummy*** and ***The Phantom Menace*** (1999). The decade—and the millennium—in visual effects was capped with four popular effects-oriented films: the stylish ***The Matrix,*** winner of the 1999 AMPAS award for Best Visual effects, ***Stuart Little*** with its innovative combination of cartoon and realistic action (Figs. 14.3.3–14.3.4), the sleeper hit ***The Mummy,*** and the much-heralded

Star Wars prequel ***The Phantom Menace***. The visual effects for the former movie were done at Mass Illusion, the later two movies were done at Industrial Light & Magic. ***La Cité des enfants perdus*** (The City of Lost Children) was a 1995 French movie with ground-breaking visual effects and ray tracing rendering done with Mental Ray software (Fig. 1.4.6). The same year ***Casino*** used Lightscape radiosity software (Fig. 6.7.3) to create realistic set extensions, ***Waterworld*** incorporated water simulated with Areté software (Figs. 5.5.10 and 12.3.3), and ***Jumanji*** rendered fur on a scale larger than ever before. ***Babe*** advanced the techniques for removing, tracking and replacing talking animal heads. During 1996 the computer-generated creature in ***Dragonheart*** was the co-star of the movie, RenderMan shaders were used in ***Mission Impossible*** to match the look of the film stock used, and a massive dynamics simulation was used to create tornados for ***Twister***. During 1997 award-winner ***Titanic*** used computer-generated water, massive digital compositing, and motion capture to create digital extras on the deck of the ship, ***Spawn*** achieved a dramatic effect in the cloth animation by combining realistic rendering with exagerated keyframe animation, ***Mars Attacks!*** included amusing slpstick comedy and extensive cloth animation. In 1998 ***What Dreams May Come*** perfected camera tracking techniques to facilitate the *animated painting* look developed for the movie, and ***Mighty Joe Young*** perfected hair rendering techniques. The 1999 award-winner ***The Matrix*** used image-based rendering as well as the *frozen time* visual effect (see Chapter 13), ***Star Wars: Episode One*** had memorable spacecraft racing and battle scenes, with some of the best crowd simulation work done until then, ***Stuart Little*** brought new life to the live action movie with a computer-generated hyperrealistic cartoon character with simulated wet cloth and wet fur, ***Fight Club*** used image-based modeling and rendering (before ***The Matrix***) with several impossible camera moves through walls.

When compared to films of previous decades the visual effects films of the late 1990s had more and more complex digital and traditional effects shots. ***Terminator II***, for example—a landmark 1991 production that redefined the use of computer animation in live action movies—had approximately 150 visual effects shots including 44 digital effects. In 1995 ***Batman Forever*** had about 250 visual effects shots. In 1997 ***Titanic*** had close to 550. In 1998 ***Armageddon*** had around 240, and ***Godzilla*** had close to 400. In 2000 ***How the Grinch Stole Christmas*** had about 600 visual effects shots with about 300 of them computer-generated, including falling and melting snow; and ***The Perfect Storm*** had around 225 shots with computer-generated virtual stunt actors, 40 of them, and 33 minutes of computer-generated waves.

Production of computer animation and visual effects for feature film during the late 1990s was mostly dominated by the companies that had established themselves as leaders during the previous ten years. The major newcomers include Foundation Imaging (1992), Blur Studios, Banned from the Ranch (both opened in 1995), and

1.4.6 The flea from 1995's *La cité des enfants perdus*. (© Claudie Ossard. Directors: Jeunet & Caro. Visual effects: Buff.)

1.4.7 Some of the main characters in Chris Landreth's *Bingo*, one of the earliest computer animations rendered in a realistic style, based on improvisational theater techniques. (© Alias|Wavefront, a division of Silicon Graphics Limited.)

1.4.8 The future of location-based entertainment is being defined by computer-generated rides like *Seafari*, a hyperrealistic computer-generated motion ride that takes the audience on an underwater rescue mission. (© 1994 MCA/Universal. Courtesy of Rhythm & Hues Studios.)

Centropolis (1996). Continuing the trend set by Sony earlier in the decade with the creation of its internal visual effects and computer animation facility, in 1996 DreamWorks purchased an interest in Pacific Data Images, Fox purchased VIFX, and Disney purchased industry pioneer Dream Quest Images. A year later Fox purchased Blue Sky Studios. Warner Digital was active from 1995 to 1997.

Some of the most polished short computer animation works that we have ever seen were also produced during this period. This includes ***Geri's Game*** by Jan Pinkava at Pixar in 1997 (Fig. 1.2.9), ***Bunny*** by Chris Wedge at Blue Sky Studios (Figs. 7.2.4 and 10.1.1) and ***Bingo*** by Chris Landreth at Alias Research in 1998 (Figs. 1.4.7 and 4.2.7), and ***Tightrope*** by Daniel Robichaud at Digital Domain in 1999 (Figs. 12.5.5 and 12.5.6). Not only were these shorts produced by different groups, but each had a recognizable style that made it unique. Both ***Geri's Game*** and ***Bunny*** won AMPAS awards in the Best Animated Short category.

The games industry, fueled by the new game platforms, grew tremendously. In 1998, for example, Nintendo released ***The Legend of Zelda: Ocarina of Time*** for the N64. Between its launch date of November 23 and the end of the year, Nintendo reported $150 million dollars in sales of 2.5 million copies. As a point of reference, one of the higher-grossing movies during that year was Disney/Pixar's ***A Bug's Life***, which collected $114 million dollars at the box office. A few games from this period with innovative character computer animation include ***Soulblade***, my personal favorite fighting game from those years, Nintendo's ***Super Mario 64***, adventure and role-playing ***Ultima Online***, strategy and wargame ***Age of Empires*** and ***Civilization***, sports games ***NHL 98*** and ***NBA Live 97***, action games ***Duke Nukem 3D*** and ***Tomb Raider***, the arcade version ***Virtua Fighter 3***, and a few installments in the ***Final Fantasy*** series by SquareSoft (Fig. 1.4.10).

Some of the notable three-dimensional computer animation for early **location-based entertainment**—or **LBE rides** as they are known—include ***The Volcano Mine Ride*** (1995), and ***Seafari*** and ***Race For Atlantis in Imax 3D*** created by Rhythm & Hues Studios in 1994 and 1998, respectively (Figs. 1.4.8 and 1.4.9). Arcade games got away from shooting and fighting, and experienced growth in the areas of sports simulations like skiing, snowboarding, and jet skiing.

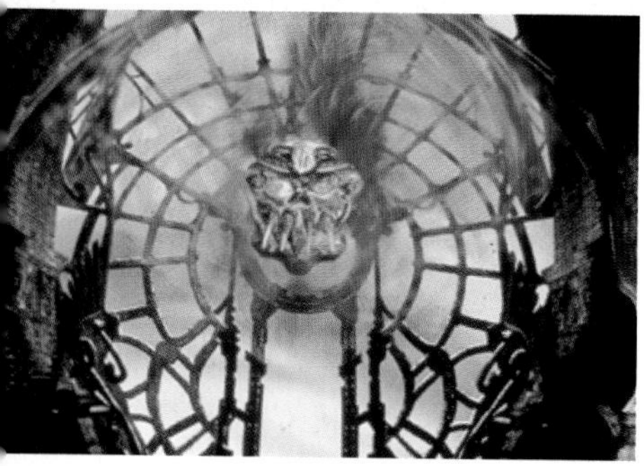

1.4.9 View of *Race for Atlantis* projected on the curved surface where the ride takes place. (Courtesy of Forum Ride Associates.)

A couple of the more memorable commercials included the ***Dance Fever*** commercials of dancing cars created by R/Greenberg Associates for Shell Oil in 1995, and ***Virtual Andre*** created from a motion-captured Andre Agassi by Digital Domain in 1997. There was also a lot of activity in the area of animated television series, with new all computer-animated series like ***Beast Wars*** and ***Reboot*** by Mainframe Entertainment (Figs. 9.4.5 and 10.4.7), ***Rednecks*** by Foundation Imaging, and charming ***Rolie Polie Olie*** (premiered in 1998) by Nelvana and Paris-based Sparx. Likewise, feature-length direct-to-video releases grew significantly during the decade.

Throughout the late 1990s traditional animation production at Walt Disney Feature Animation moved closer to three-dimensional computer animation, resulting in several examples of blending tradition with innovation. The rough animation for the canoe that *Pocahontas* (1995) rides down the river, for example, was created with three-dimensional computer animation techniques and match-moved to other elements in the scene. The face of the wise Mother Willow character was also animated with three-dimensional computer animation. Disney's 1996 production of *The Hunchback of Notre Dame* showcases three-dimensional computer-generated confetti and crowds, motion blur effects and a few props. In the final shot of the "Sanctuary!" sequence where Quasimodo rescues Esmeralda from being burned at the stake and carries her to the top of Notre Dame the three-dimensional model of the rosetta and its architectural details add dimensionality to the shot.

The 1997 release *Hercules* includes a memorable segment where the hero fights a multiple-headed Hydra monster. As he cuts some of the heads others immediately pop up in a menacing and fierce way. In addition a morphing technique was used in the opening shots of the movie to blend still paintings of clouds, columns, and other background paintings. *Mulan* (1998) displays a large variety of three-dimensional computer-animated props that blend seamlessly with the hand-drawn elements and hand-painted backgrounds. These props include flags, arrows, and carts. There is also a fair amount of effects animation like the smoke and fire from the flaming arrows and, of course, the Hun charge, which is somewhat reminiscent of moments of the wildebeest sequence in the 1994 blockbuster *The Lion King*. The Hun charge sequence, however, is enhanced with a couple of low-flying traveling shots that add drama to the danger and uncertainty of the sequence. Hand-drawn two-dimensional characters as well as some background elements were applied to three-dimensional billboards in order to populate scenes in this movie. The 1999 production of *Tarzan* offered lush jungle environments created with Disney's proprietary software Deep Canvas to recreate 2D brushstrokes on three-dimensional geometry. Many of the procedural effects animation (including water) also add to the story. From the beginning the movie was produced keeping in mind that it would be released in theaters both as a film print and as a pioneer in the digital cinema, or D-cinema, projection technology. For that reason all the final frames in the film are 100 percent digital, including the 540 feet of rolling animated credits at the end of the movie.

1.4.10 Two of the main characters from the *Final Fantasy* videogame. (© 1998 Square Co., Ltd. All rights reserved.)

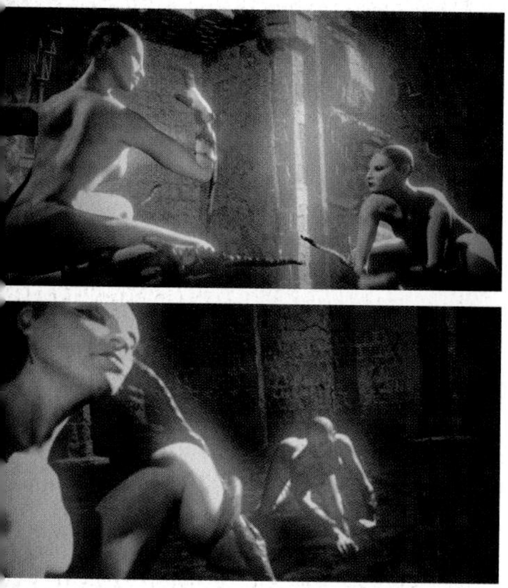

1.4.11 *Synchronicity* by Hans Uhlig was one of the earliest independent shorts to make extensive use of motion capture. (© 2000 Bay Vista Productions.)

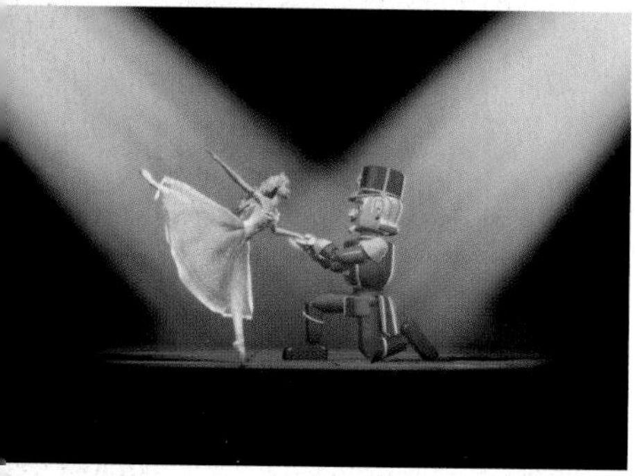

1.4.12 The Nutcracker and Barbie strike a pose in this scene from *Barbie in the Nutcracker*, a direct-to-video computer animated movie that combines motion capture with keyframe techniques. (BARBIE and associated trademarks and trade dress are owned by, and used with permission from, Mattel, Inc. © 2003 Mattel, Inc. All rights reserved.)

A couple of refinements and additions to the ratings systems took place during this decade. In 1990 the MPAA renamed their X rating to NC-17. In 1994 the Entertainment Software Ratings Board issued a ratings system for computer games, and a new system for rating television programs based on the existing MPAA categories was put in place in 1997 (Fig. 1.3.1).

Early 2000s

The early years of this decade witnessed growth in the quantity of movies incorporating visual effects as well as the total number and quality of effects shots per show. The statistics of ***Star Wars: Episode II***, for example, are impressive: 2,200 visual effects shots, 10,200 visual effects elements, 5 million frames, 929 animated shots, 20 different cuts of the movie, and a crew of over 250 digital artists who completed every day of the production the equivalent of one Man-Year of work. The choreography of the camera and the action is one of the most complex ever produced for a live action effects production. George Lucas, the director, also pushed to its limits the high-definition (HD) and bluescreen technologies available in 2002, proving that a feature movie can be made entirely with virtual sets, extensive previsualization, and compositing techniques. ***Spy Kids 2*** was another movie that followed with great results a smaller scale of the same production pipeline: shoot on HD taking advantage of greenscreen techniques, digitize the live action, create computer-generated visual effects, composite all elements using the digital intermediate process, and output to desired media (Figs. 2.4.1c and 13.1.1).

The first two installments of ***The Lord of the Rings*** (2001 and 2002) showcased stylized environments and creatures created with myriad effects techniques, ranging from in-camera effects to computer animation. Of special note are the eerie and emotionally convincing ***Gollum*** character (Fig. 12.2.7), the crowd animation system (Fig. 12.6.1), the superb color timing, and the fact that elements for the three episodes of this saga were shot simultaneously. The 2001 movie ***Pearl Harbor*** used massive amounts of computer-generated set extensions and props to replicate many of the ships and most of the airplanes. Billions of particles were also used to simulate the smoke and fire of bomb explosions. An effective rigid-body dynamics system was developed to make the crafts' explosions more real.

Because of the increased availability of high-quality visual effects this was also a period that saw a rise in the number of feature movies with excellent and subtle supporting visual effects that do not "carry the picture" but provide important accents to the storytelling. A few examples include the rain of frogs in ***Magnolia*** and the rose petals in ***American Beauty*** (1999), the boulder plunging into the swimming pool in ***Sexy Beast*** (2000), ***Amélie***'s visible heart (2001); and in 2002 the dream sequences in ***Frida***, Lechter removing the scalp in ***Hannibal***, and Adrien Brody's head digitally composited onto the body of a piano virtuoso in Polanski's ***The Pianist***.

Synchronicity was one of the first independent shorts to use motion capture techniques (Fig. 1.4.11). ***Final Fantasy*** marked the first attempt to create an entire animated feature movie with motion capture techniques (Figs. 5.5.13, and 9.2.4), and in spite of stunning visuals the commercial results were mixed. A pair of movies featuring ***Barbie*** also made use of motion capture techniques (Figs. 1.4.12 and 12.2.9). Five years in the making, Disney's ***Dinosaur*** blended live action backgrounds with computer-generated characters. Fox's ***Ice Age*** presented a mixture of slapstick comedy and drama in a beautifully rendered saga (page I and Fig. 10.5.11). DreamWorks' ***Spirit*** made innovative use of three-dimensional computer animation techniques and "cartoon-style" non-photorealistic rendering. Disney's ***Atlantis*** and ***Treasure Planet*** display spectacular integration of 2D and 3D animation techniques, but the latter fails to capture the interest of audiences during its initial release.

Partly because of the growth in quality and quantity in animation production the American Academy of Motion Picture Arts and Sciences (AMPAS) added a new category in 2001 for Best Animated Feature Movie in their yearly competition. DreamWorks' ***Shrek***, with its mixture of irreverent humor and unique stylized rendering, was the winner of the first award in this category (Figs. 2.4.4 and 12.3.7). Pixar's ***Monsters Inc.*** featured a green one-eyed monster, a blue-haired monster with 3 million hairs (Figs. 2.4.4 and 5.5.12), and a lovable girl. DNA's ***Jimmy Neutron Boy Genius*** proved that medium-size companies could deliver good-quality three-dimensional animation with off-the-shelf software, NewTek's Lightwave, and within reasonable budgets (Fig. 1.4.15). Japanese animation master Hayao Miyazaki's ***Spirited Away*** was the 2002 winner in this category (see the timetables at the end of this chapter for a listing of all nominated movies). A few years earlier the SIGGRAPH Conference also created the Best Animated Short and Jury Honors awards, which were won in 1999 by Chris Wedge's ***Bunny*** and Piotr Karwas' ***Masks*** respectively (Figs. 10.1.1 and 8.4.3); in 2000 by the cinematic opening in the ***Onimusha*** PS2 videogame (Fig. 12.7.4) and ***Stationen*** by Christian Sawade-Meyer; in 2001 by Van Phan's ***Values*** and Jason Wen's ***f8***; and in 2002 by Tomek Baginski's ***The Cathedral*** (Figs. 8.3.7 and 8.6.5) and ***Le Déserteur*** by Olivier Coulon, Aude Danset, Paolo de Lucia, and Ludovic Savonniere. The Visual Effects Society (www.ves.org) instituted in 2002 an awards program to recognize the different visual effects specialties (Fig. 1.4.14).

Computer animation and visual effects production was active and grew internationally during this period. The Spanish company Dygra, for example, completed ***El Bosque Animado***, the first European three-dimensional computer animated feature (Figs. 15.2.1 and 15.2.5). Paris-based Duran completed memorable supporting effects for ***Amélie*** and a number of music videos including ***It's Not the End of the World*** by the Super Furry Animals, and embarked in the production of ***La femme piège***, an all-computer animated feature based on the work of comic book and graphic novel artist Enki Bilal (Fig 4.2.6). ***Kaena, la***

1.4.13 More affordable digital technology and more qualified professionals have spawned visual effects companies throughout the world. (Images of *Duel* courtesy of Menfond. © China Star Entertainment Limited / Win's Entertainment Limited.)

The Visual Effects Society Award Categories

Visual Effects in an Effects Driven Motion Picture
Supporting Visual Effects in a Motion Picture
Visual Effects in a Television Miniseries, Movie, or Special
Visual Effects in a Television Series
Visual Effects in a Commercial
Visual Effects in a Music Video
Character Animation in a Live Action Motion Picture
Character Animation in a Live Action TV Program, Music Video, or Commercial
Character Animation in an Animated Motion Picture
Special Effects in a Motion Picture
Matte Painting in a Motion Picture
Matte Painting in a TV Program, Music Video, or Commercial
Models and Miniatures in a Motion Picture
Models and Miniatures in a TV Program, Video, or Commercial
Visual Effects Photography in a Motion Picture
Effects Art Direction in a Motion Picture
Effects Art Direction in a TV Program, Video, or Commercial
Compositing in a Motion Picture
Compositing in a TV Program, Music Video, or Commercial
Performance by an Actor in an Effects Film

1.4.14 The twenty new categories that the Visual Effects Society (VES) introduced in 2002 to recognize the visual effects work from a variety of creative fields and media (winners at www.ves.org).

1.4.15 Jimmy Neutron and friends having a snack. (© 2003 Viacom International Inc. All rights reserved. Nickelodeon, *The Adventures of Jimmy Neutron Boy Genius* and all related titles, logos and characters are trademarks of Viacom International Inc.)

Prophétie is another French computer animated feature scheduled for 2003 completion (Fig 8.3.11), as well as ***Free Jimmy*** by Norwegian AnimagicNet (Fig. 6.1.4). London-based Aardman Studios continued their relationship with DreamWorks, and newcomer Vanguard Animation struck a multi-picture distribution deal with Disney for several computer-animated features. Framestore and the Computer Film Company (CFC), also in London, merged in 2001 and created memorable TV commercials for Microsoft's X-Box and Levi's jeans (Figs. 9.8.4, 13.3.1 and 13.7.2). Hong Kong–based Menfond and Centro Pictures continued their innovative visual effects and computer animation work (Figs. 1.4.13 and 13.6.1).In spite of increased production during these years the industry also went through a series of ups-and-downs, with significant layoffs everywhere. Fox Studios sold VIFX to Rhythm and Hues, and Walt Disney Feature Animation closed The Secret Lab, its visual effects group. In New York City R/Greenberg Associates closed its computer animation and visual effects division, and London-based Mill Film, the company that won a 2000 AMPAS award for visual effects in ***Gladiator***, closed in 2002.

During the beginning of the decade most shows used computer technology in one way or another, and the next few years promise to be as active. As reported in the trade periodicals several animated feature films are in production as this book goes to press. The working titles of some of these animated projects at press time are ***Shrek 2, Sharkslayer, Madagascar,*** and ***Over the Hedge*** at DreamWorks/PDI; ***Bears, My Peoples, Chicken Little,*** and ***Home on the Range*** at Disney; Brad Bird's ***The Incredibles*** (2004) and John Lasseter's ***Cars*** (2005) at Pixar; and ***Robots*** at Blue Sky/Fox. Visual effects movies released or scheduled to be released during 2003 include ***Daredevil, The Hulk, Lara Croft: The Cradle of Life, The Lord of the Rings: The Return of The King, The Matrix: Reloaded, The Matrix: Revolutions, Charlie's Angels: Full Throttle, Terminator 3: Rise of the Machines, Haunted Mansion, Pirates of the Caribbean,*** and ***The League of Extraordinary Gentlemen.*** Other major visual effects movies in production, both at Sony Imageworks, include ***The Amazing Spiderman*** and Warner Bros.' ***Polar Express***, a movie based on extensive motion capture. Passion Pictures and Double Negative in London start production on a ***Captain Scarlet*** TV series.

The game industry continued its competition with movies as the premier form of entertainment, with multiplayer online games gaining acceptance. In 2001 ***Lara Croft Tomb Raider*** became the highest-grossing movie based on a videogame. Sony's ***EverQuest***, for example, launched in 1999 and reported hundreds of thousands users by 2003 (Fig. 4.7.2). Other multiplayer online games launched in 2002 include Electronic Arts' ***Ultima*** and ***Majestic***, and Maxis' ***The Simms. URU: Ages Beyond Myst***, the online version of the popular game, is slated to launch in 2003 (Fig. 4.7.3). The game platforms started to offer additional online services, and the new graphics cards for PCs fostered the development of innovative games by a wide number of developers and publishers. A few of the PC and platform games that gained critical recognition and or economic success during 2000

Timeline Categories

Visual Effects Movies

Animated 2D/3D Feature Movies

Independent Shorts

Video and Computer Games

Computer Technology and Industry Events

Related Technologies and Events

Television Programs

1.5.1 Color coding for each of the categories in the timeline charts on the following pages. In green are the live action feature movies with computer-generated visual effects. Winners of the AMPAS award for visual effects are marked with an asterisk, the runners-up are listed right next to it. Other VFX Movies includes the ones not nominated for an AMPAS award. In magenta are animated feature movies, most of which include three-dimensional computer animation. Independent productions and short computer animations are in blue boxes. Video, computer, and platform games are in brown. A selection of computer technology milestones and related industry and business events are grouped under red. A variety of related events and technologies and facts are indicated in yellow. Television animated series and a few related events are presented in deep blue.

include, for the PC ***Deus Ex*** by ION Storm Austin, ***The Sims*** by Maxis, ***Diablo II*** by Blizzard, and ***No One Lives Forever*** by Monolith; for the Dreamcast: ***Jet Grind Radio*** by Smilebit, ***Shenmue*** by Sega AM2, ***Samba de Amigo*** by SEGA Sonic Team, ***Seaman*** by Vivarium, and ***Crazy Taxi*** by Hitmaker; ***Spyro: Year of the Dragon*** by Insomniac for the PS2, and ***Legend of Zelda: Majora's Mask*** by Nintendo for the N64). In 2001 some of the games that received critical acclaim or public recognition include, for the Playstation 2: ***Grand Theft Auto III*** by DMA Design-Rockstar Games, ***Jak & Daxter: The Precursor Legacy*** (Fig. 7.4.6), ***Final Fantasy X*** by Square, ***Ico*** from Sony Computer Entertainment, ***Rez*** from United Game Artists, and Konami's ***Metal Gear Solid 2: Sons of Liberty***. For the X-Box, ***Halo: Combat Evolved*** by Bungie Studios, ***Cel Damage*** from Pseudo Interactive, and ***Oddworld: Munch's Oddysee*** (Fig. 7.6.2); for the PC: ***Max Payne*** from Remedy Entertainment, and Activision's ***Return to Castle Wolfenstein***; and ***Black & White*** from Lionhead Studios for Dreamcast (Fig. 7.3.2).

1.5 Timeline Charts

These timeline charts offer a chronological overview of the development of three-dimensional computer animation and related events during the last four decades of the twentieth century. The charts are limited to selected events and landmarks, and additional historical details can be found in the body of this chapter or at the website *www.artof3d.com.* To make the information easier to read I have organized the charts in five categories, explained in Figure 1.5.1.

1890s–1950s Timeline of Animation and Visual Effects

Categories
VFX Movies
Animated Fea
Independent S
Computer Ga
Technology /
Related Tech./
Television

1895...

- **The Execution of Mary, Queen of Scots**, 1895
- Lumiere Brothers' **Train Arriving at Station**, 1895
- George Méliès **A Trip to the Moon**, 1902
- Edwin Porter's **The Great Train Robbery**, 1903
- Winsor McCay's **Little Nemo** is first animated short, 1911
- Eastman Kodak provides **acetate film** to Edison for use in home kinetoscopes, 1912

1914...

- Winsor McCay's **Gertie The Dinosaur**, first short with live action and animation, 1914
- D. W. Griffith's **The Birth of a Nation**, 1915
- Max Fleischer invents **rotoscoping**, 1915
- Kodak introduces **16 mm** reversal film, 1923
- First Version of **The Thief of Bagdad**, 1924
- Willis O'Brien's animates dinosaurs in **The Lost World**, 1925
- Lang's **Metropolis, '26**

1927...

- **The Jazz Singer** first talkie film, 1927
- Disney's **Steamboat Willie** is first animated cartoon with synchronized sound, 1928
- **The Skeleton Dance** by Ub Iwerks, first Disney **Silly Symphony**, 1929
- Fleischer Brother's **Betty Boop**, 1930
- **TV set** patented, 1930
- **Frankenstein**, 1931
- Disney's **Flowers and Trees** is first color animated short, 1932

1932...

- Kodak's **8 mm** film and equipment, 1932
- **King Kong**, and **The Invisible Man**, 1933
- Fleischers' **Popeye the Sailor** debuts, 1933
- **The Bride of Frankenstein**, 1935
- **Things to Come**, 1936
- **Snow White and the Seven Dwarfs**, first animated feature, 1937
- Academy of Motion Picture Arts and Sciences creates Special Effects category, 1939

1939...

- VFX Movies 1939: **The Rains Came** * **Gone with the Wind** **Only Angels Have Wings** **The Private Lives of Elizabeth and Essex** **Topper Takes a Trip** **Union Pacific** **The Wizard of Oz**
- Fleischer Brothers' **Gulliver's Travels** and **Felix the Cat** 1939
- Disney's **Pinocchio**, and **Fantasia**, 1940

(* AMPAS Award Winners)

1940–41

- VFX Movies 1940: **The Thief of Bagdad** * 13 other finalists, incl.: **Dr. Cyclops** **Invisible Man Returns** **Rebecca** / **Typhoon** **Swiss Family Robinson**
- VFX Movies 1941: **I Wanted Wings** * 7 other finalists, incl.: **Flight Command** **The Invisible Woman** **The Sea Wolf** Other Movies w/VFX: **Citizen Kane**

1941–42

- Disney's **Dumbo, 1941**
- **Superman** animated series debuts with a 9 minute episode, 1941
- VFX Movies 1942: **Reap the Wild Wind** * 9 other finalists, incl.: **The Black Swan** **Flying Tigers** **One of our Aircraft is Missing** **Invisible Agent**

1942–43

- Disney's **Bambi**, 1942
- Paul Terry creates **Mighty Mouse** as a **Superman** spoof, 1942
- VFX Movies 1943: **Crash Dive** * 5 other finalists, incl.: **Air Force** **Bombardier** **The North Star**
- Disney's **Saludos Amigos**, 1943

1944–45

- VFX Movies 1944: **Thirty Seconds Over Tokyo** * 6 other finalists, incl.: **The Adventures of Mark Twain** **Secret Command**
- VFX Movies 1945: **Wonder Man** * **Captain Eddie** **Spellbound** **They Were Expendable** **A Thousand and One Nights**

1945–47

- Disney's **The Three Caballeros**, 1945
- VFX Movies 1946: **Blithe Spirit** * **A Stolen Life**
- VFX Movies 1947: **Green Dolphin Street** * **Unconquered**
- Disney's **Make Mine Music**, 1946
- Disney's **Fun and Fancy Free**, 1947

1948–49

- VFX Movies 1948: **Portrait of Jennie** * **Deep Waters**
- Disney's **Melody Time**, 1948
- VFX Movies 1949: **Mighty Joe Young** * **Tulsa**
- Disney's **The Adventures of Ichabod and Mr. Toad**, 1949

1950–52

- VFX Movies 1950: **Destination Moon** * **Samson and Delilah**
- VFX Movies 1951: **When Worlds Collide** * (only nominee)
- Disney's **Cinderella**, 1950
- Disney's **Alice in Wonderland**, 1951
- VFX Movies 1952: **Plymouth Adventure** * (only nominee)

1953–55

- VFX Movies 1953: **War of the Worlds** * (only nominee)
- Disney's **Peter Pan**, 1953
- VFX Movies 1954: **20,000 Leagues Under the Sea** * **Hell and High Water** **Them!** Other Movies w/VFX: **Gojira (Godzilla)**

1955–57

- VFX Movies 1955: **The Bridges At Toko-Ri** * **The Dam Busters** **The Rains of Ranchipur**
- Disney's **Lady and the Tramp**, 1955
- VFX Movies 1956: **The Ten Commandments** * **Forbidden Planet**
- VFX Movies 1957: **The Enemy Below** * **The Spirit of St. Louis**

1958–59

- VFX Movies 1958: **Tom Thumb** * **Torpedo Run** Other Movies w/VFX: **Vertigo**
- VFX Movies 1959: **Ben Hur** * **Journey to the Center of the Earth**
- Disney's **Sleeping Beauty**, 1959
- Ub Iwerks improves **optical film printer** to shoot successive exposures, 1959

1960s Timeline of Animation and Visual Effects

Categories
VFX Movies
ated Features
endent Shorts
nputer Games
ology / Events
Tech./Events
Television

1960

Visual Effects Movies:
The Time Machine *
The Last Voyage
Other Movies w/VFX:
Psycho
Spartacus

John McCarthy develops the **LISP** programming language for artificial intelligence applications.

Kodak introduces the **Ektachrome 7386** reversal print film stock.

Warner Bros.' (WB) **The Bugs Bunny Show** animated series debuts on ABC primetime.

Hanna-Barbera's **The Flintstones** is the first animated series to debut on primetime TV (ABC, 166 episodes).

1961

Visual Effects Movies:
The Guns of Navarone *
The Absent Minded Professor

Disney's **One Hundred and One Dalmatians**

John Whitney's **Catalog**, 16mm, 7min.

Fairchild Camera and Semiconductor Instrument manufactures the first integrated circuit on a chip.

Hanna-Barbera's **Top Cat** animated series debuts on ABC.

1962

Visual Effects Movies:
The Longest Days *
Mutiny on the Bounty
Other Movies w/VFX:
Dr. No (first 007 film)

Sketchpad system for interactive computer graphics developed by Ivan Sutherland at MIT.

MIT students Slug Russell, Shag Graetz, and Alan Kotok create **SpaceWar!** the first interactive computer game on a DEC PDP-1.

Mr. Computer Image ABC, created by Lee Harrison III with the Scanimate System.

Hanna-Barbera's futuristic **The Jetsons** animated series debuts on ABC (24 episodes).

1963

Visual Effects Movies:
Cleopatra *
The Birds
Other Movies w/VFX:
Jason and the Argonauts

The stop-motion skeletons animated by Ray Harryhausen in **Jason and the Argonauts** become effects classic.

Disney's **The Sword in the Stone**

John Whitney's **Lapis**, 16mm, 8min.

IBM introduces the 360 models, the first family of computers, a Fortran-based time-sharing system.

Polaroid introduces instant color film.

1964

Visual Effects Movies:
Mary Poppins *
7 Faces of Dr. Lao

Mary Poppins live action movie with 2D animated sequences.

Atboftb Carrier Landing, a 3D animation with plotted drawings by William Fetter and W. Bernhart at Boeing in Seattle

Thomas Kurtz and John Kemeny develop the **BASIC** programming language.

Instant replay and slow motion debut on televised sports.

Hanna-Barbera's science-fiction action-adventure **Jonny Quest** series debuts on ABC (26 episodes).

1965

Visual Effects Movies:
Thunderball *
The Greatest Story Ever Told

Stereo computer animations by Michael Noll and Bela Julesz at Bell Laboratories

Kodak introduces **Super 8 mm**, a new amateur film format.

Charlie Brown's Christmas debuts as the first animated special on television.

The Thunderbirds series breaks new ground in marionette TV animation.

1966

Visual Effects Movies:
Fantastic Voyage *
Hawaii
Other Movies w/VFX:
One Million Years B.C.

Hummingbird by Charles Csuri, first examples of computer-generated representational animation

Final episode of the original **The Flintstones** series airs.

1967

Visual Effects Movies:
Doctor Dolittle *
Tobruk

Disney's **The Jungle Book**

Cockpit Simulation by William Fetter at Boeing has a 3D computer-animated human.

Artist R. Rauschenberg and Bell Labs physicist Billy Klüver found **Experiments in Art and Technology** in N.Y.C.

Hanna-Barbera's **The Fantastic Four** and **Shazzan** debut on ABC.

Marvel Comics' **Spiderman** animated series debuts on ABC.

52 animated episodes of animé **Speed Racer** dubbed to English.

1968

Visual Effects Movies:
2001: A Space Odyssey *
Ice Station Zebra
Other VFX Films:
Planet of the Apes

The Yellow Submarine by George Dunning presents a radically new visual style.

Permutations by John Whitney

Evans & Sutherland opens.

The Motion Picture Producers of America's (MPPA) new movie **rating system**.

Kodak introduces **Eastman 5249** color reversal intermediate film, for a one-step duplicate of original.

1969

Visual Effects Movies:
Marooned *
Krakatoa, East of Java

A Boy Named Charlie Brown, by B. Melendez

Pas De Deux, by Norman McLaren

Sony's 3/4 in. **U-matic** video cassette

Kenneth Thompson and Dennis Ritchie develop **UNIX** at AT&T Bell Laboratories.

Warnock's area subdivision hidden surface removal algorithm

Hanna-Barbera releases the **Scooby-Doo Where are You!** series.

The **Pink Panther Show** animated series debuts on NBC.

1970s Timeline of Computer Animation and Visual Effects

1970

Visual Effects Movies:
Tora! Tora! Tora! *
Patton
Other Movies w/VFX:
Airport
M*A*S*H

Minicomputers are this decade's tool of choice for 3D computer animation, including Digital Equipmrent Corporations's PDP and VAX models.

Watkins' **scan line** hidden surface removal

IMAX projection premieres at the Osaka Expo 70 in Japan.

1971

Visual Effects Movies:
Bedknobs and Broomsticks *
When Dinosaurs Ruled the Earth
Other Movies w/VFX:
Silent Running

Fritz the Cat by Ralph Bakshi

Animated Faces, by Fred I. Parke at University of Utah

Robert Abel & Associates opens.

Intel releases its 4-bit **4004** microprocessor.

IBM invents the 8 in. floppy diskette.

Dolby techniques reduce noise in recorded sound in Kubrick's **A Clockwork Orange.**

1972

Visual Effects Movies:
The Poseidon Adventure *
(only nominee)

Heavy Traffic by Ralph Bakshi

Atari releases **Pong** arcade game.

MAGI animates computer-rendered polygonal objects.

Newell's **depth sort** hidden surface removal

Intel releases 8-bit **8008** microprocessor.

Polaroid's **SX-70 camera** brings one-step instant photography.

Phillips and MCA demonstrate **videodisc** recorder and player system.

1973

(No AMPAS Visual Effects Award given this year).
Visual Effects Movies:
The Exorcist
Westworld

The Savage Planet by René Laloux

Warner Bros. and Hanna-Barbera's **Charlotte's Web**

Hanna-Barbera releases **The Adams Family** animated TV series.

Cable TV goes into the mainstream during this decade.

1974

Visual Effects Movies:
Earthquake *
(only nominee)
Other Movies w/VFX:
Chinatown
The Towering Inferno
Young Frankenstein

Hunger by Peter Foldes, National Film Board of Canada.

Intel and Zilog release the **Intel 8080** microprocessor.

The first **SIGGRAPH** conference is held in Boulder, Colorado, with 600 attendees.

Technicolor stops U.S. production of **dye-transfer** film prints.

1975

Visual Effects Movies:
The Hindenburg *
(only nominee)
Other Movies w/VFX:
Jaws

Sony introduces the **Betamax** videotape format.

The University of Utah becomes a center of innovative research in computer graphics.

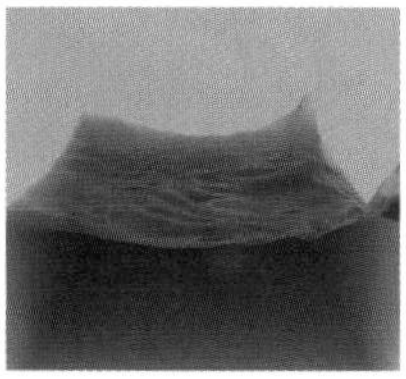

1976

Visual Effects Movies:
King Kong *
and **Logan's Run** *
(dual award)

Shugart Associates develops the 5.25 in. **floppy diskette**.

The 64-bit **Cray I** supercomputer solves 166 million floating point operations per second.

Steve Wozniak designs the **Apple I.**

The **Steadicam**, a camera stabilizing system, used for the first time in the film **Rocky**.

Canon's **AE-1** is first 35mm film still camera with built-in microprocessor.

1977

Visual Effects Movies:
Star Wars *
Close Encounters of the Third Kind
Other Movies w/VFX:
Airport '77
The Spy Who Loved Me

Voyager animated simulations of space exploration by Jim Blinn at Jet Propulsion Lab.

Atari introduces its **VCS 2600** videogame home system.

The **Apple II** microcomputer is released.

Radio Shack's releases its **TRS-80** computer.

Matsushita releases **VHS** (Video Home System) videotape format.

1978

Visual Effects Movies:
Superman *
(only nominee)
Other Movies w/VFX:
Capricorn One

The Lord of the Rings by Ralph Bakshi

Midway imports Taito's **Space Invaders** arcade game into U.S.

Digital Equipment releases the **VAX 11/780** minicomputer.

Artist **Leroy Neiman** uses a CG system to create 2D images in real-time during the CBS broadcast of the Super Bowl.

1979

Visual Effects Movies:
Alien *
The Black Hole
Moonraker / **1941**
Star Trek–The Motion Picture
Other Movies w/VFX:
Apocalypse Now

Galaxy Express 999, animé by Rintaro and Kon Ichikawa

Hayao Miyazaki's **The Castle of Cagliostro**.

Atari releases **Asteroids** arcade game.

Motorola releases 32-bit **68000** processor.

Voyager 2 visualizations by James Blinn at the Jet Propulsion Lab

Digital Effects opens in New York. Computer group starts at **ILM**.

Early 1980s Timeline of Computer Animation and Visual Effects

Categories
VFX Movies
ated Features
endent Shorts
nputer Games
ology / Events
Tech./Events
Television

1980

Visual Effects Movies:
The Empire Strikes Back *
(only nominee)
Other Movies w/VFX:
Escape from New York
Battle Beyond the Stars
Xanadu

The Empire Strikes Back takes "effects movies" to a new level of complexity and accomplishment.

Paul Grimault's **Le roi et l'oiseaux** (The King and Mr. Bird).

Vol Libre, animation of fractal landscapes by Loren Carpenter

Atari releases **Space Invaders** for its VCS 2600 system.

Namco releases **Pac Man**, most popular arcade game ever.

Seagate Technology releases **hard disks** for microcomputers.

Pacific Data Images (PDI) opens.

Pioneer markets their **videodisc players**.

Microcomputers become popular during this decade.

1981

Visual Effects Movies:
Raiders of the Lost Ark *
Dragonslayer
Other Movies w/VFX:
An American Werewolf in London
Clash of the Titans
Looker

Looker, becomes first film featuring the first virtual actor, "Cindy," made from simulated body scans of actress Susan Dey.

The Secret of Nimh, by Bluth Productions

American Pop by Ralph Bakshi

Philips develops the optical **CD-ROM**.

IBM releases its 8088-based **PC computer** with the MS-DOS operating system.

Sony introduces 3.5 in. diskettes.

Adam Osborne develops the 24 lb. **Osborne I**, the first portable computer.

Wavefront opens in Santa Barbara. **Digital Productions** opens in L.A. **R/Greenberg Associates** (RGA) opens in New York.

Quantel introduces its **Paintbox** digital paint system.

MTV goes live on cable television.

Hanna-Barbera's **The Smurfs** series debuts on NBC.

(Images courtesy of Areté Entertainment, Inc.)

1982

Visual Effects Movies:
E.T. the Extra-Terrestrial *
Blade Runner
Poltergeist
Other Movies w/VFX:
Firefox
Star Trek II–The Wrath of Kahn
TRON

TRON is first live action film with over 20 minutes of 3D computer animation.

ILM's **Genesis Effect** created for **Star Trek II**, is the first all computer-animated visual effects movie shot.

Jim Henson creates **The Dark Crystal** with puppetry, stop motion and animatronics.

Le maitres du temps by René Laloux

Carla's Island by Nelson Max at the Lawrence Livermore National Lab

SubLogic develops the **Microsoft Flight Simulator** computer game for the Apple II, later for the PC.

Silicon Graphics (SGI) opens. **Alias Research** and **Omnibus Computer Graphics** open in Toronto.

Non-Edge Cloud and Smoke Simulations by Geoffrey Gardner at Grumman Data Systems

CT5 Flight Simulator by Evans & Sutherland

Canon demonstrates first **electronic still camera**.

1983

Visual Effects Movies:
Return of the Jedi *
(only nominee)
Octopussy

Fire and Ice by Ralph Bakshi.

Growth: Mysterious Galaxy, the first in a series of semi-abstract animations by artist-programmer Yoichiro Kawaguchi.

Arcade game **Dragon's Lair**, animated by Don Bluth, first to use laserdisc technology.

The inexpensive **Commodore 64** computer outperforms videogame consoles.

Compaq introduces the first **PC-clone** computer.

SGI introduces the **IRIS 1000** terminal based on a Motorola 68000 with 10 or 12 **Geometry Engines**.

Tippett Studios opens in Berkley, **Polygon Pictures** in Tokyo.

During the mid-1980s commercial production is led by Pacific Data Images (PDI), Digital Productions, Cranston-Csuri, Sogitec, Toyo Links and Omnibus.

MIDI (Musical Instrument Digital Interface) introduced by electronic instrument manufacturers.

1984

Visual Effects Movies:
Indiana Jones and the Temple of Doom *
Ghostbusters
2010

Nausicaä of the Valley of the Wind by Hayao Miyazaki.

Bio-Sensor created at Osaka University and Toyo Links, is an early example of modeling with blobby surfaces and figure locomotion.

Still Life Etude, an early simulation of light, fog, rain, and skies created at Hiroshima University.

Trailer for **The Works**, an unfinished New York Institute of Technology movie.

Apple Computer releases the **Macintosh**.

Pixar opens its doors.

IBM releases its 80286-based **PC-AT**.

MPPA rating system is expanded to include a **PG-13** category.

Hanna-Barbera's **The New Scooby-Doo Mysteries** TV series debuts on ABC.

Herbie Hancock's music video **Rockit** receives Best Special Effects award at MTV's first Video Music Awards.

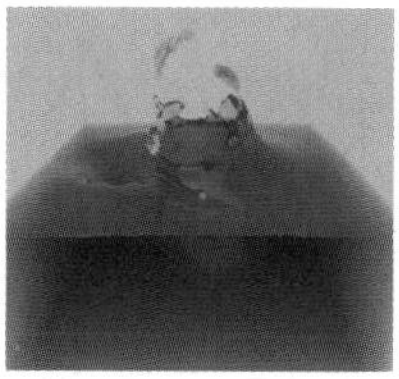

Late 1980s Timeline of Computer Animation and Visual Effects

1985

Visual Effects Movies:
Cocoon *
Return to Oz
Young Sherlock Holmes
Other VFX Movies:
The Last Starfighter
Back to the Future

The Last Starfighter created with a Cray supercomputer at Digital Productions, first live action feature film with realistic computer animation.

The Black Cauldron, first Disney animated feature film to use 3D CG technology

Brilliance commercial by Abel and Associates features sexy female robot with convincing realistic motion.

Growth III by Yoichiro Kawaguchi

Tony de Peltrie by Pierre Lachapelle and team.

U.S. release of 8-bit **Nintendo Entertainment System (NES)** with Super Mario Brothers.

SEGA releases 8-bit **Master** game system.

Kleiser-Walczak opens. **Digital Effects** closes. **The Moving Picture Co.** starts 3D production in London.

Bell Labs' Bjarne Stoustrup develops **C++** prog. language.

First wave of user-friendly 3D computer animation software.

The National Science Foundation creates **NSFNET,** a 56 Kbps network (future Internet), for research and academic work.

1986

Visual Effects Movies:
Aliens *
Little Shop of Horrors
Other VFX Movies:
Flight of the Navigator

In Disney's **The Great Mouse Detective** the moving gears in the chase sequence are created with 3D computer animation.

Laputa: Castle in the Sky by H. Miyazaki

An American Tail by Don Bluth

Jim Henson's **Labyrinth**

John Lasseter's **Luxo Jr.** nominated in AMPAS Animated Short Films category.

The still image **Road to Point Reyes** redefines realism by compositing graftals and fractals to portray a landscape.

Visitor on a Foggy Night by the CG Research Group at Hiroshima University

Softimage opens in Montreal, **Mac Guff Ligne** in Paris, **VIFX** in L.A., and **Framestore** in London. **Omnibus** declares bankruptcy.

Intel releases the 32-bit, 4-million-operations-per-second **Intel 80386** microprocessor.

SGI introduces the **IRIS 3000** series, with a MIPS single processor, and a 10 MHz **Geometry Engine**.

Quantel introduces component digital video processing with the **Harry** system.

1987

Visual Effects Movies:
Innerspace *
Predator

Akira by Katsuhiro Otomo popularizes animé, feature-length sci-fi Japanese animation, with international audiences.

Stanley and Stella: Breaking the Ice by Symbolics Graphics and Whitney Demo Productions, early flock animation

Red's Dream by Pixar

Baloon Guy by Chris Wedge at Ohio State University

Rendezvous in Montreal by Nadia Magnenant Thalmann and team.

Nintendo releases **Legend of Zelda** NES cartridge in the U.S.

Blue Sky Studios opens in New York, **Side Effects Software** (SESI) in Toronto.

Research in the simulation of natural-looking hair and fur, rigid body dynamics, and modeling fabric with visible threads starts in the late 1980s.

Bill Atkinson at Apple Computer develops **Hypercard** as an interactive software development tool.

Hanna-Barbera releases 13 new episodes of **Jonny Quest**.

1988

Visual Effects Movies:
Who Framed Roger Rabbit *
Die Hard
Willow

Who Framed Roger Rabbit breaks new ground by combining live actors with animated characters.

Many cars in Disney's **Oliver & Company** are 3D CGI models.

My Neighbor Totoro by Hayao Miyazaki

Stop motion, puppetry and live action in Jan Svankmajer's **Alice**

The Land Before Time by Don Bluth

Graveyard of the Fireflies by animé director Isao Takahata

Pixar's **Tin Toy** by John Lasseter and William Reeves wins AMPAS award.

Technological Threat by William Kroyer and Brian Jennings

Locomotion, a Pacific Data Images short, early example of 3D squash-and-stretch.

Nintendo releases portable **Game Boy** at 140 × 120 pixels, 2.14 MHz, with **Tetris** game.

RenderMan shading language released and awarded U.S. patent.

NAMCO purchases the Japan Computer Graphics Lab.

The Sky, simulations of light and skies at Hiroshima University.

Waldo C. Graphic animated in real time for the **Jim Henson Hour**.

1989

Visual Effects Movies:
The Abyss *
The Adventures of Baron Munchausen
Back to the Future Part II
Other VFX Movies:
Indiana Jones and the Last Crusade
Field of Dreams
Ghostbusters II

The Abyss includes first convincing 3D character animation.

The Little Mermaid is Disney's last film to use traditional ink and paint, CG closing shot.

Kiki's Delivery Service by Hayao Miyazaki opens in Japan.

All Dogs Go to Heaven by Don Bluth

Knickknack by Pixar, **Don't Touch Me** by Kleiser-Walczak, early motion capture character animation

Preview of NYIT's **The Works, The Little Death** by Matt Elson at Symbolics, **Eurythmy** by Susan Amkraut and Michael Girard

SEGA releases 16-bit **Genesis** game system.

Maxis releases **SimCity**.

Intel releases its 32-bit **80486** microprocessor.

CA Scanline opens. Sogitec and TDI merge into **Ex Machina.**

Letraset releases **Color Studio** image retouching software for Macs.

Matt Groening's **The Simpsons** TV debut.

Categories
VFX Movies
Animated Fe
Independent
Computer Ga
Technology /
Related Tech
Television

Early 1990s Timeline of Computer Animation and Visual Effects

1990

Visual Effects Movies:
Total Recall *
(only nominee)
Other VFX Movies:
Back to the Future III
Die Hard 2: Die Harder
Dick Tracy
Ghost
The Hunt for Red October

Disney's **The Rescuers Down Under**, first Disney animated feature film done entirely with the first version of the CAPS System

Hanna-Barbera's **Jetsons: The Movie** includes computer-animated vehicles and environments.

Karl Sims' **Panspermia**, early particle systems computer animation.

Origin Systems releases **Wing Commander**, a cinematic space adventure PC game.

Nintendo releases **Super Mario 3**, the all-time best-selling video-game cartridge.

Santa Barbara Studios opens in Los Angeles, **The Mill** in London.

NewTek's **Lightwave** software bundled with "Toaster" hardware.

Adobe releases **Photoshop** for Apple Macintosh computers.

Tim Berners-Lee at CERN develops the HyperText Markup Language (**HTML**).

MPAA renames their X rating to **NC-17** (No one 17 and Under).

Warner Bros. releases **Steven Speilberg's Tiny Toon Adventures** animated series.

1991

Visual Effects Movies:
Terminator II: Judgment Day *
Backdraft
Hook
Other VFX Movies:
Star Trek VI

Terminator II is the first mainstream blockbuster movie with multiple morphing effects and simulated natural human motion.

The animated camera in Disney's **Beauty and The Beast** travels in 3D space; first animated film nominated for AMPAS Best Picture.

Mutations by William Latham and IBM UK
Don Quichotte by Video System uses keyframe character animation techniques.

Primordial Dance by Karl Sims uses particles.
Leaf Magic by Alan Norton uses motion dynamics animation.

U.S. release of 16-bit **Super Nintendo Entertainment System (SNES)** with real-time scaling, transparency.

Spectrum Holobyte's **Falcon**, multiplayer jet combat simulation game. Capcom's **Street Fighter II** arcade game.

Motorola's 32-bit **68040** microprocessor.

Apple Computer releases **QuickTime.**

LINUX v. 0.01 Open Source OS released to Net by Linus Torvalds.

Kodak's **Professional Digital Camera System**

Peter Greenaway's **Prospero's Books** integrates windows with traditional film editing.

1992

Visual Effects Movies:
Death Becomes Her *
Aliens 3
Batman Returns
Other VFX Movies:
Bram Stoker's Dracula
The Lawnmower Man

Early 1990s defined by succesful revival of live action feature movies with visual effects.

Aladdin is Disney's first use of fully computer-animated character and 3D organic surfaces.

Porco Rosso by Hayao Miyazaki

Kroyer Films' hand-drawn **Fern Gully... The Last Rainforest** uses edge-detection filters to draw outlines around 3D objects.

Cool World by Ralph Bakshi

Liquid Selves, particle systems animation by Karl Sims

The Seven Wonders of the World by Electric Images pushes the boundaries of architectural visualization.

Foundation Imaging and **Sony Imageworks** open.

SimmGraphics' facial motion capture system **Facetracker** used to animate **Super Mario**.

NSFNET upgrades to 45 Mbps **T-3** lines.

Warner Bros. releases the **Steven Speilberg Presents Animaniacs** series.

Warner Bros. releases **Batman: The Animated Series.**

1993

Visual Effects Movies:
Jurassic Park *
Cliffhanger
The Nightmare Before Christmas
Other VFX Movies:
The Fugitive

Jurassic Park sets new standards for realism, inverse kinematics and digital compositing.

Tim Burton's **The Nightmare Before Christmas** takes stop motion to new heights and becomes a classic.

Computer animation for **Babylon 5** TV series is produced with off-the-shelf microcomputer systems.

First **Polar Bears** commercial for Coca-Cola by Rhythm & Hues.

Myst pushes the limits of a CD-ROM interactive visual experience.

George Romero and id Software release **Doom**. First-person shooting games are forever changed.

Pixar receives an AMPAS Technical Award for RenderMan.

Adobe releases Windows **Photoshop**.

SGI unveils the **Onyx** with **Reality Engine2** and VTX graphics, with 2 to 24 MIPS R-4400 processors.

Digital Domain and **WETA** open.

Cartoon Network goes live on cable TV with **Moxy**, an early real-time virtual TV host.

WB releases the **Two Stupid Dogs** series.

1994

Visual Effects Movies:
Forrest Gump *
The Mask
True Lies
Other VFX Movies:
The Flintstones
Speed

The wildebeest stampede in Disney's **The Lion King** is a tour de force in the integration of traditional with 3D computer animation.

Jan Svankmajer's **Faust**

Thumbelina by Don Bluth

Listerine Arrows TV commercial by Pixar

Sony's **Playstation** and SEGA's **Saturn** 32-bit platforms are introduced in Japan (U.S. in '95), reinvigorate electronic game industry.

Immersion, an early experiment in image-based rendering

Supermicrocomputers, or workstations, based on 32-bit or 64-bit CISC and RISC processors gain popularity early in the decade.

Apple releases **PowerPC** computers.

NewTek starts selling **Lightwave** as stand-alone software.

The Entertainment Software Rating Board issues **rating categories** for video and computer games.

DVD format debuts.

Late 1990s Timeline of Computer Animation and Visual Effects

1995

Visual Effects Movies:
Babe *
Apollo 13
Other VFX Movies:
Batman Forever
Casper / **Congo**
La Cité des enfants perdus
Crimson Tide
Goldeneye
Judge Dredd
Jumanji / **Stargate**
Species
Twelve Monkeys
Waterworld

Toy Story is first fully 3D computer-animated feature movie.

The canoe and Mother Willow sequences in Disney's **Pocahontas** created with 3D CG.

Mamoru Oshii's **Ghost in the Shell** (U.S in '98)

First-person point of view animation in New Wave's LBE **The Volcano Mine**

Dance Fever commercial for Shell Oil by R/GA squashes and stretches cartoon cars.

Chris Landreth's **the end**

id Software releases online game **Quake.**

Nintendo 64 64-bit platform introduced in Japan (U.S. in '96).

Sparx* opens in Paris, **Blur** in Los Angeles. SGI buys **Alias/Wavefront**.

The **Internet** becomes a self-supporting commercial operation.

Warner Bros. releases the **Pinky and the Brain** TV series.

DV videotape format introduced by consortium of 55 companies.

MPEG-2 format and spec published.

1996

Visual Effects Movies:
Independence Day *
Dragonheart
Twister
Other VFX Movies:
Mission Impossible
The Rock
Star Trek: First Contact

James and the Giant Peach combines stop motion and computer animation techniques.

Disney's **Hunchback of Notre Dame** has 3D confetti, crowds, and architectural details.

Warner Bros.'s **Space Jam** features the Loony Tunes characters.

The Fight by Acclaim Entertainment proves viability of mocap for character animation.

Joe's Apartment Roach Rally by Blue Sky Productions.

Nintendo's **Super Mario 64** (N64), Capcom's **Resident Evil** (PS), Namco's arcade **Soul Edge**. Core Design's **Tomb Raider**.

Dreamworks buys an interest in **Pacific Data Images**. Disney buys **Dream Quest Images.** Fox purchases **VIFX**.

Microsoft releases **Windows 95.**

Visual Effects Society (VES) is founded.

Hanna-Barbera's **Dexter's Laboratory** and **The Real Adventures of Jonny Quest** series debut on Cartoon Network.

Warner Bros. releases **Superman** series.

1997

Visual Effects Movies:
Titanic *
The Lost World: Jurassic Park
Starship Troopers
Other VFX Movies:
Air Force One
Alien: Resurrection
Batman & Robin
Con Air / **Contact**
Dante's Peak
The Fifth Element
Flubber
Mars Attacks!
Men in Black
Spawn / **Volcano**

Princess Mononoke by Hayao Miyazaki opens in Japan (U.S in '99).

Hydra sequence and morphed clouds in Disney's **Hercules**.

Fox's **Anastasia** by Don Bluth

I Married a Strange Person by Bill Plympton

Pixar's **Geri's Game** by Jan Pinkava wins AMPAS award, with subdivision surfaces.

Virtual Andre commercial by Digital Domain uses mocap.

Great animation in Namco's **Soulblade** weapon-fighting game.

Activision's **Mech Warrior** (PS). Rare's **Golden Eye 007** (N64). Capcom's **Street Fighter III** and Namco's **Tekken III** to arcades.

NVIDIA launches a 128-bit Direct3D processor.

Sony introduces **HDCAM** format.

South Park and **King of the Hill** premiere on MTV and Fox. HB's **Cow and Chicken** and **Johnny Bravo** debut on Cartoon Network.

Mainframe's **ReBoot** is early all-CG TV series.

1998

Visual Effects Movies:
What Dreams May Come *
Mighty Joe Young
Armageddon
Other VFX Movies:
Deep Impact
Deep Rising
Godzilla
Lost in Space
Mouse Hunt
Pleasantville
Small Soldiers
Sphere
X-Files: The Movie

Disney/Pixar's **A Bug's Life** and DreamWorks/PDI's **ANTZ** present all-CG insect worlds.

CG Hun crowd simulation and props in Disney's **Mulan**.

DreamWorks' **Prince of Egypt** with stylized characters and superb effects animation.

Nickelodeon's low-budget **Rugrats Movie** is box-office success.

Kirikou et la Sorcière, by Michel Ocelot, signals revival of French animated features.

Chris Wedge's **Bunny** at Blue Sky Studios wins Animated Short AMPAS Award.

Bingo by Chris Landreth explores neo-Dada theatre. IMAX-LBE **Race For Atlantis** animated by Rhythm & Hues.

Namco's **Tekken 3** (PS), Nintendo's **Legend of Zelda: Ocarina of Time** (N64), **Quake 2** for PC.

Double Negative opens in London.

Rolie Polie Olie all-CG 3D series premieres.

Hanna-Barbera's **The Powerpuff Girls** debut on Cartoon Network.

Kodak's **SFX 200T** film

1999

Visual Effects Movies:
The Matrix *
Star Wars Episode I– The Phantom Menace
Stuart Little
Other VFX Movies:
End of Days
Fight Club
The Mummy
Sleepy Hollow
Wild Wild West

2D brushstokes recreated on 3D geometry in Disney's **Tarzan**.

Toy Story 2 takes Buzz and Woody to new levels of comedic and technical achievement.

Disney's **Fantasia 2000** in IMAX, with 3D CG.

Fresh animation style and NPR rendering in Brad Bird's **Iron Giant.**

Le Château des Singes, by Jean-F. Laguionie.

South Park: Bigger, Longer & Uncut, uses 3D billboard technique.

Daniel Robichaud's **Tightrope**, playful jester confronts suit.

Bjork's **All is Full of Love** music video.

NPR rendering and surreal comedy of spatial errors in PDI's **Fishing** and **Spatial Frames**

Fiat Lux by Paul Debevec, a landmark in image-based rendering

Piotr Karwas' **The Mask** receives first SIGGRAPH Jury Honors award.

SGI's **Pentium** workstations. **Discreet** opens.

Futurama animated series debut on Fox.

Framestore's **Walking with Dinosaurs**.

Star Wars: Episode I, Tarzan, and Miramax's **An Ideal Husband**, early digital cinema.

Early 2000s Timeline of Computer Animation and Visual Effects

2000

Visual Effects Movies:
Gladiator *
Hollow Man
The Perfect Storm
Other VFX Movies:
102 Dalmatians
The Adventures of Rocky & Bullwinkle
Cast Away
The Cell / **Dinosaur**
Dr. Seuss' How the Grinch Stole Christmas
Mission: Impossible 2
Mission to Mars
O Brother Where Art Thou?
Pitch Black
Red Planet / **X-Men**

Disney's **Dinosaur** combines live action backgrounds with realistic 3D computer animated characters.

Aardman Sudio's/ DreamWorks stop motion **Chicken Run**

DreamWorks' **The Road to El Dorado**

Fox's **Titan A.E.** by Don Bluth

Disney's **Emperor's New Groove** and **The Tigger Movie**

Nickelodeon's **Rugrats in Paris**

Pixar's **For the Birds** by Ralph Eggleston wins AMPAS award.

Onimusha is Best Animated Short at SIGGRAPH 2000.

Victor Navone's **Alien Song** is widely viewed on the Web.

Debut of **Playstation 2**, **X-Box**, and **Gamecube**.

Intel's **Pentium 4** debuts at 1.5 GHz.

NVIDIA's **GeForce2**, per-pixel shading GPU.

2001

Visual Effects Movies:
The Lord of the Rings: The Fellowship of the Ring *
Artificial Intelligence
Pearl Harbor
Other VFX Movies:
Black Hawk Down
Cats & Dogs
Enemy at the Gates
Evolution
The Fast and the Furious
Harry Potter and the Sorcerer's Stone
Jurassic Park III
Lara Croft Tomb Raider
Monkeybone
The Mummy Returns
Planet of the Apes
Spy Kids
Swordfish

The AMPAS creates new category for Best Animated Feature.

Animated Movies: '01
Shrek *
Jimmy Neutron Boy Genius
Monsters Inc.
Other:
Atlantis: The Lost Empire
Final Fantasy: The Spirits Within
Marco Polo: Return to Xanadu
Mutant Aliens
Osmosis Jones
The Prince of Light
Recess: School's Out
The Trumpet of the Swan
Waking Life

Shrek combines irreverent comedy with cutting-edge rendering, wins AMPAS Animated Feature first award.

Pixar's **Monsters Inc.** story turns the tables on who scares who.

Metropolis, animé directed by Rintaro

2001 (cont.)

Nickelodeon's **Jimmy Neutron Boy Genius** delivers using off-the-shelf software and below-average budget.

Square's **Final Fantasy: The Spirits Within** displays dazzling CG technique but fails to capture the mainstream box office.

Mainframe motion-captures American Ballet Theatre dancers to animate characters in Mattel's all-CG direct-to-video **Barbie in the Nutckracker**.

Pixar short **Mike's New Car** by Pete Docter and Roger Gould.

Van Phan's **Values** is Best Animated Short at SIGGRAPH 2001.

Sega discontinues **Dreamcast** platform.

Rockstar's **Grand Theft Auto III** is a huge hit.

Framestore and **CFC** merge in London. **La Maison** opens in Paris.

GeForce3, NVIDIA's programmable GPU.

Intel releases 64-bit **Itanium** processor.

Foundation Imaging completes a US $20 million 26-episode CG series **Dan Dare: Pilot of the Future** based on the British 1950s comic book hero.

2002

Visual Effects Movies:
The Lord of the Rings: The Two Towers *
Spiderman
Star Wars: Episode II - Attack of the Clones
Other VFX Movies:
Astérix & Obélix: Mission Cléopâtre
Blade 2
Clockstoppers
Die Another Day
Eight Legged Freaks
Harry Potter and the Chamber of Secrets
Men in Black 2
Minority Report
Panic Room
Reign of Fire
Resident Evil
Scooby-Doo
The Scorpion King
Solaris
Spy Kids 2: Island of Lost Dreams
Star Trek: Nemesis
Stuart Little 2
The Time Machine
xXx

The Lord of the Rings 2 uses a combination of performance capture and keyframe techniques to animate the Gollum character, superb crowd simulation software.

Star Wars: Episode II is shot on HD video with massive amounts of blue screen and virtual characters.

Robert Rodriguez's **Spy Kids 2** uses HD and desktop production to benefit an independent production model.

Hayao Miyazaki's **Spirited Away** wins AMPAS award with fantastic story.

Fox's **Ice Age** by Chris Wedge mixes physical comedy with refined ray tracing rendering.

Mattel's direct-to-video **Barbie as Rapunzel**

2002 (cont.)

Animated Movies: '02
Spirited Away *
Ice Age
Lilo & Stitch
Spirit: Stallion of the Cimarron
Treasure Planet
Other:
El bosque animado (The Living Forest)
Hey Arnold!
Mutant Aliens
The Powerpuff Girls First Feature
Return to Never Land
The Wild Thornberrys

Disney's **Lilo & Stitch** pairs a Hawaiian girl and her alien pet, luscious retro watercolors.

Disney's **Treasure Planet** displays sophisticated 2D/3D technique, fails at box office.

Sylvain Chomet's **Les Triplettes de Belleville** is released in France, combines 2D/3D.

Memorable commercials for **Blockbuster's Carl and Ray**, **Levi's**, **X-Box Mosquito**, and **Game Boy Advance**.

Eric Armstrong's **The ChubbChubbs** wins AMPAS Short Award.

Tomek Baginski's **The Cathedral** is Best Short at SIGGRAPH 2002.

Medal of Honor: Allied Assault for PC; **Kingdom Hearts** for PS2; **Animal Crossing** for N64; and **Munch's Odyssey** for XBOX.

NVIDIA's Cg programming language.

Apple Computer buys Nothing Real's **Shake**.

Mill Film and **The Secret Lab**, Disney's VFX group, close.

Framestore/CFC's **Dinotopia** TV series.

Early 2000s

2003

Visual Effects Movies:
Daredevil
The Hulk
Kangaroo Jack
Lara Croft: The Cradle of Life
The League of Extraordinary Gentlemen
The Lord of the Rings: The Return of the King
The Matrix: Reloaded
The Matrix: Revolutions
Spy Kids 3: Game Over
Terminator 3: Rise of the Machines
X2: X-Men United

The Visual Effects Society holds first awards competition.

Feature releases include Pixar's visually spectacular underwater adventure **Finding Nemo**, DreamWorks' **Sinbad: Legend of the Seven Seas**, and Disney's **Piglet's Big Movie** and **Jungle Book 2.**

Shows in production: DreamWorks' **Shrek 2** and **Sharkslayer, Over the Hedge**, a Wallace and Gromit movie, and **Madagascar**. Disney's **My Peoples, Chicken Little, Home on the Range, Bears.** Warner Bros. **Looney Toones Movie**. Fox/Blue Sky's **Robots**.

Scheduled French releases: all-CG **Kaena, la Prophétie** by Chris Delaporte; **La Prophétie des Grenouilles**, by Jacques-Rémy Girerd; **Les Enfants de la Pluie**, by Philippe Leclerc.

Sony's **HDCAM-SR** format for HD video.

CHAPTER 1

Key Terms

Academy of Motion Picture Arts and Sciences (AMPAS)
CADAM
CAPS
Cinefex
Codecs
Computer-aided design and manufacturing
Computer intranets
Computer graphics technology
Computer games
D-Cinema
Digital cinema
Digital environment
Digital imaging techniques
Digital information
Digital movie projectors
Digital video
Dreamcast
GameCube
Genesis effect
Geometry Engine
HDC-F950
High definition digital vide
Kinetophones
Kinetoscope
LBE rides
Linux
Location-based entertainment
Mac OSX
Mainframes
Massively parallel computer
Microcomputers
Minicomputers
Motion Picture Association of America (MPAA)
Music videos
Nintendo 64
Platform games
Playstation
Playstation 2
RenderMan
Scanimate
Seventh art
SIGGRAPH
SIGGRAPH Video Review
Silicon chip
Sketchpad
Supermicrocomputers
Supercomputers
Synthavision
Time-sharing
UNIX
Viper
Windows NT
Workstations
www.artof3d.com
X-Box

(Image courtesy of NVIDIA Corp.)

CHAPTER 2

2

The Digital Production Process

Summary

THERE ARE MANY DIFFERENT WAYS TO DESIGN and produce a sequence of three-dimensional computer animation or a visual effects shot. There are as many production methods as there are different types of projects with different resource allocations and different creative goals. This chapter presents several methodologies for digital production and explains what makes each one of them unique and best suited for.

QUICK INDEX

2.1 Production Strategies

Planning the **production strategy** for any computer animation project starts with a review of the type of production, the technical complexity, and the basic resources, such as budget, schedule, personnel, and computer systems. Production strategies will vary depending on the unique combination of these factors. Production trends also change from time to time and place to place. In years of economic growth, production budgets are usually generous, but in other years budgets are tight as clients look for savings everywhere. In the late 1990s, for example, many of the Hollywood studios set guidelines to lower production costs by as much as 20 to 40 percent per movie. Imagine the effect of that on visual effects production.

Type of Production

Computer animation projects can differ a lot from each other depending on what **type of production** they are. An experimental animation short, a visual effects shot for a live action film, a commercial production, an episode for an animated series for television, a real-time platform game, and a feature movie production all have very different purposes and project dynamics. Figure 2.1.1 lists some of the categories of computer animation projects that are common today. Think of the differences that exist between the two extremes: the production of a one-person experimental computer animation and the

3D Computer Animation Sample Projects
• 90-minute all-computer animated feature movie • 30 minutes to complement a hand-drawn feature movie • 15-minute all-computer animated episode in a weekly series • 10 minutes of cut-sequences for a role-playing computer game • 4-minute independent movie • 10 minutes of visual effects shots for a live action movie • 2-minute weekly low-res animation for online streaming • 30-second interstitial for a weekly television show • 15 seconds for a live action TV commercial • 300 moves for a real-time fighting computer game

2.1.1 Some of the most common types of three-dimensional computer animation projects.

production of a computer animation for a feature movie. An experimental computer animation seeks to explore techniques, topics, or treatments that are not commonly used in mainstream productions. Most experimental works are not developed to be crowd pleasers so the director, who often is also the screenwriter and animator, has great freedom to experiment even though production resources in experimental production are usually limited. This fact may have a negative impact on the technical sophistication and amount of computer systems and personnel that may be employed, but it also may have a positive effect in the form of a relaxed production schedule and creative freedom.

Once completed, computer animations have a wide range of durations. There is no **standard length** of time that determines what is a short or a long piece of computer animation. Usually anything over 30 minutes is considered long. Thirty minutes is not such a long time, especially when one considers that the average length of a feature movie is around 90 minutes, but the huge amount of work and computer time required to produce a 30-minute segment of computer animation qualify it to be called a long work from the production point of view. Short-length computer animations under one minute long are commonly created for experimental pieces, student projects, TV commercials, TV station identification sequences or program openings, and movie titles. Computer animation productions that fall in the medium-length category include episodes of an animated series, a collection of special effects to be inserted in a feature film or TV series, sequences for an amusement park motion ride or other types of location-based entertainment, or special creative projects funded by industry or government.

Technical Complexity and Delivery Media

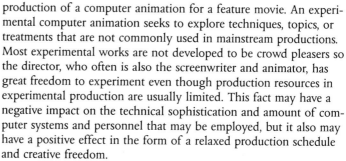

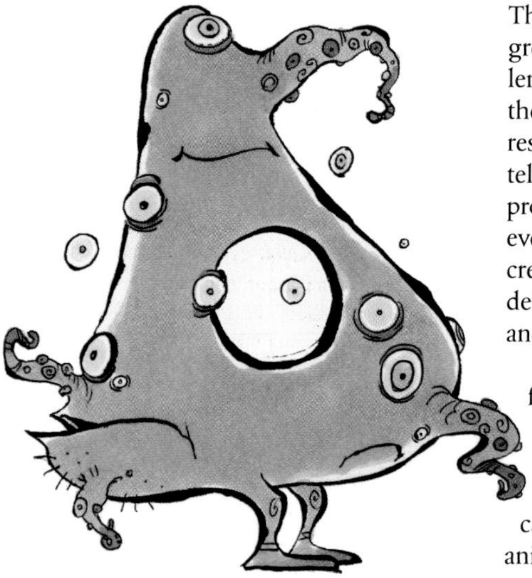

The technical complexity of experimental computer animations varies greatly from project to project, but in all cases, the technical challenges in a computer animation have to be chosen carefully so that the production may be completed successfully with the available resources. A feature computer-animated movie is usually produced to tell a story that may be appreciated by a mainstream audience. Most productions of this type are quite complex and require a careful plan even when the resources are significant. This allows for ambitious creative and technical challenges, but it also implies great pressure to deliver a product that will sell and will generate returns to partners and investors, and bonuses for the employees.

The **technical complexity** of a computer animation may range from the very simple to the extremely complex. A computer animation project that is technically simple may involve a few objects that are animated with just a single or a few simple motion techniques. For example, many television station identifications or news program openers created with three-dimensional animation may be complex from the choreographic point of view but technically simple from the point of view of the motion techniques used. These animations typically involve keyframe animation enhanced with beautifully crafted models and outstanding rendering. A special effects segment produced for a live action feature movie that includes computer animation typically requires several motion techniques such as keyframing, inverse kinematics, and motion dynamics. In this type of project the computer-generated motion has to be perfectly synchronized and aligned with the live action, the live special effects, and the traditional cel animation.

The **delivery media** is usually established early in the project since it usually has a significant impact on schedule and budget. It is imperative to clarify the delivery media specifications early on in the project since these specs will determine, among other things, the pixel resolution and the aspect ratio of the images to be rendered (see Chapter 15 for output considerations).

Meetings, Meetings, Meetings...

The best way to deal with technical complexity is by planning thoroughly before production starts. Preproduction planning starts with **meetings** usually with the producers or directors of the project. The goal of these initial meetings is to gather project information related to the technical strategies that may be necessary to generate the desired results. Producers and directors can provide information such as **creative vision**, visual style, budget, and deadlines that affects technical complexity. Effects supervisors, supervising animators, project managers and others also contribute greatly to these early discussions. Once the sequences to be animated are storyboarded it is necessary to meet with the technical directors who are responsible for clarifying complex technical issues, providing technical support, and developing new tools that may be necessary to complete the project. The goal of having these meetings and developing the storyboard is to narrow down the possibilities and to develop a precise **plan of action**. This plan must contain a **technical implementation** for every shot in the computer animation as well as a crystal-clear creative vision that will guide the production. The production plan should also contain a set of **deliverables** including number of frames, complexity of models, and number of effects. The plan also contains **milestones** that help the team set priorities and strategies. Later in the production process meetings become the forum for presenting work in progress and launch the **review** and **approval** cycle.

Planning the Production Workflow and Shots

Choosing one technical implementation—or a specific combination of techniques—over all the others usually requires finding a balance between the best way to achieve the desired result and the least expensive way to do so. This balance should take into account not just one shot but all the shots in the project. The technical imple-

Breaking Down a Shot or a Digital Production

Creative Issues
- Type of project? (see Fig. 2.1.1)
- Clear creative direction?
- Direction likely to change throughout production?
- Context of shot? What happens before and after?
- Length in seconds or minutes?
- Have to match look of live action? Visual effect or stylized animation?

Technical Issues
- Is client likely to understand technical issues?
- Nature of action?
- Type of motion?
- Complexity of geometry?
- Number of primary and secondary characters? Major and minor elements?
- Type of lens and lighting sources?
- Characteristics of final output medium and process?

Logistical Issues
- Budget amount?
- When is the delivery deadline?
- When are the preliminary review deadlines? Likely to change?
- Size and type of team?
- What computer animation tools and computing power?
- Other materials required before project can start or finish? Likely those will be on time?

2.1.2 Breaking down a visual effects shot or an animation sequence is one of the most important moments during preproduction. This process starts by considering the main creative goals of the project, as well as the major variables that might impact production. The goal of breaking down a shot or project is to end up with specific production tactics that will accomplish the best results within the limitations.

2.1.3 Planning a shot must take into account all its different components—in this case, a shot incorporating multiple elements. A computer-generated *Rapier* spaceship composited against a live action set (top), was assembled from multiple elements (opposite page) including live action, rendering computer-generated elements in layers, and compositing. (Images from *Wing Commander* courtesy of Digital Anvil Visual Effects, a division of Digital Anvil.)

mentation for each shot starts with an analysis of the elements in the shot and the ways in which they interact with each other. This analysis results in a **written description** of the plan for the shot that covers the elements of the shot, the interactions between them, and the specific techniques that will be used to create them. It is at this stage when the abstract goals and the director's vision have to be translated into lists of specific deliverables (Fig. 2.1.2).

Designing production workflows is part art and part science. Some of it is based on the analysis of the hard facts like budgets and deadlines. Some of it is based on the careful evaluation of subtler issues like creative goals, and even issues like the personalities of the members of the team, the group dynamics, and the overall production experience of the team. For example, what might work in a large production company might spell disaster in a small studio; what might work in a computer animated character film might not be an option for a visual effects live action film.

Building a successful production flow is not done in a vacuum, but by looking at the specifics of the production—and more important—by sharing the proposed flow with the core members of the team, seeking their feedback, and incorporating their feedback into the production plans. In these days of quickly changing production tools, one hears too often about digital productions that miss their goals because of a poorly structured production flow or because of an inflexible producer or production manager who did not listen to the suggestions of more experienced members of the production team.

The responsibility for coming up with the best production flow for a specific project is usually shared by several individuals involved in the production. This group may include the artistic and technical leads for the project, the assistant producer, the production manager, and other members of the art and animation production teams. It is not uncommon for an art director or an assistant producer in a small production to be suckered into doubling as a project manager when a dedicated production manager is not within the budget.

Most experienced production managers or sequence supervisors can structure the best production flow, partly because they have done it before, have made mistakes—and hopefully learned from them—and because they understand the production process. Many experienced production managers, animation directors, or visual effects supervisors are able to intuitively draft a fairly accurate and reasonable production flow just as an experienced *chef de cuisine* is able to cook a delicious dish without measuring the ingredients or even following the steps in a recipe (Fig. 2.1.3).

Two key words to keep in mind when designing a production flow are **on-target** and **compromise**. Any production flow seeks to optimize the elements and process involved in a project so that the execution and completion of the goals is on-target. The challenge though is that the concept of being on-target often means very different things to each member of the production team or to each group within a larger production. For example, to the person responsible for the finances of the production, on-target usually means "within budget." To the producer or account manager in the case of a commercial for TV, on-target is almost always equated with "the client liked it." To the artist on-target rarely means something other than "I am satisfied with it," in which case projects tend to drag on forever. It is therefore important that the individuals who are in charge of deciding how the team is supposed to deliver a project that is on target (by the deadline and within budget) understand how to balance the different aspects of the project and also how to reach a viable compromise between the forces that drive a project. If that production balance is missing from a project, then one or several of the groups who are responsible for a specific deliverable might find the process quite grueling.

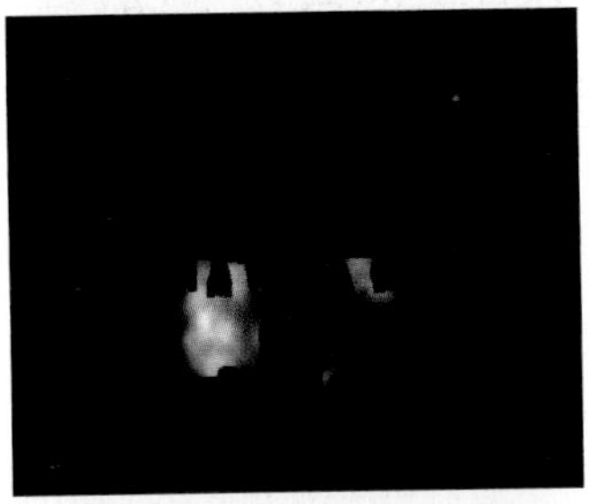

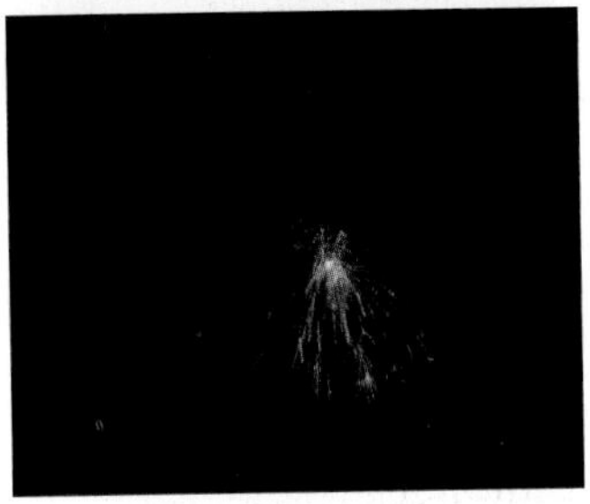

Creative Goals

Defining the creative goals of a project is sometimes a straightforward and transparent process, others an elusive recurring nightmare. In general, defining the **creative goals** of a project that involves three-dimensional computer animation is best done by an individual, an art director for example, who sets a **visual style** and a small group of individuals who have a common creative vision. But there are no rules that govern the best way to develop the creative goals of a project. One thing that is sure is that it helps to lock them down as early as possible, and it is best not to change them too many times or too drastically. A word of caution: Changing the creative goals of a project once production has started almost always has a negative ripple effect that leads to delays, complications, additional expense, and frustration.

Budget, Schedule, and Resources

A computer animation project is defined to the greatest extent by the **resources** allocated to it. One of the main tasks, for example, of a director of visual effects or supervisor of computer animation consists of making sure that the **budget** allocated to the project by the producer and director is adequate to produce the desired results. Equally important is that the production **schedule**—also set by the producer or director of the project—is based on realistic deadlines and that it provides sufficient time to achieve the desired results. Both the budget and the schedule of a production drive much of the daily dynamics of the production because they determine the number and expertise of the **personnel** that can be hired and the amount and power of the **computer resources** that can be used.

The amount of time that is necessary to complete a computer animation depends on the type of production and its technical complexity. The typical duration of the production of a simple commercial computer animation is between one and two months, and such a production may employ only a couple of animators and computers. A short production with complex technical requirements and compositing—for example, a television commercial—can last between two to three months and may require half a dozen animators and computers and a couple of supervisors. A longer computer animation production that involves dozens of shots and requires a lot of interaction with live action, special effects, and compositing—for example, a feature movie—may take more than one year to complete. This type of production may involve a production staff of over 100 individuals and a rendering farm with dozens of computers. The technical challenges of experimental computer animations vary greatly. Some are produced during the course of a year by a couple of animators working after hours on a couple of borrowed computers. Other experimental computer animations—those with better funding—may be completed in six months and employ half a dozen individuals working on several computers.

Components of a Computer Animation Studio

- Creative personnel
- Production personnel
- Technical personnel
- Administrative and sales personnel
- Turnkey application software
- Proprietary software
- Processing power
- Peripheral storage
- Computer network and communications
- Input and output equipment
- Business plan and funds
- Clients
- Space

2.2.1 Basic components of a 3D computer animation facility.

2.2 The Digital Computer Animation Studio

Most computer animation projects require the collaboration of many individuals with different skills, talents, personalities, and working habits. Computer animation projects are **team efforts** where **collaboration** is a key ingredient for success. The production of any computer animation requires lots of **planning** and constant **supervision** because of the number of individuals involved, the short production cycles, limited budgets, and the unpredictable and changing nature of cutting edge technology. Improved network communication, more standard software and better understanding of production flows have made possible the production of computer animated projects in multiple locations through **remote collaboration**.

The creation and production of computer animation takes place in environments where most of the tools and processes are computer-based. There are many ways to configure a **digital studio** depending on the type and volume of work that needs to be done and the number of people working in the studio. All digital animation studios include personnel, software, and computer systems with a specific configuration of processing power, storage, networks, and input and output peripherals (Fig. 2.2.1). Last but not least, a digital studio needs to be backed up by a **business plan** that clearly defines—among other things—the balance between income and expenditures, how to deal with significant equipment and software upgrade costs, and the means by which to achieve growth.

Personnel

The **personnel** of a computer animation studio or production house includes creative, technical, production, and administrative positions. The number of individuals employed is in direct proportion to the size and volume of a particular project or a studio. Small studios may employ only 5 individuals, medium-sized studios may have around 20 employees, and some of the large studios can have as many as

100 employees. Large studios sometimes include creative and technical personnel from areas other than computer animation, such as traditional character animation, live action film, optical compositing, sculpture, and model making. Likewise, the administrative positions in a large studio might include specialists in accounting, sales, training, human resources and distribution. Figures 2.3.1 to 2.3.6 list some of these technical and creative positions for various kinds of projects. The quality of the creative and technical personnel in a computer animation team is usually measured in terms of their talent, experience, dedication, and productivity.

Turnkey Software

In addition to the operating system and all the utility programs associated with it, a digital studio is often centered around its **applications software** (Fig. 2.2.2). This type of software may include programs as diverse as three-dimensional computer animation, image compositing, motion capture, and digital ink and paint (visit **www.artof3d.com** for a list of software resources). A large number of computer animation facilities use **turnkey software**. This type of software, also called **off-the-shelf software**, is commercially available from a variety of vendors and is ready to use on virtually all computer platforms. Turnkey software systems can range in price from under $1,000 to several tens of thousands of dollars depending on their capabilities, sophistication, and speed. Small turnkey systems are usually sold as a single unit, but large turnkey systems are usually sold as a collection of stand-alone modules that can be purchased in different configurations. Oftentimes the functionality of application software can be enhanced through the addition of **plug-ins** which are essentially add-on programs with a specialized set of functions. Plug-ins may range in price from a few dollars to several thousands.

When selecting turnkey software it is important to consider its upgrade policies, and its upward and downward compatibility. Turnkey software is upgraded periodically. Upgrades consist of adding new functionalities, optimizing existing features, and fixing problems—also called software bugs. In general, **software upgrades** are offered to owners of the upgraded software at a nominal fee, but on occasion the extent of the software upgrade is such that the software is considered a new version of the product. In the latter case, the upgraded software is sometimes offered to owners and new buyers at the same price. **Upward compatibility** exists when files created with previous versions of the software are compatible with new software upgrades. **Downward compatibility** exists when files created with a new software upgrade are compatible with earlier versions of the software. In addition to applications software, computer animation and visual effects houses use **operating systems** which are programs that manage each individual computer system in the network. A few of the operating systems most widely in use today include Linux, Windows, OS X, Irix, and Solaris.

Types of Software

- 2D scanning
- 2D animation
- 2D paint and retouching
- Ink and paint
- Flipbook player
- Rotoscoping
- Matting
- 3D surface modeling
- 3D scanning
- 3D paint
- 3D rigging and animation
- Motion capture/clean-up
- Shading and rendering
- Compositing
- Color calibration
- File compression
- Video editing
- Web access
- Media asset management
- Data backup
- Network manager

2.2.2 Some of the most common types of applications software found in computer animation and visual effects studios.

2.2.3 Two views of a rendering farm with 250 dual-processor 1 GHz Pentium III computers, 2 GB of RAM each, 4.3 TB of Fibre Channel RAID storage, and 1000- and 100-Base T network switching equipment. (Images courtesy of Render Core, Hollywood.)

Creative Team (TV Commercial)

Creative Director
Art Director
Copywriter
Producer
Account Executive
Animation Director

Production Team (TV Commercial)

Animation Supervisor
Senior/Junior Animators
Technical Directors:
Modeling, Rigging,
Lighting, Rendering
Roto Artist/Compositor
Producer
Production Manager
Technical Assistant

2.3.1 Sample creative and production teams in the production of a small all-computer animation TV commercial.

Proprietary Software

Much of the sophisticated computer animation software is often produced with a combination of commercially available software and custom, or proprietary, software. **Proprietary software** is developed in-house to provide tools and techniques that are not available in commercial turnkey systems. Proprietary software can also be used in conjunction with turnkey software; for example, it can be used to preprocess motion-capture data before it is sent to the turnkey animation module. Proprietary software is often quite costly because it requires a team of specialized and dedicated programmers to develop, maintain, and upgrade it. Using proprietary software in a project that is being split between several production houses can sometimes create complications and limit production flexibility.

Processing Power

The **processing power** of a computer animation facility is determined by the power, speed, and number of computers dedicated to compute the animation. The power and speed of a single computer system is dictated by the configuration of the computer's central processing unit, coprocessors, clock, bus, and internal memory. The exact configuration of a computer used to create animation depends both on the budget available and on the type of task assigned to that machine, for example, modeling, rendering, or compositing.

Today's production of computer animation is dominated by microcomputers and super-microcomputers. Most of the **microcomputers** used today for professional computer animation usually have one or two 32-bit CPU processors, clock speeds above 2 GHz (gigahertz), and powerful graphics cards with sophisticated hardware rendering capabilities. Popular microcomputers include Pentium-based PCs and Apple Computer's G-line. Intel's 64-bit Itanium processors have been introduced to the market. The **supermicrocomputers**, or workstations, that a decade ago dominated this field are still in use but mostly as servers or components of rendering farms. Popular supermicrocomputers include a variety of models from Silicon Graphics (SGI) and Sun Microsystems, among others, and are usually configured on one or several 32 or 64-bit custom graphics processors. Years ago microcomputers were considered too low-end for professional production, but that is no longer the case, especially as the processing power of microcomputers continues to increase and be configured as multiprocessor graphics workstations and rendering-servers. Microcomputers are also being increasingly used as the building blocks of **computer rendering farms** that include dozens or hundreds of individual processors splitting a rendering job and communicating through a fast speed network (Fig. 2.2.3). In 2001 the movie ***Final Fantasy: The Spirits Within***, for example, employed rendering farms with 960 CPUs running in the Linux environment and more than 300 CPUs in Irix.

Peripheral Storage

The type of **peripheral storage** used in a computer animation facility is also based on the volume, quality, and complexity of the work done at that facility. The frames of a computer animation are stored in digital form as they are generated and until they are recorded on film or video. Online storage is necessary so that it is possible to preview an animation in progress or to retouch and to composite some frames in the animation. The size of a single frame of high-quality computer animation may range from 4 to 50 MB depending on its spatial, temporal, and chromatic resolution. The online storage capacity of a production facility may be measured in megabytes (MB) or millions of bytes, gigabytes (GB) or billions of bytes, or terabytes (TB) or trillions of bytes. The ***Final Fantasy*** movie, for example, employed about 10 terabytes of online storage for three-dimensional data and 5 TB for two-dimensional data. A standard PC computer used for production may have a 200 GB hard disk, or access to a compact desktop 1 TB array of hard disks. **RAID disk arrays** (Redundant Array of Independent Disks) are a popular way to store data safely. A RAID array is a group of drives that act as a single storage system with high-levels of redundancy and fault-tolerance. There are several levels of RAID redundancy. Level 1, for example, creates a mirror image of all data using two hard disks. RAID Level 5, saves data across several drives, including the parity information that allows recovery from the failure of any single drive.

Bunny Team	
Writer/Director	1
Producer	1
Digital Effects Supervisors	2
Lead Animators	2
Animators	12
Lighting Lead	1
Technical Directors	19
Modelers	16
Digital Paint Artists	3
Editor	1
Production Coordinator	1
Software Tools	6
Research and Development	6
Systems Support	2
Technical Assistants	2
Production Executive	1
Production Manager	1
Production Assistant	1
Production Accountant	1

2.3.2 Partial listing of screen credits and statistics from *Bunny*, a film directed by Chris Wedge at Blue Sky Studios that won a 1998 Academy Award in the Animated Short Films category. Notice the medium-size team required to complete the award-winning short film.

Networks

The main function of a computer **network** is to bring information to the processors from storage and the peripheral devices, and vice versa. Networks usually have one or several computers—called **network servers**—whose main purpose is to help the other computers on the network fetch and send data. **Internets** are networks that connect computers in locations across the globe, whereas **intranets** connect computers that belong to a single company or might even be located in the same building. The **bandwidth**, or transmission capacity, of a network is a crucial issue that determines its functionality. Some popular network bandwidths include **T-1** or **DS-1** (Digital Signal Level One) at 1.544 megabits per second, Xerox's **Ethernet** at 10 megabits per second, **FDDI** (Fiber Distributed Data Interface) at 100 megabits per second, and **ATM** (Asynchronous Transfer Mode) at 154 megabits per second. Networks are commonly used in production environments to share files and to keep as many computers on the network as possible busy at all times. Very high-bandwidth networks are starting to be used for transferring computer animations between studios in different cities and even different countries.

Creative Team (Effects Feature Movie)
Director
Scriptwriter
Production Designer
Visual Effects Director
Art Director
Storyboard Artist
Producer

Administrative Team (Effects Feature Movie)
Executive Producer
Production Assistant
Production Manager
Director of Postproduction
Director of Finance
Production Accountant

2.3.3 Sample creative and administrative teams in a large production, a live action feature film with visual effects sequences.

Input and Output Equipment

The **input capabilities** of a computer animation studio are used for a variety of purposes. Flatbed scanners or digitizing cameras are used mostly for scanning images that may be used as texture maps or backgrounds during the rendering process. Film digitizers are used for digitizing entire live action sequences that are composited digitally with the computer animation. Three-dimensional scanners are used for digitizing the shape of scale models and full-size environments or the actions of human actors to be used as motion templates for an animation. The **output capabilities** of a computer animation facility include a variety of devices to record motion tests and the finished animations. High-resolution electronic and laser film recorders are used to output computer animation onto film. Digital disk recorders are used to output animation onto a variety of video formats. Digital disk recorders are also a popular form of peripheral storage because they can record video in digital format and play back computer animation at standard video rates on video output devices.

2.3 Creative, Technical, and Production Teams

Most computer animation projects require one or several teams of individuals with a variety of skills and talents. Computer animation teams are put together in different ways depending on the nature and needs of the project. Often several teams are involved in the creation of a single project, especially when the project is complex and requires the participation of several companies. In some cases, a single team may handle both the creative and production responsibilities, but often these two stages of a computer animation project are implemented by separate creative and production teams. The members of both of these teams are often credited in the closing credits that may be shown at the end of an animated piece.

The **creative team** is usually represented by the individuals, design studio, communications company, or advertising agency that developed the concept and the visual treatment. This team is typically responsible for creating a script or screenplay and a storyboard. The main responsibility of the **production team** is to execute the ideas provided by the creative team and to deliver a finished animation. The production team may be based in one or in several production and postproduction companies, or groups within the same company. Some of the multiple responsibilities of the **technical team** include providing technical support to the production crew, maintaining the computer systems in working order, and developing custom software for special production requirements.

2.3.4 (opposite page) Sample production team in a large production, a live action feature film with visual effects sequences.

Small Projects

Depending on their nature small projects may range from just a few individuals to thirty or forty people. Projects with very polished technical production values usually require significant crews. This is often the case with slick commercials for television, music videos, and even independent productions. **Crossing over** between different production roles is still common in small teams where a single individual may perform different roles and be in charge of different tasks. For example, in a small project an animator might also be in charge of modeling some of the characters and building their inverse kinematics chains, while in a larger project these three different tasks are usually performed by three different individuals. The creative and production teams for a short computer animation project, a **television commercial** for example, may include the positions listed in Fig. 2.3.1. The production team may also include a visual effects supervisor and an editor if the project involves a significant amount of live action and compositing. The production team for the commercial shown in Figure 13.2.2, for example, consisted of 12 people including modelers, trackers, animators, and lighters; the schedule for the project was three months and the live action was shot in five days. Figure 2.3.2 lists most of the team members in *Bunny*, a 1998 award-winning **independent short**.

Large Projects

The production of long computer animations may require a relatively small creative team but an extensive production team with specialized groups. Three different types of large-scale projects involving three-dimensional computer animation would include the visual effects for a live action feature movie, an all computer-animated feature movie, and a traditional (2D) animated feature movie with significant three-dimensional computer animation.

The creative team behind the **visual effects for a feature movie**, for example, may consist of about half a dozen individuals including the positions listed in Fig. 2.3.3. Having a large production team is one way to handle both the tight production schedules and the volume of work contained in a computer animation feature movie. A production team for this type of project may include several groups and positions (Fig. 2.3.4), but under some circumstances a few responsibilities may be assigned to a single individual. Crossing over between production roles, however, is still rare in large projects, where individuals tend to be more locked into their specialties.

The **visual effects** group is responsible for the overall production of all the special effects in the project, including the supervision of the computer animation. Usually the director decides the creative treatment for every single shot that requires special effects. A visual effects producer develops production guidelines, as well as a budget and a schedule for the project. A visual effects supervisor specifies the **production techniques** to be used and is also in charge, along with the visual effects producer, of making sure that the production guidelines, budgets, and deadlines are followed by the different production groups and subgroups. He or she functions as the liaison between the live set and the digital facility. (See Chapter 13 for additional informa-

Production Team (Effects Feature Movie)

Visual Effects Group
- Visual Effects Producer
- Visual Effects Supervisor
- Visual Effects Editor
- Visual Effects Assistant Editor
- Visual Effects Coordinator
- Stage Technicians

Computer Animation Group
- Computer Animation or Digital Supervisor
- Computer Animation Shot Supervisors
- Computer Animators
- Computer Animation Production Coordinator

Modeling and Lighting Group
- Computer Modeling Supervisor
- Modeling TDs (Technical Directors)
- Lighting Supervisor
- Lighting TDs
- Rendering Wranglers

Computer Technical Support Group
- Computer Graphics (CG) Department Manager
- CG Software Developers
- CG Technical Assistants
- CG Systems Support

Digital Compositing and Postproduction Group
- Digital Supervisor
- Digital Coordinator
- Digital Artists
- Compositors
- Digital Transfer Operator
- Scanning Supervisor
- Scanning Operators
- Rotoscoping Supervisor
- Rotoscopers
- Camera Trackers
- Digital Output Supervisor
- Digital Color Timing Supervisor
- Negative Cutter

A Bug's Life

Department / Credit	Number
Animation	**61**
Animation Manager	1
Animators	33
Assoc. Animation Manager	1
Additional Animation	23
Fix Animator/Coordinator	1
Production Assistants	2
Lighting Team	**40**
Lighting Manager	1
Lighting Artists	38
Lighting Coordinator	1
Information Systems	**33**
Director	1
Managers	2
Sys. Admins. and Support	30
Modeling Team	**31**
Modeling and Shading Mgr.	1
Modeling Artists	30
Add. Software Dev.	**30**
Director	1
Software Engineers	26
Documentation and Support	3
Crowd and Effects Team	**27**
Crowd Technical Supervisor	1
Effects and Crowd Mgrs.	2
Effects Technical Artists	13
Crowd Technical Artists	7
Add. Crowd Tech. Support	3
Crowds and Effects Coord.	1
Art	**26**
Art Department Manager	1
Shading Design	1
Lead CG Painter	1
CG Painters	3
Sketch Artists	6
Sculptors	2
Character Design	1
Additional Character Design	7
Visual Development	1
Art Development Coord.	1
Art Department Prod. Asst.	2
Postproduction	**26**
Postproduction Supervisor	1
Postproduction Consultant	1
Postproduction Assistant	1
Recording Mixers	2
Original Dialogue Mixer	1
Supervising Sound Editor	1
ADR Editor	1
Sound Effects Editor	1
Foley Editors	2
Assistant Sound Designer	1
Assistant Sound Editor	1
Foley Artists	2
Foley Mixer	1
Foley Recordist	1
Effects Assistant	1
ADR Assistant	1
Mix Technicians	2
Add. Dialogue Recording	4
Add. ADR Voice Casting	1
Executive/SupervisingTeam	**23**
Director	1
Co-Director	1
Producers	2
Screenplay	3
Story Supervisor	1
Supervising Film Editor	1
Supervising Technical Directors	2
Director of Photography	1
Production Designer	1
Art Directors	2
Supervising Animators	2
Shading Supervisor	1
Supervising Layout Artist	1
Production Manager	1
Production Supervisors	3
Editorial	**22**
Second Editor	1
First Assistant Editor	1
Second Assistant Editors	4
Editorial Coordinator	1
Film Coordinator	1
Production Assistant	1
Temporary Music Editor	1
Temporary Sound Editors	2
Add. Second Asst. Editors	6
Additional Editing	4
Production	**21**
Scheduling Coordinator	1
Production Accountant	1
Disney Prod. Representative	1
Asst. Prod. Accountants	2
Executive Asst. to Directors	1
Executive Asst. to Producers	1
Production Office Coordinator	1
Production Asst. to Directors	1
Production Assistants	3
Production Interns	7
Add. Production Support	2
Layout	**19**
Layout Manager	1
Senior Layout Artist	1
Layout Artists	9
Lead Set Dresser	1
Set Dressers	2
Additional Set Dressing	4
Layout Coordinator	1
Rendering Software Dev.	**19**
Director	1
Special Rendering Techniques	3
Production Support	2
Software Engineers	13
Shading Team	**19**
Shading Artists	17
Modeling and Shad. Coord.	2
Story Team	**19**
Story Manager	1
Story Artists	10
Additional Storyboarding	6
Production Assistants	2
Camera	**12**
Camera Manager	1
Photoscience Manager	1
Camera Supervisor	1
Camera Software and Eng.	3
Camera Technicians	3
Color Science Engineers	2
Department Administrator	1
Rendering Team	**12**
Lead Render Tech. Director	1
Rendering Manager	1
Render Tech. Directors	9
Optimization Consultant	1
Crowd Animation Team	**7**
Crowd Animation Supervisor	1
Crowd Animation	6

2.3.5 Partial listing (by size) of screen credits and statistics of some of the major departments involved in the production of *A Bug's Life*, a 1998 all computer-animated Disney/Pixar production.

The Prince of Egypt

Final Line Animation 111
(for all characters)
Department Lead 1
Sup. Character Lead 1
Character Leads 18
Senior Key Assistants 2
Key Assistants 39
Assistants 14
Breakdown/Inbetweeners 36

Effects (by sequence) **90**
2D Department Lead 1
Chariot Race, Sequence Lead 2
Animators 3
Digital Effects 4
Assistants 5
Burning Bush, Sequence Lead 2
Animators 5
Digital Effects 1
Playing with the Big Boys, Sequence Lead 1
Animators 2
Assistants 2
Players, Sequence Lead 2
Animators 2
Digital Effects 1
Assistants 9
Red Sea, Sequence Lead 2
Animators 6
Digital Effects 8
Assistants 4
Effects Breakdown/Inbetw. 19
Natural Phenom./2D CGI 2
Additional Effects Animation 4
Graphics Soft. Developers 5

Character Animation 83
(by character)
Sup. Animator, Old Moses 1
Sup. Animator, Young Moses 1
Animators, Moses 20
Sup. Animator, Old Rameses 1
Sup. Animator, Yng. Rameses 1
Animators, Rameses 4
Sup. Animator, Tzipporah 1
Animators, Tzipporah 5
Sup. Animator, Jethro 1
Sup. Animator, Hotep & Huy 1
Animator, Hotep & Huy 1
Sup. Animator, Miriam 1
Animators, Miriam 2
Sup. Animator, Aaron 1
Sup. Animator, Queen 1
Animator, Queen 1
Sup. Animator, Seti 1
Animator, Seti 1
Sup. Animator, The Camel 1
Sup. Animator, Yochevet 1
Sup. Animator, Horses 1
CG Crowd Animation 7
Additional Animators 15
Additional Animating Assts. 13

Production Management 66
(by group)
Digital Color Prod. Mgr. 1
Digital Operations Manager 1
Production Supervisors 7
- Animation/Final Line 2
- Effects/Story 1
- Production Accountants 2
- Assistant Accountants 2

Senior Coordinators 2
- Editorial 1
- Sweatbox 1

Coordinators 20
- Story 1
- Layout 2
- Scene Planning 1
- Animation 2
- Final Line 2
- Backgrounds 1
- Effects/CGI 2
- Scanning 2
- Plotting 1
- Checking 1
- Color Models/Visual Dev. 1
- Digital Paint 2
- Film Recording 1
- Script Continuity 1

Assistants 9
Production Assistants 25
Publicist 1

Editing 42

Digital Paint 41
Paint Checkers 2
Painters 39

Layout 29
Department Lead 1
Key Layout/Workbook 6
Layout 19
CGI Layout 2
Blue Sketch 1

Background 20
Background Artists 17
CGI Digital Backgd. Artists 3

Story 16
Writer 1
Writers 8
Add. Screenplay Material 1
Additional Story 6

Anim. Digital Final Check 14

Executive/Supervising Team 13
Directors 3
Executive Producer 1
Producers 2
Associate Producer 1
Art Directors 2
Production Designer 1
Sup. Editor 1
Sup. Production Manager 1
Production Manager 1

Artistic Supervisors 13
Story 2
Layout 1
Background 2
Visual Effects 2
Scene Planning 1
Color Models 1
Scanning 1
Anim./Digital/Final Check 2
Digital Paint 1

Character Design 10
Designers 3
Additional Char. Design 5
Sculpting 2

Visual Development Design 9

Color Models 8
Colorists 5
Color Markup 3

Scene Planning 7

Scanning 6
Scanners 5
Background Scanner 1

2.3.6 Partial listing (by size) of screen credits and statistics of some of the major departments involved in the production of *The Prince of Egypt*, a 1998 2D hand-drawn and 3D computer-animated DreamWorks production.

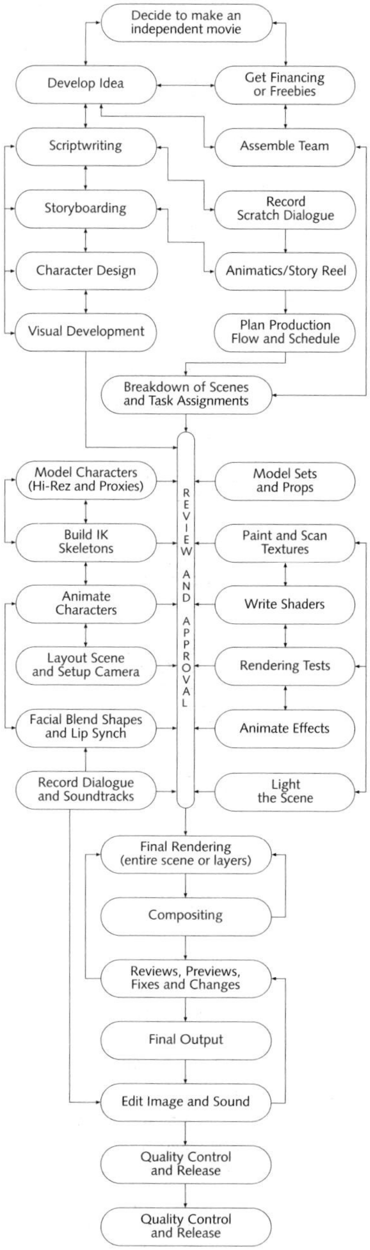

2.4.1a This flowchart presents a possible production flow for a small team working on an independent computer-animated short. The vertical bar in the center represents the production management system. (© Isaac V. Kerlow.)

tion on the visual effects production process.)

The **computer animation** group is responsible for the production of the computer animation sequences. In the case of a visual effects movie, the computer animation supervisor primarily makes sure that all the visual effects guidelines are understood and implemented by the animator. In the case of a computer animated movie, the animation director sets the tone and the target for the performances that animators have to extract from their characters. The computer animation shot supervisors are in charge of subgroups that are responsible for completing a single shot or a series of shots. The computer animators develop the imagery and motion tests until the sequences are approved by the visual effects director. The computer animation production coordinator makes sure that everybody has what they need to do their job; this individual also schedules equipment, personnel, and meetings. **Shot assignments** and footage quotas are usually made by a group of people that may include the animation director, producer, and project manager. Animators are assigned shots based on skill, sensibility, workload, or continuity. Some animators are better at action scenes or physical comedy, while others might be better at emotional delivery and subtle introspective moments. Animators are sometimes assigned to a single character throughout the movie (Fig. 2.3.6) or be allowed to animate all the characters in the shot (Fig. 2.3.5). **Footage quotas**, also known as frame or animation quotas, are the number of frames (there are 16 frames in one foot of 35 mm film) that an animator is expected to deliver on a weekly basis. Footage quotas are usually related to the experience of the animator, the quality of the animation tools, the complexity of the scene, and the schedule. In ***A Bug's Life***, for example, the quota averaged 2.5 feet a week (40 frames) per animator, while in ***Monsters, Inc.*** it averaged 4.5 feet (72 frames) a week.

Last but not least, the **digital compositing and postproduction** group may be responsible for scanning backgrounds, retouching, tracking cameras, rotoscoping, compositing, and outputting the different layers of visual effects, computer animation, and live action.

In addition to the creative, technical, and production teams, the **administrative team** oversees many of the financial, legal, and marketing issues related to the production of a complex computer animation project. An administrative team typically involves the positions listed in Figure 2.3.3. The members of the administrative team also work with the group directors in the creative and production teams to make sure that production budgets, deadlines, and strategies are adequate to complete the project successfully. Figure 2.3.5 lists some of the team members in an all **computer-animated feature movie**. Figure 2.3.6 also lists some of the team members in the production of a **hand-drawn animated feature movie** with significant three-dimensional computer animation. Notice the different approach to having animators animate characters: in one case animators are assigned specific characters for the entire production while in the other one animators may work on whichever characters appear in the scenes they are assigned to animate.

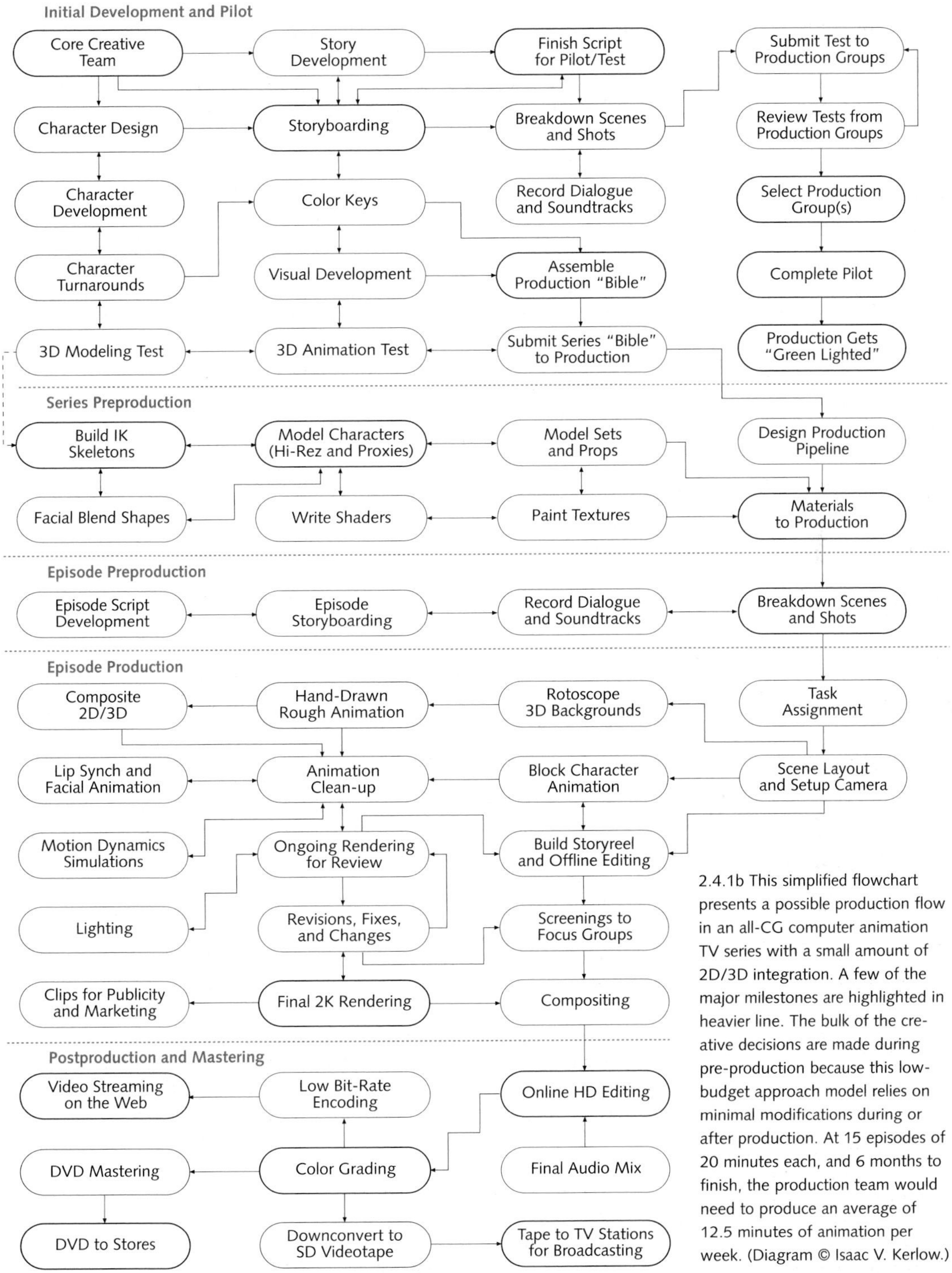

2.4.1b This simplified flowchart presents a possible production flow in an all-CG computer animation TV series with a small amount of 2D/3D integration. A few of the major milestones are highlighted in heavier line. The bulk of the creative decisions are made during pre-production because this low-budget approach model relies on minimal modifications during or after production. At 15 episodes of 20 minutes each, and 6 months to finish, the production team would need to produce an average of 12.5 minutes of animation per week. (Diagram © Isaac V. Kerlow.)

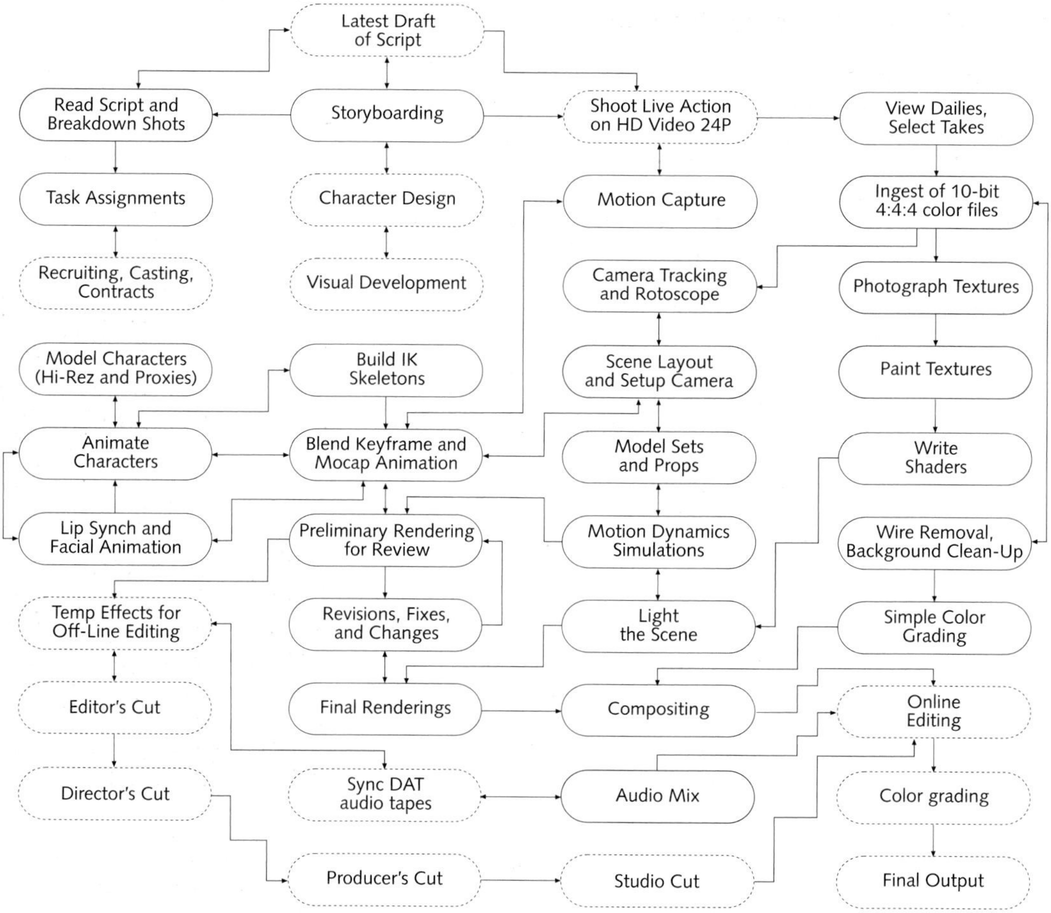

2.4.1c This flowchart presents a simplified production flow in a visual effects movie shot on HD with 3D animated characters, motion capture and camera tracking of the live action HD background plates. Notice how many of the major tasks are interrelated, and most of them run in parallel. Tasks inside the dotted line globes are performed by individuals outside of the core computer animation group. The horizontal color lines in the simplified timeline (right) represent parallel tasks on a weekly basis from beginning (left) to completion (right). (Diagrams © Isaac V. Kerlow.)

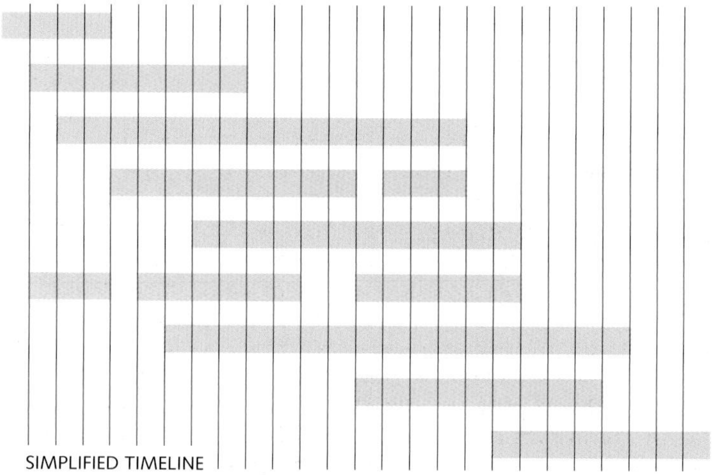

2.4 Overview of the Computer Animation Process

The process of creating computer animation or digital visual effects shots constantly evolves based on factors like creative goals, budget, schedule, and resources as well as other specifics of the production. In practice this process or **production pipeline** adopts different forms and variations, but the basic stages include preproduction, production, and postproduction. In Figures 2.4.1a–c you can notice a few obvious differences between the production flow in a computer animation movie and a visual effects-oriented live action movie.

Preproduction involves all the conceptualization and planning that takes place before a computer animation or effects project is produced. This stage in the process includes nonvisual tasks such as screenwriting, casting, and planning the management of the project, as well as visual tasks such as storyboarding, developing the overall visual look of the project. A project involving live action would also require meetings with the cinematographer and scouting for locations. Preproduction is the foundation of a project. Inadequate or erroneous preproduction usually results in delays, cost overruns, and creative deficit.

2.4.2 Concept sketch of an environment created during the visual development stage of production.

In simple terms the **production** stage in the process of three-dimensional computer animation involves a series of standard steps: modeling, rigging, animation, and rendering. First, the characters, objects, and environments used in three-dimensional computer animations are modeled. This computer **modeling** can occur with a wide range of computer-based three-dimensional techniques such as using virtual modeling tools to sculpt objects, or using a three-dimensional digitizer to capture the shape of a physical model directly into the computer program. Once the virtual actors and objects are modeled, they can be attached to the motion skeletons that will be used to animat them with a wide variety of techniques, this is called **rigging**. Computer **animation** techniques range from keyframing animation where start and end positions are specified for all objects in a sequence, to motion capture where all positions are fed to the objects directly from live actors whose motions are being digitized. The results of the animation can be previewed in the form of digital flipbooks displayed on the screen. Once the objects are modeled and animated, they can be rendered. To minimize time and budget complications, **motion tests** are often produced to preview the computer animation sequences before the final production takes place. Computer **rendering** is the process of representing visually the animated models with the aid of a simulated camera. The lighting of the scene and the shading characteristics are often specified before the animation is laid out, but the rendering itself, the calculation of the finished computer-animated images, always happens after the modeling and animation parameters have been defined.

Once the images have been rendered, a variety of **postprocessing** and **postproduction** techniques can be applied to the images before they are recorded. For example, computer-generated images

can be digitally composited or mixed with other computer-generated images or with live action. Computer animation can also be distorted, retouched, processed, or color corrected using postproduction techniques. When computer animations are completed, they are usually recorded on videotape or film so that they can be shown later on a TV screen or in a movie theater. Each film and video format has unique requirements and characteristics. For example, the standard rate of display of animated images recorded on videotape is 30 frames per second; on film it is 24 frames per second. In many instances computer animation is delivered in a **digital format** that may be played back in real time as part of a PC, game platform, or online interactive game.

2.4.3 Color keys help to define the palette and mood of a particular shot. (© 1999 Oddworld Inhabitants, Inc. All rights reserved.)

Following is an overview of the major stages in digital production of three-dimensional computer animation and computer-generated visual effects. Keep in mind that there are many ways to implement each of these tasks and that the order of execution may vary depending on a variety of factors. The production process is never entirely linear, and many tasks are interdependent, overlap and take place in parallel. A few of the main differences between a computer animation flow and a visual effects flow are highlighted in Figures 2.4.1a–c.

Story Development, Scriptwriting, and Recording Dialog

Behind any great visual project there is a strong idea and a great story. The stage of **story development** takes place before production begins, especially in small projects where the writer develops the story before any other preproduction has started or any budget has been committed to the project. In larger projects story development marks the beginning of development. During this process the writer or game designer (or story/design team in a larger project) has to focus on developing the characters and the plot, but also has to adapt it to the strengths and limitations of the visual medium in question. Usually a few creative cycles and/or revisions exist between a story or a game idea and the final **script** or the game design document. Before production can start the script needs to be broken down, or translated, into a sequence of shots. In the case of a character animation project, actors are cast this early in the process so that the **dialogue** can be recorded, especially because dialogue drives so much of the animation work.

2.4.4 The look of the main characters in *Shrek* and *Monsters, Inc.* was developed through an iterative process of intuition, design, creativity, selection, critique and refinement. (Opposite page, top: Shrek™ and © 2001 DreamWorks L.L.C. Above and opposite, bottom: © Disney Enterprises, Inc./Pixar Animation Studios.)

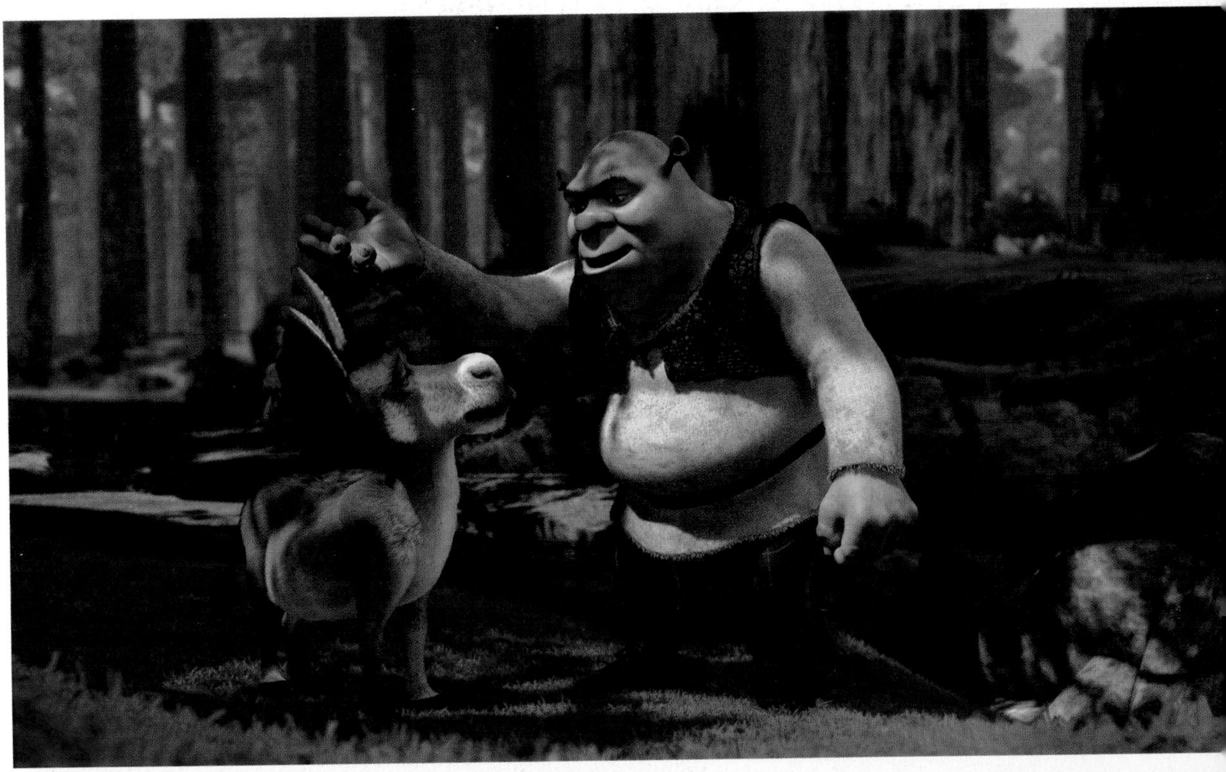

Visual Development

Visual development is about setting a visual direction and style for the project. This stage includes the creation of the characters, the types of environments and props, the overall styling, atmosphere and visual look, and even the color schemes for the project (Fig. 2.4.2). The visual development team is charged with creating concept art (as opposed to production art) usually includes painters, sculptors, and illustrators, and it is most active during the preproduction stage. Creating color palettes and the **color keys** for every scene of the project is an important aspect of the visual development process that will set much of the visual mood of the project (Fig. 2.4.3). The color keys must complement visually the goals of each part of the story. Imagine the difference in mood between a shot that has harmonious soft colors, and the same shot with loud contrasted colors.

Character Design

2.4.5 A skeleton study and development sketches of facial expressions, head shape, and neck details. Sculptures on traditional materials are also used to better define details of the character during the development process.

After the story, the characters are perhaps the second most important aspect of an animated project. The look and personality of characters is developed through drawings, sculptures, maquettes, and even computer-generated renderings (Figs. 2.4.5–2.4.6, and all unlabeled hand-drawn characters in this chapter). Visually speaking, it is important to determine early on the type of look for the character in question: cartoony, stylized, or realistic (see Chapter 10 for more details on character development.) Character sheets and character turnarounds are two important deliverables from this stage of preproduction (Figs. 10.5.1 and 10.5.7). The former consist of sets of drawings that define the attitudes and poses of the characters in the form of body positions and facial expressions, and the later show the key features of a character from different points of view.

In developing the look of characters for computer animation one must keep in mind which techniques will be used to animate it and deliver it to an audience. A character for a real-time action computer game, for example, would have to be designed very differently from a character in a feature animated film. A secondary character in an all computer-animated film would be designed differently from the starring virtual actor in a visual effects movie. **Props** used in a scene ranging from a small utensil to a vehicle are often designed by assistant character designers or industrial design specialists (Figs. 2.4.7 and 9.8.7). It is of critical importance for the character designers to consult with the technical directors who are in charge of modeling, setting up the animation controls, and rendering the character.

Storyboards

The creation of storyboards is usually the first attempt to translate the story and the script into images. In that sense, creating the storyboards is an important tool for breaking down the script into manageable production units, and it is also an indispensable tool for doing a technical breakdown of each shot. During story development the storyboards are also used to evaluate whether the storytelling needs fine-tuning. The storyboards developed early in preproduction tend to focus more on fleshing out the storytelling, general composition, actions, and camera moves and less on the technical details (Fig. 2.4.8). As this process evolves the storyboards generally include more production-oriented detail. (Read Chapter 10 for more information on the different types of storyboards.)

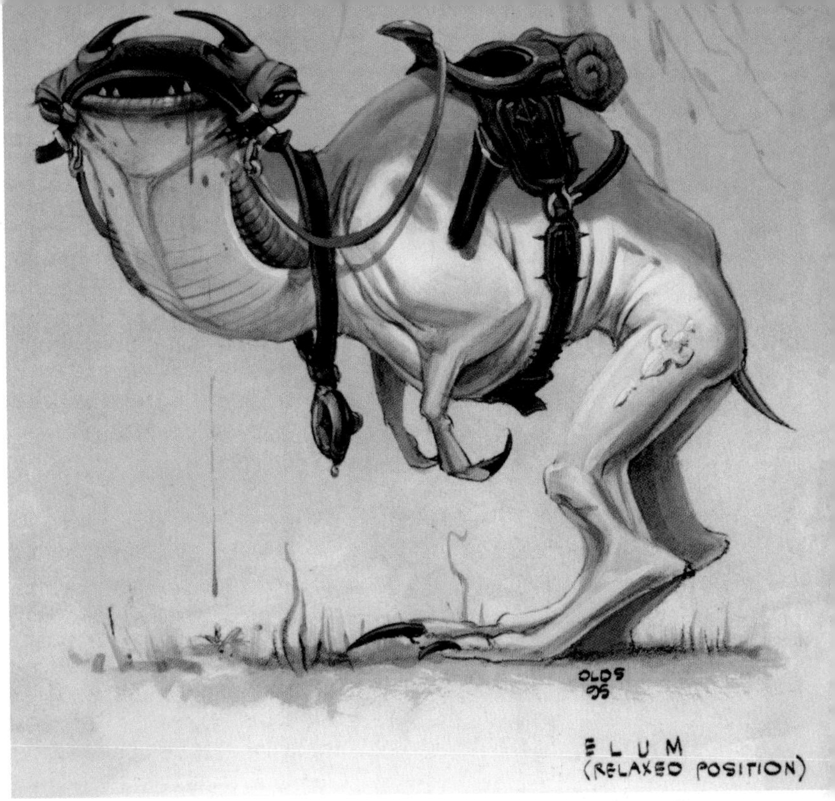

2.4.6 Concept painting indicating the shape, coloring, texture, and resting pose of a character. (© 1999 Oddworld Inhabitants, Inc. All rights reserved.)

Animatics, Previsualization, and Story Reels

Storyboards are often used to put together an animatic, which is a collection of simple moving images used to visualize how the final project may be structured and timed. A **two-dimensional animatic** can be created by scanning single drawings from the storyboard and creating a sequence of images in time. This type of animatic often includes simple camera moves (like pans and zooms) to enhance the narrative and flow of action. A **three-dimensional animatic** goes a step further by using preliminary visual materials like wireframe or low-resolution motion tests to visualize a rough cut of a computer animation. None of the special effects in an animatic are meant to be final, and often they are implemented with techniques that are cruder and less expensive than the techniques that are planned for the finished project (Fig. 2.4.9). Simple hand-drawn sketches and still photographs are common replacements for complex dynamic effects when these are presented in the form of an animatic.

Most animatics are not concerned with having a great level of motion detail, but some turn out to be quite polished. These animatics with additional detail are used for previsualizing one or several sequences in a movie, such as ones that may be particularly complex to produce on a technical level. The motion of an animated character in a regular animatic, for example, may be jerky and only insinuated, while the same motion in a **previsualization,** or **previz test**, must be as close as possible to the final motion. Animatics are like motion sketches, while previz tests present the actual action that has already been laid out and is in the process of being refined. Animatics are

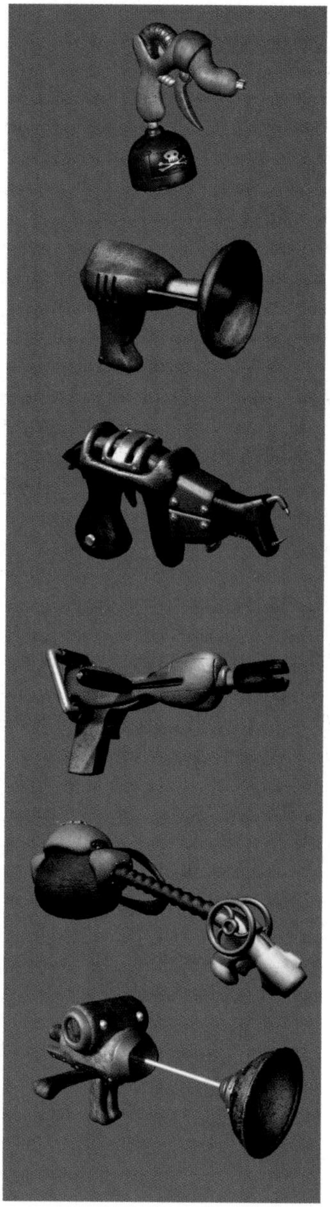

2.4.7 Designing the look and functionality of props like weapons is an integral part of the visual development process. (© bekchoi, Blueline/ Dongwoo Animation.)

commonly shown to a client or an executive producer before the final production starts. In today's production environment, animatics are usually assembled from digital flipbooks and simple live-action sequences that are composited digitally. It is partly for that reason that animatics are increasingly produced in-house at the same place where computer animation is created; both exist in a digital format. A **story reel** is essentially an animatic that is matched to the dialogue track. Story reels, also known as **Leica reels** in the days of hand-drawn animation, evolve with the production and are often updated by an editor who replaces early versions of the artwork with the most current and eventually the final version of the project.

Modeling

The task of modeling the geometry in a computer animation project is usually divided by type of model or by scene. In the former approach, popular with large projects, the models of the primary and secondary characters are assigned to a set of individuals or team while the props and the environments, called set dressing, is assigned to others. In the latter approach, which is perhaps better suited for simpler projects, the building of models for a particular shot is the responsibility of the individual or team in charge of that shot (Fig. 2.4.10). It is common to build **proxies**, or placeholder geometry, early in the process so that animators, riggers, and others can get started while the final models are completed.

Scene Layout

While final models for the characters, props, and environments are being built (sometimes even before) the positions and motions of the characters and the camera are blocked out using **placeholder geometry** (Fig. 2.4.14). This stage is called **scene layout** (Fig. 2.4.8) and it is increasingly being done directly in the computer with simplified digital models. During layout the main action is blocked out with the intention to convert a story reel into three-dimensional animatics. This **animation blocking** may include the torso, simple arm movements, and head turns; anything that has to do with body language, pose, posture, and gesture. Animation is usually done from inside out: first the torso, then the arms, hands, fingers, and facial animation is last. The motion of the characters and the camera is usually indicated in these drawings with directional arrows (Fig. 3.4.9). Some productions still make use of the traditional approach to scene layout, which is based on drawings that detail the composition of the shot within a specific animation field (Fig. 7.2.2).

Rigging or Set Up of Animation Controls

The internal skeletons that are most often used to animate characters are called **animation controls**. These controls are also called **motion**

rigs or **IK chains** (IK is short for *inverse kinematics*) because the skeletons are rigs or chains of controls that use the inverse kinematics animation technique (Fig. 2.4.11). In projects with a large volume of animations the setting up these animation controls is usually the responsibility of a **technical director** while the animators devote themselves to animating after the basic controls are set up (Fig. 12.5.5).

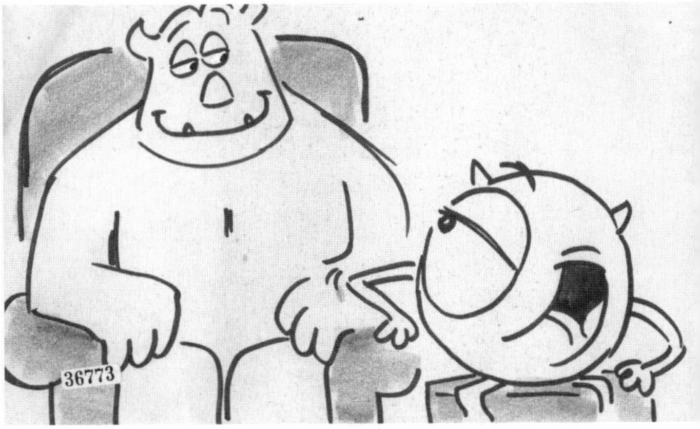

2.4.8 Storyboard drawings that emphasize facial expression, character pose, intention, and scene layout. See Figure 2.4.4 for the rendered version of the *Monsters, Inc.* top drawing and Figure 12.4.1 for the *Shrek* bottom drawing. (Top: *Monsters, Inc.* © Disney Enterprises, Inc./Pixar Animation Studios. Bottom: *Shrek*™ and © 2001 DreamWorks L.L.C.

Live Data Capture

The live data capture stage is critical in visual effects projects that revolve around the footage and data captured on the live action set, whether it is a remote location or a sound stage. Most live data capture requires specialized equipment and software specialized in motion capture (Fig. 2.4.12); three-dimensional scanning of actors, props, or terrain (Fig. 5.6.1). Live action cinematography is usually recorded with film or video cameras (Figs. 13.1.1–13.1.2). Normally these data and imagery capture tasks are done by dedicated units external to the animation team.

Rotoscoping and Camera Tracking

Once the live action elements are handed over to the digital production team the rotoscope and camera tracking specialists analyze it (Figs. 13.2.1–13.2.2 and 13.3.1). The position and motion data they extract is used by the animators and effects artists as guidelines and essential reference for their work. Both rotoscoping and camera tracking can be done manually or in a semi-automated mode. (See Chapter 13 for more details on these techniques.)

Texture Painting

Most three-dimensional computer animation projects make extensive use of textures for the geometry. Many of these textures are painted by hand directly with a digital paint system or with traditional materials and then scanned (Fig. 2.4.13). Photographic textures that are captured on film need to be scanned, and those captured with digital cameras can be transferred digitally to the system. In any case all photographic textures usually require some sort of touch-up or color balance work before they can be applied to the geometry. **Texture painting** and touch-up is usually done by painters, often from the visual development team. In some instances the texture painters have to work with the technical directors who are in charge of developing procedural textures (Figs. 9.6.4 and 9.6.8).

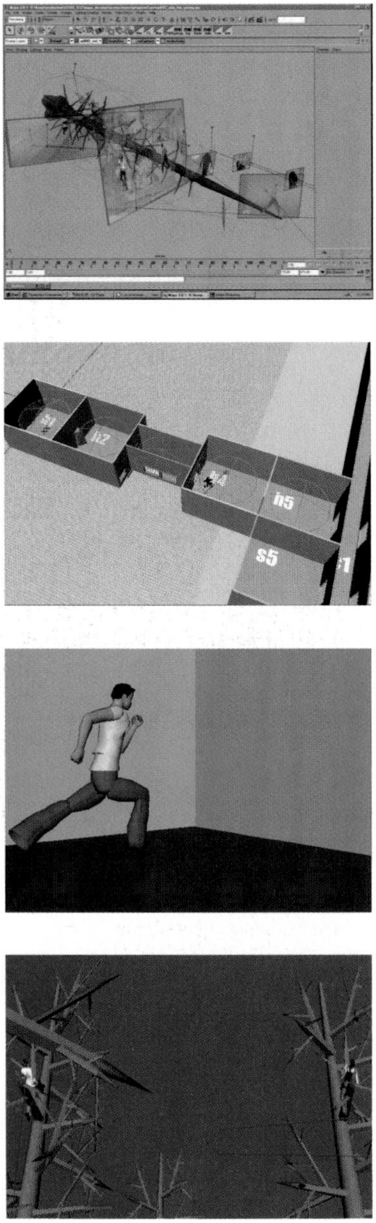

2.4.9 The computer animation for the Levi's commercial shown in Figures 13.1.3, 13.3.1, and 13.7.2 was choreographed and previsualized with these animatics. (Images courtesy of Framestore CFC and Bartle Bogle Hegarty.)

Character Animation

Character animation is done in stages, starting with rough animation and ending with animation clean up. The broad motions are usually blocked in first using placeholder geometry (Fig. 2.4.14). The secondary actions and the facial animation are added next, and finally the details are cleaned up and the timing of overlapping motion is fine-tuned. Like modeling, the animation tasks are also usually divided among different individuals or teams. A common way to parcel out the animation deliverables is by character or by scene. The animation of crowd scenes is usually assigned to a separate group, which is often part of the effects animation team. **Flipbooks** contain many still frames and are useful to preview and fine tune the animated sequences (Fig. 2.4.15).

Effects Animation

The effects animation team is in charge of animating the natural phenomena like rain, wind, and fire. Most of the techniques used to animate natural phenomena today are procedural, so often the **effects animation** team is largely composed of technically oriented animators. In some productions the animation of crowds is taken care by the effects animation group (Figs. 2.4.16 and 12.3.4).

Lighting, Shading, and Rendering

Lighting and shading are sometimes done by different teams. **Lighting** involves the placement and fine-tuning of all the light sources in every shot of the film. In many productions the lighting stage represents the first time that all the detailed models are placed together in the scene. **Shading** involves developing the shaders that are used throughout the production (Fig. 2.4.16). As with the creation of procedural textures, some aspects of lighting and shading are often done by programmers or by technically inclined artists who are able to write shaders. This process is often a direct result of the **look development** stage when most components that impact the final look of the rendered images are defined. Often with the aid of queuing software, jobs are sent for **final rendering** when all the rendering variables are set (Fig. 2.4.17). Small files are often rendered in one pass, and all the elements are rendered at the same time. Larger files with complex geometry or complex renderers are often rendered in layers, each with a different element of the shot, that require further compositing.

Compositing, Postprocessing, and Final Output

After the elements of a shot or a scene have been rendered, they are assembled and composited before the final recording takes place (Fig. 6.12.5). Stills or sequences that might need retouching or mistakes fixed are also taken care of during this stage (compositing and retouching techniques are described in Chapter 14). The logical culmination of the computer animation production process is the recording of the image onto a wide variety of media including film, videotape, DVDs, and paper (the basic concepts of output are covered in Chapter 15).

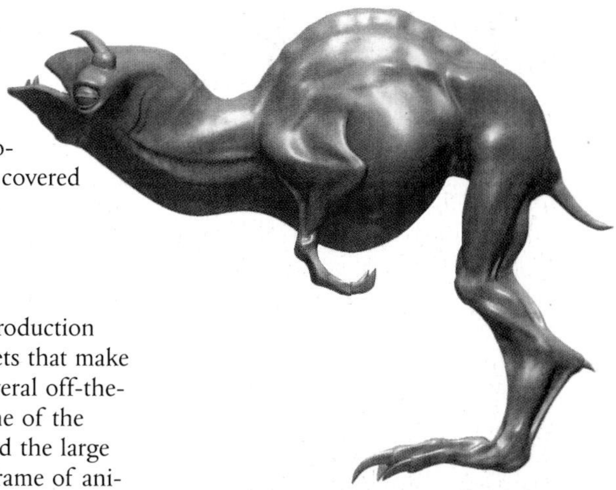

Media Asset Management and Technical Support

An often invisible but crucial component of the digital production flow is the management of the different art or media assets that make up a computer animation production. While there are several off-the-shelf **media asset management** software programs, some of the main challenges remain the constant revision of assets and the large number of people often involved in generating a single frame of animated action or visual effects. Media asset management requires daily discipline; an easy-to-understand system for identifying files from different scenes, shots, and revisions; and frequent **digital backups** of the data. The technical support group is a key component in all computer animation productions. These individuals are not directly involved in the creation of the art assets—or, in Hollywood lingo, they do not "touch the product." But without their diligence, vigilance, and quick response to technical problems, most computer animation projects would be truly unmanageable. They make sure everything works so that the production can be completed on time.

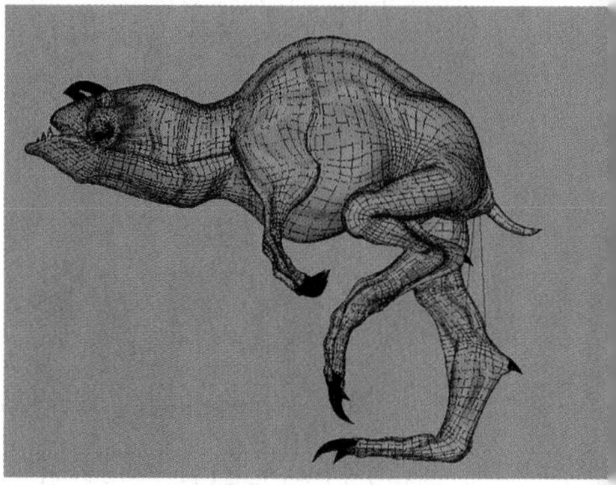

2.4.10 Wireframe and simple shading versions of a walking keyframe. (© 1999 Oddworld Inhabitants, Inc. All rights reserved.)

2.5 Ten Career Tips for Computer Animators and Digital Artists

Digital technology has been changing the face of art and animation production in a significant way since the late 1980s. Some of these changes were temporary and kept evolving until a good balance was found between the old and the new production techniques, but many of the fundamental day-to-day aspects of animation production changed for good (Fig. 2.5.1).

Being a successful three-dimensional computer artist or animator requires a lot of different skills and talents. Some are in the creative front, a few in the technical area, and many in a variety of other areas. The specific balance of skills required varies among the industries that use three-dimensional digital technology for art production: feature and television animation, platform and location-based interactive games, and websites. But for the most part there are some basic strengths that every artist and animator in this field aspires to have or is looking for in potential employees. The ten tips offered here have been distilled from years of experience and conversations with young and old practitioners. These tips might help you achieve your professional goals faster, make your career path smoother and more successful.

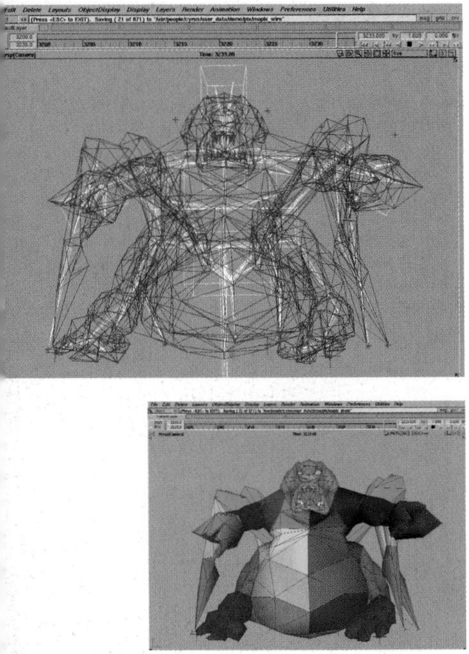

2.4.11 The inverse kinematics chain is overlaid on the geometry, which is also color-shaded to represent the different parts and functionalities associated with it. (Turok 2™ and Acclaim®, © 1999 Acclaim Entertainment, Inc. All rights reserved.)

Be Prepared for Change

The daily realities of working as a three-dimensional artist or animator in the digital production environment are in constant flux. This is not a new phenomenon. During the last decade many of the factors that define the flavor of the professional practice of digital production artists have changed. These factors—including technical developments, artistic styles, and business cycles—are still changing, and it is very likely that they will continue to change in significant ways still for several years to come.

Technical developments, for example, have a profound impact on the realities of working in digital production because they define many of the skills that are needed to complete a project. **Artistic styles** are critical because productions often hire artists based on the style of their work. In the case of three-dimensional modeling a difference in artistic style might be a cartoony approach versus a realistic approach. In the rendering area, for example, lighting scenes that will be composited with live action shots may require a stylistic approach that is different from the one needed to light scenes that will define standalone environments where virtual three-dimensional characters engage in real-time battles.

Business cycles often determine project budgets and deadlines, and both of these conditions have a major role in defining the potential of any project. Budgets usually determine the size of the creative and production teams, the type of tools (hardware and software) used to make the project a reality, as well as the period of time that the team has to complete the project. More than anything else, deadlines define the overall pressure that exists on the members of the production team. This pressure is a very real factor that governs the quality of the work experience in the life of a three-dimensional digital artist or animator.

Focus on a Realistic Goal

It is not uncommon for individuals who want to pursue a career in digital art production to have immediate goals that are clearly beyond their reach. Many who enter the field have dreams of earning fat paychecks and winning international awards within a couple of years. Many of us know that while some successful veteran three-dimensional artists and animators do make a good living and adorn their studios with awards, it is usually the result of a lifetime of effort and dedication. In this industry there have been periods that resemble the 1849 California Gold Rush. A few adventurers hit the jackpot and then thousands follow expecting to hit it with the same magnitude and within the same time frame. You have to ask yourself if you are interested in the field of three-dimensional art and animation field because of the vocation or because of some sort of a Computer Animation Gold Rush fever. A good way to focus on a **realistic goal** is by identifying a job that you both like and are qualified for. This process may start by identifying the type of place where you would like to work. Would you be more interested in joining a small shop, a medium-sized one, or a large studio? Each has pros and cons that include issues like pay scale, ability to learn from others, scope of work, and the type of projects that you would be working on. As you think about the type of place where you would like to work, you could also make a list of companies that fall within the category (or categories) that interest you. The next step would be to decide what type of positions within those companies are the ones that interest you the most. You should pay close attention to the positions that your skills and talents are best suited for.

All this preparation may mean a significant amount of research. Whether you obtain this information from magazines, instructors, friends, or at professional events, you can be sure that in most cases it pays off to be well-informed. A few lucky ones, of course, are able to land great first jobs without following this step-by-step approach but it is best not to assume that you will be that lucky. Once you have identified the type of job you are looking for, you can customize your demo reel and portfolio to meet their requirements and then start the application process.

2.4.12 The motion of this athlete is captured and will later be applied to a three-dimensional animated figure. (Courtesy of Angel Studios.)

Know Your Digital Craft

The craft of a visual artist is what allows his or her ideas to be expressed in the form of images. The craft of a digital artist or animator includes things as diverse as knowing how to get expression out of lines, shapes, color, and composition; knowing how to navigate through the different software programs being used for production; being able to work with elements created by others and, in turn, submit your own elements to the next person in the production pipeline; and being able to keep a creative focus through a production process that can be complex and removed from the final product. The **digital craft** of three-dimensional artists and animators has not been around for centuries; it is still being defined, so do not be surprised if sometimes you feel like you or your team are trying a digital production approach for the first time—you might be.

In very few other creative fields is the craft as important to the work of an artist as it is in the digital realm. When creating in some of the areas that still have not gone into a fully digital production environment, the pressures on the artist to be in full command of the craft are usually not overbearing. In those cases the production process usually involves a single artist, tools that have been around for a while (like watercolor paint), and a fairly stable production process that all participants understand.

In areas that follow the digital art production model the creative and production team is usually made up of several artists and animators. These individuals are required to use tools that are in constant change: hardware reconfigurations and software upgrades are constant. To make matters more challenging, today's digital production

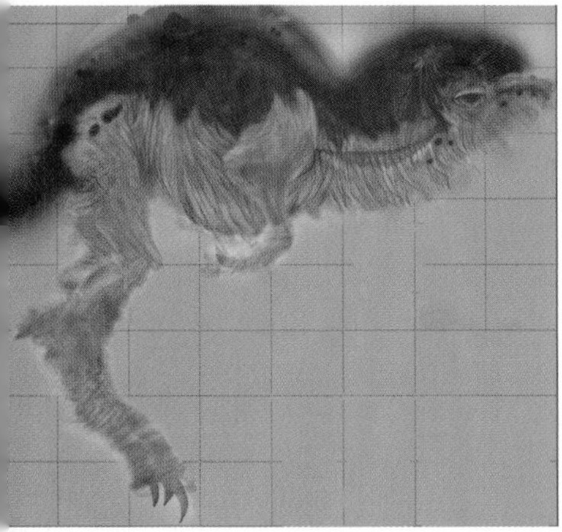

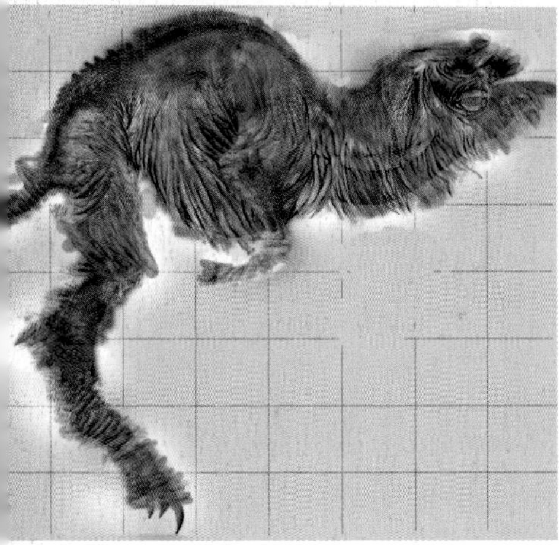

2.4.13 An image map on the left (1,200 × 1,095 pixels) and a bump map on the right to be applied to the model in Figure 2.4.10. (© 1999 Oddworld Inhabitants, Inc. All rights reserved.)

processes are still not quite standardized because many projects present such novel challenges that the process has to be adapted to those specific challenges. Staying up-to-date in the area of your artistic craft is doubly important because digital techniques are still evolving quickly. This rate of change will probably start to slow down at some point. In the meantime, continue to update your skills, perhaps by taking a professional education workshop regularly and by **sharing knowledge** with your peers on a continuous basis. Your technical knowledge and creativity can always be complemented with new specific software skills.

Update Your Demo Reel and Portfolio

A **demo reel** is a compilation of your best animation and effects work. It almost goes without saying that the most important thing about an **art portfolio** or a demo reel is that it represents your specific talents and skills in the best possible way. Traditionally demo reels are presented on videotape, but it is now common to use personal websites or DVDs to present samples of work. A website works best when it offers versions for slow and fast connections, and for a variety a players. The second most important thing—as far as getting the job that you want—is that your portfolio or demo reel contains the types of items that the potential employer is interested in seeing. For example, your portfolio or demo reel may be of high quality but if the work is not the kind that your potential employer is looking for then your high-quality portfolio will not be an effective tool for getting that job. All this basically means one thing in respect to maximizing your chances of getting the job that you want.

While you should focus your energy on developing a demo reel or portfolio that is of high quality, you should also spend some energy customizing it to the specific preferences and requirements of the company that you are applying to. Find out as much as you can about the specific demo reel and **portfolio requirements** of the companies that you want to submit your work to. Some companies will mail or fax their guidelines, others post that information on their website recruiting pages, and a few will provide it over the phone.

The fact that different companies have unique demo reel requirements might mean that you end up with a couple of slightly different versions of selections of your best work. For example, one company might prefer to review videotapes containing any kind of work of any length while, while another company might only want to see reels that are under three minutes long, that start with wireframe motion tests and end with fully rendered animated sequences, and that contain exclusively character animation created with motion capture techniques. Some companies require notes clarifying the work that you were responsible for in group projects. You do not have to **customize your reel** to get a good job, but it certainly increases your chances and your options. The specific components of a demo reel are described at the end of this chapter.

Be Prepared to Work as a Member of a Team

Virtually all digital projects are team efforts. Whether the project is a website, a videogame, or an effects shot for a live action show, the complex nature of these projects almost makes it a condition that the production process be collaborative.

In the case of an effects shot, for example, the sheer number of steps in the process requires a team of several individuals to handle the workload. On occasion some of the steps have to happen in parallel. For example, someone might have to build the extensive three-dimensional environments, while someone else builds a detailed three-dimensional character, while yet another member of the team paints the textures that will be applied to the rendered version. In the case of a website, even if the visual content is simple and requires only straightforward techniques, there is always the ever-present pressure of tight deadlines. Because websites are commonly refreshed every day or every few days, the best—and often the only—way to meet deadlines is by dividing the workload among several people.

In predigital production times many artists were able to complete their works of art by themselves. A painter working on a small painting is probably the paramount example of a traditional visual artist who doesn't really need the help of other artists to complete the work. The painter sketched the composition, primed the canvas, mixed the colors, laid down the underpaint, rendered the details, and varnished the finished work. In a similar vein, even many of the pioneering experimental animators or videomakers of two or three decades ago were able to complete many of their projects by themselves. But the complexity of the work often calls for a team approach. When paintings became too complex—as was the case with murals—the master painter had assistants who mixed the colors, prepared the painting surface and even applied the paint. As animators developed works where the action became more complex, subtle, or longer in duration or as they strove for more realistic effects the production model had to include several individuals who took care of specialized tasks.

But in today's digital environment, teams of creators working in unison are often required to complete many of the personal artwork projects that traditionally were made by a single individual. Only the simplest of short computer animations today could be designed, modeled, painted, rendered, animated, and composited by a single individual. The same can be said of almost any interactive or multimedia digital project.

Teamwork is not always what we are taught in art and animation schools. The emphasis there still tends to be on developing our own artistic voice as we master a few techniques. Perhaps we will soon see the fruits of innovative art teachers who are devising new approaches to teaching art and animation that allow students to develop their artistic vision in parallel with developing and strengthening their teamwork skills.

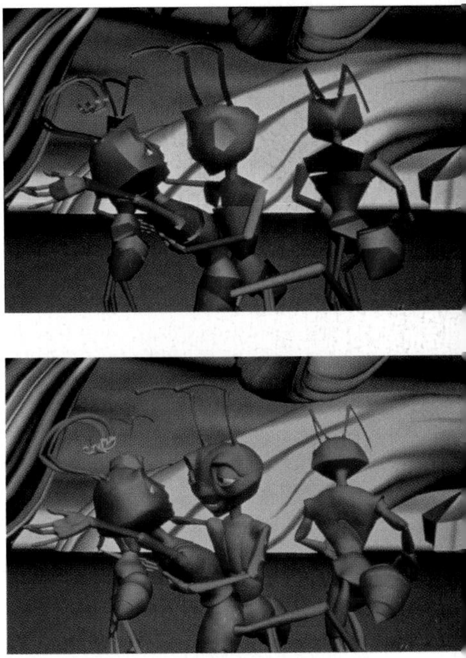

2.4.14 Proxy models are used to sketch the primary animation (top), and more detailed models are used to animate the facial expressions (bottom). (Images from the motion picture *ANTZ*™. © DreamWorks L.L.C. and PDI, reprinted with permission of DreamWorks Animation.)

Develop an Appreciation for Preproduction

Digital productions are usually complex because they require many steps to complete the work. Many of these steps often have to take place in parallel or in a very specific sequence. Experience has taught us that the best way to tackle **complex productions**—digital or not—is to analyze them and break them down into their simplest components. This analytical and planning process takes place mostly during the preproduction stage of a project. In a digital production environment preproduction is not a matter of choice. It is a requirement, especially if we want to complete the project **within budget** and **by the deadline**.

Getting used to planning ahead is a key factor for success in your digital art production career. From the production point of view you will be invaluable to others on your team by having a plan of action that you can present to them and also by sticking to the plan of action that you all agreed to follow. Find out what the next step in the process will be. That way you will be more likely to stay one step ahead, and you will be able to be more flexible and more efficient. Finally, take the preproduction meetings as seriously as you can by contributing your best ideas to them even if others do not realize the importance of the meeting. In the long term this is likely to win you the respect of your peers and will contribute to the success of the projects that you work on.

Focus on Issues that May Impact Your Health

As with any other profession being a three-dimensional animator has potential **health risks**. Fortunately most of them can easily prevented by paying attention to some basic rules and work habits. A significant number of today's artists who work with computers seem to suffer from work-related health issues ranging from simple backach-

2.4.15 Two versions of an animated 12-frame walk cycle. The right leg in the top version stays in the air a little longer than the version in the bottom. (© 1999 Oddworld Inhabitants, Inc. All rights reserved.)

es to **carpal tunnel syndrome**. The later is a condition that results from overuse and/or abuse of the arms, wrists, hands, or fingers. This typically creates swelling in the tendons that travel through the narrow carpal tunnel in the wrist, and the pressure applied to the nerves creates discomfort, pain, and even disability. In working with computers artists face unique health threats that differ from those present when working with other tools. We have to learn faster—as a community of digital artists and as individuals—to take preventive measures in a systematic way.

Let's think for a second of a few of the preventive measures that artists working in other media have developed to minimize the chance of physical injury every day. Sculptors who use power tools or who work with high-temperature metals in foundries have learned to wear goggles, gloves, and heavy boots. Dancers and athletes who submit their musculoskeletal systems to a daily eight-hour routine take the time to warm up and to cool down so that their bodies stay relaxed and limber. Painters who use toxic pigments do not lick the tips of the brushes to make them pointy. Photographers handle with care corrosive chemicals in the darkroom and when in the studio they try to give their eyes a break as they trigger multiple flash units hundreds of times throughout the day.

It is clear that artists throughout the decades and centuries have developed ways to preserve their health in the workplace. It is time for us to do the same, and it is up to us to not only come up with some simple health guidelines but to follow them every day and to share them with our peers. We can be very proactive in preventing stress-related problems and even **repetitive stress injuries**, commonly known as **RSI**. More than anything else it is a matter of stretching before we start using the mouse and keyboard, taking breaks once in a while, and keeping the right posture while we spend hours sitting down (Fig. 2.5.2). Exercising once in a while doesn't hurt either. Use common sense.

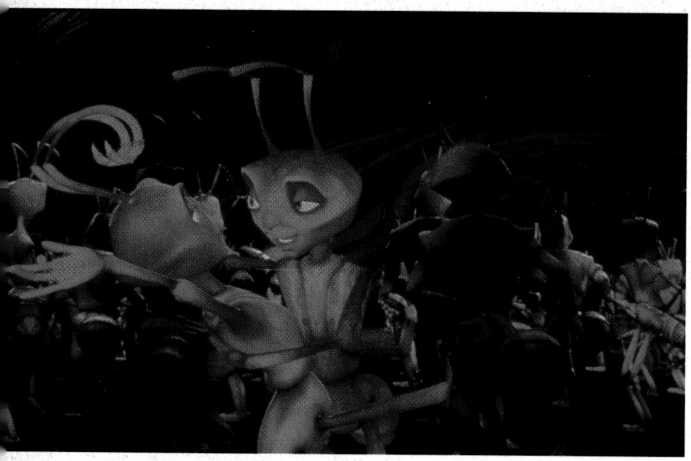

2.4.16 The lighting of the scene is finalized and rendered after most or all of the animation is in place. The frame on the opposite page includes motion blur and depth of field rendering refinements. (Images from the motion picture *ANTZ*™. © DreamWorks L.L.C. and PDI, reprinted with permission of DreamWorks Animation.)

Learn About the History of Digital Creation

As you go about creating the next masterpiece of digital art or digital animation remember that other individuals have been working toward the same goal since the 1960s. If you have been studying the three-dimensional computer art and animation created by others, you already know how much you can gain from it. If you haven't yet then this is a good time to start; by now you have probably read Chapter 1 of this book, right? : -) . Looking at other efforts can teach you a lot about which techniques work better than others or when a technique is matched appropriately to the creative goals of a project. If nothing else, knowing some of the important works that have defined the field of three-dimensional art and animation can save you from making the same mistakes that others have already made.

Learn About the Business Aspect of Your Career

If you read the newspapers or trade magazines you are probably familiar with the impact that the digital distribution of content is having on the **intellectual property** and trade laws that govern our society and the world. In a similar way many of the standard practices that used to regulate or define the employment of artists and animators are changing. Now would be a good time to invest some of your valuable time in learning about some of the most common employment and business issues that may shape your career. For example, being hired as a freelancer instead of as a staff employee has some pros and cons. Which of the two is best for your situation? Other examples in this area include the terms of an employment contract that are standard in the creative industries that employ digital art production, the benefits associated with employment, the role played by a labor union in your benefits, and the ownership of the intellectual property that is the result of your work. These issues might not be as delightful and inspiring as creating the actual images or animation that fill you with passion, but they are equally important in shaping your career as a digital artist or animator. Take the time to learn more about them; some resources can be found at the *www.artof3d.com* website.

Continue to Develop Your Artistic Vision

Last but not least, it is important to remember that your **artistic vision** and your personal sensibilities are probably the most valuable long-term aspect of your creativity. Often three-dimensional artists and animators get so caught up in the technical aspects of digital art production that they forget to develop their creative minds and polish their ideas. Continue to foster your artistic vision as you learn from

others and as you absorb the experience of digital art production. Whether you are a member of a creative team or an independent creator keep in mind that one day your voice may find a resonance in the mainstream that you never expected.

2.6 Assembling a Demo Reel

As mentioned earlier a demo reel is a compilation of your best animation and effects work, and it shows a prospective employer, client, or colleague what you are capable of both technically and creatively. The first step in putting together a demo reel is deciding what content and techniques you want to showcase. This, of course, depends on what type of skills you have and what type of positions you are applying for. Your demo reel should include a lot of character animation if, for example, you are interested in a character animation position. A demo reel with examples of compositing and technical rendering is unlikely to get you a job as a computer animator.

The second step consists of finding out what the employers' application requirements are and what job openings or skills might be looking for when you apply. You can easily do this research on the Web or by phone, and from it you should get useful information

2.4.17 Final rendering of the character, incuding the model, textures and lighting. (© 1999 Oddworld Inhabitants, Inc. All rights reserved.)

about the type and length of work to include.

The third step consists of reviewing the material that you would consider including in the demo reel, and selecting the segments that work best and represent you the best. Show it to others, especially individuals not familiar with your work, and get their opinions and reactions. After the initial selection you have to decide what would be the most effective sequencing to showcase the work. Editing a demo reel is a process that requires some expertise with video editing programs. Fortunatelly this can be done digitally with programs such as Apple Final Cut Pro, Adobe Premiere, Avid DV Express or Media 100. The selection and editing process might take several days and it usually requires a couple of different cuts before you find the one that looks good. Selecting a music soundtrack that works with your sequence of images and creating titles at the beginning and end of the reel are also part of putting the demo reel together. These titles should be easy to read and should include your name, telephone number, and email address.

The fourth step in putting together a demo reel is to record and duplicate the edited materials on a particular media. You can present your demo reel on a videotape, DVD-ROM, CD-ROM, or a website. If you go for the traditional videotape keep in mind that VHS is still the most popular video format for demo reels because practically everyone in the computer animation and visual effects industries has easy access to a VHS player. Other video formats including DV, DVCAM, Betacam SP or SX, and Digital Betacam offer better quality than VHS but not everybody has an easy way to play them: double-check before sending them. Also keep in mind that different countries use different video standards. In a nutshell the NTSC standard is used in the U.S.A., Japan, and most of Latin America. The PAL standard is used in most countries in Europe and much of the world. SECAM is used in France and a few other countries. Multi-standard players are common in Europe but rare in the U.S.A. (See Chapter 15 for more information on video output.)

If you choose to present your work on CD-ROM or DVD-ROM do your best so that the versions you burn can be played on different players, ideally a consumer DVD player, a PC, and an Apple computer. If your digital media will only play on a specific type of player or computer, make sure to indicate those restrictions on the label or the box. If you choose to display your work on a website you will probably need to go through an additional step of compression. This will help to optimize the material for playback and/or to fit all the material in a particular media or bandwidth. Always try to create materials that will easily play on as many players and browsers as possible. Quicktime, for example, is a popular

Ten Career Tips for Computer Animators

1. Be prepared for change.
2. Focus on a realistic goal.
3. Know your digital craft.
4. Update and customize your reel and portfolio.
5 Be prepared to work as a member of a team.
6 Develop an appreciation for preproduction.
7 Focus on issues that may impact your health.
8 Learn about the history of digital creation.
9 Learn about the business aspects of your career.
10. Continue to develop your artistic vision.

2.5.1 Ten career tips for computer animators and digital artists.

2.5.2 The ideal posture to avoid repetitive stress injuries, backaches, or eye strain includes keeping your wrists straight, shoulders relaxed, monitor at eye-level, and frequent stretching.

and relatively cross-platform file format for delivering demo reels on CD-ROMs and websites.

In addition to the visuals it is useful to include some written materials that complement your demo reel. These include the cover letter, the resume, and the technical notes. The **cover letter** or introductory email helps employers understand what type of a job you are looking for and what special skills or needs you might have. The most effective cover letters are short and to the point. The **resume**, or curriculum vitae, provides information about your professional experience, education, and computer proficiency among other things. Listing what specific tasks you were responsible in a specific job or project is important. Listing software programs that are part of your creative toolbox is useful, especially when you also specify your level of expertise. For example: "I am an expert user of Alias | Wavefront Maya 6.2, quite good at Adobe Photoshop 10, and have used a Discreet Inferno system a few times." **Technical notes** are often quite effective in providing information that may enhance the viewers' understanding of your work. These notes may include technical or practical information, for example, about circumstances or techniques that defined, constrained, or propelled your projects. Written details about the modeling, lighting, rendering or compositing process, for example, can shed a lot of light on your skills and understanding of the technique.

Demo Reel Checklist

- ❑ Select only your very best work.
- ❑ Include work that shows your creativity.
- ❑ Include work that shows your technical skills.
- ❑ Include work relevant to the position(s) that you are applying for.
- ❑ Highlight the work that might be of most interest to the reviewers.
- ❑ Minimize editing that may distract from your work.
- ❑ Include opening and closing titles with your name and contact information.
- ❑ View the copies before you send them to make sure the are of good quality.
- ❑ Include a few technical notes that might help to understand the work.

2.6.1 Simple checklist to prepare a demo reel.

(Next page: Characters from *El Bosque Animado*. © 2001 Dygra Films.)

CHAPTER 2

Key Terms

Administrative team
Animatics
Animation
Animation blocking
Animation controls
Applications software
Approval
Art portfolio
Artistic styles
Artistic vision
ATM (Asyncronous Transfer Mode)
Bandwidth
Budget
Business cycles
Business plan
By the deadline
Carpal tunnel syndrome
Collaboration
Color keys
Complex productions
Computer animation
Computer-animated feature movie
Computer rendering farms
Computer resources
Cover letter
Creative goals
Creative team
Creative vision
Crossing over
Customize your reel
Deliverables
Delivery media
Demo reel
Dialogue
Digital backups
Digital craft
Digital format
Digital compositing and postproduction
Digital studio
Downward compatibility
DS-1 (Digital Signal Level One)
Effects animation
Ethernet
FDDI (Fiber Distributed Data Interface)
Final rendering
Flipbooks
Footage quotas
Hand-drawn animated feature movie
Health risks
IK chains
Input capabilities
Internets
Intranets
Intellectual property
Leica reels
Lighting
Look development
Media asset management
Meetings
Milestones
Microcomputers
Modeling
Motion rigs
Motion tests
Network
Network servers
Output capabilities
Operating systems
Peripheral storage
Personnel
Placeholder geometry
Plan of action
Planning
Plug-ins
Portfolio requirements
Postprocessing
Postproduction
Preproduction
Previsualization
Previz test
Processing power
Production
Production pipeline
Production strategy
Production team
Production technique
Proprietary software
Props
Proxy
RAID disk arrays
Realistic goal
Remote collaboration
Rendering
Repetitive stress injuries (RSI)
Resources
Resume
Review
Rigging
Scene layout
Schedule
Script
Shading
Sharing knowledge
Shot assignments
Independent short
Software upgrades
Standard length
Story development
Story reel
Super-microcomputers
Supervision
T-1
Team efforts
Teamwork
Technical complexity
Technical developments
Technical director
Technical implementation
Technical notes
Technical team
Television commercial
Texture painting
Turnkey software
Type of production
Upward compatibility
Visual effects
Visual effects for a feature movie
Visual style
Within budget
Written description
Written materials

SECTION II

Modeling

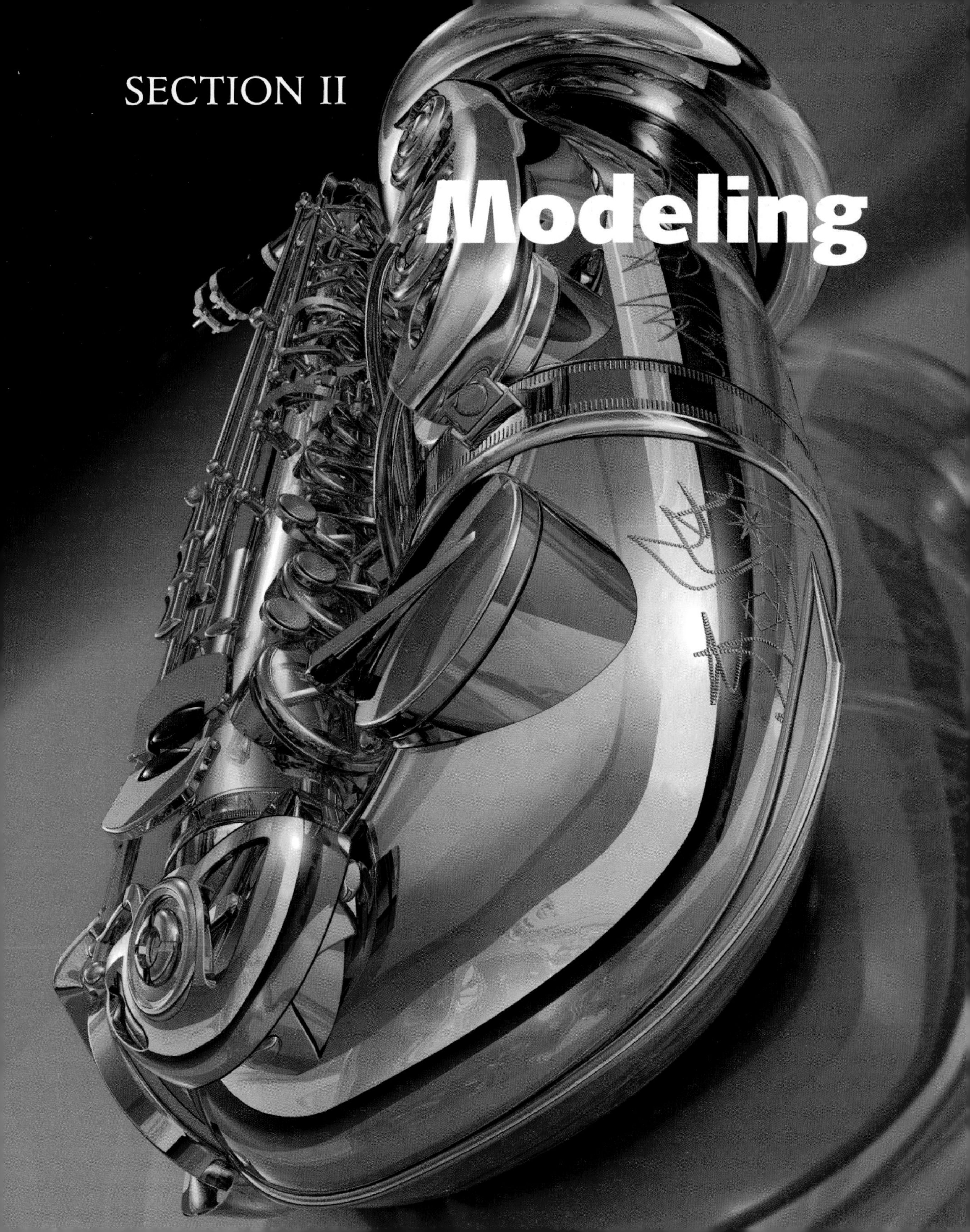

(Previous page) Saxophone modeled with myriad techniques. (Courtesy of Toru Kosaka, STUDIO EggMan.)

3.1.1 This surreal scene illustrates the concept of gluttony with an unusual assortment of objects and creatures created with multiple modeling techniques. (© Jim Ludtke.)

CHAPTER 3

Basic Modeling Concepts

3

Summary

THE SPATIAL DESCRIPTION AND PLACEMENT of imaginary three-dimensional objects, environments, and scenes with a computer system is called **modeling**. This chapter explores the basic concepts of the modeling process, including the numerical description of objects, moving and resizing objects in three-dimensional space, common file formats, and advice on getting ready for a modeling session.

QUICK INDEX

3.1 Space, Objects, and Structures

We live in a three-dimensional world. We move among other people, climb mountains, run on the beach, and admire the landscape around us. We go in and out of buildings, walk up and down the stairs, drive through bridges, and grab utensils for writing, cooking, and combing ourselves. Our daily life happens in three-dimensional environments and is full of three-dimensional objects and characters (Fig. 3.1.1). We see and feel three-dimensionality all the time. But unless we are involved in an activity or profession that is related to building things, like silverware or furniture, buildings or bridges, we rarely concern ourselves with how our three-dimensional reality was put together and what techniques were used for building it.

When it comes to the modeling of our reality we usually take a lot of things for granted. But if we want to model three-dimensional scenes with a computer program, we have to familiarize ourselves with the large selections of computer software tools that can be used for modeling objects and environments. In three-dimensional computer modeling it is quite common to use a combination of tools for building just one object. For example, think of the difference between a chair that was built using just two tools—a manual saw and a hammer—and a chair that was built with six tools—a thick saw, a thin saw, a lathe, a curved chisel, a hammer, and a sanding tool. It is obvious that while the first chair could have an interesting design the variety of shapes would be limited. The second chair would have richer

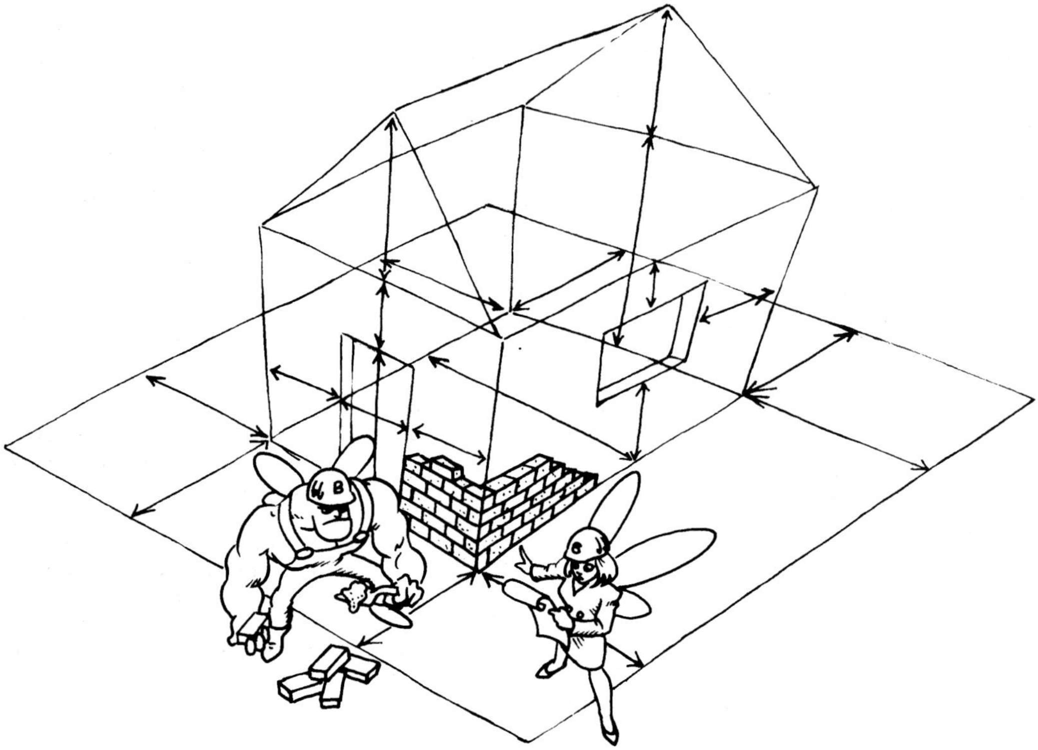

3.1.2 Building a simple rectangular room requires taking measurements that include the orientation of the walls, the location of the doorway, the windows, and the distance between the walls.

and more refined modeling. The simple computer-based modeling tools are described in this chapter, and most of the advanced modeling tools are covered in Chapter 4. Now let's step back and talk about some general issues involved in modeling in three dimensions.

Many of the basic conventions used in three-dimensional modeling software describing three-dimensional scenes are based on traditional conventions used in various disciplines. For example, to convey space in a clear and concise way, architects use conventions related to measuring, composition, and sequence. Even the design of a simple rectangular room requires measuring many times so that all the components of the room end up where they were planned to be (Fig. 3.1.2). Furthermore, to interpret accurately an architect's drawing and build it, masons need to take measurements. Over the ages masons and architects have developed conventions so that they can be precise and clear about measuring **spaces**, building **objects**, and arranging them in **structures**.

We use similar conventions to describe the dimension, placement, and sequence of objects and environments in a three-dimensional space simulated with a computer program. A beginning builder will soon find out that there are many different methods available for measuring space, and at first this variety can be confusing. But experienced builders usually find this richness of methods very empowering and have the option of using one or another depending on the requirements of the project. Let's start our definition of three-dimensional space with the boundaries that define our **workspace** or **scene**. The simplest way to do this is to imagine that we are working inside a large cube. We can think of this cube as our world or environment. Objects that exist within the cube are visible, those that fall outside are invisible (Fig. 7.2.1).

The main point of reference in this world is called the **world origin**. The origin is usually located in the center of the space, but it can also be placed or repositioned elsewhere depending on the modeling needs and strategies (Fig. 3.1.3). For example, if we were building a model of the solar system, it would make sense to have the world origin where the sun is, in the center, because all the other objects in the system are placed around the sun, and can be easily described in terms of the sun. If we were building an underwater scene that included both fish under the water and boats above the water, we might want to position the origin at the point where air and water meet. In the case of a three-dimensional model of an airport, the world origin could be placed at ground level, matching the position of the control tower. All three-dimensional spaces have three basic **dimensions**: width, height, and depth. A common method for representing these dimensions in a three-dimensional space is by using arrows or **axes** (Fig. 3.1.3). It is common to label the **axis** representing the width of a **three-dimensional space** with the letter X, the height axis with the letter Y, and the depth axis with the letter Z. The point in space where these three axes intersect, or cross each other, is the world origin.

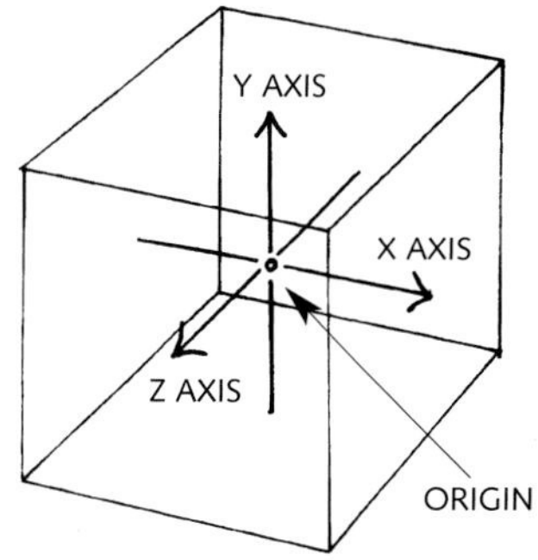

3.1.3 The origin is a point of reference usually located in the center of the three-dimensional space. It can also be located elsewhere in three-dimensional space. A three-dimensional space has width, height, and depth dimensions each represented by the three axes in the Cartesian coordinate system. The numerical values in the figure correspond to those in a right-handed coordinate system.

The **rectangular coordinate system** can be used to define specific locations and accurately position the points of objects in three-dimensional space. René Descartes, an eighteenth-century French philosopher and mathematician, formalized the idea of using three axes labeled X, Y, and Z to represent the dimensions in three-dimensional space. The coordinate system he devised is commonly referred to as the **Cartesian** (or rectangular) **coordinate system**. Each axis in the system can be divided into many units of measurement. In principle these units are abstract values that can represent different units of measurement and scales of dimension. On each axis the values to one side of the origin are positive, and the values on the other side are negative. As shown in Fig. 3.1.3, the positive direction of each axis in a right-handed coordinate system is represented with an arrowhead.

There are many ways of representing the direction of an axis and, consequently, the directions in which values on that axis are positive or negative. Usually though, in what is called a **right-handed coordinate system**, the values on the X axis become larger to the right of the origin, the values on the Y axis increase as they move above the origin, and the values on the Z axis grow as they get close to us. In a **left-handed coordinate system** the values on the Z axis decrease as they get closer to us. There are several variations of the directionality of the rectangular coordinate system, but most three-dimensional modeling programs use the right-handed coordi-

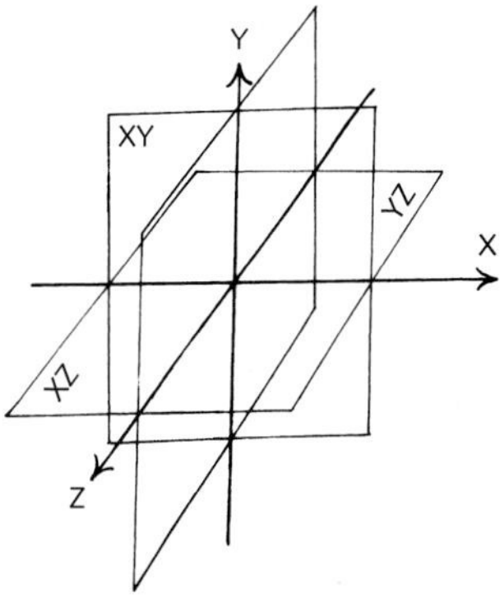

3.1.4 The three planes, or views, that can be defined with the XY, XZ, and YZ pairs of axes are useful for building models from different points of view.

nate system to describe the virtual world.

The three axes in the rectangular coordinate system can be paired with each other in three different ways so that each pair of axes defines a plane or a view. The XY axes define the **front plane**, the XZ axes define the **top plane**, and the YZ axes define the **side plane** (Fig. 3.1.4). There are other coordinate systems in addition to the popular rectangular coordinate system. The **spherical** or **azimuthal coordinate system** is also widely used because it provides a simple way for placing objects in a three-dimensional world in terms of their distance to the object, their angle around the point of interest, and their altitude angle above the point of interest. The spherical system is especially useful for placing and moving cameras and light sources in a three-dimensional scene (Fig. 3.4.8).

Any **world** or **global coordinate system** is useful for placing or moving objects in the world or in relation to each other. World coordinates are absolute values that are relative to the origin of the world. These coordinates do not depend on any specific object in the world and are applied to all objects in the world indistinctly. (Global transformations, as we shall read later in this chapter, are easily expressed in terms of the world coordinate system.) In addition to the world coordinate system, however, each object in the world can have its own **object** or **local coordinate system** (Figures 3.1.4 and 3.1.5). Object coordinate systems are values relative to the origin of the object, which is sometimes placed in the center of the object. For all practical purposes object coordinate systems are used only to specify positions, orientations, or transformations of the object in question. (Local transformations are almost always expressed in the coordinate system of the object.)

3.1.5 The world coordinate system is used to place and move objects, the entire building for example, in relation to the world origin. The objects' coordinate systems are useful for performing transformations only on specific objects, for example a single column. (Sainsbury's, view from Blackfriars Road South. © Hayes Davidson.)

3.2 Building with Numbers

Throughout time we have developed a sophisticated vocabulary for describing with the spoken or written word the shape of three-dimensional objects and their relative positions to one another. We can use that vocabulary for communicating with others about three-dimensional objects and their positions in space. But, even though verbal descriptions of objects can be very concise, they lack precision. Verbal descriptions of objects can be interpreted in a variety of different ways, not only for the obvious issues of dimension but also for the subtle issues of proportion and shape. As you read the following description of a flower vase try visualizing it in your mind or by drawing it with pencil and paper.

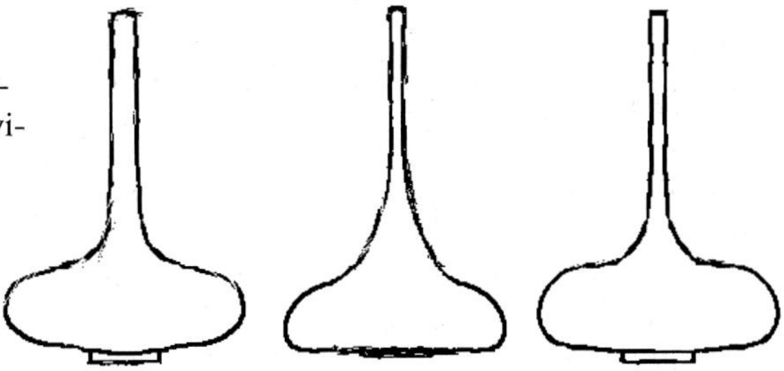

If you have some experience with modelmaking or pottery you were probably able to follow the description of the shapes in the vase and the relation between them, and your flower vase might look similar to the results shown in Fig. 3.2.1. But if you have little experience with three-dimensional models, your sketch may be quite different, or you may have been unable to finish reading all of the description. Maybe you lost interest because you found it difficult to visualize all the shapes and the ways in which they were attached to one another.

Most individuals and today's computer systems are incapable of recreating in detail verbal descriptions of complex three-dimensional shapes. Computer modeling in three dimensions requires very precise and unequivocal descriptions of shape. The method of choice for precise and unequivocal descriptions of shape and their location in space consists of using numbers. With numerical description we can specify the position of an object in space and the details of its shape: height, width, depth, diameter, curvature, and number of sides. Figure 3.2.2 illustrates most of the numbers required for describing a fairly simple three-dimensional shape.

Much of the success in modeling three-dimensional objects and environments with a computer system lies in understanding how a particular computer system describes a shape with numbers. The exact numbers can mean different things to different software programs. For example, some systems give great attention to the decimal, or floating point, numbers (i.e., 5.379) that describe the subtle shape of a small curve, while other computer systems may ignore those numbers completely and recreate the curve based on a whole numerical value (i.e., 5). We must also keep in mind that some of the numbers that describe a shape might be of little value to us if we were building the object with traditional materials, such as wood, but the same numbers often provide the computer system with crucial information for building the object with computer modeling techniques. For example, the order in which we number points in a shape can yield very different results.

The essence of all software-based three-dimensional modeling techniques consists of creating a **data file**, or a list of numbers, that defines models in a way that can be understood by the computer program. Whether we create a simple cube or a collection of computer shapes representing a human hand, the numbers describing the object are kept in a file so that the program can load them into memory, display them, modify them, display them again, save them, and so on. The files that contain the data describing the object are

Verbal Description of a Vase

- The vase has a very long neck and a short, round base.
- The neck is about five times the height of the base, the width of the base is about twice its own height.
- The cylindrical neck grows out of the base slowly.
- At the point where the neck touches the base it has a width that equals the height of the base.
- As it moves upward the neck gets narrow, and as it passes the first fifth of its height the neck reaches a thin, delicate width that remains constant until the end of the neck.
- A small section of the oval shape that constitutes the base of the vase is sliced off so that the bottom of the base is flat.
- The resulting sharp edge at the bottom of the base is rounded off just a little bit.
- Halfway between the edge of the base and its center, a thin slice of a short cylinder is attached to the base.

3.2.1 Different interpretations of the verbal description of a flower vase.

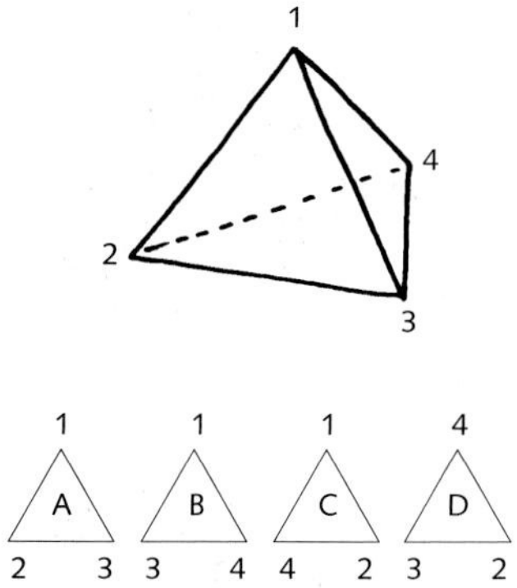

Geometry Format #1

Point	X	Y	Z
1	0	0	0
2	-1	-2	1
3	1	-2	1
4	0	-2	-1

Face	Point	Point	Point
A	1	2	3
B	1	3	4
C	1	4	2
D	3	4	2

Geometry Format #2

Face	XYZ	XYZ	XYZ
1	0 0 0	-1 -2 1	1 -2 1
2	0 0 0	1 -2 1	0 -2 -1
3	0 0 0	0 -2 -1	-1 -2 1
4	1 -2 1	0 -2 -1	-1 -2 1

3.2.2 The difference between two geometry formats for the same object is quite evident here. These two listings were generated with two different types of modeling software.

called **geometry files**. Examples of all geometry file formats are discussed later in this chapter.

In most modeling systems, three-dimensional objects can be modeled by typing the numbers that describe the object directly into the system. This method of **direct numerical description** can be quite tedious and time-consuming. We rarely use it unless we are looking for an extremely specific shape or a detail that can be hard to model with regular modeling tools. Even when we use the interactive modeling tools provided by the software it is still possible to peek at the numerical information that the software uses to describe and manipulate three-dimensional shapes. Most systems allow us to get this numerical information in varying degrees of detail (Fig. 3.2.2). Both the shape of an object and its position in three-dimensional space are expressed in terms of numerical values (Fig. 4.6.1). From the computer's point of view, numerical values are easy to manipulate and easy to repeat. This facilitates the building of three-dimensional objects with modeling software, as well as the duplication of objects using the **cut-copy-paste** techniques used by most of today's programs.

3.3 Points, Lines, and Surfaces

Now that you have learned how to locate points in three-dimensional space and how to create and edit lists of numbers that represent XYZ spaces you are ready to start thinking about building a simple model. The three-dimensional object illustrated in Fig. 3.3.1 is defined by four points, six lines, six edges, and four planes.

Points, lines, and surfaces are among the basic elements that can be used to build three-dimensional objects. A **point** can be easily defined by its XYZ location. A **line** can be defined by the XYZ location of its two endpoints. An **edge** is defined by two adjacent surfaces. A planar **surface** can be defined by the position of its bounding lines. An object is usually composed of several points, lines, and surfaces. A three-dimensional object can be described to software as a list of numbers. This list is usually generated automatically by the computer program, but it can also be generated directly by the user. As stated earlier, it is not necessary in most cases to input all of these numbers by hand. In fact, we do not need to be aware that all this number-shuffling is taking place. But once in a while you will encounter modeling situations when it will be paramount that you understand the meaning and proper structure of these numbers. It is for those occasions when the information in this section will come in handy.

Simple objects like the one pictured in Figures 3.2.2 and 3.3.1, and even much more complex objects, can be easily described or edited in most modeling software providing their point XYZ positions and the connectivity lists to the three-dimensional program. Whether this is done by typing their numerical values directly on the keyboard or by transferring the XYZ data collected by a three-dimensional scanner, a simple methodology can be followed. First, label all the points and all planes in your sketch or printout—if one is available (Fig. 3.2.2, top). Then write down the XYZ position of each of the points in list form (Fig. 3.2.2, Format 1 points). Finally, make another list that includes each of the planes and all the points that must be connected to define them. It is important that all the points in each plane are connected in the same direction—either clockwise or counterclockwise (Fig. 3.2.2, Format 1 faces). Some computer programs require that you connect the points clockwise, while others require counter-clockwise, but usually all programs require that the order be consistent throughout the entire object.

The planar surfaces that define most three-dimensional objects are also called **facets**—as those in a cut diamond—or polygons. The word polygon has its roots in the Greek word *polygónon*, which means "with many angles." Polygons are closed planes bounded by straight lines. Polygons can be regular or irregular. Many of the three-dimensional shapes created with three-dimensional computer software are made of polygons. Simple geometric shapes may be defined with dozens of polygons. Objects like a teacup that require a fair amount of detail may also require hundreds of polygons to model that detail. Complex objects, such as the detailed model of a human, may require thousands of polygons (Fig. 3.3.2). The modeling of natural phenomena, such as a forest or simulation of the explosion of a supernova star, may require millions of polygons.

Sometimes we can define objects with curves instead of straight lines, and curved surfaces instead of flat polygonal surfaces. At first building objects with curved surfaces can be more demanding than using polygonal surfaces because curved surfaces are more complex. Read Chapters 4 and 5 for additional information on curves and curved surfaces.

3.3.1 Three-dimensional objects are defined by points, lines, and planes. This simple pyramid has a total of four vertices and four sides.

3.4 Moving Things Around

Once we have built some objects we can move them around in three-dimensional space and create a composition or a scene. Sometimes it becomes necessary to move some of an object's components—a group of points, for example—before the modeling is completed.

The functions used for modifying the shape of objects, their size and proportions as well as their position in space, are called **geometric transformations**. The name of these simple but powerful tools obviously comes from the fact that they can be used to transform—to change, to move, to modify—the geometry of objects. In effect, these **mathematical operations** can modify the numerical information that describes the objects that we build in the environment and even the environment itself. The most widely used geometric transformations are translation, rotation, scaling, and perspective projection.

Geometric transformations can also be applied to the camera that "looks" at the scenes we model and arrange, and also to the lights that reveal our creations to the camera. See Chapter 7 for more information on camera motion, and Chapter 8 for more on moving lights around. In general, when specifying transformations to be applied to a single object or a group of objects it is important to specify the type of transformation, the axis or axes in which the transformation is to take place, the point around which the rotation or series of rotations will occur (whether the transformation is local or global), and the order in which transformations are to take place in a sequence of several of them. Geometric transformations are usually calculated by most programs with the aid of a **transformation matrix**. This 4×4 matrix is used to calculate the new XYZ values after a transformation is applied to all the points of a three-dimensional element. A few programs allow users to manipulate XYZ values directly in the matrix in addition to, or instead of, using more user-friendly tools.

Global or Local Transformations

Geometric transformations can be performed on single objects or on entire environments. Transformations that are applied to the objects using the environment's axes and/or origin are called **global transformations**. When transformations are applied to a single object—or a limited selection of objects—using the object's own axes and origin, they are called **local transformations**.

In general, software programs offer two basic techniques for specifying whether a transformation—or a series of transformations—is global or local. It can be done by selecting the objects directly with the mouse or by typing the names of the objects on the keyboard.

We can start to define a local transformation by selecting or activating one or several objects—but not all of them. In such instances, the transformation will be applied to the active objects only. In general, when one object is selected as the recipient of a local transformation, the object's center and axis are usually used as the centers of rotation and scaling, and the axis of translation, rotation, and scaling. (The centers of rotation or scaling are usually located in the center of the object unless specified otherwise.) Some programs, however, offer the option to apply local transformations to an object based on the environment's center and/or axis instead of the object's center and/or axis. The results can be quite different (Fig. 3.4.1). For example, an object scaled along its axis after being rotated retains its shape, while an object scaled along the world's axes will not retain its shape. Check the manuals of the software you use to find out how local and global transformations are implemented. Having a clear understanding of this is crucial to the correct operation of your software.

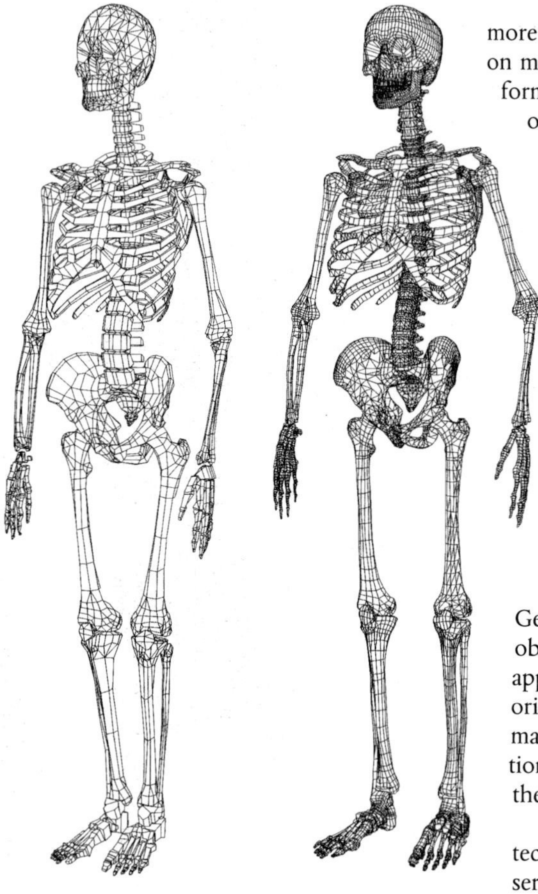

8,979 POLYGONS   35,305 POLYS

3.3.2 The first skeleton model is built with 8,979 polygons, the second one is built with 35,305, and the third one (opposite page) with 141,788 polygons. Notice the higher density of polygons in areas of the surface that have more modeling detail. (© Viewpoint Datalabs, used with permission.)

When performing global transformations, or local transformations that occur along or around the global axis, the order in which transformations are applied to an object or a series of objects can affect the final result. For this reason rotation and scaling sequences should be planned carefully, although translation sequences can be applied in any order. **Concatenated transformations** is the name sometimes given to a series of global transformations applied in sequence. Figure 3.4.2 illustrates the different results obtained by applying the same global transformations to a trio of objects but in a different sequence each time.

In general, if all objects in a scene are active, the transformation is global and applied to all objects. Most software programs apply transformations to all the active objects. When performing a global rotation or global scaling, the center of the environment usually doubles as the center of rotation and scaling for all the objects unless specified otherwise.

Absolute or Relative Values

When working with most interactive modeling programs, applying transformations to one or several objects is as easy as selecting them and dragging them to a new location in three-dimensional space. It is quite common to use the mouse and the mouse button to control the position, orientation, and size of the models in the environment. However, it is sometimes necessary to type specific values on the keyboard for controlling the exact position, orientation, and size of models. When typing values becomes a necessity one must keep in mind that all transformations can be specified as **absolute values** or as **relative values**.

Absolute values, or numbers, always refer to an exact position in space where the object must be relocated regardless of where the object was located in space before the transformation. Relative values, as their name indicates, are numerical values that express the number of units that must be added or subtracted to the current position of the object. Relative values are relative to an existing absolute position. For example, if we have a sphere with a center located at XYZ coordinates 30 30 30, the command *trans sphere 0 20 0* (if the numbers were relative) would reposition the sphere's center at XYZ coordinates 30 50 30 because 20 units would have been *added* to the sphere's position. However, if the numbers being used were absolute numbers, the sphere's center would be relocated to the 0 20 0 XYZ position, regardless of the fact that the sphere's center was previously located at 30 30 30.

Translation

Translation is the simplest of all geometric transformations. This operation is used to move an object or group of objects in a linear

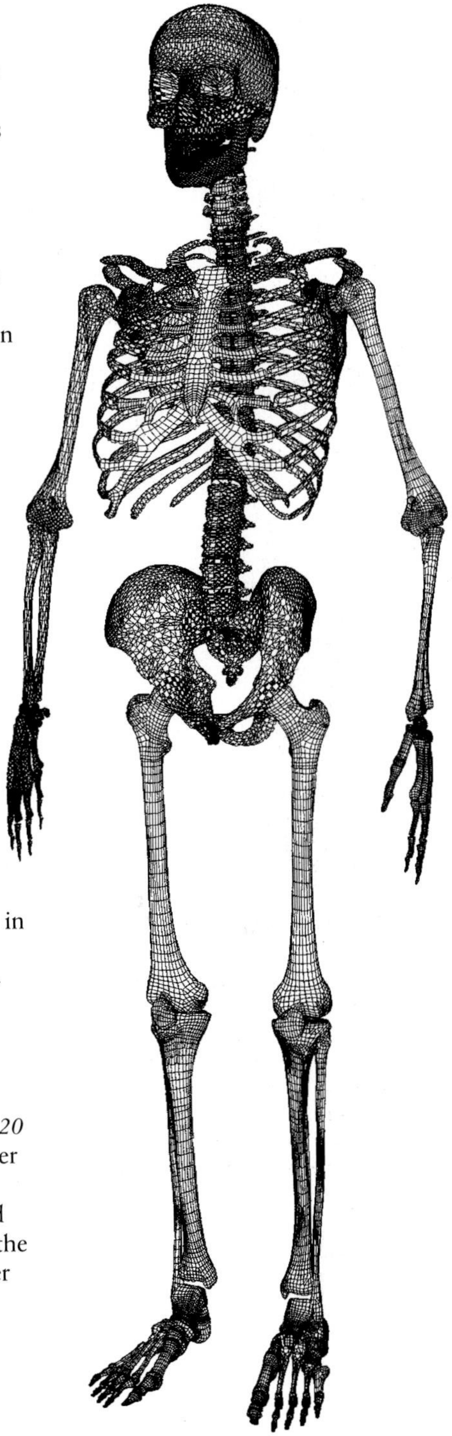

141,788 POLYGONS

way to a new location in three-dimensional space (Fig. 3.4.3). Translation is the simplest and easiest to control of all geometric transformations. Translation can occur along one axis or along several axes at the same time. The order in which several global and local translations are applied to one object does not affect the final position of the object. For example, an object that is translated 5 units along the X axis, then 10 units on the Y axis, and finally -7 units on the Z axis would end up in the same positions as an object that is translated first 10 units along the Y axis, then -7 units on the Z axis, and finally 5 units on the X axis.

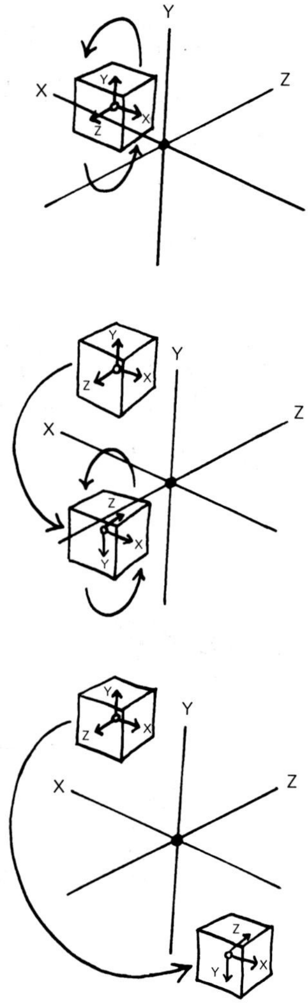

3.4.1 The position of an object's center has very important implications in the results of the transformations applied to it. The first cube has been rotated locally around its own X axis and its own origin. The second cube has been rotated around the world's X axis and its own local origin. The third cube has been rotated globally around the world's X axis and origin.

Rotation

Rotation is the geometric transformation used to move an element or group of elements around a specific center and axis. The amount of rotation is usually specified in terms of an angle of rotation (measured in degrees) and a direction of rotation (Fig. 3.4.4).

Depending on whether the rotation is global or local, objects can be rotated around their own center, the center of the environment, or even the center of their "parent" in a **hierarchy** of objects (for more on transformation of model hierarchies see Chapters 5 and 11). When rotating an object around its own center it is possible with many programs to reposition that center. Consequently, the center of rotation of an object may not always be placed in the geometric center of the object.

Rotations can be used to present different sides of an object to the camera. Rotations are very effective for arranging subtle details in a scene, such as to expose sides of a model with the most interesting shapes or detail, to simulate motion, or to emphasize the perspective of the objects in the scene.

Because rotations always happen around an axis, it is important to know which way rotations are supposed to occur. Depending on the value (positive or negative) that defines a rotation, the rotation can be clockwise or counterclockwise. In a right-handed coordinate system, positive rotations are always counterclockwise and negative rotations are clockwise. A simple method for remembering the direction of rotations consists of representing the axes on which the rotation is taking place with our extended right hand thumb as shown in Figure 3.4.5. If the thumb points to the positive direction of the axes, the direction of a positive rotation is defined by the direction in which we close the hand and make a fist.

Scaling

Scaling is a geometric transformation used to change the size and/or the proportion of an element or a group of elements. Scaling can be applied to an object in a proportional or a nonproportional mode. **Proportional scaling** consists of resizing an object along each axis in equal amounts. The result of proportional scaling is always a larger or smaller object with the same proportions as the original object. With **nonproportional scaling** the object may be resized by different factors along each axis. Nonproportional scaling can be used to change the proportions of a three-dimensional object so that it becomes taller or shorter, wider or narrower, or deeper or shallower (Figs. 3.4.6 and 3.4.7). Because of its ability to easily modify the shape of objects, nonproportional scaling is widely used in computer animation to simulate the "squash and stretch" distortions typical of three-dimensional objects in motion.

When a scaling operation is performed, not on a single object but on all the objects in the environment, we get an effect that is similar to a camera zoom.

Perspective Projection

Perspective projection is a transformation of critical importance because it makes possible the representation of three-dimensional environments on the flat surface of the computer's monitor or a sheet of paper. A perspective view of a three-dimensional scene is created by projecting each point of an object from the viewpoint onto the picture plane. The points in the three-dimensional object coordinate system are then transformed to the two-dimensional image coordinate system.

Perspective projection is a transformation that happens automatically in virtually all three-dimensional software. It is not necessary that we ask for perspective projection each time we do something to our scene. The three-dimensional environment is constantly being transformed into a two-dimensional view using perspective projection techniques. The final two-dimensional images obtained on the screen can be modified by moving the objects in the three-dimensional environment or by altering the camera. See Chapter 7 for more information on perspective projection.

Navigation

Navigation usually refers to the motions that place the camera in different parts of the scene. Navigation can be used during the modeling process for looking at the models from points of view that show the model in more detail. Navigation can also take place before the rendering process to focus on areas of interest, or before the animation process to place the camera where it helps tell a story more effectively.

The spherical or azimuthal coordinate system is often used to navigate through the world by specifying camera positions in terms of the camera's angle around the horizon, its angle above the horizon, and its distance from the object (Fig. 3.4.8).

Navigating through three-dimensional space by moving the camera can take place on any of the four view windows provided by

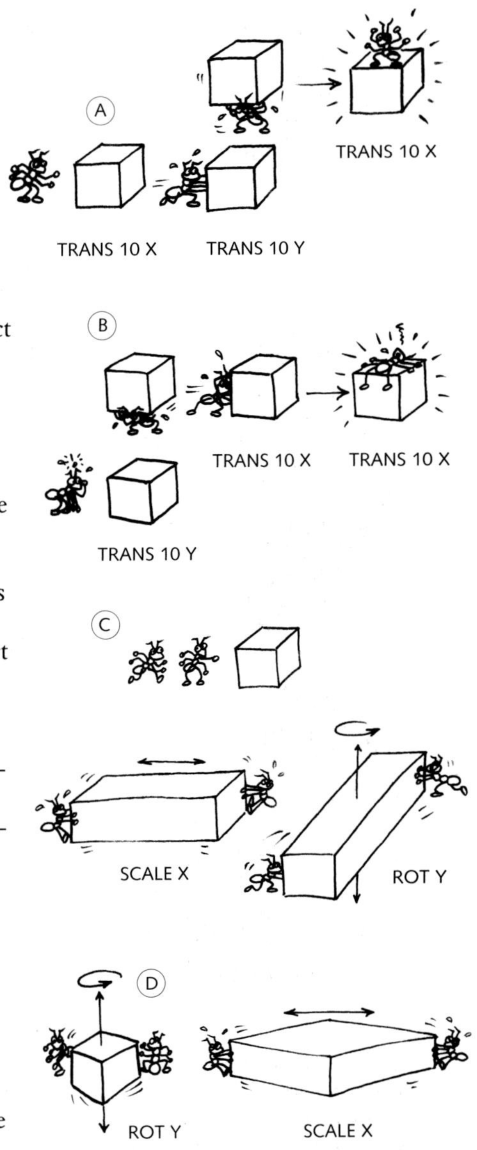

3.4.2 The first two examples (A and B) show the same translations applied to the same object in two different sequences. The results are identical; in both cases the object ends up in the same place. Examples C and D show two different resulting shapes after applying the same rotation and scaling to an object, but in a different sequence.

3.4.3 An object being translated.

almost all three-dimensional software. These windows include the perspective view and the three orthographic views: top/bottom, front/back, and right/left. All the camera motions described here can take place in the perspective window, but in some programs some camera motions—such as yaw/pitch or azimuth/elevation—cannot be viewed in the orthographic views because these motions can be calculated only in three-dimensional space, and not on a flat surface.

The basic characteristics of a virtual camera in three-dimensional space (what the camera sees) are defined by the camera position, its point of interest, and the camera lens. These characteristics can be quickly set by typing numerical values on the keyboard. These characteristics can also be set interactively by clicking on the control buttons provided by some programs, or by directly manipulating the camera with a variety of input peripherals that include the mouse, graphics tablet, trackball, joystick, or dial box.

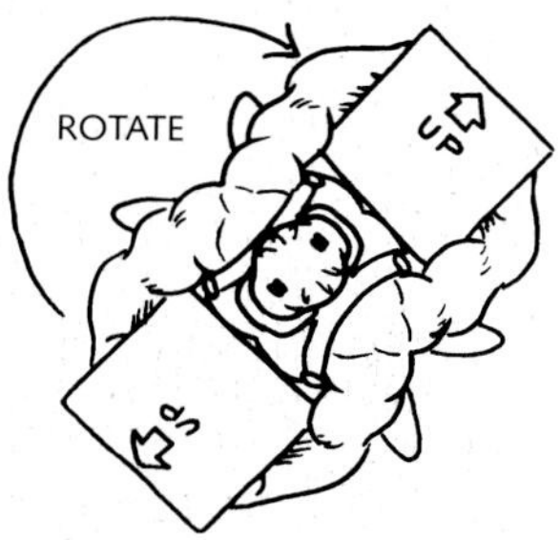

3.4.4 A bird's-eye view of an object being rotated.

Even though all camera positions and moves can be input from the keyboard, it is a lot more practical and fun to position and move the camera interactively. In any case, each possible camera move will result in the modification of at least one of the camera's three basic values: position, orientation, and focal length.

The motions of computer animation virtual cameras are based on the camera moves defined in traditional cinematography. Most programs use the same camera names used in traditional cinematography, but some use a different nomenclature. All of the camera moves, even the most complex ones, can be expressed in terms of translations or rotations around one or several camera axes (Fig. 3.4.9). A **dolly** is a translation of the camera along its X axis, a **boom** is a translation along its Y axis, and a **truck** is a translation along its Z axis. A **tilt** is a rotation of the camera around its X axis, a **roll** is a rotation around its Z axis, a **pan** is a rotation around its Y axis. Sometimes a tilt is called a **pitch** (as in airplanes pitching), and a pan is called a **yaw**. A **zoom** is a special type of camera move where only the camera's simulated focal length is modified but its position and orientation remain untouched. (Read Chapter 7 for additional information on cameras and camera moves.)

3.4.5 In a right-handed coordinate system the direction in which your hand closes to make a fist is the direction of a positive rotation around any axis represented by the extended right-hand thumb.

3.5 File Formats for Modeling

There are many formats for saving the information contained in three-dimensional geometry files. Many of the existing **file formats** containing descriptions of object geometry are exclusive to specific computer programs and are not portable. This means that the information contained in these files is formatted according to conventions that are particular to the software in question, and the files are not compatible with other programs. A few geometry file formats are **portable**, which means that they can be exchanged among several programs. All three-dimensional models created within a modeling program can be save and retrieved in the application's own **native file format**. A specific three-dimensional software, for example, can save all of the three-dimensional models created with it in a file format that has been optimized for its own requirements.

The obvious advantage of using native, or custom, file formats is that it is easy and fast for any particular program to read files in its own native format. Files saved in native formats usually load faster and require less space for storage. There are a number of **conversion utilities** that can translate geometry files in native formats between applications in varying degrees of accuracy. Models that have been built with standard techniques or that have a simple topology can usually be converted in this way very successfully (Fig. 3.5.1). But trying to convert complex modeling files from one native file format to another might modify some subtle details—or destroy them altogether—and might require a fair amount of manual adjusting. Solutions to the format incompatibility problem include using "universal" file formats for saving information about three-dimensional models or converting one native file format directly to the native file format of another program.

The file formats used for transporting geometry information between modeling programs are often called **universal file formats**, and two of the most popular ones include OBJ and DXF. The **OBJ** or **.obj** format, short for object, was popularized by Alias | Wavefront software products for high-end computer animation and visual effects production. The **DXF** format, short for **Drawing Interchange Format**, was developed by Autodesk, Inc. for handling both two- and three-dimensional geometry information, and is widely used in computer-aided design (CAD) applications. Even when using universal file formats to save three-dimensional information, there can be minor differences in the ways different programs interpret the information. This latitude in interpretation is due to the fact that many of the universal file formats describe three-dimensional information in a very general way. The DXF files, for example, contain some two-dimensional information that is often discarded when imported by three-dimensional software. It is also common for three-dimensional programs to interpret in different ways the precision and/or the curvature of a line that defines a surface.

Virtually all three-dimensional modeling programs offer some degree of **file conversion.** That capability is found either inside the standard file management options (under a command or menu option name such as Import or Retrieve) or as a standalone utility conversion program that can be executed outside of the modeling program. Most programs can also **export** its three-dimensional modeling data into other native or universal file formats.

Many of today's three-dimensional modeling programs offer some degree of **foreign-to-native** file format conversions. The number of data formats that a particular three-dimensional program may

3.4.6 These buildings and tunnels were created by duplicating and scaling a variety of shapes and an extruded arc. (Top: aerial view of St. Botolph's House. © Hayes Davidson. Bottom: © Jim Ludtke.)

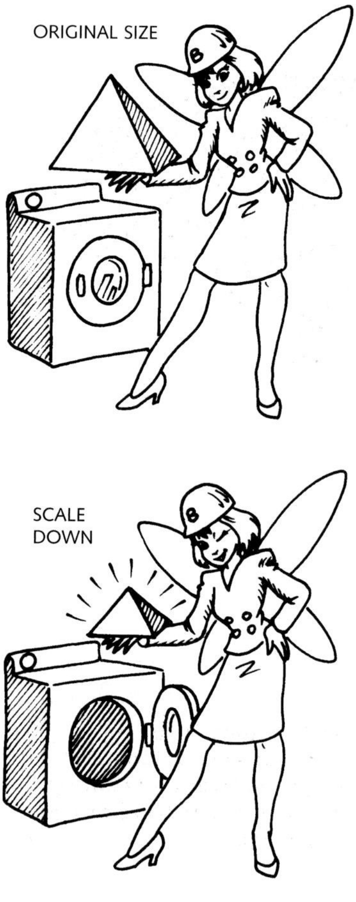

3.4.7 An object being scaled, in this case by using a shrinking machine.

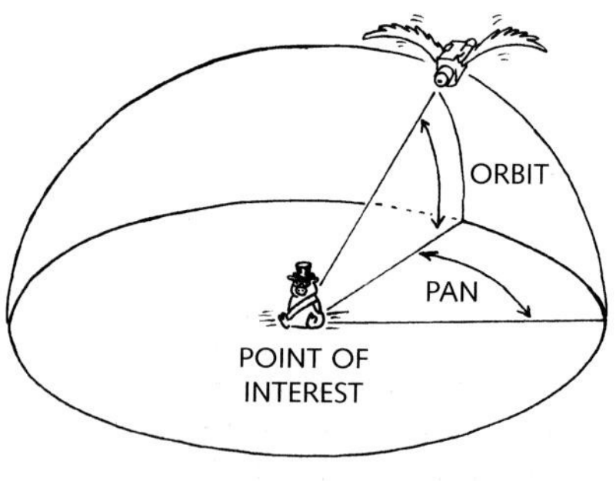

3.4.8 The spherical or azimuthal coordinate system allows for orbiting or panning the camera around the subject.

be able to convert may range from just a couple to several dozen formats. All file format conversions are controlled by **import filters,** which are tables that instruct the conversion utility program how to translate each of the elements encountered in the original—or foreign—file. Figure 3.5.1 shows how a particular file conversion program exports a data file into three different formats. Even when the most reliable file formats and conversion filters are used there are always small variations between the results obtained with different programs. Figure 3.5.2 illustrates the wide range of options available in software when importing or exporting data in the DXF format. One of the reasons for offering so many options in a conversion to a "standard" format is because not all the aspects—or options—of the DXF format are supported by all programs that are capable of reading DXF files. Figure 3.5.3 illustrates how a specific program deals with one aspect of the native-to-DXF file format conversion.

The results obtained with different file conversion utilities vary widely. Some file conversions are almost flawless (with only minor details requiring adjustment), while others rarely produce desirable results. There is no easy way to know if a file conversion program will work perfectly or not: each has to be tried and evaluated.

During the early 1990s the **Virtual Reality Modeling Language**, widely known as **VRML**, gained popularity as a convenient way to describe in a portable format three-dimensional environments for real-time online display. VRML is barely used today, but it brought forth several innovations that are now being implemented in other fledgling streaming three-dimensional standards for use in the Web and other online applications. One of VRML's innovations was to allow for the creation of virtual reality environments where multiple participants can interact with each other in three-dimensional spaces. **X3D**, for Extensible 3D, is a newer open-source standard for implementing interactive three-dimensional environments on the Web and in embedded devices. X3D is a newer **scene description language** that addresses object geometry, as well as rendering, navigation, interaction, and networking of virtual environments. Other file formats used for real-time display are covered at the end of Chapter 5.

3.6 Getting Ready

Modeling can be a time-consuming activity because of the great attention to detail that is required. This can only be accentuated if one encounters a lot of unexpected hurdles along the way. In spite of the flexibility offered by many computer modeling systems, trying to fix complications caused by poor planning sometimes can be more time-consuming and headache-inducing than starting over again. For this and other reasons—also related to practical issues such as time and budgets—it is very important to consider some of the preproduction guidelines listed below. All of these strategies are to take place before one actually starts building the three-dimensional models.

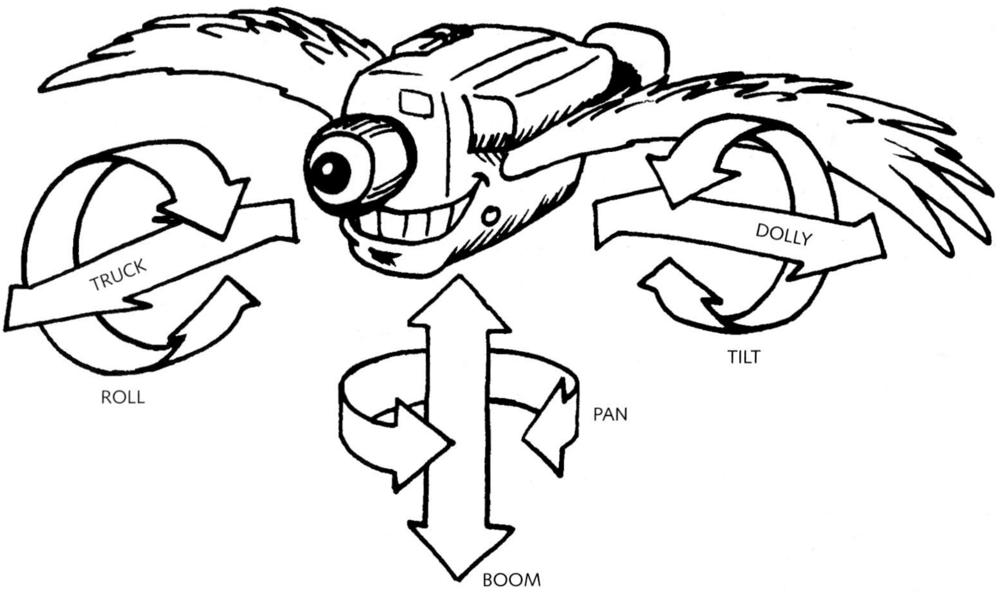

3.4.9 Navigating through three-dimensional space can be done by using the traditional cinematography camera moves: dolly, boom, truck, tilt, pan, and roll.

Sketch Your Ideas First

Sketching your modeling ideas on paper or modeling them in clay can sometimes be faster and more economical than starting to model directly on the computer. While there is nothing intrinsically negative about creating three-dimensional models without having a sketch at hand, in most cases starting that way increases the chances of running into small problems that might have been easy to avoid. Small details such as the ways in which two complex shapes will blend into one another, for example, can be visualized faster and cheaper on paper or modeling clay. In most cases, it is not an issue of whether something can be sketched and visualized directly on the computer, but one of economics: It can be much more expensive to sketch with the computer system than with a number two pencil, plain white paper, and an eraser.

Another advantage of developing three-dimensional ideas on paper or with modeling clay is that both media are absolutely portable and do not present any type of compatibility problem. This is especially important when you are required to present your work to others before actual production starts. It is very easy to show someone a sketch on paper; that can be done anytime and anywhere. There is no need, for example, for your client to travel to your location because they do not have computers or for you to have to reserve one of the workstations in your company so that your client can see your ideas. There are few techniques for sharing your visual ideas with others as direct, portable, participatory, and friendly as a sketch on a piece of paper or a clay scale model.

3.5.1 (Next page. Credits: ApeBot model © 1999 Matt McDonald, Vision Scape Imaging, and Newtek, Inc. Respective screen shots © 1999 Newtek, Inc., Kinetix, Inc., Avid Corp., and MultiGen-Paradigm Corp. Images courtesy of Okino Computer Graphics.)

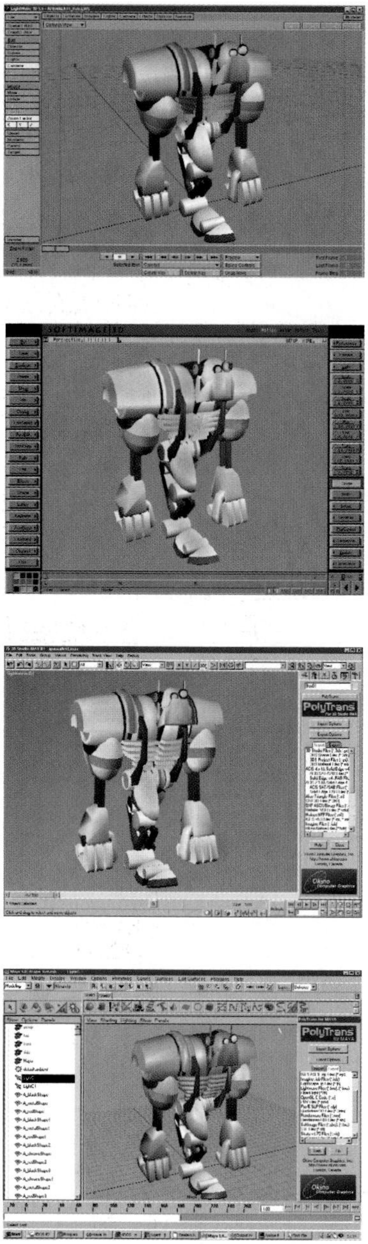

3.5.1 Four images show how a geometry file originally created with Lightwave™ is converted with PolyTrans v. 2 software into three other native file formats: 3D Max, Softimage, and Maya.

If you are still unconvinced, keep in mind that a sketch is just a quick study, a rough drawing, a draft, a preliminary outline. A sketch is not a polished rendering or detailed sculpture. A sketch for a three-dimensional model should take just a few minutes to complete; it should be tentative but also offer enough detail in the more complex areas of the object. Sketches are meant to be aides in the production process, not works of art to be framed and admired by museum-goers. In some instances, it can be useful to complement the drawn sketches with short, explanatory notes regarding details such as the proposed modeling technique or the number of polygons needed to define the curvature of a part, or the advantages and disadvantages of the solution proposed in the sketch (Fig. 3.6.1).

Use Multiple Camera Views While Modeling

It is often quite advantageous to model a three-dimensional object with multiple camera views. A sculptor, for example, walks around the sculpture as he works on it in order to have a clear mental picture of how all the parts and shapes relate to one another. As soon as some of the shapes change, others require reshaping and fine-tuning. In much the same way, it is convenient for an individual using a computer three-dimensional modeling system to look at the object from multiple points of view as it evolves. This can be easily accomplished by constantly rotating the object around its own center. But it can be more convenient to have several views—often called windows—active while modeling. That way one can get immediate feedback from different points of view while concentrating on the modeling.

Most three-dimensional modeling systems allow having four active views open at once (Fig. 3.6.2). It is common to use a front view, a side view, a top view, and a camera view. The camera view usually allows for total control of the point of view: the simulated camera can be placed close to the object being modeled—for examining details—or far away—for evaluating the overall shape. Some viewing positions such as 60-0-30, 45-0-45, 20-0-120, 45-0-220, and 30-0-60 are popular for positioning cameras during the modeling process because these positions resemble the angles of some of the standard three-dimensional projections commonly used in drafting.

In certain situations, the more views required from the computer program, the longer it will take to process the information and to update the screen. This may force you to work with just the camera view and one other view that can be switched between front, top, and side views as needed. (Read Chapter 7 for more information on setting the camera.)

Write Your Numbers Down

Writing your numbers down can often help both before you start modeling and throughout the modeling process. Initially it is important to write down (on a simple piece of paper, in the project spec sheet, or in your production journal) the numbers that describe general but important things such as: the general dimensions of your object, its position in three-dimensional space, and the boundaries of the active area or workspace. Writing down this type of information can be especially useful when you return to a project that was put on hold for a long time or when somebody who is not familiar with the project has to take over because you have decided (or somebody has decided for you) to work on something else.

Do Not Lose the Blueprints

Blueprints are a necessity in cases where the objects to be modeled are too complex and detailed for improvisation and memory. In those instances, it becomes paramount to hold on to the original blueprints (Fig. 3.6.3). Even after you think the models are finished, you or someone else on your team (or on the opposite team) may decide that the models are not finished after all. In such an event, you or someone else may need the blueprints again.

Polygons or Curves?

Most of today's three-dimensional modeling programs are exclusively polygon-based, but many are curved-based, and some offer both capabilities. Choosing between polygons or curves for modeling a three-dimensional object has obvious implications as far as the model's shape is concerned (for more on these implications see "Geometric Primitives" in Chapter 4). However, the rendering implications of modeling with polygons or curves are less obvious but critical in some cases (Fig. 3.6.4).

As we will learn later in Section III: Rendering, many rendering programs require polygonal structures from the modeling programs. This means that whenever curves are used—but before the three-dimensional model can be processed by most rendering programs—the curves have to be converted to polygonal structures. In most cases, this conversion is not a problem: Many programs perform this conversion automatically. However, in some cases, whether to start modeling with polygons or curves can become an issue that requires planning. For example, some curve-based modeling programs do not accept polygonal models, and likewise, some polygon-based modeling programs will have a difficult time reading files of models that have been specified with curves. Furthermore, in many three-dimensional modeling programs—even those that offer both polygonal and spline-based modeling techniques—some advanced functions such as bevelling or clipping will work only on polygonal meshes. Most of the sophisticated programs that offer two-way conversions between polygon meshes and spline surfaces do so at the expense of the shapes involved. When these conversions are performed there is always a significant amount of distortion that sometimes requires time-consuming, point-by-point rearranging.

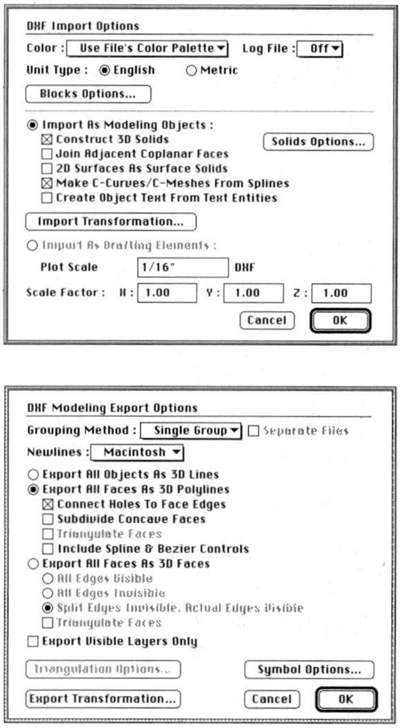

3.5.2 Dialog boxes to control the import and export of files in the DXF format. (Dialog boxes from form•Z. © 1991–1995 auto•des•sys, Inc.)

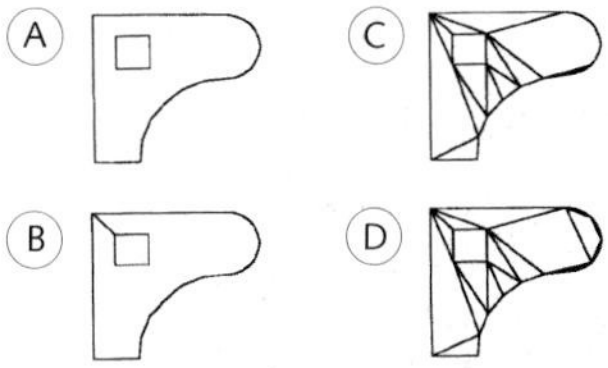

3.5.3 The decomposition process of a concave shape with a hole (A) when exported to the DXF file format. First all holes are connected to the edges of the shape (B), then the concave shape is decomposed into several convex parts (C), next all parts are further decomposed into four-sided parts (D), and finally, the shape is triangulated so that all the component parts become elements in a triangular polygonal mesh. (Courtesy of auto•des•sys, Inc.)

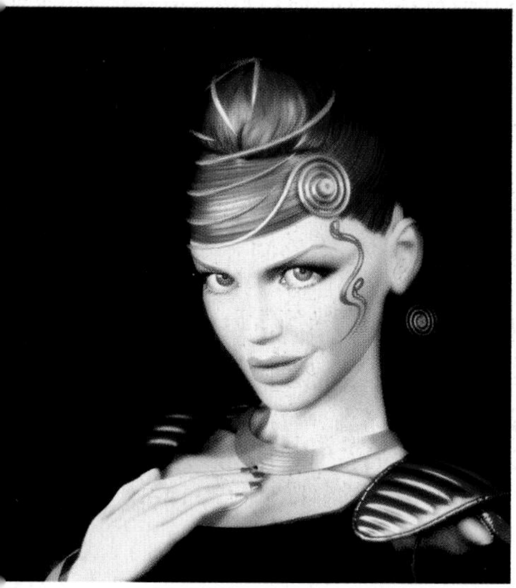

3.6.1 Sketching your ideas and trying different poses, gestures, and variations can help to refine your ideas before the beginning of modeling production. (Sketches and rendered image from *Thomas in Love*, © 2002 Aentre Chien et Loup/JBA/RTBF.)

Will the Model Be Used for CADAM?

Objects that are modeled just to be rendered or animated are built very differently from objects that will serve as models for **computer-aided design and manufacturing** (CADAM). It is extremely important to know whether one's models will be used for CADAM. If so, a specific modeling methodology has to be chosen and followed consistently throughout the project. Figure 3.6.5 shows a three-dimensional model that was used to fabricate a sculpture with stereo lithography techniques (Fig. 15.8.3).

The two significant differences between modeling for CADAM projects or modeling for animation projects lie in the modeling technology used, and in the fabrication and structural implications of the objects modeled. Very few computer systems offer both modeling techniques. The majority of software is either just boundary-based or solid-based. In those situations this issue is automatically solved by the limitations of the software. It is in cases when the software has both capabilities that we have to choose between object shells or solid objects. When we build three-dimensional objects for rendering or animation purposes, we are almost always interested in the surfaces of the objects and very rarely in their inside volume. For that reason, when we model objects for rendering and animation, we usually use **boundary** and **geometry modeling techniques**. Boundary geometry focuses on the surface or **shell** of objects, and ignores the **volume** and inner structure.

This is similar, for example, to making a photographic portrait of a person. We are mostly interested in capturing expression, gesture, skin texture, posture, eye color, and other details. In general, we are quite uninterested—as far as completing a successful portrait—in whatever is under the skin of this person: muscles, bones, and organs.

On the other hand, when we build three-dimensional computer models for the ultimate goal of fabricating them—with a computer-controlled milling machine or stereo lithography system—we are fundamentally interested in the inside of the object, its structural soundness, and whether the shapes we have included in our model can actually be fabricated efficiently (Figs. 15.1.1 and 15.8.4–15.8.5.) For all these reasons when we model objects for CADAM projects we often use **constructive solid geometry** (CGS) techniques. These techniques are not concerned with how fast a three-dimensional model would render, how realistic it would look, or how efficiently it would animate. Instead, CGS techniques focus on whether our three-dimensional model meets structural criteria, whether it has the exact required dimensions, and whether it contains the specified amount of material.

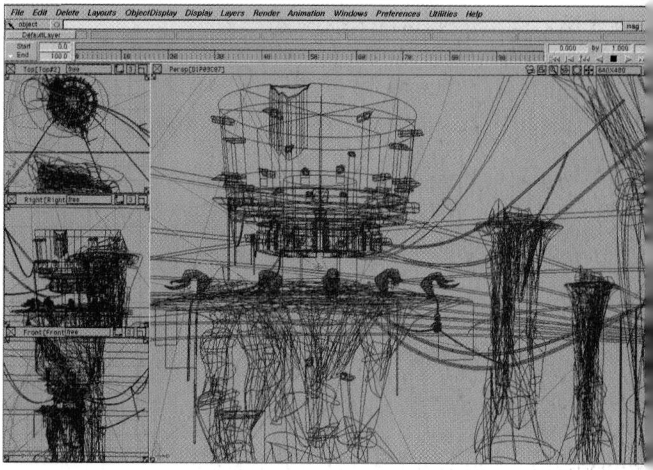

3.6.2 Most three-dimensional programs can display multiple projections of the camera view. Shown here are the perspective projection, and the top, front, and side orthographic projections. See the sketches for this environment in Figures 2.4.2 and 2.4.3.

Modeling Is Related to Rendering and Animation

The life of a three-dimensional computer-generated model rarely ends with the modeling process itself. Most three-dimensional models go on to be rendered, and many continue through the production process to animation.

As you will read later in this book many creative and technical decisions made during the modeling process can simplify, complicate, or even paralyze the rendering or animation processes or both. It would be premature to explain which modeling solutions are more likely to complicate a certain rendering technique or an animation sequence. (It is certainly hoped that you will gain this information by reading the entire book.) For now, keep in mind that before you embark on future modeling projects, you should get as much information as possible about the plans regarding the rendering and animation of the objects, if any.

For example, a certain rendering technique, production deadline, or camera position may require that you cut in half the number of polygons used to define a section of the object, or the animation script might require that you group the objects a certain way (Fig. 3.6.6). If you know about either of these conditions in advance, you will avoid the difficulty of taking apart a model that is finished in order to try to reduce the number of polygons or having to undo a complex five-level hierarchical structure with hundreds of objects in order to reestablish some basic links in a different way. Figure 3.6.7 shows the same geometry at two different **levels of detail (LOD)** created with a **polygon reduction** software.

Keep the rendering and animation requirements of your project in mind during the modeling process. This will help to keep wasted time to a minimum.

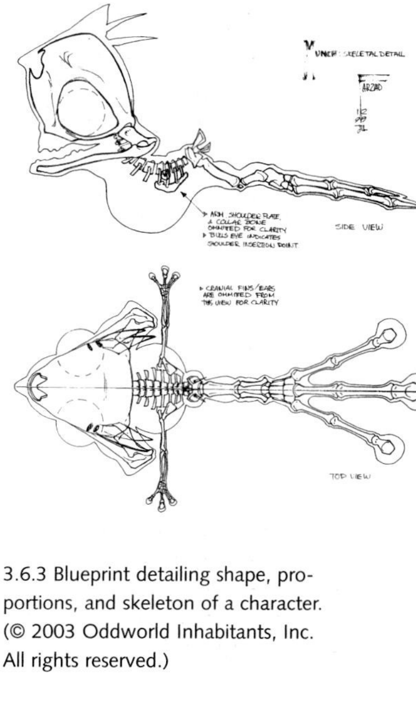

3.6.3 Blueprint detailing shape, proportions, and skeleton of a character.

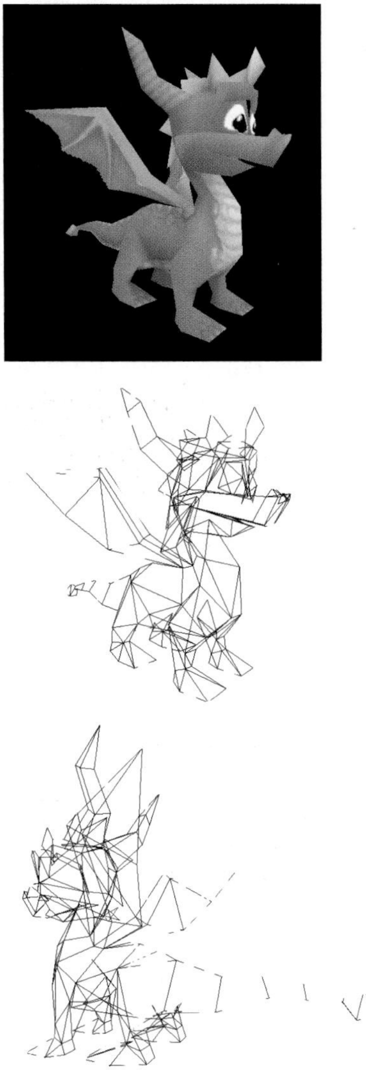

3.6.4 The real-time model of *Spyro the Dragon*™ has 352 polygons and 230 vertices. The modeling started in Alias Power Animator 8.5 with a couple of polygonal geometric primitives and continued by pulling points. Individual polygons were added for features like the eyes, feet, and interstices between joints. (Spyro the Dragon™. Images Courtesy of Universal Interactive Studios, Inc. and Insomniac Games, Inc.)

Check the Preferences File

Remember that both the three-dimensional modeling program that you are using as well as your computer's operating system keep their preferred, or default, settings in a **Preferences file**.

The contents of the Preferences file are important because they control directly and indirectly the result of many operations, functions, and tools. Some of the settings contained in a Preferences file may include, for example, the units used to specify the dimension of objects being modeled, or whether a tool for creating cubes will define by dragging from the center of the cube outwards or from one corner of the cube to the opposite corner. As you can see, some of these settings may affect the result of your three-dimensional modeling, rendering, and animation.

In general, the last person who opened a file or who used the program or the computer system is capable of altering the files by changing the Preferences file. In some systems, Preferences files are attached to the three-dimensional computer program and in some cases to the model files themselves. Check your system for details.

Check Your Memory Requirements

Most of today's three-dimensional modeling software will allocate enough of the system's memory (RAM and/or virtual). This means

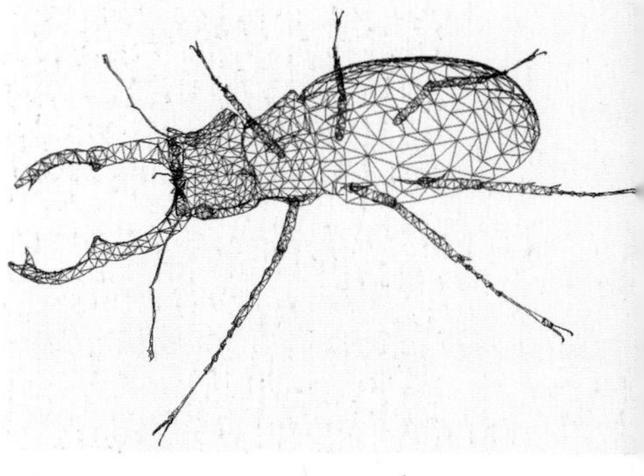

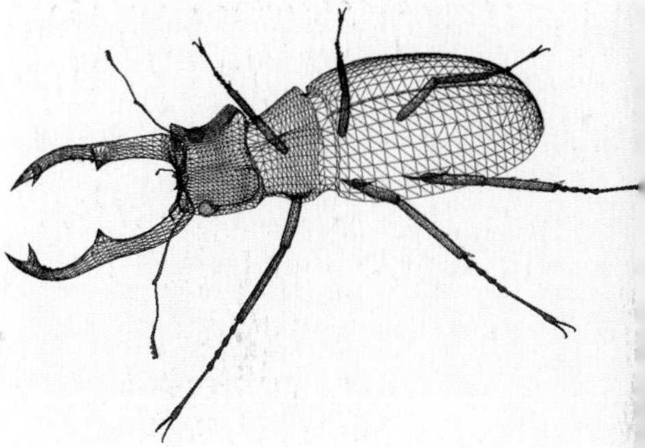

that in most cases you do not have to be concerned about whether there will be enough space in the computer's memory for you to build your model. But sometimes, especially when complex three-dimensional models are being created in small computer systems, the issue of not having enough memory can become a problem. Most professional three-dimensional software today is comfortable with about 512 MB of RAM, but happier with one GB or more. Sometimes when the system does not automatically make sure that there is enough memory for you to keep building, the system will unexpectedly run out of memory and freeze. Also keep in mind that many modeling programs can recover from errors very gracefully (and will allow you to restore all your data), but others cannot.

Save Your Work Often

Save your work often, every 15 minutes or so, and make periodic backups of your important data files. Some applications automatically save the file(s) that you are working on at regular intervals specified in advance. Take advantage of such features.

3.6.5 (opposite page) Computer visualization of a model built with Rhinoceros software. The stereolithographic model and the bronze casting are shown in Fig. 15.8.3. (© 1999 Bathsheba Grossman.)

3.6.6 (top left) Projects created within tight deadlines requires an efficient approach to modeling and animation rigging. (*Mr. Digital Tokoro* by Polygon Pictures. © TPVN.)

3.6.7 The beetle low-resolution geometry model (above, top) might be suitable for scenes where the beetle is far away from the camera, but the high resolution version (above, bottom) might be better for close-up shots or for scenes where the beetle is the main character in the scene. (Polygon reduction and rendering by VSimplify software. © 1999 Virtue Ltd.)

CHAPTER 3

Key Terms

Absolute values
Axes
Azimuthal coordinate system
Boom
Boundary modeling techniques
Cartesian coordinate system
Computer-aided design and manufacturing
Concatenated transformations
Constructive solid geometry
Conversion utilities
Cut-copy-paste
Data file
Dimensions
Direct numerical description
Dolly
Drawing Interchange Format
DXF
Edge
Export
Facets
File conversion
File formats
Foreign-to-native
Front plane
Geometric transformations
Geometry files
Geometry modeling techniques
Global coordinate system
Global transformations
Hierarchy
Import filters
Left-handed coordinate system
Levels of detail, LOD
Line
Local coordinate system
Local transformations
Mathematical operations
Modeling
Native file format
Navigation
Nonproportional scaling
Object coordinate system
OBJ, .obj
Objects
Open Inventor
Pan
Perspective projection
Pitch
Point
Polygon reduction
Portable
Preferences file
Proportional scaling
Rectangular coordinate system
Relative values
Right-handed coordinate system
Roll
Rotation
Scaling
Scene
Scene description language
Shell
Side plane
Spaces
Spherical coordinate system
Structures
Surface
Three-dimensional space
Tilt
Top plane
Transformation matrix
Translation
Truck
Universal file formats
Volume
Virtual Reality Modeling Language
VRML
Workspace
World coordinate system
World origin
X3D
Yaw
Zoom

(ReBoot® and © 1997 Mainframe Entertainment, Inc. All rights reserved.)

CHAPTER 4

Basic Modeling Techniques

4

Summary

THE BASIC TECHNIQUES FOR MODELING three-dimensional objects with a computer system are covered in this chapter. The chapter starts with a short but important note about lines, their use in the creation of surfaces, and the general differences between polygonal meshes and curved surfaces. Following that is a discussion of the simplest geometric modeling tools available in most of today's systems. After that comes a survey of several derivative techniques including revolving, extrusion, and sweeping. Techniques for creating terrains and simple free-form objects are followed by a survey of utilities that are useful to modelers of all levels. An overview of modeling for real-time display concludes this chapter.

QUICK INDEX

4.1 Introduction

Just like traditional modeling techniques, the computer-based three-dimensional modeling process begins with an idea. Before the modeling process can start we try to visualize this idea of what we want to create, perhaps by creating some sketches or even detailed blueprints.

The conceptualization and design of the three-dimensional model usually constitutes the first stage in the simulation of a three-dimensional scene with a computer. From an artistic point of view this step is probably the most important one in the process because it is here where the basic characteristics of the scene are laid out: the shape, position, and size of the objects; the colors and textures; the lights; and the position of the camera. It is also at this stage where the basic ideas have to be analyzed and the best modeling methods chosen for each task.

I usually prepare the initial sketches that describe the three-dimensional objects and environments with traditional media, such as colored pencils or markers on paper. These sketches indicate the general characteristics of the objects such as size, relative position, color, and lighting effects. Once the sketches are finished, I analyze

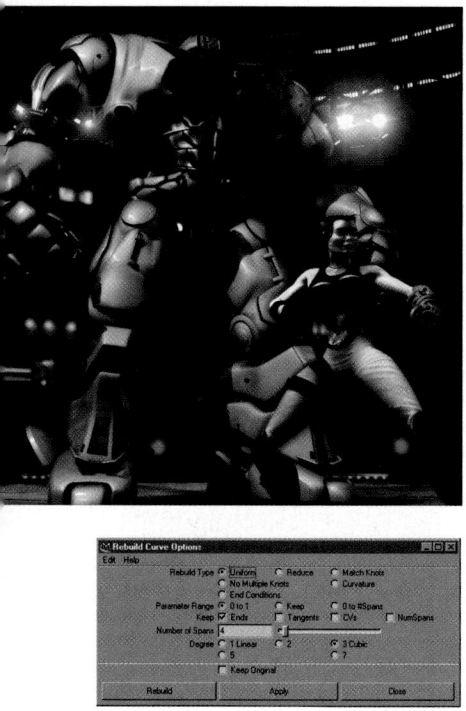

4.2.1 The characters from this X-Box commercial are built with different types of lines and surfaces. The dialog box shows conversion options between different types of lines. (Top: Image courtesy of Blur Studio. Bottom: © Alias|Wavefront, a division of Silicon Graphics Limited.)

them and prepare a set of blueprints containing one or several detailed views of the object with dimensions.

There are many ways of translating the visual information contained in the sketches into numerical information suited for computer manipulation. Most three-dimensional modeling software allows users to build the model interactively. This means that the models that are being worked on can be displayed on the screen. Any and all model changes made by the user are displayed on the screen almost instantly. This interactive quality provides the visual feedback that is so important in developing the shapes of objects and the layout of three-dimensional spaces. Because of the lack of immediate tactile feedback when creating three-dimensional models with software, the real time visual feedback on the screen becomes almost indispensable.

When the modeling process is complete we usually end up with a file that contains a detailed description of the objects in our environment including information regarding their geometry, position, and hierarchy. Realistic images of the files can be obtained by rendering the file with some of the techniques presented in Chapters 6–9. There are many techniques for describing three-dimensional structures, and each produces different results and requires a different type of approach (Figs. 4.2.6–4.2.7).

Unless otherwise specified, all modeling techniques described in this chapter are based on boundary geometry and not on constructive solid geometry. As explained in Chapter 3, this means that the three-dimensional objects are built as hollow shells only and not simulated as true solid objects.

4.2 A Note About Lines

Lines are used to define the shape of the object and many of its surface characteristics. Lines are a fundamental component of all three-dimensional objects. For this reason it is important that we understand differences between types of lines, as well as their attributes and limitations. This section offers a brief characterization of some of the standard lines most commonly used in three-dimensional modeling. Keep in mind that the names used here are as general as possible, but your computer system may have a different name for a specific type of line or a line tool. The classification presented here is based on the practical characteristics of different types of lines, on their advantages and disadvantages, and also on their mathematical nomenclature. The following paragraphs explain some of the differences between types of lines. Please read them carefully. These concepts are crucial for understanding much of the material presented in the other chapters about modeling and rendering.

One obvious difference between lines is that some are straight and some are curved. Straight lines are concerned with defining the shortest distance between two points, but curves are concerned with subtlety of change and elegance of design. There are many differences between straight lines and curved lines: their mathematical description, their behavior as they are used to model, the type of three-dimensional structures they yield, and in most cases, their visual appearance. Some three-dimensional modeling computer programs are capable of converting curved lines to straight lines and vice-versa, but in many cases the results of these conversions are sometimes surprising and might require considerable work before they can be used (Figs. 4.2.1 and 6.4.1).

Straight lines—as their name implies—do not have any curvature. Straight lines are defined by two endpoints only, and may have a slope but no change in angularity. In other words, the slope of curves is variable, but the slope of straight lines is not. In three-dimensional modeling programs, straight lines are sometimes called **polygonal lines** because they can be used to build polygons and polygonal meshes. The three-dimensional modeling computer programs that use exclusively straight lines are capable of building models only with polygonal meshes (and not with spline-based surfaces). The three-dimensional modeling computer programs that use curves are capable of building models with both curved surfaces and polygonal meshes.

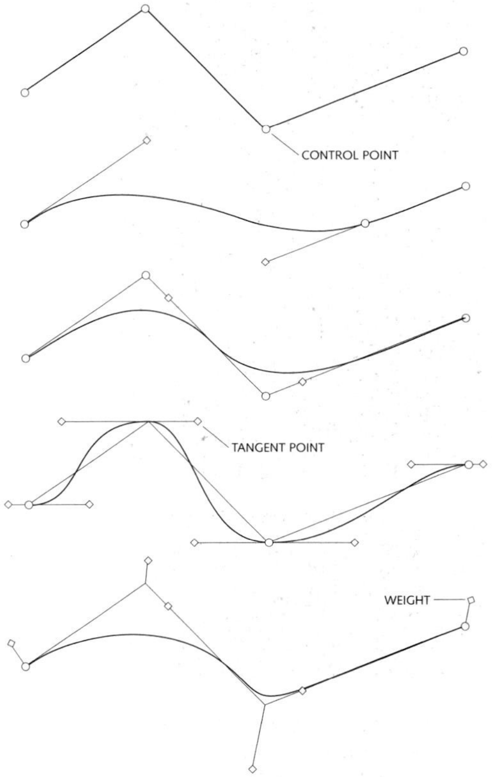

4.2.2 Five popular types of splines are illustrated here: linear splines, cardinal splines, b-splines, Bézier curves, and NURBS, or non-uniform rational b-splines.

Many programs offer two different line drawing tools. One draws straight lines and one draws curved lines. While it is difficult for a straight line to turn into a curve (because straight lines just do not have a variable for change of angularity), it is easy for a curve to turn into a straight line (just by setting the change in angularity to nothing). For this reason, many three-dimensional modeling programs offer just one single—and powerful—tool that draws just curves of all kinds, including curves that look like straight lines.

Curved lines are usually defined by several points and deviate from a straight path without any sharp breaks in angularity. Curved lines are sometimes called curve segments and can be used to define curved surfaces and build meshes of curved surfaces.

Curves are also often called **splines** because they resemble the physical spline—a long narrow strip of wood or metal—used by a draftsperson or construction worker to shape or fit curves between various points. The spline, traditionally used in the design and construction of ships' hulls, is shaped by lead weights. By varying the number and position of weights the spline can be turned into a smooth curve that passes through the required points. Even though not all curves fall into in the mathematical category of spline curves, some three-dimensional modeling programs use the term generically. That generalization is, of course, inaccurate.

There are many types of curves, and they can be catalogued based on their mathematical and geometric characteristics. In this text, however, we shall limit our summary to five of the more popular types of splines used in mainstream three-dimensional modeling: linear splines, cardinal splines, b-splines, Bézier curves, and NURBS

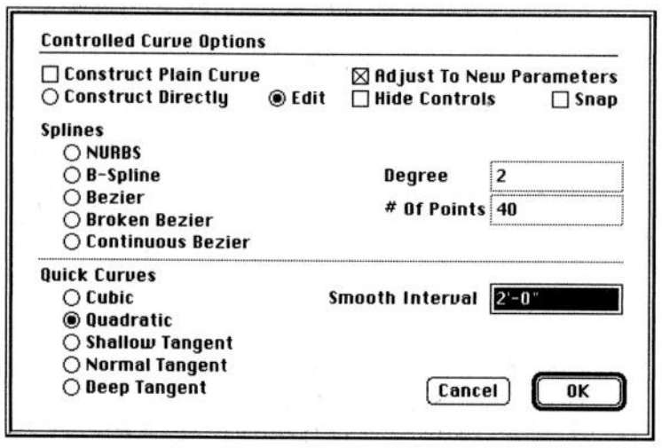

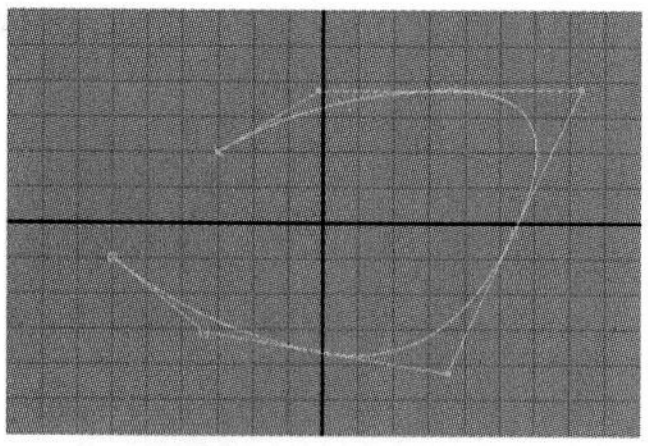

SECOND DEGREE

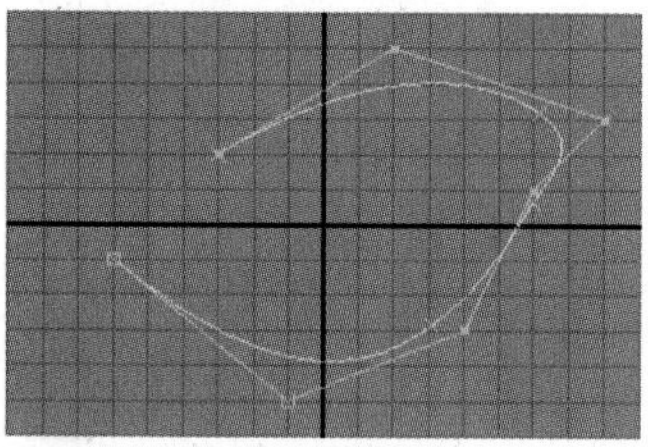

THIRD DEGREE

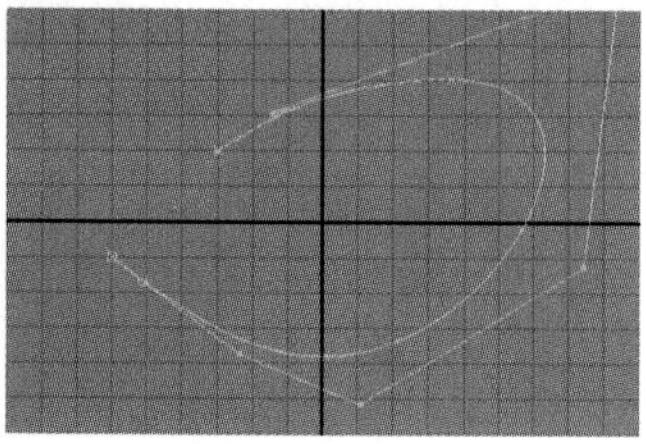

FIFTH DEGREE

4.2.3 The dialog box illustrates a few curve controls available in off-the-shelf software; and NURBS curves of second, third, and fifth degrees. (Top, dialog box from form•Z. © 1991-1995 auto•des•sys, Inc. Bottom, © Alias|Wavefront, a division of Silicon Graphics Limited.)

or nonuniform rational b-splines. Figure 4.2.2 illustrates these five types of curves.

All splines are generated from a defining polygon. Because of this fact splines are called **controlled curves**. The structures that control the splines are invisible—they are displayed only while we shape the spline—but they contain important information that can be used to reshape the spline.

The controls found in splines of different types include the control line or control polygon or hull, the control points or control vertices, the tangent points, the knots, and the weights. Keep in mind that different software programs use different nomenclatures and slightly different implementations of the controls. Figure 4.2.3 shows some of the controls for modifying splines provided by different software programs.

Each of the spline curves can be quickly characterized by the way in which it is controlled by the **control points** or **control vertices**. A **linear spline** looks like a series of straight lines connecting the control points. A **cardinal spline** looks like a curve that passes through all of its control points. The **b-spline** looks like a curved line that rarely passes through the control points. A **Bézier curve** passes through all of its control points. A **NURBS,** or nonuniform rational b-spline, does not pass through its control points.

Another easy way to characterize splines is to look at their controls other than the control line and the control points. Control points can control the **curvature** or **tension** of a curved line mainly by how close they are to one another and, in some cases, by how close they or their tangent points are to the curve (Fig. 4.2.4). The Bézier curve differs from the three splines mentioned here so far mainly because it has **tangent points** in addition to the control points. Tangent points are used to fine-tune the degree of curvature on a line without modifying the control points.

NURBS offer a high degree of local curve control by using weights and knots. These controls allow a portion of the spline to be modified without affecting other parts of the spline. One **weight** is attached to each control point, and they determine the distance between the control point and the apex of the curve. By default, all control vertices on a spline have the same weight factor, and that is called a **nonrational curve**. (B-splines, for example, are NURBS with equal weights.) When the values of the weights on the curve are modified then the curve is called a **rational curve**. Manipulating weights on a NURBS curve may improve the subtle shaping of a line, but it usually also slows down the rendering of the final model. Another disadvantage of working with different weight values is that many systems will ignore the data when model files are exchanged. In many cases, results similar to using different weight values can be obtained by placing two control points very close to each other.

The **knots** on a NURBS determine the distribution and local density of points on a curve. The minimum number of knots required to form a curve segment is equal to the degree of a curve plus one plus the number of control points. The **degree of curve** refers to the high exponent in the mathematical formulas that generate curves. Each curve type (b-spline, Bézier, and NURBS) has a different mathematical formula, and each curve type may be created at different degrees (Fig. 4.2.5). The higher the degree of a curve the more computation is required to create it. Curves of the first degree correspond to linear segments, curves of the second degree correspond to quadratic curves, and curves of the third degree correspond to cubic curves. The higher the degree of a curve, the more control points and knots are required to form a curve segment.

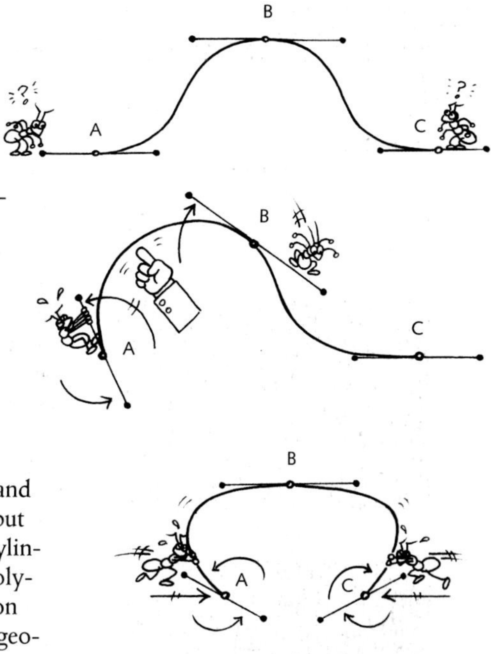

4.2.4 This sequence illustrates how control and tangent points affect the tension of a spline. In the middle drawing only the tangent points are moved. In the bottom drawing the control points are moved closer to one another and the tangent points change along to make the final curvature smoother.

4.3 Geometric Primitives

Virtually all three-dimensional modeling computer programs provide a collection of tools for creating simple shapes with a fixed structure known as **geometric primitives.** The number and type of geometric primitives varies from program to program, but the following list is a representative selection: cubes, spheres, cylinders, cones, toruses, regular polyhedra, and two-dimensional polygons. Figures 4.3.1 and 4.4.1 include some of the most common geometric primitives. Expressive characters can be built out of geometric primitives (Fig. 10.2.4).

In some programs, the different geometric primitive tools will appear all as a single menu selection while in others each or some of the tools may appear separately. In all cases, however, the feature that relates all geometric primitives to one another is the fact that they are standard shapes that the modeling program can create and manipulate effortlessly and usually from a simple predefined mathematical description. In principle, all geometric primitives may be created as polygonal structures or as curved patches.

Geometric primitives can be used to represent simple shapes, or they can be used as the basis for more complex, composite three-dimensional shapes. In the former case, the shapes provided by the tool would require almost no modification except for changes to their position in space, size, and proportion in some cases. In the latter case, geometric primitives may be modified or used to build more complex objects with a variety of utility tools for trimming, attaching, and blending, among others. As most other tools, geometric primitives may be modified on-screen directly using the mouse, trackball, or electronic pen, or by typing the appropriate values in a dialog box.

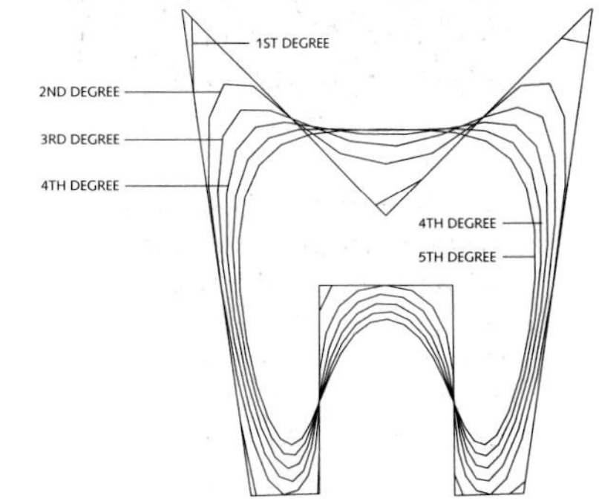

4.2.5 In general, the higher the degree of a spline, the further away it is from the controlling polygon (the outer shape with sharp angles).

Cubes

Cubes are usually modeled as six-sided, closed, three-dimensional objects. Since all sides of a cube have the same length, usually the only variable required for modeling cubes is the length of a side. Sometimes a number of subdivisions can be specified along each of the three axes. Cubes are almost always created as polygonal structures.

4.2.6 The characters and city in the movie based on Enki Bilal's *La femme piège* graphic novel are modeled with a combination of curved surfaces and geometric primitives. (Image courtesy of Duran.)

Spheres

4.2.7 The main character in *Bingo* is modeled with a variety of techniques. (© Alias|Wavefront, a division of Silicon Graphics Limited.)

Spheres, like cubes, are also modeled as symmetric, closed, three-dimensional objects. In order to be defined, all spheres require a variable of **radius** or **diameter**, and they can be modeled as a polygonal structure or as a patch of curves. When modeled as polygonal structures, drawn with straight lines, a sphere's definition requires a number of divisions along the longitude (top to bottom) or latitude (around). These divisions resemble the parallels and meridians on a globe, and their number has a proportional effect on the geometric smoothness of the final shape. When modeled as curved patches, spheres require a type of spline to be specified in addition to the information listed above. Spheres are also very popular as the starting point for free-form modeling (Fig. 4.5.1).

Cylinders and Cones

Cylinders and **cones** are commonly defined as polygonal objects, and they may be shaped by the following variables: radius, height, number of longitudinal divisions, number of latitudinal divisions, and whether they are "capped" or not. The number of subdivisions used to build cylinders and cones defines the amount of modeling detail of the these objects. Objects with a small number of subdivisions can be rendered more quickly than objects with many subdivisions. When planning to render objects with image maps it is best to model them with a large number of subdivisions. Doing small rendering tests is essential to determine the optimum number of subdivisions that should be modeled into any geometric primitive. **Capping** determines whether the round sides of cones or cylinders are open or whether they are closed.

Toruses

A **torus** is a three-dimensional, closed shape that resembles a donut. A torus is like a cylinder that has been bent and stretched so that the two bases touch each other. The variables required to construct a torus are almost the same as those required for building a sphere, plus one additional variable, which is the interior radius. A full listing of modeling variables for a torus includes whether polygons or patches will be used, size of exterior radius, size of interior radius, number of latitudinal divisions, and number of longitudinal divisions. A torus is a geometric primitive that can also be built with radial sweeping techniques (Fig. 4.4.1).

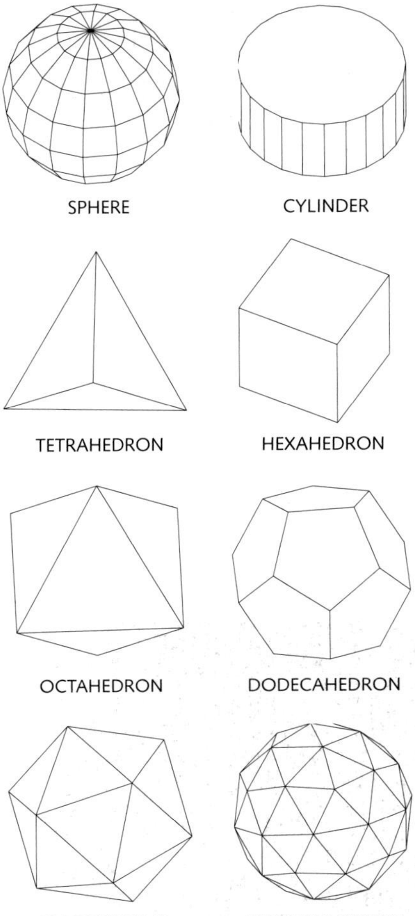

4.3.1 A sphere, cylinder, and regular polyhedra including a tetrahedron (4-sided), a hexahedron (6-sided), an octahedron (8-sided), a dodecahedron (12-sided), an icosehedron (20-sided), and a geodesic sphere.

Regular Polyhedra

Many three-dimensional objects belong to the category of **regular polyhedra**, or objects with multiple facets. A polyhedron (singular of polyhedra) refers to a three-dimensional object that is composed of polygons. Some of the most common regular polyhedra include the 4-sided **tetrahedron**, the 8-sided **octahedron**, the 12-sided **dodecahedron**, and the 20-sided **icosahedron**. Regular polyhedra are usually modeled as polygon meshes and can be built by specifying a radius and a number of facets required.

Two-Dimensional Shapes

Two-dimensional shapes can be used to generate three-dimensional shapes by using derivative techniques such as extrusion or sweeping. Two-dimensional shapes usually include arcs, circles, spirals, triangles, squares, and other polygons.

Circles are two-dimensional, closed contours and require a radius or diameter, a number of control points, and a type of spline. **Arcs** are two-dimensional, open contours and require the same information that circles do plus the starting point and the ending point, both specified in degrees. **Spirals** are also two-dimensional, open contours and require a starting and an ending radius, a starting and an ending angle, a number of control points, and a height. **Polygons** (including triangles and squares) are two-dimensional, open contours, are almost always built with polygonal or linear splines, and can be defined by a number of sides and radius.

4.4 Sweeping

Sweeping is perhaps the most powerful derivative modeling technique, especially when you consider the complexity of the three-dimensional shapes created with it in relation to the simplicity of the input that is required for generating them.

The basic idea behind all sweeping modeling techniques consists of defining a two-dimensional outline that is swept along a prede-

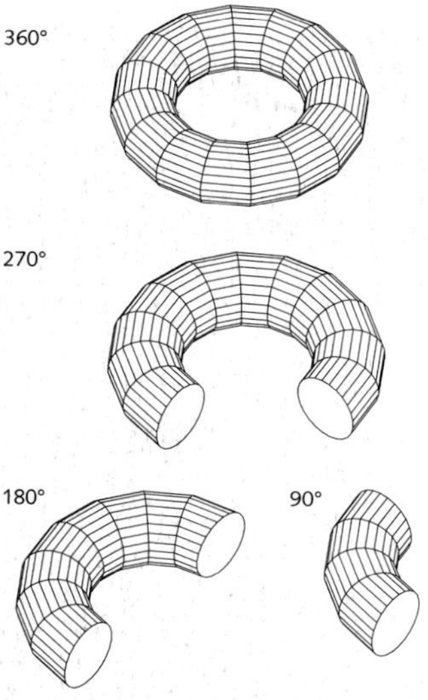

4.4.1 Toruses and other geometric primitives can be created by sweeping a two-dimensional outline around an axis. Slices of geometric primitive shapes created this way are usually easier and faster than the equivalent shapes created with the geometric primitive tool and then sliced with a trimming tool.

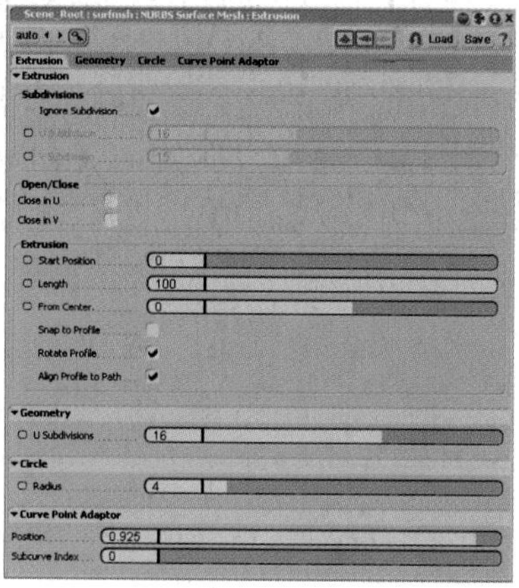

4.4.2a The dialog box shows the type of controls used to create an extrusion along a straight path. (Image courtesy of Softimage Co. All rights reserved.)

fined path. As the outline is swept it defines a shape in three-dimensional space. The resulting three-dimensional model depends largely on the complexity of the **seed outline** and the complexity of the path (Fig. 4.4.2b). The three most popular sweeping techniques are extrusion, lathe or revolve, and free-form sweeps.

Simple Extrusion

In the conventional lingo of industrial design and manufacturing, **extrusion** stands for the process of shaping a material (such as plastic or metal) by forcing it with heat and pressure through a **die**. A die is a tool used for shaping or stamping different materials. The process of industrial extrusion is usually based on a stationary die just because of the limitations in handling both the hot materials and the heavy die. Meat grinders or pasta machines, for example, extrude the ground meat and the pasta through dies of different shapes.

Most three-dimensional modeling computer programs offer simple extrusion tools that—like their heavy industry counterparts—create three-dimensional shapes by starting with a two-dimensional outline and extruding or extending it along a straight path along one axis (Fig. 4.4.2a). Simple extrusion happens along any one axis. The two-dimensional outlines to be extruded can be created with geometric primitive tools or exported from other programs in highly portable file formats such as EPS (Encapsulated PostScript). Extrusion is sometimes called **lofting** because the two-dimensional outlines are duplicated and moved a level up.

Free-Form Sweeping

Some programs also offer the ability to extrude objects along paths of any shape and along any axis or combination of axes. An extrusion that takes place along several axes is sometimes called a sweep, sometimes called an extrusion on a path, or a **free-form extrusion** (Fig. 4.4.3). The results of free-form extrusion that is either scaled along the path or that is based on two paths are similar to those obtained with the skinning modeling technique decribed in Chapter 5.

Modeling by extrusion has been quite popular for centuries for creating meringue and ornaments on pastries, cookies, and cakes. The pastry extrusion tool, or die, moves with a sweeping motion along a decoration path. The motions of the pastry tool usually extend on a surface in a single continuous action, such as that of a broom or a brush, and in a wide curve or range.

Lathe

One very popular sweeping variation is commonly referred to as a **lathe** or a **revolve**. This form of sweeping is so popular that it is almost always presented as a standalone tool, separate from the general-purpose sweeping tool. The surfaces created with this technique are usually called **surfaces of revolution**. The software-based lathe tool simulates a real lathe, which is a tool composed of a rotating base on which you place a cylinder of wood that is shaped by placing a steel blade on its surface as the base rotates around its vertical axis. A potter's wheel is used to perform an almost identical operation on a slab of clay. The clay or wood are cut uniformly around the cylinder as a blade or sharp tool moves in and out following a predefined path. The software lathe sweeps a two-dimensional outline around one axis; the two-dimensional outline may be open or closed. A new three-dimensional shape emerges as the two-dimensional outline is swept along a circular or radial path; it usually remains perpendicular to the sweeping path as they are swept. The resulting three-dimensional object is defined by the areas enclosed within the revolved two-dimensional outline. Surfaces of revolution require an angle of rotation and a number of steps or facets. The number of subdivisions is usually determined by the number of points on the outline used to generate the shape.

Surfaces of revolution that result from a 360-degree sweep are frequently closed, three-dimensional shapes. Sections—or slices—of three-dimensional shapes can also be created by sweeping less than 360 degrees. Two-dimensional outlines that do not touch the axis of sweeping will result in three-dimensional objects with holes (Fig. 4.4.4). In these cases, or when only a slice of a shape is created, the resulting shapes can be capped or uncapped.

The lathe modeling technique can also be used to recreate some of the geometric primitive shapes such as the cylinder and the cone (Fig. 4.3.1). Using the lathe for this purpose offers the advantage of increased control and economy of steps when trying to model a special version of a geometric primitive.

4.5 Free-Form Objects

Some projects require the creation of **free-form three-dimensional objects**. Creating these types of models can be time-consuming because they must be sculpted out of a mesh in a way that is very similar to sculpting or modeling a piece of soft clay. Simple free-form objects usually require a lot of point-picking, pulling-and-pushing, and overall "massaging" of the surface mesh (Fig. 4.5.1). The meshes may be planar, curved, or even based on subdivision sufaces. Planar or polygonal meshes, which are covered in this section, are particularly well suited for gaming projects where real-time rendering almost requires that polygons are used. Medium resolution polygonal meshes look smooth at a distance, especially when mapped with detailed image maps, but the illusion of smoothness breaks down as the model gets closer to the camera. High-resolution polygonal meshes like those obtained by scanning a three-dimensional maquette usually result in fairly large files, and they are sometimes used for animated feature films.

Free-form modeling—also called free-form deformation—is

4.4.2b The outline of the different floors were defined on the XY (top) plane, and the resulting outline was extruded along the Z axis. Details were added later using a variety of techniques including trimming and Boolean operations. The finished rendering was composited with an open shutter still photograph of the area where the building was scheduled to be built. (110 Bishop Gate. © Hayes Davidson.)

4.4.3 Fluid shapes can be created with free-form sweeping, which is based on an extrusion along a complex path and a multitude of axes. These wolves have a primitive quality that makes them very different from both the cartoon and the realistic styles of modeling. (Pastilles Vichy. Agency: EURO RSCG BETC. Director: Pierre Coffin. Illustrator: Jean-Christophe Saurel. Production and Computer Graphics: Ex Machina. Images courtesy of Ex Machina.)

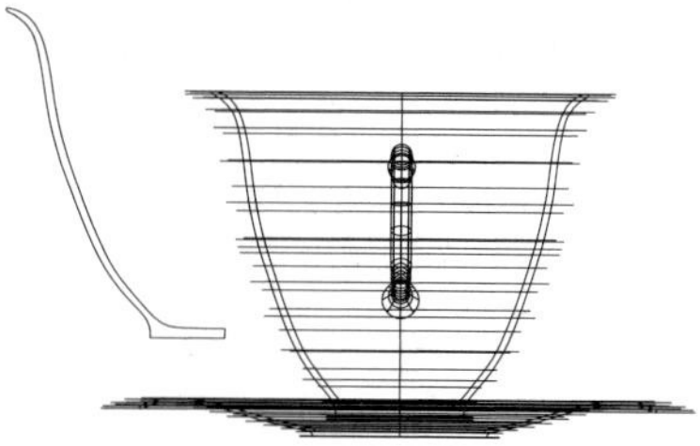

SWEEPING A 2D OUTLINE

used when other modeling techniques are too rigid for building a specific scene or when using a combination of other tools would get the job done but would also require additional production time and a larger production budget. Free-form objects are also sometimes used because of the creative preferences of the individuals who design the look of the three-dimensional scene. Figure 4.5.2 illustrates a free-form technique that uses a simple polygonal mesh to generate and control a curved surface. In this case the mesh is created by extruding new polygons and welding them to one another. A flat polygon is extruded to create the basic torso, and the points are pulled to refine the shape (A). The breast shape is created by pulling points on a lathed spline (B and C). Extra edges on some torso polygons are created to weld to it the 8-sided breast object, which is duplicated and attached by welding vertices and deleting the interior faces (D and E). The bottom torso polygons are extruded to create the pelvis area, and the vertices are sculpted (F). The bottom facets are sliced, extruded, and sculpted to create the legs (G and H). Additional facets are created on the back by dividing the edges of some polygons and rounding the mesh manually, and the arms are created by forcing some edges on the sides of the torso into a 5-sided shape, extruding them, and moving points to sculpt detail (I, J, and K). The torso area is sliced to create a navel indentation, the faces on the bottom of the body are extruded downwards and adjusted to create the legs (L). The feet and hands are created by extruding down the bottom ankle, extruding some of the front faces, and creating additional polygons to define the toes and fingers (M and N). More detail is sculpted with additional polygons, and finally the spline surfaces are generated from the polygonal mesh (O). The finished model can be seen in Figure 10.5.11.

Free-form modeling techniques can also be used in conjunction with other techniques—especially those described in Chapter 5. The technique of free-form modeling has a couple of variations including direct point manipulation, deformation with lattices, and terrains.

4.4.4 This cup was modeled by sweeping a two-dimensional outline 360 degrees around the Y axis (opposite page), and adding a handle later. (Courtesy of Iris Benado.)

Virtual Sculpting with Polygonal Meshes

The most common and easiest way to create three-dimensional free-form shapes usually starts with an existing three-dimensional structure that is to be "sculpted" and transformed into the desired free-form object. This **virtual sculpting** process is, in essence, quite similar to the process of modeling fresh clay with one's hands. The initial shape of the clay is fairly unimportant in terms of the desired final three-dimensional shape. But as our hands massage, push, pull, and rub the shapeless clay, it is slowly transformed into a meaningful structure. A simple primitive like a sphere can be the starting point, or we can start from a three-dimensional scan of a real scale model. Some techniques for sculpting with free-form curved surfaces and for fitting curved surfaces to polygonal meshes are described in Chapter 5.

The **direct point manipulation** modeling process, as virtual sculpting is also known, starts by identifying the points—or control vertices—in the wireframe structure that can be displaced in three-dimensional space. Most three-dimensional modeling programs offer simple ways of picking a single point or a group of points. Direct point manipulation in the case of curve lines can be done directly to a point on the curve or to a control or a tangent point. Usually the selection is done by just clicking and dragging one or several points. Once the points have been selected they can be dragged in any direction. Some programs offer excellent tools for picking and manipulating single points, while similar capabilities in other programs leave a lot to be desired. Some of the most useful direct point manipulation options include the ability to select several points that are not contiguous, or the ability to lock the position of points in some parts of the object while other points are being manipulated. Figures 4.5.1 and 4.5.2 illustrate the result of free-form modeling.

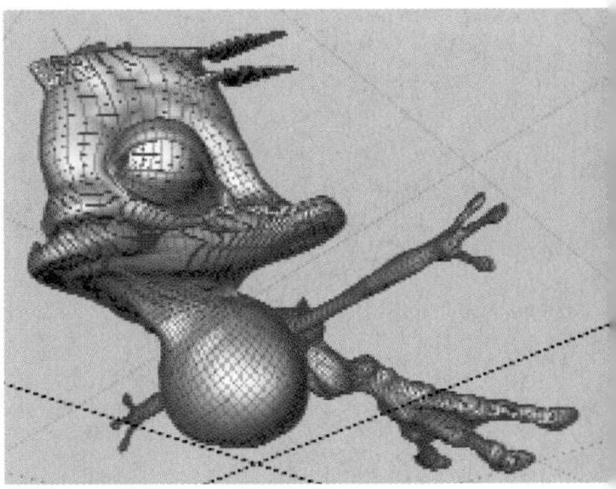

4.5.1 This wireframe character was created with NURBS patches, including simple free-form modeling techniques that pull and push individual points in a mesh. Simple meshes like spheres are commonly used as virtual clay in free-form modeling both because they are easy to create and because they offer a good number of points to work with. (© 2003 Oddworld Inhabitants, Inc. All rights reserved.)

Deformation with Lattices

Direct point manipulation can be a very efficient technique when only a few points need to be manipulated or when the user is really skilled at free-form sculpting. There is another free-form modeling technique that can be more appropriate for the task than direct point manipulation—especially in cases where a uniform global deformation is desired or when the user does not have the skill or the time to manipulate a large number of points one at a time. This technique is called **deformation with lattices**. (Lattices are sometimes called bounding boxes, not to be confused with the boundary boxes described later in this chapter.)

A lattice is a structure of points and lines that controls the points in the model. We can think of the lattice as a structure of grids that is connected to the points in the model with imaginary springs. Therefore, when the grids—or points on the grids—are moved, they drag the object's points with them (Fig. 4.5.3).

Every point on the lattice is connected to one or several of the model's points. The ability to control the deformation of the object by moving one or several grid points in the lattice depends directly on the number of lattice points. A small number of points on the lattice results in very rough or global distortion. Lattices with a large number of control points can be used to apply very subtle—or local—distortion on the object controlled by the lattice.

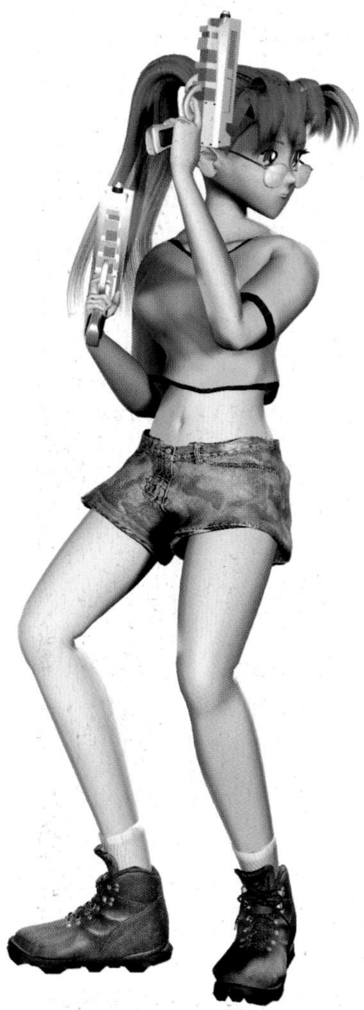

4.5.2 This Animé-inspired character is an example of straightforward modeling with the Mesh Smooth tools in 3D Studio MAX. Keeping a low polygonal count was as important as maintaining all polygons four-sided to create this human body. (© 1999 Michael B. Comet. All rights reserved.)

Simple Terrains and Functions

A great variety of techniques is available for creating **terrains** that simulate or recreate natural or imaginary landscape surfaces. A great variety of other techniques use **mathematical functions** for distorting those terrains.

The simplest technique for creating a terrain consists of using a flat two-dimensional plane with XY subdivisions. Obviously, the more subdivisions on a plane, the more detail will appear on the final terrain model. As mentioned earlier, the position of points on the plane can be modified by direct point manipulation or by lattice deformation. Either of these techniques would be appropriate if the shape was supposed to resemble a natural terrain. But if you are trying to create a more fantastic terrain, the basic plane could be deformed with a mathematical function. Figure 4.5.4 shows terrains created by distorting a terrain with different functions.

Another technique for creating terrains consists of building a three-dimensional mesh based on two-dimensional contours that define an imaginary or real landscape. This technique is very data-intensive but also very efficient for creating accurate models of terrains. Because of their topological detail, terrains created with this technique are rarely distorted with mathematical functions (Fig. 5.1.4). A simpler technique for quickly building terrains consists of applying a black-and-white image as a displacement map to a three-dimensional flat plane (Fig. 9.6.2).

4.6 Basic Modeling Utilities

In addition to basic modeling tools, virtually all three-dimensional modeling programs offer a set of basic utilities meant to complement the modeling process. Among them we find such useful techniques as naming objects and getting information about them, duplicating, snapping to grid, mirroring, displaying as a bounding box, calculating volumes, and creating text.

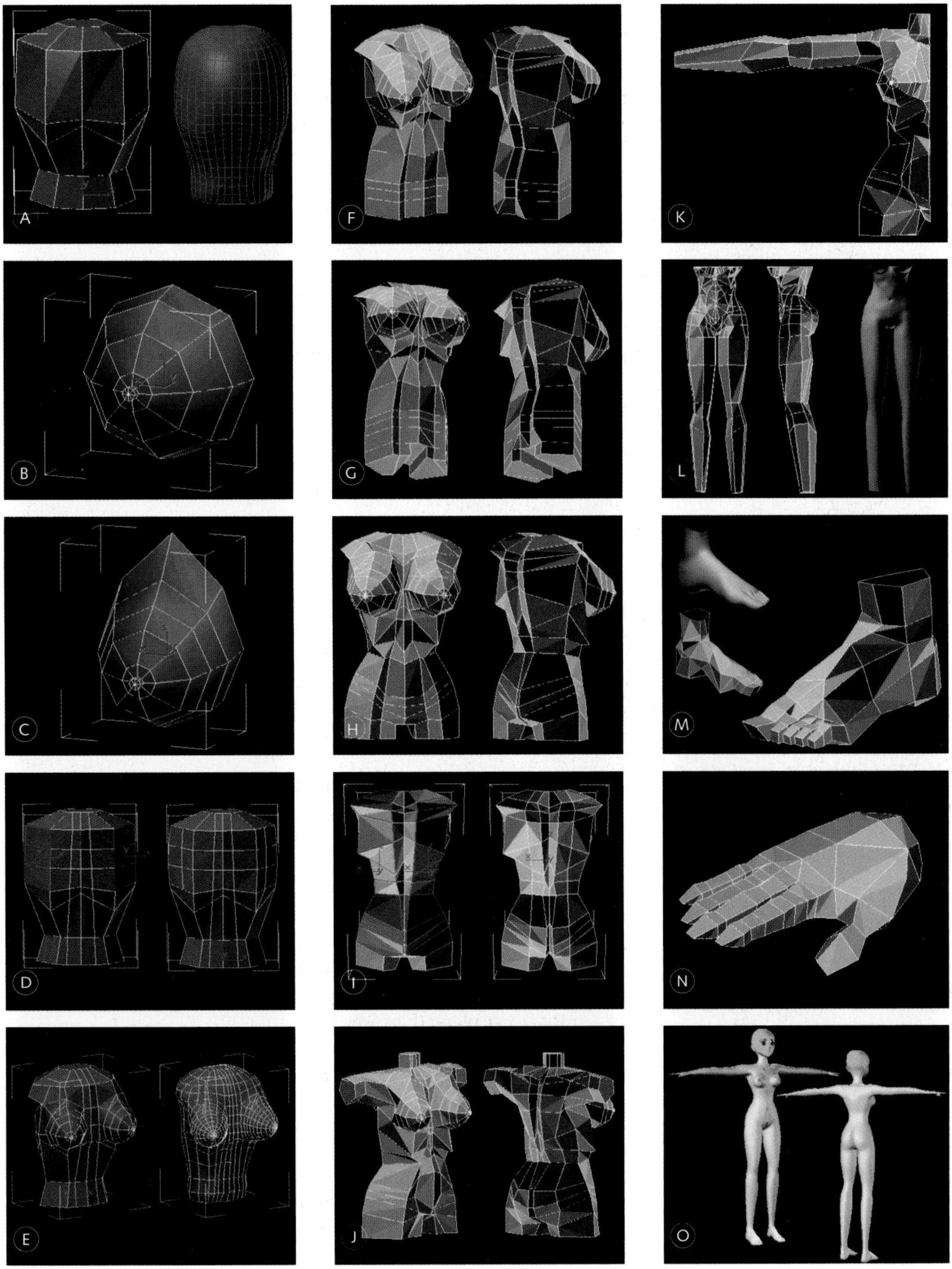
A
B
C
D
E
F
G
H
I
J
K
L
M
N
O

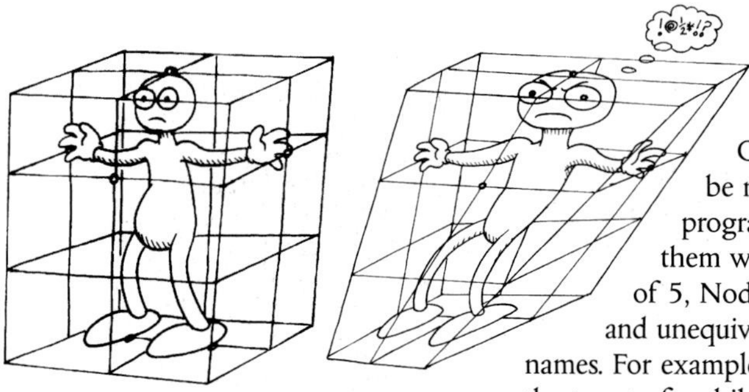

4.5.3 These drawings illustrate the effect of lattices on the shape of a three-dimensional object. Every time the lattice is moved the model is deformed because each of the grid points on the lattice is connected with imaginary springs to the object's points.

Getting Information and Naming Objects

Objects and components of objects in some cases can be named so that we can identify them faster. Many programs will automatically name objects as we create them with names like Cube 1, Cube 2, Cube 3, or Node 1 of 5, Node 2 of 5, and so on. But in some cases where quick and unequivocal identification is required it is best to use unique names. For example, when one of 50 ellipsoids representing balloons is the target of a child's dart, naming it "target balloon" instead of "Ellipsoid 37" could be useful to quickly identify it during the explosion sequence (Fig. 4.6.1).

Another useful feature for quickly assessing detailed information about a specific object—such as its position, dimensions, and orientation—is the Get Information feature that presents information about the active object in numerical form.

Locking

Objects can be locked in a specific position, orientation, size, or spatial range. **Locking** an object or an object's element that is not supposed to move can help streamline the modeling process. In most cases, objects can be switched from the locked position to the unlocked position without losing or modifying any other attributes.

Duplicating and Instancing

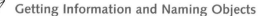

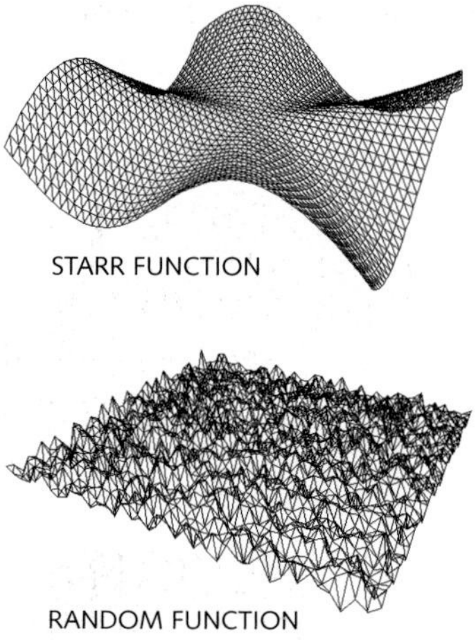

4.5.4 A plane terrain with a resolution of 40 × 40 units is deformed with different mathematical functions: a Starr function, a random function, and on the opposite page versions of the Julia and Mandelbrot fractal functions.

Models can be easily duplicated without having to build them from scratch. **Duplicating** creates a single independent copy of the selected model or group of selected models. The copy can be created in the same location as the original or in a new position defined by an XYZ offset value. The duplicating utility can also create multiple copies of an object. The values needed to create multiple copies of an object typically include the number of copies, as well as the XYZ values for translation, rotation, and scaling (Figs. 4.6.2 and 4.6.3). Creating copies of an object creates more three-dimensional elements in the scene, increases the file size, and demands more computing time.

Instancing is an alternative to duplicating that is available in many systems. **Instancing**—also called **cloning** in some systems—creates multiples of an original object by using its numerical description and cloning it elsewhere in the scene. The multiples created with instancing are like "living clones" that continue to be related at all times to the original object. If the original changes shape or is scaled, its dependent instances are also transformed. Because instances of a model do not increase the size of a file they are convenient for creating large armies of objects that look alike and that display a consistent group behavior. Instancing, however, may not be appropriate if a project requires each multiple to undergo a different shape transformation.

Setting a Face

Two-dimensional outlines drawn with free-form or curve tools are not really three-dimensional objects. When they are first drawn, two-dimensional outlines that are closed are just lines with a hole in the middle. Therefore, in order for two-dimensional outlines to be rendered properly it is necessary to turn them into planes. This process is called **setting a face** to an outline.

Mirroring

Mirroring a three-dimensional model is a useful technique when building an object composed of two identical (or almost identical) halves. The **mirroring** technique is implemented in a number of ways by different software, each with particular requirements and subtle functional differences. Three-dimensional objects can be repositioned in space with the mirroring technique. In such cases the object is entirely moved to where its mirror image would be. In general, however, mirroring works by copying an object, placing the copy in the same location as the original, and finally repositioning the copy. This way, the object remains in its original position, and its copy is placed where the mirror image of the original object would be.

Mirroring works by either providing a scaling value of -1 along the axis on which the mirroring is to take place, specifying a two-dimensional plane (XY, XZ, or YZ) on which the object is to be mirrored, or by establishing an axis of reflection by clicking a line perpendicular to the object to be reflected (one end of the line represents the base point of reflection, the other end represents the beginning of the axis reflection). Mirroring is illustrated in Figures 4.6.2 and 4.6.4.

Setting the Center of Objects

Most three-dimensional programs keep track of where the centers of objects are placed. By default, these centers are automatically placed in the objects' geometric centers. These points become very important—especially during the animation process because many operations are calculated based on the spatial position of the center of the object. These operations include scaling, rotation (global and local—the latter is also known as pivoting), linking, and simulations of motion dynamics related to center of gravity. Being able to interactively reposition the center of an object is a powerful modeling and animation utility (Fig. 4.6.1).

Snapping to the Grid

By forcing the object's or its components' points, for example, to **snap to a grid**, three-dimensional modeling programs can help to simplify the construction of regular shapes or precise details within larger shapes (Fig. 4.6.3). Grids can usually be defined by the user.

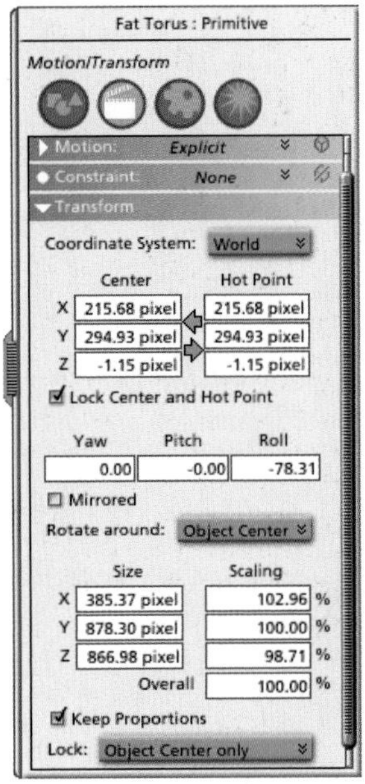

4.6.1 This dialog box provides quick numerical information about the position, orientation, size, and ranges of motion of an object. (Carrara dialog box © 2001–2003 Eovia Corporation.)

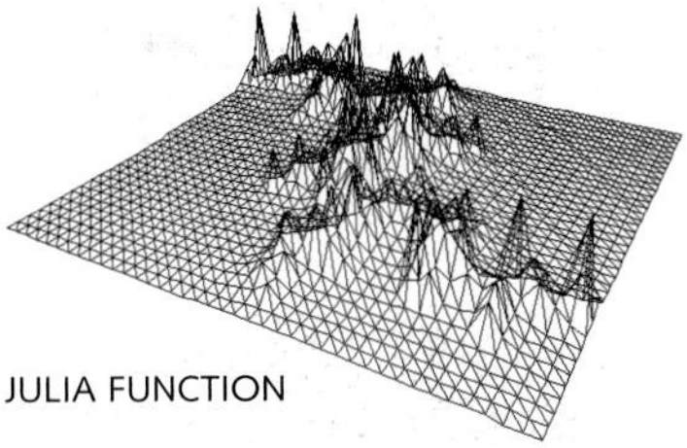

JULIA FUNCTION

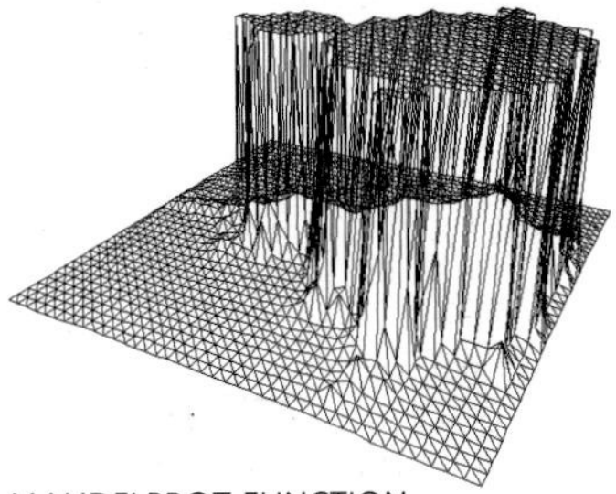

MANDELBROT FUNCTION

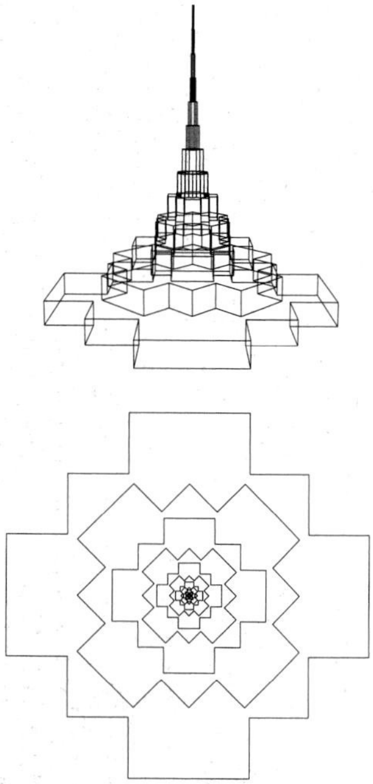

4.6.2 This object was created by duplicating the original shape at the bottom 12 times. Each instance of the original shape was mirrored by rotating 45 degrees and translating one unit on the Z axis.

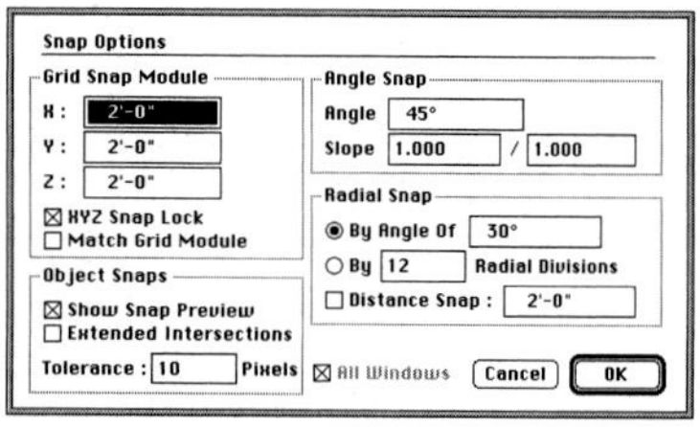

4.6.3 Controls for the snap to grid option. (form•Z Dialog box. © 1991–1995 auto•des•sys, Inc.)

This includes the size of the grid unit, whether the points snap to the grid, whether the object's center or edges snap to the grid when the object is moved, and whether the snap to grid function is applied to all objects in the scene or only to some.

Setting Text

The text tool is capable of automatically producing two-dimensional outlines or three-dimensional objects extracted from the two-dimensional outlines of fonts (or typefaces) installed in the computer system. The sophistication and variety of two-dimensional text outlines varies greatly from software to software, and so do all the additional features associated with letterforms, such as letterspacing, kerning capabilities, and point-editing features (Fig. 4.6.5).

Most of today's three-dimensional modeling programs extract the text outlines from spline-based descriptions (often in the PostScript language) resident in the system software. Some three-dimensional programs extract this outline information from a font database—sometimes in curve format, other times in polygonal format—that is provided with the three-dimensional program itself. The shapes of the letterforms are usually smooth and detailed when the outline information is brought in as a series of curves. However, when the outline information is brought in as a series of polygonal lines, the resulting shape may be jagged and unrefined, especially in the portions of the outline with the most curvature.

Most text tools work in conjunction with the keyboard. Any character that can be typed from the keyboard will show up in the three-dimensional environment as a two-dimensional outline. When an extrusion value is specified for the two-dimensional outline, the letterform can be three-dimensional. As with all objects modeled with extrusion, bevelling can be applied to letterforms modeled with extrusion-based text tools (Fig. 5.4.1–5.4.2). (See Chapter 5 for additional information on bevelling.)

Volume Calculation

The calculation of volumes and unfolding of planes are two modeling specialized techniques that can be useful when designing three-dimensional models that eventually get fabricated out of real materials. Volume calculation tools allow users to find out the total volume and area of the inside, outside, or parts of any three-dimensional object. Knowing the exact volume of liquid that can be contained in a new bottle design can be very important to an industrial designer. Likewise, an engineer in charge of supervising the actual production of the bottle needs to know the volume of glass needed to fabricate the bottle. Some of the volume calculation tools can also be used to extract data related to the object's mass or its center of gravity and inertia. This information can be used later in the animation of models using motion dynamics animation software.

Being able to unfold the plans that bound a three-dimensional object can be quite useful when it is necessary to fabricate either a cardboard scale model or prototype of the three-dimensional object or the final object itself in more durable materials, such as plastic or sheet metal. Figure 15.8.1 shows three-dimensional objects that were built with a variety of modeling techniques and then unfolded into two-dimensional patterns.

4.6.4 The components in this engine were created by duplicating and mirroring a few custom objects. (Courtesy of Toru Kosaka, STUDIO EggMan.)

Bounding Box

When modeling a scene with multiple complex objects many computer systems may slow down because of the huge number of calculations needed to redraw the image of the models on the screen. Using bounding boxes to represent objects is a convenient technique for speeding up their display. **Bounding boxes** are usually rectangular, and they are defined by the points most distant from the center of the model. Bounding boxes can also be used to define the collision volumes in a videogame (Fig. 4.6.6) or a dynamics simulation (Fig. 13.3.1). Bounding boxes are not to be confused with lattices, which can be used to distort the three-dimensional objects contained within them. Bounding boxes and the lattices used to deform free-form objects look similar but behave differently.

Making objects invisible or **ghosting** them are two options similar to the bounding box. Making objects invisible removes them from the display but not from the information contained in the file. Objects made invisible with this method are usually not displayed regardless of the rendering method until made visible again—usually by just clicking a choice in a checkbox. The ghosting option offered by some programs is similar to the bounding box. In some implementations of the ghosted display the model is represented with dotted lines, and the display of the ghosted model is only updated when the mouse button is released at the end of an interactive manipulation. In other implementations of ghosting it does not speed the display of images on the screen but instead facilitates working with complex models by making ghosted portions unselectable.

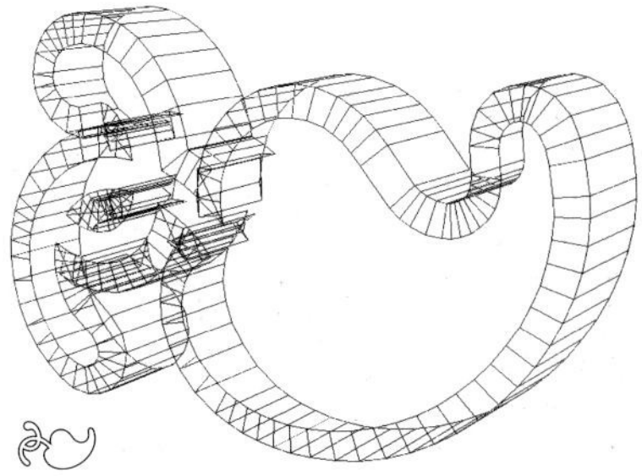

4.6.5 Two-dimensional text outlines can easily be converted into three-dimensional type.

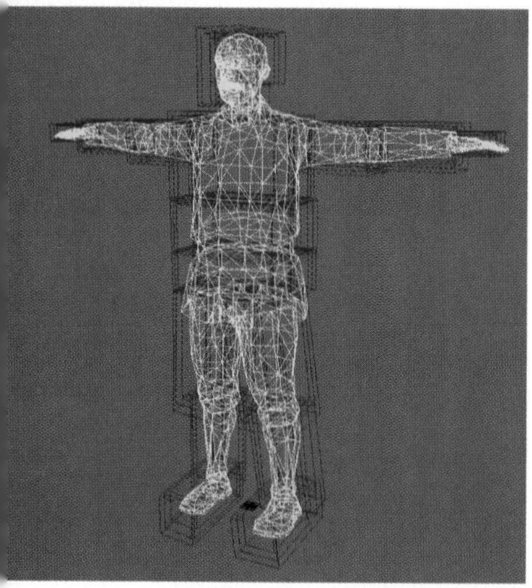

4.6.6 The collision detection volumes in dark blue define the areas of vulnerability of a soldier in the game *Medal of Honor*, and trigger hit reactions. The larger boxes are used for the easy playing mode while the smallest boxes offer a greater degree of difficulty. (© 1999 Electronic Arts Inc. All rights reserved.)

4.7 Real-Time Polygonal Models

The ability to render polygonal models in real-time is almost as old as three-dimensional computer animation, but today's systems offer more realistic rendering and more complex models than what was possible a decade ago. Gaming is the area that takes the most advantage of real-time rendering, whether it takes place on game platforms or computers. Interactive online websites with three-dimensional navigation and functionality also take advantage of polygonal models rendered in real-time. Both gaming and online websites require an approach to modeling for real-time that emphasizes efficiency and portability.

Improved hardware rendering, as explained in Chapter 6, has fueled the feasibility and popularity of ever more complex real-time polygonal models. Powerful graphics cards and GPUs, faster clock speeds, and increased memory continue to raise the bar for real-time polygonal models. But there are always limits to what a powerful graphics system can do, and for that reason it is important to **optimize polygonal models** for real-time rendering. Designing and building polygonal models and their textures for real-time rendering is about compromise and optimization (Fig. 4.7.6). There is always a compromise between visual detail and speed in a real-time environment. Real-time models may range from a few hundred polygons to thousands of polygons. ***Spyro the Dragon***, for example, has 352 polygons (Figs. 3.6.4, 10.5.10 and 11.1.1) while ***Dawn*** (Fig. 6.10.1) is built with 203,741 triangles. A "heavy" model with too much geometrical complexity could slow down the real-time rendering and the frame rate would drop, lessening the illusion of natural motion. Same would be true for a model with image maps, textures, too large for the available memory, graphics card, or GPU in question. Keep in mind that the geometry and size of image maps that might be optimal for one environment might be overkill or not enough for another. This is a common challenge when "porting" or adapting a computer game from one platform to another, from platform to PC or vice versa: models and image maps sometimes require significant revision and optimization.

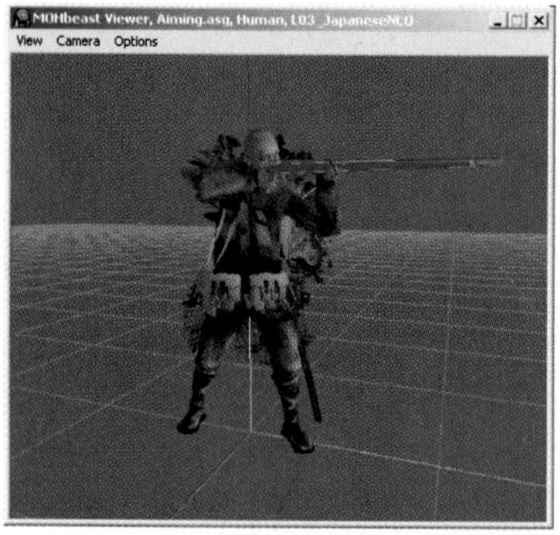

4.7.1 The blending of animation cycles as calculated by the game engine is previsualized on a PC in real-time with the *MOH Beast* utility. (© 1999 Electronic Arts Inc. All rights reserved.)

Most computer or platform games use their own custom **rendering engine** to render polygonal models in real-time (Fig. 4.71). The engine is fed with highly optimized polygonal and image map information. Because different game engines use a variety of different rendering and animation techniques the polygonal model and image maps formats may vary between engines (Figs. 3.6.4, 4.7.5, 7.4.6, and 11.5.4). For this reason it is always a good idea to keep a lowest-common denominator model that can be adapted and converted for different game platforms and engines.

Most online websites that use real-time polygonal models require a **player** or plug-in. Most multiplayer gaming websites use their own formats and engines (Figs. 4.7.2–4.7.3, and 4.7.8). But a wide variety of off-the-shelf three-dimensional players for real-time rendering is also available. These can usually be downloaded to the

4.7.2 The multiplayer game *EverQuest* has characters ranging between 500 and 3,000 polygons, a minimum of two 256 x 256 textures, and bump maps. (EverQuest® courtesy Sony Online Entertainment Inc. EverQuest is a registered trademark of Sony Computer Entertainment America Inc. © 1999-2002 SCEA Inc. SOE and the SOE logo are registered trademarks of Sony Online Entertainment Inc. All rights reserved.)

4.7.3 *URU, Ages Beyond Myst* (left) is the multiplayer online version of *Myst*. The high-resolution avatar is roughly 5,000 polygons, but level of detail (LOD) techniques are used to lower its resolution for long shots. The environment is several thousand polygons, but the total may surpass 15,000 polygons when the degree of tessellation of the water increases due to ripple and flow. (© 2002 Cyan Worlds, Inc. All rights reserved.)

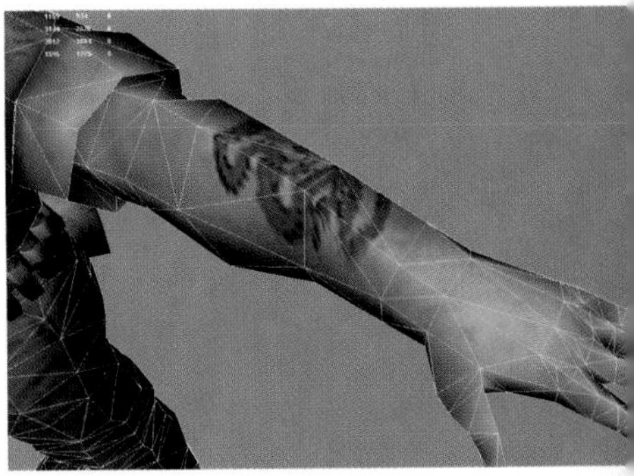

4.7.4 (above) Using UV coordinates a high resolution image map of a tattoo is placed on a dozen polygons on the arm. (© 1999 Electronic Arts Inc. All rights reserved.)

user's computer from the World Wide Web, sometimes free of charge. Some of the most popular off-the-shelf formats and players include Shockwave 3D, Viewpoint, Cult 3D, Wild Tangent, Pulse 3D, and more recently MPEG-4. This file format is used primarily for encoding moving images, but it also provides tools for encoding three-dimensional polygonal meshes that can be used for low resolution real-time character facial and body animation. MPEG-4 uses visual lip configurations, called **visemes**, that are equivalent to speech phonemes. Three-dimensional files in general may include compressed geometry, connectivity, shading normals, color, and texture coordinates.

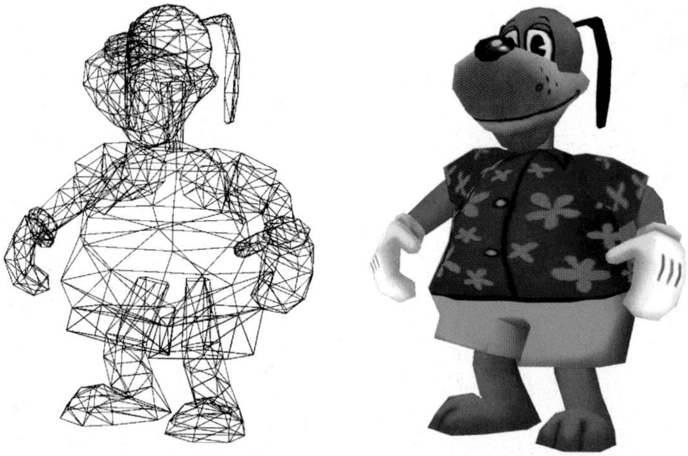

4.7.5 Sample character in wireframe and shaded versions from Disney's *Toontown* Online multiplayer game. Model is within the 1,000 polygon average, including a 392-polygon head, 476-polygon torso, and 158-polygon legs. (© Disney Enterprises, Inc.)

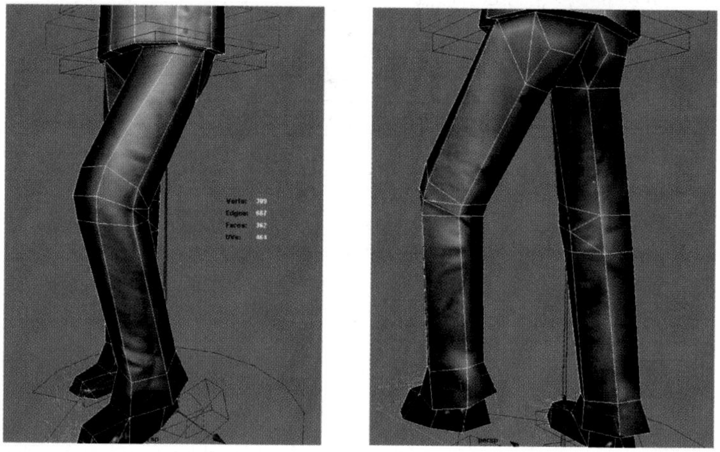

4.7.6 This polygonal mesh has been designed to optimize the folding of the pants at the knees. (© 1999 Electronic Arts Inc. All rights reserved.)

4.7.7 First-level playground in the *Toontown* multiplayer game, with two avatars that players can create interactively from a catalog of parts (torso, legs, head, muzzle) and clothes. (© Disney Enterprises.)

In addition to using powerful graphics cards or simplifying the geometry and the image maps, there are a few tricks and shortcuts that can be used to accelerate real-time rendering. A few of the most common are levels of detail, billboards, and Flash animations. Levels of detail are useful in situations where the same three-dimensional character or prop appears very close and very far from the camera. Levels of detail, also called LODs, consist of having the same model at different resolutions that can be seamlessly loaded as the object or character moves closer or away from the camera (Fig. 3.6.7). Image maps with different levels of detail can also be used to highlight details such as the tattoo in Figure 4.7.4. Billboards are a few polygons that define a flat surface used to project image maps. Billboards have the same function that painted backgrounds have on a theatre stage or a movie set (Figs. 4.7.7 and 4.7.9). (See Chapter 9 for more information on billboards for visual effects.) Using Flash MX files to deliver three-dimensional animations online is another common shortcut. In this case the three-dimensional animation is rendered

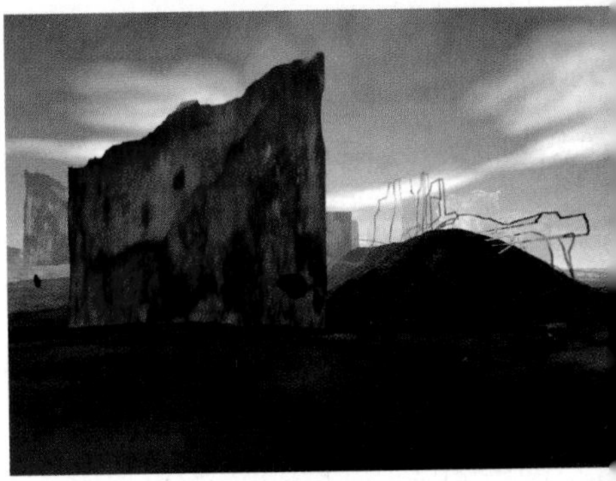

4.7.8 In addition to the 8,192-polygon terrain in *Purbeck Light Years* there are 128 models in this Shockwave 3D world, each consisting of 2 polygons for a world total of 8,448 triangles. A higher resolution model, 131,072 polygons, was used to capture these images. The castle image maps are 32-bit color and 1024 × 512 pixels, and the maps for the planes, ground and sky are 512 × 512 pixels. (© 2003 Jeremy Gardiner. Programming by Anthony Head, research by Veronica Falçao.)

and saved as a two-dimensional SWF file or Flash movie. The advantages of this approach, or "cheat," are that Flash files are generally compact and download fast, and also that the Flash player is ubiquitous worldwide. Three-dimensional animations saved in the SWF format are usually contained in small windows, 200 × 200 pixels for example, that can be imported into a Flash movie and easily played within larger scenes.

Computer and platform games are the most pervasive applications of real-time rendering, but certainly not the only one. Fine artists are increasingly creating interactive worlds and virtual reality installations using off-the-shelf players or repurposed game engines; the latter approach is called **game moding**. Figure 12.7.3 shows a virtual reality installation that requires users to wear a VR helmet. Figure 4.7.8 shows ***Purbeck Light Years***, a real-time computer animation and immersive virtual reality based on paintings and drawings. The land mesh in this installation was created from a satellite image of Dorset, England, and the grayscale values used as a displacement map on a 8,192-polygon terrain. The ground and sky are covered with bitmap textures. To simulate day or nighttime the ground and sky textures blend gradually into other textures. The skies are chosen at random to represent the unpredictable nature of real weather, and during the daytime there is a 30% chance of rain. The textures for the rectangular vertical planes, or billboards, are from drawings and paintings of Corfe Castle and an alpha transparency channel is used to display their irregular shapes. A flocking system governs the movement of birds, a theatrical element in the project. A polar coordinate system (Fig. 3.4.8) is used to keep the castle in the middle of the scene at all times.

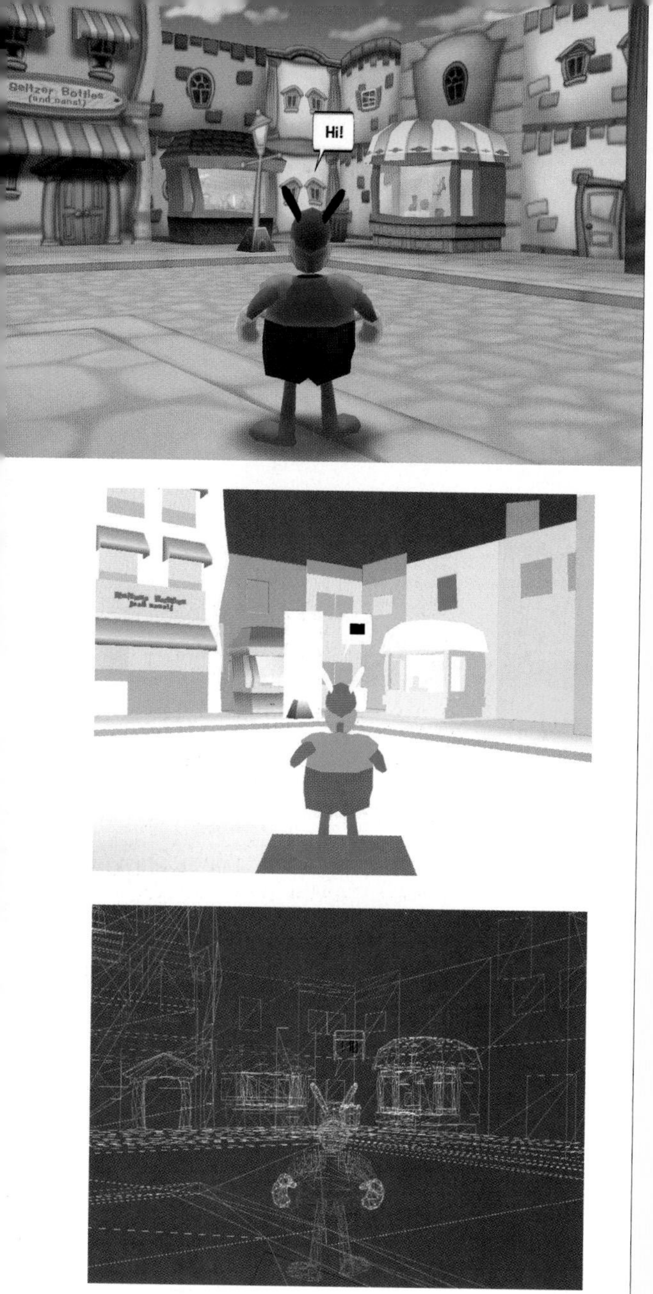

4.7.9 Wireframe and shaded versions of a corner in *Toontown*, where real-time environments typically range between 2,000 and 3,000 polygons excluding characters. The Panda3D proprietary engine can display geometry in real-time using either OpenGL or DirectX. (© Disney Enterprises, Inc.)

Chapter 4

Key Terms

- Arcs
- B-spline
- Bézier curve
- Bounding boxes
- Capping
- Cardinal spline
- Children
- Circles
- Cloning
- Cones
- Control points
- Control vertices
- Controlled curves
- Cubes
- Curvature
- Curved lines
- Cylinders
- Deformation with lattices
- Degree of curve
- Diameter
- Die
- Direct point manipulation
- Dodecahedron
- Duplicating
- Extrusion
- Free-form extrusion
- Free-form modeling
- Free-form three-dimensional objects
- Game moding
- Geometric primitives
- Ghosting
- Icosahedron
- Instancing
- Knots
- Lathe
- Linear spline
- Locking
- Lofting
- Mathematical functions
- Mirroring
- Nonrational curve
- Non-uniform rational b-splines
- NURBS
- Octahedron
- Optimize polygonal models
- Parents
- Player, plug-in
- Polygonal lines
- Polygons
- Radius
- Rational curve
- Regular polyhedra
- Rendering engine
- Revolve
- Seed outline
- Setting a face
- Snap to grid
- Spheres
- Spirals
- Splines
- Surfaces of revolution
- Sweeping
- Tangent points
- Tension
- Terrains
- Tetrahedron
- Torus
- Two-dimensional shapes
- Virtual sculpting
- Visemes
- Weight

CHAPTER 5

5

Advanced Modeling and Rigging Techniques

Summary

SOME OF THE ADVANCED MODELING TECHNIQUES used for building three-dimensional objects and environments are covered in this chapter. These techniques include complex curved surfaces and blobby surfaces, logical operators and trimmed surfaces, a variety of utilities like surface blending, procedural description used mostly to model natural phenomena, and image-based modeling. An overview of animation rigging techniques concludes the chapter.

QUICK INDEX

5.1 Free-Form Curved Surfaces

Free-form curved surfaces have been a popular modeling technique since the mid-1980s. Their smoothness and curvature are easy to manipulate with the mesh of control points associated with all curves. Unlike polygonal meshes that allow the free addition or deletion of single poygons, adding local detail to curved surfaces can sometimes be a task with multiple steps because curved surfaces must start with a checkerboard pattern where only entire rows or columns can be added or deleted. In the absence of great local modeling control, curved patches are commonly stitched to one another to create complex shapes. In the case of a hand modeled with curved surfaces, each finger, the thumb, and the palm would be modeled as separate partches and then stitched together.

Free-form curved surfaces allow a great degree of surface control. They are mathematically defined and are also called **parametric curved surfaces** because each coordinate is a function of one or more parameters, such as a control hull, control points, tangent points, knots, and weights. **Free-form curved surfaces** and complex free-form surfaces are the generic names given to bicubic surface patches, Bézier surfaces, b-spline surfaces, and skinned surfaces. Each of these types of surfaces is based on different types of curves.

As explained in Chapter 3, curved lines are defined by several points and deviate from a straight path without any sharp breaks in angularity. Curves are used to define free-form curved surfaces and to build meshes of curved surfaces. There are many types of curves, and the most popular types include linear splines, cardinal splines, b-splines, Bézier curves, and NURBS (Fig. 4.2.2).

Each of the curved surfaces can be characterized by the way in which its curvature or tension is controlled by the control points. Curved surfaces defined by Bézier curves, for example, pass through all of its control points, and their degree of curvature is fine-tuned with tangent points. Curved surfaces created with b-splines rarely pass through the control points, and those created with NURBS do not pass through the control points, but rely on weights and knots for increased local curve control. (Read Chapter 4 for more information on curved lines.)

Cubic splines make use of curve-fitting techniques and pass through all of the specified points. They also use parabolic blending and require numerical specification of both direction and magnitude of the tangent deviations. In the case of Bézier curves, the shape and order of the curve can be varied by the use of parameters. The first and last points are used to define the curve, which is defined by an open polygon. If any points are moved, then the entire curve is altered because it is an average of all its vertices. B-spline curves offer more local control than Bézier curves.

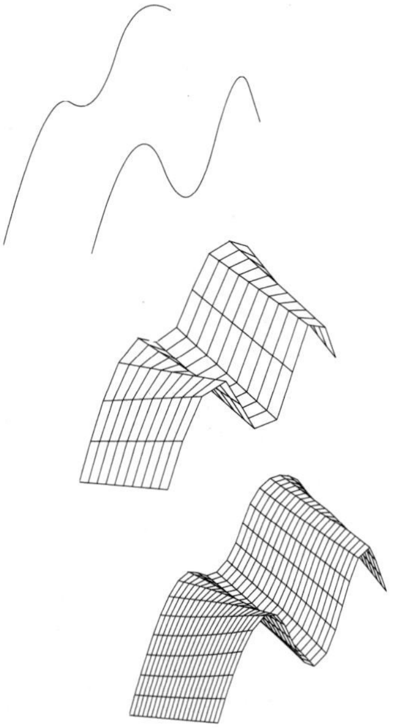

5.1.1 Two curves were used to create patches of different resolutions.

Curved Patches

A curved patch is a small curved area that can be created from two or four curves. When a patch is created from two curves, they are positioned opposite to one another (Fig. 5.1.1). Four curves can also be used to define a rectangular area. Complex free-form surfaces are created by **merging** (two or more) **curved patches**. When curved patches that have the same number of rows and columns are merged, the results are fairly predictable. But merging patches with different numbers of rows and/or columns requires the use of interpolation techniques that modify one of the two patches being merged (Fig. 5.1.2). This merging can also be controlled with great detail by specifying manually which points in the first patch merge into which points in the second patch. Having patches that merge into each other seamlessly is important to create a crisp rendering of the new patch, especially when the surface contains an image map on it.

Merging patches is one the most powerful modeling techniques that can yield detailed models with subtle shapes (Fig. 5.1.3) However, the large number of points or vertices in a model created with patches is often a concern. This can be addressed by either making sure that the patches throughout the model have a small number of subdivisons, or by using a modeling utility that purges some of the points according to criteria such as the angle or distance to other points. Curved patches can be further manipulated and refined by using some of the utilities described both in this chapter and in Chapter 4.

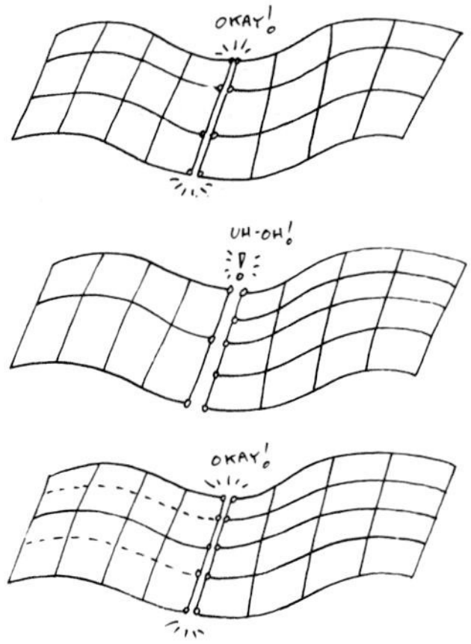

5.1.2 Merging two patches usually requires matching their number of columns and/or rows.

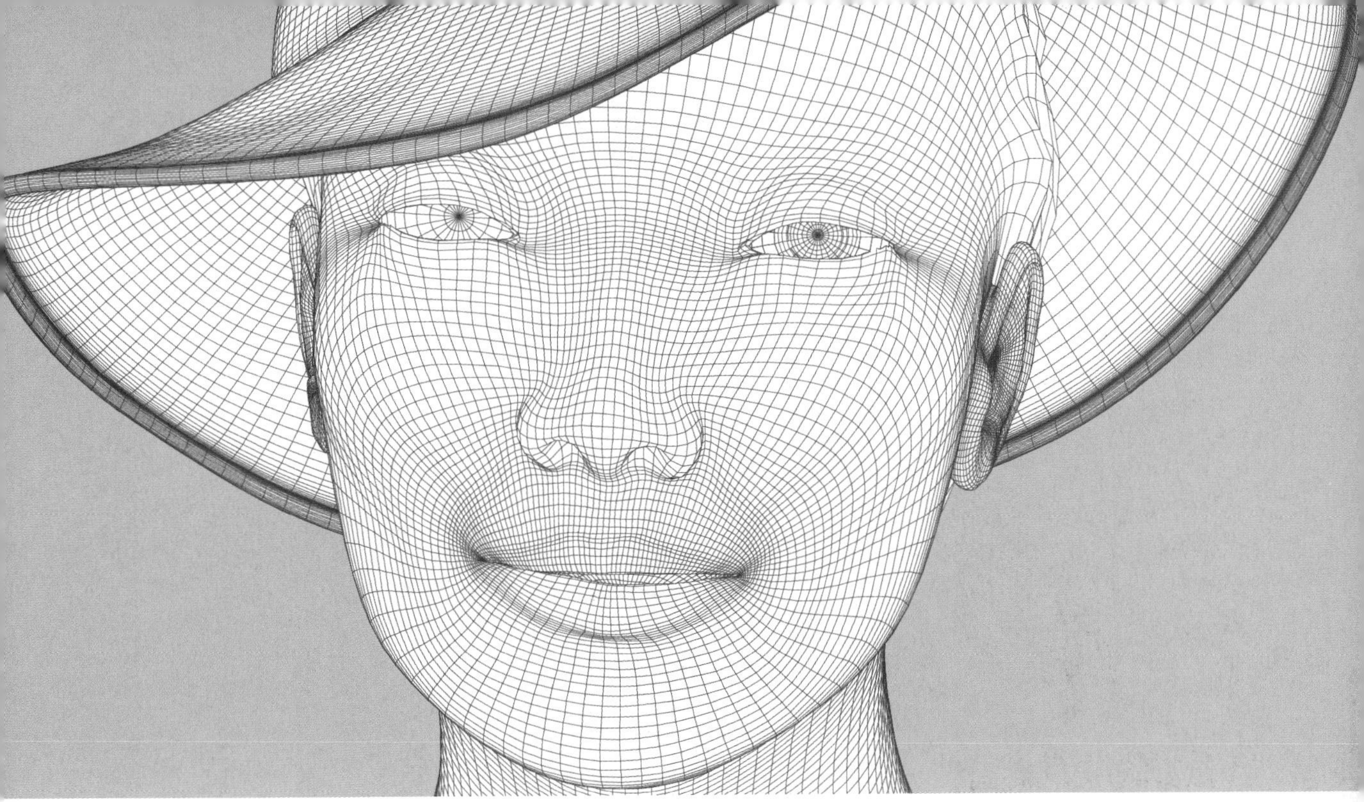

Skinning

A unique way to create curved surfaces that fit predefined closed curves in three-dimensional space is called skinning. This technique creates three-dimensional objects by connecting a sequence of two-dimensional **cross sections**, also called **slices** or **outlines**, with curves. Skinning is somewhat similar to free-form extrusion because the modeling follows a path, but it is different because the shape of the cross sections being skinned is predefined. Most skinning functions usually require that the two-dimensional outlines are closed and that they all have the same number of points. Some skinning functions, however, can skin outlines with different numbers of points by creating points as needed based on guessing what the best skinning would be. Topographic data that includes altitude information is commonly used to generate terrain models using the skinning technique (Fig. 5.1.4).

The technique of skinning is also called **cross section extrusion** or **serial section reconstruction** because entire objects can be reconstructed from cross sections or slices that can be obtained with a variety of methods. Skinning is particularly useful to create models of humans because these are easily described as series of two-dimensional contours. A variety of technologies, such as three-dimensional laser scanners and magnetic resonance (MR) scanners, for example, are used to gather precise data about the outside and inside shapes of

5.1.3 This model of a famous actress was created by making a physical bust, scanning it, converting it to a NURBS surface, and then pulling points with Softimage, the software that was also used for animating the model. The single surface has openings at the mouth, the ears are separate surfaces, and the eyelashes were created with bump maps. (© 1999 Virtual Celebrity/Marlene Inc.)

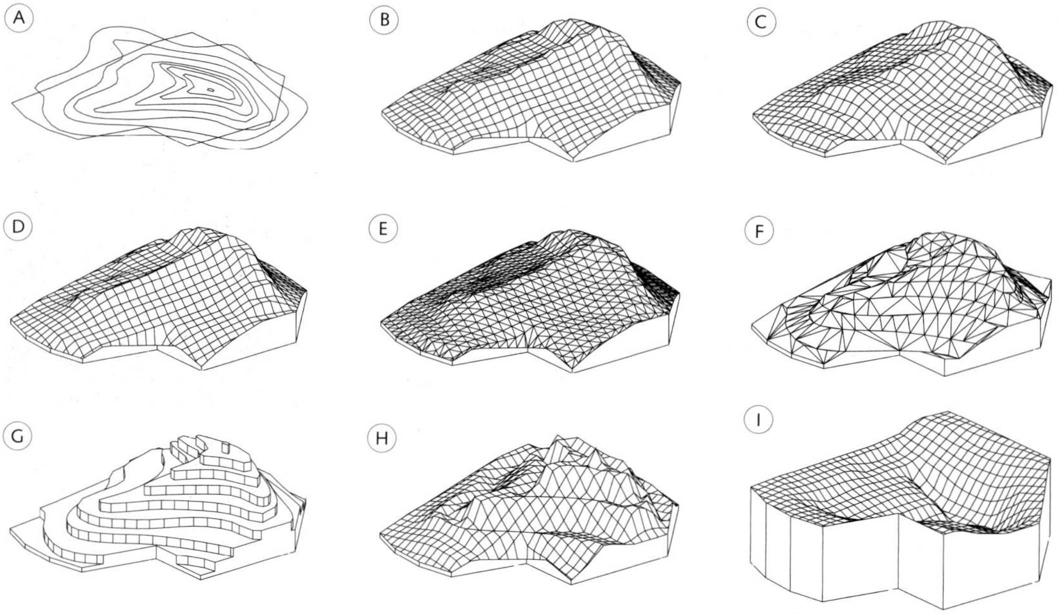

5.1.4 Different three-dimensional objects can be created by connecting, or skinning, two-dimensional outlines (A) in a variety of ways. A mesh based on both XY directions (B) looks slightly different than meshes weighted along the X or the Y axis (C and D). The outlines in (E) and (F) are connected by two triangular meshes of different resolutions and by simple steps in (G). The altitude of every other outline has been shifted up or down in (H), and in (I) the altitude of the outlines has been inverted.

human bodies (Fig. 5.1.5). The three-dimensional data used to create the stereo pair of a human thorax, illustrated in Figure 5.1.6, comes from a person who did 45-second breath holds in a magnetic resonance (MR) scanner. At each breath hold, a series of scans of a single coronal slice were taken at ten different phases of the heart cycle. This was achieved by coordinating the scanning process—or data acquisition—with the electrocardiogram signal of the subject. This process was repeated about 50 times at different cross sections of the heart. The complete acquisition took about an hour, and it yielded 490 slices, comprising ten groups of 49 slice-volumes at ten different phases of the heart cycle. The flowing blood appears as the brightest object in the images.

The contours that define a skinned object can also be traced manually on a digitizing tablet. This technique is especially useful for obtaining three-dimensional skinned objects that have the irregularities typical of handmade objects. The number of digitized cross sections needed to describe an object is in direct proportion to the complexity and detail desired in the final object. The sections on the X and Y planes represent a sample in the horizontal and vertical levels of the original object. Some objects are easier to describe by their horizontal cross sections, while others are easier to define by their vertical cross sections. The number of sections that are necessary to describe an object accurately can range from half a dozen to more than a hundred. A loss of data is apparent when the skinned objects are sampled at large intervals and the cross sections are too far apart from each other. Once the cross sections have been digitized, it is sometimes necessary to edit the database to adjust individual sections within the three-dimensional object. Geometric transformations can be performed on the contours to change their relative spatial position.

The technique chosen to define the outer surface of an **articulated skeleton** defines the final appearance of the animated three-dimensional model. Ideally the geometry attached to an articulated skeleton should follow the motion of the **articulated chain** segments, and also deform automatically. Rigid geometry usually behaves like hard shells around the skeleton and can only be deformed with keyframe animation techniques, laboriously pulling individual points on the mesh. **Attaching rigid models** to an articulated chain is possible. The procedure usually consists of creating a hierarchical structure by clicking on one chain segment and one model at a time. However, three-dimensional rigid models that are assigned to a skeleton do not deform automatically with rotations of the joints.

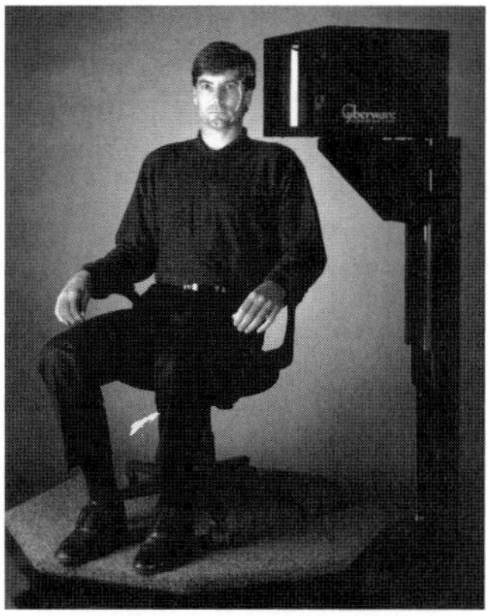

5.1.5 A three-dimensional scanner can quickly gather precise modeling data. (Courtesy of Cyberware, Monterey, CA.)

Most software programs provide tools for generating a skin-like surface that wraps the skeleton or articulated chain. The surfaces covering the skeleton are called **skin surfaces** because they are continuous and flexible like skin; they deform in response to the movement of the skeleton that they cover. A clear advantage of using skin surfaces over rigid models to envelop the skeleton is the greater degree of deformation control that the former have over the latter. When bound properly to the animation rig skin surfaces may automatically adjust to modifications in the translation, rotation, and scaling of the skeleton. The realistic effect of skin that stretches with motion—especially at the joints—is often achieved only with a combination of animation techniques that may include motion dynamics of flexible bodies, attaching the skin to the bone and muscle systems using spring-like simulations (Fig. 12.1.7), and free-form shape animation in the form of flexible lattices.

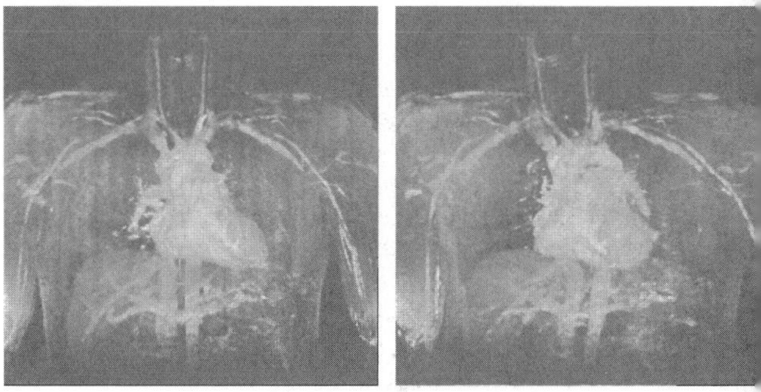

5.1.6 This stereo pair of the organs and structures inside a human thorax was created by reading the 49 slices comprising this volume into a volume rendering program. The images were processed with opacity settings to emphasize the bright flowing blood. The left image is a frontal volume rendering projection, and the right image was made by rotating the volume 10 degrees counterclockwise to the first image. (Data set by Dr. Paul Margosian et. al., Picker Inc., Cleveland, OH. Rendering software by ISG Technologies, Toronto, Canada. Data formatting and presentation by Irwin Sobel, HPLABS, Palo Alto, CA. Courtesy of Irwin Sobel.)

There are two common techniques for creating a skin surface that surrounds an articulated figure or a simple articulated chain. The automatic method involves creating a three-dimensional surface based on the chain itself. The manual method consists of assigning predefined three-dimensional surfaces, curved or polygonal, to a chain or specific segments of the chain. Skin surfaces can be generated automatically by creating an outline shape and letting the software extrude it along the skeleton (Fig. 5.1.7). Just like standard extrusion techniques, automatic skin surface generators allow the animator to specify the number of times that the outline being extruded may be repeated along a segment of the articulated chain, and also whether the resulting shape will be capped. In most cases, the surface that results from **automatic skin generation** can be edited manually.

Skin surfaces can also be created manually with a variety of modeling techniques and then positioned around the skeleton (Fig. 5.1.7). **Manual creation of skin surfaces** offers two main advantages over automatic generation. More detail can be modeled with

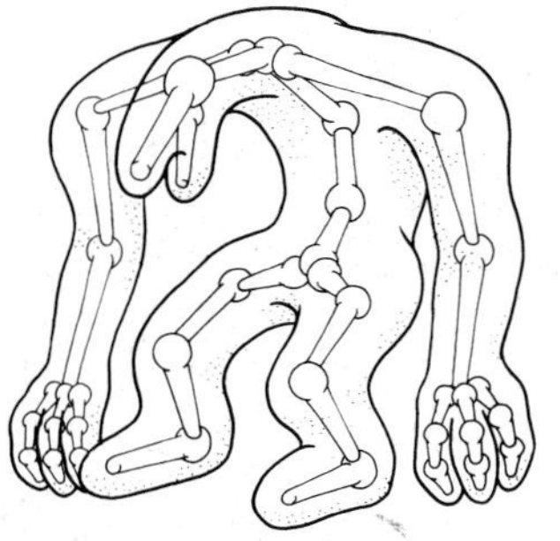

SKELETON AND AUTOMATIC SKIN

SKELETON AND MANUAL SKIN

SHREK MANUAL SKIN

5.1.7 Skeletons with hierarchy information, with skins created automatically and manually. Skins modeled manually have more detail than those generated automatically. (Bottom: *Shrek*™ and © 2001 DreamWorks L.L.C.)

manual techniques, and skin surfaces generated manually can also be positioned more accurately over the skeleton to optimize the way in which the skin deforms. It is common practice to model more detail in the parts of the skin surface—usually the joints—that will bend under skeleton control. This can minimize unnatural stretching effects or extreme distortion of the skin (Fig. 5.1.8).

Once the skin surfaces have been assigned to different segments of an articulated chain or skeleton they can be further refined and controlled by specifying their **deformation parameters**. These parameters allow animators to control the various properties of bending skin and to manipulate single vertices or groups of vertices on the skin's surface. The deformation parameters include the amount of bulging or rounding of a portion of the skin surface as a result of a joint bending. These parameters also control the weight that defines how the vertices will respond to deformation, the way adjacent regions blend with one another, and the assignment of vertices on the skin surface to a specific segment in the articulated chain (Fig. 5.1.9). See the end of this chapter for additional information on the rigging skeletons that control the surfaces around them.

In some cases, the skin of three-dimensional models is not defined as a **continuous surface** but instead as a series of independent surfaces that are related to each other through a hierarchical structure. In these instances, the surfaces representing the skin should be arranged with care to minimize the number of **gaps on the surface** of the animated model. Gaps on the surface of a model are obviously not an issue if the figure is designed in such a way that the surfaces are not connected—for example, a cartoon character with unconnected floating body parts. In many cases, gaps on the skin surface tend to look like modeling mistakes. Two simple techniques that can be used to minimize the gaps on the skin of objects built with several surfaces consist of using filler shapes at the joints, and plain-shape interpolation. **Filler objects** are usually spherical and positioned at the joints that have wide rotation angles, which is where gaps in butting surfaces are most likely to occur. **Simple-shape interpolation** can also take reasonably good care of small gaps that may develop on the surface of models during simple rotations. But simple shape interpolation offers far from perfect results because it also generates unexpected skin distortion when applied to gaps created with rotations that happen around several axes simultaneously.

Blobby Surfaces

Blobby surfaces are usually defined as spherical objects that change shape depending on how close they are to other blobby elements. The magnitude of the **attraction force** of blobby elements is usually defined by their volume, but their **area of influence** can also be set independently from their size. In an animation, **blobby surfaces** are dynamic and constantly regenerate as they move in and out of the areas of influence of other blobby elements (Fig. 5.1.10). When two or more of these touch one another they can fuse into a single object, just as two drops of oil or mercury merge into one another when they meet on a surface. The way in which blobby objects, also called **implicit surfaces**, fuse into each other is determined by the explicit or random links that are established between each of the objects in a blobby system (Fig. 5.1.11).

Fitting Curved Surfaces to Polygons

The techniques of fitting curved surfaces to polygonal meshes have gained popularity due to the increased use of three-dimensional scanners to capture physical models and maquettes. Scanners usually capture three-dimensional geometry in the form of polygonal meshes, and specialized software has been developed to help convert the polygonal information into curved surfaced. The purpose of this type of software is to convert the data in an efficient way but also to allow a human modeler to specify how the patches should be positioned and oriented on the polygonal mesh (Fig. 5.1.12).

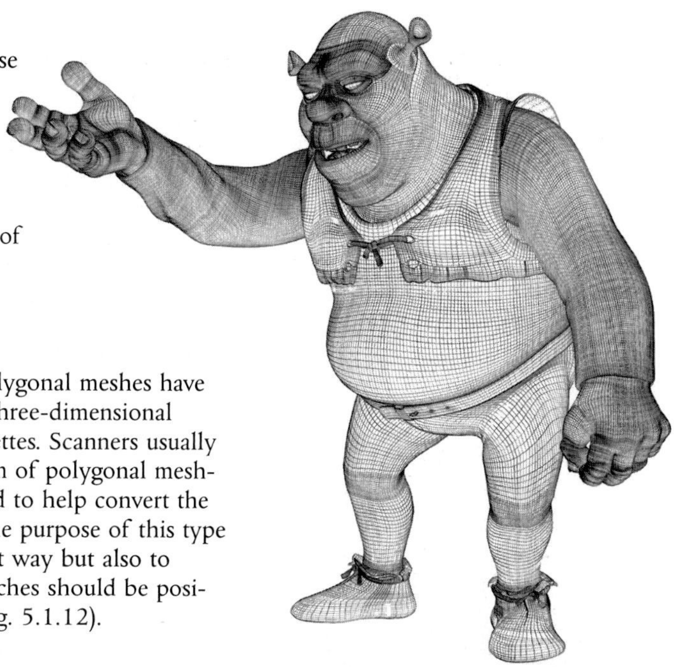

5.1.8 The skin model of *Shrek*, including clothing. Figure 5.7.4 shows some of the muscle and bone rigging system used to animate the skin surface of the character. (*Shrek*™ and © 2001 DreamWorks L.L.C.)

5.2 Subdivision Surfaces

Subdivision surfaces are popular as a flexible solution for modeling surfaces. These surfaces are something of a cross between polygonal meshes and patch surfaces, and they offer some of the best attributes of each of these traditional modeling techniques. Subdivision surfaces have the flexibility of polygonal meshes but without the faceted look typical of low resolution polygonal geometry. Subdivision surfaces can also yield smooth curved surfaces without the topological restriction of patches where the number of columns and rows has to be identical before two patches can be merged with one another.

Instead of having a constant density of points throughout the model, subdivision surfaces allow for different resolutions on arbitrary sections of the surface. Subdivision surfaces inherited their property of subdivision from curved patches, but they excel at modeling creases and cracks that are difficult to manage with b-spline curved surfaces, for example. But subdivision surfaces are not parametric (as curved surfaces are) because their topology is irregular and is not defined with a formula in a explicit way. Subdivision surfaces are defined algorithmically, and many of the algorithms that produce more polygons do so in two steps: first split each surface into four facets and then reposition the vertices by doing **local weight point averaging**. As shown in Figure 5.2.1 this procedure can be applied multiple times to create more detail. There are many ways to go about subdividing a surface including interpolation, averaging, approximation, and insertion of new points. But for these approaches to be efficient, they are usually based on **adaptive approximation**, which means that the surface will subdivide only

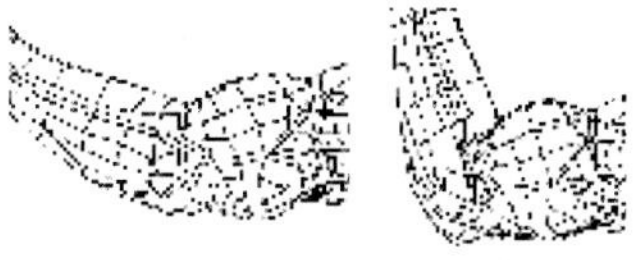

5.1.9 The skin that represents the biceps muscle swells as a secondary action because it is linked to the bone rotation. (Courtesy of Acclaim Entertainment, Inc., Advanced Technologies Group.)

5.1.10 Detail of a rendering of characters created with blobby surfaces. See page 181 for a wireframe view of the main character. (Image courtesy of Tim Cheung.)

5.1.11 (below right) The Cloud character in *The Stormriders,* played by Aaron Kwok, has the martial craft of pulling water from the surroundings and turning it into a deadly weapon. The liquid attack was created with Softimage Metaball. (Images courtesy of Centro Digital Pictures Ltd.)

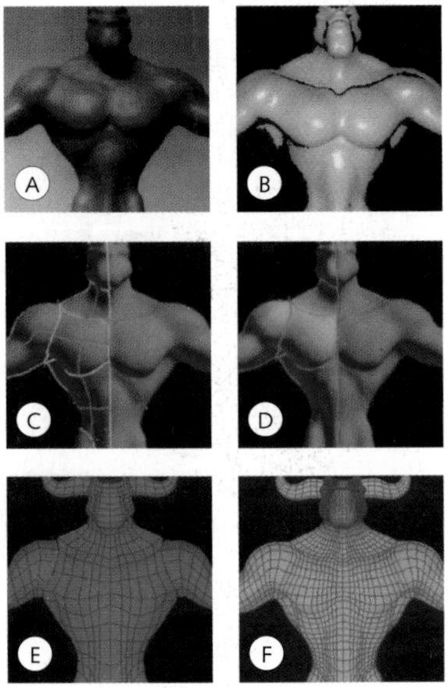

5.1.12 The modeling process of fitting curved surfaces to a polygonal mesh starts here with (A) a scaled sculpture that was digitized with a laser scanner. (B) The raw scans are integrated. (C) An internal patch feature structure and control curves are created with Paraform software. (D) The fitted NURBS surfaces. A low-resolution (E) or a high-resolution curved surfaces model (F) can be generated. (Images courtesy of Domi Piturro.)

where the topology of the surface requires additional detail. Subdivision surface techniques were first used in production in ***Geri's Game*** and ***A Bug's Life.*** Each of Geri's hands, the head, the jacket, and the pants was a single subdivision surface (Figs. 5.2.2 and 1.2.9). The faces and the hands of Flick and Hopper were also modeled with subdivision surfaces, while the sets were done with curved surfaces. The techniques for mapping image maps with UV techniques onto subdivision surfaces are yet to be perfected. Often the image maps can only be accurately placed onto the subdivided surfaces if the texture coordinates are subdivided in texture space exactly like the models were subdivided.

5.3 Logical Operators and Trimmed Surfaces

Logical operators are used to create models by adding and subtracting shapes in a variety of ways. The most common logical operators include **union, intersection,** and **difference.** The union operator is also known as **and,** intersection is called **or,** and difference is called **not.** The union and the difference of a sphere and a cross are illustrated in Figure 5.3.1.

The logical operator of difference is usually referred to as **trimming**, and the surfaces created with it are called **trimmed surfaces**. The modeling technique of trimming is especially useful for creating three-dimensional objects or **surfaces with holes**. The sequence illustrated in Figure 5.3.2 shows this operator in action along with the union operator. The union of a cylinder and a box (a, b) results in a box with a rounded top. The difference between the rounded box and a cube (c) yields a rounded base with a rectangular trim. Finally, the difference between the base and a cylinder (d) results in a base with two round holes (e). Many implementations of trimming require at least one pair of intersecting three-dimensional objects as illustrated in Figure 5.3.1. But others can trim surfaces or objects with just a line or a two-dimensional shape—the hole—that intersects the shape or that is projected through the object.

5.4 Advanced Modeling Utilities

Many modeling utilities like beveling, fitting, blending, and spline deformation are used to further manipulate surfaces, and to complement the advanced modeling techniques.

Beveling, Rounding, and Fillets

The edges between adjacent surfaces can be customized with great detail with a variety of beveling techniques. Simple **beveling** usually works by truncating the hard edge between adjacent surfaces—usually two or three—and replacing it with a slanted plane. The amount of beveling can be controlled by a distance, radius, or angle value between the edge being beveled to the place where the bevel is to be placed. **Rounding** is a delicate form of beveling that literally rounds the straight edges or points of an object. The degree of rounding is controlled by the number of segments or facets that are used to define the smooth transition between adjacent surfaces (Fig. 5.4.1).

Utilities for creating fillets also modify the junction of surfaces. **Fillets** create a custom trim that extends along the edge. This trim is more ornate than plain beveling or rounding. Fillets are like the decorative strips of molding that are often placed at the corners or edges of furniture, or like the functional molding that is used to protect the edge where walls meet the floor. Some software programs create fillets by trimming the surface, and others by sweeping a custom two-dimensional outline along the edge that is being modified (Fig. 5.4.2).

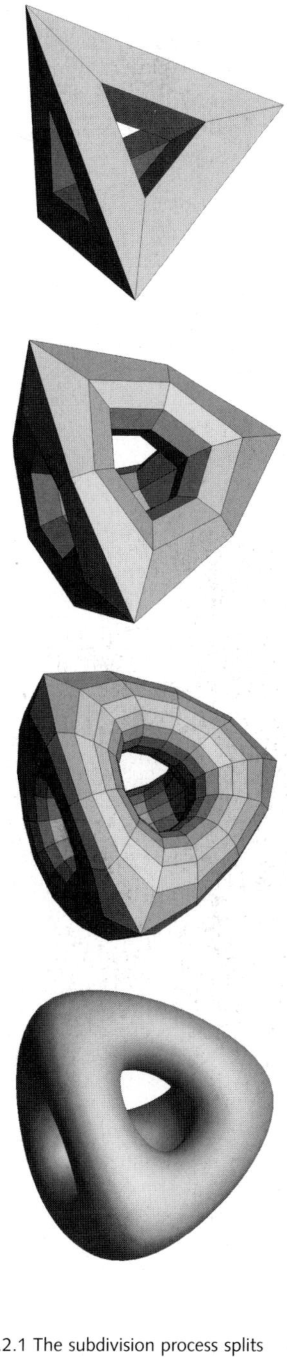

5.2.1 The subdivision process splits each surface into four facets by adding edge midpoints and face centroids. (© Pixar Animation Studios.)

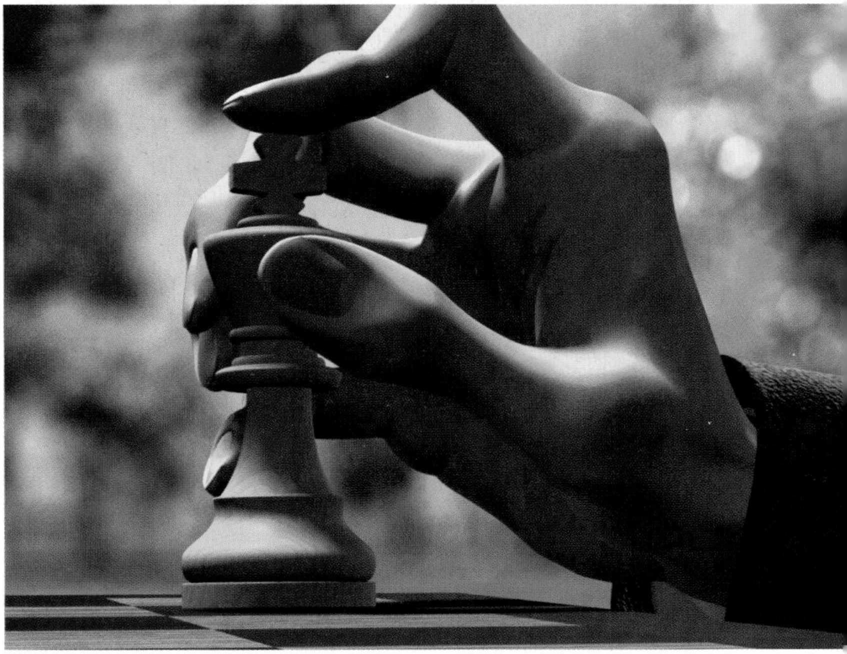

5.2.2 The short film *Geri's Game* was a technology test bed for subdivision surfaces and clothing dynamics. Each hand is a single seamless subdivision surface with a few sharp edges, which are obtained by subdividing just along the edge but not across. Notice the sharp crease along the thumbnail, and several softer creases with variable sharpness as it moves around the area. The model of Geri's head (opposite page) shows the adaptive point density typical of subdivision surfaces. The vertices where more local detail was desired were selected, and then the subdivision procedure was applied to them (see rendered version in Figure 1.2.9). (© Pixar Animation Studios.)

5.2.3 The models for the *Medicus* project were created as subdivision surfaces with Lightwave software. (© 2002 Dan Platt, Solid Image Arts, LLC.)

Aligning, Fitting, and Blending

Software programs with advanced modeling provide utilities that are especially useful for fine-tuning curved patches. Utilities like aligning, fitting, and blending manipulate the edges of curved patches—and also polygonal surfaces—to refine and clean up the shapes of three-dimensional models. **Aligning** two patches usually works by selecting the two patches to be aligned and then moving and rotating them until they are aligned a certain way. **Fitting** utilities get rid of small gaps between surfaces by dragging the two surfaces that are not quite touching each other until their edges match each other perfectly. Fitting is almost always used prior to merging two patches. **Blending** is a special way of merging two surfaces. Instead of merging two surfaces by first making them touch each other and then merging them, blending creates a new surface that extends from each of the two surfaces being blended. The new surface created by blending connects the two surfaces, and the smoothness of the blending is controlled with a function curve or by manipulating the control points of the blended surface (Fig. 5.4.3).

Purging Points

Three-dimensional models created with curved patches often have a large number of points or vertices. This results in models that may be too complex for the requirements of the project and also increases rendering time and file size. **Purging** utilities are useful for auto-

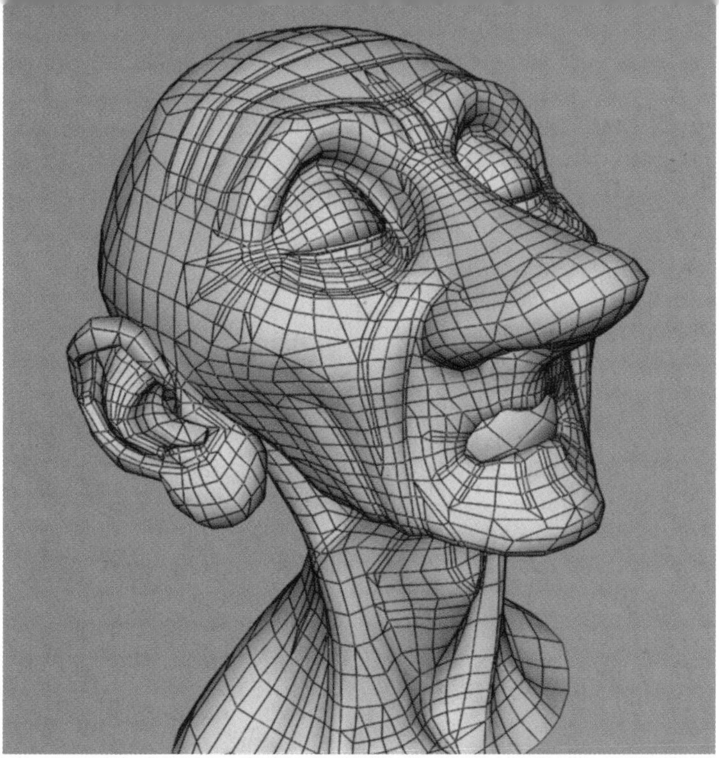

matically eliminating excessive vertices in complex three-dimensional models. This is usually done by identifying pairs of points that are too close to each other—based on a minimum distance—and deleting one of them. Manual point-editing is often used in conjunction with purging utilities to fine-tune and adjust the distribution of points in the model.

Deformed and Randomized Surfaces

In addition to using lattices for deforming the shape of three-dimensional objects, it is also possible to deform them with splines, patches, functions, or random numbers. (Deforming objects with lattices and functions is covered in Chapter 4.)

The technique of **deformation with splines and patches** consists of using a spline or a patch as the agent that deforms the object that is associated with them (Fig. 5.4.4). Deforming an object with a spline offsets the points in the object according to the shape of the spline. Deforming an object with a patch pulls the object to the shape of the patch in those areas where the object overlaps the patch.

Interesting deformations can be achieved by offsetting the vertices of three-dimensional objects with functions or random values (Figs. 4.5.4 and 5.4.5). The technique of **random distortion** is especially useful for creating models of terrains that have so many irregularities that it would be difficult to model them with other techniques. Random distortion can also be used to animate the effect of shaking by animating the displacement of points back and forth through time.

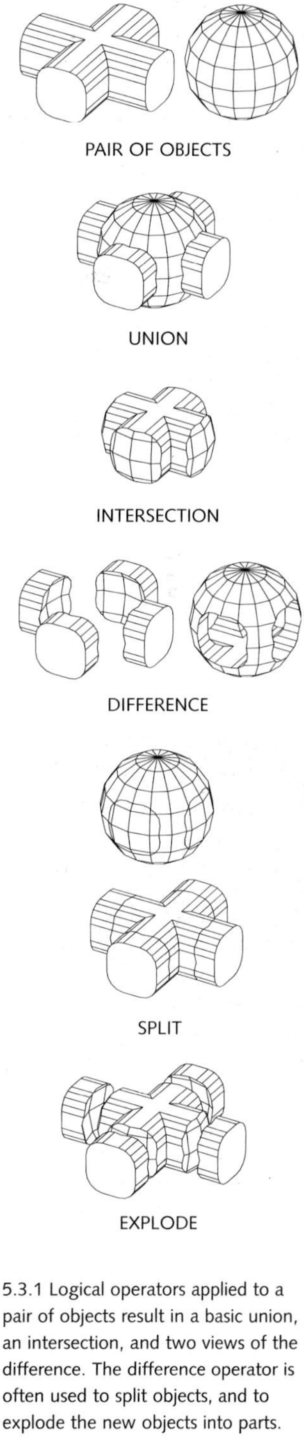

5.3.1 Logical operators applied to a pair of objects result in a basic union, an intersection, and two views of the difference. The difference operator is often used to split objects, and to explode the new objects into parts.

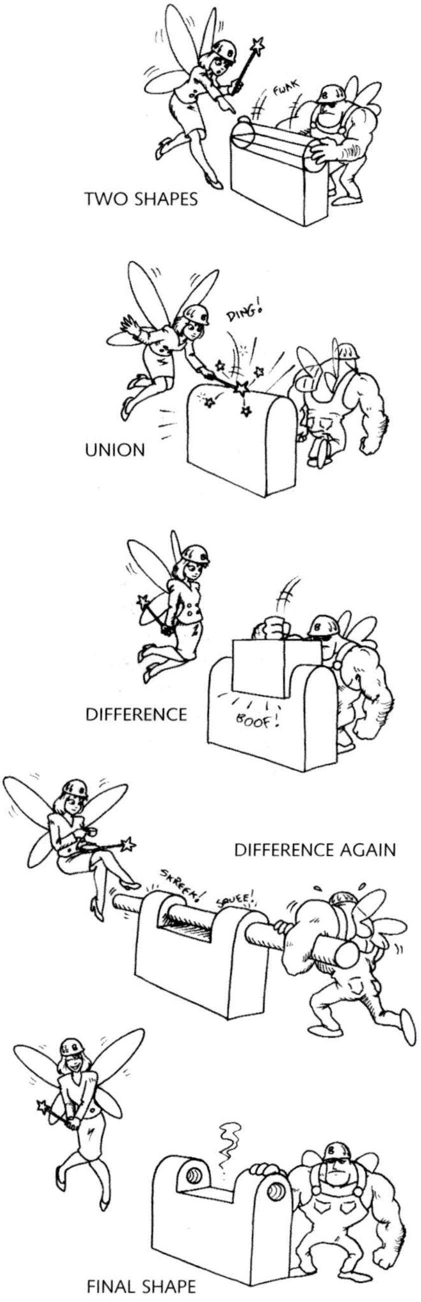

5.3.2 This sequence illustrates the logical operators of union and difference being used to model a complex three-dimensional object from four components.

5.5 Procedural Description and Physical Simulations

Procedural descriptions of three-dimensional models—especially those found in nature—are effective alternatives to the regular and sometimes rigid shapes obtained with geometric modeling systems. With procedural description objects are not modeled by sculpting their exterior shell. The modeling techniques of **procedural description** get their name from the fact that, with them, objects are modeled by simulating, for example, their natural growth process that is described in the form of procedures (Fig. 5.5.1). Fractal geometry and particle systems, for example, are two procedural description methods that create a modeling complexity that is difficult to obtain with geometric modeling. Both of these methods are well suited for the generation of natural-looking forms because they allow for randomness, recursion, and accidents of shape like those typical of natural shapes. A wide variety of plants can also be described with a combination of procedural description techniques. Finally, the shape of many natural phenomena that we do not think of as having a three-dimensional shape—waves, clouds and smoke, for example—can be built by simulating their physical behavior.

Fractal Geometry

Fractal geometry is especially effective for creating random and irregular shapes that resemble shapes found in nature (Fig. 5.5.2). This modeling technique was developed by Benoit Mandelbrot in the 1970s. It can be applied to existing three-dimensional meshes, or it can be used to generate entirely new models or parts of models. When applied to an existing model, **fractal procedures** work by dividing the polygons in the object recursively and randomly into many irregular shapes that resemble those found in nature. The amount of subdivision is usually expressed in the form of a factor or **level of recursion** (Fig. 5.5.3). Fractal geometry can also be used to create objects from scratch by using random seed values or iterations of algebraic formulas (Fig. 5.5.4).

Particle Systems

Modeling with **particle systems** is based on employing simple shapes, usually small spheres or points in three-dimensional space. These shapes, or particles, have **growth attributes**. When these attributes are simulated, the particles have specific behaviors that result in specific particle **trajectories**. As the particles grow over time their trajectory defines a certain shape that results in a three-dimensional model. The growth process of many of the attributes of the particles, including their height, width, branching angle, bending factor, number of branches, and color, can be controlled or randomized. Figure 12.4.2 shows a scene that was modeled by simulating feathers of birds or petals of flowers by creating particles that grow

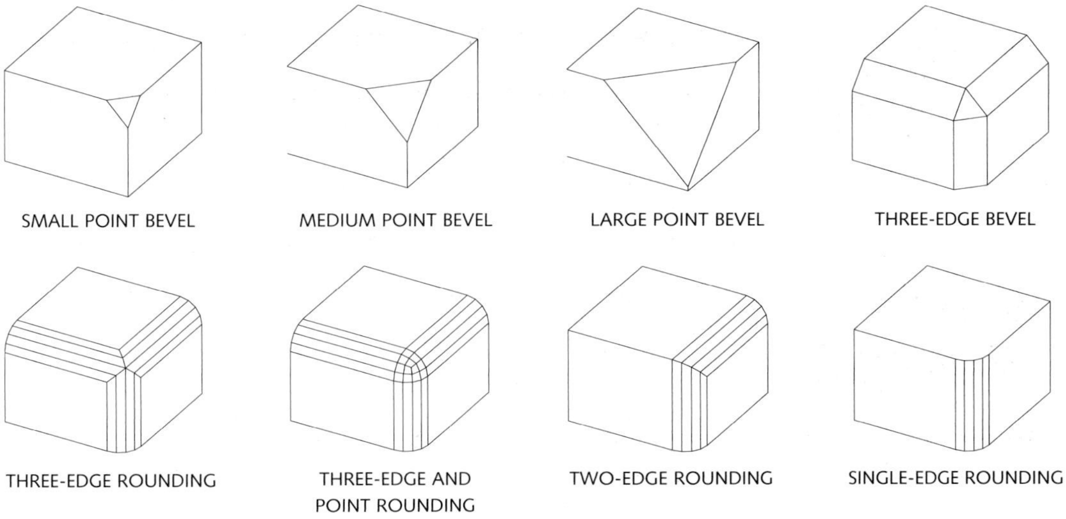

5.4.1 The first three shapes display a point bevel of different magnitudes. The second group of shapes includes a three-edge bevel, a three-edge rounding, and a three-edge and point rounding. The last two shapes are examples of a two-edge rounding and a single-edge rounding.

densely on the surfaces of three-dimensional objects. In this project, colored maps were applied to the feathers, the bird is animated with a skeleton deformation technique, and all the feathers grow at their positions as the body moves. (Read Chapter 12 for more examples and information about animating with particle systems.)

Procedural description, and particle systems in particular, are used to create a variety of natural materials and phenomena whose shape constantly changes throughout time. This includes, for example, snowstorms, clouds, flowing water, moving soil, and fire. When particles are used to recreate the motion of water, for example, they each represent a drop of water with attributes like density, cohesion, transparency, and refraction. Particles have a life span during which they behave a certain way, and then fade away or merge with other particles (Fig. 5.5.6). Of all the procedural modeling techniques, particle systems is the one that best recreates the dynamic shapes of natural elements. This technique produces large numbers of particles that do not have a specific shape and are usually spheres or dots. But the particles are grouped in shapes that change through time according to rules that define the behavior of elements such as water and fire. Particle systems are a very popular and powerful technique for the animation of effects both in animated and live action movies (Figs. 12.3.4, 12.4.1, and 13.7.1–2).

Modeling Plants

Three-dimensional models of plants and trees created with procedural techniques offer increased modeling control and more efficient modeling than most other techniques. This is due to the large number of elements and surface detail contained in a plant, as well as the complexity of shapes. Polygonal modeling techniques are often less than adequate for modeling realistic plants. Curved surfaces are

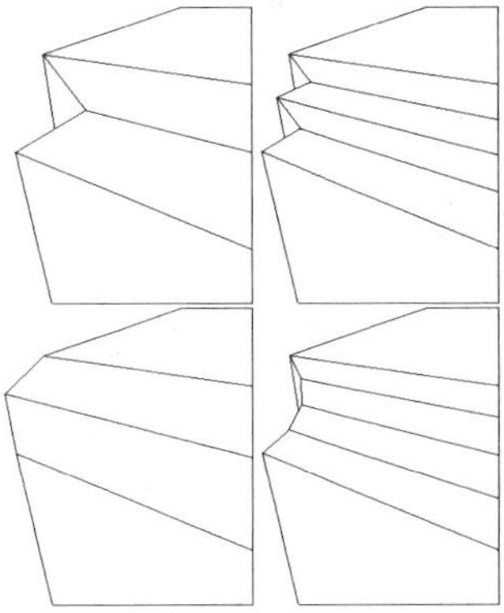

5.4.2 This figure shows the results of four different fillet styles applied to the corner and edge of a cube.

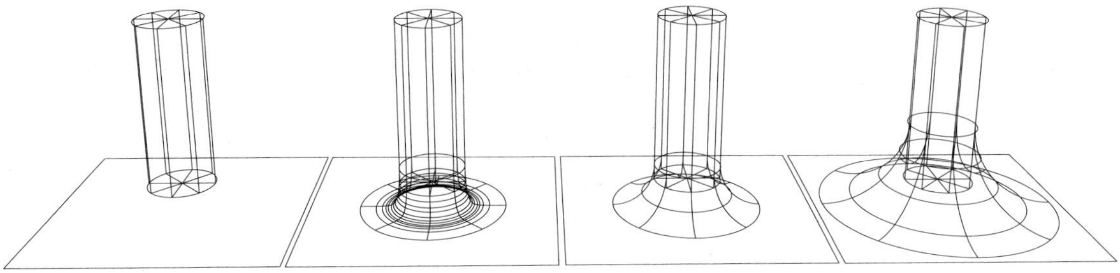

5.4.3 Blending a cylinder and a plane with different degrees of transition between the two surfaces.

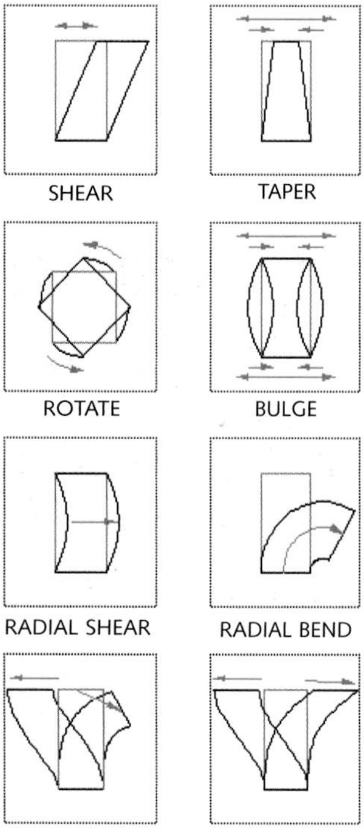

5.4.4 Sequence of icons illustrating different techniques for controlling patch deformation. (form•Z icons, © 1991–1995 auto•des•sys, Inc.)

capable of modeling the shapes found in plants, but when done this way modeling plants quickly becomes time consuming.

Models of plants can be built by encoding their characteristics in a series of rules or procedures that are used as the basis for a growth simulation. This method can also be used to animate the growth process of plant models in a scene. There are several ways to generate models of plants with procedural techniques. These general techniques can be classified as either space-oriented or structure-oriented.

Space-oriented procedural techniques for modeling plants and animating their growth are based on the effect of the environment on them. **Structure-oriented procedural techniques** techniques, on the other hand, are based on the conditions that are internal to the plant, more specifically the growing process of the plant and the resulting structure that is characteristic of a plant species. Many of the procedural modeling techniques centered on the growth process of plants are often expressed in terms of the mathematical models formalized by biologist Aristide Lindenmayer during the late 1960s. These structure-oriented models describe the growth process of plants at the level of cellular interaction and are known as **L-systems**, short for Lindenmayer systems. L-systems are especially suited to represent structures that **branch in parallel**, just like a tree trunk splits into several branches at the same time (Fig. 5.5.7). Another characteristic of L-systems is that at each branching cycle, the branching procedures generate **successor modules** that replace the **predecessor modules**.

There are many variations of L-systems. Some are defined by parameters that represent exclusive conditions under which the L-system can bloom. Others are based on **stochastic** (or somewhat random) **values**. **Context-sensitive L-systems** are those whose performance is defined by the characteristic of the preceding module. The technique of **graftals** is an example of context-sensitive L-systems that allows the creation of complex images from small databases, a technique known as **database amplification**. Graftals are based on production rules and generation factors; they avoid random number generators, and can employ geometric or nongeometric objects—spheres, cylinders, or fuzzy objects with smooth edges.

Environmentally sensitive L-systems are defined by environmental characteristics, such as exposure to light and collision with objects. Pruning is an example of three-dimensional models based on a simulation of a growing plant whose shape is determined by an environmental variable (Fig. 5.5.8).

Some of the main techniques for controlling the simulation of a structure-oriented plant system include lineage and the interaction between the components of the growth process. **Lineage** is the transfer of attributes from one level of the plant to another at the time of branching. The interaction of the components of the growth process includes, for example, taking into account the watering conditions or the availability of nutrients that define the way in which plants grow. The plants modeled with procedural description are more faithful to the real plant based on the number of components that are considered into the derivation of the plant shapes.

Techniques that seek to find efficient ways to process the large amount of data neccessary to model and render realistic plants are actively explored. The obvious challenges include dealing with billions of geometric primitives, distribute them throughout the terrain in a realistic way, and render all the subtle light and shadows effects that one observes in natural landscapes. Figure 5.5.9 illustrates the result of a technique that can populate the environment with a combination of ecosystem simulation and gardening techniques where the location of plants is done by hand. The figure also contains the statistics of instancing and geometric compression for the scene. This technique also makes extensive use of **model approximate instancing** where plants or groups of plants are replaced by instances of representative objects before the scene is rendered. In exploring complexity the researchers behind this technique found out that when one of the scenes approaches 100,000 plants each plant is visible on average only in ten pixels of a 1000 × 1000 pixel image.

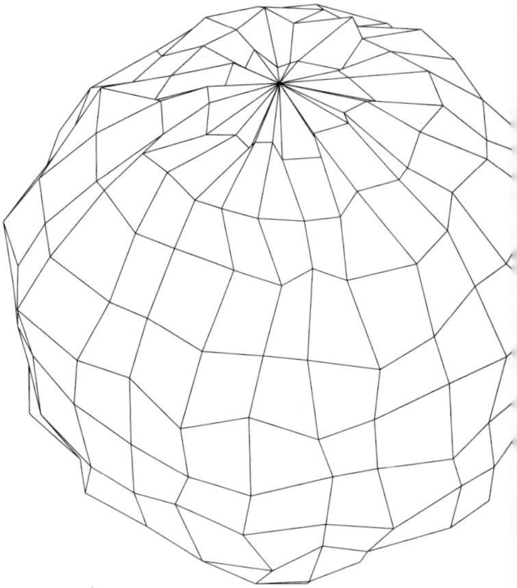

5.4.5 Random distortion of a sphere.

5.5.1 This ray-traced scene, entitled *Crop Circle*, contains more than 100 million primitives. It was specified using a technique called procedural geometric instancing, which represents the field of wheat by hierarchically instancing a single wheat stalk. At instantiation, each stalk of wheat examines its position to determine if it should bend over or remain upright. (© 1994 John C. Hart, Washington State University.)

Modeling with Physical Simulations

The easiest way to model natural materials whose shape is in constant change is not to sculpt them but to simulte them. Physical simulations are used extensively to model natural phenomena like rain, fire, smoke, and even wind; some of those techniques are covered in Chapter 12. Figure 5.5.10 shows a dialog box that allows users to animate a grid of waves with the basic variables of average wave height and slope, direction, frequency, and speed. Other global settings determine the complexity of the waves, the wave patterns, and underwater shots. Secondary motion in the simulation can be controlled at different levels of detail in the form of ripples, swells, and boat wakes (Fig. 11.2.8). The shading parameters in a physical simulation of water may include variables such as glitter, mapping of two-dimensional image and bump maps on the surface, reflection blurring, and index of refraction (Fig. 5.5.10). Depth and visibility fading is often used for underwater scenes. Figure 5.5.5 shows a simulation of pouring water in a glass, and Fig. 5.5.10 shows the result of a daytime ocean simulation.

5.5.2 Details from *Seasons of Life* illustrate how fractal procedures can express the roughness and fragmentation of natural phenomena. (Courtesy of Midori Kitagawa De Leon.)

The shape of solid but flexible objects can also be controlled with physical simulation software tools. Figure 5.5.11 shows two pieces of fabric whose shape has been defined by a simulation of gravity and other forces that affect them. Natural-looking hair is usually simulated with multiple strands of particles that are guided by a few control hairs (Figs. 5.5.12 and 5.5.13).

5.6 Photogrammetry and Image-Based Modeling

Photogrammetry techniques allow us to reconstruct three-dimensional enviromnents by extracting three-dimensional information from a series of photographs of an environment from known locations. The reconstruction process in many **photogrammetry** programs starts by indicating in the scanned photographs the corners or main edges of the major shapes. Photogrametry software reconstructs a simple version of the geometry by analyzing and comparing perspective lines and shading information in several related photographs of the same environment. Figures 6.8.1 and 6.8.2 provide a stunning example of image-based modeling.

Another technique that can be very effective in modeling large-scale three-dimensional environments is **laser scanning**. This technique often uses a linear laser scanner to collect three-dimensional point data which is then converted into a polygonal mesh. An interesting use of laser scanning is coupled with traditional film or video cameras to capture high-resolution image maps that can be applied to the geometry (Fig. 5.6.1–5.6.2).

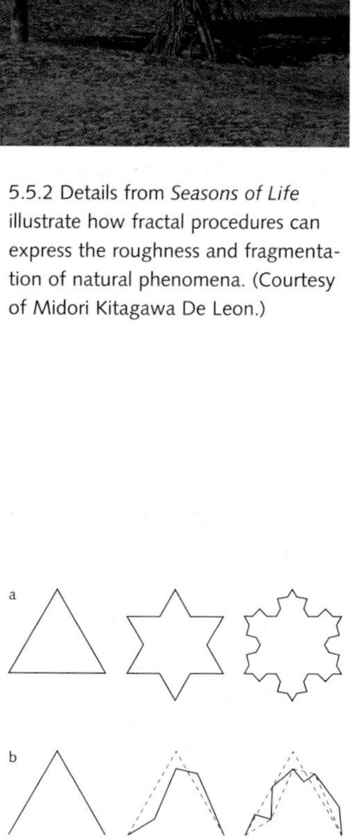

5.5.3 A fractal recursive subdivision is applied to a regular polygon (top), and to the detail of a three-dimensional mesh (bottom).

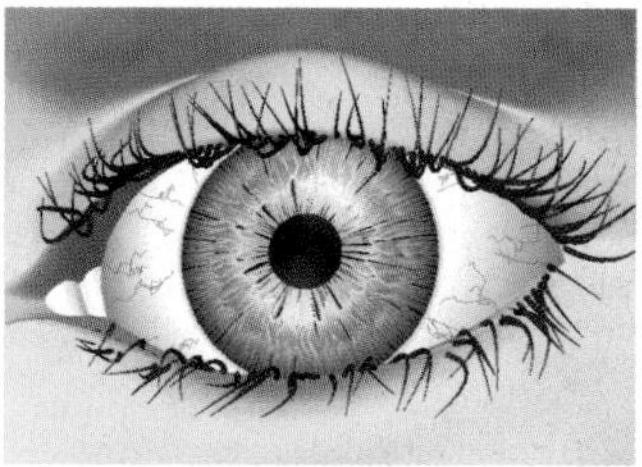

5.5.4 Rendering of an eye. (From "A Virtual Environment and Model of the Eye for Surgical Simulation," in the SIGGRAPH '94 Conference Proceedings. Courtesy of Mark Sagar, Department of Mechanical Engineering, University of Auckland, New Zealand.)

5.5.5 This dynamic simulation models the water surface and allows for interactions between objects and fluids. (© 2002 Next Limit SL.)

5.5.6 This still from the animation *Flow* shows a particle system combined with a water mesh simulation system. (Rendering and animation by Gavin Miller, modeling by Ned Greene. © Apple Computer, Inc.)

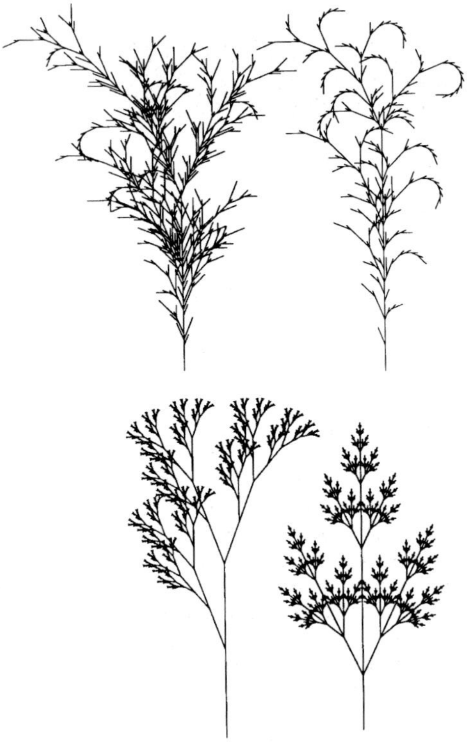

5.5.7 These plants clearly show the transfer of attributes, called lineage, from one level of the plant to another at the time of branching. (From "The Algorithmic Beauty of Plants," by P. Prusinkiewicz and A. Lindenmayer, Springer Verlag, New York, 1990. © 1994 Przemyslaw Prusinkiewicz.)

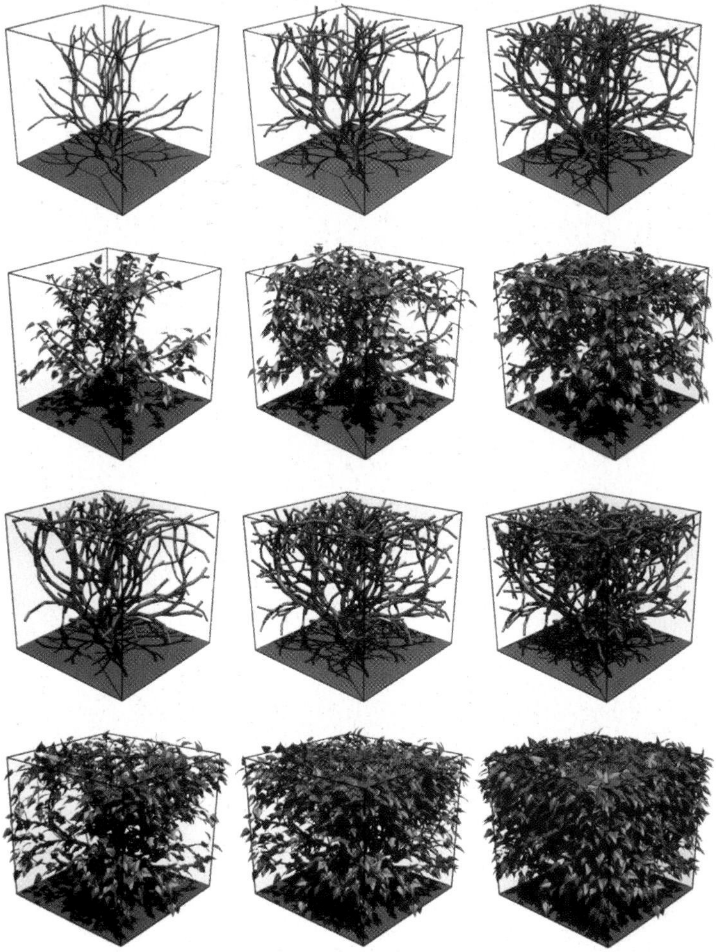

5.5.8 (top right) Simulated response of a tree to progressive pruning. The branches grow more densely near the edges of the cube used to clip the model. The leaves are defined as Bézier surfaces. Shown in red is the vigor of the reiterated branches on the appearence of the pruned tree. (© 1994 P. Prusinkiewicz, M. James, and R. Mech.)

5.7 Animation Rigging and Hierarchical Structures

Three-dimensional objects can be grouped together in a limitless number of ways in order to create structures that define the ways in which these models behave when animated, how they relate to each another, and how they are rendered. Groups of three-dimensional objects are usually called **hierarchical structures**, because within these structured groups some objects are always more dominant than others. (See Chapter 11 for additional information on levels of precedence, joints, and degrees of freedom.) Hierarchical structures are the most basic layer of an animation rig.

Objects within hierarchical structures have defined levels of importance and the objects within this hierarchy inherit attributes from the dominant objects. The object or objects at the top of the hierarchy are called **parents**, and the objects below are called **children** and grandchildren: Children inherit their parents' attributes.

Tree Statistics

Plant	*Objects*	*Instances*
Apple trees	1	4
Reeds	140	140
Dandelions	10	55
Grass tufts	15	2577
Stinging nettles	10	430
Yellow flowers	10	2751

5.5.9 The images representing each species of plant in the top image were rendered separately and later composited. The table lists the number of prototype objects and their instances for each species. The compute time on a 195 MHz R-10,000 8-processor SGI Onyx with 768 MB of RAM was 75 minutes. The poplar tree in the top image is 16KB when saved as a procedural model but 6.7 MB in a standard text geometry file format. (Copyright Bernd Lintermann. Software by Oliver Deussen and Bernd Lintermann.)

Hierarchical structures can also be visualized as an inverted tree structure where the highest level of importance in the structure corresponds to the trunk of the tree. The branches that come out of the trunk are the next level of hierarchy, branches that come out of the main branches are the next level, and so on until we get to the leaves, which are in the last level of the hierarchical structure.

In most cases, there is just one set of hierarchy diagrams per scene, and these diagrams control all the modeling, rendering, and animation information about the objects. Some programs, however, provide several sets of hierarchy diagrams, and therefore hierarchy configurations, so that **modeling links** can be independent and different from the **rendering links** and the **animation links**. Modeling links, for example, make sure that the shape of all the children throughout the hierarchy changes when the shape of the child's parent is modified. Rendering links transmit the rendering attributes of the parent down the structure. Animation links automatically update the spatial position of the children when the parent is transformed.

The relations between objects in hierarchical structure are often complex and can be better visualized by a schematic representation

5.5.10a Surface of the sea modeled by simulating the motion of the water, and on the next page a NatureFX software dialog box used to control the the simulation of water surfaces. (Courtesy of Areté Entertainment, Inc.)

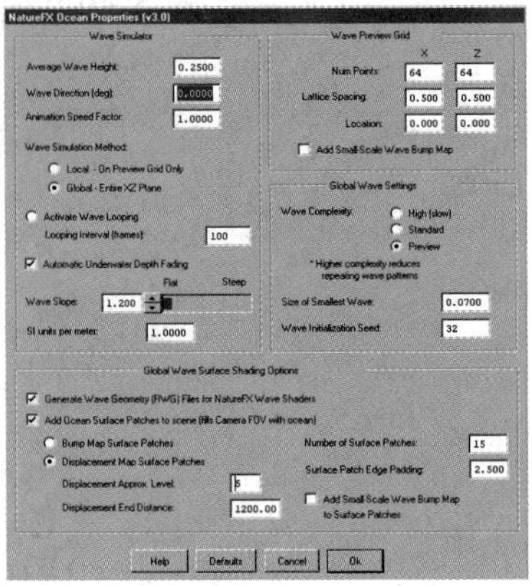

5.5.10b NatureFX software dialog box used to control the the simulation of water surfaces. (Courtesy of Areté Entertainment, Inc.)

5.5.11 (right) Fabrix simulation software was used to shape the purple fabric and the gold backdrop. Clusters were positioned and scaled to gather a 20 × 40 Nurbs mesh into the hands of the high-resolution human modeled by Zygote. The simulation also tested for self-collisions. (*Fab-girl* by Shawna Olwen. © 1999 Reflection Fabrix Inc.)

5.5.12 (opposite page, top) Sully from *Monsters, Inc.* used 10,000 control hairs to define the placement, orientation, and animation of between 2.8 and 3.2 million blue hair strands. (© Disney Enterprises, Inc./Pixar Animation Studios.)

in the form of a line diagram. These diagrams are often built with boxes representing items in the structure and lines representing their place in their hierarchy and their relations with other items.

As shown in Fig. 5.7.1 there are many ways to group objects or nodes in a hierarchical structure. The best choice of hierarchy is usually one that takes into account the rendering and animation requirements of the scene. (See Chapters 11 and 12 for more details on how hierarchical structures affect the object's rendering and transformation attributes.) A node in the hierarchy that does not contain an object but holds several children together is called a **null parent**, or null for short. A null parent is used, for example, when two or more objects are grouped at the same level in the hierarchy. Nulls are often represented with italics or as empty boxes in the structural diagrams. Figures 5.7.1 and 5.7.2 illustrate the use of a null cell that can be used to keep the four legs and the wheels in one group so that they can be manipulated independently of the ring.

The specific steps required to establish hierarchical relationships between objects vary from software to software. But the basic concept has two variations. Clicking on the three-dimensional objects themselves in any one of the camera views, or clicking on the boxes representing the objects in the diagram representing the links between them. Some programs require users first to click on the object that is to be the parent and then on the children. With other programs the object that is to represent the children must be clicked before the parent. Hierarchical structures are more significant to the

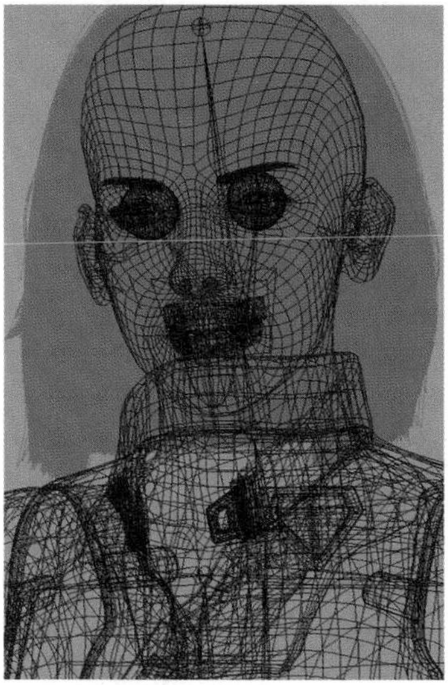

stages of rendering and animation, they are usually created during the modeling process in the form of animation rigs.

An animation **rig** is a hierarchical control structure that is custom-designed to animate characters. The animation rig is the motion engine of the character; all the joints and all the motion logic of the character are contained in the rig. Very complex rigs require significant computation and when manipulated by animators they take longer to update, so it is best to include in only the essential features. In most large-scale projects control rigs are usually designed and assembled by specialized technical directors called riggers. For a small

5.5.13 (bottom left and right) Between 30,000 and 60,000 strands were used to create Aki's hair, which accounted for 25% of the total rendering in *Final Fantasy: The Spirits Within*. The hair appears in 611 shots, almost half of the total. Aki's body and head model has up to 100,000 subdivided polygons. (© 2001 FFFP.)

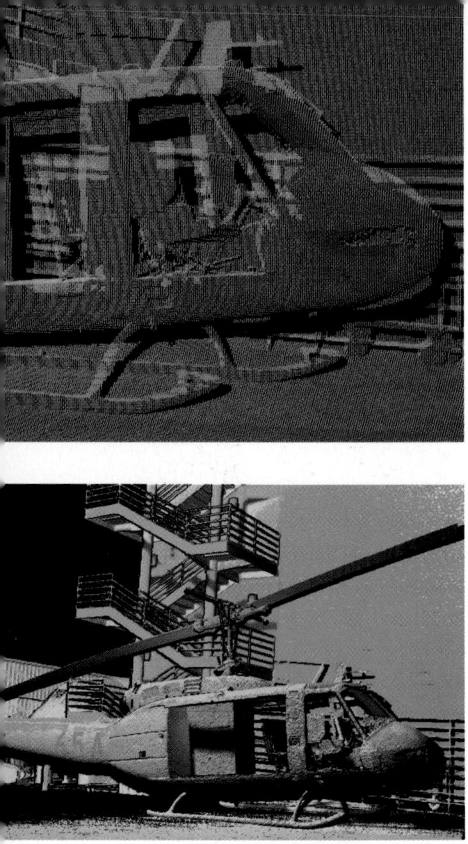

5.6.1 Wireframe geometry and shaded version of a helicopter and the environment surrounding it as modeled with the *Panascan*™ laser scanning process. (Courtesy of Panavision.)

5.6.2 Dialog box from Image Modeler, a software that allows three-dimensional reconstructions from photographs. (© Realviz®.)

production with limited resources a simple rigging and skin binding structure can be more efficient and minimize rendering times.

Animation rigs can be visualized in different ways: as a hypergraph or hierarchy chart (Fig. 5.7.2b), as a rig skeleton showing bones and joints (Fig. 5.7.3), or as the set of controls that animators use to manipulate the rig system. These animation controls are represented with icons and color-coded (Fig. 12.5.6) so that animators recognize faster what controls do or what parts they control. During the animation process the rig skeleton is usually turned off as animators pose the character with a proxy, low resolution, version of the skin and with the animation handles (Figs. 5.7.3 and 5.75). Sophisticated rigs are capable of notifying the animator through visual cues when a limit is reached or when the animator is trying to do something that the character is not supposed to do, like trying to bend a knee backwards or pass a foot through the ground.

Animation controls in a rig can consist of a point, a curve or a complex surface. For ease of use animation controls often include multiple controls, a foot control, for example, might include foot pivoting, toe lifting, wiggling, and twisting. The legs and feet are crucial in animating a character since they are so important in walking. Most leg-feet rigs include joints for hip, knee, foot, ball of the foot and toe end (Fig. 12.1.8). Facial animation rigs also include multiple bones as shown in Figure 12.5.5.

One of the basic issues in setting up a rig is defining the order in which rotations take place. The **order of rotations**, as explained in Chapter 3, is important because the sequencing of axis rotations creates different results (Figs. 3.4.1–3.4.2). Software programs usually require an order of rotations to be specified in a rig, with the Y axis commonly being first followed by X or Z in worlds where Y defines the vertical axis. This way characters can turn around in any direction around Y and move sideways or lean without reaching **gimbal lock**, which is a point at which the model runs out of rotations.

Skin Deformers

The animation rig controls and deforms the skin geometry of the character in a variety of ways: with simple joint attachments, using the actual bone geometry, or a complete muscle system. Binding skin points to one or several joints is the simplest technique for skin deformation. In order to increase the complexity of their translations these skin points can be weighted, or influenced by the rotations of multiple joints.

The skeleton geometry itself (not the abstract hierarchical skeleton) can also be used as a skin deformer. In this case the bone geometry is parented to the IK joints and used as skin weights. Using bone geometry as a skin deformer serves the dual purpose of being a useful visual aid for positioning skin, joints and muscles in the proper place. The bone geometry is only used to extract weight values and "baking" them into the skin, after which point the skeleton

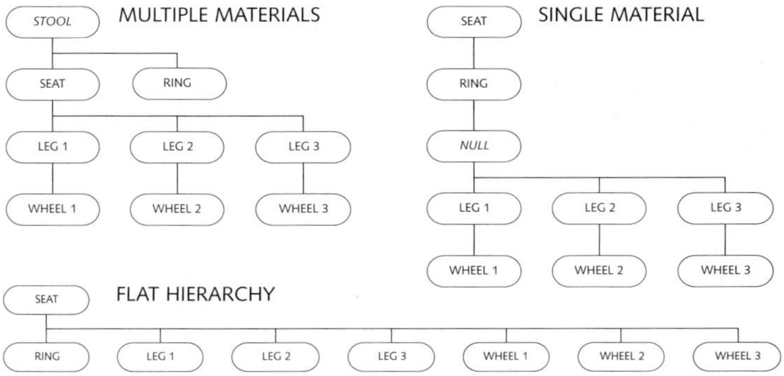

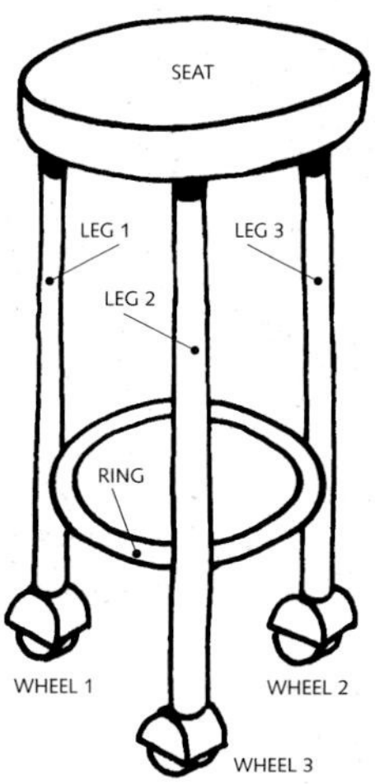

5.7.1 The diagrams show three possible variations of the hierarchical structure for all of the stool's components. The first arrangement (top left) would be the most practical one if the stool (opposite page) were to roll on its round wheels, and if the seat, legs, and wheels were each to be rendered with a different material. The second option (top right) would be best if the entire stool was made out of just one material. The third option (bottom) has the seat at the top of the hierarchy and everything else below the seat at the same level.

geometry can be removed. Baking can be done by assigning the weight information to the skin without the bone geometry, saving the skin weights to a file, removing the skeleton, and reassigning those values to the skin without the bones.

A more sophisticated technique for skin deformation consists of building geometry that simulates muscles. The geometry of these virtual muscles is usually designed with several control points so that it maintains its volume as it flexes. The muscles are usually connected to the skeleton by following its hierarchy: the start of the muscle is connected to parent bone and the end to the child. Collision detection is used to set-up the muscles so that they slide along or bulge as they press against a bone or other muscles (Figs. 5.1.9 and 5.7.4).

Muscle rigs can have different degrees of realistic motion depending on the complexity and functionality of the geometry used to simulate them. Muscles built from a single piece of geometry can be set-up to twist along with a bone twist. Spheres are useful simple shapes for modeling a large variety of muscles, but groups of muscles often need to be modeled with more complex shapes (Fig. 4.5.1). Several geometry strands can be used to achieve more detailed motion of the muscles and the skin attached to their surface. Multiple curves and lattice deformers can also be used to control more subtle deformations of the muscle surface. Lattices are easy to set-up (Fig. 4.5.3) but can be less precise than a carefully constructed cluster of control curves.

5.8 Getting Ready

Overlapping Edges and Gaps

Many three-dimensional software programs have trouble rendering objects with **overlapping edges** or overlapping facets. Clean up your three-dimensional models before you pass them over to the team members in charge of rendering them or before you render them. Use modeling utilities such as aligning or blending to eliminate overlapping objects. In critical situations automatic aligning tools may not be available to fix the misalignment of two elements and the resulting

5.7.2a A portion of the internal hierarchy of this real-time animated character grasping an object is represented by the diagram on the next page. (© Motion Factory.)

5.7.3 Animation rig of the gunnery Sergeant in *Medal of Honor*. Notice the animation control handles used by animators to pose the character. Three of his core poses are shown in Figure 10.5.12. (© 1999 Electronic Arts Inc. All rights reserved.)

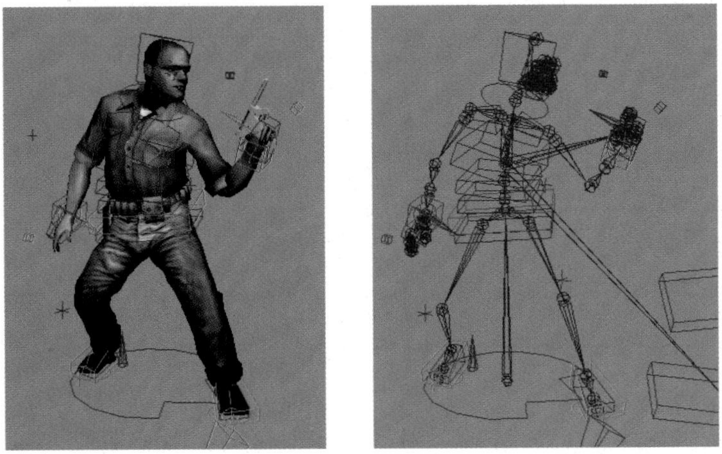

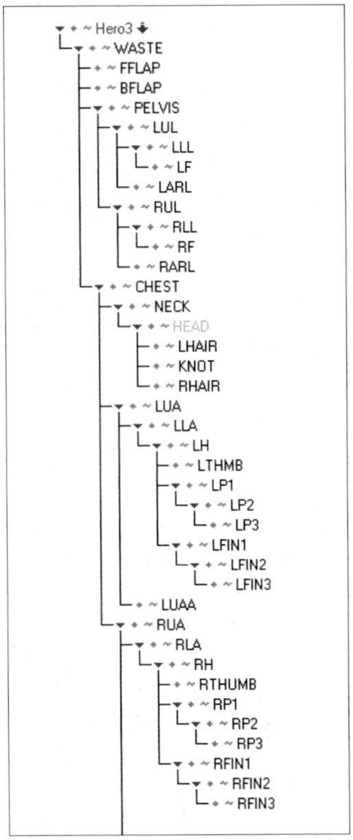

5.7.2b Notice how the root of the diagram controls the pelvis and the chest. The pelvis drives the upper and lower legs, and the feet. The chest drives the neck, the upper and lower arms, and the hands. (© Motion Factory.)

gaps on the rendered surface. In those cases it is often preferable to align the objects by typing their exact XYZ position in space instead of trying to drag them into position with the mouse.

Disable Polygons that Face Away

When building a large model that is to be rendered only from a single fixed point of view—front view only, for example—it is wise not to model the **surfaces facing away** from the camera and to disable the **back faces**. This technique is reminiscent of stage sets that are perfectly finished on the sides that face the audience but are raw and unpolished on the sides that cannot be seen from the theater. Some programs allow users to turn off the rendering of individual polygons or groups of them. Other programs require users to slice off the unwanted surfaces and discard them altogether from the three-dimensional scene. Either technique is useful for single-point of view renderings because it yields simpler models, more compact file sizes, and faster renderings.

Keep Heavy Motion Rigs Separately

Complex rigs can become cumbersome and may require significant computing to apply all the controls to the skin. For this reason "heavy" motion rigs may be kept as separate components or layers. This offers more flexibility and allows animators to start animating with a lighter rig while the technical director refines the skin mesh and the muscle deformers of the final rig.

Stay Away from Overmodeling

Creating too many elements, or **overmodeling**, is a bad habit that usually has negative consequences in the stages of rendering and animation. Streamline the size of your models and data files by keeping

5.7.4 Muscle and bone rigging system used to animate *Shrek*. Figure 5.1.8 shows the clothed skin model that was attached to this hierarchical system. (*Shrek*™ and © 2001 DreamWorks L.L.C.)

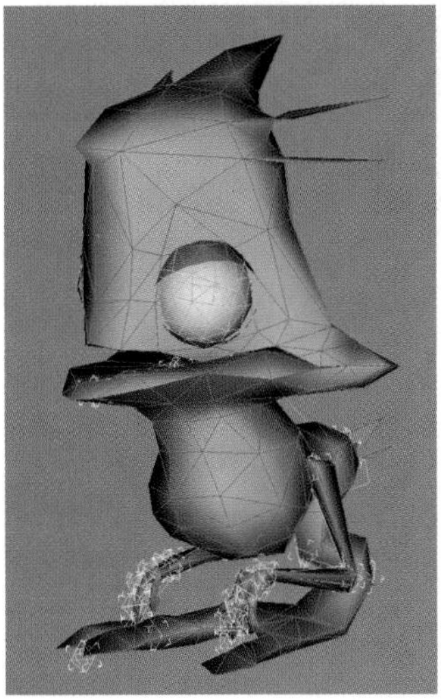

5.7.5 Wireframe model (1,272 polygons) showing the rigging skeleton. A blueprint with structural and motion analysis of the character is shown in Figure 3.6.3 (© 2003 Oddworld Inhabitants, Inc. All rights reserved.)

the number of polygons, curves, or points on the curves down to an absolute minimum. If necessary, use purging or blending utilities or edit your models manually. The numerous complications created by overmodeling are never obvious during the modeling process, but they become painfully clear later, during animation and rendering.

Take Advantage of Modeling Mistakes

During the modeling process, one often encounters tools or functions that do not quite behave the way they are supposed to. This is particularly true of **derivative modeling techniques**, such as skinning and logical operators, that create objects from other existing objects. The limitations of these modeling tools is apparent when one tries to build unusual surfaces such as zig-zagged shapes, overlapping concave areas, or a large number of acute angles. Modeling mistakes or accidents also happen when we try to get the tool to do something that it was not intended to do. For example, asking a skinning tool to first connect the two contours on opposite edges of the object and then proceed inward until all the contours are connected in this fashion insead of just skinning the adjacent contours serially and in sequence from one side of the object to the other. While the malfunctions of modeling tools are disappointing at first—like any other defect or "bug" in a program—we can learn to look at them in a fresh way and seriously consider whether the results can be used in a creative way to enrich the scene. Think of the ways in which the painters of the Abstract Expressionist movement of the 1950s used the shapes of accidental paint dripping and the unpredictable patterns of energetic brushstrokes to build their marvelous works.

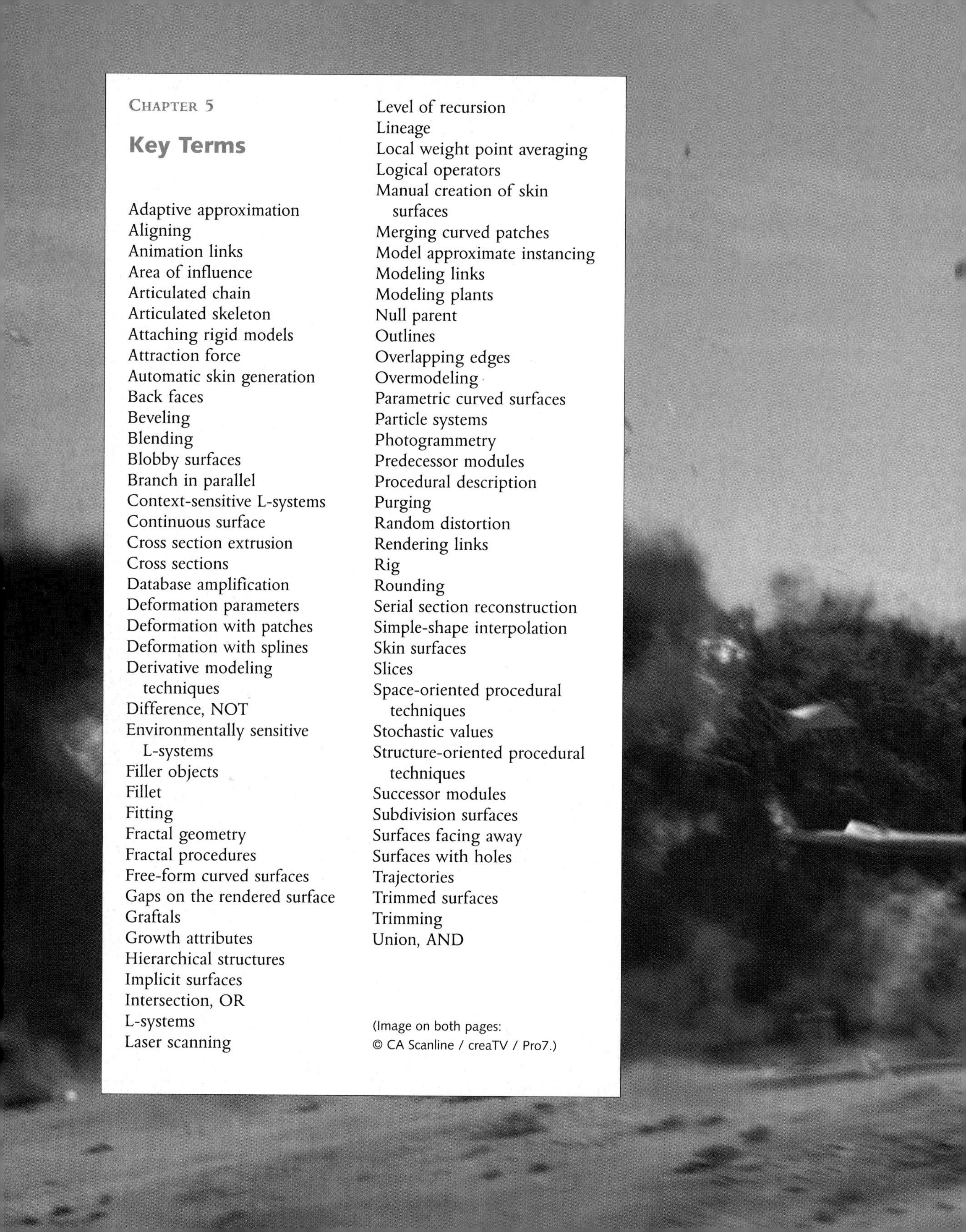

CHAPTER 5

Key Terms

Adaptive approximation
Aligning
Animation links
Area of influence
Articulated chain
Articulated skeleton
Attaching rigid models
Attraction force
Automatic skin generation
Back faces
Beveling
Blending
Blobby surfaces
Branch in parallel
Context-sensitive L-systems
Continuous surface
Cross section extrusion
Cross sections
Database amplification
Deformation parameters
Deformation with patches
Deformation with splines
Derivative modeling techniques
Difference, NOT
Environmentally sensitive L-systems
Filler objects
Fillet
Fitting
Fractal geometry
Fractal procedures
Free-form curved surfaces
Gaps on the rendered surface
Graftals
Growth attributes
Hierarchical structures
Implicit surfaces
Intersection, OR
L-systems
Laser scanning
Level of recursion
Lineage
Local weight point averaging
Logical operators
Manual creation of skin surfaces
Merging curved patches
Model approximate instancing
Modeling links
Modeling plants
Null parent
Outlines
Overlapping edges
Overmodeling
Parametric curved surfaces
Particle systems
Photogrammetry
Predecessor modules
Procedural description
Purging
Random distortion
Rendering links
Rig
Rounding
Serial section reconstruction
Simple-shape interpolation
Skin surfaces
Slices
Space-oriented procedural techniques
Stochastic values
Structure-oriented procedural techniques
Successor modules
Subdivision surfaces
Surfaces facing away
Surfaces with holes
Trajectories
Trimmed surfaces
Trimming
Union, AND

(Image on both pages:
© CA Scanline / creaTV / Pro7.)

SECTION III

Rendering

6.1.1 The masterful use of lights, cameras, and materials makes it difficult to decide what in this picture is real and what is computer generated. (Photograph by Lorey Sebastian for the motion picture *Mouse Hunt*. © 1997 DreamWorks L.L.C.)

CHAPTER 6

6

Basic Rendering Concepts

Summary

MOST OF THE VISUAL CHARACTERISTICS of a simulated three-dimensional environment are determined during the rendering process. This chapter provides an overview of adjusting the lights, setting the camera, and the main rendering techniques, including ray tracing, radiosity, and image-based and nonrealistic rendering.

QUICK INDEX

6.1 Lights, Camera, and Materials

The world of rendering by computer is populated by most of the attributes of our visual realm where the shapes of objects are revealed by light and obscured by shadow, where color creates moods of subtle tranquility or explosive happiness, where textures are as delicate and lyrical as fine sand or as dramatic and forceful as malachite, where the restless translucency of rain distorts the features of the world and the mirror of transparent water puts them back together. Rendering worlds of reality or fantasy with the computer can create results as artistic as with any other medium (Fig. 6.1.1).

When we use computers to render real or imagined scenes we can follow specific procedures, as we would if working with other media, that help accomplish all the tasks required before the rendering can be completed by the computer program. This fact is understood by artists who use media like paint, photography, or cinematography to depict scenes, express emotions, or tell stories with the elements of visual language. Each of these groups of image-making professionals has developed ways of doing things, basic techniques, orders of execution, and even complex procedures to do their jobs. In any case, most visual artists have to deal with some basic elements during the rendering process. These elements include composition, lighting, and defining surface characteristics such as color and texture.

Let's, for example, consider all the preparation that takes place before a professional photographer is ready to push the camera's

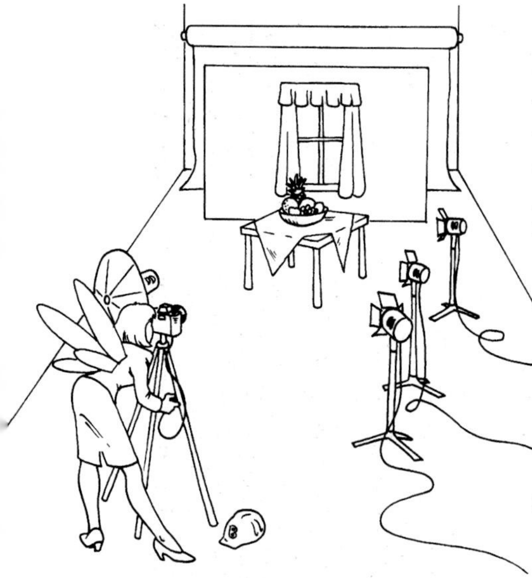

6.1.2 The still life is arranged close to the fake wall in the photo studio so that the window and the painted backdrop showing through it appear behind the table. The top view of the shoot location is below.

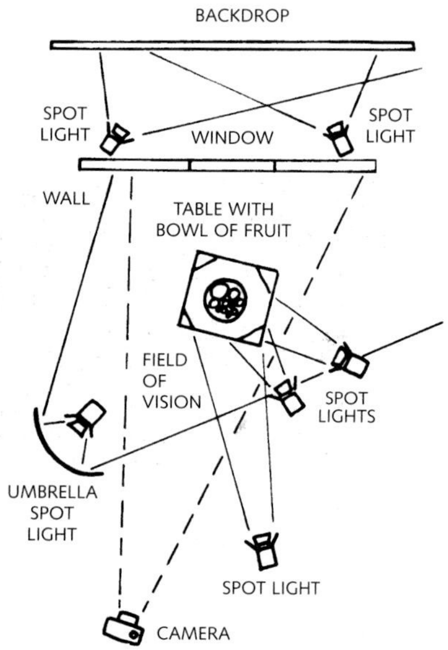

trigger and actually take a photograph. The tasks that the photographer must complete will lead to the creation of an image. Likewise, when using three-dimensional computer software to simulate a realistic or imaginary scene, many tasks and variables have to be taken care of before the program can process the information needed to generate the image we have in mind. The tasks needed when rendering by computer are similar in theory to the tasks of the photographer. But in practical detail, the tasks are carried out with very different tools and in a different environment.

The photographer in our example is photographing an arrangement of fruit in a bowl placed on a small table in the middle of a large room with a bright landscape showing through the only window in the room (Fig. 6.1.2). The photographer has to start by selecting the models, or "props," themselves. That includes the fruit, the bowl, the small table, and the tablecloth. The props may be procured from a variety of places that might include a farmer's market, a housewares store, and an antiques shop. Keep in mind that the objects and the fruit have to be picked according to a certain criterion that specifies the way they are supposed to look. The table and the tablecloth, for example, might have to have a certain soft antique look. The bowl, on the other hand, might have to be made of dark translucent crystal and have a very elegant and simple design. Only the freshest fruit can be used for this shot. Once all the objects have been brought to the studio, then the photographer and her assistant will arrange the objects in a specific composition.

In three-dimensional computer graphics all of the objects used in the scene are simply called **models**. We learned in Section II of this book that three-dimensional models can be built with a variety of software techniques. Once the models have been built, they can all be placed in the **virtual studio** that exists in the computer's memory and arranged in a specific way by using a combination of geometric transformations.

Let's return to the photographer, who is in the process of placing the table near the panel in the middle of the room and the camera in front of it so that the window on the panel appears behind the table. She also arranges the fruit in the bowl. She steps back, looks at the fruit through a professional photographic camera that is mounted on a tripod that is close to the subject, and returns to rearrange the fruit. At this point the photographer takes a snapshot with a hand-held camera loaded with instant film and a flash, just to get a quick preview of the composition. Because of the flash of intense light emitted by the flash lamp, the color in some areas of the instant photograph washes out, the overall illusion of depth is somewhat flattened, and the delicacy of some textures is lost. But the instant flash photograph does the job: it records the position of objects in space and the composition. It is also possible to create such quick snapshots with three-dimensional rendering software.

6.1.3 The haunting lighting and rendering effects in *The Cathedral* were rendered with the Brazil ray tracing renderer. (Copyright 2002 Tomek Baginski and Platige Image.)

All the components of the still life are now in place, and it is time to start playing with the position, intensity, color, and focus of the lights. Since the shot is taking place inside the studio, very little natural sunlight is available. Therefore, the photographer must recreate not only the sunlight but also some lights that must be focused on several areas of the fruit in order to delineate the shapes with more clarity and to accentuate the highlights and the shadows on the fruit to further the effect of depth.

Our imaginary photographer pauses for a minute, looks around the almost empty and dark room, and tries to visualize the effect of different types of lights on the fruit, the tablecloth, and the walls. After discussing some of the stylistic possibilities and production implications with her assistant, the photographer decides to start with one intense but indirect flood light for simulating the effect of warm natural light of a medium intensity. The flood light is placed between the still life and the camera, but away from the still life and into a concave portable reflective surface in the shape of an umbrella.

Then the photographer carefully maneuvers three small spotlights pointed at different fruits in the bowl. Since the three spotlights all have the same intensity, the photographer has to move some of them closer or farther away from the fruit depending on the lighting effect desired. While the photographer is still arranging the three spotlights, her assistant is busy lighting the backdrop (with a landscape painted on it) that is placed behind the fake wall and visible through its window. The photographer's assistant decides to use two small flood lights with a slight blue coloration in order to simulate the exterior light of a cold rainy day. The two small floodlights are pointed at 45-degree angles from the back of the fake wall directly onto the back-

6.1.4 Uniform ambient lighting and bright overhead lights were used to light this low angle shot, from the *Free Jimmy* animated feature. (© 2003 AnimagicNet Norway.)

drop (Fig. 6.1.2). Most three-dimensional rendering programs allow artists to select and place light sources with the same amount of intuitive trial-and-error and precision as lighting with real lights.

During the placement of the lights, the photographer and her assistant go back and forth to the camera to check through the viewfinder whether the lights are defining the image composition and mood that they had in mind at the onset of the process. At first, double-checking the lights is intuitive and purely visual. But before taking the final photograph it becomes necessary for her to measure light in a systematic and precise way. This measurement is done with a special device called a **light meter**, which provides the photographer with a precise, numerical value that represents different characteristics of the incident light at any point in the three-dimensional environment.

It is also necessary, as part of the light measuring process, to double-check and adjust the light readings against other numerical values involved in the process of photographing the still life. Those other numerical values might include, for example, the speed and chromatic characteristics of the photographic film, the chromatic value of the filter placed on the lens of the camera, and the chromatic value of the reflected light. This constant back-and-forth double-checking is not only necessary to stay on the desired track but is also an integral part of the creative lighting process.

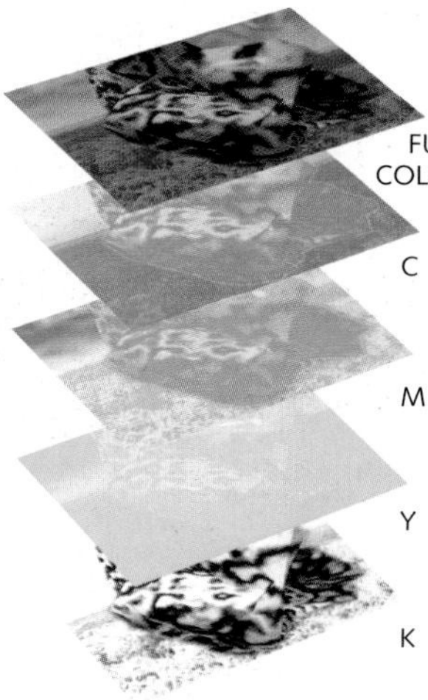

6.2.1 A CMYK full-color image is created when the four image layers are viewed together. Four-color separations (cyan, yellow, magenta, and black) are employed in most mechanical reproduction of color images in paper-based magazines and books.

During the visual checking done by looking through the viewfinder, the photographer's assistant notices that the surface of one of the fruits looks somewhat dull and slightly flat, and that is not the way fruit is supposed to be portrayed in this image. The photographer and her assistant determine that this might be because the skin of the fruit became too dry while in storage at the store. They also agree that the best way to fix this—short of getting a replacement fruit—would be to apply a thin coat of oil to the skin of the fruit. The surface characteristics of all objects can be easily determined and fine-tuned with most three-dimensional rendering software.

Once all the lights and surfaces have been fine-tuned it is time to make slight adjustments to the placement and focusing of the camera. The photographer decides to replace the lens of the camera with another one that provides a wider field of vision so that a larger portion of the scene will fit in the final image without having to move the camera further away (Figs. 7.4.3 and 7.4.4). Finally, the scene is ready to be recorded. Three-dimensional rendering software provides tools for simulating lenses of different focal lengths as well as the effects, such as depth of field, associated with them (Figs. 6.1.3–6.1.4).

6.2 Color

This section covers some of the most popular color models used in three-dimensional computer rendering including Cyan, Magenta, Yellow, and Black (CMYK), Red, Green, and Blue (RGB), and Hue, Saturation, and Lightness (HSL). See Chapter 13 for more information on color resolution and color look-up tables.

Additive and Subtractive Systems

Those of us who learned about color theory when we were kids were given three jars with red, blue, and yellow paint, and told that we had to create other colors by mixing the paint from the three jars. We were told that the three primary colors are red, blue, and yellow (RBY). But that was only part of the story. Those three colors are indeed primary colors but only in a **pigment-based** color environment. The RBY **subtractive** color system is useful for understanding color relationships in a paper-and-paint environment.

Cyan, Magenta, Yellow, and Black

Another model that is used to explain and define colors that are pigment-based is the **Cyan**, **Magenta**, **Yellow**, and **Black (CMYK)** color model. This model is widely used in the traditional graphic arts and digital printing for mechanical reproduction of color images (Fig. 6.2.1).

Red, Green, and Blue

The colors displayed on a computer screen, however, occur in a **light-based** color environment. These colors are created by combining different amounts of the three primary colors in the **additive** color system: **Red**, **Green**, and **Blue (RGB)**. In the RGB model colors are defined in terms of their amounts of red, green, and blue. Combining—or adding—all the primary colors in the RGB system yields white, therefore the name additive system. Combinations of two primary RGB colors yield results that would not make sense in a pigment-based model. For example, the combination of red and green lights in equal proportions yields yellow light. The RGB color model takes advantage of the technology used in computer monitors. It is a precise and efficient way of describing color, and it is used in all computer systems. Most software represents each of the RGB primary colors in a separate layer or channel so that each color can be manipulated independently (Figs. 6.2.2 and 6.2.4). RGB colors can be described by specifying numerical values that may range, for example, from 0 to 1, or from 0 to 255. The value of pure green is 0-255-0. The value of a greenish light blue could be 150-200-255, and a yellowish dark orange 120-80-30 (Fig. 8.3.3).

Hue, Saturation, and Lightness

Working with the RGB model can be confusing for many visual people. The **Hue, Saturation**, and **Lightness (HSL)** color model can be used as a more intuitive alternative for specifying color in a light-based environment. In the HSL model, colors are described in terms of their hue, saturation, and lightness. The HSL color model can be visualized as a three-dimensional space that simplifies the

6.2.2 These beautiful patterns display the values of color samples in the RGB, HSB, and CMYK color models. The RGB values range from 0 to 255, CMYK ranges from 0 to 100%, and HSB is expressed in degrees (hue) and pecentages (saturation and brightness). (Courtesy of Akira Kai, FOTON).

6.2.3 (top right) This diagram of the CIE color space defines the colors in the electromagnetic spectrum. Those visible to the human eye are inside the inverted D-like shape, those beyond the range of visible color—like ultraviolet and infrared color frequencies—are outside of the shape. (© Photo Research, Inc. All rights reserved.)

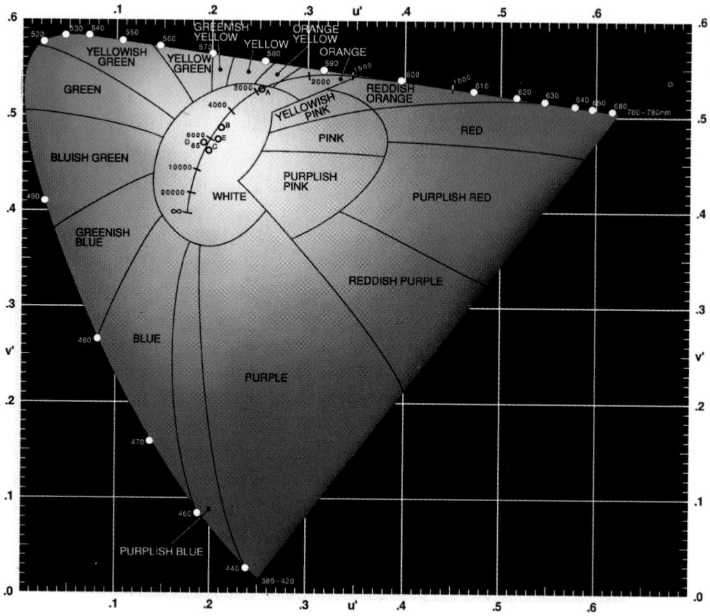

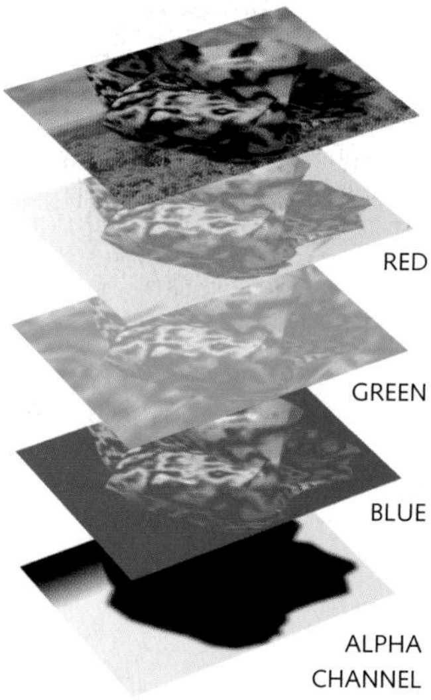

6.2.4 Each of the RGB primary colors is kept in a separate layer or channel. These image layers can also contain information other than color. An alpha channel, for example, contains a black-and-white image that can be used as a stencil to mask some areas of the layers being composited with other images.

location and description of color. This space can be defined by two cones connected at their base. The vertical axis that runs between the two peaks is used to define the **lightness**, or darkness, of a particular color. The lightness of a color increases or decreases along the direction of this axis, with the lighter colors located at the top of this space, and the darker ones at the bottom. The **saturation** of a color increases along a line that starts perpendicular to the vertical axis of the space and ends at the outside surface. The colors on the outside surface are fully saturated, while the colors close to the center of the space are washed out. The **hue** of colors in the HSL color space changes with the angular position of the color around the vertical axis. All the spectrum of hues can be found around the vertical axis, and their position can be specified in degrees.

Slicing the HSL space horizontally reveals many hues and saturation values with the same lightness value. The gray colors—neutral and "colorless"—are found on the vertical axis. Absolute white and absolute black can be found in the peaks of the HSL space. A popular variation of the HSL color model is the **Hue, Saturation,** and **Brightness (HSB)** color model. The main difference between the HSL and the HSB models is that the latter uses two cylinders—instead of two cones—to define the chromatic space. A graphical representation of the HSB color space is shown in Figure 8.3.4.

Color Conversions

When creating images with computers, it is often necessary to convert from one color space to another. This is mostly due to the fact that the creative process usually takes place in both light-based and pigment-based color environments. When we scan photographs or drawings we deal with pigment-based color. When we manipulate existing images or create new images on the screen we deal with light-based color. When we print one of our images on paper we deal, again, with pigment-based color.

In most cases this **color conversion** is done automatically by the computer software that we use. Obviously, the quality of these color conversions varies from program to program. If we are pleased with the color output of our computer system in general, we do not have to get involved in the color conversion process. If we are not satisfied with the automatic or default color conversion, however, it is important to get involved in the color balancing and correction or enlist the help of a color-experienced user.

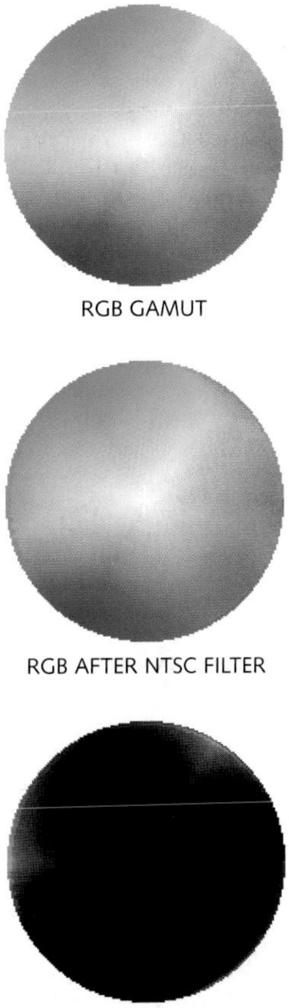
RGB GAMUT
RGB AFTER NTSC FILTER
RGB/NTSC DIFFERENCE

6.2.5 The dark areas in the lower circle represent the different chromatic ranges between the RGB and the NTSC color spaces.

Color Ranges

In the early 1930s the International Commission on Color, known as CIE (*Commission Internationale de l'Eclairage*), first presented a color space that defined all the colors in the spectrum that are visible by the human eye. The **CIE color space** is a useful aid for understanding which colors we can see—for example, ultraviolet and infrared color frequencies are beyond the range of visible color (Fig. 6.2.3). The CIE color space is also very useful for visualizing the **chromatic ranges** of different media. It turns out that not all media and techniques we use for creating color are capable of creating exactly the same colors. This explains why so often the colors we see on the screen are different from the colors we see on the printout. Knowing which color ranges do not overlap between a variety of media and formats is helpful in devising solutions to work around this physical limitations of color reproduction.

A common problem one encounters when creating computer images for output on videotape is that the colors created with RGB computer monitors are too bright and saturated for display on standard television sets. Those working in RGB for eventual output to video have to clip the RGB colors that are outside the video color range in order to avoid distortions such as color bleeding from showing in the final video recording. This is illustrated in Figures 6.2.5 and 6.2.6 where a color sample of the RGB color space is translated into the NTSC and CMYK spaces.

6.3 Steps in the Rendering Process

The overall rendering process consists of five major steps regardless of the computer system used. It is not required that these steps happen in a rigid order. In fact, some projects might require that the sequence of steps is slightly altered. More details on the entire production process can be found in Chapter 2. Because of the complex and cumulative nature of the rendering process there is usually considerable bouncing back and forth between stages before the process

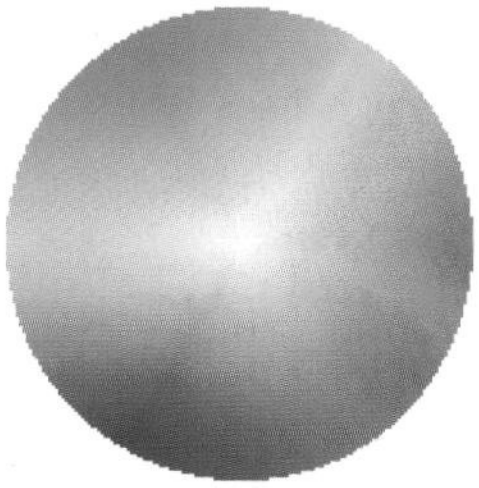

RGB GAMUT

RGB AFTER CMYK CLIPPING

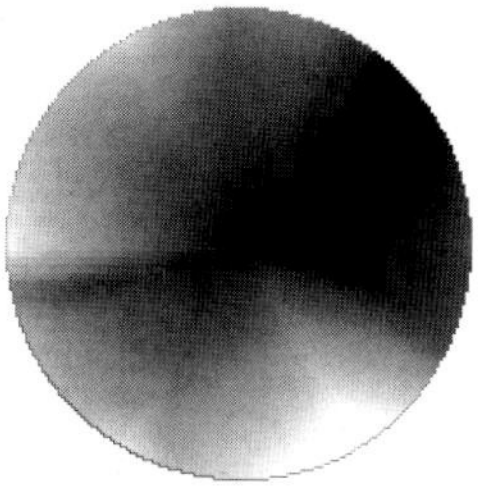

RGB/CMYK DIFFERENCE

6.2.6 The dark areas in the lower circle represent the different chromatic ranges between the RGB and the CMYK color spaces.

is completed. But keep in mind that the implementation of general techniques in different programs might require slight variations in the sequence of steps described here. Figure 6.3.1 summarizes the main steps in the **rendering process** in the form of a flowchart. Each of the steps in the rendering process is covered in detail throughout Section III of this book.

The first step in the rendering process consists of getting the models to be rendered straight from the modeling module of the program or from some kind of peripheral storage like a hard disk. These models usually include characters, props, and sets. Secondly, we maneuver the camera in XYZ space so that we look at the portion of the environment that we are interested in. We might reposition the camera, tilt it, change the focal point and the depth of field, and adjust the proportions and the resolution of the image. If necessary, we may further rearrange the objects in the scene. Third, we design and implement the lighting scheme. This can be done by drawing and specifying the arrangement of the lights and their characteristics on paper or by visualizing it in one's head. We might define and place several light sources in the three-dimensional space of the computer software.

Next, we specify many characteristics of the surfaces of the objects including color, texture, shininess, reflectivity, and transparency. Specifying surface characteristics often requires a fair amount of attention to detail. Doing a good job during this stage will have a great impact on the quality, refinement, and energy of the final rendering result.

Finally, the fifth step consists of choosing a shading method and generating the final rendered image. Specifying the surface characteristics and choosing the shading techniques are two distinct steps but they are intrinsically related to one another and often overlap with each other.

When the geometry or shading in any given scene are too complex it is common to render different components of the scene separately. This is usually called working or **rendering in layers**. A simple example of this method would consist of rendering the background by itself, then rendering the foreground elements, and finally compositing them together using the techniques described in Chapter 13 (Fig. 13.1.1).

Rendering Methods

A large variety of rendering methods can be used to turn a wireframe view of a three-dimensional model into a shaded image. In addition to the skilled placement of light sources in a scene and the assignment of surface characteristics to objects, the final shaded image is largely dependent on the type of rendering method used. It is important to keep in mind that the users of rendering systems—especially turnkey systems—are dependent on the capabilities of the rendering method, or algorithm, used. This is partly because most rendering methods are usually supplied as "black boxes" that only accept geometry data and rendering variables—such as lighting, shading and surface characteristics—and cannot be modified by the user. The **RenderMan shading language** is an exception to this rule because it provides a rendering environment that can be tweaked by the user. Some rendering programs provide extensive technical notes explaining how they work, and such notes can provide useful insights about the ways in which the program renders. This information can prove invaluable when setting up a scene to be rendered. But in most cases it takes a fair amount of practice to get a feel for or to understand how a specific program renders. Knowing the strengths and weaknesses of a rendering program can be very advantageous for many stages of the three-dimensional creative process with computers, ranging from the sketching and storyboarding stage all the way through final output and recording.

You should keep a couple of practical ideas in mind about rendering in general. Each of the rendering methods described in this section has particular strengths and weaknesses. Often the same rendering method is implemented slightly differently in different software programs, so the results of using the same rendering method with the same variables in two different software programs cannot be expected to be the same. Finally, keep in mind that several rendering methods can be used in conjunction with one another. This is usually called **hybrid rendering**. Figures 6.7.4 and 6.12.4 show the result of rendering a scene in layers and with both ray tracing and radiosity rendering techniques.

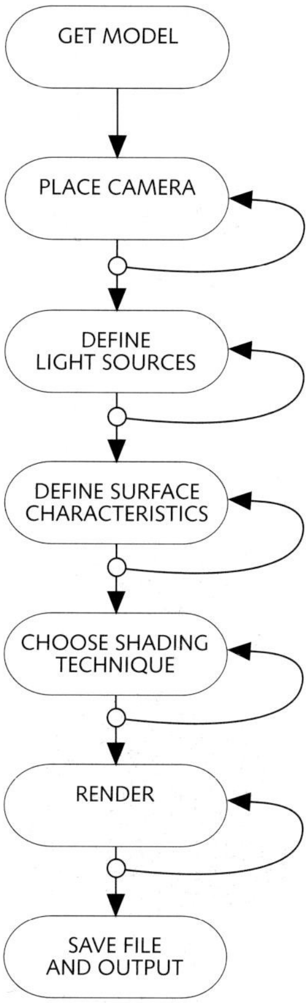

6.3.1 The steps of a fairly standard rendering process. After some of the steps a test is made to see if the results are on track. If not, the variables are adjusted. See the flowcharts in Chapter 2 for other digital production processes that are fine-tuned to a specific type of project, team configuration, budget, or deadline.

6.4 Hidden Surface Removal

The hidden lines and surfaces of the object that are not visible from the point of view of the camera must be removed before the three-dimensional wireframe models can be rendered. Several algorithms have been developed to sort all the points, lines, and surfaces of an object and decide which of them are visible and which are not. Then the **visible surfaces** are kept and the **hidden surfaces** are removed (Fig. 6.4.1). Before the polygonal meshes and free-form curved surfaces can be rendered, they are subdivided into triangles; this process is called **tessellation**. As explained in Chapter 9, the removal of hidden surfaces is determined by the relationship between the orientation of their surface normals and the position and orientation of the camera. There are many methods for hidden surface removal, and they can can be separated into the general categories of object space and image space. A few hybrid rendering methods operate in both object and image spaces.

Object space methods for hidden surface removal make the calculations in three dimensions. These algorithms require intensive computing but are unique because they generate data that can be used to improve the rendering of textures, shadows, and antialiasing. Ray tracing is an example of object space rendering methods, and it is the standard rendering method of many of today's rendering programs. Ray tracing follows the rays of light—emitted by the light sources in the scene—as they bounce off or travel through objects and eventually reach the camera.

Image space methods for hidden surface removal retain the depth information of the objects in the scene, but sort from a lateral position, and only to the resolution of the display device. Image space rendering methods render a three-dimensional scene by projecting the models onto the two-dimensional image plane (Fig. 6.4.1). Image space algorithms are generally efficient but discard some of the original three-dimensional information that can be used for shadowing, texturing, and antialiasing enhancement. Many of the image space methods for the removal of hidden surfaces were first developed in the early 1970s, and include Warnock's **area subdivision** (1969), Watkins' **scan line** (1970), and Newell's **depth sort** (1972). (The latter is generally considered a hybrid image/object space algorithm.)

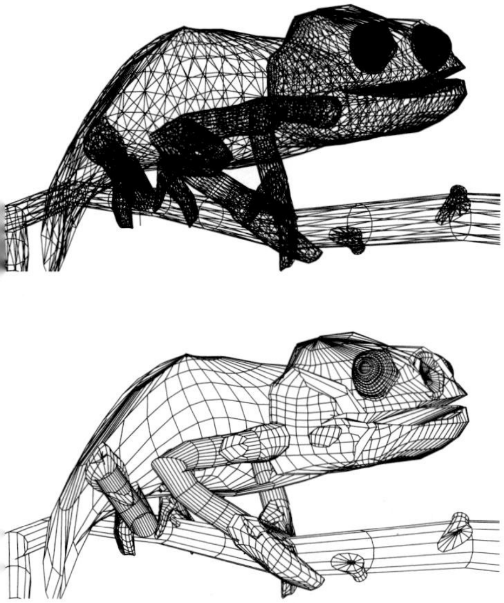

6.4.1 A chameleon modeled with curved surfaces and then converted to a polygonal mesh. Rendered in wireframe mode and with the hidden lines removed. (Courtesy of Tim Cheung.)

Multiple improvements and refinements to each of the original image space rendering procedures have been made by several others. Very few of today's programs that use image space rendering methods identify the specific type of method they use, but in general, there are no significant differences in quality between images created with different image space rendering methods of equal sophistication. However, some of the limitations of image space rendering methods include the fact that some work only with polygonal meshes but do not work well—if at all—on models created with parametric curved surfaces.

6.5 Z-Buffer

The Z-Buffer rendering method is an example of an image space rendering technique, but it also incorporates some concepts used in object space rendering. **Z-Buffer** rendering gets its name from the fact that all objects in the scene are sorted by their Z position, or depth, in the scene. This depth information is kept in a buffer, and made available to the rendering process as the hidden surface removal calculations are performed.

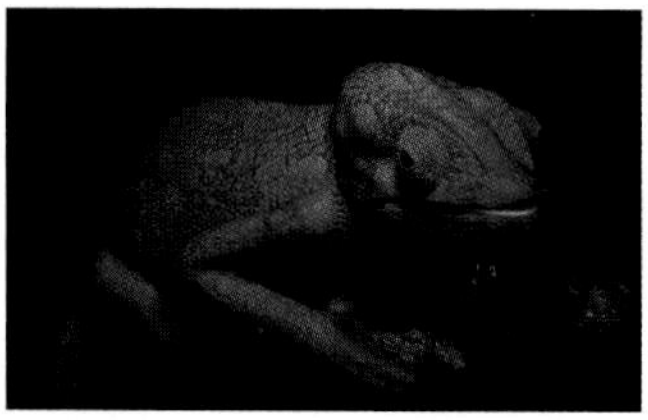

6.5.1 The color on the visible surfaces of this chameleon was calculated at each pixel. The total Reflected Light that bounces off the surface of the model equals the product of the Incident Light multiplied by the Surface Reflectivity.

The Z-Buffer rendering method makes the hidden surface removal one object and one pixel at a time. This method determines whether an object is visible from the point of view of the camera at each pixel, and one pixel at a time. If the object is visible, its depth information (or distance from the camera) is checked, and this determines whether the object is the closest one to the camera up to that point in the sorting process. If it is, the object is shaded at that pixel, and this visibility test is repeated for the same object at all pixels on the screen. When the visibility of one object is completed, another object is chosen, and the visibility process is performed at all pixels all over again (Fig. 6.5.1). It is easily determined whether a new object is closer to the camera than the object tested earlier by checking the depth information of the new object. If the new object is closest to the camera, its shading values replace the previous shading values at that pixel. The Z-Buffer rendering is completed when the visibility of all objects in the scene has been tested in all the pixels.

6.6 Ray Tracing

Ray tracing is a rendering technique that is capable of creating photorealistic images of three-dimensional scenes. Ray tracing is one of the most advanced and accurate methods of rendering, in part because it calculates every ray of light in the scene by following each one through the scene until it each reaches the camera. Ray tracing creates images with very accurate reflections and refractions of light as well as detailed textures and shadows.

In general terms, **ray tracing** works by creating a ray for each pixel on the screen and tracing its path—one ray at a time—all the way back to the light source. A ray is an imaginary straight line that travels through three-dimensional space and collects rendering information. The values for the ray of light are calculated as it bounces off—or travels through—different surfaces in the scene with a variety of characteristics (Fig. 6.6.1). Ray tracing rendering techniques are based on the way in which rays of light travel from the light sources to our eyes, bouncing off surfaces that affect their characteristics along the way. However, it would be impractical to trace all the rays of light emitted by a light source in a scene because many of them never reach the camera. For that reason ray tracing programs trace the rays of lights **backwards**, from the camera to the light source, to minimize the number of wasted calculations.

6.6.1 The ray tracing process.

The main strength of the ray tracing rendering method comes from the fact that the image of a three-dimensional scene is calculated in three-dimensional space. The traced rays travel in three-dimensional space and often bounce from object to object. These rays are able to deal with processes—such as images being reflected on a surface, or the light being bent by a transparent object—that can best be simulated in a three-dimensional space. Unlike image space rendering methods, ray tracing is precise about simulating the behavior of light in three-dimensional space.

The primary controls in a ray tracing rendering are related to the depth of the ray tracing, the number of pixels in the image, and the number of light sources in the scene. The **ray tracing depth** is related to the number of times that a ray will be allowed to come in contact with surfaces in the three-dimensional space. Most subtle details in a ray-traced image are controlled by the depth of the ray tracing. Most ray tracing programs use different controls for the reflection rays, the transparency or refraction rays, and the shadow rays. Each of these types of rays calculate different components of the rendering of a three-dimensional scene. The depth of these three different types of rays is independent from one another. Figure 6.12.2 shows versions of a ray-traced image based on different combinations of tracing depth. The first image contains no reflections and the transparent surfaces are not rendered as such. The second image contains a fair amount of reflections on the reflective surfaces, and refraction in the transparent surfaces, but no shadows. The third images contain shadows, plus an increased amount of reflection and refraction. It is important to keep in mind that when using the ray tracing rendering method, a surface that is made very reflective becomes like a mirror and, as a consequence, loses many of its other surface characteristics.

Reflection rays travel through the scene in a straight way, and they bounce off the reflective surfaces they hit at the same angle at which they hit them. Once a point in three-dimensional space has been hit by a ray and the value of that surface has been calculated, a **shadow ray** is shot from that point to the center of each light source in the scene. That point in three-dimensional space will only be visible if the shadow ray does not encounter another object before reaching the light source. When the ray tracing process encounters transparent surfaces in the scene, **refraction rays** are generated to calculate the amount of light refraction. In most ray tracing programs refraction is only enabled when the surface that is supposed to be refractive has a **thickness** defined by the distance between the front face and the back face of the surface (Figs. 6.6.2 and 6.6.3).

The number of rays traced in a scene—regardless of their tracing depth—is related to the spatial resolution of a scene, which is determined by the total **number of pixels** in an image. A single ray is traced backwards to a light source through every pixel in the image. Therefore, an increase in the number of pixels will result in an increase in the number of rays traced and in the length of time that will be required to complete the rendering of an image.

The **number of light sources** in a scene also influences the number of rays that are traced through the scene and, consequently, the length of the ray tracing rendering calculation. This is due to the fact that ray tracing works by tracing backwards each ray of light that reaches the camera.

Due to the intense computations required by the ray tracing rendering methods many software programs provide simple ways to preview just a portion of the three-dimensional scene in the ray tracing mode (Fig. 6.12.3). Some programs also estimate the length of time that will be required to complete a rendering and let the user know so that other tasks can be pursued in the meantime. In most cases the color of the light that is reflected by a surface is calculated as the combination of red, green, and blue light. The color of the reflected light is based on the color of the surface, the color of the incident

6.6.2 Detail of a ray-traced scene including reflected light sources and refracted objects and environments. (Courtesy of Charles Csuri.)

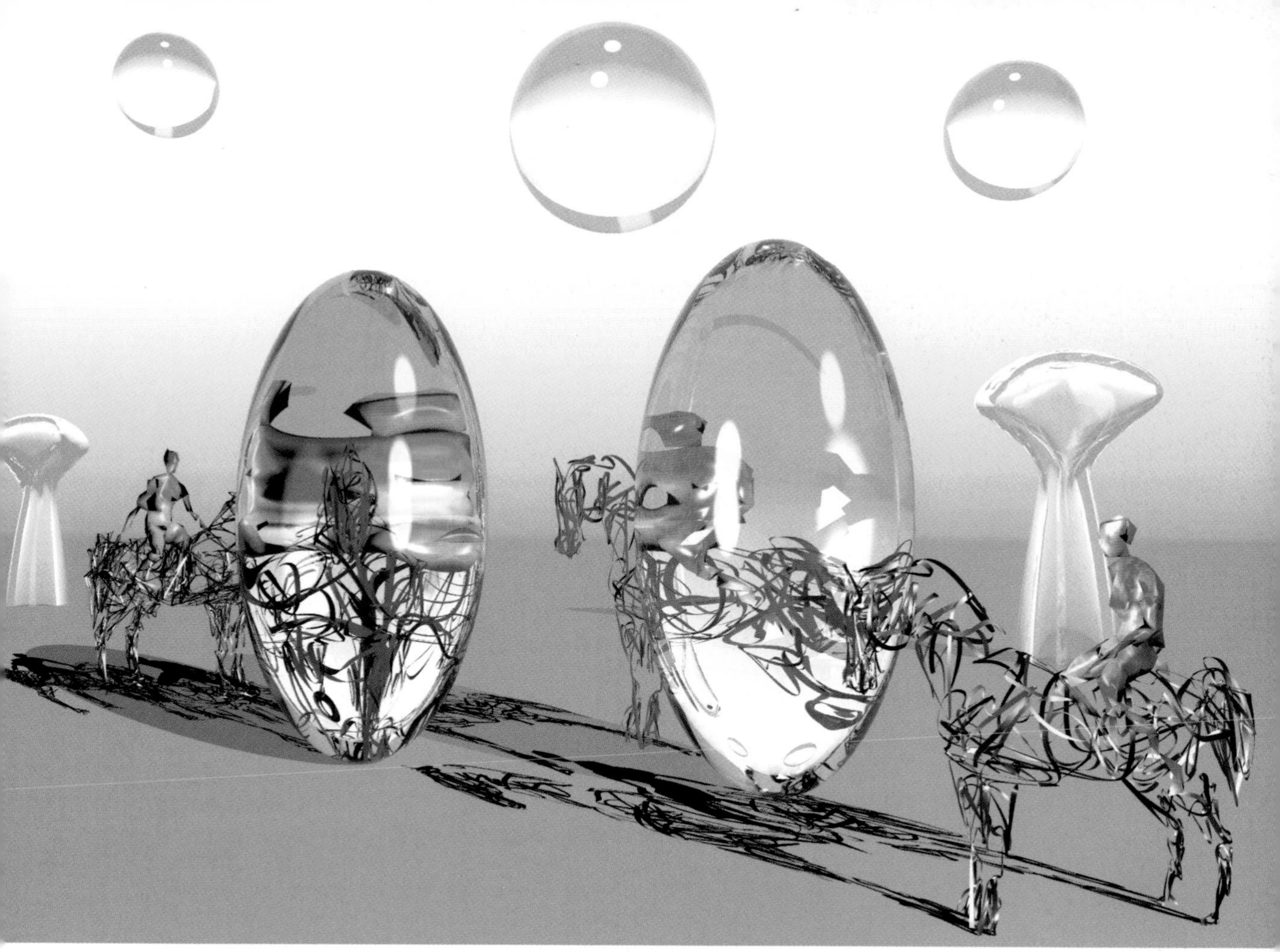

light that reaches the surface, and on the reflectivity of the surface for each of the red, green, and blue components of light.

6.6.3 A ray-traced image with effects of reflection and refraction. Notice the ribbon-like structure that was used to define the horses. (Courtesy of Charles Csuri.)

6.7 Global Illumination and Radiosity

Global illumination can create images that are more physically accurate than any other rendering technique because it calculates indirect illumination on objects, including diffuse, glossy and specular **interreflection** between surfaces and transmission of light from other objects (Fig. 6.7.2). The global illumination rendering methods are based on the principles of illumination engineering theory and energy transfer. There are a few variations of global illumination rendering, including radiosity and photon maps.

Radiosity rendering focuses on diffuse interreflection between surfaces, and it typically divides the geometry in the environment into areas, or clusters, of polygons according to the way in which light affects them. The polygons in a radiosity calculation are typically cata-

6.7.1 In this radiosity rendering the three-dimensional space is subdivided with an overlaid mesh that simplifies the calculations into a sequence of small clusters of source, receiver, and blocker polygons. (From "Partitioning and Ordering Large Radiosity Computations," by Seth Teller, C. Fowler, T. Funkhouser, and P. Hanrahan. University of California Berkeley Walk-Through Group, and Princeton University Computer Graphics Lab. Courtesy of Seth Teller.)

6.7.2 (opposite page) The XSI global illumination dialog box. (Courtesy of Softimage Co. All rights reserved.)

logued into light sources, light-receiving surfaces, and light-blocking surfaces. By using iteration techniques, radiosity rendering calculates the amount of light that is transferred from one surface to another. This iteration or repetition is continued until the light energy is fully absorbed by the surfaces and/or it dissipates in space. With radiosity rendering the subdivision of the three-dimensional space is based on the amount of light that is emitted or transferred between surfaces. The cataloguing of surfaces that is necessary to perform radiosity calculations generates a data structures that look like **subdivision grids** when displayed on the screen (Fig. 6.7.1). These data structures typically require large amounts of main memory (RAM), and of raw computing. Once a grid of subdivisions has been established then the energy that is emitted by each light source can be followed throughout the environment based on the geometry of the surfaces. The distance between surfaces and their angular position are two important factors used in establishing the amount of light energy that can be transferred. Before light dissipates in space, much of it bounces off between surfaces if they are parallel to each other. But less energy is transferred if the surfaces are perpendicular, and none is transferred if they face away from each other. Likewise, more energy is transferred between surfaces if they are close to one another than if they are further apart from each other (Fig. 6.7.3). One of the most striking lighting effects achieved with radiosity is **color bleeding**, which happens when colored objects pass some of their color through diffuse light to the neighboring objects.. When rendered with radiosity a bright red sphere, for example, will cast a pale red diffuse interreflection on an adjacent white wall.

Radiosity may be combined with other rendering techniques to achieve striking and innovative results. In the award-winning film ***Bunny***, radiosity was used to render the set and the props while the two main protagonists were ray-traced and later composited into the environment as if they were live action models (Figs. 6.7.4 and 6.12.4). The direct lighting on the characters does not include any radiosity, because rendering fur with radiosity techniques would have been impractical. An interesting side effect of using radiosity was achieved by limiting the number of times that light was allowed to bounce within the environment. In this case the one or two cycles that light bounced were not enough to resolve all the detail in the environment because there was not enough radiosity sampling. Interestingly enough, the resulting image artifact yields a look that is similar to the emulsion grain on photographic film. The creators of the film took advantage of this stochastic sampling artifact and made it serve an aesthetic purpose. The radiosity grain varies from shot to shot, and it varies based on many factors.

Photon map rendering is another version of global illumination. **Photon maps** are collections of small energy packets that are emmited into the scene to represent the way light travels through space. The values of photons as they are reflected, absorbed or transmitted through surfaces and volumes are used to compute global illumina-

6.7.3 Lighting simulation of the main lobby of the Eli Lilly Library in Indiana University at Bloomington. One of the earliest images rendered with radiosity techniques, this image was created in the early 1990s with Greg Ward's Radiance version 2.2. The geometry was created with AutoCad Release 12 for the IBM RISC 6000. (Courtesy of Reuben Mcfarland and Scott Routen, Artifex, Bloomington, IN.)

tion (Fig. 8.3.2). Caustics are a striking lighting effect rendered with this technique. **Caustics** are created when specular light is focused or dispersed by reflection or refraction, and are typically seen when light travels through crystal or water (Figs. 8.1.6–8.1.7).

6.8 Image-Based Rendering

Image-based rendering (as well as image-based modeling) works by extracting geometry, image texture, and global illumination information from analyzing photographic data. In essence this type of rendering can recreate a three-dimensional environment uses photographic sample images. Generally speaking, a more ambitious image-based recreation of three-dimensional environments will require a more complex analysis of the photographs and longer rendering times (Figs. 6.8.1 and 6.8.2).

Some of the earliest experiments with image-based rendering used photographs of real environments to extract depth maps of the environment and reproject pixels in three-dimensional space. The quality of these early examples of image-based renderings was very dependent on the number of views taken of the environment. A few photographs would yield gaps and errors in the rendering, but newer techniques can calculate the missing information and fill in approximate data (Fig. 6.8.3).

Gathering the information to be used in the image-based rendering is an important step because it will define the quality of the final results. This information includes the images recorded photographically or digitally with as much quality and resolution as possible. This

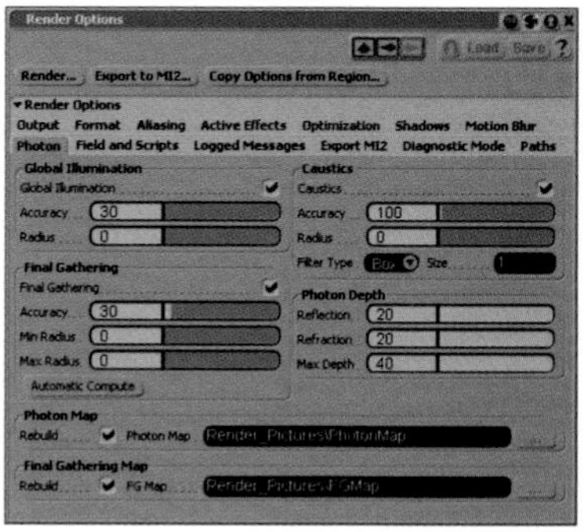

6.7.4 The set and props in Chris Wedge's *Bunny* were rendered with radiosity techniques, while Bunny and the moth were ray-traced. In lighting this shot a bounce card was placed above the sink (and out of the frame) to emphasize the light from the light bulb and to help focus it on the sink. Notice the film-like grain that results from limited radiosity sampling. (© 1998 Blue Sky Studios.)

data gathering also seeks information about the exposures and lens apertures or **finite dynamic range**, samples of the intensity of light or **radiance**, information about the position of the camera and the distance to some of the key points in the scene (done with **point sampling**), and last but not least general information about the type of light that falls on the objects—for example, direct or filtered sunlight or incandescent light from bulbs.

The animation ***Fiat Lux*** is a good example of a comprehensive test-bed project created with image-based modeling, rendering, and lighting techniques. The geometry, appearance, and illumination of the environments were acquired through digital photography. The environments and the lighting were extracted from the photographs shot on location at the Basilica of Saint Peter in Rome. Different views were recorded with **high dynamic range** (**HDR**) photography in order to capture the full range of illumination; some of these seed images have a dynamic range of over 100,000:1. Several exposures taken with varying shutter speeds were combined into a single linear response radiance panoramic image (Fig. 6.8.1). Then the props were modeled from scratch with an off-the-shelf three-dimensional modeling program that was also used to build a simple three-dimensional model of the Basilica of Saint Peter in Rome from the photographs using the Façade photogrammetric modeling system, and the image maps were projected onto the geometry (Fig. 6.8.2). Next, the position of the illumination sources recorded in the photographs was recreated in three-dimensional space, and the light probe images were used to create three-dimensional light sources of the correct

6.8.1 (opposite page) The appearance and illumination of the real environment was recorded and point light measurements were taken. Each light probe measurement was made by taking one or two telephoto radiance images of a 2-inch mirrored ball placed on a tripod. Each of these images provided an omnidirectional illumination measurement at a particular point in space. The dynamic range of some of the resulting radiance images was stabilized, and the images processed to diminish glare. (Courtesy of Paul Debevec, University of California at Berkley, 1999.)

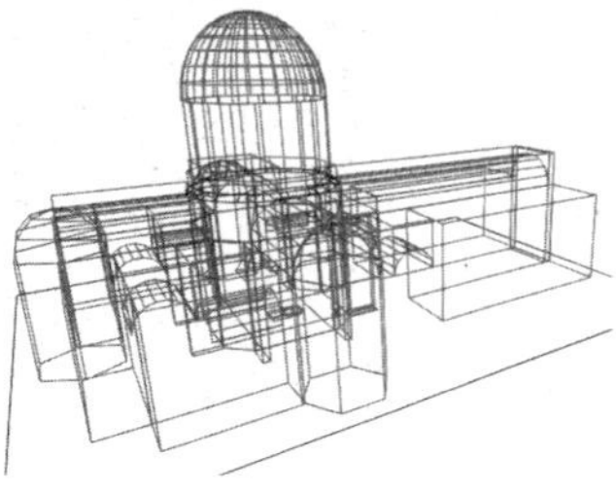

6.8.2 The rectangular slabs and the spheres in *Fiat Lux* were animated procedurally or with the dynamic simulator in Maya software. The final renderings were created on a cluster of workstations using the Radiance global illumination system to simulate the photometric interaction of the objects and the environments. The final look of the film was achieved using a combination of blur, flare, and vignetting filters applied to the high dynamic range renderings. (Courtesy of Paul Debevec, University of California at Berkley, 1999.)

intensity and location. The original illumination information was also used to remove the highlights, reflections, and ground shadows in the original photographs, allowing the synthetic objects to cast shadows and appear in reflections throughout the final rendering (Fig. 6.8.3).

6.9 Non-Photorealistic Rendering

Non-photorealistic rendering techniques became increasingly popular during the late 1990s to create three-dimensional computer animation and still images that look as if they were created with traditional techniques. There are many approaches to **non-photorealistic rendering**; some are based on three-dimensional rendering techniques and others on two-dimensional image processing techniques. The latter are essentially post-processing filters that can be applied to a three-dimensional model after it is rendered with realistic techniques (Fig. 13.2.9). The non-photorealistic rendering, or **NPR**, techniques that operate in three-dimensional space calculate the amount of light that reaches the three-dimensional surfaces but the shading is done through simulations of how traditional materials like paint pigments are distributed on a surface or with modified versions of existing shading techniques. Non-photorealistic rendering techniqes are sometimes called **toon shaders** because they are reminiscent of the comic book drawings with a black outline and somewhat flat colors. Some hybrid renderers are able to combine realistic and NPR techniques in a

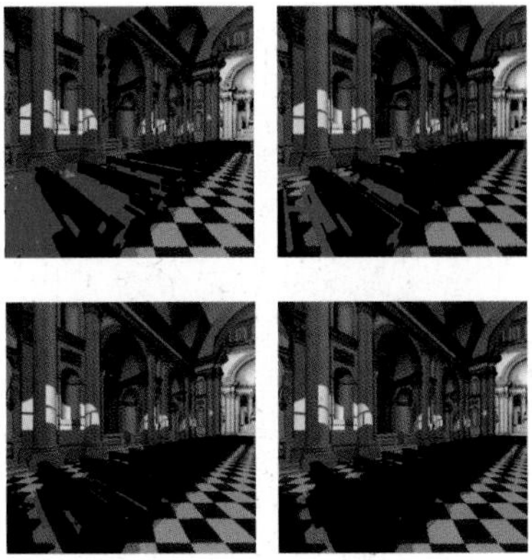

6.8.3 The top left view shows some of the geometric detail (shown in blue) that was not captured in the original photographs. The rest of the views show steps in the process of approximating the data and filling it in with the reconstruction software. (Courtesy of Chun-Fa Chang, G. Bishop, A. Lastra, N. O'Brien, and ACM.)

single pass or multiple passes. Figure 6.9.1 shows a test comparison of simple shading and NPR flat color rendering. The three final frames have a variable width outline and narrow color palette (Fig. 6.9.2).

Figure 6.9.3 shows an image from the animated short ***Fishing*** rendered in a watercolor simulation process that begins by creating a two-dimensional matte from the three-dimensional target object. Within the matte the different behaviors of fluid watercolor pigments and binders are simulated on surfaces that have different absorbency and reflectance qualities. With this process geometry can be rendered with some of the effects typical of watercolor painting including superimposed glazes in complementary colors (as in Fig. 6.9.3), dry brush effects, the edge darkening typical of wet-on-dry brushstrokes, the backruns that happen when a puddle of water spreads back into a damp region of paint, granulation and separation of pigments, and the flow patterns typical of wet-in-wet painting. The final effect was varied over time to reflect the changing time in day as well as the mood of the main character. The rendering in Figure 6.9.4 has the look of gouache paint, and uses transparency maps to map irregular shapes like the broom onto rectangular geometry. Figure 6.9.5 shows two variations of a nonrealistic rendering technique that changes the color hue along with the light shading information and also adds an outline edge similar to the drawing outlines used in hand-drawn traditional animation. The variations show shading and highlighting variations achieved with different versions of shading models.

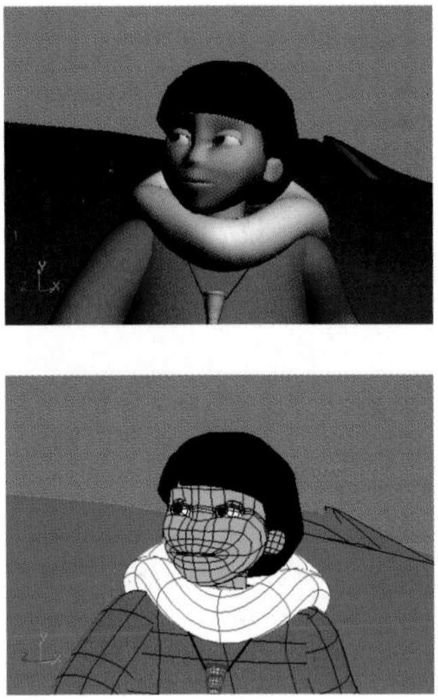

6.9.1 A boy rendered with simple shading and a non-photorealistic shader that applies a flat color to entire areas. (Based on the artwork of Marc Tetro. Directed by Phillip Stamp. © Tube Nunavut Inc. © Marc Tetro.)

6.9.2 These landscapes are rendered by dividing the geometry in groups with different Z-depths. Notice the variable width line used to outline the shapes. (Based on the artwork of Marc Tetro. Directed by Phillip Stamp. © Tube Nunavut Inc. © Marc Tetro.)

6.10 Hardware Rendering

In the majority of projects complex rendering operations were traditionally calculated by the software, and only the simplest operations were simulated in hardware. Computer systems in the early 1990s, for example, rendered only in batch mode but also had the ability to create an instant **hardware preview** with limited features. Hardware previews then were limited to simple shading techniques, and rarely included image or bump maps. But rendering in real-time changed with the advent of powerful and affordable graphics cards such as those manufactured, for example, by NVIDIA, ATI, and 3D Labs. These cards add significant rendering power to computers used for three-dimensional computer animation as well as computer game platforms (Fig. 6.10.1). The rendering capabilities of the popular game platforms are impressive: the Sony Playstation 2, for example, renders 66 million triangles per second; the NVIDIA-powered Microsoft's X-Box renders 125 million triangles; and Nintendo's GameCube renders 12 million triangles per second (Fig. 1.2.10). Figure 6.10.2 shows an environment from the game ***Spyro the Dragon*** rendered on a Playstation, and Figure 6.12.7 shows screens from the ***Oddworld: Munch's Oddysee*** game rendered on an X-Box.

Many of today's graphics cards are capable of significant rendering complexity. This is possible not only because of an increased number of microelectronic components in the card itself, but also because some rendering algorithms have been built into the silicon chip. The rendering power of the newer generations of graphics cards is exemplified, for example, by ATI's Radeon 9800 Series technical specifications: programmable vertex and pixel shaders in hardware, up to eight parallel rendering pipelines, up to 16 textures per pixel rendering pass, up to 128-bit per pixel color resolution, shadow volume rendering acceleration, over 18 billion full-scene antialiasing samples per second, fast Z-Buffer sorting, support of high-degree complex curved surfaces, and continuous tessellation levels per polygon for dynamic levels of detail (LOD). In addition to their three-dimensional rendering features, several high-end graphics cards are also capable of processing video with real-time features like capturing video at standard and high-definition and decoding MPEG-2 files. **Vertex shaders** are routines in the graphics card pipeline that can process the vertex data passed on by the three-dimensional game engine. This vertex data ultimately describes the triangles in the polygonal mesh, and it includes the position of the vertex, the diffuse color, the specular color, up to four pairs of texture coordinates, and the range of fog. Some graphics cards offer programmable vertex shaders, and this makes possible to customize the operations on vertex data. Vertex shaders are versatile and can even be used to calculate automatic skinning of a motion skeleton.

In addition to their built-in hardware rendering rendering features a few graphics cards are fully programmable. This means that custom rendering shaders may be developed and then rendered in

6.9.3 The colors in this watercolor simulation are animated to reflect the changing time in day as well as the mood of the Fisherman. (*Fishing*, a PDI Short Film by David Gainey.)

hardware in real-time. The **Cg graphics language** and the CgFX file format developed by nVIDIA, for example, can be used to create and save platform-independent shaders for hardware rendering. Figure 6.10.1 shows a realistic character rendered on an nVIDIA GeForce FX card with shaders written in the Cg language. In general terms the shaders written in Cg are compiled, or translated, by the graphics card to the graphics API used by a particular computer system. An **API**, or Application Program Interface, is the set of low-level commands used to display images on the computer screen. **Open GL** and **DirectX** are the two most popular APIs used today.

Many programmable hardware shaders are as versatile as some of the nonreal-time software rendering. The realistic character in Figure 6.10.1, for example, includes several Cg hardware shaders. Two vertex shaders drive her motion: a branching skeletal shader where the body mesh is driven by the animation rig, and a blend shape shader that deforms her face based on control parameters. A skin shader uses a complex combination of color maps, specular maps, and blood characteristic maps to produce human-like realistic skin. This shader calculates the oiliness of the skin surface and the amount of blood that runs just beneath the surface. Lighting subtleties are accomplished with a series of maps for diffuse specular and highlight skin lighting. An anisotropic hair shader calculates different values for hair strands depending on their orientation and external stimuli. A translucent wing shader modifies the color reflected off the wings as well as the amount of light passing through the wings based on viewing and light angles.

6.11 File Formats for Rendering

All three-dimensional rendering programs can save and retrieve rendered images—also called **picture files**—in their own native file format. Some rendering programs also have the capability of saving rendered image files in one or more standard file formats. This capability enhances the software's ability to share image files with other application programs or across computer platforms. For that reason we shall focus here briefly only on the file formats that can be used to exchange image files with other programs or with other computers (Fig. 6.11.1). Consult your software's manual for information about its own native rendering file format. (See Chapter 15 for additional information on file formats.)

Image or picture files are not to be confused with model files. Image files contain only two-dimensional information and can be

6.9.4 Zoe the girl is rendered in a style that resembles *gouache* painting. (© 2002 Sparkling*, CGI by Sparx*.)

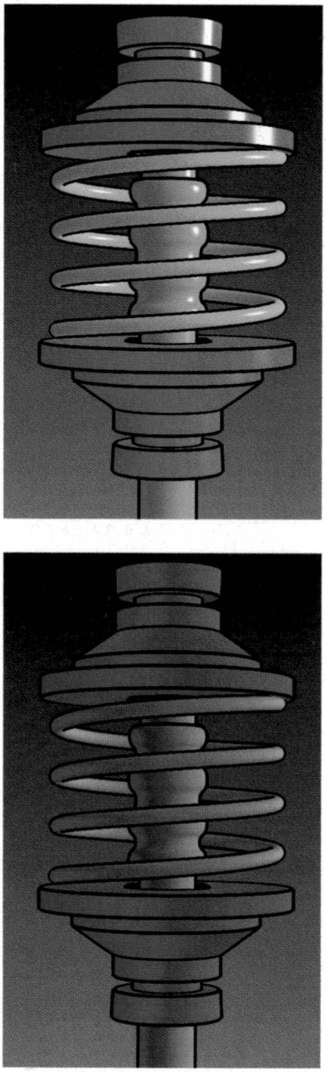

6.9.5 Non-photorealistic rendering showing the results obtained with a new shading model with highlights, a cool-to-warm hue shift and edge lines (top), and an approximation of this technique using conventional Phong shading, two colored lights, and edge lines. (© 1998 Amy Gooch.)

manipulated in three-dimensional space only by being mapped onto an object. In addition to their own native file formats, the majority of rendering programs offer one or all of the most popular picture file formats including: TIFF, TGA, JPEG, QuickTime, EPS, and Cineon. Each of these file formats has been designed with a specific goal in mind and, therefore, each is suited to a particular task (Fig. 15.3.1). It is also possible to translate files from one format to another. Sometimes this can be accomplished within rendering programs that have internal picture file conversion capabilities. But especially when large amounts of picture file conversion are needed, it is common to use a specialized file conversion program like Adobe Photoshop or one of several standalone utility conversion programs.

Generally speaking, in an everyday production environment and when translators for exotic file formats are not available or do not work, the following standard formats would be good choices. For example, the TIFF format for best halftone detail quality, the EPS format for high-quality line drawings of wireframe renderings, the QuickTime format for compressed and portable animated sequences, and the Cineon format to store wide dynamic ranges. In theory—and most of the time in practice too—these file formats are portable both across platforms and operating systems (Fig. 6.11.2).

The **TIFF** file format (Tagged Image File Format) is popular with prepress and publishing software and useful when the rendered image will be reproduced in a publication. The TIFF format preserves detailed grayscale information that can be very useful for generating the high-quality halftones (grids of dots of varying size) commonly required in publications. TIFF files tend to be large in size so many applications usually provide options or utilities for compressing and uncompressing them. The **TGA** file format is very popular with video-oriented software and is very efficient and quite convenient for transferring files into the video environment. TGA is short for TARGA, the name of a family of graphics boards developed in the early 1980s that pioneered video input and output with microcomputers. The **JPEG** file format uses a very efficient image compression technique, which can affect the resolution and quality of the image (Fig. 15.3.3). Because of their compact sizes JPEG files are commonly used to transfer low-resolution images through the Internet. The **QuickTime** file format is useful for saving still images, animated sequences, and sound in a variety of levels of image compression and quality (Fig. 15.3.4). QuickTime also supports different rates of frames per second, video streaming, and sound MIDI compatibility. The **EPS** file format, or Encapsulated PostScript, is popular in prepress applications, and can be quite useful and effective when high-quality line wireframe drawings are needed. EPS files usually require significant amounts of memory for storage and transfer. The **Cineon** uncompressed file format is commonly used to capture the subtlety and dynamic range of images originally recorded on motion picture film, and it typically allocates 10 bits of color depth for each RGB channel. (Read Chapter 15 to learn about additional image file formats.)

6.10.1 This character was rendered in real time using custom shaders with an NVIDIA GeForceFX graphics card. *Dawn* has 203,741 triangles, a 98-bone skeleton, and 50 morph targets for facial animation. (© 2002 NVIDIA Corporation. All rights reserved.)

6.12 Getting Ready

Rendering can be a complex process because of the large number of factors that play a role in it. That is not to say that rendering is necessarily complicated. Most of the individual steps in the rendering process are actually simple. But when the steps are all taken into account and added up, the result requires a thorough understanding of the process and some basic management skills to keep track of all the subtleties and implications buried in our choices of tools and techniques. The recommendations presented here are meant to make the rendering process as successful and effective as possible.

Take Notes and Don't Throw Them Away

Even the simplest three-dimensional scene contains a large number of variables that define how the rendered objects will look when the rendering is calculated by the computer. It is always useful to write all or some of these numbers down in a notebook or a production log. It is also, of course, very important not to misplace this notebook and to have it handy at all times during the rendering process. Writing all the rendering information on a small piece of paper is not good practice, since this can easily be lost. Sometimes while a scene is being rendered by the computer we want to review the informa-

6.10.2 On average there are about 7,000 polygons per environment (not including the characters) in the *Spyro the Dragon*™ game, rendered on a Playstation game platform. (Image courtesy of Universal Interactive Studios, Inc. and Insomniac Games, Inc.)

tion we fed into the program. Depending on the computer system we are using, it is possible to get this information even while the program is rendering. Obviously, in those situations it is not necessary to have a notebook at hand, but the book really comes in handy when the computer system cannot be interrupted for us to browse through the information we need while the program renders. It could be important to have a book in cases when our access to the computer is restricted by reasons beyond our control: the system is being backed up and cannot be accessed, we might be traveling and the batteries of our portable computer suddenly lose charge, we are at our client's location and their telnet connection to our computer system just went down, or we are at the beach for the weekend, thinking about our project with just a bathing suit and a towel at hand.

6.11.1 Image files are translated many times from one format to another during the course of production. This image was saved in multiple file formats and computers, transferred via networks, and output to a digital film recorder. You would never know that the file was transferred from format to format and from system to system just by looking at it!

File Formats for Still Images

.bmp	Bitmap
.cin	Cineon
.eps	Encapsulated PostScript
.gif	GIF
.jpg, .jpeg	JPEG
.pic, .pict	Picture
.qt	QuickTime
.tga	TARGA
.tiff	TIFF

6.11.2 Some of the most popular file formats (and their name extensions) for still images are listed here. Read Chapter 15 for a full description of these and other file formats.

6.12.1 (opposite page) This dialog box illustrates the importance of checking the global preferences of the rendering program before starting the rendering of a model. (© Alias|Wavefront, a division of Silicon Graphics Limited.)

Rendering Is Related to Modeling

As explained throughout Section II of this book, many of the decisions we make during the modeling process have a direct impact on the performance of the rendering software. In general, and under the same rendering conditions, models that were built properly render quicker than models that were built clumsily. When we are in charge of building the models, it can be easy to diagnose the cause of rendering problems that might have their origin in inadequate modeling decisions. But as you probably know by now, in some cases, due to production deadlines or lack of skills, we might not have modeled the objects that we are in charge of rendering. In those cases it is imperative that we find out what techniques were used to build the models, whether they were used properly or not, and whether the rendering requirements were taken into account during the modeling process.

Some modeling situations that can be the source of rendering headaches—this may vary from software to software—include intersecting polygons, concave polygons, open polygons, surfaces with holes that have not been built properly, surfaces that are supposed to be aligned with each other but have small cracks between them, models with more control vertices or polygons than the rendering software can handle, models that were exported between modelers where some original modeling attributes got lost or altered during the translation process, and objects containing other objects that were not supposed to be there. Sometimes we can work around these modeling deficiencies by modifying the rendering variables or by switching to another rendering technique. But it is not uncommon to have to go back to the modeling stage, fix the modeling problems, and then return to the rendering stage with a proper model file.

Rendering Is Related to Animation

There is a big difference between rendering just one view of a three-dimensional scene and rendering hundreds of frames of that scene as part of an animated sequence or an interactive walk-through. In general, when using the identical rendering technique—and regardless of the computer system being used—rendering just one view takes a lot less time than rendering many views of the same scene. This means that often we can overindulge in rendering sophistication when we are working on just one scene. We can set complex lighting arrangements, multiple texture layers and many levels of ray tracing. If it does not look good, we can try it again, twice, five, or ten times until we get it right. But when we work on dozens or hundreds of frames we have to be realistic and choose rendering settings that can be completed by our system within our deadline or within a reasonable period of time. When choosing the rendering specifications for an animation, be cautious and consider the capabilities and rendering speed of your equipment. Test how long it takes to render one frame and multiply it by the number of frames that need to be rendered. Make sure that the frame you choose is representative of the rendering complexity in the animated sequence. It is common for the rendering specifications to vary throughout a sequence. For example, lights could be added or complex models could enter halfway through the scene.

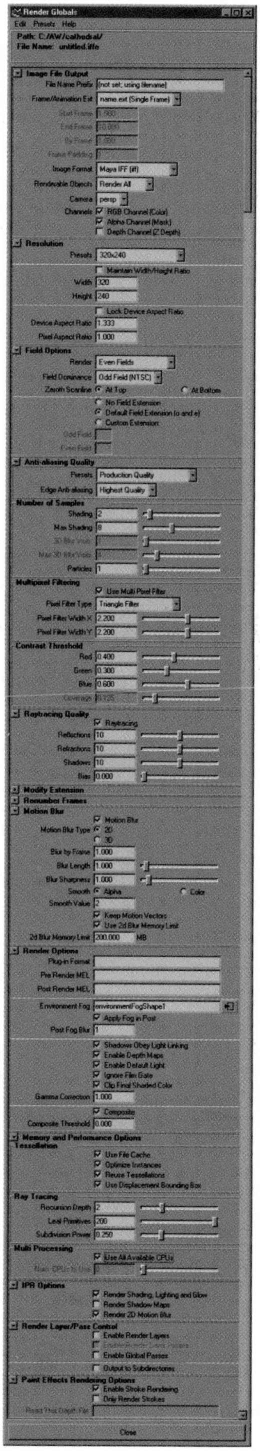

Consider the Limitations of Your Computer System

It is extremely rare to work in an environment where hardware resources are not an issue. No matter how powerful our computers may be it is always possible to overwhelm them by submitting them to a taxing rendering. It is sensible to work within rendering specifications that are based on your system's capabilities. Unless you have unlimited supply of funds to upgrade your computer system on a weekly basis, it makes sense to work and be creative within your system's limitations.

Rendering Is Related to Output

Unlike finished three-dimensional models that can be changed without having to build them from scratch even after we thought they were finished, finished renderings that we want to change have to be re-rendered all over again. Renderings are always created at a specific output resolution. Before completing a rendering—especially one that is expected to require a lot of computer processing—it is wise to consider all the output options and choose the most appropriate one. Output issues, as explained in Chapter 15, almost always have to do with issues of color, spatial, and format resolution of the rendered image or rendered sequence. Ask yourself how many images need to be rendered. One? One hundred? One thousand? Will it be viewed on an RGB monitor or a television screen? Will it be projected in a theater with a film projector or a digital projector?

Check the Preferences Files

If you work at home or if you have a dedicated computer at work, you might be the only person using your rendering program or your

REFLEC: 1, REFRAC: 0, SHAD: 0

REFLEC: 3, REFRAC: 1, SHAD: 0

REFLEC: 5, REFRAC: 3, SHAD: 1

6.12.2 These three versions of the same ray traced image are based on different combinations of ray trace depth. The depth values of reflection, refraction and shadows are in the first image 1-0-0, in the second image 3-1-0, and in the third image 5-3-1.

6.12.3 The small square area in this image is previewed in the ray tracing mode while the rest of the image was rendered with faster and less accurate techniques.

entire computer system. In that case you probably know what is contained in both the system's Preferences file and the rendering Preferences file. The settings contained in both files control many fundamental aspects of the rendering process. As shown in Figure 6.12.1 the Rendering Preferences File may be altered in ways that absolutely cancel certain operations that you might have specified within other parts of the program.

Make Rendering Tests

One advantage of using a computer for rendering three-dimensional models is that we can preview our work as we develop it. This ability to preview is very useful throughout the rendering process, especially when the final rendering is complex (Fig. 6.12.2). Making rendering tests at low resolutions or with simple shading techniques is a good way to check as we go along that all of the basic rendering specifications, like color, are being applied as we want. As we start applying more demanding rendering variables, like texture, it is useful to test again with a better shading model or higher color and spatial resolution. Finally, after we have specified in all objects the complex rendering attributes, such as refraction or motion blurr, then it might be time to make the last rendering test to visually check everything before the final rendering is produced. Remember that making rendering tests before the final rendering will save you a lot of work later trying to fix mistakes that could have been avoided (and that might require a lot of computer processing time to fix).

There are other strategies for testing rendering specifications that, unlike previewing at low resolutions or with simple shading techniques, allow us to preview the scene or part of the scene in full detail. One strategy, which is supported by several programs, consists of selecting only some objects to be rendered. For example, we might opt not to render some of the three-dimensional objects in the scene whose surface is too complex. Another strategy consists of turning off some secondary or tertiary light sources. Usually the number of light sources in a scene is proportional to the time that it takes the computer to render the scene. Finally, a third strategy, which is supported by many rendering programs that use ray tracing rendering techniques, consists of rendering just one small area of the scene but with all objects, lights, and shading attributes turned on (Fig. 6.12.3).

One of the best ways to understand both the potential and the limitations of a rendering program is by actually using it. Additional insight can also be gained by reading the technical notes—when available—that explain how a specific rendering program works. But the best way to learn and really know how the rendering tools behave is by using them. Making rendering tests and comparing the results of different rendering tests while paying attention to the different variables that were used in each case is a good way to get a feel for what the numbers—or numerical values assigned to rendering variables—mean.

Save Your Work Often

Save your work often, every fifteen minutes or so, and be sure to make frequent backups of your important data files. Data accidents occur when least expected, usually right around the time of a scheduled crucial delivery.

6.12.4 This high angle shot of *Bunny* was rendered with a combination of ray tracing techniques for the charaters and radiosity techniques for the environment and props to produce stunning results. (© 1998 Blue Sky Studios.)

Learn the Strengths of Your Software and Use Them

After you read the three chapters in this section on Rendering (or even if you decide just to look at the illustrations) it will be obvious that every software for rendering has a unique approach to different aspects of rendering. In some cases, the differences are as obvious as different names given to the same tool or different ways of presenting the information in the dialog boxes that we use for specifying values. But often the differences between rendering software are very significant, and it is often those important differences that are poorly explained in the manuals or not documented at all. In many cases it is up to you, the user, to find out some of the wonderful things that your software—and not the other programs—can do best. Explore this and take advantage of it.

6.12.5 Final composite and several shot elements (page 181) of the Tiger Claw jump effect from the feature film *Wing Commander*. (Courtesy of Digital Anvil Visual Effects, a division of Digital Anvil.)

6.12.6 This still from *Invisible Ocean*, a film by François Garnier, shows how effective carefully placed light sources can be in revealing the attributes of materials, surfaces, and objects. (Executive Production: Ex Machina. © 1998 Monaco Inter Expo. Special thanks to the Oceanographical Museum of Monaco.)

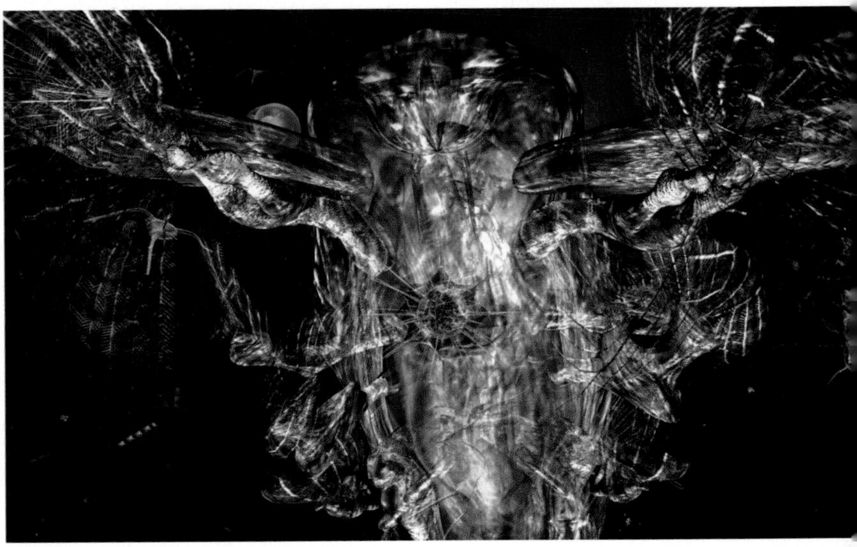

Optimize Your Renderings

6.12.7 This screen from the game *Oddworld: Munch's Oddysee*, is rendered in real-time on an X-Box game platform. (© 2003 Oddworld Inhabitants, Inc. All rights reserved. Some ™ and/or ® designate trademarks or registered trademarks of Oddworld Inhabitants, Inc. in the United States and/or other countries.)

A professional artist of three-dimensional computer rendering and animation can be defined not only by the beauty and communication power of his or her images, but also by how often he or she completes projects within the deadline. Optimizing the rendering time of an image is directly related to completing projects within deadlines, and this is done by choosing techniques in a way that creates the desired results in an efficient way (Fig. 6.12.4).

Opportunities for optimizing the rendering can be found throughout the stages of modeling and rendering stages. Use compositing techniques to assemble separate renderings into one (Fig. 6.12.5). Try using texture-mapping techniques when possible for simulating transparency, reflectivity, and roughness of a surface instead of ray tracing techniques, especially in complex scenes (Fig. 6.12.6). When ray tracing is a must, try to keep the ray tracing depth value down. Try keeping down the number of polygons or the geometric resolution of patches in a three-dimensional model (Fig. 6.12.7).

As mentioned in Chapter 8, use only the amount of light that is really necessary to create the desired mood. This principle should be kept in mind throughout the entire creative process, not only for the final rendering but also during the rendering tests created throughout. Making rendering tests before the final rendering is submitted to the computer is essential in avoiding rendering settings that might be wasteful. Try rendering critical portions of the scene before rending the entire scene. Read Chapters 13 and 15 to learn about further optimizing possibilities by using two-dimensional techniques, and by previewing the final image in the final delivery medium and not only on the RGB monitor.

(Opposite page, left: Wireframe version of a character created with blobby surfaces; see Fig. 5.1.10 for rendered version. Image courtesy of Tim Cheung. Right: Shot elements from the feature film *Wing Commander*.)

CHAPTER 6

Key Terms

Additive
API, Application Program Interface
Area subdivision
Backwards
Blue
Brightness
Caustics
Cg graphics language
Chromatic ranges
CIE color space
Cineon
CMYK
Color bleeding
Color conversion
Cyan, Magenta, Yellow, Black
Depth sort
DirectX
EPS file format
Finite dynamic range
Global illumination
Green
Hardware preview
Hidden surfaces
HSB, HSL
HDR, high dynamic range
Hue
Hybrid rendering
Image-based rendering
Interreflection of light
JPEG file format
Image space
Light-based
Light meter
Lightness
Models
Non-photorealistic rendering, NPR
Number of light sources
Number of pixels
Object space
Open GL
Photon maps
PICS file format
PICT file format
Picture files
Pigment-based
Point sampling
QuickTime
Radiance
Radiosity
Ray tracing
Ray tracing depth
Red
Reflection rays
Refraction rays
Rendering in layers
Rendering process
RenderMan shading language
RGB
Saturation
Scan line
Shaders
Shadow ray
Subdivision grids
Subtractive
Tesselation
TGA file format
Thickness
TIFF file format
Toon shaders
Vertex shaders
Virtual studio
Visible surfaces
Z-buffer

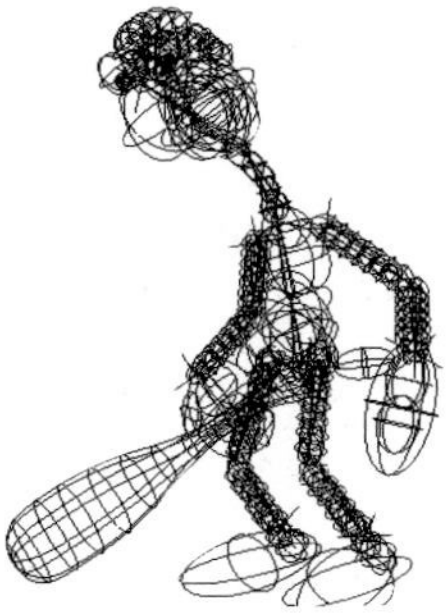

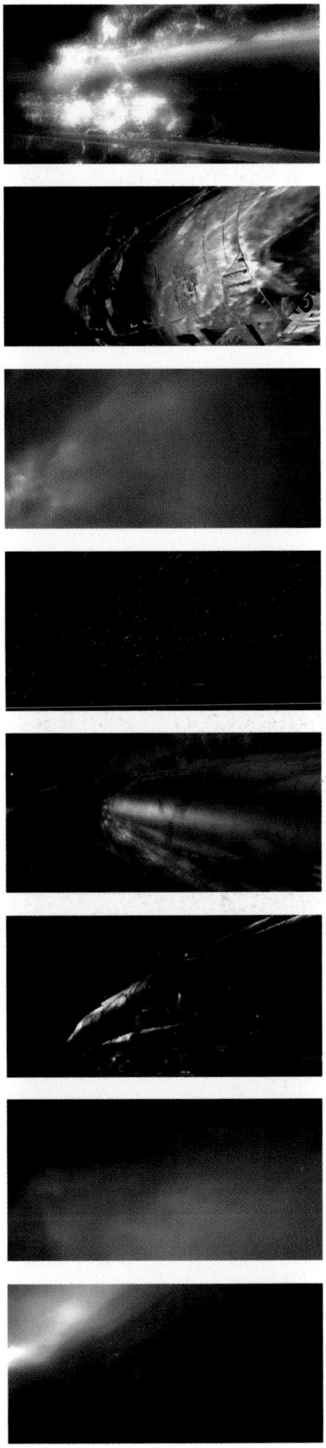

CALLEGARI BERVILLE
ExM
BONDEX
BONDEX
BONDEX
BONDEX
BONDEX
VERNIS
BONDEX
COULEUR
BONDEX

CHAPTER 7

7

The Camera

Summary

THE TECHNIQUES FOR SETTING THE CAMERA within a three-dimensional scene, and for controlling and adjusting all of its parameters are covered in this chapter. The most popular types of camera shots and lenses are also examined in this chapter.

QUICK INDEX

7.1 Types of Cameras

For more than a century we have used cameras to select and record our reality. Throughout the years cinematographers have developed a variety of camera techniques to prioritize the elements in the frame as well as the flow of the storytelling. When creating a virtual three-dimensional environment we use many of those techniques. The composition of each shot helps the audience to understand the characters in the story and their actions in the shot. Without a **virtual camera** our computer-generated worlds and stories could not be seen or shown, let alone recorded.

Cameras are a small but essential detail in the rendering process mostly because they define what we see in the shot, where we see it from, and how we see it (Fig. 7.1.1). And while many of the steps in composing the shot have to do with arranging and defining the objects in front of the camera, defining and positioning the camera itself marks the beginning of the rendering process.

In general, and for the sake of convenience, all three-dimensional rendering programs provide a **default or standard camera**. This camera is usually placed not too far from and aimed at the origin (or center) of the imaginary three-dimensional world. This virtual camera is also usually equipped with an imaginary lens of medium focal length. The lens represents the scene in front of it using **perspective projection**, which projects all objects in the three-dimensional environment onto the image plane. This is done by projecting every point in space toward the camera until the projection intersects the image plane (Fig. 7.2.1). Other views of the default camera are

7.1.1 (opposite page) This sequence of still frames from a commercial shows how camera points of view, composition, and lighting are used to guide the viewer's eye to the desired points of interest. The placement and positioning of the camera has a hand-held feeling. (Bondex *The Fashion Parade*. Images courtesy of Ex Machina. Director: Majid Loukil. Agency: Callegari-Berville. Production: Ex Machina.)

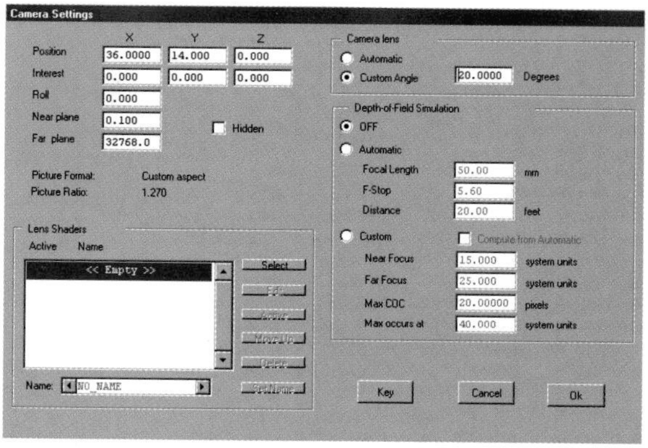

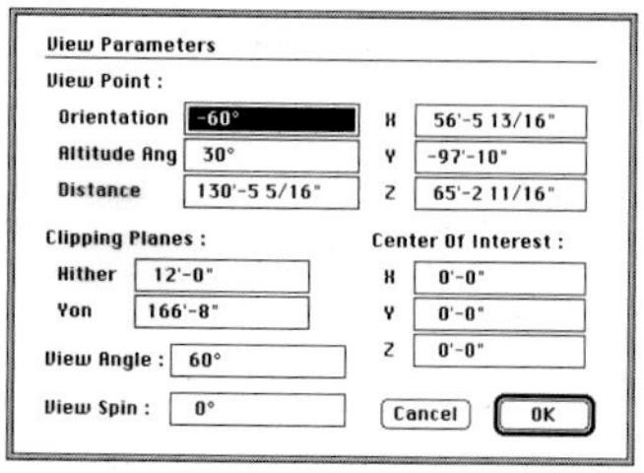

7.1.2 The numerical values that define the position and characteristics of a camera can be edited through the use of dialog boxes like these. (Top dialog box from Nature FX, courtesy of Areté Entertainment, Inc.; bottom dialog box from form•Z. © 1991–1995 auto•des•sys, Inc.)

commonly shown in the form of flat front, top, and side views known as **orthographic projections** (Fig. 3.6.2). The default camera can be modified or edited with mouse movements or through numerical input. Most three-dimensional rendering programs usually provide both methods. Figure 7.1.2 shows some dialog boxes for editing the numerical values that define a virtual camera.

Once the default camera has been customized, it can be named just like any other object in the three-dimensional environment, and its parameters and position can be saved in a file independently from the geometry of the other objects in the world. This ability to save and retrieve the name of the camera and related information makes it possible to apply any **predefined position** with ease to the **active camera** in the scene. It is also possible to create other cameras in addition to the default camera, but when **multiple cameras** are present in three-dimensional space only one camera can be active at a time. An animated sequence or a collection of still images can be created with multiple cameras that become active one after the other as the action in the scene develops and the camera moves around or switches in sequence between different points of view.

In the wireframe display mode, cameras are usually represented with graphic icons that resemble cameras. When multiple cameras are placed in a scene, the secondary cameras placed inside of the field of vision can be seen by the main camera, unless they are made **invisible**. In many programs, all cameras are visible by default, and when the scene is rendered they appear in the image as small three-dimensional icons that usually look like little cameras.

What a virtual camera sees in three-dimensional space is defined by the type of shot, the image aspect ratio, and the type of lens. These characteristics can be set by typing numerical values on the keyboard, by clicking on the control buttons provided by some programs, or by directly manipulating the camera with a variety of input peripherals that include the mouse, graphics tablet, trackball, joystick, or dial box.

7.2 The Pyramid of Vision

The **pyramid of vision**, also called the **cone of vision,** can be defined as the portion of the three-dimensional environment that is seen through the camera. The pyramid of vision provides a simple way to understand some of the technical concepts involved in rendering. The pyramid of vision is defined by several parameters that are essential for controlling the position and characteristics of the camera. This numerical information includes the point of view and the point of interest, the line of sight, the near and far clipping

7.1.3 (opposite page) The composition of this shot from *Polygon Family* is balanced and also dynamic. The vertical elements anchor it and the diagonals give it motion. (© POLYGON PICTURES/IPA/NK-EXA.)

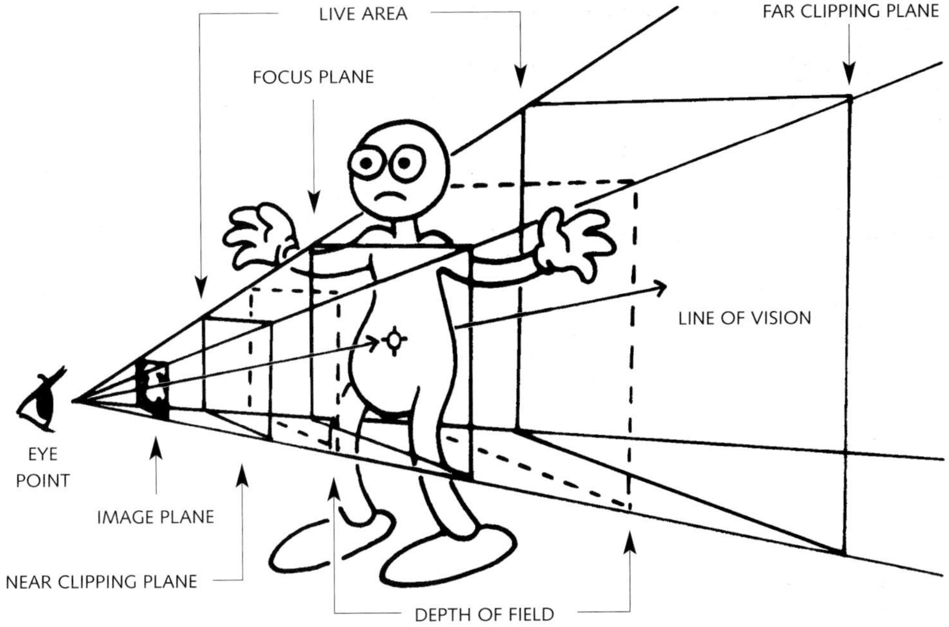

7.2.1 The pyramid, or cone, of vision shows the visible space defined by the near and far clipping planes, and within it the depth of field area. Also shown are the image and the focus plane, the eyepoint, and the line of vision representing the position of the camera and its orientation. The point of interest is represented by the target on the belly of the character. (Next 2 pages: frames from *Alien Song*, © 1999 Victor Navone.)

planes, the field of vision, the viewing angle, the focal length, and the depth of field (Fig. 7.2.1).

The pyramid of vision can be represented as a four-sided pyramid that grows out of the camera in the direction in which the camera is pointing. As mentioned earlier, the objects that are located inside of this pyramid can be viewed by the camera. The objects—or parts of objects—that happen to be outside of the pyramid of vision are not seen by the camera.

Points of View and Interest

The **point of view (POV)**, or viewing point, is the location in the scene where the camera is placed. The **point of interest (POI)**, or center of interest, is the location in space where the camera is focused. The **line of sight** in the pyramid of vision is defined as a perpendicular line that travels away from the camera, from the point of view to the point of interest.

Clipping Planes

The clipping planes are perpendicular to the line of sight. The **far clipping plane**, also called the **yon plane**, defines the most distant area that can be seen by the camera. Think, for example, of a landscape with fog in the distance when we cannot see beyond the fog. In that case, the fog would be the far clipping plane in our field of vision (see Chapter 9 for more information on fog). The **near clip-**

(*Alien Song*. © 1999 Victor Navone.)

ping plane, also called the **hither plane**, represents the area closest to the camera that is visible to the camera. Think, for example, of your own eyelashes. Your eyes cannot see them because your eyelashes are placed before your own eyes' near clipping plane and, therefore, outside your field of vision. The **viewing angle** defines the size relation between the near and the far clipping planes. The viewing angle also defines the width spread of the pyramid of vision and, consequently, the focal length.

Field of Vision

The clipping planes truncate the pyramid of vision and define the **field of vision** and the **image plane**. The objects contained inside the field of vision are projected onto the image plane to create a two-dimensional image of the three-dimensional environment. This projection process is quite similar to the way in which a real scene is projected by the optical lens used in a photographic camera onto the film that is loaded inside the camera. The relation between the width and the height of the image plane defines the **aspect ratio**, or proportion, of the image. **Media formats** such as film, video, or still photography each have their own characteristic aspect ratio. With the exception of a few square formats used in still photography—2.25 × 2.25 in., for example—all computer-simulated cameras have a rectangular aspect ratio usually in a horizontal orientation, also called **landscape format**. The **portrait format**, as its name indicates, evolved as the most convenient way to frame portraits of individuals and focus on their faces and/or figures. Some of the most common media formats and their aspect ratios are shown in Figure 15.5.1. **Field guides** are grids of concentric rectangles used to position the still elements and the action within the frame (Fig. 7.2.2). In animation production, field guides can be used to specify zooming of the camera and to "block" the areas of the shot that can safely contain important action, titles, or credits.

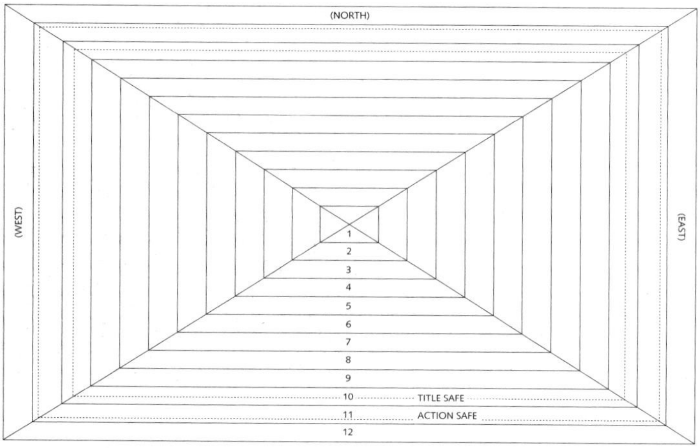

7.2.2 A field guide of 1:1.377 ratio (35 mm Academy format) consists of 12 concentric rectangles that help position the still elements and the action within the frame. The title safe and action safe areas for field 12 are shown with dotted lines.

Focal Length

The focal length of a camera controls the way in which three-dimensional objects are seen by the camera. The **focal length** in a virtual camera is defined by the relation between the near clipping plane and the far clipping plane. This relation defines the way in which the objects in a three-dimensional environment are projected onto the projection plane of a virtual camera—or the surface of the

film in a real camera. The focal length in a photographic camera is determined by the curvature and shape of the lens, and by the distance between the lens and the image plane. Standard camera lenses have a fixed focal length, except for zoom lenses that are capable of variable focal lengths by gradually changing, in real time, the distance between the near and the far clipping planes. Virtual camera lenses can simulate almost any focal length (Figs. 7.4.2–7.4.3).

Depth of Field

The **focal plane** of a lens is the plane perpendicular to the camera that is resolved into a sharp image. Only one plane in three-dimensional space can be in perfect focus when seen through any lens, but the areas that neighbor the focal plane are in focus. The **depth of field** is the portion of the scene in front of the camera that appears focused, and it is defined by the area between the near and the far focal planes. In renderings with a shallow depth of field, many elements appear out of focus (Figs. 7.2.3 and 7.2.4), while scenes with ample depths of field yield images with an overall sharpness that spans from the foreground to the background (Fig. 7.2.5).

7.2.3 The shallow depth of field, the tight framing, the soft lighting, and the tilt of the head all contribute to a feeling of intimacy. This is also an example of facial animation with a single model that was deformed, without blend shapes, using facial motion capture data as a guide for deformation. (© NAMCO Ltd. All rights reserved.)

7.3 Types of Camera Shots

Cameras, like other objects in three-dimensional space, can be placed in specific spatial locations in a variety of ways. The process of finding a position for a camera is called **interactive camera placement,** and sometimes **navigation** because we navigate through three-dimensional space looking through the camera. Stationary cameras that can be used to render still images can be placed with numerical input, interactive mouse movements, or predefined positions (dynamic cameras are described in Chapter 11). Navigation is essential for framing the objects, virtual actors, and scenery in an effective way. This process can take place during or before the rendering process in order to focus on specific areas of interest and tell the story more effectively.

7.2.4 Notice the narrow depth of field in this low angle view of Bunny that emphasizes the tension and prepares the viewer for a surprise. (© 1998 Blue Sky Studios.)

When using the numerical input method, cameras can be positioned and repositioned by specifying two absolute XYZ locations: camera position or point of view (POV), and camera point of interest. Cameras can also be positioned and repositioned using interactive mouse movements. This activates two of the basic geometric transformations: translation and rotation. All of the camera moves, even the most complex ones, can be expressed in terms of translations or rotations around one or several camera axes. But in some cases, the spherical or azimuthal coordinate system illustrated in Figure 3.4.8 is used to specify the camera's position and orientation in terms of its angles around and above the horizon and its distance from the object. (See Chapter 3 for more information on geometric transformations.)

Navigating in some programs is often accomplished by clicking buttons and dragging tools that control the camera. Other programs offer a menu of complex camera motions that can be chosen and controlled by dragging the mouse. Another technique for focusing the camera in a specific orientation consists of choosing **predefined** points of interest. These are available from pull-down menus, usually in the form of an absolute XYZ position, or an absolute angle such as $X=45^\circ$ $Y=30^\circ$ $Z=60^\circ$, or the name of an object in the scene, such as, point at the table.

There are several types of **stationary camera shots**. Each one has a specific name and an inherent **narrative and psychological effect**. Most stationary camera shots can be described in terms of their point of view, point of interest, the distance to the subject, and the type of lens used. Some of the most common camera shots are listed in Figure 7.3.1. (Animated camera moves are described in Chapter 11.)

Both the point of view and the point of interest are used to define the traditional camera shots: point of view (POV), low angle,

7.2.5 The golden hour lighting effect typical of sunset is recreated in this shot. A tilted camera accentuates the perspective. (© NAMCO Ltd. All rights reserved.)

high angle, and reverse angle shot. The distance from the camera to the subject and the type of lens used defines the area of the scene that is captured by the camera. The camera shots based on the area of the scene that is framed within the image are illustrated in Figure 7.3.2 and include extreme close-up, close-up, medium close-up, waist, medium, knee, wide, long, medium long, and extreme long shots. Many software programs use the same names used in traditional cinematography to define camera shots, but some use a different nomenclature.

Point of View Shots

Point of view shots often place the camera at eye level looking straight into the action, because in many circumstances it is assumed that the active character is standing in front of the action. But generally speaking, a point of view shot cannot be pegged to an absolute spatial position, because by definition its location is always relative to where the active character happens to be. A **point of view shot** shows what the active character, narrator, or virtual cameraperson sees. This type of shot places the camera wherever the eyes of the active character happen to be and sets the orientation of the camera according to the direction in which the active character or narrator is looking (Fig. 7.3.2).

7.2.6 High angle shot of a user-contolled camera in a multiplayer online game. (© 2002 Cyan Worlds, Inc. All rights reserved.)

Types of Camera Shots
Extreme close-up
Close-up
Medium close-up
Waist
Medium
Knee
Wide
Long
Medium long
Extreme long

7.3.1 Using different types of camera shots gives motion pictures their rhythm, intonation, point of view, and narrative tension.

(Credits for Fig. 7.3.2, opposite page. Extreme close-up: © Michael Koch. Close-up: ReBoot® and © 1997 Mainframe Entertainment, Inc. All rights reserved. Medium close-up: © Jim Ludtke. Waist: Copyright Westwood Studios. All rights reserved. Medium: Copyright Lionhead Studios. Knee: © 1998 Square Co., Ltd. All rights reserved. Wide: © POLYGON PICTURES, IPA/NK-EXA. Long: Copyright 1999 Oddworld Inhabitants, Inc. All rights reserved. Medium long: Copyright Lionhead Studios. Point of view: Images courtesy of Ex Machina, full credits in Fig. 10.2.2. Low angle: Copyright Westwood Studios. High angle: © 1998 Blue Sky Studios.)

Low Angle and High Angle Shots

In low angle and high angle shots, the camera is pointed at the action with a certain slant. The angle is usually defined in relation to the point of interest so that a **low angle shot** places the camera below the point of interest, looking up (Fig. 7.3.2). Inversely, a **high angle shot** places the camera looking down at the point of interest, placed above it (Figs. 6.12.4 and 7.2.6). The amount of slant in low and high angle shots is never implied and has to be defined explicitly in the form of an XYZ position or a specific angle measured in degrees. The range of low angle shots includes, for example, what a cameraperson would see if shooting lying down or in a kneeling position, or if shooting while standing up at street level and looking up at the action occurring on the roof of a house. High angle shots range from a cameraperson shooting over a crowd or perched on a ladder to a camera mounted on a helicopter hovering over a crowd.

Reverse Angle Shots

Reverse angle shots are commonly used in conversations between two people where the sequence includes shots back and forth between the two faces. A **reverse angle shot** always happens as a response to a previous shot. A typical reverse angle shot sequence starts with the camera placed over the shoulder of character A so that character B speaks to the camera. The reverse angle shot is then placed over the shoulder of character B, and it shows character A responding to what character B said in the previous shot (Fig. 7.3.3).

Close-Up Shots

A **close-up shot** places the camera at close range so that details in the subject can be appreciated. An **extreme close-up shot** is even closer to the subject than a close-up and presents delicate surface details such as the veins in the leaf of a plant or the pores of skin (Fig. 5.2.2). A close-up shot usually fills the image with the subject in question and crops all other items in the picture (Fig. 7.2.3). A close-up of a face, for example, shows nuances of expression. A close-up of a cut precious stone focuses on the delicate interplay of the facets and the refracted light. A **medium close-up shot** presents subjects close to the camera while leaving some of space between the subject and the edge of the frame to include a small portion of the background. A medium close-up of the face of a character is often called a **head shot** because it focuses on the face, neck, and shoulders. Head shots typically focus on facial expression and head movements (Fig. 10.1.1).

Medium and Wide Shots

A **waist shot** presents characters from the waist up. A waist shot focuses on the upper body language and gestures of the character,

7.3.2 Using different types of camera shots gives motion pictures their rhythm, intonation, point of view, and narrative tension. (Credits on opposite page.)

and includes a fair amount of the three-dimensional environment surrounding the character. Heads and faces are never cropped in a regular waist shot (Fig. 1.3.6). A **medium shot** frames characters from the hips up (Fig. 14.3.1). A **knee shot** crops the subjects at the knees, and is commonly used in shots of an encounter or conversation between two or three characters (Fig. 7.3.2). A **wide shot** presents enough of the scene to include the full bodies of five characters (Fig. 12.2.2).

7.3.3 A reverse angle shot showing a moment in the wordless conversation between a cowboy and a mosquito. (© 2001 Angela Jedek.)

Long Shots

A **long shot** focuses on the scenery and barely permits recognition of individual characters in the environment (Fig. 1.4.1). Wide and long shots are both used in animated sequences as establishing shots to introduce the place where a scene is supposed to be taking place. A **medium long shot** typically presents a landscape and focuses on features like the topography and the sky, the ambient lighting, the weather, and the time of day. An **extreme long shot** presents environments seen from very far away, for example, the planet Earth seen from an orbiting spacecraft.

7.4 Types of Camera Lenses

Most three-dimensional rendering software provides an infinite range of camera lenses that can be used for practical and stylistic purposes. The **practical use** of switching camera lenses is to modify the size of objects in the image without having to move the camera. The **stylistic use** of employing different camera lenses is to create different moods in the scene by simulating different perspective projections. The emotional effect of a wide angle lens, for example, is intense and can even be frightening because objects look distorted. The opposite emotion is aroused with a telephoto lens, one of tranquility and detachment because the objects in the scene are not distorted and most of the lines in the composition are horizontal and static.

Camera lenses, whether real or simulated, are perhaps the most important component in any camera system because they define the way in which the three-dimensional world is projected onto the **projection plane** of a camera. In photographic cameras, the photosensitive film is located exactly on the projection plane. The projection plane of computer-simulated rendering cameras can be positioned virtually anywhere in space.

Photographers refer to camera lenses in terms of their focal length because this characteristic controls the way in which three-dimensional objects are seen by the camera (Fig. 7.4.1). Focal length, as explained earlier, is defined by the distance from the point of view to the focal plane. Most photographic camera lenses have a **fixed focal length**, except for the so-called zoom lenses that contain multiple lenses and are therefore capable of a range of **variable focal lengths**. Figure 7.4.2 illustrates the effect of changing the focal length of a virtual camera by increasing and decreasing the distance between the point of view to the focal plane. Lenses simulated with rendering software are not limited to the standard focal lengths of photographic lenses that are listed in Figure 7.4.1.

The standard nomenclature for the focal length of lenses is expressed in millimeters (mm). There is a great variety of lenses, but the staple lenses used in traditional photography and cinematography include a normal 50 or 55 mm lens, a wide angle 28 mm lens,

Focal Lengths of Popular Lenses	
Fisheye	7.5 mm
Extreme Wide	18 mm
Wide Angle	28 mm
Medium Wide	35 mm
Standard	50 to 55 mm
Medium Long	80 mm
Long (Telephoto)	135 to 250 mm
Extra Long (Supertelephoto)	500 mm or more

7.4.1 Typical focal lengths of popular types of lenses used in photography, cinematography, and video.

| 5 mm, FISHEYE | 15 mm, EXTREME WIDE ANGLE | 28 mm, WIDE ANGLE |
| 50 mm, NORMAL | 80 mm, MEDIUM LONG | 100 mm, TELEPHOTO |

and a telephoto 135 mm lens. Each of the three standard lenses has characteristics that define the way images are projected onto the image plane and can be used for different situations. In general, lenses with a short focal length offer a wide angle of view and increased depth of field, but objects appear distant to the camera. Inversely, lenses with a long focal length have narrow angles of view and depth of field. The relation between the focal length of lenses and their angle of view is illustrated in Figure. 7.4.3.

The area of the scene that is framed within the image can be defined by three different variables: the type of lens used, by the distance between the camera and the subject, or by both. In the first case, when the type of lens is varied, it is assumed that the distance between camera and subject remains constant (Fig. 7.4.3). In the second case, when the distance between camera and point of interest is changed to include more or less of the image, it is assumed that the type of lens used remains constant. Only a small portion of the scene is contained in the frame when the camera is very close to the subject. As the camera is placed further away from the subject a larger area of the scene is contained in the frame (Fig. 7.4.4).

Figure 7.4.5 illustrates three different examples of what happens when both the lens and the point of view are changed. In the first example, a 24 mm wide angle lens is placed close to the subject. The wide angle view of the lens makes the shot very panoramic and shows a large area of the scene. In the second example, a 50 mm standard lens includes less of the background in the three-dimensional environment because its angle of view is narrower than the previous lens, but the subject occupies roughly the same amount of

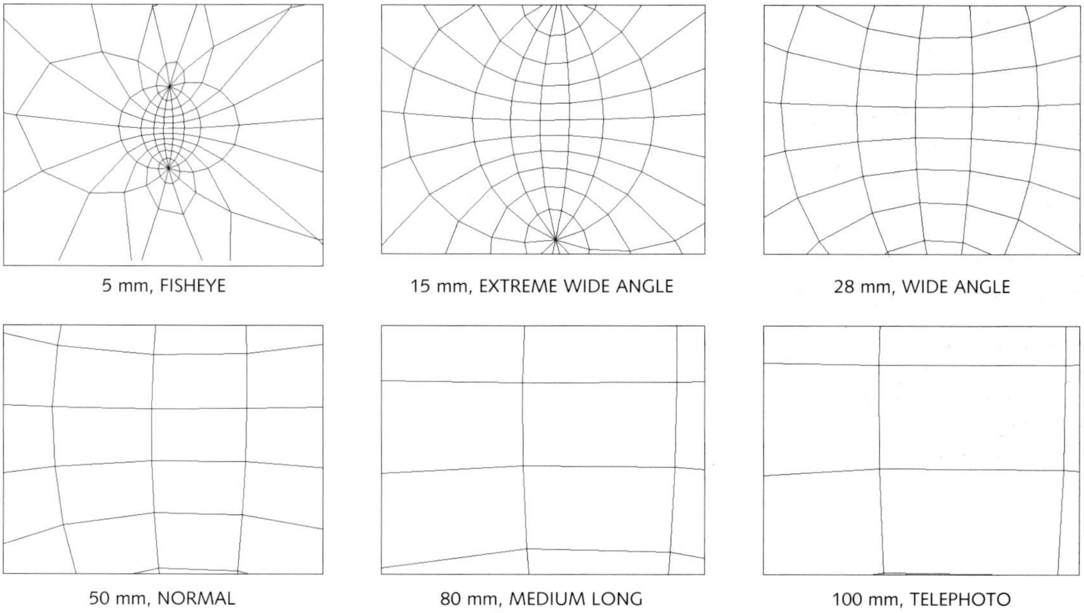

7.4.2 A camera placed inside of a sphere "sees" a different image each time a different lens is used. The scene viewed through a normal lens with a focal length of 50 mm looks similar to the way we see reality with our vision. The diagonal lines are steeper and the perspective projection is more extreme with the 28 or 15 mm lenses. The same scene viewed through a 5 mm wide angle lens looks distorted and tense. The 80 or 100 mm telephoto lenses flatten the perspective due to their narrow viewing angle and the similarity between the areas of the near and far clipping plane. The focal length of a camera can be changed by modifying the distance between the point of view and the focal plane. The magnification of the scene viewed through the lens is directly proportional to the focal length.

7.4.3 As the focal length of a fixed lens increases its angle of view decreases.

image area. In the third example, a 135 mm telephoto lens is placed far from the rings. Due to its long focus (or ability to concentrate on distant objects) the image retains as much of the subject as the previous lenses, but it includes little of the scenery.

Normal Lens

The **normal 50 or 55 mm lens** offers a standard 46-degree angle of view with average depth of field. A 50 mm lens is useful for medium to wide shots because it can fill the field of vision with foreground subjects and background without flattening or distorting the perspective—as telephoto or wide angle lenses do.

Wide Angle Lens

A **wide angle 24 or 28 mm lens** supplies a generous 83-degree angle of view, outstanding depth of field. This type of lens also provides a small amount of distortion on the edges of the picture due to the forced perspective projection typical of the wide angle of vision (Fig. 7.4.6).

Telephoto Lens

A **telephoto 135 mm lens** has excellent abilities for close framing. However, it flattens the perspective and has a narrow 5-degree angle of view and a small depth of field. On occasion the wide angle and telephoto lenses can be replaced or complemented with a zoom lens that allows for a variable focal length, for example, from 35 mm to 80 mm.

7.5 Camera Animation

The camera has a powerful storytelling effect because it leads the eyes and mind of an audience through a story. Animated camera moves can be based on both changes of position and orientation.

The **camera moves** that are based on a change of the **position** of the camera include a dolly, a truck, and a boom. A **dolly** is a translation of the camera along the horizontal axis (Fig. 11.3.1). A tracking or **traveling shot** occurs when a dolly moves along with the subject and follows it. The motion paralax effects that can happen on dolly moves are described in Chapter 11. A **truck** move is a translation of the camera along the depth axis, and it usually goes in or out of the scene. A **boom** is a translation of the camera along its the vertical axis. A **crane shot** can be implemented with a combination of boom, truck, and sometimes dolly camera moves.

The camera moves that are based on the change of the **orientation** of the camera include a tilt, a roll, and a pan. A **tilt** is a rotation of the camera on its horizontal axis. A tilt is also called a pivot and is used to look up or look down. A **roll** is created by rotating

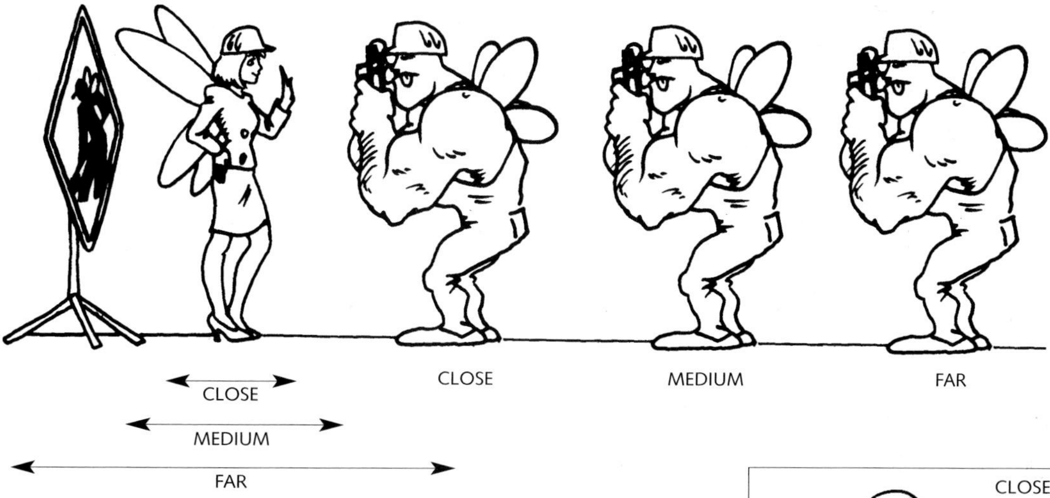

the camera around its Z axis. Roll camera moves are common when simulating fly-throughs. A **pan** is a move created by rotating the camera around its vertical axis (Fig. 11.3.2). Panning is very effective for scanning the scene from side to side while the camera remains stationary. Sometimes, especially when simulating flying cameras, a tilt move is called a pitch—as in airplanes pitching—and a pan move is called a yaw. (A zoom is a camera move that is achieved not by moving the position or orientation of the camera but by animating its focal length.)

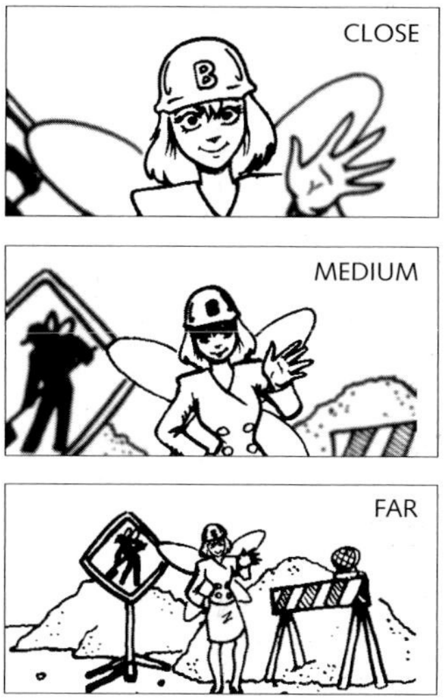

7.4.4 Both the size of the image area and the depth of field increase when a camera moves away from a fixed subject.

7.6 Getting Ready

Set the Aspect Ratio Early

The aspect ratio of a virtual camera determines the relation between the width and the height of the final image. It is important to set the correct aspect ratio of the image early on in the creative process because many decisions like composition and lighting are closely tied to it. Changing the aspect ratio in the middle of a production may mean that the placement of all the cameras, lights, and even the objects in the scene may have to be done all over again.

Composition Tips

When composing still images it is useful to remember that the arrangement of elements within the image frame plays a fundamental role in expressing the emotion or telling the story behind the image. The following composition tips can be applied to any image, regardless of the subject. Whether a composition is simple or complex, there are some basic qualities and rules that contribute to **straightforward communication**. These include the clarity of foreground subjects, the

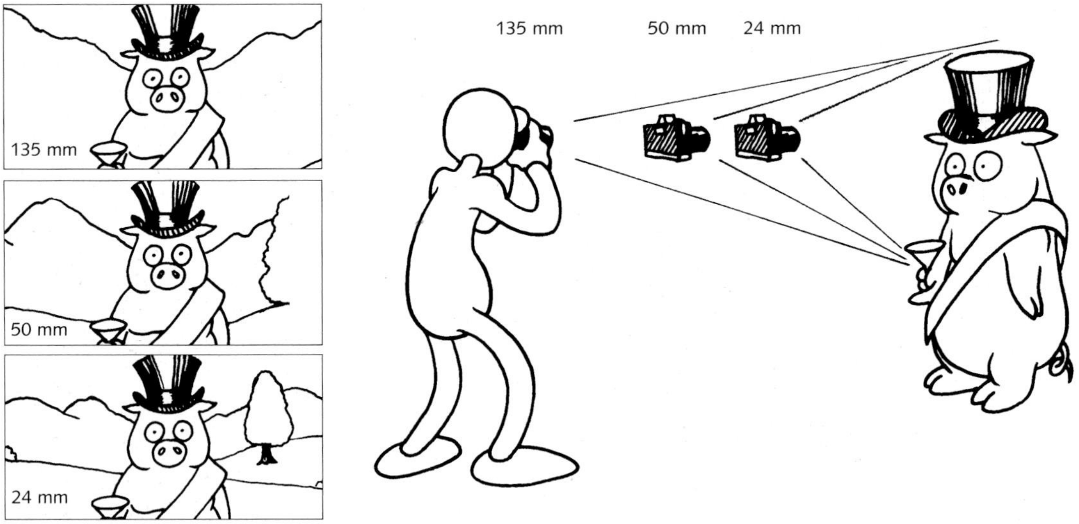

7.4.5 The pig is framed so that it occupies roughly the same amount of space in each image, but each view has been created with a different lens and distance between the camera and the pig. The subject in the foreground of the image remains within a similar scale as long as the focal length decreases or increases along with the distance between the camera and the subject. The projection of the background elements, however, is significantly different.

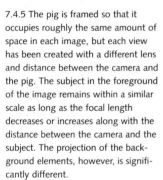

7.4.6 Wide angle lens distortion. (*Jak & Daxter* image courtesy of Naughty Dog, Inc. © 2001 Sony Computer Entertainment America, Inc.)

number of image layers between the foreground and the background, the density of the background, the relation between the foreground and the background, the relation between the center of the image and the edges, and the relation between image zones and image proportions. Figure 7.1.3 shows a shot with the main character in the foreground, walking to his destination, and the secondary characters in the middle ground as a smaller but important visual element that catches our attention. The horizontal lines in the composition add some tranquility while the perspective lines add motion.

Keep the long straight lines in the composition parallel or perpendicular to the edges of the image to avoid unwanted tension and distraction. This includes, for example, the horizon or a tall tree in a landscape tilting to one side especially when the tree is close to an edge of the image.

It is usually distracting to cut off the head of a subject in a head shot or a portion of the object in a close-up shot. However, when done skillfully, cutting off portions of the main subject can help the viewer focus on details—such as the eyes or the mouth—that may add emotion to the image.

Positioning the camera too close to an object may result in images with large unfocused areas occupied by these objects. This effect often overwhelms the rest of the image. Objects that are too close to the camera can be used to create effects of intrusion or anxiety, but they should only be used if those emotions are the right ones to present the main subject to the audience.

When image clarity is an important issue, it helps to place the main subject in a shot against plain backgrounds. Backgrounds with dense textures or with a multitude of objects and colors tend to take the attention of the viewer away from the items in the foreground.

7.6.1 The composition of this shot is balanced and also dynamic. (*Jak & Daxter* image courtesy of Naughty Dog, Inc. © 2001 Sony Computer Entertainment America, Inc. See page 328 for full credits.)

Dynamic Cameras

Unlike animated shorts or feature movies where the camera is fixed and predetermined, computer and platform games use dynamic cameras which allow game players to control what they see as they look around or as they navigate through the environment (Figs. 7.6.1–7.6.2, and 11.6.2). **Dynamic cameras** give players the ability to view the action from different points of view. At any given point in most games players may switch between multiple cameras usually located at the player's point of view, **first-person camera**, and other locations. The latter are usually called **third-person cameras** because they show other characters' point of view, but they might also include bird's eye views (Fig. 7.2.6), and cameras placed at fixed locations, the entrance to the dungeon for example. Most **dynamic cameras** are capable of six degrees of freedom: XYZ translations as the player moves, and XYZ rotations (tilt, roll, and pan) as the character looks around. Usually first-person cameras have a limited rotation range, in some games for example, it is not possible to tilt down (X rotation) a first-person camera enough to see the character's feet.

7.6.2 (Next page) Screens from the game *Oddworld: Munch's Oddysee* rendered on an X-Box game platform. (© 2003 Oddworld Inhabitants, Inc. All rights reserved.)

CHAPTER 7

Key Terms

Active camera
Aspect ratio
Boom
Camera lenses
Camera moves
Close-up shot
Cone of vision
Crane shot
Default or standard camera
Depth of field
Dolly
Dynamic cameras
Extreme close-up shot
Extreme long shot
Far clipping plane
Field guides
Field of vision
First-person camera
Fixed focal length
Focal length
Focal plane
Head shot
High angle shot
Hither plane
Image plane
Interactive camera placement
Invisible
Knee shot
Landscape format
Line of sight
Long shot
Low angle shot
Media formats
Medium close-up shot
Medium long shot
Medium shot
Multiple cameras
Narrative and psychological effect
Navigation
Near clipping plane
Normal 50 or 55 mm lens
Orientation
Orthographic projections
Pan
Perspective projection
Point of interest (POI)
Point of view (POV)
Point of view shot
Portrait format
Position
Practical use
Predefined
Predefined position
Projection plane
Pyramid of vision
Reverse angle shot
Roll
Stationary camera shot
Straightforward communication
Stylistic use
Telephoto 135 mm lens
Third-person cameras
Tilt
Traveling shot
Truck
Variable focal lengths
Viewing angle
Virtual camera
Waist shot
Wide angle 24 or 28 mm lens
Wide shot
Yon plane

CHAPTER 8

8

Lighting

Summary

THIS CHAPTER DESCRIBES THE MAIN ELEMENTS of lighting a shot, presents a variety of simple and complex lighting strategies, and covers some of the basic techniques for controlling and adjusting the lights that illuminate the environment. Lighting is an important component of the rendering process not only because it may contribute significantly to the overall processing time necessary to render the scene, but mostly because it reveals the three-dimensional world and sets the mood of the scene.

QUICK INDEX

8.1 Lighting Strategies and Mood

There are as many philosophies of lighting as there are disciplines that require lighting. This would include the performing arts—dramatic theater, musical theater, dance, opera—which usually take place indoors, and cinematography, which may take place both indoors and outdoors. Lighting designers in each of these disciplines favor particular approaches to lighting, which in turn are based on the discipline's lighting needs. Of course, within each discipline there are many different points of view. We can learn a lot of interesting lighting techniques and creative points of view by examining specific movies, plays, operas, and musicals. (Next time you have the chance to attend one of these events, pay attention to the lighting arrangements and try to figure out how they affect the mood of the moment.)

Much of the mood in any computer-generated scene is also established with the choice of lights and their arrangement (Fig. 8.1.3). Lighting can be bright and fresh, soft and intimate, multicolored and festive, or tinted and moody. Light on a scene can be even and peaceful or uneven and disturbing. The shadows created with light can be harsh and sharp or soft and slow. Many of the figures in this chapter show different moods that have been achieved mostly with the effective use of lighting. Many techniques for describing, measuring, and arranging light in the scene have been developed

Lens Aperture f/stops	
f/1	f/11
f/1.4	f/16
f/2	f/22
f/2.8	f/32
f/4	f/45
f/5.6	f/64
f/8	f/90

8.1.1 This scale lists the f/stops is used to measure the aperture of the lens, and to determine how much light will pass through it. With each additional f/stop the amout of light passing through the lens doubles. f/1 represents the lens wide open and f/90 is only a small aperture.

The Zone System	
Zone 0	3.5%
Zone I	4.5%
Zone II	6%
Zone III	9%
Zone IV	12.5%
Zone V	**17.5%**
Zone VI	25%
Zone VII	35%
Zone VIII	50%
Zone IX	70%
Zone X	100%

8.1.2 The Zone System is used to catalog the gray levels on a scale that goes from nonreflective black to absolute white. Zone V represents the average reflectance of objects.

over the years in traditional still photography and cinematography. The purpose of these techniques is to help expose the film correctly so that the shots and scenes are captured in an artistic and effective way. As of yet only a few of these basic traditional techniques have been translated into the mainstream of computer-generated lighting. While the general principles of lighting for a live action film, for example, are almost identical as those of a computer animation feature, the processes and subtleties of the craft are sometimes far apart.

The ability to control the aperture of a camera's virtual lens, for example, which is a cornerstone of everyday cinematography is just starting to be implemented in computer animation software. Perhaps one reason behind this situation is the fact that in computer animation both the camera and the lights are synthesized from scratch, while in a live action film light has to be measured in relation to the characteristics of the film stock and the desired look. A small mistake in the measurement of lighting on location can impact many other aspects of live action production in adverse ways, while in a computer animated feature there is the opportunity to interactively fine tune the lighting before commiting it to film. An important exception to this situation happens when live action and computer animation overlap in the form of a visual effect. In that case visual effects supervisors do take **light measurements on location** and the lighting technical directors do their best to replicate the lighting conditions with their computer tools. But a lot of the elements in the process of matching the live light with the computer-generated light still include a lot of trial and error. In any case, while this situation changes it is worth mentioning a couple of relevant traditional lighting concepts and techniques related to measuring the intensity of light, and a scale to measure grayscales.

The **f/stop** is a unit to measure how much light passes through the aperture of a lens. In theory an absolute aperture of the lens would allow all light passing through it to reach the film. The common scale of f/stops is roughly based on the square root of the number 2, and it represents a doubling of the additional amount of light that makes it through when the lens is opened, or the additional amount of light that does not reach the film when the lens is closed (Fig. 8.1.1). The scale of f/stops represents how traditional film reacts to light. There are a couple of additional units that are also useful to measure the intensity of light, the candela and the footcandle (Fig. 8.6.2). The **candela** represented the amount of light emitted by a certain type of light, and it is a development of the standard candle, an older unit based on the amount of light created by a candle. The **footcandle**, and its metric system equivalent the **metercandle** or **lux**, measures the amount of light that falls on a surface (one footcandle equals 10.764 lux).

The **zone system** is a technique widely used in photography to classify and balance the amount of light distributed throughout the scene. In essence the zone system, developed by photographer Ansel Adams, catalogs the grey levels in the image on a scale that goes from a pure black that barely reflects any light (Zone 0) to an

absolute white (Zone X). The grey tones of each scale between Zone 0 and Zone X are separated by one f/stop (Fig. 8.1.2). **Zone V**, which is right in the middle of the scale, is of particular importance because at about 18% reflectance of light it represents the average reflectance of objects.

8.1.3 A key light placed in front of and facing the camera is used to represent the journey of the souls in one of the last shots from the film *Bunny*. The halos around the moths helps to make them look like ghostly angels. (© 1998 Blue Sky Studios.)

Visualizing Light

Effective lighting design starts with the visualization of the effect of lights in a specific environment. Fortunately, three-dimensional rendering programs are capable of actually simulating for us specific lighting arrangements. But even when using a computer rendering program to visualize light, any lighting designer is likely to achieve a greater degree of sophistication, beauty, and efficiency if he or she spends some time imagining visualizing the effects of the planned lights before trying them with the program.

An easy way to visualize lighting consists of starting with a dark space, turning the spot lights on and then adding the ambient light in small increments. By turning on the spot lights (or any other secondary light) first, you can focus on their lighting effect because much of the scene will still be quite dark. By turning on the ambient light (or the major point light) second, and in small increments, you can visualize the blending of secondary lights with the main light. This way the overall lighting effect shows through (or builds up) while retaining at all times the light accents. If necessary, those accents—usually in the form of spot lights or colored lights—can still be turned up or down after the ambient light has been defined, and adjusted to the requirements of the scene.

The lighting design can also be visualized by starting with a space that is already lit with ambient light. In this method the lighting accents are added toward the end of the process. While the final result can be the same whether one starts visualizing a dark room or a lighted room. I find that the latter requires more concentration, greater visualization power, and perhaps a little more lighting skill.

8.1.4 The colored lighting on this nordic warrior is as dramatic as his pose and gestures. (© 1999 Midway Home Entertainment Inc. All rights reserved. Used by permission.)

White Light

Most of us assume, incorrectly, that all natural light—and artificial light to a lesser extent—is white. But light, in fact, is almost never white. Light is usually tinted. Few elements in nature (perhaps water) are as chromatically dynamic as light (Fig. 8.1.3). The color of light changes with the time of day, the weather, the landscape, and the location on earth. Just think of the chromatic differences, for example, between the light of a sunny winter afternoon in the Nordic fjords or a summer sunset in the stormy Caribbean or high noon in the clear spring skies of the Australian rocky desert. Nordic winter light might have a slight blue tint, while the light of a stormy Caribbean sunset might be the pink color of the *mamey* tropical fruit, and the spring Australian desert's light might have a slight yellow tint. The color differences in the three examples above might be subtle but very meaningful if one is trying to simulate environments like those with a three-dimensional rendering program.

The lighting effect created by a **lightning** storm can be recreated by inserting one or two white frames in the sequence just a couple of seconds before the sound of thunder is heard. After that a very strong light—placed in the area near where the lightning is supposed to have fallen—is suddenly turned up to a bright white color, and then dimmed in a flickering way.

Colored Light

We can achieve startling lighting effects by using **colored lights**. The results are always reminiscent of the performing arts where performers are literally tracked around the stage with colored lights (Fig. 8.1.4), or dance clubs where much of the festive atmosphere and visual chatter is created with constant sequences and patterns of colored lights. The visual power of colored lights is so great, however, that they must be used with prudence, especially when lighting spaces or situations where a festive atmosphere would be distracting.

A pleasing visual surprise that is very common in circus performance scenes happens when the projected lights of colored spot lights overlap with one another. This lighting resource owes its startling force to the unexpected colors that result from the mixture of colored lights (Fig. 8.1.8). Audiences are somewhat familiar with the results of mixing primary **pigment-based colors** with one another. Most have experienced this first-hand in elementary school or earlier: red and yellow gives orange, blue and yellow gives green, and red and blue gives purple. Mixtures of **light-based colors** are startling because they follow the physical rules of **additive (light-based) color systems** as opposed to **subtractive (pigment-based) color systems.** It is always entertaining to puzzle your friends with a demonstration of the basic color mixtures in a light-based, three-dimensional rendering system: green and blue make cyan, blue and red make magenta, and (my favorite one) red and green make yellow.

8.1.5 Tinted lights were used to soften and color the shadows in this shot. Based on the novel *parasite EVE* by Hideaki Sena (Kadokawa Horror Bunko). Character designed by Tetsuya Nomura.)

Tinted Light

Using tinted lights is a less dramatic but more subtle lighting effect than using colored lights. Using tinted lights is also a very common technique in the lighting of simulated three-dimensional spaces—especially in determining a mood for the scene.

Using tinted lights can be an effective method for creating a cohesive atmosphere. **Tinted lights** create an effect similar to a coat of overpaint or varnish on the layers of paint, which unifies objects of disparate colors or surface finishes (Fig. 8.1.5). Tinted lights are created by selecting a slight coloration for the light emitted by the light source. When using the HSB color model to describe a tint, the saturation values should be low so that the color is washed out, the brightness values should be high so that the tint is not too dark, and the hue values could vary depending on the coloration desired for the tint. When using the RGB color model, each of the three values (red, green, and blue) would be high, so that the resulting color would be bright and not too saturated.

Light in Water

The effect of light reflected off the surface of **moving water** can be recreated by placing spot lights shining up through a surface that represents water and that has an animated shape (Fig. 8.1.6). Some rendering programs have the ability to accurately simulate the effects seen when light travels through a volume of water (Fig. 8.1.7). These light patterns, called caustics, are caused when multiple focused rays of light are reflected or refracted onto one another.

8.1.6 This image was created with a lighting model that is based on optical phenomena such as the scattering and absorption of the light in the water. This model is capable of creating subtle details of the reflection and refraction of light on the water surface, the scattering and absorption of light in the water, and the shadows cast on the water surfaces. (Courtesy of Hideo Yamashita and the Computer Graphics Research Group of Hiroshima University.)

8.1.7 (opposite page, top) These underwater scenes display some of the caustic effects of light being refracted by the volume of seawater. (*Invisible Ocean*, a film by François Garnier. Executive Production: Ex Machina. © 1998 Monaco Inter Expo. Special thanks to the Oceanographical Museum of Monaco. Images courtesy of Ex Machina.)

8.1.8 (opposite page) Scene from the *Egg Cola* trailer where colors were added with light, resembles the traditional painting approach. Between 20 and 25 Maya's dome and sphere light sources were used for the control room, and sphere lights only for the background. Characters were modeled with NURBS. (© Independence, Inc.)

Animating Light

The position and attributes of light sources in a scene can be animated using the keyframe interpolation techniques described in Chapter 11. These techniques include the interactive specification of key poses, the editing of parameter curves, forward kinematics, and motion paths. A wide variety of lighting effects that affect the mood of a scene can also be created by animating the intensity of a light source as well as its color, cone angle, and falloff. Moving lights in a three-dimensional environment, however, should be done with great restraint because poorly animated light sources can be a great source of visual distraction in any animated sequence.

8.2 Types of Light Sources

There are several basic types of light sources according to the way in which they irradiate light. Simulated light sources generally include point lights, spot lights, linear lights, area lights, infinite lights, and ambient lights (Fig. 8.2.1). All of these types of light can be created and modified by the user. In addition most rendering programs automatically create one or several **default lights** in the three-dimensional scene. Default lighting schemes can usually be customized and may consist of an ambient light source, an infinite light that simulates the intensity and position of the sun, or a point light that is placed above and behind the camera or in any other XYZ position. Some default lights automatically turn themselves off as soon as we specify any light source in the scene; others remain on until they are turned off manually. Some rendering programs do not provide default lights, which means that if it is rendered without any new lights, the result will be like looking into a windowless room without any lights. As you practice creating computer-generated lights try to learn as much as you can about the major types of traditional lights and their characteristics (Fig. 8.6.1).

Point Light

A **point light** casts light evenly in all directions. For this reason a point light is also called an **omnidirectional** light (literally "in all directions"). Point lights are the simplest type of light source, and they can be placed anywhere in the scene. Point lights can be placed, for example, outside of the field of vision of the camera, behind an

Common Types of Computer-Generated Light Sources
Point Light Spot Light Infinite Light Area Light Linear Light Ambient Light

8.2.1 The basic types of computer-generated lights are defined by the characteristics of the source, the direction and angle of the beam, their shape and placement in space.

object in the scene, or even inside of objects. The effects of point lights placed inside of objects varies between software programs, but in many cases the light will shine through the walls of a transparent object as in the case of a light bulb. An incandescent light bulb is a simple example of a point light. A star, a candle, and a firefly are also point lights but require additional effects.

Spot Light

A simulated **spot light** is like a point light to which "barn doors" of the type commonly used in the performing arts have been added. Spot lights cast light in a cone shape and only in one specific direction. Spot lights have some unique characteristics: a variable-angle cone of light, and a light fall-off factor (Fig. 8.3.5). Flashlights, lamps with shades, jack-o-lanterns, and the light reflectors used in stage or movie productions are all examples of spot lights (Fig. 8.2.2).

Spot lights that are dimmed or turned up produce a very effective way of attracting the attention of the audience to a specific area or situation in a three-dimensional scene. A narrow soft-edged spot light can be especially effective for highlighting the action when the **illumination level** in the scene is low. A spot light in a dark scene can add a feeling of suspense or fear to the shot because the lighting effect might remind the audience of a search for something—or someone—that is hiding, or trying to hide from someone—or something—that is looking for us.

Infinite Light

Infinite lights are so far from the elements in the scene that their light rays reach the scene parallel to each other. **Infinite lights** are also called **directional lights**, and they behave like stars in the sky. But unlike stars, computer-simulated infinite lights can be placed anywhere in the environment, are massless, and their intensity can be modulated (Fig. 8.2.3). In many programs infinite lights have a constant intensity, and do not decay as they travel through space. The **sun** is a special case of an infinite light source that can be accurately placed above the scene by typing the latitude and longitude of the location plus the exact time of day and date when the simulated scene is taking place (Fig. 8.5.1).

8.2.2 Flashlights are an example of a spot light. They sometimes have a visible cone of light and a visible light fall-off factor.

Area Light

Some programs provide **area lights** in the form of multiple lights grouped together, or a single large area of light (Fig. 8.5.3). Area lights can be scaled to almost any size but are more efficient when kept small, and are usually rectangular or round in shape. Area lights are especially useful for lighting small areas uniformly like the way, for example, in which custom jewelry is photographed by professionals by being placed on a translucent light box or between two light boxes. Area lights can also be used to simulate the reflection of light coming into an interior space through open windows.

Linear Light

The light of the fluorescent tubes used to light so many public spaces can be simulated with linear lights (Fig. 8.2.4). **Linear lights** have length but no width, and they can also be scaled to any size. Using linear light sources should be exercised with care because their computation in some cases can be much more time-consuming than the combination of several point lights.

8.2.3 The sun is a good example of an infinite light.

Ambient Light

The light radiated by the **ambient light** source is distributed evenly throughout the entire scene. The term ambient light is often used very generically by different software programs, and technically speaking, it does not always refer to an ambient light source. In some cases it refers to a point light source that is created automatically by the program for each scene. Even though an ambient light source can be placed in a specific XYZ position in three-dimensional space, it is best to think of an ambient light as coming from all directions. The ambient light source often determines the general **level of illumination**, or shade, of a scene and almost always there is only one ambient light source per scene.

8.3 Basic Components of a Light Source

The main elements of all simulated light sources include position, color and intensity, decay and fall-off, glow, and shadows. In addition, spot lights are also defined by their orientation and cone angle. These components are listed in Fig. 8.3.1. All lighting software makes it possible to edit each of the individual components of a light source separately. Some programs also allow users to group several of these attributes and save them together in a file, called a **light shader**, that can be applied to any light source (Fig. 8.3.2).

8.2.4 The fluorescent tube is the classic example of a linear light.

Position and Orientation

Both the **position** and **orientation** of a light source can be controlled with the standard navigation or geometric transformation tools provided by all rendering programs. In general, the tools for placing light sources in a simulated three-dimensional space are the same as the tools used for placing cameras: simple and combined translations and rotations. In the wireframe display mode, light sources are usually represented with a variety of graphic symbols; for example, a light bulb for a point light, a lantern for a spot light, a sphere attached to a straight line for an infinite light, and so on. But when a scene is rendered, the actual light sources themselves (not the

Basic Components of a Computer-Generated Light

Position and Orientation
Color and Intensity
Decay and Fall-Off
Beam Angle
Glow
Shadows

8.3.1 A list with the basic components of standard light sources simulated with three-dimensional computer animation software.

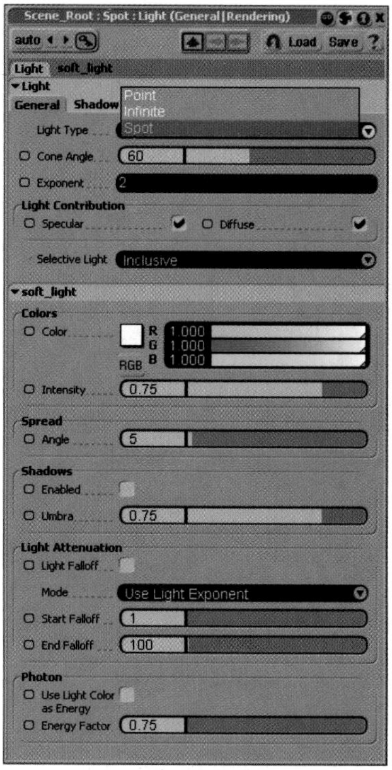

8.3.2 Powerful tools for editing light sources, including photon emitters on next page. (Image courtesy of Softimage Co. All rights reserved.)

light coming from them) can usually be seen, unless they are made into **invisible lights,** in which case they do not appear in the final rendering. In many programs, the light sources are visible by default, and when rendered they appear in the image as bright spots or as small three-dimensional objects that look like the graphic symbols commonly used to represent the light source in the wireframe mode.

Color and Intensity

Simulated light can have virtually any **color**. In most rendering programs, the color of lights is usually specified using a light-based or **additive color model**. The RGB (Red, Green, Blue) model and the HSB (Hue, Saturation, Brightness) model are both additive color models (both are described in Chapter 6). Some programs provide both color models to work with, other programs provide only one of them. In the RGB color model, a color can be specified by its individual red, green, and blue components. The numerical ranges used to specify color also vary from program to program. They can range, for example, from 0.000 to 1.000, 0 to 255, or 0 to 65,535 depending on the color resolution and precision of the system. Unlike pigment-based color models, where the color mixture gets darker as more color is added, in the RGB color model the color of the light will become lighter as the amount of color mixed increases (Fig. 8.3.3). Note that in a three-dimensional environment, the color assigned to objects is always influenced by the color of the light sources as well as the position of the object in relation to them.

When using the HSB color system it is possible to specify the intensity of a light source independently from its color or hue. For this reason it is easier for most people to quickly define the color of lights with this color model than when using the RGB model. One of several tools for selecting colors visually within the context of the HSB color system is illustrated in Figure 8.3.4. Most three-dimensional rendering programs provide dimmers to control the **intensity** or **brightness** of a light source. Intensity values commonly range from 0.000 to 1.000 with maximum intensity represented by a number one and minimum intensity (or OFF) being represented by zero when using the HSB color model (Fig. 8.3.11). Some programs offer simple tools for boosting the intensity of a light source (Fig. 8.3.5). The intensity of the light source can be controlled independently of its color, but since the intensity and the color of light influence each other, almost any change in the color of a light affects its intensity. For example, if we have two red lights with the same intensity but one of them has a dark red color and the other a light red color, the latter will appear to be a light with a higher intensity.

Decay and Fall-Off

The **decay** value of light controls the force of a light source and, as a result, how far from the light source the light travels. A weak light decays rapidly, while a strong light decays slowly and travels far. In the real world the decay of light is always linked to the intensity of the light source that created the light, but in computer-simulated lighting decay is often independent of the intensity parameter.

In most programs the decay parameter defines the force of the light—regardless of its type—as it travels away from the light source. The light created from point lights decays equally in all directions. The light created from spot lights, however, decays as it moves away from the light source, but also as it moves from the center of the beam cone **toward the edges**. This type of decay is sometimes called **fall-off**. Decay and fall-off can be controlled with linear interpolation for slow fading effects or with exponential interpolation for abrupt fading. The sharpness or softness of the edges of spot light beams are controlled with the fall-off value.

Beam Angle

The **beam angle** feature of lights is unique characteristic of spot lights only. The cone angle of a spot light defines the diameter of the beam of light and also the surface area covered by the light. This parameter simulates the barn doors in real spot light lamps that control the **spread** of the light beam (Fig. 8.3.5).

Glow and Cone of Light

It is possible with some programs to simulate a variety of glowing lights. The **glow** of a light is a circle of light that forms around the light source because the light is refracted and reflected by particles in the environment—generally ice, dust, or smoke. In some instances the glow of light is calculated based on the **bleeding** displayed by very bright light sources, instead of the refraction of light in a three-dimensional environment. The light bleeding effect is very common in situations when a photographic camera is pointed directly at a light source, and the resulting photograph has a bright spot with light bleeding around it. The difference between these two methods of creating a glow in computer-generated lights is that one (refraction) is based on three-dimensional calculations, while the other (bleeding) is based on two-dimensional calculations.

The glow of a point light usually occurs as a **circle** or **halo** around the light source. The glow of a spot light occurs in the form of a **cone of light**. Circular and conical light glows are often called **volumetric lights**, and they are both defined by the decay of the light source. Linear decay results in a gradual fading of the glow effect, while exponential decay results in a sudden vanishing of the glow. Conical light glow is further controlled by the spread or beam angle of the light source. The thickness or frequency of the particles in the environment that cause the light glow is controlled with parameters that simulate the size, orientation, motion, and opacity of the particles in the environment that cause the light glow (Fig. 8.3.6).

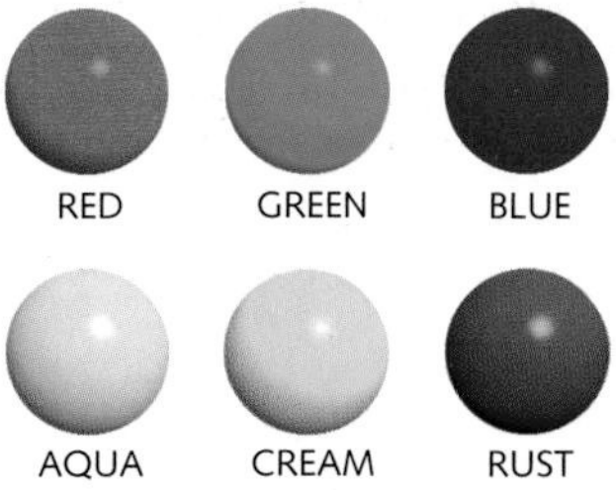

Color	*0-255 Scale*	*0-1 Scale*
Red	255-0-0	1-0-0
Green	0-255-0	0-1-0
Blue	0-0-255	0-0-1
Aqua	161-255-238	.631-1-.933
Cream	252-255-103	.988-1-.403
Rust	141-43-17	.552-.168-.066

8.3.3 Two columns with RGB numerical values expressing color in two different ways, using a scale of 0–255 and a scale of 0–1.

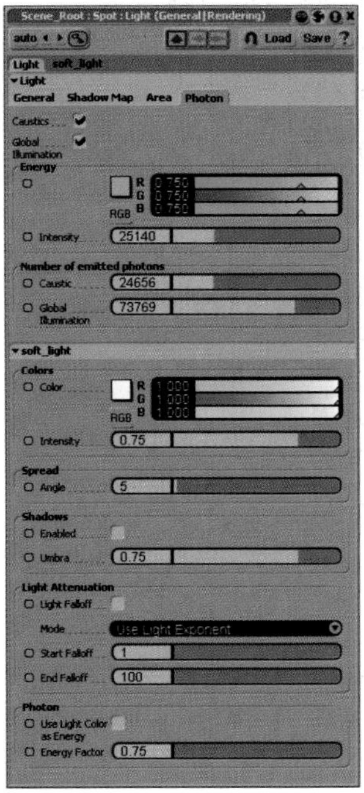

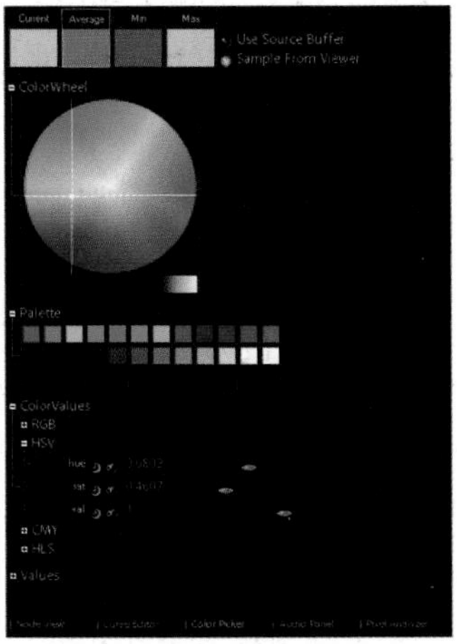

8.3.4 The Shake Color Picker simplifies the visual selection of color within the ranges of the HSB (Hue, Saturation, Brightness) color model. Color can also be selected by inputting numerical values in HSB or RGB (Red, Green, Blue) formats. (Courtesy of Apple Computer.)

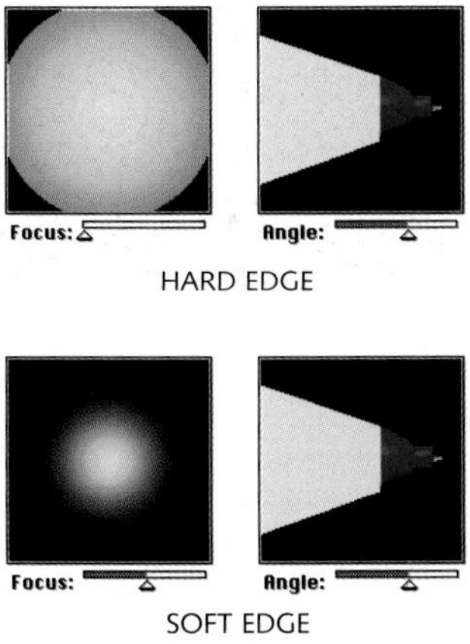

8.3.5 These two pairs of images compare two spot light beams with the same cone angle values, but the one on top has sharp edges or almost no fall-off, and the lower one has soft edges or lots of fall-off. (Graphs from Infini-D 2.6. © 1991–1995 Specular International, Ltd.)

Lens flare is an effect that is related to light glow, and it simulates the refraction of light inside of a camera lens. Lens flare creates the rings or stars caused by the refraction of light inside camera lenses, and it is also a two-dimensional effect commonly available in many postprocessing and compositing programs.

Global and Local Lights

Global light sources shine on all objects in the scene that are directly exposed to the light sources. The light sources in a scene are global by default. Rendering methods like radiosity are used when even the three-dimensional surfaces that are not directly exposed to a light source receive some light in the form of penumbra or **diffuse interreflections**. The illumination effect of global lights is largely dependent on their position and orientation in the scene and their brightness, but objects directly exposed to global lights always reflect some of that light.

A different situation occurs with **local light sources**, also called **linked** or **selective light sources**. A local light source sheds its light on the objects linked to it, and this link can be exclusive or inclusive. An **exclusive link** between the light source and the objects limits the light projected by a local light source to fall only on the objects linked to it. In some programs an exclusive link may override the fact that a linked surface may not be exposed directly to the light source. This is as if the light source could magically travel through opaque objects that would ordinarily block light from reaching the linked object without affecting them. An **inclusive link** allows a local light source to always illuminate the objects linked to it as well as other objects in the scene that may be directly exposed to it.

Establishing links between light sources and three-dimensional surfaces can be an effective way to achieve complex lighting situations, but it can also increase the management complexity of a scene. Local light sources are implemented in different ways by different programs. For this reason local light sources should be used with restraint. From the point of view of an object that is linked to one or several local light sources, the object will be illuminated only by them and not by any other light sources that may be active in the scene.

Shadows

In principle, all light sources cast **shadows**. But shadow-casting is a feature of lights that can be turned on or off. Since shadow-casting is also an optional attribute of objects and shading techniques, the final visual appearance of shadows is determined not only by the attributes of the shadow but also by the attributes of the shadow-casting object and the rendering method employed. Shadows can be defined by several parameters, including color of the shadow, color of the penumbra, and softness of the shadow edge (Figs. 8.3.7–8.3.9, 8.5.5, and 8.5.6).

The portion of a shadow that blocks direct light altogether is called **umbra**. It is the inner part of the shadow. The area in the edges of the shadow that blends with other lights in the environment is called **penumbra**. The **softness** of the edge of a shadow is controlled in a variety of ways. With many rendering methods—excluding ray tracing—the soft edges of a shadow can be controlled by the distance between the light source and the shadow-projecting object. The shadow edges will be sharp as the light source moves further away from the object. The number of levels of shadow tracers influences the softness of a shadow when ray tracing is used. When using radiosity-based rendering the shadow edges are soft when the surfaces in the environment create a lot of diffuse inter-reflections (Figs. 7.3.2, lower right, and 10.1.1).

Patterns of shadows are often used to create a mood in the scene. A common way to create these patterns is by projecting light through cutout stencils, also known as **gobo lights**.

8.3.6 Reflectors with glow pointing to the skys in this architectural visualization of the Samsung headquarters building in Seoul, Korea. (Courtesy of Rafael Viñoly Associates.)

8.4 Lighting the Scene

Those who realize the importance of lighting can appreciate the importance of a systematic approach to lighting. Without light the entire contents of the world could not be appreciated visually. Without adequate lighting, shapes, colors, and textures can only be experienced halfway. Think, for example, of some of the elements of a beautiful face: the features, the proportions of the shapes and their curvatures, the evocative color of the eyes, the subtle coloration and the texture of the skin, and the weight and flow of the hair. A successful lighting arrangement can reveal all of these elements and present them in a harmonic way. But a poorly designed lighting scheme will fail to bring up the full experience and depth of the beautiful face. Strong shadows in the eyes, for example, may obscure or hide the eye color. Unbalanced shadows around the nose might distort its delicate balance. Lighting the face from certain angles might flatten the jawline or

8.3.7 *The Cathedral* tells the story of a pilgrim who arrives at a magical place on the edge of the world. The lighting contributes to the staging of the action and the suspense of the storyline. (© 2002 Tomek Baginski and Platige Image.)

dilute the seductive meaning hidden in the shape of the lips.

Next we will review some ideas about the placement of light sources based on concepts borrowed from traditional stage lighting. Amazingly enough, most stage lighting concepts can be easily adapted to the lighting of computer-simulated environments because in both situations the scene is totally dark unless we turn the lights on. We will approach lighting here from two points of view: the areas in the scene that require lighting and some of the basic positions of light sources.

From the point of view of stage lighting design there are some constant areas or aspects of the scene that require lighting. Throughout the ages many lighting methods and techniques have been developed for the different formats and genres presented on a stage, ranging from drama to comedy. The following categories of lighting summarize a variety of traditional lighting methods that can be adapted to the design and production of computer animation. These categories of lighting are the main action area and key lights, the secondary action areas, the backgrounds, ambient or fill-in lighting, visible light sources, and moving lights.

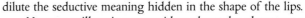

8.3.8 The character in the background is turned into a shadow by using lighting from behind. The venetian blind shadow patterns on the foreground character are created with gobo lights. (Images created by Mondo Media, CA. © 1999 Pulse Interactive.)

Main Action Area

The **main action area** is the area in the scene where most of the action takes place. The main action area may consist of a small area, for example, if a molecular interaction is being rendered, or a large area in the case of a car chase in an underground parking lot. The main action area in a dialogue scene between two characters would be where the action takes place. In computer-generated scenes the main

8.3.9 The sunlight floods this shot that evokes the simple pleasures of lunching in the backyard. In spite of their well-defined edges, the inside value of the shadow is quite light. By simply making the shadows a darker value this scene would have a very different connotation. (*Polygon Family*, © POLYGON PICTURES/ IPA/ NK-EXA.)

action area might be located in a quiet indoor space or extend over firewalls and colored rain. A couple of spot lights might be enough for a simple shot of a mostly static scene, but several point lights and spot lights might be needed to delineate the motion of ten fantastic characters dancing back and forth on the stage. A specific lighting arrangement of the main action area may require several variations in cases when the scene is shot from different points of view to emphasize different aspects of the subjects to cameras placed in different locations. In many situations the lighting of the main action area defines the overall mood of the scene. For that reason the light sources used to light the main action area on a theatre stage are often called key lights and are often used in conjuction with the fill lights described shortly. In traditional stage lighting design it is not uncommon to divide the main action area into several sections, depending on the action that is to take place, and to assign each section a certain number of lights, for example, between two and five spot lights per section (Fig. 8.4.1).

Secondary Action Area

The **secondary action area** is the place in the scene into which some of the action eventually spills. For example, two characters in a scene that takes place in a living room spend most of their time sitting on the couch (main action area). But at some point one of the

8.3.10 The lighting in this shot of a businessman waiting for the train to return home is simple but interesting. Notice the presents for his kids, and how the light shadows add warmth to the moment. (*Polygon Family*, © POLYGON PICTURES/IPA/NK-EXA.)

8.3.11 The contrast between the sharp light reflections and the fill lights emphasizes the dramatism of these scenes from *Kaena* (opposite page, bottom). (© 2003 Xilam Films–StudioCanal–Group TVA Inc.)

characters gets up and walks to the bookshelf (secondary action area), picks a book, and returns to the sofa. The lights illuminating the bookshelf and the book may be on at all times throughout the scene, or only turned up as the character starts walking to the bookshelf and dimmed down as the character sits back down. The number of lights needed to illuminate the secondary action area—especially in a small environment—is usually smaller than the number of lights required to light the main action area.

Background

The **background** in computer-generated environments, also referred to in computer simulations as the **stage**, the scenery, or the surroundings. The background usually consists of the props surrounding the action areas. Scenery might consist of horizontal or vertical planes with texture maps—of bricks, for example—or convex surfaces with procedural maps of animated clouds or even a photographic background that has been composited. Scenery—especially backdrops with texture maps—is very sensitive to colored light. Very minor chromatic changes in the lights that illuminate the scenery will have significant effects on the color of the scenery.

Key Lights

The **key light** is the main light on the subject or point of interest, and it also may be the only light in a scene. There may be one or several key lights in a shot, especially when the subject moves or when there are multiple subjects,, and they may be positioned almost anywhere on the scene. Key lights delineate and define the subject (Fig. 8.5.6) and they also project shadows that are sometimes softened by the fill lights.

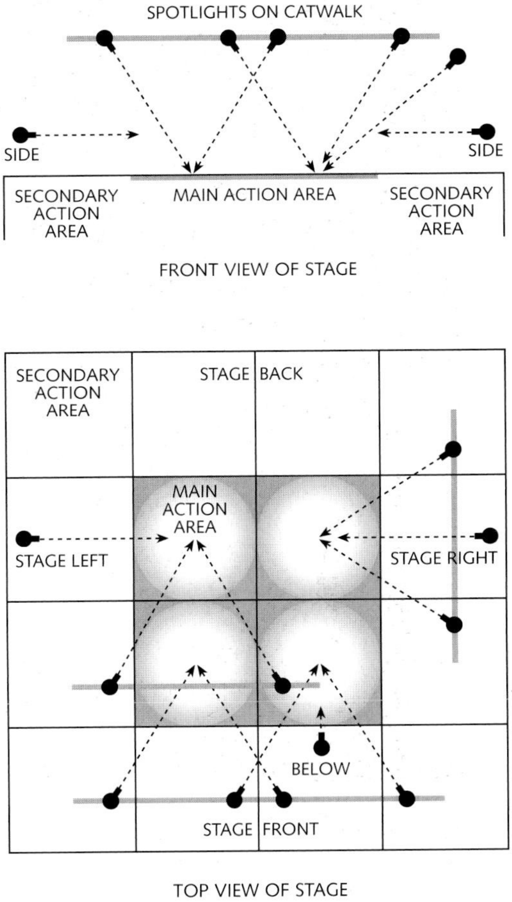

8.4.1 This diagram shows a lighting layout of the main and secondary action areas. In traditional stage lighting the size of each grid subdivision corresponds to an area that can be filled by a spotlight beam.

Fill Lights

The **fill light** has the dual purpose of defining the overall color tone of the entire scene, as well as blending some of the other multiple lights in the scene. Computer-generated fill lights are usually created with spot lights, and directionless or ambient fill can be created with infinite light sources. Depending on the lighting effect desired, fill lights can be soft and tinted or quite bright, but almost invariably fill lights do not project shadows. Two specialized versions of fill lights include the **eye-light**, which is used to draw a twinkle in actors' eyes, and the **kicker light** or **rim light**, which is used to accentuate and define the outlines of a face or an object.

Visible Light Sources

Visible light sources are sources of light that can be seen by the camera and, therefore, the spectators. Visible light sources might include lamps, fireplaces, reflectors, candlelight, televisions, refrigerators, fireflies, and comets (Figs. 8.4.2–8.4.3 and 8.5.7). These light sources are called **practical lights** in traditional film and video production, and they are usually important from the dramatic point of view when they play an important storytelling role. Often, relevant events happen near visible light sources, and that is why this type of light is commonly emphasized in the visual composition of a scene. Computer-simulated visible light sources can be simulated with point lights, and their effect can be accentuated by placing them inside of a sphere that is rendered with transparency and glow. The effect of a visible spot light can be accentuated by using a transparent cone to emphasize the cone of light of the spot light.

The sun or the moon, for example, are commonly represented as light sources. They can be easily defined as point lights, but they can also be ambient light sources. The point light sources recreating celestial bodies can have medium to high intensity and little or no fall-off. The color of these lights may have a warm tint in the case of the sun, for example, or a slightly cool tint in the case of the

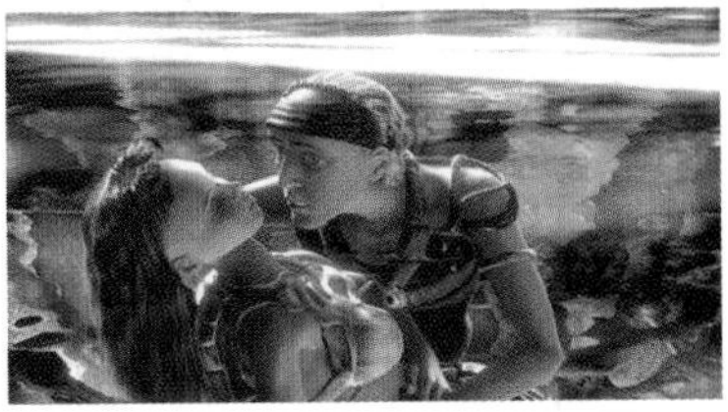

8.4.2 The practical light held by this icon of filmmaking dominates this image that also includes a significant amount of digital painting and compositing techniques. (Produced by Kleiser-Walczak Construction Co. for First Light, Inc. and Columbia Pictures. Animated by Jeff Kleiser, Diana Walczak, and Ed Kramer. Courtesy of Kleiser-Walczak Construction Co.)

moon. One advantage of using ambient light to simulate distant light sources is that the objects cast soft shadows if any at all. The light of many celestial bodies may include some flickering that can be recreated by animating the intensity or the glow of a point light source. This quality is especially apparent when the camera is pointed directly at the light source.

Moving Lights

Unlike a theater stage where most lights are fixed, all lights in a computer-simulated scene can be easily moved. But there is always a category of **moving lights** that move a lot or have motion as their main characteristic. Moving lights can be used to emphasize special aspects of the scene. For example, a very focused spot light that moves very subtly over one object can reveal a highlight or emphasize its transparency, or a series of spot lights can be mounted on the camera and can follow the action by trailing the camera. A number of moving lights fall within a subcategory of special lighting effects that can be used to emphasize certain dramatic moments or to impose dominant moods. Fireworks, explosions, haze and fog, and lightning are all examples of special lighting effects (Fig. 8.4.4).

Many lighting effects encountered in nature can be simulated with combinations of moving light sources (see Chapter 11 for more details about animation of light sources). Some of these lighting effects include the light emitted by lightning, fire, natural explosions like a volcano, the light reflected off the surface of moving water, and refracted through moving water like a waterfall.

Fire lighting effects that are off-screen can be achieved with a group of point lights and spot lights placed within an area that corresponds to the dimensions of the fire being recreated. The intense and constant lighting motion generated by a fire can be achieved with wiggly parameter curves for position, cone angle, and each of the RGB colors in order to achieve maximum irregularity. Other techniques to simulate fire are described in Chapter 11. The lighting effects created by light travelling through colored glass—for example, the effect created in an interior space by exterior lights traveling through stained glass—require a translucent image map, or a rendering technique like radiosity or ray tracing that calculates the effects of light traveling through transparent or translucent surfaces.

8.4.3 The light from the lamp (a practical lightsource) carries the lighting in this shot, while the flood light is kept very low. This lighting adds intimacy and mystery to this moment when a metaphysical character searches for his identity by trying on different masks. *Masks* won the first SIGGRAPH Electronic Theatre Jury Honors Award in 1999. (Image courtesy of Piotr Karwas, writer/director/animator/designer.)

8.5 Basic Positions of Light Sources

When compared to traditional stage lighting, computer-simulated lighting has the great advantage that lights can be moved around without having to worry about clamping them to spot light bars or poles. Computer-simulated lights have the ability to float in space. Most three-dimensional rendering programs use standard XYZ notation for positioning lights in three-dimensional space. However, some programs offer the **spherical coordinate system**—instead of or in addition to the Cartesian coordinate system—for placing lights. The spherical coordinate system, as mentioned in Chapter 3, specifies the position of objects in three-dimensional space in terms of their altitudinal and azimuthal angles (above and around) in relation to a center of reference. The position of the sun, for example, can be described in terms of its altitude and its azimuth (Fig. 3.4.8). The **altitude** is defined by the angle of the light in relation to the horizon. The **azimuth** is defined by projecting the angle of the sun onto the east-west axis. This technique is especially convenient in architectural projects where the position of the sun has to be defined for calculating both the amount of shadow cast by a building and its surroundings, as well as the amount of direct sunlight received by the structure at any time of the day (Fig. 8.5.2).

Once light sources are positioned they can be aimed at specific objects or areas in the environment in a variety of ways. Centers of interest can be specified **numerically** by typing XYZ values, **visually** by pointing the **light vector** displayed by some light sources at

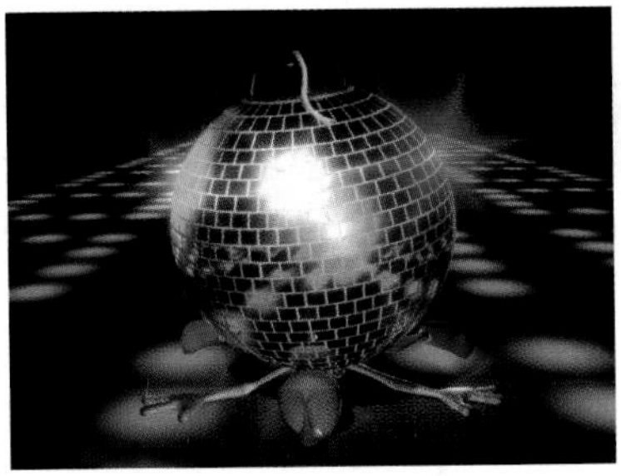

8.4.4 The disco ball, an example of moving lights, plays a heavy role in the conclusion of *Alien Song*. (See Figure 10.5.4 for another disco ball.) (© 1999 Victor Navone.)

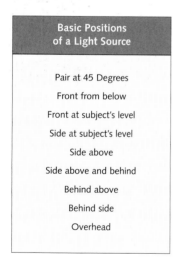

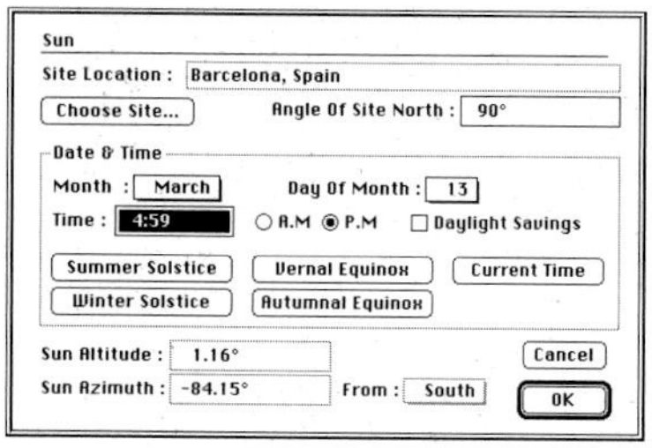

8.5.1 The position of lights—especially the sun or other stars—can also be specified using the spherical coordinate system. This dialog box provides an easy way to define the position of the sun in relation to earth anywhere and anytime. (form•Z dialog box. © 1991-1995 auto•des•sys, Inc.)

Basic Positions of a Light Source

Pair at 45 Degrees

Front from below

Front at subject's level

Side at subject's level

Side above

Side above and behind

Behind above

Behind side

Overhead

8.5.2 The basic positions of light sources are listed on top, and illustrated on the opposite page as they focus on a sphere.

the object in question, or **procedurally** by choosing commands (provided by some programs) that will automatically point one object—usually a light source or a camera—to another.

In principle there is no limit to the **number of light sources** that can be placed in a three-dimensional scene. In computer-simulated lighting, just as in real physical lighting, the only limitations to the number of light sources lighting a scene are of a practical nature. The budget and timetable of some projects may determine the number of light sources. Both in computer-simulated lighting as in real lighting, to create, place, and fine-tune lights requires time and money. But lighting requirements—whether real or simulated—have a wide range of complexity. Compare the lighting requirements of an indoor large-scale sports event to those of the close-up photography of a diamond ring.

Lights can be placed in a variety of places in relation to the subject that needs lighting and the camera. Five basic positions of light sources and their corresponding variations as they focus on the subject are examined here: pair of spot lights at a 45-degree angle, front (below and subject's level), side (subject's level, above, and above and behind), back (above and side), and top. Figure 8.5.2 provides a visual summary of these basic lighting positions using only spot lights to accentuate each lighting effect. It is important to keep in mind that not all situations need all these lights present at all times. Use your judgment and preview to finalize a lighting arrangement.

45-Degree Pair

One of the most common lighting arrangements (in fact, it is usually called **ordinary lighting** by stage lighting designers) consists of two spot lights placed above, in front, and to the sides of the subject. In this common lighting configuration the lights are both focused on the subject at a 90-degree angle in relation to each other. Both lights are rotated 45 degrees around the vertical and horizontal axis. This ordinary **45-degree angle spot light pair** represents a simple and effective way to have a generous amount of light that reveals the features of the subject as well as some detail in the form of shadows (Fig. 8.5.3).

Frontal Light

Frontal light from below is very effective for casting pronounced shadows both on the subject and the environment. Since we rarely encounter this type of light in natural surroundings, frontal lights from below can look very artificial or overly dramatic. But they can also be quite effective for accentuating truly dramatic, scary, or other-worldly moments (Fig. 8.5.4). **Frontal light at the subject's level** tends to flatten the subject because it usually eliminates most of the deepest shadows, but it can also be used as a low intensity fill light for blending other spot lights in the scene.

PAIR AT A 45-DEGREE ANGLE

FRONTAL FROM BELOW

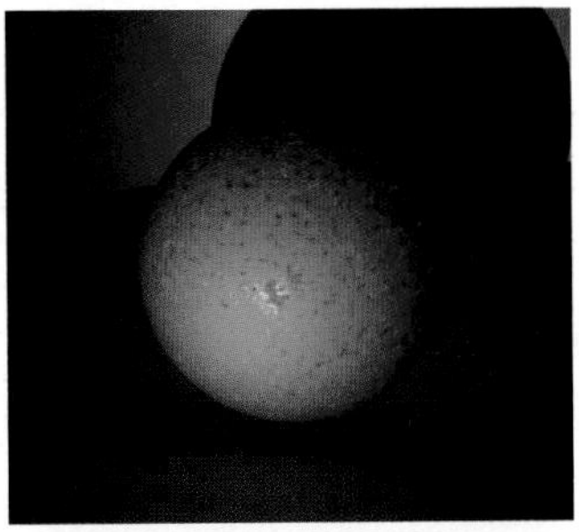

FRONTAL AT SUBJECT'S LEVEL

LATERAL AT SUBJECT'S LEVEL

LATERAL ABOVE SUBJECT

LATERAL ABOVE, BEHIND SUBJECT

BACK ABOVE SUBJECT

BACK SIDE OF SUBJECT

OVERHEAD

Lateral, Top, and Back Lights

A **lateral light at the subject's level** is useful for increasing the contrast between light and dark. The accentuated shadows created with lateral light can have a powerful dramatic effect and add a lot of depth to the scene. Lateral lights should be used with care because they can easily overpower other more delicate lights in the scene (Fig. 8.5.5).

A **lateral light from above**—especially when used in pairs, one on the left and one on the right—creates an effect that is similar to the 45-degree spot light pair described earlier but with slightly more pronounced shadows. One advantage of creating pronounced shadows with lateral lights from above is that the shadows created by the main subject are usually projected on the floor and not on

8.5.3 A pair of lights at a 45-degree angle (one stronger than the other) delineate the edges of the delicately shaped legs of this insect and make its hair glow. (Courtesy of Akira Kai, FOTON.)

other objects in the scene, as would be the case when using frontal lights from below or lateral lights at the subject's level.

A **lateral light from above and behind** is an effective way to outline a subject against a background. This position combines some of the advantages and limitations of all lateral, overhead, and back lights. It models the actor with contrasted shadows (lateral), and it also creates a halo of light on the top of the subject that clearly differentiates it from the background (back and overhead). Both the side and top **back lights** create halos of lights on the subject's edges. Back lighting can be an effective way to create depth in a scene.

Overhead lights also create dramatic halos around the top of a subject. As with back lights, overhead lights can also add depth and drama to a scene (Fig. 8.5.6).

8.6 Getting Ready

Check the Default Light

Do not forget to check whether the rendering software that you use creates a default light automatically. If it does not, you must define a light source before you render. The default light in most programs is an ambient light source that lights all the objects in the scene uniformly. Default ambient lights can be modified when the original settings are not suitable to the scene in question.

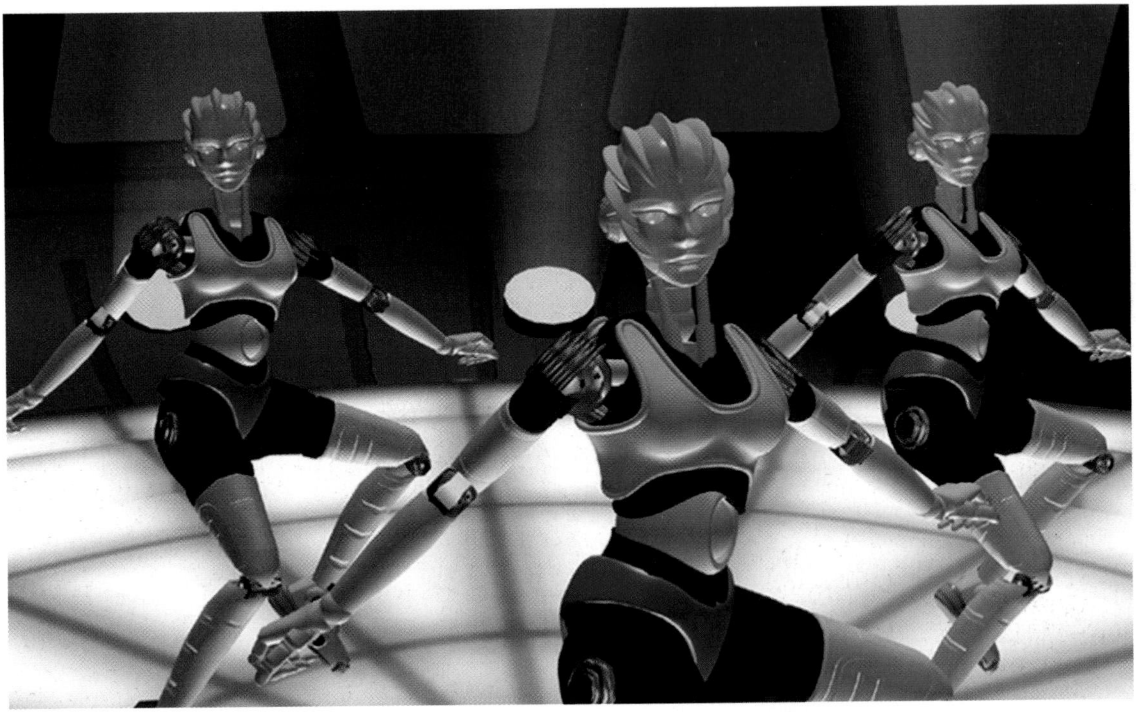

8.5.4 The soft area lighting from below gives these dancing robots a light and sublime look. (*Aerobot*, © POLYGON PICTURES/IPA/NK-EXA.)

Invisible Light Sources

Do not forget to make the computer-generated light sources (the lamps, not the light) invisible after they have been defined and positioned in three-dimensional space. Otherwise, they will show—usually in the form of small boxes, arrows, or brilliant dots—in the final rendered image.

8.5.5 The lateral lighting projects a harsh shadow on this smoking creature who wonders what his luck will be. (© Jim Ludtke.)

Missing Shadows

Sometimes an object that is meant to cast shadows does not do so even though the light source has been defined as a shadow-casting light. This problem might occur because the shadow-casting preference has been turned off either in the object itself or in the shading technique or in both.

Simulated Shadows

Transparent planes can be used to create shadows on objects in the scene, and even on photographic backgrounds that are composited, or blended, with a three-dimensional environment. In the latter case the transparent planes have to be aligned with elements on the background through a series of trial and error alignment tests. (For more information on image compositing read Chapter 13.)

8.5.6 A single overhead light cascades onto the subject's hair and reveals the outline of her body while keeping the rest in the penumbra (*Bondex, The Fashion Parade*. Director: Majid Loukil. Agency: Callegari-Berville. Images courtesy of Ex Machina.)

Minimize Rendering Time

Try to minimize rendering time by keeping the number of lights down to a minimum. Most scenes can be properly lighted with a couple of well-placed light sources. Many inexperienced designers create more light sources than necessary to light a scene. A lot of rendering time can saved by studying the scene first and placing only those light sources that are essential to the lighting effect sought. Large numbers of light sources should be reserved for creating special lighting effects in critical shots that will receive lots of attention (Fig. 8.6.1).

Learn About Traditional Lighting

Learning about traditional light sources can give you ideas on how to better use lighting in a computer-generated scene. Some of the main differences between lights used for motion picture, theatre, and television production include the color light emitted by the lamp, the power of the lamp, the number of lamps, the shape and surface of the source, and features like reflectors, lenses, and barndoors.

The power of the lamp is measured in watts but the amount of light emitted is measured in footcandles. Figure 8.6.2 lists the difference between light output by a similar lamp at different distances and in two different source configurations. Notice how the focused beam of a spotlight outputs many more footcandles than the more diffuse light of a flood light source. Light sources of 10,000 watts (10K) or more are used for large sets and are usually fairly large in size and surface. Light sources between 2,000 and 5,000 watts are used for medium sets. Lights at 1,000 watts or less are versatile because they can be placed almost anywhere in the scene, and are often used to add light-

8.5.7 (opposite page, right) The lighter is an example of a practical light shining from the front and below. (© 2002 Avalon/ Sparkling*.)

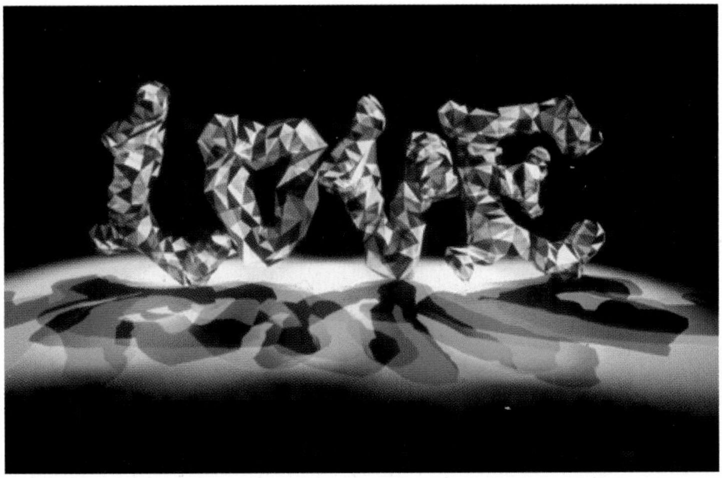

8.6.1 This rendering of three-dimensional lettering recreates the shadow effects that are typical of colored theatrical lights. (*Dancing Love* © Toshifumi Kawahara/POLYGON PICTURES.)

ing accents. Most light sources have one lamp—but a few have groups of lamps, usually in the form of a rectangular matrix, or rigs of fluorescent tubes. As far as the shape of light sources goes, most spotlights are round and flood lights are rectangular or round. **Reflectors** consist of a highly reflective material inside of the light source that helps to amplify the amount of light emitted. Lenses and **barndoors** are used to focus and shape the beam of light. **Fresnel lenses** have concentric lens sections, and are especially effective at focusing sharp beams of light from light sources that have a large diameter. All kinds of diffusion materials and bounce cards are also used to direct light.

The traditional lighting sources are listed in Figure 8.6.3. Tungsten fresnels are effective at creating a sharp and intense beam because of their built-in reflector and lens. The 2K fresnel has been widely used as a key light on a single actor. HMIs are also widely available with fresnel lenses. Xenons are very powerful lights with the highest ratio of lumens-per-watt of all light sources, and they emit a flicker-free light that makes them suitable for high-speed cinematography. Open face lamps, as their name indicates, have no lens to focus the light, but they do have a wide reflector that spreads a lot of light. Open face lamps are often used to bounce light off other surfaces, and their output can be controlled with barndoors. The PAR light sources are similar to car headlights because the lamp includes a self-contained bulb, lens, and reflector. PARs are often used in groups of five, nine or twelve lights; the 9-light version, for example, is a matrix of 3 × 3 lamps. Some PARs are available with interchangeable lenses and with different light spread characteristics. Softs have different characteristics that diffuse their light, ranging from frosted lenses or lamps (like fluorescent tubes) to white (instead of silver) reflectors. Broads are rectangular reflectors often used as powerful fill lights or footlights on a theatre stage. Last but not least, lekos are the highly focused theatrical spotlights often used to project patterns (called gobos) on the set.

Light Output in Footcandles of HMI Fresnel Sources

Spot	@ 10 ft.	@ 20 ft.	@ 30 ft.
12K	45,000	16,000	7,300
6K	49,000	12,250	4,400
4K	28,000	7,150	2,500
2.5	13,200	3,450	1,200
1.2	7,150	2,230	670
575	1,150	706	228
Flood	**@ 10 ft.**	**@ 20 ft.**	**@ 30 ft.**
12K	5,800	1,650	730
6K	4,100	1,000	370
4K	2,000	510	195
2.5	1,800	410	150
1.2	490	168	54
575	300	64	19

8.6.2 This list compares the illumination of a popular type of light for film and video, the HMI fresnel source, used both as a spotlight and a flood light. The distance to the subject is measured in feet, and the illumination is measured in footcandles. Notice the large difference in intensity between the spotlight and the flood light versions.

Traditional Lighting Sources

Tungsten Fresnels
200-250 watts (inkie), 500-750 (tweenie), 1K (baby or ace), 2K (deuce or junior), 5K, and 10K

HMIs
575 watts, 1.2, 2.5, 4K, 6K, 8K, 12K, and 18K

Xenons
75 watts, 1K, 2K, 4K, and 7K

Open Faced Units
600 watts, 650, 1K, 2K, and 5K (skypan)

PARs
650 watts (PAR 36), 1K (PAR 64); 575, 2.5K and 4K (HMI PAR)

Softs
1K and 2K (zips); 2K, 4K and 8K (studio softs); cone lights; flourescent rigs

Broads
750, and 1K

Lekos
1K, and 2K

8.6.3 A list of the most popular lighting sources used in film and video production. These units are often referred to by the watt power of their lamp (1K stands for 1,000 watts).

8.6.4 (top right) The computer-generated lighting on the computerized pet was carefully matched to the soft lateral light above the young actor in *Spy Kids 2* (© 2002 Hybride. Images courtesy of Dimension Films.)

8.6.5 (right) The lighting on this character from *The Cathedral* accentuates the camera's depth of field, and brings up the texture detail. (Copyright 2002 Tomek Baginski and Platige Image.)

Lighting is Related to Shading

It is challenging to talk about the effects of lighting in computer-simulated three-dimensional environments because so much of it is determined by the shading technique or techniques that are used to render a scene. This is especially true in shots where the computer-generated lighting must match the live action lighting (Fig. 8.6.4–8.6.5). In this chapter we limit the discussion of lighting to the elements directly associated with the process of lighting: the light sources, their lighting characteristics, and their positions in three-dimensional space. For more information on shading and rendering techniques read Chapters 6 and 9.

Chapter 8

Key Terms

- 45-degree angle spot light pair
- Additive (light-based) color system
- Additive color model
- Altitude
- Ambient light
- Area lights
- Azimuth
- Back lights
- Background
- Barndoors
- Beam angle
- Bleeding
- Brightness
- Candela
- Circle
- Color
- Colored lights
- Cone of light
- Decay
- Default lights
- Diffuse interreflections
- Directional lights
- Exclusive link
- Eyelight
- Fall-off
- Fill lights
- Footcandle
- Fresnel lenses
- Frontal light at the subject's level
- Frontal light from below
- f/stop
- Global light sources
- Glow
- Gobo lights
- Halo
- Illumination level
- Inclusive link
- Infinite lights
- Intensity
- Invisible lights
- Key light
- Kicker light
- Lateral light at the subject's level
- Lateral light from above
- Lateral light from above and behind
- Lens flare
- Level of illumination
- Light measurements on location
- Light shader
- Light vector
- Light-based colors
- Lightning
- Linear lights
- Linked light sources
- Local light sources
- Lux
- Main action area
- Metercandle
- Moving lights
- Moving water
- Number of light sources
- Numerically
- Omnidirectional light
- Ordinary lighting
- Orientation
- Overhead light
- Penumbra
- Pigment-based colors
- Point light
- Position
- Practical lights
- Procedurally
- Reflectors
- Rim light
- Secondary action area
- Selective light sources
- Shadows
- Softness
- Spherical coordinate system
- Spot light
- Spread
- Stage
- Subtractive (pigment-based) color system
- Sun
- Tinted lights
- Toward the edges
- Umbra
- Visible light sources
- Visually
- Volumetric lights
- Zone system
- Zone V

9.1.1 *Kiss That Frog* is a rock video based on the music of Peter Gabriel. A rich array of shading techniques was used to portray exotic creatures in an environment that also contains live action characters. (© 1993 MEGA/ Real World. All rights reserved. Courtesy of Angel Studios, Carlsbad, California.)

CHAPTER 9

9

Shading and Surface Characteristics

Summary

THE MAIN TECHNIQUES USED FOR SHADING three-dimensional surfaces by calculating the effect of light on the objects in the scene are the focus of this chapter. This chapter also presents how surface shaders and image mapping work. The characteristics of three-dimensional surfaces including reflectivity, color, texture, and transparency and different ways of defining them are also explained.

QUICK INDEX

9.1 Surface Shading Techniques

The visual appearance of a simulated three-dimensional environment is determined mostly through the shading process. The shading process creates surfaces on the wireframe structures created during the modeling process. Surface shading is calculated based on the relative position and distance of the object from the light source, and it also takes into account the surface characteristics of the objects.

Shading is the moment in the rendering process when visible surfaces are assigned a **shading value**. This value is calculated based on the relationship between the surface normals and the light sources that reach the surface. **Surface normals** are vectors or straight lines with a specific direction, and they are located on the vertices, or corners, of each polygon of the surface. A large number of software programs convert all surfaces to polygonal surfaces for the purpose of shading. The surface normals are used to define the orientation of a surface, and they have a paramount role in the calculation of surface shading. (Surface normals are also used in some rendering methods to determine whether surfaces are visible or hidden.)

Each shading technique is based on different representations of light and surface. These shading representations are contained in mathematical models that process the variables associated with shading in different ways. Some of the most popular surface shading techniques with local illumination include faceted, smooth, and specular shading. Shading techniques are sometimes also referred to by the last name of the individual who authored a specific version of the technique.

Often it is difficult to understand shading techniques because there are many different implementations of each of the basic shading techniques. Each rendering program offers its own version of the generic shading models, and sometimes the differences between implementations are significant. On occasion the basic shading models are mixed with each other or modified—for example, by adding new variables into the shading equation—resulting in **hybrid shading models** (Fig. 9.1.1). Therefore, when discussing shading techniques it is best to be specific and to discuss the implementation of a shading technique in a particular rendering program.

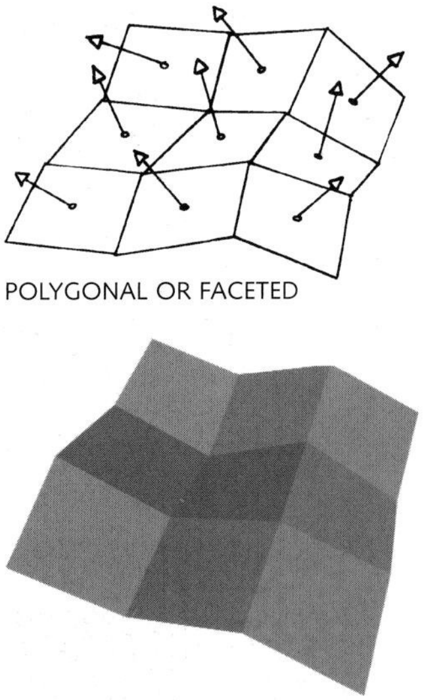

9.1.2 The shading of each polygon with faceted techniques is determined by one surface normal per polygon.

Faceted Shading

Faceted surface shading assigns a single and constant shading value to each visible polygon on the surface according to the angle of its normal in relation to the light source. This technique usually assigns a shading value to each polygon on the surface by measuring the amount of light that is received at the center of the polygon or in just one of the vertices. Most faceted shading models measure the amount of light received at the center of the polygon only. But some models measure the light received at the vertices of the polygon—usually three or four vertices—and the average value is applied uniformly to the entire polygon. Faceted shading, as indicated by its name, results in three-dimensional models with a faceted appearance that show each visible polygon in the model clearly distinguished from the rest. For this reason, faceted shading techniques are sometimes called polygonal shading, or constant value faceted shading. Most faceted shading techniques take into account parameters of ambient light only, but some also compute diffuse shading. Faceted techniques do not handle complex surface characteristics such as texture and transparency well—and sometimes not at all (Fig. 9.1.2). Faceted shading is the simplest type of shading and also the fastest because it uses only one surface normal per polygon to determine the shading for the entire polygon. The **Lambert shading model** is a popular form of faceted surface shading.

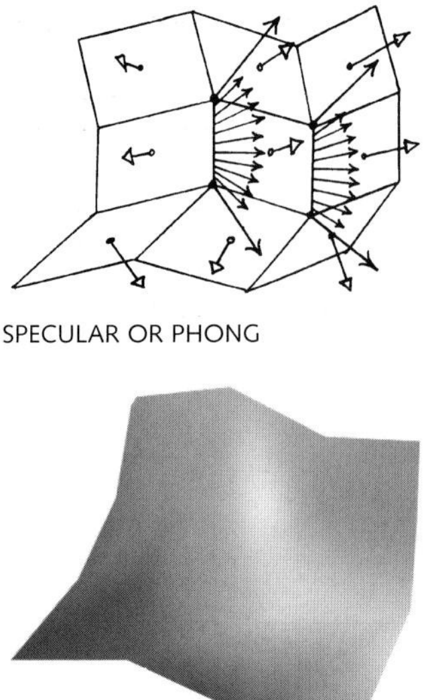

9.1.3 In specular shading, the vertex normals are interpolated across the surface of the polygon, and then shading is calculated at each point on the surface.

Smooth Shading

Smooth surface shading assigns a continuous shading value that blends throughout the visible polygons on the surface. The basic idea behind this technique is to average the surface normals of adjacent polygons, creating a smooth transition of shading between polygons. This is often done by first sampling the amount of light reaching the surface normals in the center of polygons, then by creating a vertex normal that averages the values of the surface normals of adjacent polygons, and finally by blending the intensities of the vertex normals in a polygon (Fig. 9.1.4). For this reason, smooth shading techniques create the appearance of smooth shading even with polygonal three-dimensional objects that have a small amount of modeling detail. Smooth shading is also called intensity interpolation shading. Some programs allow users to define the angle ranges for smooth shading to occur. Only when the angle between normals is less than the specified limit will this type of shading create a continuous blend throughout polygons on the surface. A popular shading model on which many smooth shading techniques are based is the **Gouraud shading model**. Smooth shading techniques do not compute the highlight values that are typical of reflective surfaces and as a result, create only surfaces with a matte finish. Smooth shading techniques take into account ambient and diffuse lighting parameters, and handle some of the complex surface characteristics well.

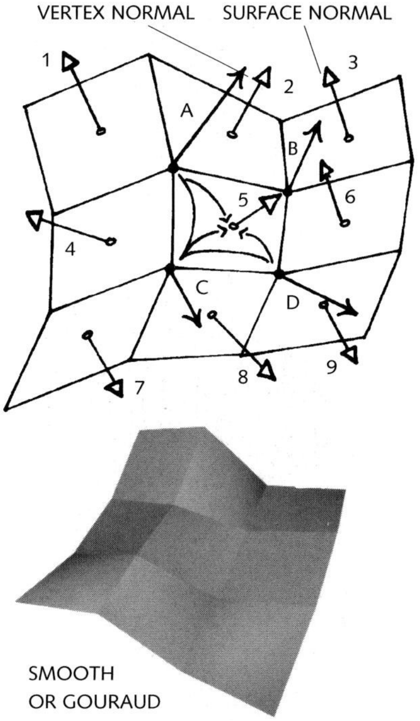

9.1.4 In smooth shading, the surface normals of four adjacent polygons are averaged to determine the four vertex normals of a single polygon. This process occurs four times in this illustration. Surface normals 1, 2, 4, and 5 are averaged to created vertex normal A. Surface normals 2, 3, 5, and 6 are averaged to create vertex normal B, and so on. Finally, the intensity values of the vertex normals are interpolated across the polygon.

Specular Shading

Specular surface shading techniques create surfaces with highlights that are found in reflective surfaces. The word *specular* means mirror-like. In addition, specular shading techniques create a smooth continuous shading across polygons by using normal interpolation techniques that are more detailed than those used by smooth shading methods. Specular shading is also called normal vector interpolation shading because it calculates the shading at every point on the surface of a polygon. This is done by interpolating the vertex normals and shading every point on the surface of the polygon by computing the relation between the angle of its normal and the angle of the incident light. This process differs from smooth shading, which calculates only the shading values at the vertices of the polygons, and then blends them across the points on the surface of the polygon (Fig. 9.1.3).

Many shading models on which specular shading techniques are based include the **Phong shading model** and its Blinn and Cook variations. Specular shading techniques take into account ambient, diffuse, and specular lighting, and they deal with detailed surface characteristics extremely well. This technique can create more accurate renderings than the other two shading techniques can, but it is also more computationally intensive.

RenderMan Shading

RenderMan is a collection of rendering tools that includes a shading language and a renderer or rendering program. The shading language is, in fact, a C-like programming language. It can be used to describe how things look, and it is especially well suited to create new looks and complex appearance on simple geometry. One of the main innovations of the **RenderMan shading language** is the fact that users have the ability to extend the **renderer** by writing shaders and shading capabilities with its shading language. As seen later in this chapter, a shader is a collection of shading characteristics and rendering techniques that are applied to an object during the rendering process. There are four basic types of RenderMan shaders: surface shaders (probably the most widely used type), light shaders, volume shaders, and displacement shaders. Shaders can be applied in layers as illustrated in Figure 9.2.5.

RenderMan can handle most types of geometry including polyhedra, parametric curved surfaces, patches, NURBS, and—more recently—point clouds (dots that can move like particles), blobby implicit surfaces and subdivided surfaces that have arbitrary topology, smooth interpolation, controllable creasing, improved motion blur, particles that have the ability to reflect light towards the camera, and soft shadows that fade out in the distance. RenderMan shaders written for general use can be saved as templates or library subroutines and incorporated as modules in other projects. Special-purpose shaders are often times customized for a particular geometry or production pipeline and therefore are not suitable for recycling (Figs. 1.2.7. and 1.3.2). In addition to the official release of the shading language, **Photorealistic RenderMan** (PR), there is a shareware version called **Blue Moon Rendering Tools** (BMRT) that has ray-tracing rendering capabilities.

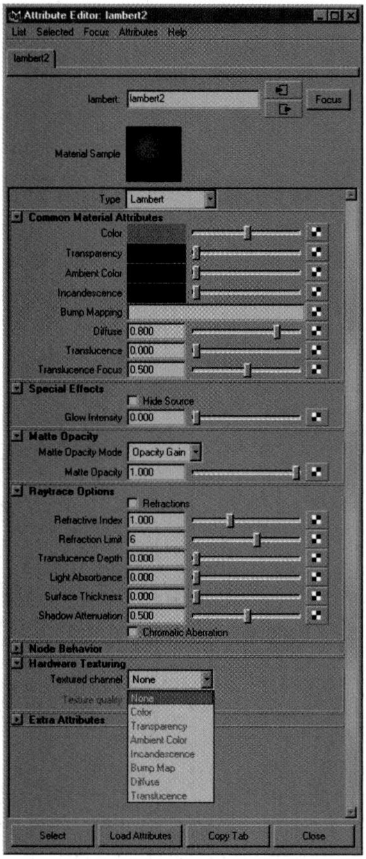

9.2.1 Surface properties can be edited by typing the numerical values or by dragging the appropriate sliders with the mouse. (Maya dialog box. © Alias|Wavefront, a division of Silicon Graphics Limited.)

9.2 Surface Shaders

A convenient way to think of all the variables that influence the rendering of a three-dimensional scene consists of grouping all of them in a shader. A **surface shader** is a collection of the surface characteristics and shading techniques that are applied to an object during the rendering process. Surface shaders are used to define the **surface finish** of the **simulated material** that a three-dimensional object is made of. The basic surface characteristics contained in most shaders include reflectivity, color, texture, and transparency. Surface shaders are used to determine the amount and color of light that is reflected by three-dimensional surfaces. Shaders also represent a flexible way to manage the large number of variables that are used to render three-dimensional objects. Ideally, shaders should be defined in such a way that different rendering methods can interpret the shaders according to their own rules.

The number of rendering methods available in different software varies between programs—some offer several rendering methods, while others offer just a few. As explained in Chapter 6, each rendering method has a particular approach to rendering three-dimensional objects. Some rendering methods may ignore variables that are not necessary for their calculations. This would be the case, for example, with a rendering program that is based on the Z-buffer method and that uses faceted or constant shading ignoring the transparency values contained in a shader. Ideally, even when a specific rendering method ignores some shader values it would still use the values that are relevant to it. Other rendering methods may require values that are particular to them but meaningless to other rendering methods. That would be the case, for example, with the reflection depth values that are meaningful only to a ray tracing program and not to other rendering techniques. The concept of shaders has slightly different meanings in different programs. In general, it means a collection of surface characteristics and shading techniques. Sometimes rendering programs provide all the information that is usually contained in a shader but scattered throughout several dialog boxes. In such cases, the surface characteristics and shading techniques applied to a three-dimensional object cannot be found and edited all together in the same place. Instead, the user has to look for them in different menus and work with multiple dialog boxes. While this approach may be less convenient than working with shaders that can easily be edited and applied to different objects, the end result in most cases is the same, as long as all the shading variables are available.

Sometimes shaders include only surface characteristics that can be applied to the three-dimensional objects independently from the shading techniques used to render them (Fig. 9.2.1). When shaders include only the characteristics of the surface material and not the shading technique to be used for rendering they are often called **surface libraries** or **material databases**. Shaders are usually applied to entire objects or groups of objects, but they can also be assigned to parts of an object, for example, a group of polygons as shown in Figure 12.1.7. In general, surface shaders use some or all of the following information to determine the shading of a surface: shader name, shading technique and parameters, surface characteristics and parameters, and rendering method and parameters (Fig. 9.2.2). Shaders can be edited by typing numerical values, by dragging sliders, or by modifying function curves. The ranges of shader values are often between zero percent and 100 percent, from 0 to 255, or from 0 to 1. Figure 9.2.3 shows interfaces for defining shader information.

Specifying surface characteristics often requires a fair amount of attention to detail. Doing a good job in the simulation of surface materials has an impact on the quality, refinement, and energy of the final rendered image. Specifying the surface characteristics and choosing the shading techniques are two distinct steps, but they are intrinsically related to one another and often overlap with each other.

When defining surface shaders and when applying them to three-dimensional surfaces, it is important to consider the lighting characteristics that the shaders will be used under. Lighting conditions have a powerful effect on the appearance of shaders to the extent that the same shader can look very different under two different lighting conditions.

Surface Layers

One of the great advantages of using surface shaders or surface libraries is that complex surface characteristics can be defined in the form of **surface layers**. This method builds the surface characteristics of a three-dimensional object by adding layers and compounding

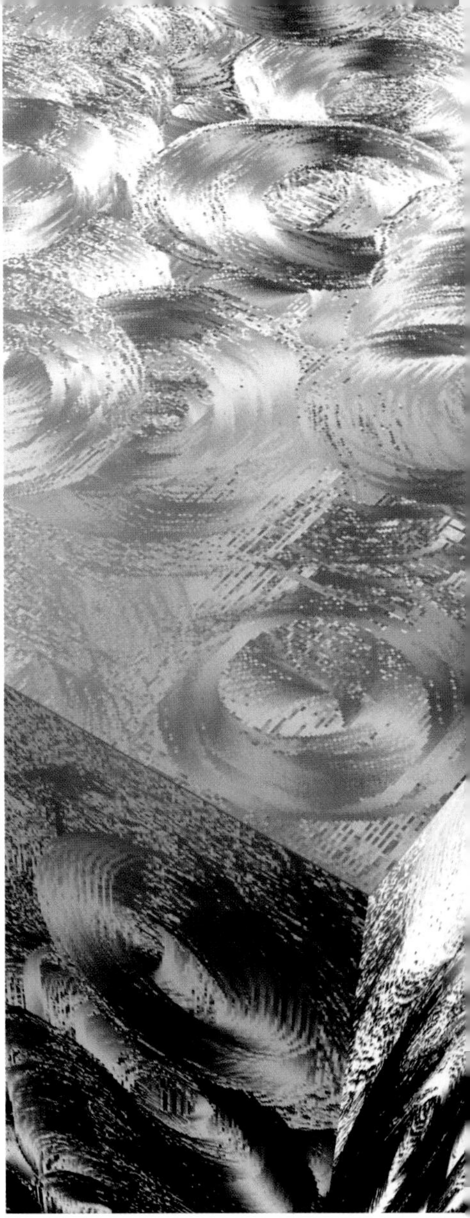

9.2.2 This image of brushed metal was created with a reflection model for metallic surfaces. The model handles the effects of diffraction by taking into account the wave nature of light, and it was implemented in the form of Maya software shaders. The directions of anisotropy, different values reflected in different directions, were texture mapped to add visual detail. (© 1998 Jos Stam, Alias|Wavefront.)

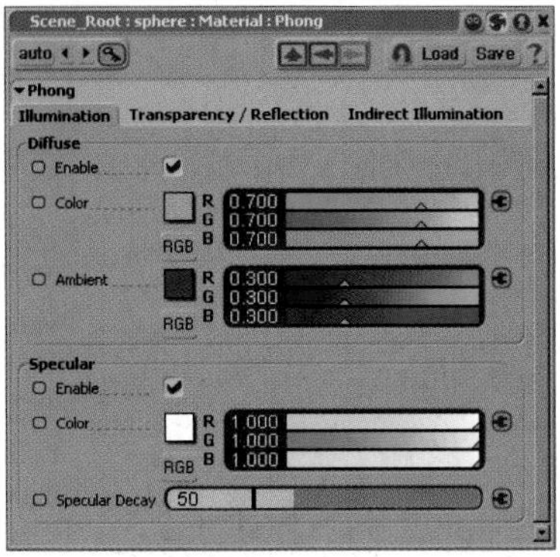

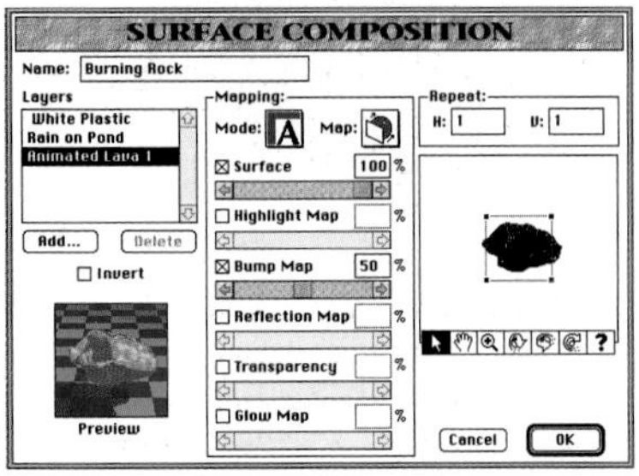

9.2.3 An editor of shading parameters (top), and editor for the composition of surface layers, mapping projection, and interactive map placement (bottom). (Top: XSI dialog box courtesy of Softimage Co. All rights reserved. Bottom: Infini-D 3.0 dialog box. © Specular International, Ltd.)

9.2.4 (top right) Still from Final Fantasy rendered with multiple layers of two-dimensional maps and three-dimensional lights and geometry. Motion capture was used for about 90 percent of the human motion, using 16 camera system from Motion Analysis in an 8 x 10 x 2.5 meter capture area, resulting in over 2,000 motion capture elements. Only body data was captured, not including hands and faces.(© 2001 FFFP.)

their effects to determine the final look of the surface. Fig. 9.2.3 shows an interface to compose complex surfaces with layers. This method is similar to the way, for example, in which painters during the Renaissance created their paintings by first priming the surface with a white mixture, and then applying, one at a time, multiple coats of opaque and transparent paint and varnish. On occasions the **underpaint** coats contained colors that were not directly visible but that influenced the translucent colors from upper layers in particular and the overall color effect in general. At the end of this process the dry surface was burnished to compact all the layers of paint and varnish, and also to create a smooth, shiny outer surface. There is a great variety of techniques for layering surface shaders, just as there are many techniques for painting (Figs. 9.2.4–9.2.5). Surface layers can also be used in the rendering of **surface subscattering** effects. A few renderers have the ability to calculate the distribution and behavior of light as it travels back and forth through translucent surfaces. This technique allows for realistic rendering of skin that takes into account multiple layers of skin, fat and capillaries.

9.3 Image Mapping

Image mapping is a very important component of the surface shading process, and it is also a rich technique that deserves to be examined separately. The basic idea behind **image mapping** consists of taking a two-dimensional image and mapping it on the surface of a three-dimensional object. There are many mapping techniques, for example, projecting or wrapping, and each creates a distinct result. But the real power of image mapping lies in the fact that two-dimensional images can be used to very efficiently simulate not only the texture of a three-dimensional surface, but also other surface attributes such as reflectivity, and roughness.

Image mapping techniques are often used as shortcuts for simulating surface characteristics. In fact, the exact same image can be mapped in different ways onto a surface for simulating attributes such as color, texture, and transparency (Figs. 9.3.1). Each of these attributes can also be simulated with a unique image map.

Image maps can modulate the surface characteristics by linking the brightness or color of a pixel in the image map to the characteristics of the point in the surface where that pixel is mapped. For example, the brightness of a pixel in an image map can control the reflectivity of the point on the surface where the pixel is mapped, or its color, or its transparency. Different image maps can also be combined to control different aspects of the surface characteristics of an object. The types of image maps covered in this chapter include reflection and environmental maps, color maps, procedural maps, bump and displacement maps, and transparency maps. The nomenclature used here to describe image maps is quite generic and is used in many three-dimensional software programs. The reader should be cautioned, however, that once in a while the same name is used by different programs to indicate different types of image maps.

9.2.5 The surface in the top layer is composed of the four separate layers below it. The second layer from top to bottom is translucent and refracts the image of the layers below (see the top edge of the third layer from top to bottom). The different layers of a planet's atmosphere or a human's skin can be easily rendered using this layering technique.

Creating the Map

Two-dimensional images that can be mapped onto three-dimensional surfaces include painted images, photographic images, and abstract patterns. As explained shortly, each of these images is best suited for a specific purpose. Image maps can be created directly with computer paint systems and brought into the rendering program in a variety of file formats (Figs. 9.3.2 and 9.3.3). **Digital painting** software—commonly called paint systems—provides many of the tools found in the studio of a traditional painter, such as brushes and sticks of different types, paints of different colors and densities, and papers with different degrees of texture and absorbency. These painting tools and media are simulated by the computer system, but in many cases these simulated tools behave like their physical counterparts, especially when a **pressure-sensitive** graphics tablet is used instead of a mouse. Painted images that are to be used as maps can be created from scratch with the computer paint system, or they can be based on a sketch or photograph that is scanned into the program.

Images that can be mapped onto three-dimensional surfaces can also be captured directly into the computer system with a variety of input devices. This includes recording a live image with a **digital camera**, scanning an existing photograph or painting with a flatbed or laser **digital scanner**, or loading an image file that was previously scanned and saved on a **CD-ROM**.

Scanners and digital cameras transform the visual information into numerical information that can be easily processed by the computer software. This conversion is done by converting the **continuous visual information** that we find in reality, a color photograph, or a painting into a series of **discrete numerical values**. This conversion is based on an **averaging** of the values found in the original image. The scanning process starts with a **sampling** of the color values in the image. The number of samples taken from an image directly determines the spatial resolution of the image map.

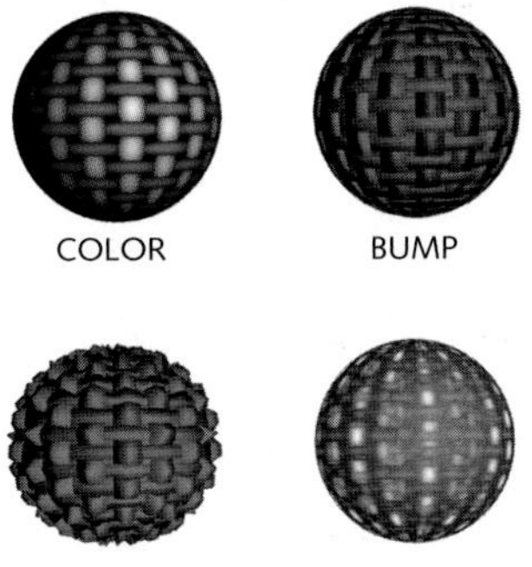

9.3.1 The same two-dimensional image is used as a map to control different surface attributes including color, two types of texture (bump and displacement), and transparency.

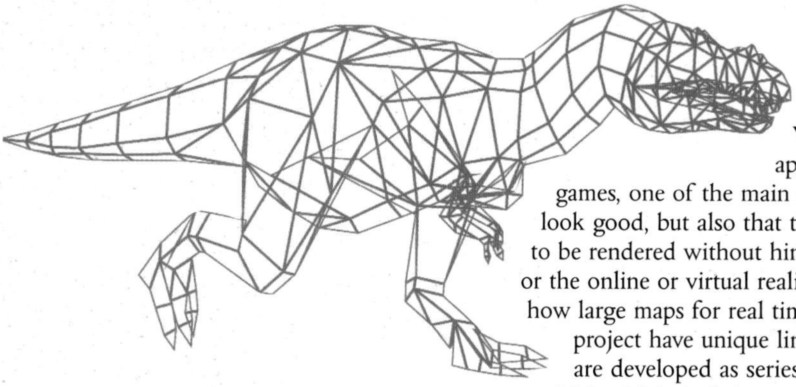

Maps for Real-Time

When creating maps for real-time applications like computer or platform games, one of the main concerns is making sure that they look good, but also that they are efficient and compact enough to be rendered without hindering the performance of the game, or the online or virtual reality experience. There is no set limit to how large maps for real time should be; each system and each project have unique limitations. Usually maps for real time are developed as series of small panels or tiles of all sizes: 256 × 256 pixels is a common one. Each of the panels may contain different images that are usually assembled and mapped onto the model in real time. Sometimes a single panel will be repeated—or tiled—to fill a large surface. The character in Figure 9.3.4, for example, uses almost a dozen 256 × 256 panels, while the character in Figure 9.3.5 uses a single 128 × 256 map. Some panels from Fig. 9.3.4, the hair panel for example, are tiled over large surfaces. The middle left section in the rectangular map from Figure 9.3.5 is mirrored and also stretched along the shirt. A basic principle when tiling image maps is to make sure that the texture seams or outer borders match, so that the resulting texture will appear to be a large single map as opposed to many small off-sync tiles.

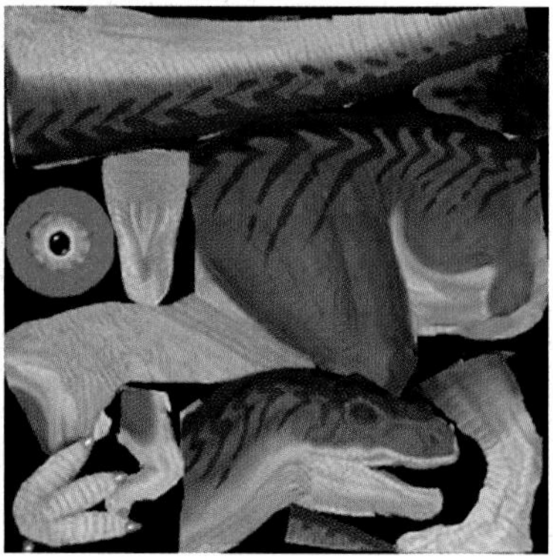

9.3.2 Different color maps were painted for different sections of a T-Rex low resolution polygonal model. The game engine takes care of mapping the different sections of the image onto the right area of the geometry. See Fig. 10.5.5 for the inverse kinematics skeleton for this polygonal model. (Courtesy of Angel Studios.)

The maps used in the real-time character shown in Figure 11.1.1 have a surface of only 32 × 32 pixels, which translates into a total file size of 3.7 Kb. But after the bitmaps are converted to the Playstation .sif texture format they shrink down to 572 bytes. The main character in the Spyro the Dragon™ game uses about 20 of these texture maps, while most of the supporting cast uses up to 10 maps each. In fact, the majority of the characters in this and other games have texture maps that cover only about 15% of their body surfaces, while the rest of their bodies is rendered with smooth shading only in order to conserve precious memory—VRAM in particular—during gameplay.

Generally speaking the painting style used to develop image maps for real time should be kept simple, somewhat graphic, and usually within a fairly limited color palette—especially if color look-up tables will be used in the rendering of the game (Fig. 9.3.6). As seen in Figure 13.1.4 the use of color lookup tables for rendering tends to limit the range of color, even if the original image map had rich and subtle color values. On the other hand, increasing the amount of detail painted in the texture7 map usually softens the look of low resolution geometry. Deciding what the right balance is between too much detail and too little detail is often based on previous experience and understanding what works best in the target playback platform.

Image maps for real-time applications are rarely layered due to the limitations of the real-time rendering, but they are often times used in conjunction with procedural textures of the kind shown in Figures 9.6.3 and 9.6.4. In those cases when real-time procedural

textures are not feasible—because they require a fair amount of computing—a great shortcut consists of generating a procedural texture, saving it as an image map, and apply it onto the geometry.

9.3.3 This rendering of a virtual actress (can you guess who?) was created by mapping different types of texture maps onto spline-based geometry. The color map used can be seen in Figure 9.5.1, the bump map in Figure 9.6.2, and the geometry in Figure 5.1.3. (Director: Daniel Robichaud, Animation Supervisor: Stéphane Couture, Art Direction: Michelle Deniaud. © 1999 Virtual Celebrity/ Marlene Inc.)

Maps for Feature Film

When creating maps for feature film the main and overriding concern is that they look good; rendering times usually are of secondary importance. The size of image maps for feature film ranges from a couple of megabytes to dozens, even hundreds, of megabytes. The image map in Figure 9.5.1, for example, is 3072 × 3072 pixels and over 36 megabytes and was used along with the maps in Figure 9.6.2 to render the headshot in Figure 9.3.3. The two key factors in deciding how large a map for feature film should be are the size of the area to be covered by the map, and the distance of the map to the camera. The closer a map is to the camera, the larger its size and the more detail will be required. A map for a close-up shot of the main character is going to be much more detailed that a facial map for a virtual extra sitting in the background.

The style used to develop image maps for feature film is usually very detailed since these tend to be rendered accurately. Image maps for animated features often use a lush painterly style since that translates well into the three-dimensional environments. Sometimes por-

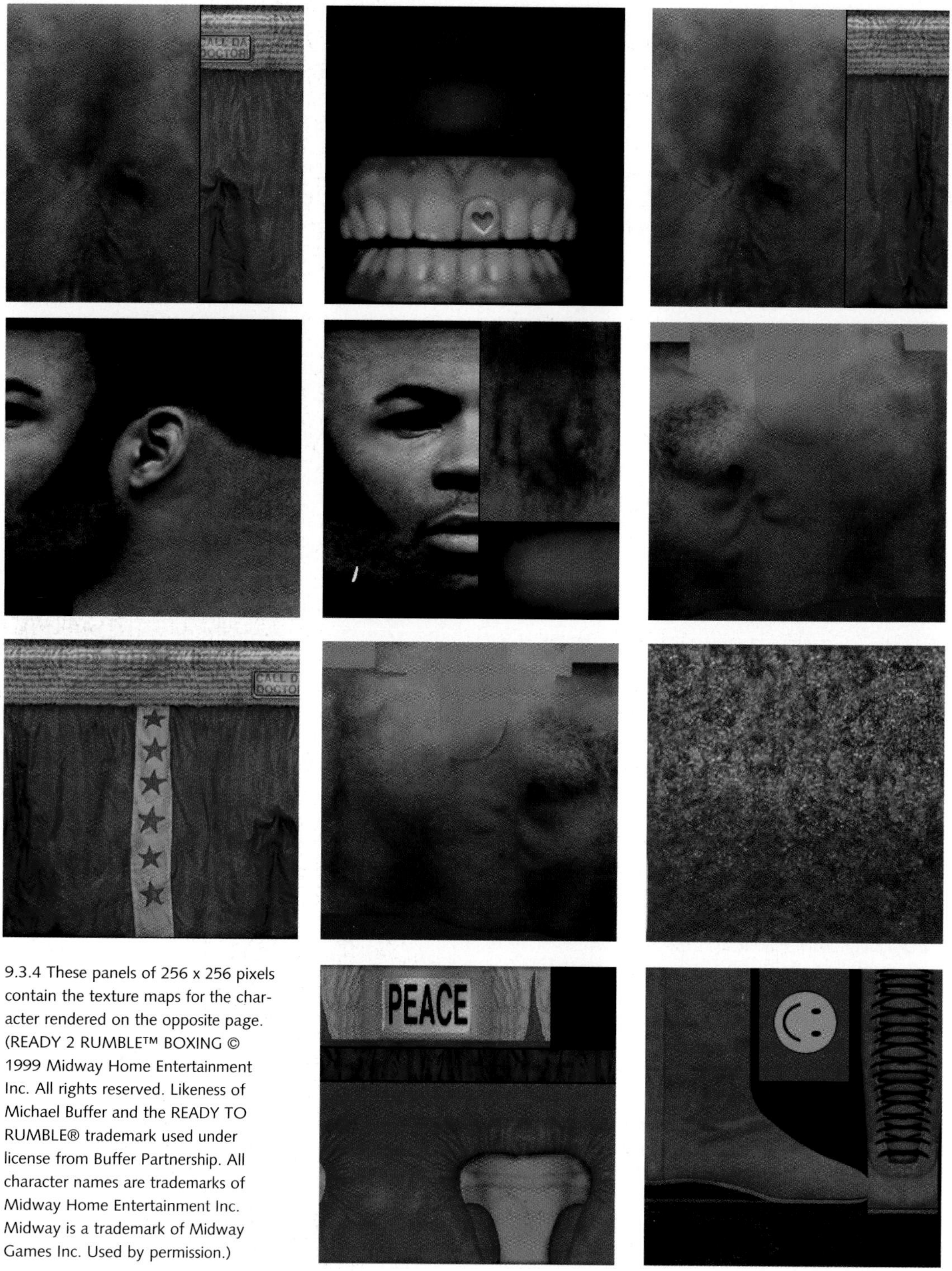

9.3.4 These panels of 256 x 256 pixels contain the texture maps for the character rendered on the opposite page. (READY 2 RUMBLE™ BOXING © 1999 Midway Home Entertainment Inc. All rights reserved. Likeness of Michael Buffer and the READY TO RUMBLE® trademark used under license from Buffer Partnership. All character names are trademarks of Midway Home Entertainment Inc. Midway is a trademark of Midway Games Inc. Used by permission.)

tions of photographic reference are cut and pasted into the digital paintings for added effects. In the case of live action feature films most image maps usually come from photographs, often taken on location. In most visual effects shots for live action films it is imperative that the image maps closely match the look of the background plates and live elements. Figure 9.3.7 shows a creature rendered with very detailed image maps that also match the coloring and lighting of the live background plate.

Image maps are rarely tiled for feature film because of their tendency to reveal a uniform pattern over large areas that may look unnatural. A trick that is often used to soften the look of tiled image maps consists of adding a certain degree of random image noise to the regular pattern or patterns that are being tiled. This technique was used effectively for rendering portions of the road's asphalt in the feature film ***Toy Story 2***. Image maps for feature film are often layered to achieve a richer look. The skin of virtual characters, for example, can gain realism and depth by rendering it in translucent layers as pictured in Figure 9.2.5. Going from the inside out these layers could have, for example, the blood vessels, the flesh, the freckles, the skin oil on the surface, and the makeup. Image maps for film are also often used in conjunction with procedural textures. The later provide an excellent solution to mapping convoluted geometry that might make the wrapping of the image maps very difficult. Finally, the techniques of image-based rendering and modeling described in earlier chapters take the concept of photographic image maps to a new level that actually derives most illumination and modeling information from the photographs and measurements taken on location (Figs. 5.5.12, 6.8.1, and 6.8.2).

Projection Methods

There are many ways to project image maps onto three-dimensional surfaces. Some projection methods are simple and others are complex; some create realistic effects and others create surprising results. Choosing a **mapping projection method** should be based on creative considerations without ignoring production concerns. Some projection methods may express the ideas behind a rendered image better than others. Some of the most useful projection methods

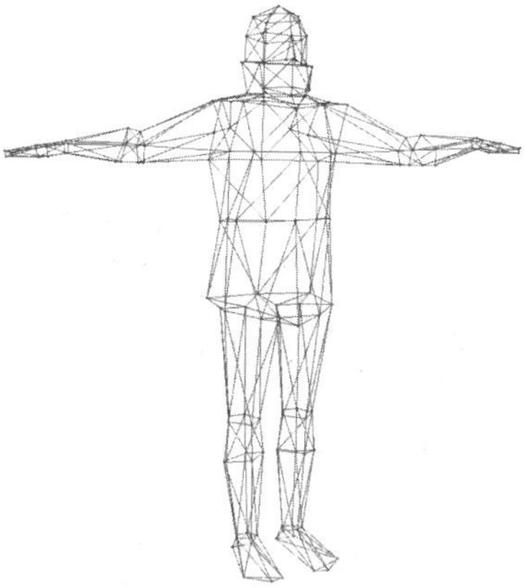

9.3.5 The rectangular mosaic of textures contains the color maps for the three-dimensional low resolution model shown in wireframe (top) and shaded modes (opposite page). Notice the economy and effectiveness of the maps once applied to the character. The mosaic is 128 × 256 pixels, and at 72 ppi is roughly 1.8 × 3.5 in. (Created by Mark Lizotte. © 1998 Looking Glass Studios.)

include flat and cubical, cylindrical, and spherical.

The **flat projection** method applies maps onto surfaces in a flat way. This projection method is ideal for applying image maps onto flat surfaces because the results are totally predictable, and the potential for distortion is minimal as long as the three-dimensional surface is parallel to the projection plane. In principle, flat projection can occur on any plane—XY, XZ, and YZ—with identical results as long as the three-dimensional surface is parallel to the projection plane. But flat projection can also be used on curved objects to simulate the effect of slide or film projectors because this method projects a flat image in a perpendicular way onto whatever is in front of it (Fig. 9.3.8). Another useful application of flat projection is the creation of **backdrops** and simple **dioramas** that include three-dimensional objects and characters placed in front of a painted or photographic backdrop.

The **cubical projection** method is a variation of the flat projection method that repeats the map on each of the six sides of a cube. This projection method is particularly effective with cubes but only as long as one of the planes of the cube is parallel to the projection plane. Cubical projection can also be used on curved or irregular objects to achieve unexpected results (Fig. 9.3.8).

The **cylindrical projection** method applies maps onto surfaces by wrapping the sides of the map around the shape until the two ends of the map meet behind the object (Fig. 9.3.8). This projection technique is useful for mapping textures around elongated objects like a carrot or a glass bottle. Cylindrical projections are designed to wrap around the object and to cover its entire surface, but wrapping of cylindrical projections can be customized so that the opposite sides of the map do not meet, and cover only a portion of the object. This is controlled by specifying the **angle of mapping** around the object with a degree value. A cylindrical projection can also be customized by determining whether the top and bottom of the object are to be left uncovered or whether they are to be covered with a cap. A cap in a cylindrical projection uses the same texture wrapped around the object unless specified otherwise.

The **spherical projection** applies a rectangular map by wrapping it around a surface until the opposite sides meet, and then pinching it at the top and bottom and stretching it until the entire object is covered. This technique is useful for projecting maps onto round objects, such as a basketball or a football. Spherical projections wrap the map around the entire three-dimensional object unless the projection is customized to cover just a portion of the object. This can be controlled—as it is in cylindrical projections—by specifying an angle of mapping (Fig. 9.3.8).

The **wrapping** projection method—as it is called in some programs—allows textures to be projected onto three-dimensional objects in a straight way, but also to be stretched until the four sides of the map are pressed against each other. This projection type is useful for placing texture maps over objects that may require stretching throughout the map for a good fit—such as terrains or complex surfaces. This

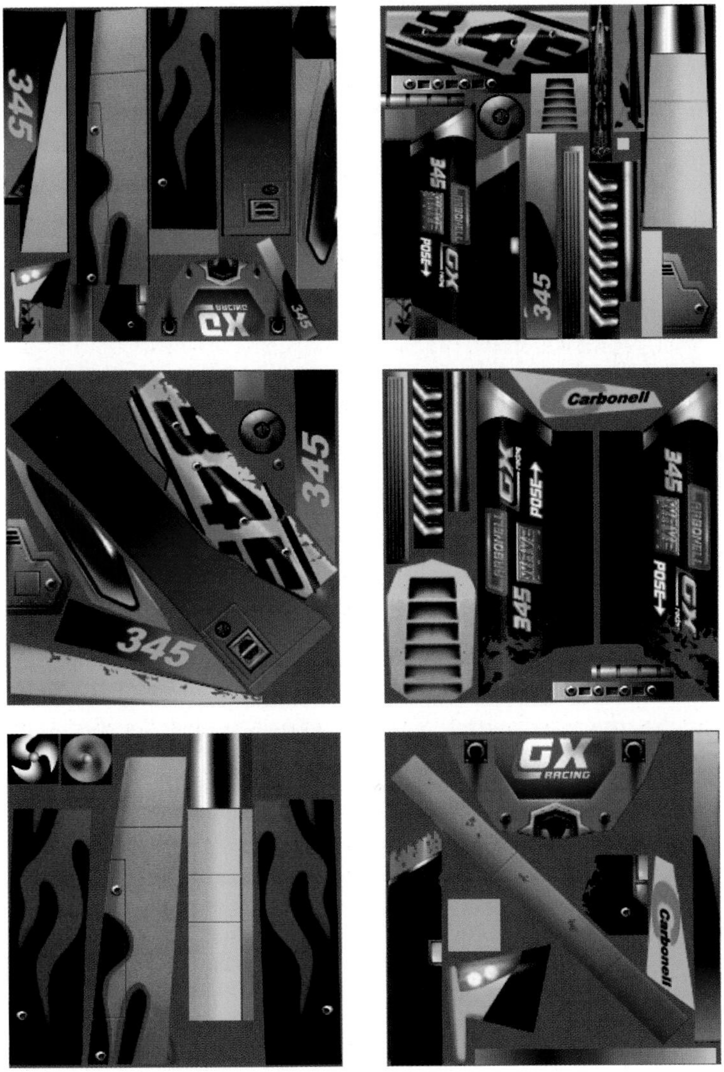

9.3.6 Finished vehicle from *Hydro Thunder* and the six 256 × 256 image maps used on the surface. (© 1999 Midway Home Entertainment Inc. Midway is a trademark of Midway Games Inc. Used by permission.)

technique is also effective for applying textures to small portions of three-dimensional objects in the form in which decals are applied to model airplanes (Fig. 9.3.9).

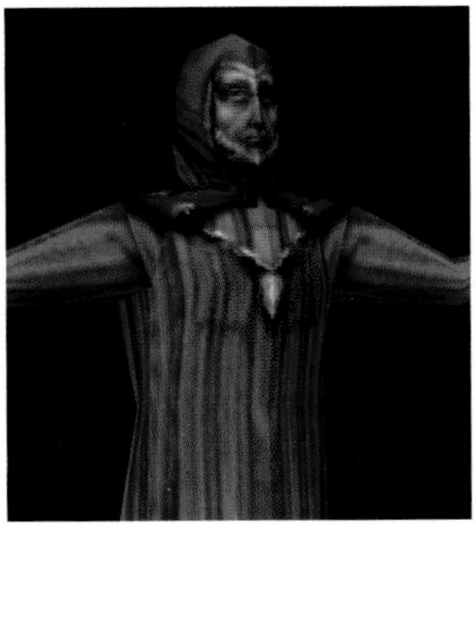

Positioning the Map

There are a variety of techniques that facilitate the placement of texture maps on three-dimensional surfaces. Ideally, maps should cover the entire three-dimensional surface unless a specific project requires a different approach. Texture maps are always **rectangular images** that are applied to polygonal or curved surfaces, and they can be defined by tagging their four corners. The nomenclature for identify-

9.3.7 A three-dimensional computer-generated creature was composited with the live-action plate in this sequence of *Deep Rising*. Notice the matching of the computer-generated lighting with the lighting on the live set. (Images courtesy of The Walt Disney Company. © Hollywood Pictures Company. All rights reserved.)

ing the corners of a texture map is simple whether the surface is made of polygons or curved patches (Fig. 9.3.10). The upper left corner of the map is designated as the origin (0, 0), the lower left corner is (0, 1), the upper right corner is (1, 0), and the lower left corner is (1, 1). In some cases, the lower left corner is designated as the origin, and the upper right corner is designated (1, 1).

Ordinarily a texture map is pinned by default to the origin of a surface, wherever the origin may be (origins can be located, for example, in one corner of the surface or in its center). This procedure is straightforward in cases when the three-dimensional surfaces are simple, and when the maps are supposed to cover the entire shape. However, placing texture maps on three-dimensional surfaces requires some fine-tuning when the surfaces are complex, when the proportions of the map and the surface differ, or when special effects are sought. It is important to keep in mind that the tools for positioning of the texture maps over three-dimensional surfaces vary greatly between programs.

Some programs allow interactive placement of texture maps over three-dimensional surfaces. Texture maps can also be positioned very accurately over three-dimensional surfaces by inputting **numerical values**. With this method a map can be moved with precision over the surface. In the cases of polygonal objects, **XY coordinates** are used to **offset the map** over the surface. The default position of maps aligns them at (0, 0). If the map is offset by (.5, .5), it will be moved horizontally and vertically halfway across the surface.

In general, the **parameter space** used to position image maps on curved patches is based on the rectangular coordinate system used when maps are applied to polygonal models. But points on curved surface are defined in terms of their **UV coordinates** instead of their XY values. The parameter space of a curved surface is defined by a U (or u) horizontal value that stretches from 0 to 1, and a V (or v) vertical value that also ranges from 0 to 1. The value of U is commonly 0 on the left edge of the parameter space, and 1 on the right edge. The value of V is 0 at the top of the parameter space, and 1 at the bottom. All the points located within this rectangular parameter space are defined in terms of U,V coordinates. The rectangle is twisted and bent to match the shape of curved patches or quadric surfaces, which are built from a curve that is swept in three-dimensional space around an axis, like a surface of revolution. In quadric surfaces, the U axis represents longitude, and it runs approximately the circumference of the revolution; the V axis represents latitude, and it runs along the curve that is used to define the surface (Figs. 9.3.11 and 9.3.13).

Positioning image maps with UV coordinates is a very precise method that allows you to match specific pixels on the mapped image with specific vertices on the surface of the three-dimensional object. When mapping textures on curved surfaces it is common to use UV parameters. Similar accurate placement techniques are also available for positioning image maps onto polygonal structures. Image textures that are mapped with UV techniques usually stretch in a way that follows with little distortion the shape of the three-dimensional object. This is due to the extreme control of image pixel-to-object vertex matching offered by UV mapping. Textures mapped with UV techniques are like elastic surfaces—a silk stocking, for example—that stretch over three-dimensional objects.

In addition to all the controls for accurately placing a two-dimensional image map on a three-dimensional surface, there are other techniques for controlling the map once it has been placed on the surface. These techniques include scaling and tiling. **Scaling** image maps can be used when the maps need to cover more or less of the surface of an object. Image maps that are too small to cover the entire object can be scaled up. Likewise, image maps that are too large to be seen in their entirety when placed on the surface of the object can be scaled down. Maps can also be scaled in cases where the software automatically scales a map of any dimension to fit the object, but the desired effect requires that the map only covers a portion of the object.

Tiling an image allows you to create patterns based on repeating a tile or single rectangular image map. A large number of three-dimensional software programs can repeat an image in a variety of arrangements along the vertical and horizontal axes. Some tiling permutations commonly available are plain repetition without any image flipping, repetition with horizontal flipping on every other tile only, repetition with vertical flipping only, and repetition with both horizontal and vertical flipping (Fig. 9.3.14).

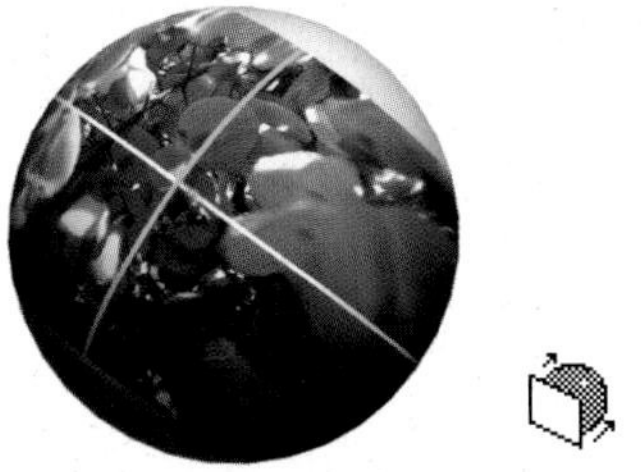

FLAT OR STRAIGHT PROJECTION

CUBICAL PROJECTION

CYLINDRICAL PROJECTION

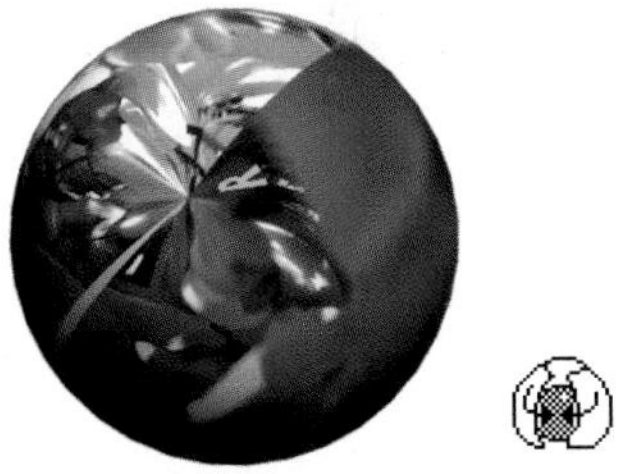

SPHERICAL PROJECTION

9.3.8 An image map (previous page, lower left) applied to a sphere with four different projection methods. Notice how cubical projection repeats the map six times, and how spherical projection stretches the map toward the poles as it wraps it around. (Infini-D 3.0 icons. © Specular International, Ltd.)

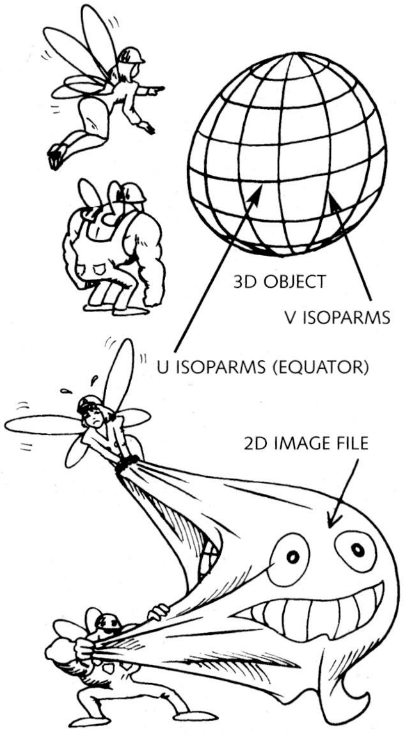

9.3.9 Wrapping projection is useful for fitting image maps with maximum coverage onto three-dimensional objects.

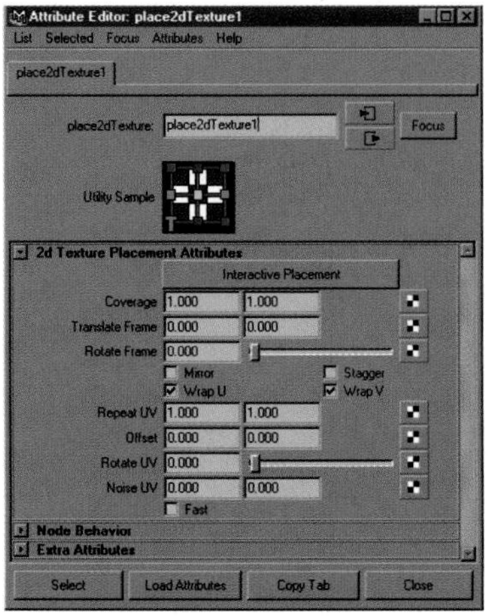

9.3.10 Dialog box with parameters for placing interactively maps on a surface. (© Aliasl Wavefront, a division of Silicon Graphics Limited.)

Map Blending

Map blending techniques determine the way in which surface layers, including image maps, blend with the surface of the object as well as with other surface layers. The blending of an image map with other surface characteristics can be controlled in a variety of ways. Some map blending techniques include overall blending, blending by types of illumination, blending with the alpha channel, and blending with matting techniques. **Overall blending** allows to control the degree by which the image map blends uniformly with all the attributes of the surface. Overall blending is usually expressed in percentages of visibility, ranging from blending where only the map is visible to blending where only the surface is visible (and the map is totally invisible). Intermediate stages of overall blending allow for different degrees of blending. Blending by type of **surface illumination** controls the degree by which the maps blends with the surface by splitting it in terms of ambient, diffuse, and specular areas of surface illumination.

Blending with **matting techniques** allows you to control the degree of blending using different parts or aspects of the image map as a mask. A **mask** is an image that masks or protects a surface, or portions of it, and it determines the degree by which different portions of the image map blend with the surface. Masks can be high-contrast or continuous. **High-contrast masks** have sharp edges and solid areas, while **continuous masks** have soft edges and different shades of gray. Blending with matting techniques can be done by using all the pixels in the image map to mask out the surface, or by using only the black or white pixels in the map as a mask. Overall blending controls can be used in conjunction with matting techniques for creating a wide variety of blending possibilities (Fig. 9.3.12).

Blending or compositing with an alpha channel allows you to control the blending of the surface and the image map according to an additional image file that is used as a mask in the matting process. An **alpha channel** is a black-and-white image file that is linked to an image map. Alpha channels can be saved with an image file in the form of a fourth channel in a standard RGB image file. An alpha channel can be used to determine the degree of blending of the image map with a surface based on the intensity of brightness values of the pixels in the file used as alpha channels. Total blending (transparency) can be assigned to the black pixels in the alpha channel, and lack of blending (opacity) to the white pixels; the reverse is also possible. The pixels with gray values are always assigned different degrees of blending. (Read Chapter 13 for more information on matting techniques and the alpha channel.)

9.4 Surface Reflectivity

Light can be reflected off reflective surfaces in different ways depending on the proportion of the types or components of surface reflectivi-

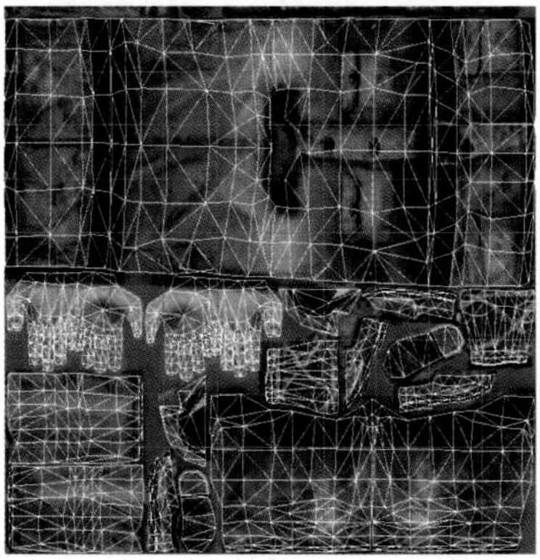

9.3.11 An image map with the clothing for one of the *Medal of Honor* characters is placed on the polygonal surface using specific UV locations. (© 1999 Electronic Arts Inc. Medal of Honor and Electronic Arts are trademarks or registered trademarks of Electronic Arts Inc. in the U.S. and/or other countries. Medal of Honor is a trademark or registered trademark of Electronic Arts Inc. in the U.S. and/or other countries for computer and video game products. All rights reserved.)

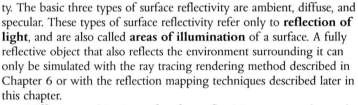

ty. The basic three types of surface reflectivity are ambient, diffuse, and specular. These types of surface reflectivity refer only to **reflection of light**, and are also called **areas of illumination** of a surface. A fully reflective object that also reflects the environment surrounding it can only be simulated with the ray tracing rendering method described in Chapter 6 or with the reflection mapping techniques described later in this chapter.

Different combinations of surface reflectivity types can be used to simulate the surfaces of different materials. **Matte surfaces**, for example, can be simulated by using a combination of ambient and diffuse reflections. **Metallic surfaces** can be simulated with ambient and specular reflections. **Plastic surfaces** are typically simulated with a combination of ambient, diffuse, and specular reflections (Fig. 9.4.1). Most shading software programs provide accurate controls to vary the sharpness and decay of the specular reflection in both metallic and plastic surfaces.

Ambient Reflection

The type of surface reflection that reacts to the intensity and color of the ambient light sources only is called **ambient reflection**. A unique characteristic of ambient reflection is that its intensity is independent of the distance between the reflective surface and the light source and also of the angle of the surface in respect to the

9.3.12 Blending with matting techniques can be used to reveal or cover portions of the image layers on the surface of an object. In this example the final result (top) was obtained by layering an image map and its own alpha channel onto a blue sphere, and revealing the dark blue surface of the sphere only through the black pixels in the alpha channel. A similar result can be obtained with a simpler image map without an alpha channel and using the white pixels in the map to reveal the dark blue surface underneath.

light source. This means that light scatters evenly in all directions and that, as a result, all the polygons in three-dimensional models that are shaded with just ambient reflection end up with the same intensity. As a result, the three-dimensional models appear as a completely flat silhouette when only this type of reflection is used to shade them. But when ambient reflection is used in conjunction with other types of reflection, it contributes to the overall intensity of the object. (Fig. 9.4.1).

Diffuse Reflection

A surface with **diffuse reflection** reacts to incident light in different ways depending on the position and orientation of the light source in respect to the surface. Naturally, a light source that is very close to a surface with diffuse reflection will reflect more than a light source that is far away. But the most important factor in diffuse reflection is not so much the distance between the light source and the object as the angular position of the light source in relation to the object. Diffuse reflection is greater in areas of the surface that face the light source in a perpendicular way. The amount of light reflected with diffuse reflection decreases as the angle between the incident light source and the reflective surface becomes more oblique. Areas of a surface with diffuse reflection that are not reached by the light reflect very little or not at all (Fig. 9.4.1). The size of the surface area that faces the light source is also a factor in the intensity of the reflected light when using diffuse reflection.

Specular Reflection

Surfaces with **specular reflection** appear very shiny because they reflect light the way a mirror does. Specular reflection light does not scatter evenly throughout the surface. Instead, it is reflected in a focused and concentrated way, a characteristic known as **highlight sharpness**. In determining the amount of light reflected by surfaces with specular reflection the position of the light source alone with respect to the surface is not as critical as it is in diffuse reflections. Instead, the apparent intensity of light reflected off surfaces with specular reflection depends mostly on the relation between the angle of the reflected light and the angle of the camera that is looking at the object. The intensity of the reflected light is greater when these two angles coincide. As the two angles move farther apart, the intensity of the reflected light decays sharply, a characteristic known as **highlight decay** (Fig. 9.4.1).

Reflection Maps

The visual effects of reflection can be used effectively to render shiny materials such as glasses, metals, or plastics, and varnished surfaces. When applied to objects that are not ordinarily reflective in the real world, reflectivity attributes can effectively simulate virtual realities. Realistic reflection effects can be best obtained with ray tracing rendering, which simulates with precision the amount of reflectivity on a three-dimensional surface. Another strategy for creating reflective surfaces is based on reflection maps.

A **reflection map** consists of a two-dimensional image that is applied to a three-dimensional surface with the purpose of making the surface—or portions of it—reflective. A surface with a reflection map reflects the image of the three-dimensional models that are placed in front of the surface. The brightness values in a reflection map are used by the software to determine which parts of the surface are reflective and which are not. The dark values in a reflection map are used by some programs to determine which parts of the object will be fully reflective, but sometimes the light values in the map are used for the same purpose. Either way, the final results are the same.

Reflection maps are usually monochromatic and not in full color because the brightness values drive the simulation of reflectivity. Chromatic information in reflection maps is irrelevant and can be misleading to the individual who fine-tunes the subtle degrees of reflection in the map. Reflection maps can be projected onto three-dimensional surfaces with any of the standard projections used in texture mapping.

9.3.13 Characters for *Loco Rodeo* created with organic shapes and image maps painted with traditional watercolor. (Image created by Mondo Media, San Francisco, CA. © 1997 The Locomotion Channel.)

Environment Maps

Environment maps, like other types of image maps, are used to compute the color of light reflected by the surface of the map. **Environment maps** can be thought of as a special type of reflection map because they reflect not only the objects surrounding the mapped object but the environment surrounding the reflective surfaces (Figs. 9.4.2 and 9.4.5). But the main characteristic of environment maps is that they are projected on all the objects with reflective surface characteristics in the scene and not just on one particular object. (Reflection maps are usually applied to one three-dimensional surface at a time.) The reflections of the surroundings on a group of objects can also be calculated with ray tracing rendering, but environment maps are often a cost-effective way to achieve similar results that are appropriate and sufficient in a large number of rendering projects. This technique is a favored alternative for creating the

9.3.14 An example of tiling using the spiral image map on Figure 9.6.2.

AMBIENT REFLECTION

DIFFUSE REFLECTION

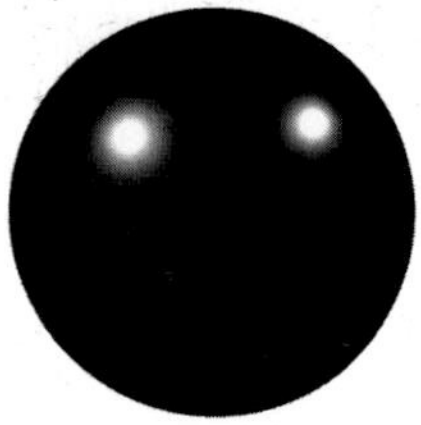

SPECULAR REFLECTION

ALL THREE REFLECTION TYPES

9.4.1 A sphere rendered with four different combinations of surface reflectivity. The first image is rendered with ambient reflection and an ambient light source. The second image is rendered with diffuse reflection only, one spotlight and one point light. The third image is rendered with specular reflection, one spotlight and one point light. The fourth image combines the three types of surface reflectivity and the three light sources.

appearance of global reflections when ray tracing rendering methods are not used. When both ray tracing and environment mapping are active simultaneously, most rendering programs calculate the two parameters. However, in such cases, priority is usually given to the ray-traced reflections by placing them closer to the objects, and in front of the environment map reflections.

Environment maps create an image of the environment that surrounds the object as seen from the object itself. The appearance of the reflection of the environment is achieved by preparing a simplified version of the three-dimensional environment in the form of two-dimensional images and then projecting those images onto the object with reflective surfaces as if they were the environment being reflected. Environment maps can be created with a variety of techniques. Two popular choices include a technique that resembles the spherical projection method and a technique that is an interesting variation of cubical projection of maps. In both cases, an image of the environment is first mapped inside the spherical or cubical space that contains the reflective object, and only then is the environment mapped onto the object or objects inside of the space (Figs. 9.4.3 and 9.4.4). Other environment mapping techniques that include procedural generation of environments are described next.

Spherical environment mapping is based on a flat image that is first projected on the inside of a sphere that represents the environment. The sphere is defined as a longitudinal space that goes from 0 to 360 degrees, and a latitudinal space that ranges from -90 to 90 degrees. Once the image representing the environment has been applied to the sphere it is then projected onto the object or objects that need environment mapping and that are placed inside the sphere. When an image is mapped inside a spherical environment, its left and right edges of the image end up butting against each other, and its top and bottom edges are crimped. It is necessary to keep these mapping distortions in mind when preparing the image map for environmental spherical mapping. It usually works best when the left and right edges of the image map match perfectly with one another; this way their projection can be seamless. It is also useful to keep the top and bottom areas of the image map uncluttered to avoid extreme distortion when the images on the top and bottom of the spherical space are somewhat compressed when crimped (Fig. 9.4.3).

The process of assembling an image suitable for **cubical environment mapping** is somewhat more demanding than preparing one for a spherical environment map. This is largely due to the fact that an environmental map based on the modified cubic projection is created by assembling six views of a scene. These six different views of a three-dimensional scene must represent a simplified view of the environment as if seen from inside an object that is placed at the center of this environment. The six views of the environment are the four side views, a top view, and a bottom view. The four side views are created by looking from the center of the environment toward the outside in angular increments of 90 degrees. In addition, each of the four side views must capture a full 90-degree view of the environment, so that when the four side views are assembled in sequence next to each other the result is a full 360-degree view of the environment (Fig. 9.4.4). The six panels required for a cubical environmental map can be painted from the imagination of an artist or photographed in a real environment. These six panels can also be created by rendering six different 90-degree views of a computer-generated three-dimensional space. The images used in an environment map can also be generated with procedural techniques. Simple **color ramps**, for example, can be generated procedurally in the form of smooth gradations or blendings of color and are commonly used to represent clean skies or the chromatic effects of the sunrise or sunset on horizon lines. Clouds and an assortment of lighting effects can also be created procedurally and used as environment maps (Figs. 6.12.1 and 9.4.6).

Environment maps can be animated to represent the motion that may happen around objects with mapped surfaces. The activity in a busy café can be simulated, for example, by mapping on a reflective sugar bowl a movie of people walking, drinking coffee, and interacting with each other. Another example of an animated environment map would consist of a movie of people dancing on the floor of a discotheque. This sequence could be mapped on the rotating silver sphere that is used to deflect light in all directions, or the eyeglasses worn by an observer.

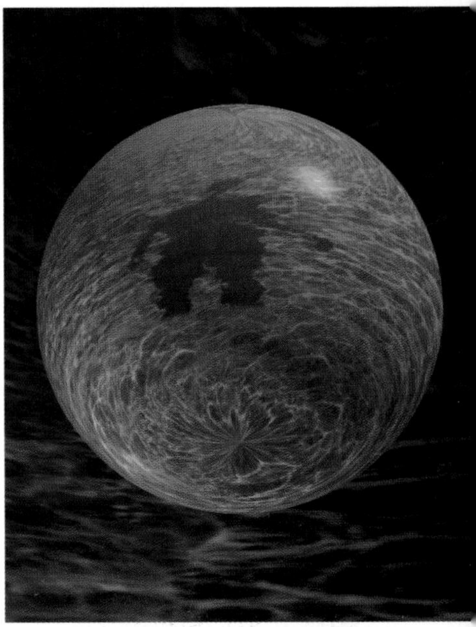

9.4.2 An environment map is mapped onto a sphere with 100 percent reflectivity, 90 percent specular highlights and two wave functions on its surface. (© Isaac V. Kerlow.)

Some programs provide tools for accurately placing the environment map on the surface. This interactive preview is commonly done in low resolution or in the wireframe mode, and it can save a lot of rendering tests that are otherwise necessary to find out how an environment map falls on a three-dimensional surface.

Some programs provide rich procedures for generating environment textures of skies that take into account not only the position and brightness of the sun and whether the sky is cloudy or not, but also atmospheric parameters such as the curvature of the planet and the densities of the air and dust particles. (Shading that takes into account atmospheric characteristics is related to the volume shaders mentioned later in this chapter).

Glow or Incandescence

Surface **glow**, sometimes called **incandescence**, is a surface characteristic that is associated with reflectivity. Incandescence makes objects glow in ways that resemble a variety of naturally glowing objects. Incandescent objects may appear as if they have an internal light source, like a fiber optic transmitting light, for example, or as if they generate a glow because of their extremely high temperature, such as molten lava (Fig. 9.4.7). This surface characteristic also resembles the opalescence of some gems that results from the reflection of iridescent light. Glow can be created as a uniform color across a surface or with an image map that determines which areas of the surface display glow. Glow or incandescence, however, is not

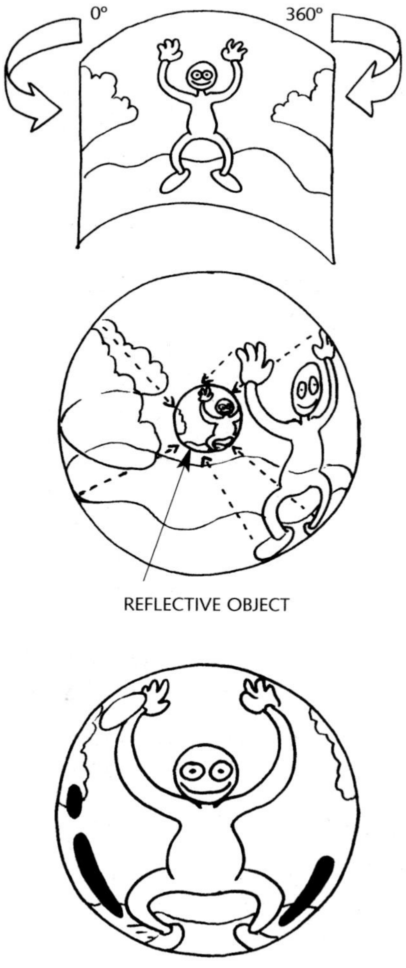

9.4.3 In spherical environment mapping, a flattened image of the environment is created and then mapped inside a spherical space that contains the reflective objects.

9.4.5 (opposite page, bottom) Character with the look typical of environment mapping. (ReBoot® and © 1997 Mainframe Entertainment, Inc. All rights reserved.)

related to the light sources in the three-dimensional scene, and it does not turn the glowing object into a light source either. A surface glow is quite different from a light glow, and objects with surface glow do not cast light on the surrounding objects.

9.5 Surface Color

Surface color is one of the most obvious of all surface characteristics. Color attributes are easier to identify and remember than most other surface characteristics. Surface color contributes to the personality of a three-dimensional character or the mood of a scene. When assigning a specific color to a three-dimensional surface it is important to keep in mind that the final color of the surface will also be greatly influenced by external factors such as the angle and color of the lighting applied to the surface, and even the color of the surrounding objects when rendering techniques such as radiosity or ray tracing are used.

Surface color can be defined with a variety of color models, many of which are covered in Chapter 6. Additive or light-based color models, like RGB or HLS, are used to define the colors in images displayed on computer monitors. Subtractive or pigment-oriented systems, such as CMYK, are used to define the colors in computer printouts. When defining surface color, it is important to keep in mind the **color shifting** that occurs when a computer-generated image is moved from an additive color environment—like an RGB monitor—to a subtractive color environment—like a printout on paper (see Chapter 15 for more details on minimizing color shifting).

Color Maps

A great variety of subtle or loud color effects can be created by mapping two-dimensional images onto the surface of three-dimensional objects. Like other types of image maps, **color maps** are used to compute the color of light reflected by the three-dimensional surface on which the color map has been placed (Figs. 9.5.1–9.5.2 and 9.3.13). Color maps are also called **picture maps** because they often involve photographic images. Color maps are often used to represent the images and labels that we find on packages and containers such as a cardboard cereal box, a glass wine bottle with a paper label glued on, or a plastic shampoo bottle with lettering printed directly on the plastic surface.

When color maps are applied to three-dimensional models of cardboard cereal boxes, for example, six different images are usually mapped with flat projection onto each of the six panels in the box. In cases such as this, when the label or printed graphics cover the entire surface of the packaging, there is no need to use other types of maps in conjunction with the color map.

It is common to use the cylindrical projection method when color maps are applied to three-dimensional models of glass containers. This projection method allows the label to be mapped onto the side of the bottle or jar. If the label being simulated is rectangular and made of an opaque material, there is usually no need to use other types of maps in addition to the color map. But a transparency map may be necessary to define, for example, a label made of translucent paper or an opaque label with a shape that is not strictly rectangular. In the latter case, a label with a triangular shape, for example, has to be contained within a rectangular color map because virtually all three-dimensional shading programs require that image maps be rectangular. In such case, a transparency map would also be used to specify the triangular area of the label as opaque, and the excess or unused areas within the rectangular map as fully transparent. (For more information on transparency maps see the "Surface Transparency" section later in this chapter.)

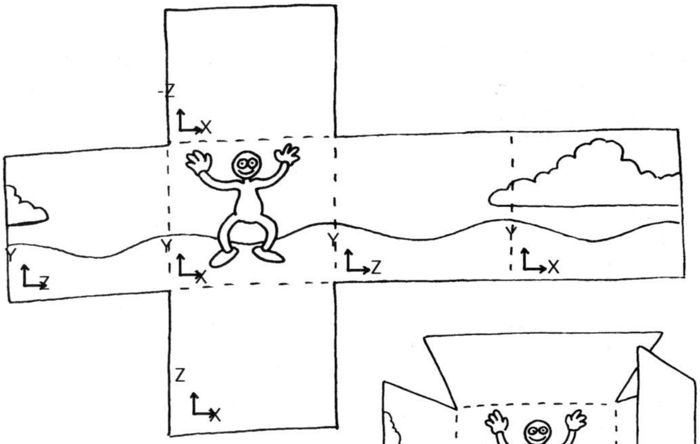

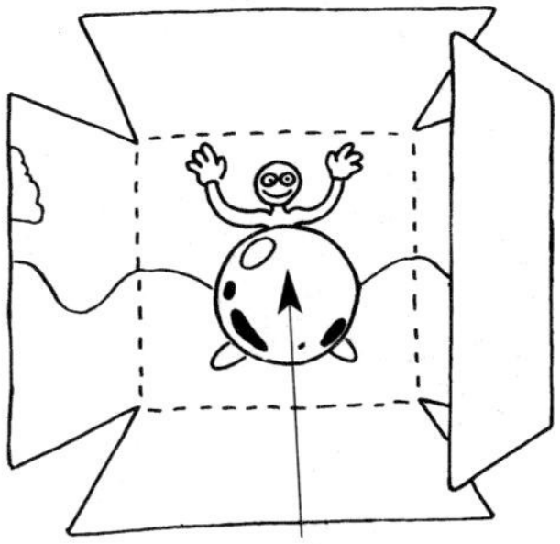

9.4.4 In cubic environment mapping, a six-panel view of the environment is created and then mapped inside a cube that surrounds the reflective objects. The small diagram indicates the orientation of each of the six two-dimensional views of the simulated environment.

Color maps can also be applied to three-dimensional models of plastic containers, like a shampoo bottle, for example. This type of container often requires that the lettering be printed directly on the plastic surface of the container, and no paper label is involved. In such cases, it is common to use the cylindrical projection method and a transparency map in addition to the color map. The transparency map is used to determine the opacity and transparency of different areas in the color map. The lettering and other graphic elements would be opaque, and the background (or areas in the map without lettering or graphic elements) would be transparent so that the plastic surface of the bottle can show through the transparent areas in the color map. Displacement maps (described later in this chapter) can be used to simulate the slight relief of the lettering and graphics that are silkscreened on containers with thick ink, enamel, or varnish.

Color maps can be projected and placed onto surfaces by using any of the standard techniques described earlier in this chapter: flat, cubical, cylindrical, spherical, wrapping and UV coordinates. Interactive positioning of color maps is useful for accurate placement of labels and lettering on three-dimensional surfaces. Some systems provide a wireframe mode for positioning labels, which is usually much faster than any rendering test would be.

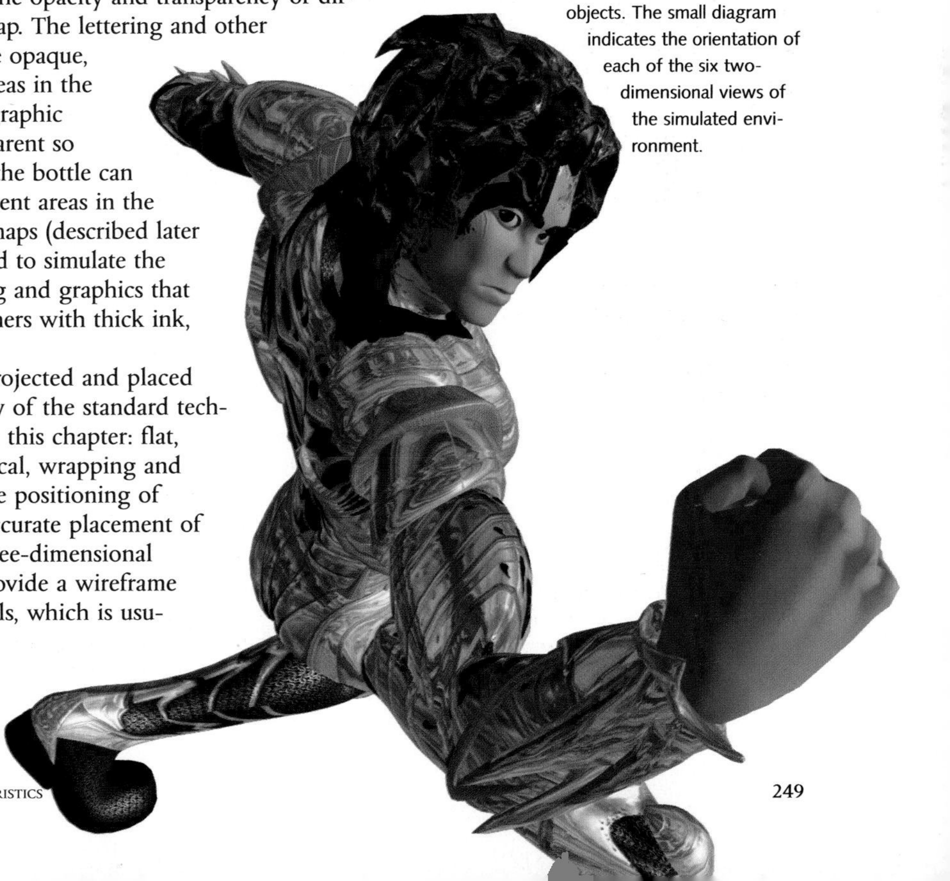

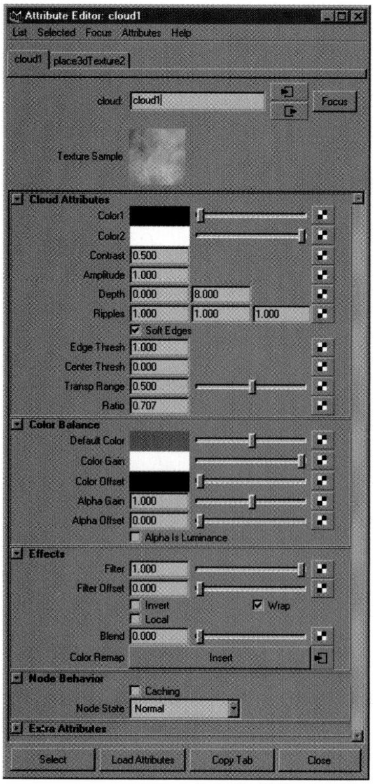

9.4.6 The Maya cloud dialog box. (© Alias|Wavefront, a division of Silicon Graphics Limited.)

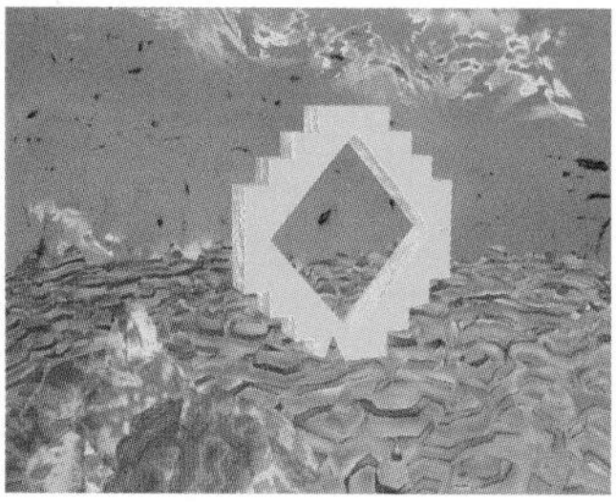

WITH GLOW

9.4.7 These images show the effects of shading the incandescent object (in the center) with and without (opposite page) a surface glow.

9.6 Surface Texture

It is possible to create very interesting visual effects by applying textures onto the surfaces of three-dimensional objects. Surface textures can be modeled so that they have true dimensionality. Modeling surface characteristics, however, is usually time-consuming and also results in inefficient three-dimensional models that require a lot of rendering time. This can be especially wasteful when objects with **modeled surface textures** are too far from the camera for the surface detail to be appreciated. Surface textures can also be simulated with a technique originally known as texture mapping, which today can be more accurately described as image mapping. This method, pioneered in the mid-1970s by Ed Catmull, affects the intensity and chromatic values of a surface, but it does not affect its smoothness.

The great variety of **texturing** techniques can be grouped in visual and spatial textures. **Visual textures** are flat simulations of three-dimensional texture and do not affect the geometrical surface of the object; they look textured but they are not (Fig. 9.5.3). For example, a visual texture representing bricks is like brick **wallpaper**, and different from a real wall of bricks with relief textures that can be felt by touch. A practical benefit of using visual textures—in addition to their inherent aesthetic value—is that they make possible the creation of complex and rich textures with a minimal investment of polygons (Fig. 9.5.2). Some of the most useful visual textures include color and procedural maps, as well as environment, bump, and transparency maps.

Spatial textures exist in three-dimensional space and affect the spatial integrity of the smooth surface of an object. Spatial textures are closer than visual textures to the concept of a real tactile texture. Spatial textures can be created by modeling a detailed mesh of planar polygons. But this approach is time-consuming and impractical. More effective methods for creating spatial textures include using bump and displacement maps, or the fractal modeling techniques described in Chapter 5.

Bump Maps

Bump maps provide an effective way to simulate roughness or bumpiness on a flat surface. **Bump maps** alter the orientation of the surface normals during the shading process. Changing the orientation of the surface normals of polygons before shading then causes the light to be reflected in several directions simulating the way light would be reflected from an object with rough surfaces. This results in the appearance of a textured surface with modulations that resemble the pattern contained in the image file used as a bump map (Fig. 9.3.1). The darkest values in the image map may represent the valleys, and the lightest values simulate the peaks in the simulated texture, or vice versa. The surface, however, remains flat, and the peaks cannot project a shadow.

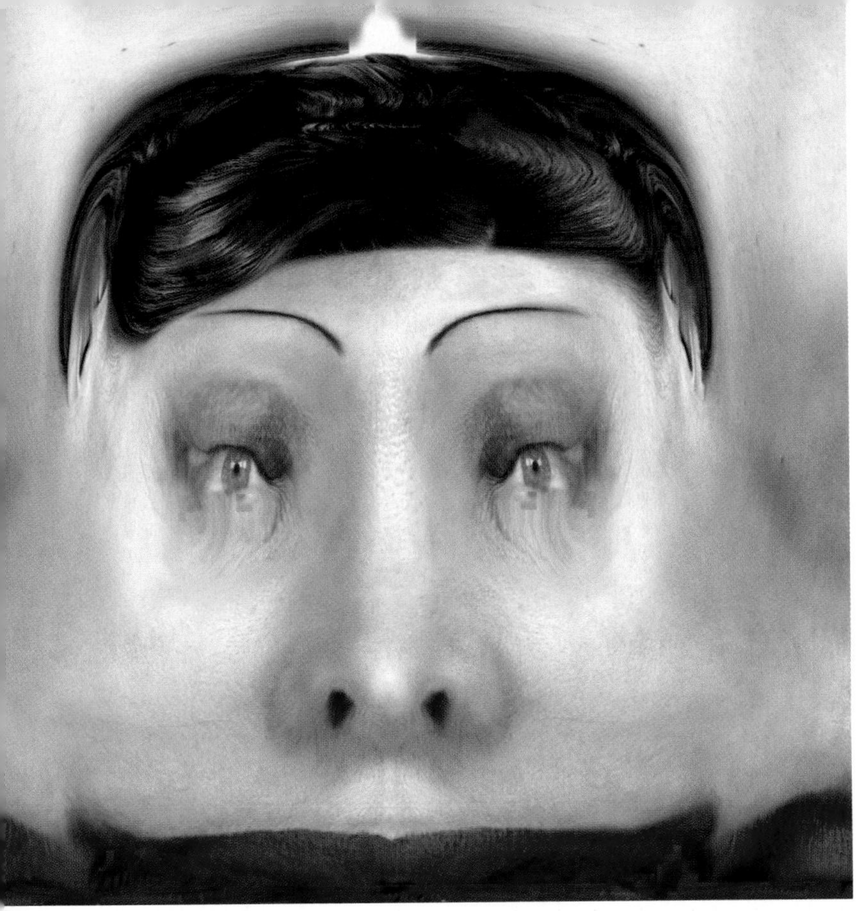

9.5.1 Color map with the skin tones applied to the virtual Marlene Dietrich in Figure 9.3.3. This color map was created with a combination of painting and scanning techniques. The lips, for example, were captured by "printing a kiss" with lipstick and scanning it. (© 1999 Virtual Celebrity/Marlene Inc.)

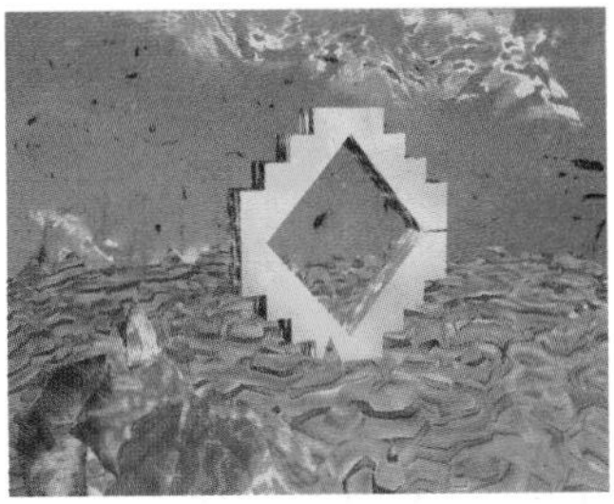

WITHOUT GLOW

Bump maps are an effective technique for creating complex and realistic textures especially in objects that are not too close to the camera or that also have a slightly irregular shape. Bump maps, however, create undesirable results when applied to objects that are too close to the camera and with their edges visible. This is due to the fact that bump maps do not create any texture on the profiles of objects. This flaw is accentuated when the bump map has a wide range of brightness values that create the impression of a lot of bumpiness and that may contrast a lot with the smooth profile of the object.

Spatial textures exist in three-dimensional space and affect the spatial integrity of the smooth surface of an object. Spatial textures are closer than visual textures to the concept of real tactile textures.

An alternate method for creating visual textures, developed by Jim Blinn and refined by several authors, simulates the imperfections on a smooth surface not by affecting the surface itself but by altering the surface normals of the object. Altering the surface normals before shading the object causes the light to be reflected in several directions, therefore simulating the way light would be reflected if the object were really textured.

Bump maps are often used in combination with parametric waves to represent the motion of water. This motion is usually limit-

9.5.2 Hand-painted color maps applied onto cutout figures and billboards. (Created and directed by Wolf-Rüdiger Bloss. © Tube Caveman Inc.–Antefilms Production.)

ed to the linear or concentric undulations created on the surface of the water by wind or objects that touch a point on the surface (Fig. 11.2.8). Parametric waves used as bump maps can also be used as displacement maps to create a more three-dimensional effect.

Displacement Maps

Displacement maps provide a unique way to use an image map to actually modify not only the shading but the geometry of the surface being mapped. **Displacement maps** alter both the orientation of the surface normals and the three-dimensional position of the surface itself. This results in a truly textured surface that has three-dimensionality as well as two-dimensional patterns mapped on it (Figs. 9.3.1 and 9.6.2).

Displacement maps are often used to create three-dimensional terrain that includes mountains and valleys. Terrains can be built with displacement maps that are based on photographic images of aerial views where the different elevations are coded with different colors or shades of gray. Three-dimensional terrains can also be built by generating two-dimensional images with fractal techniques and using them as displacement maps. Whether photographic or fractal, the two-dimensional images are usually applied to a three-dimensional surface in the form of a black-and-white displacement map and as a color map.

9.5.3 The visual maps in this image include weathered metal surfaces with rust, corrosion, bumps, and raised patterns. (© 1999 Acclaim Entertainment, Inc. All rights reserved.)

Two-Dimensional Procedural Texture Maps

As mentioned earlier, the two-dimensional images that can be mapped onto three-dimensional surfaces can be painted by hand, captured with cameras, or created with procedural techniques. **Procedural creation** relies on mathematical functions or computer programs to create images that are usually abstract. Mathematical functions that create pseudo-random or rhythmic patterns of color are popular ways to create two-dimensional procedural texture maps (Fig. 9.6.3). Two-dimensional images that are created with procedural techniques can be mapped onto three-dimensional surfaces following the standard procedures for image-mapping.

Some software programs provide tools to extract two-dimensional image maps from three-dimensional procedural texture maps. This handy function works by taking a snapshot of the surface texture on the object with solid texture and saving it as an image file that can be mapped onto other objects. This option is especially useful when rendering speed is a consideration, and in many cases image files are mapped faster than procedural textures. However, they also require more storage space since image files—especially those that are high resolution—tend to be large files.

Three-Dimensional Procedural Texture Maps

Many of the textural qualities of objects found in nature can be easily simulated with texture maps created with three-dimensional procedures. Three-dimensional procedural texture maps are **solid textures** that exist on the surface of an object as well as inside the object. These textures are based on mathematical functions or short programs that create abstract patterns. But unlike two-dimensional procedural textures that are projected onto the surface of an object, three-dimensional procedural texture maps distribute the three-dimensional patterns throughout the object being textured. A small chunk of marble is a good example of how three-dimensional solid textures behave. On the outside, marble has a very distinct texture defined by the colors and surface characteristics of the minerals that it is composed of. But the texture of marble does not occur only on its surface, it continues inside of the stone because the minerals that define the marble are all throughout the stone. The texture of marble cannot be peeled off like a two-dimensional texture map could. When the stone is chipped or cut, the surface texture changes, revealing the inner mineral composition and continued texture of the stone.

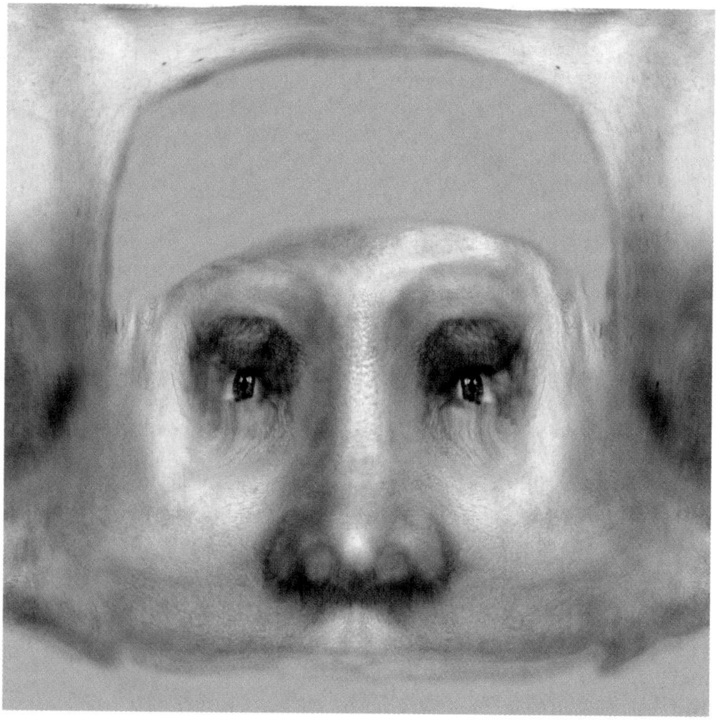

9.6.1 This bump map was used to render the pores of the skin. To capture the map, ink was rolled on faces and an imprint was made on paper. The eyelashes were created with an additional bump map not shown here. On th eopposite page, the left map on the opposite page was used to accentuate the specular highlights during rendering. The small color image map was used for the right ear of the character in Figure 9.3.3. (© 1999 Virtual Celebrity/Marlene Inc.)

Many natural and synthetic materials can be recreated with procedural solid textures. This is done by providing different values to a variety of procedural parameters, such as color, roughness, frequency, scaling, orientation, cohesion, and density. These values can be typed directly on the keyboard or controlled interactively with sliders. Some natural materials that are offered as prepackaged standard options in many software programs include a variety of stones, such as marble and granite, wood, corroded metal, leather, and even smoke and clouds (Fig. 9.6.4).

Software programs have slightly different ways for defining three-dimensional solid textures, and each produces a unique result. Figures 9.6.5–9.6.7 illustrate how marble solid textures are defined by different software. In the first example, the variables used are Color 1, Color 2, X Weight, Y Weight, Z Weight, Turbulence, and Cohesion (Fig. 9.6.5). In the second example, the variables used are Filler_color, Vein_color, Vein_width, Diffusion, and Contrast (Fig. 9.6.6). Other general three-dimensional solid texture variables associated with marble definitions include some noise parameters and the minimum and maximum levels of recursion depth. In the third example, the variables are Color 1, Color 2, Color 3, Color 4, Color 5, Spacing, Angle, Strength, Iteration, and Power (Fig. 9.6.7).

Many procedural texturing techniques are based on the idea that some degree of controlled randomness is useful, even necessary, to define the characteristics of specific textures. This randomness is often

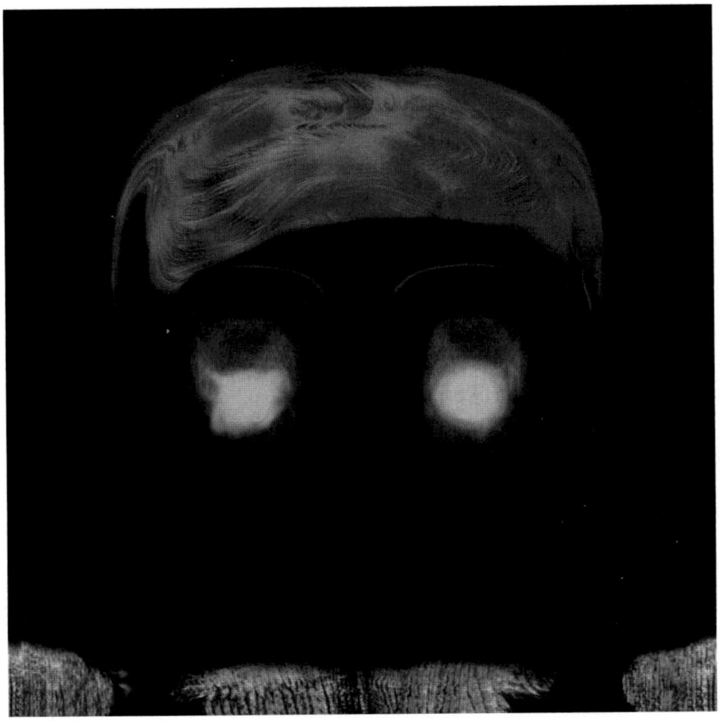

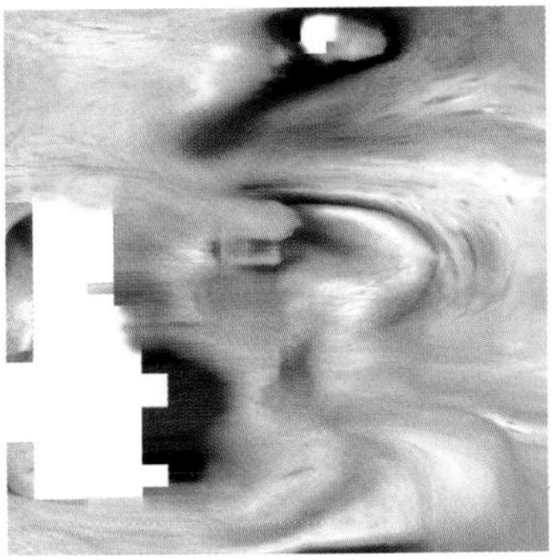

specified in the form of a **noise** function that generates stochastic (or pseudo-random) values, and feeds them to the procedure as the solid texture is calculated. Much of the parametric randomness contained in procedural textures is best defined with noise functions. One way to define the turbulence in marble-like surfaces, for example, is with patterns whose magnitude decreases with frequency. This means that as the marble texture patterns become tighter—as their frequency increases—their area on the surface becomes smaller.

Placing solid procedural textures is usually done by typing numerical values that offset the texture across the model that the solid texture is applied to. Some software programs preview how the solid texture looks on a shape (Fig. 9.6.8). Procedural solid texture maps do not use standard projection techniques. Solid textures exist throughout the object (outside and inside), and there is no need to project them.

9.7 Surface Transparency

Transparency and translucency effects are useful for rendering materials such as glass or water, and also for visualizing fantastic transformations of matter—for example, a short animation that shows how opaque charcoal turns into a transparent diamond. **Surface transparency** is represented by simulating the behavior of light on transparent materials. Realistic transparency effects are best simulated with

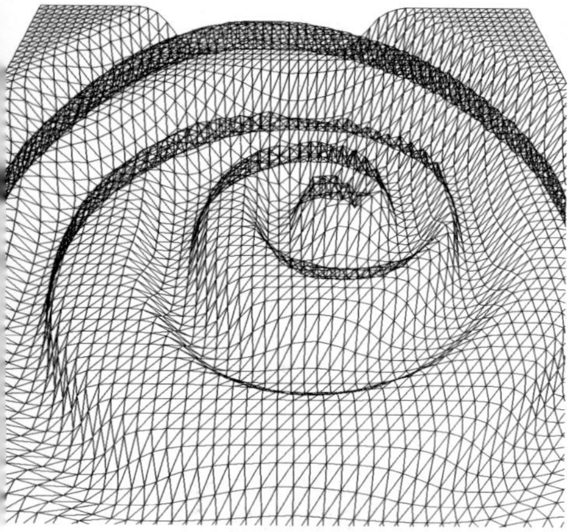

9.6.2 A terrain created by displacing the XYZ locations of a surface with an image map. This technique can be used to animate the effect of footsteps left on the ground by a walking ghost by using a sequence of black and white footprints (one at a time and in sequence) to displace down the ground.

the ray tracing rendering method (described in Chapter 6), which usually provides accurate controls for transparency and for light refraction.

Transparency Maps

Another strategy for simulating transparency consists of applying transparency maps to the surface of a three-dimensional object. A **transparency map** consists of a monochromatic two-dimensional image that is applied to a three-dimensional surface with the purpose of making all or some of the surface transparent (Fig. 9.3.12). The basic idea behind a transparency map is that the rendering program looks at the **brightness values** of the pixels in the map and uses them to determine whether the surface will be transparent, opaque, or translucent.

Some programs use the black values in the transparency map as the indicator for full transparency (Fig. 9.7.1), while other programs use the white values to activate full transparency. In either case, a gray transparency map results in a translucent surface. Creating a transparency map in full color is a waste of time because the majority of shading programs only pay attention to the grayscale brightness values when dealing with transparency maps. Furthermore, preparing transparency maps in color can be distracting and can make it more difficult for users to focus on the brightness values.

An interesting situation occurs when transparent surfaces are rendered with both reflection maps and reflectivity settings in the ray-tracing rendering method. Most rendering programs combine the ray-traced reflections with the effect of the reflection map, but the ray tracing of reflected three-dimensional objects takes precedence over the reflection mapping.

9.8 Environment-Dependent Shading

A large variety of shading attributes are determined by the characteristics of the three-dimensional environment in which the rendered objects are placed. Some of the most common tools for controlling environment-dependent variables include antialising, motion blur, and depth-fading.

Antialiasing

When the spatial resolution of an image is too low, its details are often lost. This phenomenon is called **spatial aliasing**, and it occurs when the details in the image are smaller than the size of the individual pixels used to represent the image. Aliasing, as spatial aliasing is usually referred to, is usually seen in the form of **jagged edges** of objects, especially those with diagonal and curved profiles. Aliasing effects can be found not only in computer generated images but in images generated with other media, such as painting or photography, for example, when the brush strokes or the film grain are larger than the image details. Aliasing can also be thought of as the image distortions that result from a limited or insufficient sampling of the original visual data.

The best way to eliminate aliasing is to increase the **spatial resolution** of an image, which means to increase the number of pixels in the image. However, this approach may also dramatically increase the time that is required to render a three-dimensional scene, because the number of rendering calculations is related to the number of pixels that must be created in an image. Alternative methods for eliminating aliasing effects are called **antialiasing** techniques. These are usually based on **oversampling** and **interpolation** techniques. These techniques determine the color value of a pixel by first examining the value of the surrounding pixels, then averaging those values, and finally using that average to determine the value of the individual pixel.

There are many antialiasing algorithms, and some are more efficient and accurate than others. Some antialiasing techniques can dramatically increase the quality of an image but sometimes at the expense of performance. For this reason, when choosing degrees of antialiasing, users of three-dimensional rendering systems must consider all the factors in a specific production—such as deadlines, budget, and quality desired—and apply their best judgment (Fig. 9.8.1).

Motion Blur

When recording reality with a video or a film camera we observe that objects that move too fast in front of the camera appear blurred. This phenomenon is called **motion blur,** and it occurs naturally in film or video recordings where the shutter speed is too slow to freeze an object in motion. Motion blur is a form of **temporal aliasing** that results from samples that are too far apart from each other to capture motion details. The speed of shutters in photographic still cameras is measured in the amount of seconds or fractions of a second that the camera shutter remains open. Usually speeds of 1/250th of a second are necessary to freeze fast-moving objects. The speed of shutters in motion film or video cameras is usually measured in terms of the number of frames that are recorded per second. Most motion cameras have fixed speeds of 24 frames per second (fps) for 35 mm film, and 30 fps for video. Only high-speed motion cameras are capable of high shutter speeds that can freeze the motion of objects. This is achieved by recording a large number of frames per second and, therefore, slowing down the motion of the objects.

Motion blur can add a touch of realism to computer animation because it reminds viewers of the blurring effect that occurs when we record fast-moving real objects directly with a camera (Figs. 9.8.2 and 9.8.3). But motion blur does not occur naturally in computer animation, it must be added. Motion blur is commonly defined by specifying a shutter speed expressed in seconds or frames per second, and also the rate at which moving objects are sampled while

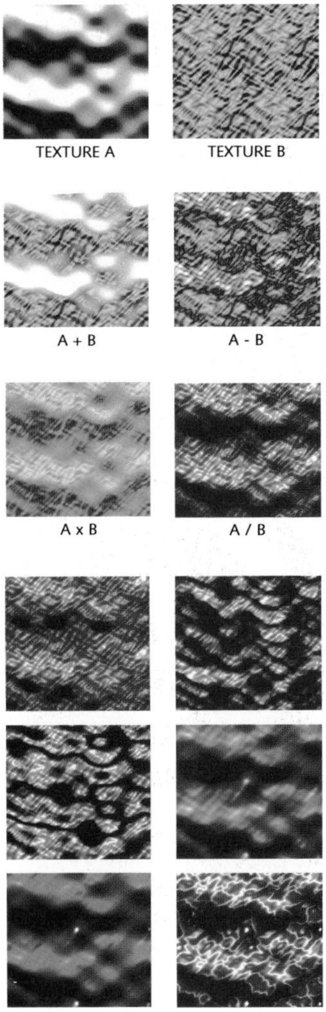

A/B AND DIFFERENT FUNCTIONS

9.6.3 Examples of procedural two-dimensional textures. The first two textures from top left to bottom right were generated with procedures based on functions with different levels of complexity, detail, twisting, and contrast. The next four textures were created by blending the two original textures with the same function curves, and the following operators: A + B, A - B, A × B, and A/B. The remainder of the textures were created with the A/B operator, and a different combination of function curves each time.

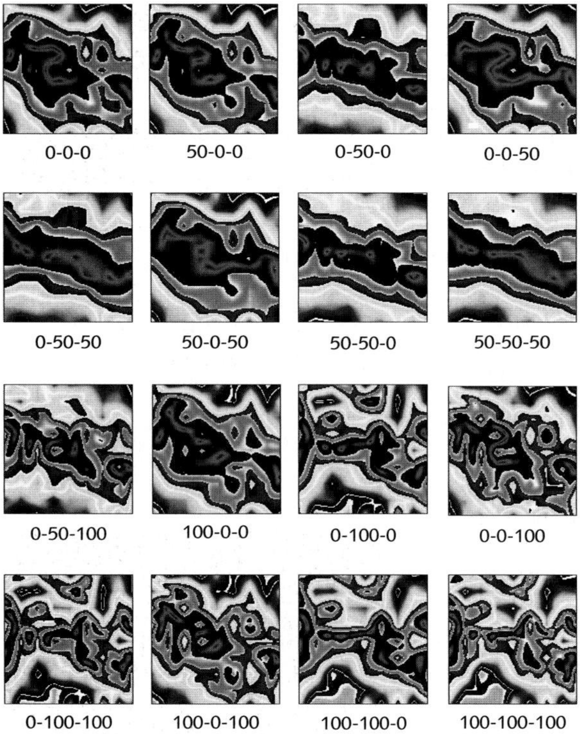

9.6.4 Variations of a solid wood texture cross section created with different values of swirling, grain density, and cutting. These previews are used to quickly visualize how a solid texture looks like before it is sent to a detailed rendering. Examine the first example with values of 0-0-0, the tenth example with maximum swirl values of 100-0-0, the eleventh example with maximum grain values of 0-100-0, the twelfth example with maximum cutting values of 0-0-100, and the sixteenth with overall maximum values of 100-100-100.

the shutter is open. For animation that is recorded at 30 fps, for example, a camera shutter that remains open for two frames has a speed of 1/15th (or 2/30ths) of a second. In most shading programs, motion blur is not directly calculated based on the absolute speed of the object but instead based on a minimum number of pixels that the object moves within the two-dimensional space of the image plane of the camera (Fig. 9.8.5). Motion blur is applied as a process that takes place after the calculation of the position of the three-dimensional object in the three-dimensional scene. Even though motion blur softens hard edges, it is not used to compensate for the lack of detail found in aliased images.

Fog

Most rendering software provides atmospheric or environmental shading tools for simulating the effect of **fog** in a three-dimensional scene. The presence of fog makes the three-dimensional images fade into the color of the fog according to their position relative to the camera (Fig. 9.8.6). Objects that are far away from the camera and deep into the three-dimensional scene blend more with the fog. For this reason this technique is sometimes called **depth-fading**. In most cases, fog and depth-fading are just two different names given to the same function, but in some programs, fog and depth-fading are two different functions.

There are many algorithms for calculating fog, and some produce more realistic effects than others. In general, the functionalities of fog tools control the starting and ending distance of the fog, its color, and sometimes its transparency. The starting and ending distances—also called minimum and maximum distances—of the fog specify the distances from the camera to the plane where the fog starts and ends. Objects that are closest to the ending distance blend more with the fog. The color of the fog can be specified with a variety of color models, and in many cases the color of the fog is related to—even determined by—the **background color**, a global shading parameter. The transparency of the fog defines the degree in which the objects placed behind the fog are visible. Opaque fogs, for example, may block everything that is placed behind them, while somewhat transparent fogs allow the objects behind them to partially show through.

Many fog functions provide a **visibility** parameter that is usually related to the depth, or thickness, of the foggy area. Visibility can be easily determined by subtracting the starting distance of the fog from the ending distance.

Both fog and depth-fading techniques can be used to create images that incorporate the principles of aerial perspective refined by Leonardo da Vinci in the sixteenth century. **Aerial perspective** techniques are used to depict depth in a two-dimensional image by simulating the atmospheric effects of light, temperature, and humidity on objects situated far away from the observer. Aerial perspective was developed to complement the realism of images represented with the principles of linear perspective. (Linear perspective techniques are implemented in the determination of visible surfaces that occurs during the rendering process.)

Many software programs provide fog and depth-fading functionalities, but often these two words represent different versions of an effect. This is the case, for example, with software programs that support the functionalities provided by the RenderMan programming language. The difference between fog and depth-fading basically lies in the way in which each of these operators adds the background color to the light that is reflected by three-dimensional surfaces. Both operators add the background color to the reflected light based on the distance between the surface and the position and orientation of the camera. But in depth-fading the color of a surface is entirely the background color if the surface is beyond the maximum distance, while in fog the reflected light always retains some of the color originally reflected by the surface.

Fog, clouds, and smoke can also be simulated as a cluster of particles with uniform density that is placed in front of the camera (Fig. 9.8.7). Small clusters of fog, smoke, or steam can be created with the solid procedural textures described earlier in this chapter.

Fog belongs to the category of volume shaders, a type of shaders that go beyond light and surface shaders. In the RenderMan environment, for example, **volume shaders** define the characteristics of materials in three-dimensional space that affect light as it travels through them. Our atmosphere, for example, contains gases and solid and liquid particles that affect light before it reaches our eyes and after being emitted by light sources or being reflected by surfaces. The characteristics of the light or imaging ray that travels through the volume can be defined based on attributes of the volume, such as density, color, and motion. Other examples of light or other types of imaging rays traveling through volumes include underwater scenes and the inside of the human body (Fig. 5.1.6). A procedure related to volume shaders is described earlier in this chapter in the section about environment maps.

In addition to fog that extends only horizontally, some programs offer the capability of simulating distant layers of fog placed at different altitudes. This is usually achieved with an image map that has a painting or a photograph of the horizontal layers of fog. This image map is used to calculate the color of light reflected by objects behind the fog plane or by a color map that is used as a backdrop. Another shortcut to rendering fog consists of mapping painted foggy scenes on flat billboard with varying degrees of translucency.

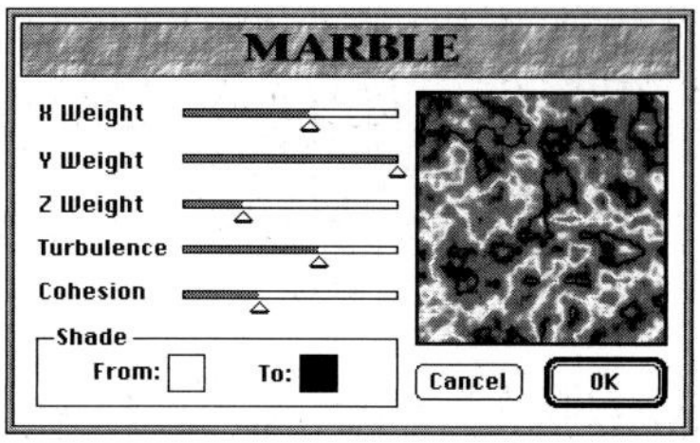

9.6.5 Dialog box for a three-dimensional marble texture. (Dialog box from Infini-D 3.0. © 1991–1995 Specular International, Ltd.)

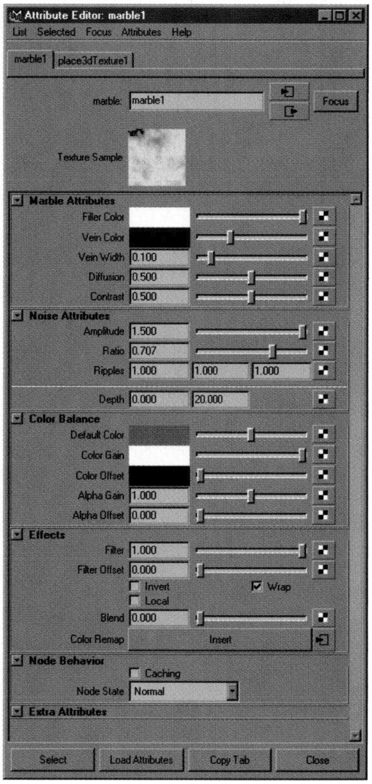

9.6.6 The Maya three-dimensional texture dialog box. (© Aliasl Wavefront, a division of Silicon Graphics Limited.

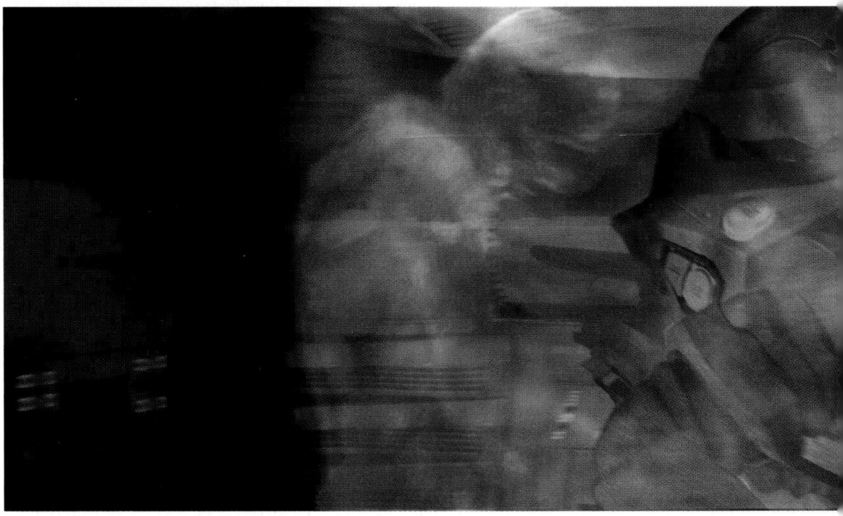

9.6.7 False color rendering and compositing were used to create the "spirit" phantoms in *Final Fantasy,* a show rendered primarily with Renderman, and Maya for ray-traced effects such as caustics. Photoshop and Amazon Paint were used to create matte paintings and textures. The modeling and animation were done mostly with Maya, and the compositing with Illusion, Shake and Flame.
(© 2001 FFFP.)

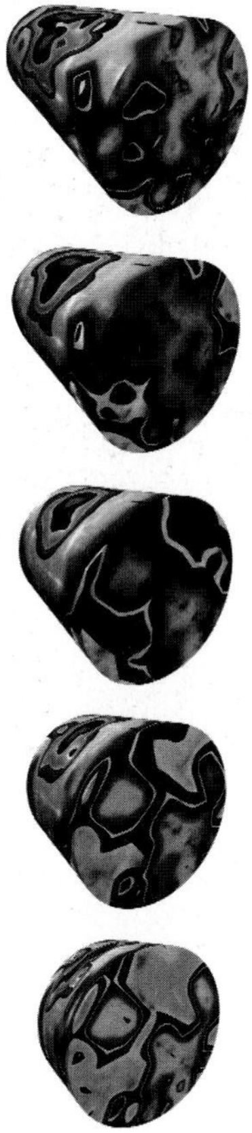

9.6.8 Slicing a cylinder reveals how solid textures exist throughout objects. See Figure 15.2.2 for a higher resolution version.

9.9 Selected Rendering Hacks

Hacks or **cheats** are shortcuts that usually yield almost the same result as the established technique with less work, time, and/or computing power. A hack is sometimes an effective way to develop a one-time solution that may be quicker and cheaper than other more established or technically solid methods. Hacks should be used with care as they tend to be fragile and unpredictable; they seem to work successfully about half of the time.

Hacks are sometimes used extensively during the rendering process because they can be a great help in reducing the computing time that a complex rendering setup might require. A few popular rendering hacks that are not covered elsewhere in the book are quickly reviewed here. Interestingly enough, many hacks are based on nonstandard solutions that eventually spawn tricks and techniques that become standard practice.

Billboards are widely used to insert in a scene image maps of more complex scenes that have been prerendered or recorded from live action. Billboards are usually flat polygons that are mapped with a still or a sequence of image maps. In real-time games for example, billboards are great for mapping prerendered animated sequences of distant characters. When used effectively this hack can look as good as having the full three-dimensional character in three-dimensional space: one polygon instead of hundreds (Figs. 9.5.2 and 11.6.2). In live action feature film, billboards are sometimes used to map live footage in an all-synthetic shot. That is the case, for example, with the actor inside the helicopter in ***Mission Impossible***'s tunnel sequence. In either case, the images are mapped on the billboard with a transparency channel, to make transparent the billboard areas that do not have an image on them. Billboards are also often used to hold single stills of distant backgrounds that have been pho-

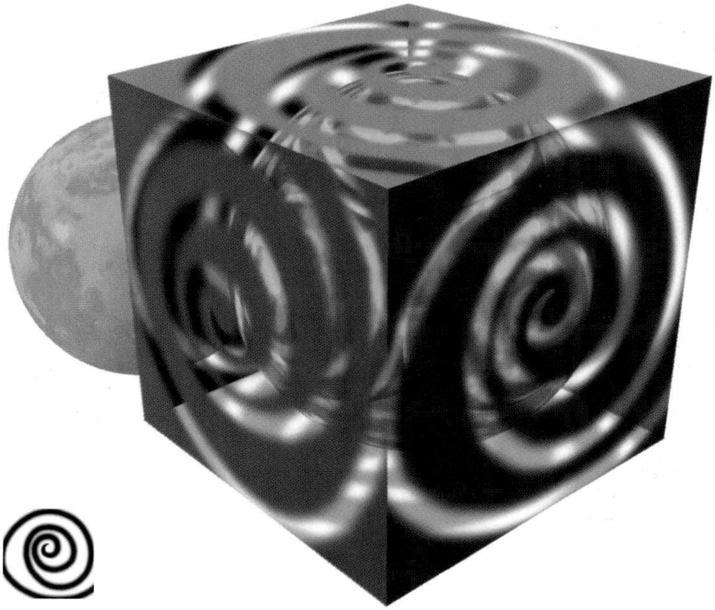

9.7.1 (top left) Transparency map applied to a cube with cubical projection, using the black and white pattern from Figure 9.6.2

tographed on location or from scale models (as was the case in the pod race sequence in ***The Phantom Menace***. Earlier in this chapter we mentioned the popular approach of applying procedural textures rendered on a flat plane as image maps to other geometry. This greatly saves rendering time.

Selective ray tracing is a good way to minimize rendering times without impacting the quality of the visual end result. In a crowd scene, for example, where the characters are scheduled to being ray-traced only those closest to the camera are ray traced, while the ones far away are rendered with faster techniques. This was the case in several shots with the little green creatures in the movie ***Flubber***. Another ray-tracing hack consists of simulating it with reflection and environment maps. Depending on the particular scene this can yield satisfactory results for a fraction of the rendering time. This hack does not always work when the reflected maps are too close to the main character or object, having them far away works best.

Simulated film grain was achieved very successfully in the movie ***Bunny*** by computing just a couple of iterations in the radiosity rendering cycle. While this may not be the cheapest way to simulate film grain in computer-generated images, it creates a beautiful and unexpected visual quality by using an established technique for doing things that it was not intended to do. ***Bunny*** is also an example of selective ray tracing since only the furry characters were ray traced while the environments were rendered with radiosity.

Simulated lens glows and flares can be quickly inserted in a three-dimensional environment by mapping preexisting images of glows and flares on a polygon that overlaps with the near clipping plane of the image. More orthodox glows and flares are achieved by

WITHOUT ANTIALIASING

LOW ANTIALIASING

HIGH ANTIALIASING

9.8.1 The same detail of a three-dimensional scene rendered with three different levels of antialiasing. Notice the significant differences in edge jaggedness in the steep diagonal edges.

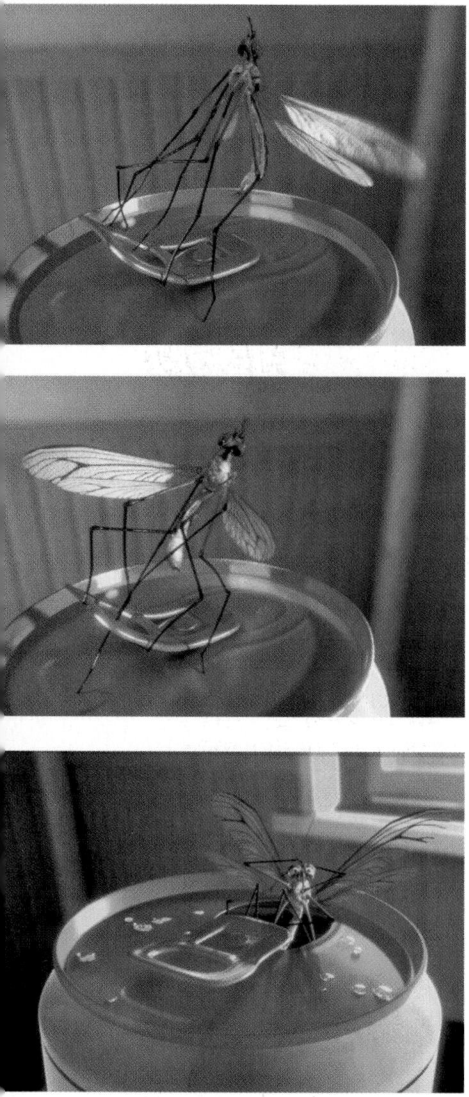

9.8.2 The effects of motion blur can be seen on the wings of this mosquito who is trying to open a beer can. Since the camera is stationary the story in this scene is carried only by the mosquito's performance. (Courtesy of Blue Sky Studios. © 1998 Tennent Caledonian Breweries, Inc.)

computing the diffraction and refraction of light rays inside the optics of the lens, but the computing overhead can be significant (Fig. 10.1.6). Using stills or sequences of photographic or pre-rendered glows and flares saves time since the main rendering challenge in this hack becomes to line them up with the scene and to blend them using a delicate transparency map with soft edges.

9.10 Getting Ready

Rendering in a Network

Computer networks offer several strategies for increasing the speed of your renderings. But keep in mind that the final performance depends not only on the specifics of the network but on the network rendering features of your software and computer. The two most common strategies for sending your rendering to other machines on the network are distributed rendering and remote rendering.

Distributed rendering consists of sending portions of a rendering job to different computers on the network, for example, rendering the top half of a scene on one machine and the bottom half on another machine. Distributed rendering requires software that is able to split a rendering job into several sections and then put the results back together. **Remote rendering** occurs when the rendering of a three-dimensional model—that may reside in your machine—takes place in one of the other machines on the network. Many companies today have **rendering farms** that consist of many computers solely dedicated to network rendering (Fig. 2.2.3). These rendering farms may be located in the same building as the rest of the company, or they may be located in other buildings, other cities, or in other countries, where rendering labor may be more economical. (See Chapter 2 for more details on rendering farms.)

Depending on how a computer network is configured, renderings can be sent to other computers with or without the permission of their respective users—also called owners. Regardless of your network configuration or technical skill, keep in mind that it is considered impolite in network etiquette to submit renderings to somebody's computer without his or her express permission. Find out what the rules are regarding remote rendering on the network you use. Not only can you be slowing down another machine on the network by sending your renderings there, but your own system may be performing below the norm because other users are rendering in the "background" on your machine. But by all means, take advantage of remote rendering whenever possible; it is a great time-saver.

Streamline Your Shading Data

Shading parameters, such as the number of surface layers or the number of image maps applied to surfaces, should be kept to a minimum, especially in productions where rendering time is of the essence. Very

often, the best rendering results are achieved with just a few well-chosen shading parameters. Too many shading parameters not only prolong the time needed to render a scene but also might not significantly contribute the visual quality of the final image. It is the responsibility of an artist, especially those working within production environments, to find a balance between the essential aesthetic needs and the practical limitations of the project, such as the rendering speed of the computer system, people's schedules, the budget, and the delivery deadlines. In general, an overabundance of shading parameters burdens not only the computers that must render the scene but all the individuals involved in the production, including the client.

9.8.3 Motion blur enhances the illusion of fast-twirling hair in this shot from *Spy Kids 2*. (© 2002 Hybride. Images courtesy of Dimension Films.)

9.8.4 Another mosquito, this one showing how depth of field increases the realism of a rendering (also next page). (Images courtesy of Framestore CFC and Bartle Bogle Hegarty.)

Rendering Glass

Many rendering programs provide users with predefined shading parameters or surface shaders for a variety of materials, including glass. Most software manuals—or digital libraries of shaders—suggest starting by selecting a specular shading technique. Depending on the color, thickness, transparency, and roughness of the glass being simulated, both the reflectivity and the transparency of the object should be set very high—values above 90 percent are not uncommon. The refractive index can be set slightly above normal to create a small amount of distortion, or it can be boosted to simulate the increased light-bending qualities of handmade glass, for example. Specular highlight values can be sharpened and focused. In cases where the software provides separate controls for the ambient, diffuse, and spec-

9.8.5 The motion blur of an object increases with its speed and as the object gets closer to the camera.

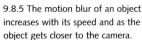

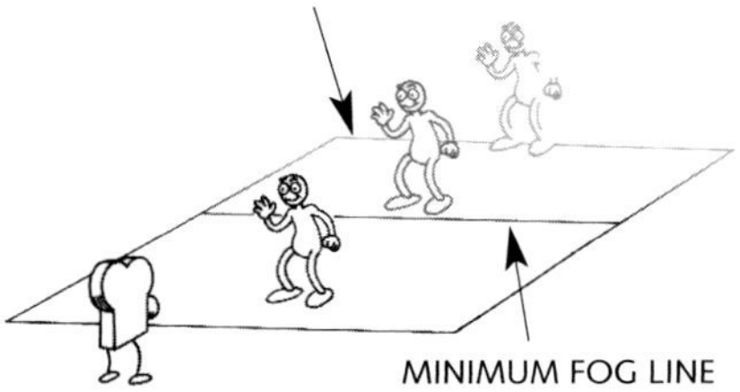

9.8.6 The shading of objects within the foggy area in this diagram gets influenced by the color of the fog.

ular areas of illumination, the specular reflection can be boosted up above 100 percent to compensate for the high values of reflectivity and transparency; ambient and diffuse reflection can be turned off altogether. The transparency and reflection depths of a ray-traced rendering must be set to a minimum value of 4 in order to capture the subtle distortions that give refraction its tantalizing qualities.

Keep Digital Backups

The preferred method for recording computer animations consists of accumulating a good number of still frames in peripheral memory and then dumping or recording them onto film or videotape. This batch mode of recording animation is usually more efficient than recording still frames one at a time as each is rendered. In any case it is very convenient to keep all the files that contain the digital still frames, even after they have been recorded on film or videotape. Keeping a **digital backup** of the animation can be invaluable if anything should happen to the master videotape or the original film negative

9.8.7 Smoke effects, motion blur, lens glows, and flares were applied in this scene from the *Command and Conquer 2* computer game. Notice the bump and displacement maps, and the hard-edge shadow on the foreground terrain. (© Westwood Studios. All rights reserved.)

before the project is delivered. Discarding the computer animation still frames as soon as they are recorded onto film or videotape is a situation that should be avoided at all costs. If this were done and the master videotape or original film negative were damaged then large portions of the project would have to be rendered all over again.

Consider the Final Output Media

Before producing your final renderings consider for a moment what the final output media is. As mentioned in Chapter 6, there can be significant color shifts when recording an RGB computer-generated image onto media with other chromatic ranges. This becomes especially critical when recording still images or animated sequences onto NTSC videotape due to its limited range of color. Special care should also be paid to make sure that the computer-generated images fall within the chromatic range of film—for example, when the computer animated characters are composited over a live action background plate (Fig. 14.1.1).

CHAPTER 9

Key Terms

Aerial perspective
Alpha channel
Ambient reflection
Angle of mapping
Antialiasing
Areas of illumination
Averaging
Backdrops
Background color
Billboards
Blue Moon Rendering Tools
Brightness values
Bump maps
CD-ROM
Cheats
Color maps
Color ramps
Color shifting
Continuous masks
Continuous visual information
Cubical environment mapping
Cubical projection
Cylindrical projection
Depth-fading
Diffuse reflection
Digital camera
Digital painting
Digital scanner
Dioramas
Discrete numerical values
Displacement maps
Distributed rendering
Environment maps
Faceted surface shading
Flat projection
Fog
Glow
Gouraud shading model
Hacks
High-contrast masks
Highlight decay
Highlight sharpness
Hybrid shading models
Image mapping
Incandescence
Interpolation
Jagged edges
Lambert shading model
Map blending
Mapping projection method
Mask
Material databases
Matte surfaces
Matting techniques
Metallic surfaces
Mirror-like
Modeled surface textures
Motion blur
Noise
Numerical values
Offset the map
Overall blending
Oversampling
Parameter space
Phong shading model
Photorealistic RenderMan
Picture maps
Plastic surfaces
Pressure-sensitive
Procedural creation
Rectangular images
Reflection map
Reflection of light
Renderer
Rendering farms
RenderMan shading language
Remote rendering
Sampling
Scaling
Selective ray-tracing
Shading value
Simulated film grain
Simulated lens glows and flares
Simulated material
Smooth surface shading
Solid textures
Spatial aliasing
Spatial resolution
Spatial textures
Specular reflection
Specular surface shading
Spherical environment mapping
Spherical projection
Surface finish
Surface illumination
Surface layers
Surface libraries
Surface normals
Surface shader
Surface subscattering
Surface transparency
Temporal aliasing
Texturing
Tiling
Transparency map
Underpaint
UV coordinates
Visibility
Visual textures
Volume shaders
Wallpaper
Wrapping
XY coordinates

SECTION IV

Animation and Effects

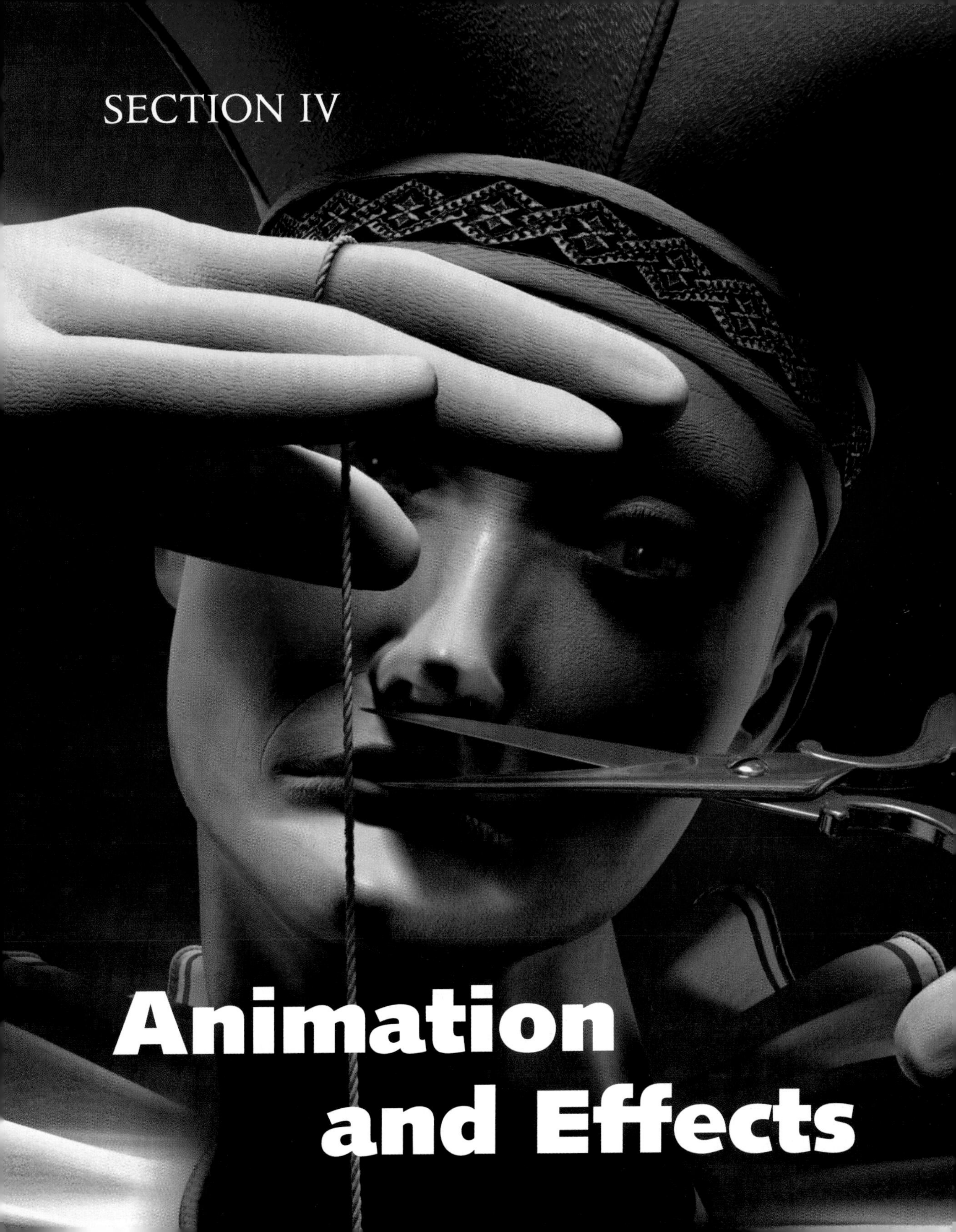

(Previous page) Still frame from *Tightrope*. (© Digital Domain, Inc.)

10.1.1 A minor event in the life of *Bunny*'s main character makes her confront her memories and her future. (© 1998 Blue Sky Studios.)

CHAPTER 10

10

Basic Concepts of Animation

Summary

USING COMPUTERS TO CREATE ANIMATED IMAGES offers animators new creative possibilities as well as potent production tools. This chapter reviews some of the basic concepts of animation, including fundamental techniques such as keyframing and in-betweening, the components of storytelling and storyboarding, and the communication of emotions and thought processes through an animated character. The artistic and creative process in preproduction and the early stages of production is also explored here.

QUICK INDEX

10.1 Types of Animation

The first animated flipbooks and films were created at the turn of the nineteenth century. But most of the principles of animation were developed during the first two decades of the twentieth century and perfected with the hand-drawn cartoon animations of the 1930s and 1940s. Some of the computer animation techniques used to create **sequences of still images** are based on the techniques of traditional cel animation, but most are unique computer-based simulations of three-dimensional worlds and characters in motion. Many three-dimensional computer animation techniques have been adapted from earlier methods such as hand-drawn, stop-motion, and performance animation. Some of these and other techniques have been fine-tuned to different specialties within three-dimensional computer animation that include character animation, effects animation, and computer-generated visual effects.

To animate means to give life to an inanimate object, image, or drawing: *anima* means soul in Latin. Animation is the art of movement expressed with images that are not taken directly from reality (Fig. 10.1.1). In animation, the illusion of movement is achieved by rapidly displaying many still images—or frames—in sequence. Computer animation is a process that begins with the development of a story through scripting and storyboarding, continues with

10.1.2 The main rock characters in *Das Rad* were animated with stop motion techniques. (© 2001 Filmakademie Baden-Wuerttemberg/ Gruber–Stenner–Wittlinger.)

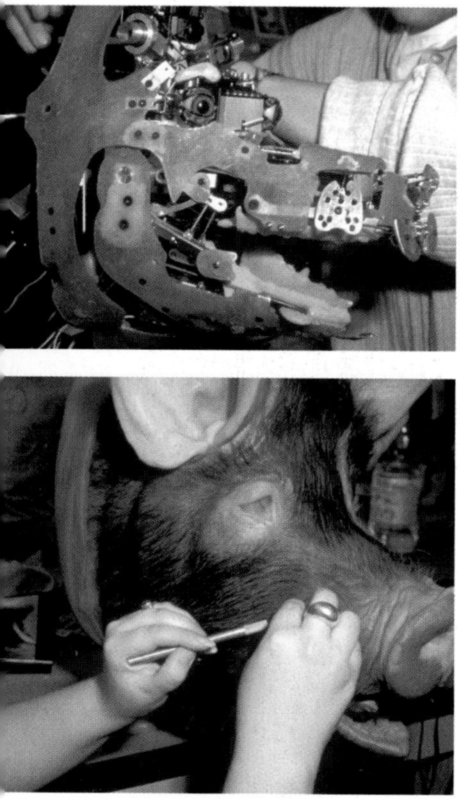

10.1.3 A servo-driven animatronic pig's head under construction (top), and the hair being punched into the synthetic skin that covers it. (Courtesy of Jim Henson's Creature Shop.)

extensive preproduction planning, and ends with the production of an animation on film, video, or digital media. The story behind the animated images is critical to the success of the project, regardless of whether the topic is a short animation of an abstract logotype or the animation of a cartoon character.

Hand-Drawn Animation

The most common technique of traditional animation is **hand-drawn animation**, often called **cel animation**. This technique starts with sequences of individual pencil drawings on paper. These drawings are recorded successively on an animation stand to create a preview of the motion, or **pencil test**. Once this rough animation is approved, the drawings are then sent for **clean-up**. The cleaned-up drawings then go to **ink and paint**, which means that the pencil lines are inked and the areas of the drawing that require color are painted. Years ago the inking and painting of animation drawings was done entirely by hand on individual acetate overlays or **cels**, but the use of cels is on the decline. Today we scan the cleaned-up drawings into a digital ink and paint system and save them as files. The digital files with the scanned drawings contain the foreground shapes that move over the background. The **foreground** may contain, for example, drawings of cartoon characters, letterforms, or scanned photographs; the **background** usually consists of painted or photographic images. In any given shot there may be several layers of drawings arranged on the background. Once finished, all the layers are composited digitally over the background. In the olden days this was achieved by placing the transparent cel overlays over the background and recording them on photographic film one frame at a time.

Stop-Motion Animation

Traditional **stop-motion animation**, also known as stop-motion photography, consists of animating a jointed model and recording the different positions on a single frame each (Fig. 10.1.2). This technique was successfully used to create landmark visual effects for live action films from the 1930s to the 1950s, including ***King Kong*** and ***Jason and the Argonauts***. Early miniature models for traditional stop motion animation were made of modeling clay, but most later models consisted of a rubber skin with a wire armature. Stop motion, a form of forward kinematics animation, can also be used to set key poses of three-dimensional computer-animated characters. This is usually done with special metal armatures that send information on the joint angles to the animation software (Fig. 11.2.2).

Animatronics

The computer-controlled models that can be animated in real time are called **animatronics**. These motion control systems have mechanical and electronic components, and they usually consist of a metal-jointed armature that is covered with a synthetic skin and that is moved with servomotors (Fig. 10.1.3). The fact that animatronics are usually placed on the set alongside live actors sometimes eliminates the need for compositing later in the production process. The motions of animatronics are usually programmed with forward and inverse kinematics software, and they may be repeated and refined since they are stored as digital information.

10.1.4 Preparing to shoot the animatronic dog with walking mechanism, mounted on a rolling rig along with the puppeteer, and towed behind the camera dolly. (Courtesy of Jim Henson's Creature Shop.)

Performance Animation

The oldest form of **performance animation** is probably found in the art of **puppetry**. *Bunraku* for example, my personal favorite form of puppetry, exposes the puppeteer alongside the puppet. Whether created with puppets or with an actor inside of a suit the basic idea is that a live actor controls the performance of the animated character (Figs. 10.1.4 and 10.1.5). When applied to three-dimensional computer animation this technique is usually called motion capture, and it has two modalities: live motion capture, which is directly applied to the computer character, and processed motion capture, where the collected data is fine-tuned and sometimes enhanced with the use of other animation techniques (Figs. 10.5.3, and 12.2.7). When executed with skill, motion capture can bring to computer animation some of the freshness and natural motion of a live performance.

10.1.5 A suit performer in an animatronic bear costume is given a rest break between shots. (Courtesy of Jim Henson's Creature Shop.)

Character Animation

Character animation seeks to bring to life imagined or virtual characters, and is considered by many the highest form of animation (Figs. 10.1.1 and 10.5.1–10.5.15). In the majority of computer animation productions a few character animators are charged with blocking out the primary motion of the character, while assistant animators are responsible for cleaning up the primary motion and adding the secondary motion. **Character animation** is usually created with a combination of inverse and forward kinematic techniques and motion capture, both of which are covered in Chapters 11 and 12.

Effects Animation

Most of the animation that is not character-oriented falls within the specialty of **effects animation**. This usually includes natural phenomena like fire, smoke, wind, dust, and water in its many forms (rain, snow, clouds, rivers, waterfalls, oceans), as well as special lighting effects like sparks and shadows (Figs. 10.1.6 and pages 150–151). Effects animation often deals with props and entire sets, such as the ball in a soccer game or the grass in a landscape. This area of computer animation usually relies on techniques that allow the animator to control vast numbers of elements over time, such as particle systems and other procedural techniques and dynamic simulations.

10.1.6 Effects animation includes animating lighting effects and the flight paths of props like the vehicles in this detail from *Lights & Water*. (Courtesy of Satoshi Kitahara.)

10.2.1 (next 3 pages) This TV commercial exemplifies parallel action, which is at the core of this work, implemented as a montage of live action and computer-generated short sequences (leaving the beach, arriving at the mansion) and single shots. At the end of the sequence the image format changes from letterbox to full screen format. (Stills from: *Lara Needs SEAT*. Client: SEAT. Agency: Callegari-Berville. Production: Ex Machina. Director: Pascal Vuong. Consultant: Eidos Interactive. Images courtesy of Ex Machina.)

Visual Effects Animation for Live Action

Animating visual effects and characters for live action requires a unique approach that is usually quite different from traditional animation. Since the main goal of **visual effects animation** is to complement live action, most animated elements must visually match the motion, colors, lighting, and perspective of the live sequence (Fig. 11.2.6). Unlike cartoon animation where the creator is free—even required—to exaggerate motion, visual effects animation must blend seamlessly with the action plates provided by the cinematographer. (See Chapter 13 for more information on effects and character animation for live action.)

10.2 Principles of Animation

Animation borrows many of its principles from older crafts and forms of expression including the visual arts, theatre, and cinema. This section reviews some of those borrowed principles as well as others which are unique to animation, including a reinterpretation of the twelve animation principes and a few new ones.

Keyframing and In-Betweening

One of the fundamental techniques used in animation is called **keyframing**. This technique is used to define an animated sequence based on its key moments. In the case of hand-drawn animation the drawings that correspond to the key moments in an animated sequence are called keyframe drawings, **keyframes** or **extremes** (Fig. 11.1.1). In stop-motion animation the key moments captured in the armatures or clay models are called **key poses**. Another animation technique called **in-betweening** is used once the keyframes have been established and drawn. In-betweening consists of creating all the transition or **in-between** drawings that fill in the gaps between the keyframes. In traditional animation, the in-betweening process is done by laboriously creating each in-between drawing by hand. In computer animation, in-betweening is usually done with a technique called **interpolation**. A variety of computer interpolation techniques can be used to create as many in-between frames as needed by using simple information, such as keypoints in a keyframe or interpolation curves. (See Chapter 11 for more information on interpolation.)

Units of Animation

Animations are made of thousands of frames, but the smallest unit of animation is the **frame**. One frame consists of a single still image, and for that reason one frame of animation is sometimes called a **still frame**, or simply a still. The number of frames that constitute one second of animation depends on the output media on which the animation is delivered. One second of animation at normal speed video equals **30 frames**; one second on film equals **24 frames**. On an interactive real-time computer the frame rate adapts itself to the hardware capabilities, ranging from 8 to 60 frames. The number of frames of animation per second is also called the **rate of display** or rate of projection, and is usually indicated with the letters **fps (frames per second)**.

Animation that is created by recording a different drawing on each frame recreates motion with the highest quality. One drawing (or image) per frame delivers the most information about motion to our perceptual system. When budgets or deadlines are tight animation is often created by recording each drawing on two consecutive frames. This is known as **shooting on twos**, and the resulting quality may range from acceptable to almost as good as when each image is recorded on a single frame. Most animated series created for television and many feature animated films today are shot on twos. When animated within high standards the quality degradation goes unnoticed by most moviegoers.

In film and video production a **shot** is a string of frames recorded by a single camera without interruption. A shot can consist of a few frames, or it can go on for several seconds or even minutes. A **sequence** consists of a succession of camera shots that are connected to each other because they develop the same aspect or moment of the action. Several sequences of shots usually add up to a scene. A **scene** can also be described in a more traditional way as continuous action in one place or as a unit of traditional storytelling. An **act** in a traditional theater play is usually made up of several scenes. In some animated productions a shot is sometimes referred to as a scene.

The style of the great majority of today's computer animations certainly relies more on the juxtaposition, or **montage**, of short shots than on a few long shots. The clarity of visual storytelling has to do as much with the composition of each shot as it has to do with the montage of shots and sequences.

Timing of the Action

Telling a story with computer animation is based on timing the actions to the story and on designing motions that convey the desired effect. The **timing of the action** is based on how the actions of the characters and the motion of the camera are timed to the story. There are many ways for the visual action to relate to the story. The action may be ahead or behind the story, or it may be shown in parallel.

The action may be **ahead of the story** in cases when, for example, an animated character reacts to a sound located off-camera by turning its head. The character's action is ahead of the story because it indicates to us that something will happen before we know what it is. The action may be **behind the story** when the audience knows before the character what is going to happen next. The action is behind the story, for example, in a long shot where the audience can

see that a piano is falling from the roof of a building right over a character who is unaware of the impending and disastrous action. ***Knickknack,*** a 1989 animation pictured in Figure 1.3.4, is a classic example of the action being constantly behind the story. Timing the action to be slightly ahead or behind the story is a good technique for keeping the interest of the audience. The effect of actions that are ahead of the story may be suspense and expectation because the audience wants to find out the outcome of the story and they try to guess what's next. The effects of the actions that are behind the story are commonly used in comedy, and audiences enjoy it because they can watch the character find out—often the hard way—what they already knew. **Interrupted action**, also called a **fake hold**, can be used to give the audience a moment to catch up with action that is ahead of the story, or to savor action that is behind the story.

Parallel action occurs when the audience is shown actions that take place at the same time but in different places. Parallel action is often shown as a series of shots that cut back-and-forth between each location (Fig. 10.2.1). Parallel action may show, for example, a man having lunch at a restaurant with his friend, while their respective wives are having lunch and talking about their husbands in a restaurant that is located around the corner from where their husbands are. Parallel action can be used to indicate a change of events or a turning point in the story. The action in an animation can also be interrupted to hold the interest of the audience for an unexpected action that is about to occur.

The skillful timing of the action in an animated project, or in any visual storytelling for that matter, can have a major positive effect on the audience—to hold their interest by having them constantly trying to guess how the story will evolve. This sense of curiosity and **anticipation** of the action is essential to all successful visual stories. Equally important to a good story is the **follow-through** of the action. Good follow-through keeps the interest of the audience by allowing them to confirm their expectations or suspicions or to surprise them with an unexpected turn of events. In any case, the visual follow-through of the action gives the audience a chance to digest and enjoy the plot of the story.

The Visual Grammar of Motion

The motions of a character help to tell the story and to define the personality and emotions of the animated character. (In cases when the computer animation is based on abstract shapes and not on characters, the motion of the shapes and the timing of the action becomes the main conduit for storytelling due to the lack of facial expressions and body gestures.) Motion is also a great tool for directing the **attention of the audience** to a specific place in the image. For example, a slight motion in the background of a calm scene will immediately draw the eyes of the audience to that area. Motion is so effective for guiding the eyes of the audience that it should be carefully choreographed. The **readability of motion** will result in action that flows, while confusing motion will result in unfocused action.

Different combinations of timing, speed, rhythm, and choreography result in different types of motion, including primary and secondary motions, overlapping motions, staggered motions, and motion holds. These types of motions apply not only to the objects and characters in the environment but to the camera. The virtual camera plays an important role in computer animation because its motions—as well as its position, point of interest, and focal length—have a powerful storytelling effect (see Chapter 7 for more information on camera animation).

To choreograph motion is to compose and arrange the motion of all objects or the parts of objects in a sequence of actions. Choreographing motion starts with planning the action and breaking it down into manageable blocks. This becomes very useful when animating characters with many parts that move at the same time and is also helpful to refine simple movements. **Simple motion** may consist of just one object or part of the object moving in a single direction, while **complex motion** may consist of several objects or their parts moving in a variety of directions, speeds, and rhythms. In computer animation, most environments with multiple models, and most models—particularly characters—with multiple joints imply complex animation.

Complex motion consists of primary or dominant motions and secondary motions. The **primary motion** in a shot is the motion that captures the audience's attention. The primary motion in a character is the motion that carries the action forward. The primary motion in an interior shot, for example, could be personified by two loud patrons in a bar who laugh hysterically while the rest of the customers watch. The **secondary motion** in a shot is the motion that echoes or complements the primary motion. The arms slowly moving closer to the body of a spinning ice skater or the snapping fingers of a jumping dancer are both samples of secondary motion. Secondary motion often starts as a reaction to a primary motion and through time becomes the new primary motion.

Motions in a sequence—whether just primary motions or a combination of primary and secondary motions—are rarely independent from one another. Motions often alternate and overlap. **Overlapping motion**, also called staggered motion, occurs when some motions start before others conclude (Fig. 10.2.9). Our world is full of overlapping motion. For example, when people walk they start moving the left foot before they have finished moving the right foot. When a tree is moved by the wind the small branches move at one rhythm, the larger branches at a different rhythm, and the leaves move at yet a different rhythm. For this reason, animations that want to replicate or echo natural motion are usually based on the principle of overlapping motion: Before one motion dies a new one starts to bloom.

A **motion hold** happens when a character interrupts or concludes one motion and pauses. The function of a motion hold is to

Techniques for Motion Control
Forward kinematics
Inverse kinematics
Motion dynamics
Motion capture
Procedural motion
Hybrid techniques and blending

10.2.2 The most popular techniques for motion control of animated characters.

Expanded and New Principles of Animation

	ACT.	DIR.	DRA.	PHY.	MOT.
1. Squash and stretch	✓	✓	✓	✓	
2. Anticipation	✓	✓			
3. Staging	✓	✓	✓	✓	
4. Straight ahead action and pose to pose	✓	✓		✓	
5. Follow through and overlapping action	✓			✓	
6. Slow in and slow out				✓	✓
7. Arcs	✓		✓	✓	
8. Secondary action	✓			✓	
9. Timing	✓	✓			✓
10. Exaggeration	✓	✓			
11. Solid modeling and rigging			✓	✓	
12. Character's personality	✓	✓	✓	✓	✓
13. Visual styling			✓	✓	✓
14. Blending cartoon with real motion	✓	✓	✓	✓	✓
15. Cinematography		✓	✓		✓
16. Facial animation	✓	✓	✓		
17. User-controlled animation	✓	✓	✓	✓	✓

10.2.3 The principles of animation developed by cartoon animators in the 1930s expanded for computer animation. These principles are about acting, directing, representing reality, simulating physics, and editing motion.

give the audience a chance to catch up with the development of the story or to indicate that a new action is about to happen (Fig. 10.5.11 and page v). The most effective way to create a motion hold is by interrupting the primary motion while continuing with a small motion. Motion holds should never result in an absolute and total interruption of the action because that results in mechanical motion or destroys the continuity and flow of the action. Secondary motions such as the turning of a head or blinking of the eyes can help carry on a motion hold.

The relation between primary, secondary, and overlapping motions and motion holds becomes an important concern when animating a group of moving objects, especially when animating articulated figures with hierarchical groupings of objects. A useful strategy for planning and refining complex motion in computer animation is based on the idea of animating the **layers of motion** one at a time. An animated scene can have several layers of motion. In a scene with primary, secondary, and overlapping motion it usually makes sense to animate first the layer of primary motion, then add layers of secondary motion, and finally go back and forth between layers to adjust all the overlapping motions. Animated objects or characters can also have several layers of motion, and the most practical way of animating them consists of starting with the primary motion and the secondary motions next. When animating an articulated figure with keyframes, this implies establishing the poses for each keyframe starting at the top of the hierarchical structure and working down to the details only after the dominant motions have been worked out. In a scene that consists, for example, of one singer and a five-character chorus it would be convenient to start animating the primary motion of the lead singer. One could continue with the dominant motions of the chorus singers. Then the secondary motions of the lead singer could be determined, followed by the secondary motions of the chorus singers. At this point fine-tuning the overlapping motions would be easy because all the primary and secondary motions would already be contained in the scene.

Animating motion in layers is convenient because it breaks a complex challenge into smaller and more manageable parts. It is also convenient and almost necessary in complex animated sequences because in many of them the keyframes in different motion layers are placed in different moments along the time line. Keyframes in an animated sequence with complex motion are usually abundant and scattered throughout the scene in an overlapping fashion.

Techniques for Motion Control

There are many computer animation techniques for controlling the motion of three-dimensional characters, objects and effects. Some of these **motion control techniques**—inverse kinematics, for example—work well within the context of keyframe animation; others, including motion dynamics, require animation methodologies that are borrowed from scientific simulations (Fig. 10.2.2). But increasingly,

10.2.4 Before throwing the ball the pitcher anticipates the target and winds up for the pitch.

however, computer animations are developed within a **hybrid framework** that combines many different motion control techniques and production methodologies into a single project. An important task of computer animators consists of selecting the most appropriate technique or set of techniques for **implementing the motions** designed for a specific project. Some of the most common computer animation motion control techniques for the arrangement of keyframes include interactive or manual, kinematic, motion dynamics, procedural, and hybrid techniques, all of which are covered in Chapters 11 and 12.

The simplest, most direct—and potentially most time-consuming—of all motion control techniques consists of manually arranging the objects in a scene. This approach has its roots in traditional hand-drawn keyframe animation, where all the information in the keyframes was originally drawn by hand, and it is based on the idea of defining keyframes, specifying the ease function, and letting the software interpolate the in-between frames. The technique of **manual arrangement** of the objects in a scene is always done interactively, and it works best when the animator is experienced and has a good eye and a good hand for animation.

Kinematic techniques for animating objects and characters are based on changing the position and orientation of models in three-dimensional space. In **forward kinematics,** the angles of the joints are manipulated to achieve a specific motion, while in **inverse kinematics** the limbs or objects are moved to a position and the software calculates the joint rotations that are necessary for the in-between positions to be created. Inverse kinematics techniques, covered in Chapter 12, are especially useful for animating complex models with a large number of joints. Inverse kinematics calculates the motion of entire skeletons by specifying the final angle positions of just some of the key joints that define the motion. **Motion capture** techniques provide the kinematic information to the software by recording the positions or angles of joints of live actors or objects in motion. Kinematic techniques in general can greatly simplify the animation of models that have to move in a realistic way, for example, a tiger running.

Animation techniques based on the physical laws of motion, called dynamics, can generate realistic motion of objects by simulating their physical properties and nature's laws of physical motion. **Motion dynamics** techniques control the motion of three-dimensional objects by applying forces to the joints and actually simulating the motion that would result in the physical world if such forces were applied to a real object with specific characteristics. Motion

10.2.5 Differences in staging can turn the same scene from happy to suspenseful.

POSE-TO-POSE, AND ARCS

10.2.6 The structured movements of a ballerina, from one key pose to another, is a good example of pose-to-pose action. Her smooth motions follow curved paths.

dynamics techniques take into account variables such as an object's weight, mass, inertia, flexibility, and collision with other objects, as well as the environment's friction, gravity, and other forces that may influence the motion of objects.

Procedural or **rule-based motion** techniques animate the objects in the scene based on a set of procedures and rules to control motion. The animation of flocks is an example of procedural motion control. Rule-based motion techniques are often scored with a special-purpose programming language so that they can be easily edited and previewed.

Applying the Twelve Principles to 3D Computer Animation

The **twelve principles of animation** were created in the early 1930s by animators at the Walt Disney Studios. These principles were used to guide production and creative discussions as well to train young animators better and faster. These twelve principles became one of the foundations of hand-drawn cartoon character animation. The twelve principles, as they are commonly referred to, also helped to transform animation from a novelty into an art form. By applying these principles to their work these pioneering animators produced many of the earliest animated feature films that became classics: ***Snow White*** (1937), ***Pinocchio*** and ***Fantasia*** (1940), ***Dumbo*** (1941), and ***Bambi*** (1942).

The twelve principles are mostly about five things: acting the performance, directing the performance, representing reality (through drawing, modeling, and rendering), interpreting real world physics, and editing a sequence of actions. The original principles are still relevant today because they help us to create more believable characters and situations. They can be applied to almost any type of animation, even though they work best for comedy. But, some of these principles require updates, and a few new additional principles are also needed to address the new techniques and styles of three-dimensional computer animation (Fig. 10.2.3).

Animation techniques and styles, and the scope of productions, have changed tremendously since the 1930s. The dominant, almost exclusive, style of animation then was hand-drawn pose-to-pose cartoon narrative animation. Today we have more styles including nonlinear interactive videogames and non-narrative music videos. In the 1930s some animation techniques and capabilities were underdeveloped, camera moves and lighting for example, or misunderstood: rotoscoping or stop-motion. Consider too the new tools that have transformed our craft: hand-held cameras, television, non-linear editing, compositing, motion capture, computer graphics and procedural tools. Other artforms have greatly evolved since the 1930s, creating new languages and new principles. It is time to do the same with animation, it is time to reinterpret and expand the original principles. We also need to create new additional principles that address today's new animation styles and techniques. This is our collective challenge.

STRAIGHT-AHEAD ACTION

10.2.7 The improvisation, spontaneity, and unpredictability in the walk of a drunken character illustrates straight-ahead action.

FOLLOW-THROUGH

10.2.8 Follow-through includes the reactions of a character after an action. These let the viewer know how the character feels about what has just happened.

OVERLAPPING ACTION

10.2.9 Multiple motions happening at the same time result in overlapping action, for example when a character falls.

SLOW-IN...

AND SLOW-OUT

10.2.10 Right before and right after kicking the ball a soccer player slows-in and slows-out; this highlights the precise moment of the kick.

TIMING

10.2.11 The timing of a response to someone calling us, or to a noise, tells a lot about our attitude, confidence and disposition.

EXAGGERATION

10.2.12 Exaggerated reactions are often comedic.

Squash and stretch, the first principle from the original twelve, 1
is used to exaggerate the amount of non-rigid body deformations usually with the purpose of achieving a more comedic effect (Fig. 1.1.3). Three-dimensional squash and stretch can be implemented with a variety of techniques: skin and muscle, springs, direct mesh manipulation and morphing. It can also be implemented in more experimental ways with weighting, especially for dynamics simulations, and unusual IK systems (Fig. 10.5.11).

The technique of **anticipation** helps to guide the audience's 2
eyes to where the action is about to occur (Fig. 10.2.4). Anticipation, including motion holds, is great for "announcing the surprise." In three-dimensional computer animation it can be fine-tuned using digital time-editing tools such as time sheets, timelines, and curves. More anticipation equals less suspense. Horror films, for example, switch back and forth from lots of anticipation to total surprise.

Staging, or *mise-en-scène* as it is also known, is about translating 3
the mood and intention of a scene into specific character positions and actions. Staging the key character poses in the scene helps to define the nature of the action (Fig. 10.2.5). Three-dimensional animatics are a great tool for previsualizing and blocking out the staging before the primary, secondary and facial animation (Figs. 2.4.4 and 2.4.14). There are many staging techniques to tell the story visually: hiding or revealing the center of interest, and a chain reaction of actions-reactions (about to happen in Figure 10.2.9) are a couple of them. Staging can also be aided with contemporary cinematic techniques such as slow motion, frozen time, motion loops, and hand-held camera moves.

Straight-ahead action and pose-to-pose are two different anima- 4
tion techniques that yield fairly different results. In the early days of hand-drawn animation **pose-to-pose action** became the standard animation technique because it breaks down structured motion into a series of clearly defined key poses (Fig. 10.2.6). In **straight-ahead action** the character moves spontaneously through the action one step at a time until the action is finished (Fig. 10.2.7). Motion capture and dynamics simulations, even three-dimensional rotoscoping, are clearly the straight-ahead techniques of three-dimensional computer animation. They can all be blended intelligently using channels.

Follow-through and overlapping action are two techniques that 5
help make the action richer and fuller with detail and subtlety. **Follow-through action** consists of the reactions of the character after an action, and it usually lets audiences know how he or she feels about what has just happened or is about to happen (Fig. 10.2.8). In **overlapping action** multiple motions influence, blend, and overlap the position of the character. In three-dimensional computer animation a lot of the common follow-through motions of clothing and hair, for example, can be animated with dynamics simulations (Fig. 10.2.9). The layers and channels in three-dimensional computer animation software allow us to mix and blend different overlapping motions from different areas of the character.

6 **Slow-in** and **slow-out** consist of slowing down the beginning and the end of an action, while speeding up the middle of it. A snappy effect is achieved when motion is accelerated and retarded in this way (Fig. 10.2.10). In three-dimensional computer animation slow-ins and slow-outs can be fine-tuned with digital time-editing tools. When using motion capture techniques for cartoon-style animated characters it is essential to remind performers to do slow-ins and slow-outs. The inverse variation of this effect, a fast-in and fast-out, is often times seen in TV commercials and music videos where the beginning and end of the sequence are accelerated while the middle is slowed down giving it a surreal or dreamy feeling.

7 Using **arcs** to animate the movements of characters helps achieve a natural look because most living creatures move in curved paths, never in perfectly straight lines (Fig. 10.2.6). Non-arc motion comes across as sinister, restricted or robotic. In three-dimensional computer animation we can use software constraints to force all or some of the motion within arcs. Even motion-captured performances can be fine-tuned with curve editors, as long as the motion is not flattened.

8 **Secondary action** consists of the smaller motions that complement the dominant action (Fig. 1.1.3). In three-dimensional computer animation we can take advantage of layers and channels for building up different secondary motions, for example, a layer for hair, a layer for the character's hat, a layer for the cape, and so on.

9 **Timing** is the precise moment and the amount of time that a character spends on an action. Timing adds emotion and intention to the character's performance (Fig. 10.2.11). Most three-dimensional computer animation tools allow us to fine tune the timing by shaving off or adding frames with non-linear time-editing. Timing can also be controlled and adjusted by placing each character on a separate track, and using sub-tracks for parts of the character such as head, torso, arms and legs.

10 **Exaggeration** usually helps cartoon characters to deliver the essence of an action (Fig. 10.2.12). A lot of exaggeration can be achieved with squash and stretch. In three-dimensional computer animation we can use procedural techniques, motion ranges and scripts to exaggerate motion. The intensity of a moment can be increased with cinematography and editing, not just with performance.

11 **Solid modeling and rigging**, or solid drawing as it was called in the 1930s, emphasizes the clear delineation of shape necessary to bring animated characters to life (Fig. 10.2.13). Solid and precise modeling helps to convey the weight, depth and balance of the character, and it also simplifies potential production complications due to poorly modeled characters. Animation rigs are at their best when they are optimized for the specific personality and motion of the character. Pay attention to silhouettes when aligning characters to the camera.

12 **Character personality,** or appeal as it was originally called, facilitates the emotional connection between character and audience (Fig. 10.2.14). Characters must be well developed, have an interesting personality, and have a clear set of desires or needs that drive their

SOLID MODELING AND RIGGING

10.2.13 Solid modeling helps to pose silhouettes that are easy to read visually, and good rigging helps animators deliver performances that are adequate to the character.

CHARACTER'S PERSONALITY

10.2.14 Understanding the motivations and desires of characters makes their personality better defined and increases their appeal.

10.3.1 The pose of Princess Fiona from *Shrek* is defined by her geometry and range of motion but also by the comedic moment. (*Shrek*™ and © 2001 DreamWorks L.L.C.)

10.3.2 The personality of this character is translated into facial expressions, body poses, and motions. (© 1999 Mitch Butler Company, Inc.)

behavior and actions. Complexity and consistency of motion are two elements of character appeal that can be easily developed with three-dimensional computer animation. Writing down the ways in which the character moves (Fig. 10.5.7), how he/she reacts to different situations, and how he/she relates to other characters can help define the main characteristics of the character's personality. Fine-tune the personality with the key poses and the character turnarounds.

A Few New Principles for 3D Computer Animation

A few of the new issues that need to be addressed by new principles of three-dimensional computer animation include: visual styling, blending cartoon physics with real world physics, using cinematography, mastering facial animation, and optimizing user-controlled animation.

Visual styling in three-dimensional computer animation means more than just how things are supposed to look. Visual styling also has a significant impact on rendering, on animation techniques, and overall production complexity. As we develop a visual look we must keep in mind that it is feasible to produce within the boundaries of the project. A certain look for the skin of a beast, for example, might look cool but might also require too complex a rig, too detailed a model and too complex an animation process.

14 It is possible today to **blend motion** from different sources, and we need to develop a clear approach for blending cartoon with realistic motion. Before production starts it is necessary to define clear guidelines for a variety of motion/animation styles including cartoon physics, realistic cartoon, realistic human motion and rotoscoping. Above all, we must direct live performers when capturing their motion to add intention to their movements.

15 Since we have absolute control over camera positions and movement in three-dimensional computer animation, we should make the **cinematography** a crucial component of our animation, not just an afterthought. The composition, lighting, and sequencing of our moving images has a huge impact on storytelling. Most of this work can crystallize during previsualization and the assembly of the three-dimensional animatics. The lighting style needs to be addressed separately, since it impacts both the look and the rendering pipeline.

16 Most of the thoughts and emotions of characters are expressed on their faces. Three-dimensional computer animation offers more **facial animation** control than ever before, including the subtle motion of eyelids and eyeballs. Establishing early in the process the level of facial control and techniques has a positive effect on the styling of the character and the design of the production flow. Building a catalog of facial morph targets or blend shapes for production and reuse is today as essential as building walk cycles.

17 Computer and platform games put much of the animation control in the hands of gamers. This poses the challenge to create great animation that works regardless of what move the gamer decides to make. Games are a combination of **user-controlled animation** and preset/narrative animation. One of the creative animation challenges is to find a balance between the narrative and the improvisational aspect of the game. Look at the model of participatory street theater (different from traditional stage theater) for ideas on how to constraint the gamer-action to establish strong staging. User-controlled animation relies on strong animation cycles with built-in anticipation that are able to branch smoothly into reaction shots. Fortunately many of today's game engines have built-in intelligence that can smooth transitions between animation cycles. The combination of preset and dynamic user-controlled cameras is also unique to games (Fig. 11.6.2).

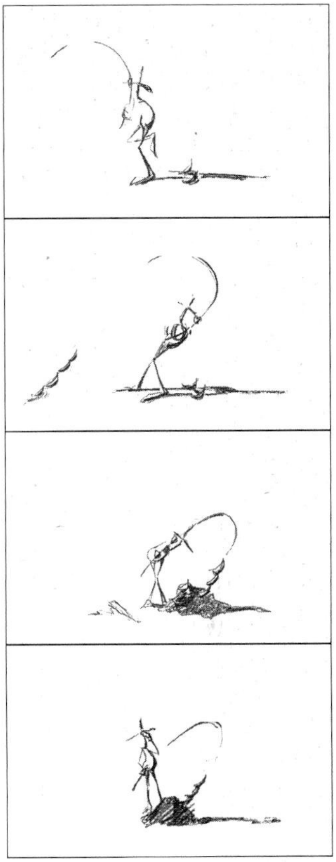

10.4.1 A conceptual storyboard indicates the essence of a shot or a sequence without getting into the details. (Images from *Fishing*, a PDI short film by David Gainey.)

Before the Computer Animation Begins

The planning stage is key to the success of any three-dimensional computer animation project. As reviewed in Chapter 2 many of the creative and practical factors that govern production are defined during the planning or preproduction stage. These creative factors include the story, the overall visual look of the project, the personalities and ambitions of the characters, and the animation style. The practical factors include the budget, the deadlines, and the overall talent of the animation team.

10.4.2 (next page) A presentation storyboard with detailed renderings including lighting effects and lens flares. (© 2003 Oddworld Inhabitants, Inc. All rights reserved.)

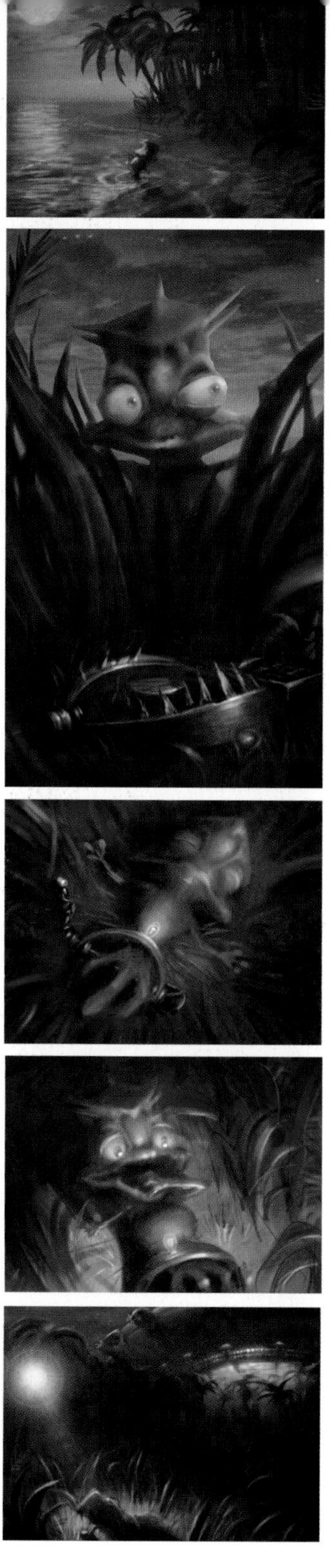

The creative development and production planning that may lead to a successful computer animation or visual effects production is often as challenging as the production itself. For that reason it is important to spend time and energy on these issues. As a general rule, the more defined the plans, the easier it will be to achieve the creative goals. The remainder of this chapter focuses on a few preproduction stages: the screenplay, the storyboards, and the development of the characters.

10.3 Storytelling

Stories are the most common and most powerful vehicle we use to talk about life. Not just one life but many lives. Life in general, and our own lives in particular. Past, present, and future lives. Real, imagined, and assumed lives. Inspiring, intriguing, tormented, or impossible lives.

Stories communicate facts. Stories provide answers to questions. Stories make us feel different emotions. Stories sometimes even provoke actions that shape reality. Whether they are linear or nonlinear, whether they depict an event with cartoon characters or a colorful dance of abstract shapes, stories are the essence of animation. Being a good storyteller requires many talents and skills. But why should anybody interested in computer animation have to learn about storytelling? Because animations are more than just moving images. Animations tell stories and communicate emotions that are initially drafted in screenplays, and later in storyboards and character sheets.

In most cases, the work of animators involves the **visual interpretation** of a story and its characters (Figs. 10.3.1 and 10.3.2). Animators translate the personality of characters into facial expressions, gestures, and motions, whether the story is a complex epic drama between nations or the simple courting of a lady sphere by a male square. Animators and other visual people involved in the production of animations, often start to sketch their visual interpretations of a story by reading and discussing a screenplay.

The Screenplay

A **screenplay** is a written document that tells a story by using descriptions, dialogue, and some production notes. Unlike a novel, which is written to be printed and read, a screenplay is not an end-product in itself. Instead, the screenplay is an intermediate work, a vehicle for the story to be retold with images in the form of an animation, a movie, or a play. For this reason, screenplays tell stories in ways that can be **translated into moving images**. One screenplay page is usually equivalent to one minute of action on the screen. Screenplays can differ by the amount of dialogue they incorporate, the number of characters they present, or the detail of their descriptions of imagery. But what all screenplays have in common is a subject and a clearly defined treatment of the subject that is adequate for the intended audience.

The **treatment of the subject** in a screenplay is defined by the point of view that the storyteller wants to convey to the audience. Treatments can be, for example, dramatic, comic, or lyrical, action-packed, or introspective. Considering the **intended audience** can make it easier to define the treatment for a screenplay's subject. This includes not only the philosophical or political treatments of the subject, for example, but also the visual treatment. This concerns animations because some screenplays may require very simple or specific computer animation techniques to achieve the desired effect or emotion. The **subject of a screenplay** is defined by what the story is about, who the characters are, and what happens to them throughout the sequence of events. Because the subject of a story is often presented through the actions of a character, it is important to develop the personality of all the characters before the story is told.

A screenplay's subject can be presented in the context of a variety of dramatic and narrative structures. The **structure** of a story holds all the parts of the story together. There are no rigid rules about the best way to structure a story, and stories can be told with a wide variety of styles and techniques. But stories that are told in the context of a **linear** medium—such as film or video—consist of a beginning, a middle, and an end, and the action in a story usually moves from one event to another.

The **beginning of the story**—also called exposition or setup—usually introduces the main characters, establishes the dramatic premise, and sets up the events and situations that will develop the story. The **middle of the story**—also called confrontation or climax—usually contains the moments when the main characters confront the conflicts that when resolved will lead to a resolution. The **end of the story**—also called resolution or *dénouement,* from the French "untying a knot"—usually contains the outcome of the dramatic sequence of events in the story.

Several variations of the traditional structure of a story are possible. For example, the structure can be altered so that the story starts with the resolution, continues with the setup, and concludes with the confrontation. But in every instance stories are always told in terms of **events** or **plot points** that make the story evolve in a particular way. These events are the moments in the story when the action takes a different turn. These moments and events help develop the story and keep the action moving.

Nonlinear Storytelling

Storytelling in most visual media happens in a linear way because images, sounds, and text follow each other in a single predetermined order. But a variety of possible sequences may be possible in an **interactive project** because users can make different requests and also follow a variety of paths. Interactive projects may have multiple endings and even multiple beginnings each time they are played. Storytelling for interactive media requires unique techniques because

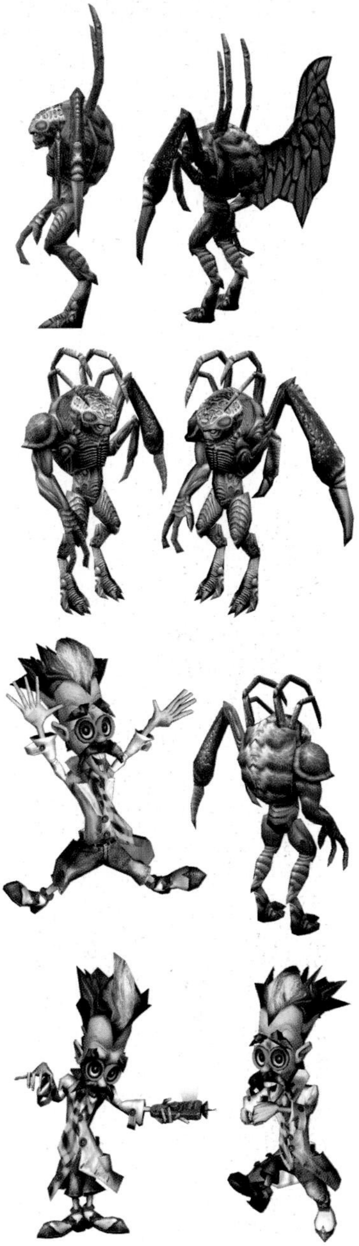

10.5.1 Character turnarounds present the key personality features from different points of view, a menacing and powerful mutant and a mad scientist. (Top: Primagen from *Turok* 2™ and Acclaim®. © 1999 Acclaim Entertainment, Inc. All rights reserved. Bottom and next page: Dr. Muto © 2002 Midway Games West, Inc.)

of the **nonlinearity** of the media.

Creators of an interactive project have in **flowcharts** a powerful tool for planning the project and for determining the many paths that the story may follow. Flowcharts are diagrams that clearly lay out all the **branching** options that may occur in the **flow of events** of interactive dialogue. The branching structure in an interactive system may be simple if few options are offered or complex if the options are multiple. Each branching node in a flowchart is controlled by a choice made by the individual or individuals interacting with the system. When a choice is made at a branching node the flow of events advances to another **hierarchy level** in the flowchart. On occasions the sequencing of events in an interactive project may be sketched out in the form of a traditional storyboard. The **interactivity** of a computer system is based on the **dialogue** established between the system itself and the individuals using it.

Individuals using interactive systems can make their choices through standard input peripherals such as mice, joysticks, and keyboards, or unique ones such as gloves and bodysuits with ultrasonic and light sensors that determine the position, orientation, and physical gestures of a person. Interactive media systems are usually built around one or several computer systems that are able to control the flow of information stored in a variety of media, formats and systems, including still and moving images, sound, and text. Hence the name interactive multimedia.

Flowcharts describe in an abstract manner the overall structure and dynamics of an interactive project. But **scripts** address the flow of events in an interactive project; they are the practical implementation of the ideas contained in a flowchart. Scripts are computer programs that collect and evaluate information about the choices made by the system's users, and then direct the program in the appropriate direction. Scripts trigger events that may include displaying an image or playing a sequence of images or sounds.

Interactive media are not made to be just watched or read; instead, they are made to be used by people. Three-dimensional real-time computer games are made to be played. For this reason, the functionality of an interactive system should always be checked with extensive **user testing**. The feedback and suggestions of users usually uncover the moments in the flow of events that may be confusing, or important functionalities that may be missing, or user's requests that crash the program and freeze the system. Only after a thorough user testing process can interactive nonlinear storytelling projects be released to the public.

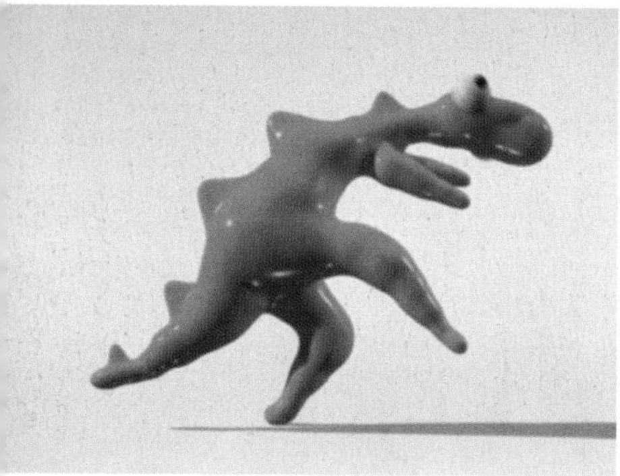

10.5.2 The external shape of these two charming characters is soft and playful. Their silhouette and internal structure is simple and straightforward. Their lack of facial expressions concentrates the expression of their vivacious and mischevous personalities on their body language. (Agency, Nickelodeon; Director/Designer, Chris Wedge. Courtesy of Blue Sky Productions, Inc.)

10.4 Storyboarding

Screenplays are converted into storyboards as they are readied for visual production. A **storyboard** is a visual interpretation of the screenplay and contains many images and production notes. A storyboard consists of a series of panels that contains in visual form the scenes and shots specified in the screenplay. There is no standard medium for storyboards, but they are usually drawn on boards, on plain paper, or preprinted paper with guides. When using preprinted storyboard paper you have to be certain that the proportion of the drawing area corresponds to the proportions of the format that the animation will be recorded on, for example, video, 35 mm film, or 70 mm film. Many characteristics of a storyboard, including its **dimensions**, are determined by whether the main function of the storyboard is to develop the concept, to present the concept to a client, or to guide the actual production of a piece.

10.5.3 Early examples of successful motion capture these two characters, opponents in a duel that will probably end in the annhilation of one of them. Their external shapes are realistic, and the internal structure that governs their motion is complex. Their facial expressions are limited in range but intense: pain and fear, determination and coldness. (Courtesy of Acclaim Entertainment, Inc., Advanced Technologies Group.)

The Conceptual Storyboard

A **conceptual storyboard** is used to develop the basic visual ideas such as the actions of the characters, the camera positions, the timing of motions, and the transitions between scenes. Conceptual storyboards are often loose, sketchy, and informal, and may contain lots of abbreviated notes (Fig. 10.4.1). These storyboards are often drawn on napkins and sketchbooks, and sometimes on letter size or A4 size plain paper.

The Presentation Storyboard

The **presentation storyboard** is used to show a detailed visual summary of the project to individuals with a decision-making authority, such as clients or supervisors. Presentation storyboards usually include important scenes of the project are often executed with great attention to detail, in color and on high-quality materials (Fig. 10.4.2). The visuals are usually large enough so that several people in a meeting room can look at them from a distance, and small enough to fit inside a portfolio. The notes included in presentation storyboards should always be very legible and descriptive without getting too technical.

The Production Storyboard

A **production storyboard** often guides the production of an animated project. This type of storyboard can be the document that everybody involved in the production process refers to, to clarify detailed questions. For this reason, they are always very detailed and precise, and they include drawings and written information about every shot in the story. It is very important to work out many of the technical details in an animation before a production storyboard is created. Otherwise, information contained in the storyboard may change a lot, rendering the storyboard useless for production purposes.

The **written information** in production storyboards may include detailed descriptions of the motion, the camera, the set, the lighting, and other rendering specs, the timing, and the transitions between the shots. Production storyboards also include soundtrack

10.5.4 The simple geometry of this face allows for an interesting and surprisingly effective approach to facial expressions. (© 1996 Felipe Lara.)

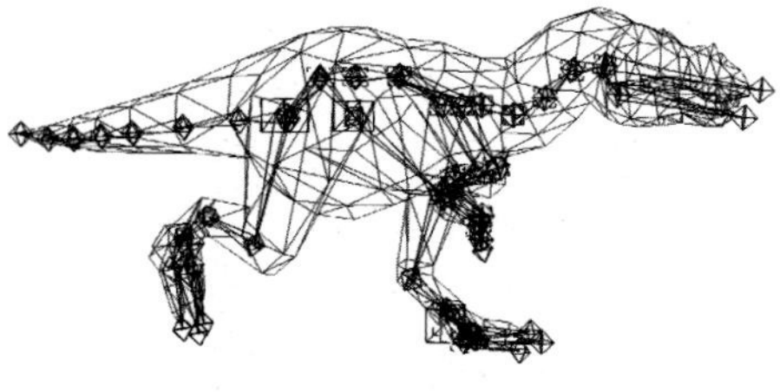

10.5.5. The inverse kinematics chains of a real-time character are shown over the wireframe skin. Notice the large amount of joints on the tail and neck, and the importance of the hips and feet in effecting motion. (Courtesy of Angel Studios.)

information such as transcripts of the dialogue and narrator's voice-over, and descriptions of the music and sound effects.

Each still frame that represents a shot in the storyboard is usually numbered with a **shot number** or with a **scene-and-shot-number**. The timing information for each shot is usually noted right below the visual representing each shot. Absolute timing values, or **elapsed time**, indicate the exact time at which the shot starts and ends in terms of hours, minutes, seconds, and frames. For example, a one-and-a-half-second long shot in the middle of the storyboard for a short video animation may start at 00:01:37:15 and end at 00:01:39:00. Relative timing values or **running time** simply indicate the total length of a shot, usually in seconds and frames, for example, the same shot may be one second and 15 frames (1 sec. 15 fr.) long.

The **drawings** in the storyboard depict the images seen by the camera. Sometimes the motions of the camera are further clarified by using directional arrows to indicate them visually over the drawing. The points of visual interest in the composition and the direction of the paths of visual interest are sometimes also overlaid on the still drawings in the storyboard (Fig. 2.4.8).

The passage from one shot or scene to the next is called a **transition**. Some of the most common transitions between shots specified in a storyboard include a cross-dissolve, a fade-in, a fade-out, or a soft-cut (these are explained in Chapter 14). Plain cuts between shots are usually not indicated in storyboards because it is assumed that most of the transitions are cuts. Aspects of the camera specified in a storyboard include the type of shot, the type of move, the point-of-view or POV, and the type of lens (see Chapter 11 for more information on camera animation). Production storyboards can be drawn in formats that can be easily pinned to a wall or carried in a binder or briefcase. Sometimes these storyboards are drawn so that the visual and written information on each shot is contained on a single piece of paper. This way a sequence of shots in a storyboard can be easily rearranged if necessary while production is underway. Other times these storyboards are drawn on letter size or A4 size paper so they can be carried by different members of the animation team.

Personality of a Character

External shape

Silhouette

Internal structure

Facial expressions

Body poses

Timing

Rhythm

10.5.6a The main components of the personality of a character.

Titles and Credits

In addition to the animation itself, many production storyboards commonly contain detailed information about the titles, the opening and closing credits, and any other text, letterforms, or graphic information that may appear in the animation. The titles of a computer animation can be simple or elaborate, but they are always storyboarded in detail. Simple titles typically consist of two-dimensional letterforms superimposed on the animated opening sequence. Two-dimensional letterforms are usually created with a **character generator** or an electronic **paintbox**, and not with a three-dimensional modeling program. The latter is used in cases when the titles are of three-dimensional nature or when they are part of the animated

10.5.6b Notice the striking differences in personality between the grumpy small characters and the large but affable intruder. The silhouettes are also quite contrasting. (*For the Birds*. © Pixar Animation Studios.)

environment. The credits almost always consist of two-dimensional letterforms. Some major credits may be superimposed on the opening sequence, but most appear at the end of the animation as **rolling credits**. (See "Creative and Production Teams" in Chapter 2 for more information about the proper way to credit those who participate in a computer-animated project.)

When designing the placement of text and graphics on the screen it is important to make sure that they are readable and that they will not be cut off by being too close to the edge of the frame. **Field guides** are graphs with concentric rectangles that can be used to specify the exact position of text and graphics within the frame (Fig. 7.2.2). The **title safety area** in the field guides clarifies what constitutes a placement of the titles and graphics that may not always be within the frame due to slight differences in vertical and horizontal positioning of the image among television sets or film projectors.

10.5 Character Development

Much of the story in an animated film is communicated through the actions of characters. For that reason a great deal of time and energy is dedicated to the character development stage in a project. In developing the look of a character for computer animation one must keep in mind the type of project that the character is intended for. Throughout this book you will find examples of cartoon characters, more stylized characters or very realistic. **Cartoon characters** are usually caricatures of someone and are especially well suited for

Drunken Pig

External Shape
Massive, uniform, even boring
Silhouette
Little detail, limbs don't show
Internal Structure
Limited joint mobility
Facial Expressions
None, just a blank stare
Body Poses
Monotonous
Timing and Rhythm
Slow, off-beat, erratic

Perky Girl

External Shape
Well defined, many shapes
Silhouette
Attractive, long limbs
Internal Structure
Lots of mobility, ample motions
Facial Expressions
Varied, multiple, distinct
Body Poses
Wide range, unique, sculptural
Timing and Rhythm
Alive, rhythmic, graceful

Paranoid Guy

External Shape
Simple but varied
Silhouette
Friendly, cartoony
Internal Structure
Very mobile, almost rubbery
Facial Expressions
Limited to eyes, effective
Body Poses
Expressive but small repertoire
Timing and Rhythm
Quick, ahead of the beat

comedies. **Stylized characters** are seen in dramatic or lyrical works, and **realistic characters** are well suited for creating virtual actors.

Character sheets are drawings used to define the main emotions and attitudes of the characters in the form of body positions and facial expressions. Character sheets are also used as templates by all the individuals involved in the **character development** that includes both drawing and building models. But before the final character sheets are completed it may also be necessary to create hundreds of studies and sketches on paper and a simple modeling material such as clay (Figs. 2.4.5–2.4.6, and Harald Siepermann's hand-drawn characters in Chapter 2). Equally important are the **character turnarounds**, which show the key features of a character from different points of view (Fig. 10.5.1). Character sheets usually present two different aspects of a character: its anatomy and its personality. In traditional animation, the anatomy of a character is related mostly to the way the character looks. But in three-dimensional computer animation the **anatomy** of a character is related to both its external shape and internal structure.

External Shape and Silhouette of a Character

The **external shape of a three-dimensional character** defines how the character looks—its visual appearance. Often the shape of a character implies much of the character's personality or the way it moves. For example, think of the difference in motion implied by a fat and heavy body shape with a small round head as opposed to a long and thin body shape with a large cubic head. Or think of the difference in personality that would be projected by a character with a slender frame shaped with a rich assortment of soft curved spaces gracefully connected to each other, as opposed to a disjointed character with a hunched frame covered with unevenly distributed sharp and irregular thorn-like shapes. Of course, appearances can be deceiving, and the personality of a character or its motion is not defined just by its shape. But also keep in mind that much of **casting**—or the assignment of dramatic roles to actors—is partly dependent on the desired appearance of the character to be represented (Figs. 10.5.2–10.5.4).

Animated characters, just like humans, animals, plants, and minerals, come in all shapes. One of the most fun aspects of developing a computer animation is designing the shape of the characters. Character design usually starts as sketches done on paper, and it takes into account the **production technique** that will be used to animate the character. For example, a computer animation developed with limited computing resources may favor characters with simple shapes, while a project developed with unlimited resources may employ human-like characters. The design of a character also takes into account the type of story that is being told and the type of emotions that it contains. For example, characters may be caricatures or realistic representations of human beings; each treatment will tell the story in a slightly different way and will also have different animation requirements. Characters may be shaped with stylized forms and ball-joints, or with a single continuous skin. When designing a character one must consider the modeling tools available to do the job, the time constraints, and all the implications of a simple or complex model in the rendering and animation stages. On occasion it is useful to make studies of the character in clay. Three-dimensional clay models complement the character drawings and help to better visualize the overall shading, facial expressions, and body gestures of the characters.

The shape of characters can be used to accentuate an aspect of the character's personality. For example, a big bouncy nose can accentuate the silliness of a character, an overly long tail can be an excuse for its clumsiness, or a slender waist can help focus on its grace and agility. However, it is always the relation between all the parts of a character—and not just a single shape—that expresses the character's personality. When designing characters it is important to consider not only the shape of its body, but also the shape of its clothing. Keep in mind that the realistic animation of cloth may require complex animation techniques.

The **silhouette** of a character helps to define its personality due to the inherent visual characteristics of shapes. Shapes with a lot of contrast tend to be more exciting than shapes with no contrast; the latter can even give a static aura to the character. Fragile shapes can emphasize a fragile personality or reveal the contrast between a fragile appearance and a strong personality. Heavy and imposing shapes can accentuate the bullyness of a character or emphasize the contrast between a huge frame and a gentle spirit.

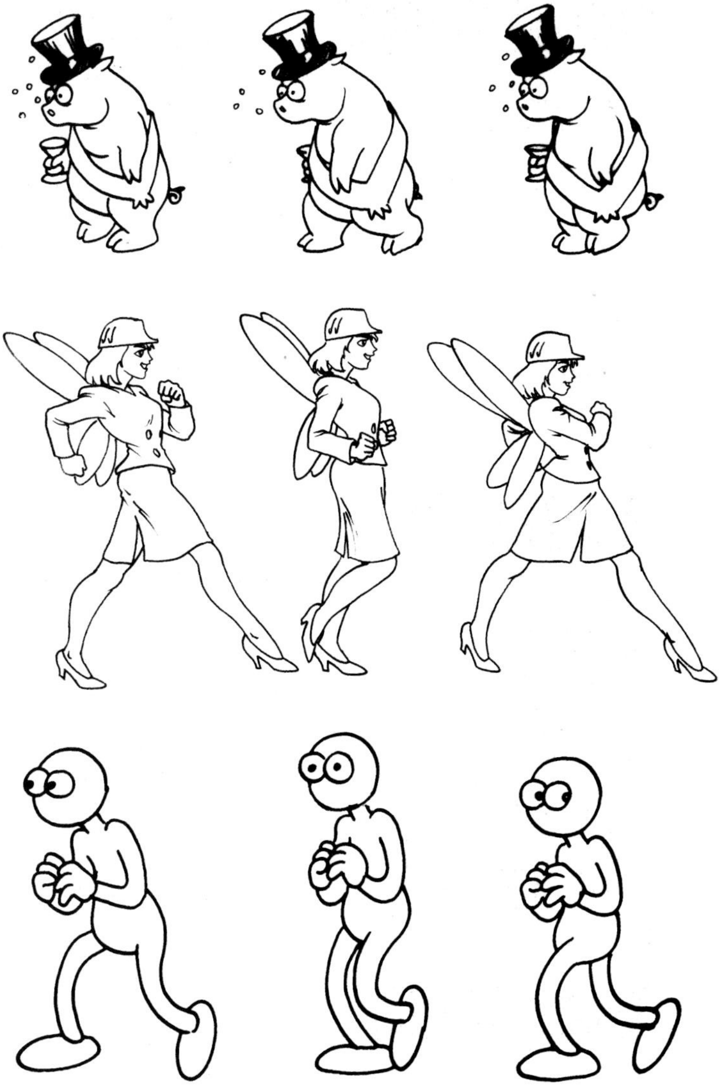

10.5.7 The personality differences of three characters walking down the road are expressed in their motions and body posture, and also listed on the opposite page.

Internal Structure of a Character

Since motion is a fundamental component of animation, the **internal structure of a three-dimensional character** is of the utmost importance in a computer animation because it defines how a character

10.5.8 These characters from the *ReBoot* television series (opposite page too) all have distinct body shapes, silhouettes, facial expressions, and body poses that give them their distinct personalities. Can you describe each of their characteristics? (ReBoot® and © 1997 Mainframe Entertainment, Inc. All rights reserved.)

moves. The structure of a three-dimensional character is often determined by its hierarchical **skeleton** and by the functionality of its **joints**. This is convenient since most three-dimensional computer animation systems provide a variety of techniques for manipulating skeletons and joints as if there were muscles moving them. The skeleton and joints of a three-dimensional character are like the frame and joints of a puppet—they define the ways in which it can move. The puppeteer animates the puppet by pulling strings. The computer animator brings the virtual characters to life by manipulating data, and by applying functions and transformations to the skeleton and joints. Hierarchical skeletons are defined in more detail in Chapters 5 and 11, including Figures 5.7.1–5.7.5 and 11.5.1–11.5.3.

The complexity of a character's skeleton and joints controls the timing of its motions (Fig. 10.5.5). A skeleton with a simple structure usually results in simple motions, while complex skeletons may yield complex motions. For example, a character that can move its shoulders independently from the lower torso will be capable of more complex—and expressive—motion than a character that can move its shoulders only in conjunction with the lower torso. Likewise, motions animated with a set of joints that have a few rotating constraints may be more convincing than the motion created with joints that have very limited angles of rotation.

Personality of a Character

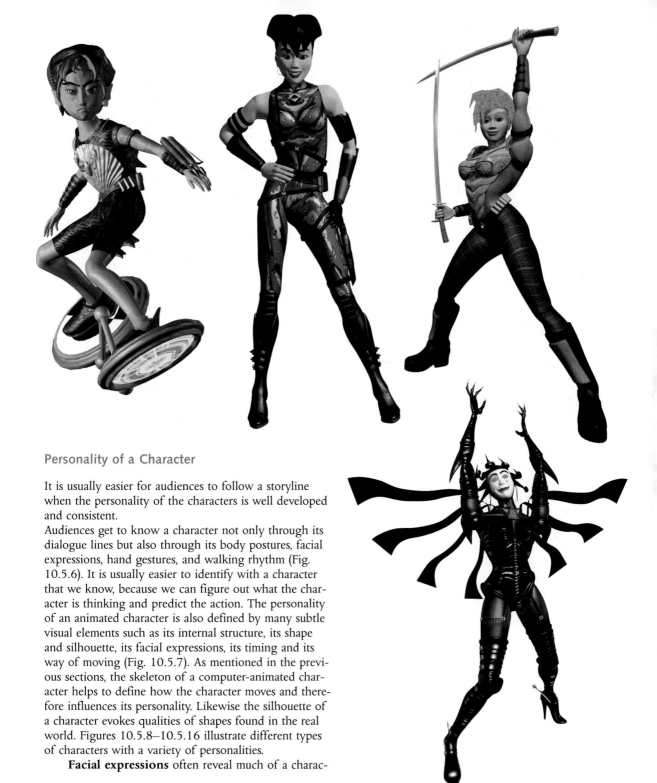

It is usually easier for audiences to follow a storyline when the personality of the characters is well developed and consistent.

Audiences get to know a character not only through its dialogue lines but also through its body postures, facial expressions, hand gestures, and walking rhythm (Fig. 10.5.6). It is usually easier to identify with a character that we know, because we can figure out what the character is thinking and predict the action. The personality of an animated character is also defined by many subtle visual elements such as its internal structure, its shape and silhouette, its facial expressions, its timing and its way of moving (Fig. 10.5.7). As mentioned in the previous sections, the skeleton of a computer-animated character helps to define how the character moves and therefore influences its personality. Likewise the silhouette of a character evokes qualities of shapes found in the real world. Figures 10.5.8–10.5.16 illustrate different types of characters with a variety of personalities.

Facial expressions often reveal much of a character's personality and passing emotions. Character sheets include the key facial expressions that define the personality of a character, but it is often necessary to develop hundreds of key facial expressions that will give the character its personality—and that will also be used as keyframes. These facial expressions can be stored in a library of expressions and used throughout the animation. Part of the research for defining those facial expressions consists of observing and drawing the expressions of others as well as making faces in front of a mirror and drawing or modeling them.

10.5.9 This sinister doctor is in the process of getting rid of the viruses who plague his lab. Notice how the lighting reinforces the creepiness of the moment. (© Jim Ludtke.)

The **timing of a character** is essential in defining its personality as well as its emotional state. Timing is about how long it takes to act or to react, and it includes tempo and rhythm. The **tempo**, or pace, of a motion can have different rates of speed, and these variations in the speed of the character's motion can be very expressive. For example, a slow tempo may express seriousness, fatigue, caution, or intimacy. A flowing tempo may project trust, elegance, or moderation. A lively tempo may express happiness or nervousness.

The rate of speed of a character is based on its skeleton but also related to its shape. **Speed** of motion can be constant, can change slowly, or can change very rapidly. A friendly and trustworthy character may move at a constant speed, while a treacherous and mean character may have sudden changes in the speed at which it moves. The speed of animated objects and characters can also be used to indicate their weight, mass, and power. A fast-moving object implies lightness only if it can stop relatively quickly. A fast-moving objects that requires a long time to stop implies lots of inertia and, therefore, great mass, and weight. The speed of animated objects can also be a good indicator of the amount of stretching and squashing to be expected if and when the object collides and bounces off some other thing in the scene.

10.5.10 *Spyro The Dragon*™ is a feisty character that combines the large head of a baby with the sharp claws of a fearsome foe. Spyro is built for real-time performance with 352 polygons and 230 vertices. (Images courtesy of Universal Interactive Studios, Inc. and Insomniac Games.)

The **rhythm** of a character's motion is the repetition or recurrence of motions performed by a character, or the pattern of motion projected by the character. The rhythm of a character's motion can be flowing or broken, regular or irregular. Motion rhythm can combine long motions with short motions, strong and weak beats, in different ways. Think of the differences in personality derived from the rhythm characteristics of three characters as they walk down the road. The first character in Figure 10.5.7, the drunken pig, barely raises its feet off the ground as it walks but keeps its arms close to its stiff torso, and its neck leans forward with the eyesight fixed on the ground. The resulting overall motion—and personality—is quite dull and uneventful. The second character, the perky girl, walks with extreme energy. The head is free and high with a radiant smile on the face. With each step, each shoulder moves back and forth echoing the motion of the opposing foot, the relaxed waist rotates gently from side to side, and the hands hang loose from the arms bouncing back and forth like the shoulders. The motion of the second character speaks for itself, and its personality seems animated and confident. The third character, the paranoid guy, limps as

he walks with short, tense steps. Every three or four steps the character stops, nervously turns his head from side to side, and looks around with quick eye movements. His arms are held close to the chest as if seeking some protection.

10.5.11 This *Ice Age* moment illustrates how a motion hold allows audiences to focus on what has just happened and think of what is about to happen. Notice how the sloth's IK system allows for extreme bending backwards. (Ice Age © 2002 Twentieth Century Fox. All rights reserved.)

Acting, Expressing Emotion, and Thinking Process

The storyline drives all the events in a computer animation, but the **acting** gets the emotions and the thoughts out of the characters. The **emotions** expressed by the character help define the mood of the story. Emotions are a powerful medium for conveying the fine points of a story or for reinforcing some of the character's traits. In addition to feeling emotions, and expressing or hiding them, characters actively think throughout the story. The **thinking process** of characters provides many clues and insight about their fate and the possible developments of the story. One of the reasons audiences follow the development of a story is because they empathize—or identify—with a character or because they anticipate the action. The emotions, thoughts, and intentions of characters are a perfect vehicle to generate empathy and anticipation in an audience (Figs. 10.5.1–10.5.16).

Motions and actions in keyframe animation are often built as a series of poses and gestures that will be used as keyframes to create the motion. When establishing these **key poses** it is important to keep in mind that the goal of the pose is to express an emotion and action and not to just be a beautiful pose. Key poses should not be built with

10.5.12 Shrek's facial expression and paused hand gesture indicate that he is thinking about what he is about to say. (*Shrek*™ and © 2001 DreamWorks L.L.C.)

the same criteria that we create, for example, a sculpture. Sculptures are made to be looked at from different angles and throughout long periods of time. Sculptures turn time and emotion into a still pose that we can contemplate. But key poses in an animation are transitory because they are just moments in continuous motion. When composing key poses for keyframe animation it is important to pay attention not only to the visual arrangement of the pose itself but also to the idea or emotion that is being expressed through motions. In computer animations that are based on cartoon characters, **exaggerated gestures** are often used to punctuate dramatic deliveries.

When composing keyframes it is useful to consider the visual line of action. The **visual line of action** determines the position and sequence of the motions in the scene that will guide the eye of the audience to different parts of the image.

10.6 Animation File Formats

Three-dimensional computer animations can be saved in a variety of file formats after they have been rendered. Those output file formats are described in detail in Chapter 15, and include QuickTime, MPEG, and AVI formats. However, before the animations are rendered they usually exist in proprietary formats that can only be processed by the application program that created them. Most computer animation programs are able to save the animation parameters and data in a **stand-alone** animation file that is independent from the files containing the modeling and the rendering information. However, unlike many modeling and rendering programs that are capable of saving data in both native and portable file formats, most animation programs only save the animation information in native file formats that are incompatible with other programs. The **FBX** file interchange format is an exception to this rule. Developed by Kaydara, FBX is a widely supported format used for acquiring and exchanging three-dimensional assets and media from a wide variety of sources. XYZ translation motion data captured with an optical system can be saved in a variety of formats including Acclaim (AMC and AMF) and Biovision (BVA and BVH). These formats provide the post-processed data once it has been applied to the skeleton. The Acclaim format is saved in two related files, an **AMC** file with the skeleton motion and an **ASF** file with the skeleton hierarchy. The **BVA** format includes nine channels of positional data with XYZ translation, rotation and scaling values. The **BVH** format saves the hierarchy and initial pose of the skeleton, and the motion data.

10.5.13 The impatient facial expression and the menacing body language of Lord Farquaad make his intentions crystal clear. (*Shrek*™ and © 2001 DreamWorks L.L.C.)

10.7 Getting Ready

The preproduction stage in all computer animations is very important to the success of the final animated piece because computer animations are team projects that require extensive planning. This is especially true of computer animations that may have a tight deadline or that may be produced by a variety of companies or groups within the same company. Failing to do adequate planning for a computer animation project or failing to follow the production schedule often results in a negative and serious impact to the budget of a production and the credibility of those involved.

10.5.14 The characters pause in this motion hold to reflect on what just occurred. (*The ChubbChubbs* © 2002 Sony Pictures Imageworks Inc. All Rights reserved.)

Check Your Three-Dimensional Models and Rigs

The success of a computer animation project depends greatly on how well the three-dimensional models and animation rigs are built. Take the time to familiarize yourself with both of them and make sure they do what they are supposed to and, if they do not, have them optimized. This may avoid many problems later in the anima-

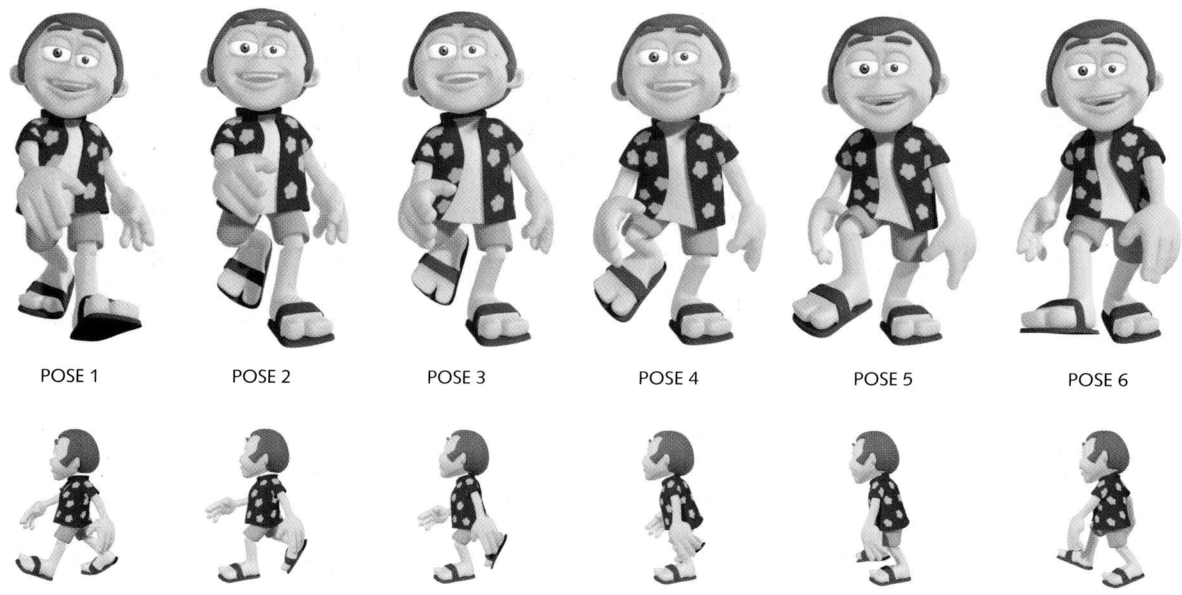

10.5.15a Top and side views of a walk cycle. Notice how the hip rotates on all axis, and how it relates to the feet. The hip moves higher on the side of a passing leg, it moves forward as the foot makes contact with the ground and down and sideways right after. (Animation courtesy of Kyle Balda. Model by Charles Beirnaert.)

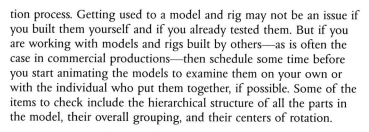

tion process. Getting used to a model and rig may not be an issue if you built them yourself and if you already tested them. But if you are working with models and rigs built by others—as is often the case in commercial productions—then schedule some time before you start animating the models to examine them on your own or with the individual who put them together, if possible. Some of the items to check include the hierarchical structure of all the parts in the model, their overall grouping, and their centers of rotation.

Check the Preferences File

The default settings stored in the preferences file or dialog box are important because they control directly and indirectly the result of many operations, functions, and tools of three-dimensional animation programs. Some of these settings include, for example, the animation rate of frames per second, the aspect ratio of the still image, and whether to load external files—such as texture maps or custom procedures—that may affect the final look of the animation project.

Make Motion Tests

One of the advantages of animating with a computer is that we can preview the motion as we develop it. The ability to create motion tests in the wireframe mode or with simple shading techniques at low resolutions provides invaluable feedback when developing complex motion sequences. Wireframe motion tests are useful mostly to check the choreography of a scene and the timing of the motions. But low-resolution shaded motion tests are often required when we want to

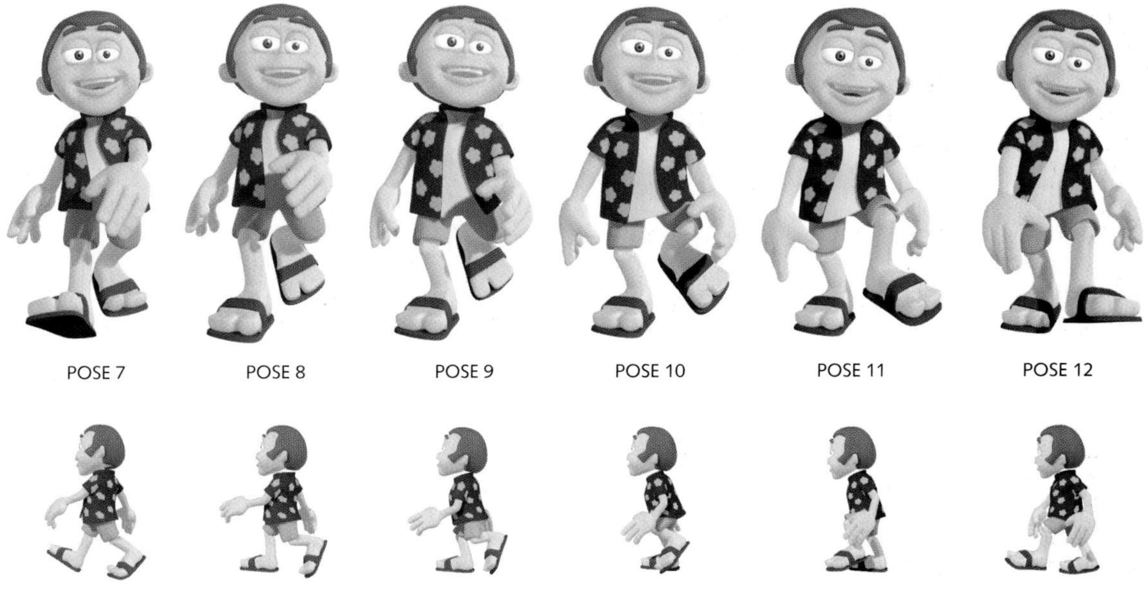

check, for example, the effect of light and shadow on the models as they move. Moving light sources may often cast undesirable hard-edge shadows on some objects or leave others looking too bright and overexposed. Virtually all computer animation programs allow for the creation of motion flipbooks that can be played back directly on the computer's screen. In cases when this is not possible, motion tests are recorded onto videotape and played back with a videotape player.

There are many strategies for testing different aspects or parts of the motion, some are useful for previewing scenes with many objects, others for previewing scenes with complex motion. One strategy for checking the speed of the motion consists of animating the objects in the scene as bounding boxes. It is also possible to render some objects in full shape and other as bounding boxes. Another strategy for focusing on the motion of just one or two objects in a crowded scene consists of turning off—or making invisible—all the other objects in the scene. Secondary objects in the scene can also be rendered in the wireframe mode with dotted lines or lines of a different color from the lines in the primary objects. A third strategy that is useful for analyzing the motion of objects in detail consists of playing the flipbook back in slow motion. This technique is often useful for discovering small mistakes such as single objects—fingers, for example—that should be moving within a hierarchy and are not, or small objects that may be colliding with each other.

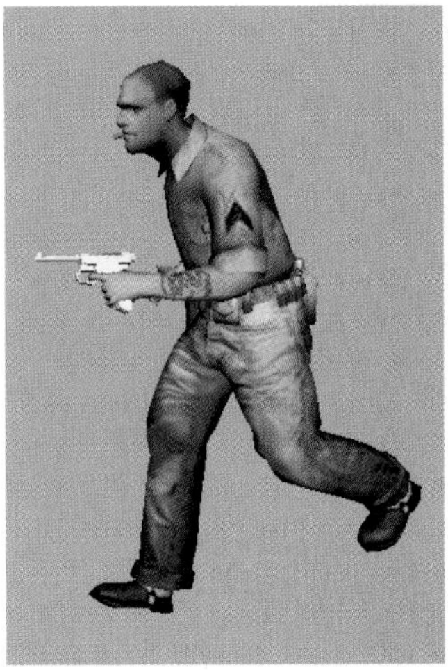

10.5.15b (above and previous page) Two core poses of Gunny, the *Medal of Honor* gunnery Sargeant: pistol standing attack and a 20-30 frame run cycle. The animation rig for this character is shown in Figure 5.7.3. (© 1999 Electronic Arts Inc. All rights reserved.)

Blocking the Animation

Blocking the motion is usually the first pass in keyframe animation. The main goal at this stage is to capture all the key moments in the

10.5.16 There is a huge disconnecct between the characters in this scene of *Mike's New Car*. Mike is pleased with his new car and unsuspecting of the trouble the he is about to unleash, while Sully is uncomfortable and not really enjoying the "special" occasion. (© Disney Enterprises, Inc./Pixar Animation Studios.)

scene, also known as **story beats**, without focusing on details or secondary motion. One common method for blocking the animation starts with the hips, letting them drive much of the body weight of the character. The translation of the hips up and down and sideways, as well as the tilting and twisting around the three axis also helps to define much of a character's personality (Fig. 10.5.15). After the hip positions are blocked one can continue with the primary motion of shoulders and arms, hand positions, face direction, and eye, eyelid and eyebrow animation.

Save Your Work Often

Save your work often, every 15 minutes or so, and make frequent and regular backups of your important data files.

(Opposite page: © 2002 Midway Games West, Inc.)

CHAPTER 10

Key Terms

24 frames
30 frames
Acclaim AMC, AMF formats
Act
Acting
Ahead of the story
Anatomy
Animatronics
Anticipation
Arcs
Attention of the audience
Background
Beginning of the story
Behind the story
Biovision BVA, BVH formats
Branching
Cartoon characters
Casting
Cel animation
Cels
Character animation
Character appeal
Character development
Character generator
Character sheets
Character turnarounds
Clean-up drawings
Complex motion
Conceptual storyboard
Dialogue
Digital backup
Dimensions
Drawings
Effects animation
Elapsed time
Emotions
End of the story
Events
Exaggerated gestures
Exaggeration
External shape of a three-dimensional character
Facial expressions
Extremes
Fake hold
FBX file format
Field guides
Flow of events
Flowcharts
Follow-through action
Foreground
Forward kinematics
Frame
Frames per second (fps)
Hand-drawn animation
Hierarchy level
Hybrid framework
Implementing the motions
In-between
In-betweening
Ink and paint
Intended audience
Interactive project
Interactivity
Internal structure of a three-dimensional character
Interpolation
Interrupted action
Inverse kinematics
Joints
Key poses
Keyframing
Keyframes
Layers of motion
Linear
Manual arrangement
Middle of the story
Montage
Motion capture
Motion control techniques
Motion dynamics
Motion hold
Nonlinearity
Overlapping action
Overlapping motion
Paintbox
Parallel action
Pencil test
Performance animation
Plot points
Pose-to-pose action
Presentation storyboard
Primary motion
Procedural motion
Production storyboard
Production technique
Puppetry
Rate of display
Readability of motion
Realistic characters
Rhythm
Rolling credits
Rule-based motion
Running time
Scene
Scene-and-shot-number
Screenplay
Scripts
Secondary action
Secondary motion
Sequence
Sequences of still images
Shooting on twos
Shot
Shot number
Silhouette
Simple motion
Skeleton
Slow-in
Slow-out
Solid drawing
Solid modeling
Speed
Squash and stretch
Staging
Stand-alone
Still frame
Stop-motion animation
Stories
Story beats
Storyboard
Straight-ahead action
Structure
Stylized characters
Subject of a screenplay
Tempo
Thinking process
Timing
Timing of a character
Timing of the action
Title safety area
Transition
Translated into moving images
Treatment of the subject
Twelve principles of animation
User testing
Visual effects animation
Visual interpretation
Visual line of action
Written information

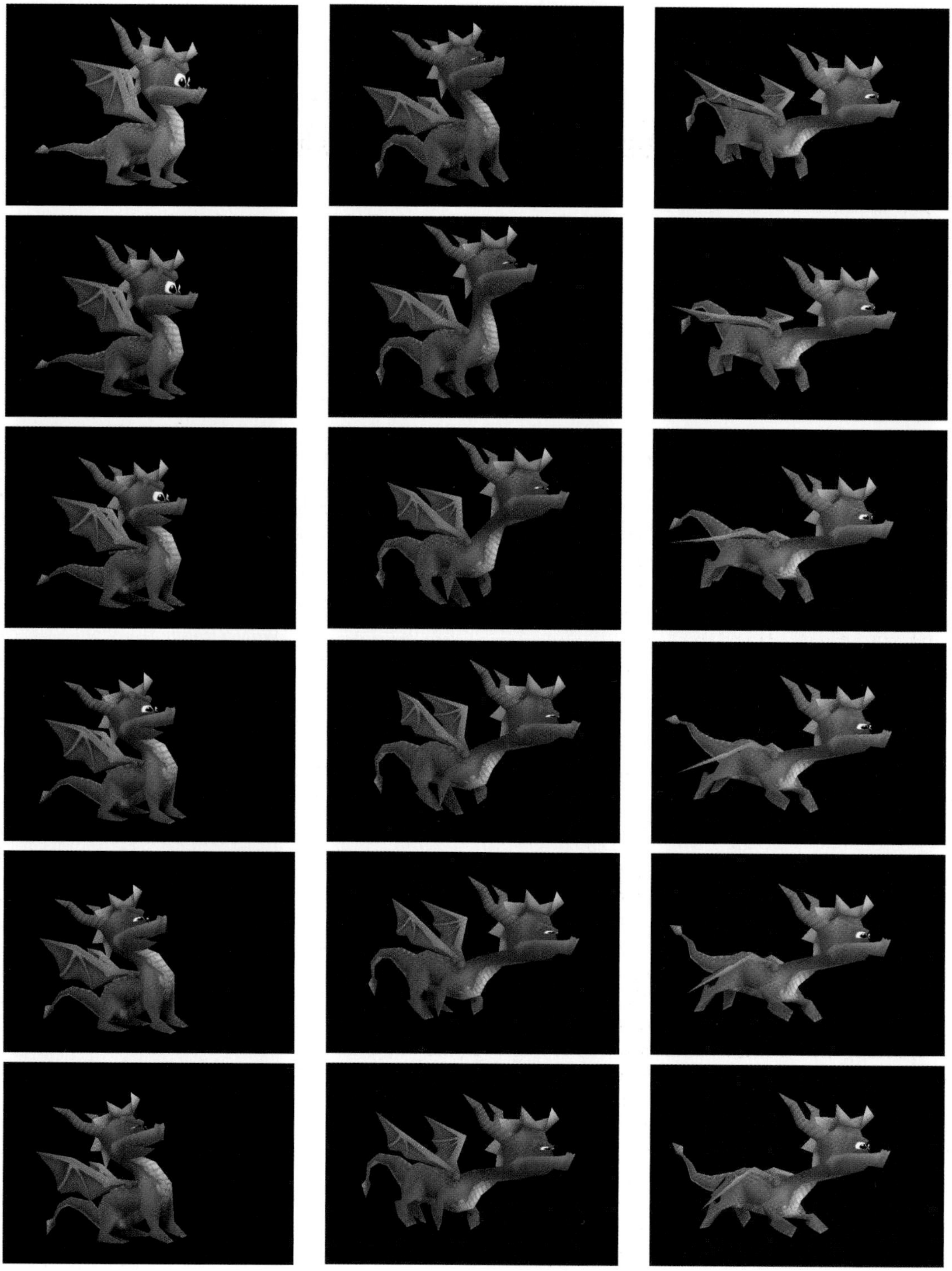

CHAPTER 11

11

Basic Computer Animation Techniques

Summary

THE PRINCIPLES OF KEYFRAME INTERPOLATION as applied to animating the position, orientation, shape and attributes of three-dimensional characters are reviewed in this chapter. A variety of three-dimensional computer animation techniques that are based on keyframe interpolation are also reviewed. This includes the spatial animation of models, cameras, and lights with interactive placement of the keyframes and with forward kinematics; the shape animation of three-dimensional models with lattice deformation or morphing techniques; and the interpolation of attributes like the surface characteristics of models, the depth of field of cameras, and the color of lights. The chapter concludes with an review of hierarchical animation and rigging, and the integration of two- and three-dimensional computer animation.

QUICK INDEX

11.1 Principles of Keyframe Interpolation

The **keyframe interpolation** technique is used in computer animation to create sequences of still frames. This computer animation technique calculates the **in-between frames** by averaging the information and key poses contained in the keyframes (Fig. 11.1.1). Interpolation techniques can be used to calculate the position of objects in space, as well as their shape and other attributes. Keyframe interpolation provides as many in-between frames as needed—depending on the length of the sequence being interpolated—but the spacing of the in-between frames varies depending on the type of interpolation used. The most common type of interpolations include linear interpolation and curve interpolation.

A **keyframe** is defined by its particular moment in the animation timeline as well as by all the parameters or attributes associated with it. These parameters include, for example, the position of an object in space, its shape, and its surface characteristics (Fig. 11.1.2). Interpolations are a simple but powerful way to express and control

11.1.1 (Opposite page) This 18-frame animation cycle shows the real-time model of *Spyro the Dragon*™ preparing to blow a flame of fire, blowing it, and returning to the resting position. Animators set the keyframes with forward kinematics, moving and rotating individual joints. (Spyro the Dragon™. Courtesy of Universal Interactive Studios, Inc. and Insomniac Games.)

11.1.2 A sequence with three keyframes and two interpolations—one quicker than the other.

the relation between the time that it takes to get from one keyframe to another and the amount of change in the parameters or attributes. The **speed** or **rate of change** is defined by the amount of time that it takes to get from one keyframe to another and by the amount of change in the animated parameters.

Interpolations are commonly expressed in the form of a graph that summarizes the relation between time and the parameter being animated. Time is usually represented by the horizontal axis, and the parameter in question is usually represented by the vertical axis. The **slope** of the path in the graph represents the speed or rate of change. A flat path, for example, indicates no change—zero speed—a diagonal path indicates constant change, and a curve path represents variable change. The steeper the slope of the path the greater the rate of change (Fig. 11.1.3). Interpolation graphs are generated automatically by most computer animation software as soon as the animator specifies the animation parameters on one or several objects in the scene. It is usually possible to edit these graphs interactively.

Linear Interpolation

Linear interpolation is the simplest and most straightforward computer animation technique for calculating in-between frames. **Linear interpolation** simply averages the parameters in the keyframes and provides as many equally spaced in-between frames as needed. However, linear interpolation techniques may produce mechanical results when applied to subtle motions unless a significant amount of work and animation skill are used to fine tune the results. Linear interpolation is based on constant speeds between the keyframes, but it produces abrupt changes in speed on the keyframes where one constant speed ends and a different constant speed starts. **Constant speed** is represented by the straight lines in the graph. Linear interpolations cannot handle subtle changes in speed because the in-between frames are created at equal intervals along the path (Fig. 11.1.4).

Curved Interpolation

Curved interpolation, also called an **interpolation ease**, is a technique for calculating in-between frames more sophisticated than linear interpolation. Curved interpolation averages the parameters in the keyframes taking into account the variations of speed over time, known as **acceleration**. When curved interpolation is represented in graphical form the increase in speed, also called an **ease in**, is represented by a line that curves up. An **ease out**, or decrease in speed, is represented by a line that curves down (Fig. 11.1.5). Therefore, the distribution of in-between frames along the path depends on whether the rate of change increases or decreases. Curved interpolation can also include motion with constant speed, and that is represented with straight lines (Fig. 11.1.4).

Working with Parameter Curves

A graph representing curved interpolations is also called a **parameter curve** or a **function curve**. As mentioned earlier, parameter curves are generated automatically by most computer animation software as the animator positions the objects in space and defines their animation parameters for each keyframe. Working with parameter curves provides animators with an additional method for modifying the animation by manipulating only the paths contained in the graphs and without having to manipulate, for example, the position of objects in three-dimensional space. Working with parameter curves is commonly used to edit and fine tune subtle aspects of an animated project.

As mentioned in Chapter 4, some of the most popular types of curves include linear splines, cardinal splines, b-splines, and Bézier curves. Each of these types of curves is shaped in a characteristic way by their control points, or control vertices. Therefore, the exact shape and functionality of function curves depends on the type of curve used (Fig. 11.1.6). A linear spline, for example, consists of a series of straight lines that connect all the control points. The animation generated by linear splines is based on constant speed between keyframes and abrupt changes of speed at the keyframes where two different constant speeds meet. The animation generated with a cardinal spline is very dependent on the placement of the keyframes in the interpolation graph because the control points in a cardinal spline force the curve to pass through all of them. The tight fit of cardinal curves to the control points often results in harsh closed curves, which translate into rough eases. The animation created with b-splines usually contains very smooth interpolation eases because the shape of the curve is loosely controlled by the control points but not forced to pass through them. Parameter curves calculated with Bézier curve functions offer the most flexible—and complex—path control because the shape of the curve is controlled by the position of both the control points and the tangent points. Bézier curves facilitate the creation of flexible curves with a wide range of characteristics that often translate into the animation. Bézier curves, for example, can be made to blend into a straight line very slowly and softly or suddenly. Another advantage of using Bézier curves for defining interpolation graphs is that their slope can be modified with just the tangent points, therefore avoiding the insertion of additional control points (keyframes) to shape the curve and the motion.

Parameter curves can represent either a linear interpolation, an ease in, or an ease out. But complex interpolations that include these three interpolation types are called **ease functions**. These complex interpolations can be defined interactively by specifying the type of curve function that the keyframe control points in the graph should use to calculate the interpolation. Ease functions are also defined by dragging a slider that represents the proportion of ease in, linear, and ease out in the function (Fig. 11.1.7). Ease functions can also be

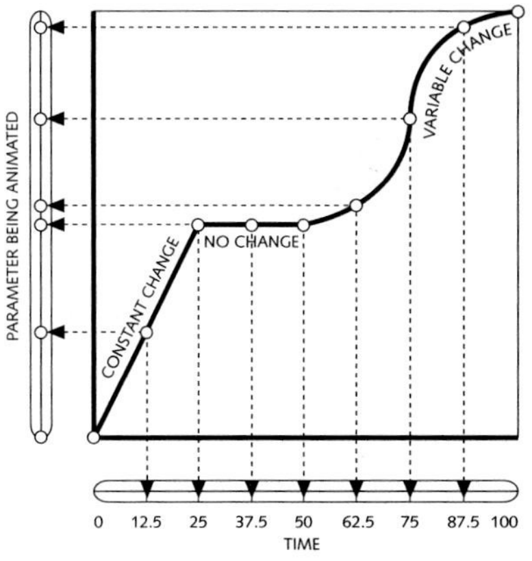

11.1.3 The slope of an interpolation path results in changes of speed or the parameter being animated.

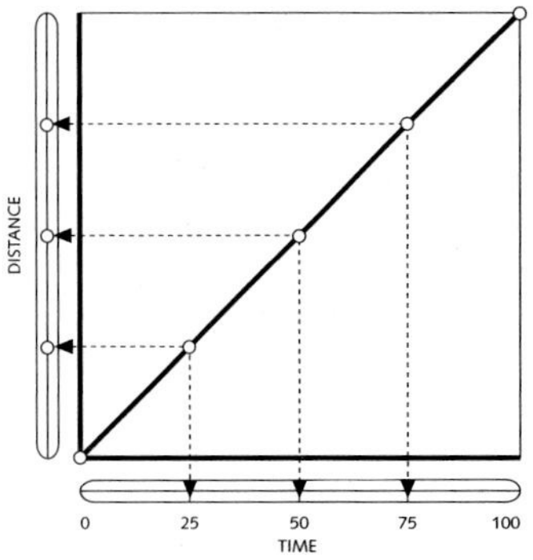

11.1.4 A linear interpolation graph using time and distance as the parameters. The diagonal line represents speed.

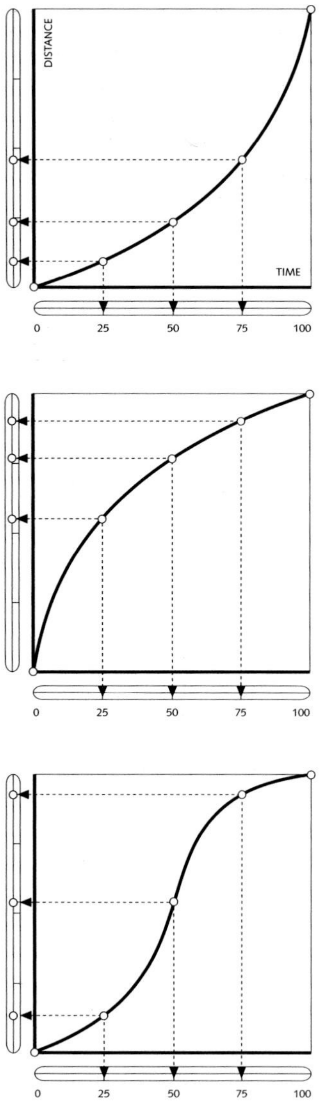

11.1.5 Three graphs for curved interpolation. Notice how the distance traveled over time by the animated model varies with the slope of the curve.

specified by inputting numerical values that range from 0 percent to 100 percent or from 0 to 1 (Fig. 11.1.8).

Interpolation of Position and Orientation

Interpolation techniques can be used to calculate the position and orientation of animated objects in three-dimensional space. This includes not only the models in a scene but also the cameras and the light sources. As mentioned in Chapter 3, the position and orientation of an object in three-dimensional space can be modified by changing the values in the **transformation matrix** that controls the translations, rotations, and scaling that are applied to the objects in the scene. When keyframe interpolation techniques are used, the values in the transformation matrices of moving objects are specified at the keyframes, and the in-between values are interpolated. Most computer animation programs provide animators with direct ways to edit the transformation matrix of an object through the parameter curves.

Interpolation of Shape

Interpolation techniques can also be used to animate the shape of three-dimensional models. The basic idea behind **shape animation** consists of transforming one key shape into another one by letting the interpolation techniques calculate all the in-between positions of the points and lines that define the shape of the model. A variety of shape interpolation techniques were used to created the image in Figure 11.2.6.

Interpolation of Attributes

The **attributes** or characteristics of models, cameras, and lights—other than spatial position and shape—can also be animated with interpolation techniques. In the case of three-dimensional models, it is common to animate their surface characteristics, such as color, texture, or transparency. Focal length and depth of field are two characteristics of cameras often animated. In the case of light sources, it is common to animate attributes such as color, intensity, cone-angle, and fall-off values. Several interpolations of attributes are covered in the next three sections in this chapter, and texture interpolation is illustrated in Figure 11.2.9.

11.2 Model Animation

Keyframe interpolation techniques are very effective for animating the position, shape, and attributes of three-dimensional models. The spatial animation of simple models can be easily controlled through the parameter curves or through motion paths placed in the three-dimensional scene. (The techniques used to animate hierarchical models are covered later in this chapter and in Chapter 12.) The shape animation of models can be implemented with a variety of techniques that include free-form shape interpolation, three-dimensional morphing, and external control structures such as lattices and functions. Finally, spectacular results can be achieved by animating the surface characteristics of models with interpolation techniques.

The most common method for specifying the **spatial animation** of three-dimensional models when using keyframe interpolation is to interactively arrange their position and orientation. This method is based on the idea of defining keyframes by placing the models in three-dimensional space and applying the geometric transformations to them, refining the motion with the ease functions, and letting the software interpolate the in-between frames. This idea is, in fact, the essence of all keyframe animation, traditional and computer-based.

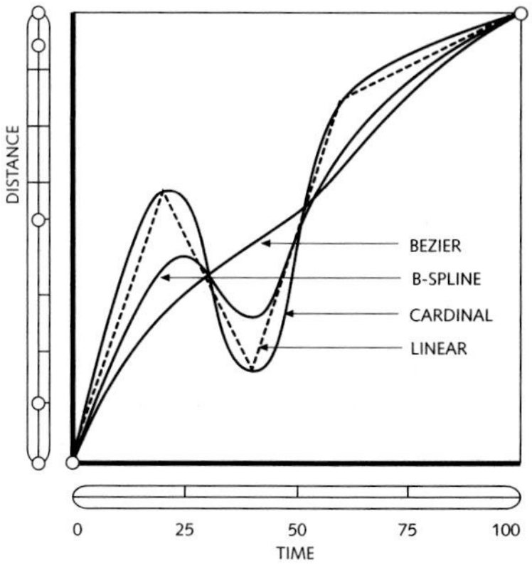

11.1.6 Four types of function curves with the same control hull have been overlapped to show the different animation results.

Interactive Specification of Keyframes

The **interactive specification of key poses** can be enhanced when the animator previews his or her work on several camera views simultaneously so that the subtlety of the motions can be examined from different points of view. As mentioned before, the interactive specification of key poses can be done by either dragging the objects interactively with the mouse, pen, or track ball, or by editing the parameter curves as described earlier. In both of these cases, it is necessary to preview the motion in order to check that the parameters specified are producing the desired results.

Forward Kinematics

Another technique that can be used to specify motion through key poses, especially with jointed figures, is called **forward kinematics**. This technique consists of determining the motion and final position of a model by first specifying the angles of its joints (Figs. 11.1.1 and 11.2.1). This can be accomplished by typing the numerical value for each joint angle directly into the appropriate fields or dialog boxes provided by the software (Fig. 4.6.1) or by using an input peripheral like the one pictured in Figure 11.2.2. Forward kinematics is a simple technique that requires a great deal of manual work, and it should not be confused with the technique of inverse kinematics that is described in Chapter 12. Forward kinematics can be used very creatively in situations when all the joint angles are known in advance and are repeated many times. Once such case is exemplified by an interactive program—like a videogame—where the positions of the characters are finite, repeated many times, and known in advance. In forward kinematics the joint angles must be input with an armature-like device or through the keyboard, and the motions have to be such that the angles are easy to establish or calculate before the motions are actually performed (Fig. 11.2.2).

The project illustrated in Figure 11.2.3 shows the results of a computer program that seeks to create interactive animated characters

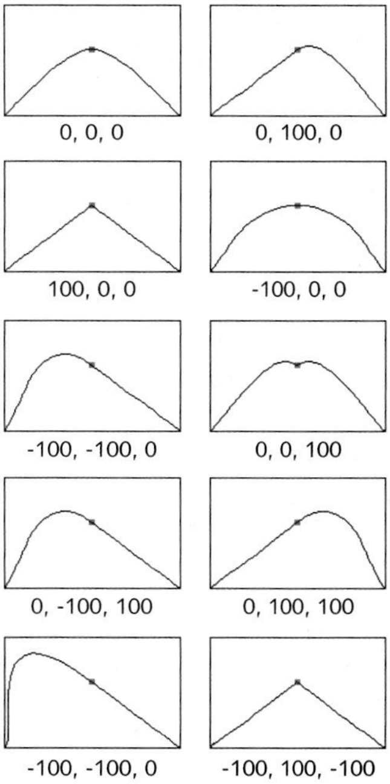

11.1.7 Motion paths can be eased in and out with sliders that control the tension, bias and continuity. These function curves illustrate a variety of settings.

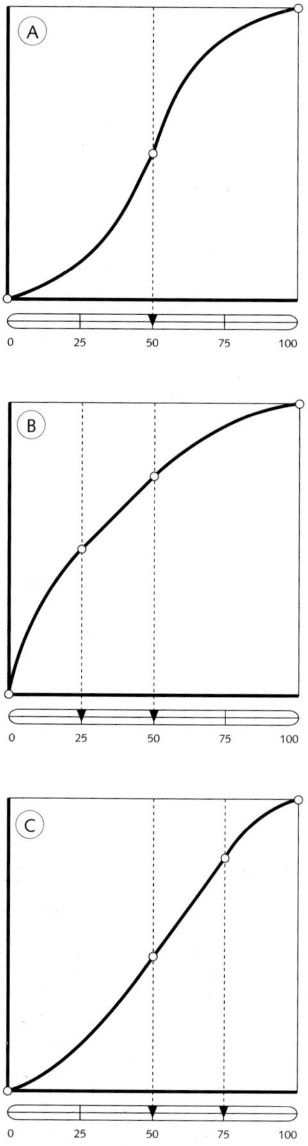

11.1.8 Ease parameter curves specified with different numerical values: 50% ease in and 50% ease out (A); 25% ease out, 25% linear, and 50% ease out (B); 50% ease in, 25% linear, and 25% ease out (C).

that dance with some sort of emotional expressiveness and a minimum number of joints. In this case, the joints were universal, four for each limb and one for each waist, neck, and head. (Even with such a small number of joints, this figure has two separate joints at the base and the top for the neck because the head position is so important for emotional expressiveness.) The figure was driven by a combination of forward kinematics expressed in the form of key actions, body constraints, and a small amount of somewhat random noise. In this example, the actions are taught to the animated character in advance, and the transitions between actions are adjusted so that the motion looks natural. Establishing the proper joint angles before the motions occur is important since most of the personality of the character and the mood of the dance step is expressed through body language.

The model of the dancer is built with ellipsoids. Some of the motion contraints include a few simple joint constraints—the head, for example, cannot turn all the way around. Obstacles in the path are avoided by turning away from them, and the supporting foot at floor level propels the character. Predefined actions such as a dance step can be stored in the form of a table of ranges for each joint involved in the action. The values used to specify the rhumba dancer are also listed in Figure 11.2.3. The lowercase letters represent a variety of functions, including a random noise generator function (n) applied to the head to simulate the character looking around as she dances. The arm joints at the chest (Rchest and Lchest) are controlled by functions in the X and Z axis that result in an elliptical motion of the shoulders. The noise function is also used to give the standing still figure of the dancer a subtle restlessness and apparent shifting of weight back and forth from one side to the other.

Motion Paths

The technique of **motion paths** provides an additional method for defining the motion of objects in three-dimensional space. This technique is somewhat similar to working with parameter curves because it also involves a path. But the actual motion path is drawn as a single path in the three-dimensional environment instead of being drawn as several two-dimensional interpolation graphs.

Three-dimensional motion paths are easy to work with because they allow the animator to define motion that may involve translations and rotations in a very quick way. Working with motion paths allows us to think of motion in terms of "go from here to there, and follow this path." This technique is especially useful to define with precision the motion of flying and swimming models because they both move by following a three-dimensional path. Motion paths are particularly useful for defining the motion of flying cameras, and they can also be used to animate objects that move by sliding over a surface. This would include, for example, sail boats and snow skiers (Fig. 11.2.4).

Motion paths are also useful to sketch or layout the motion of traction vehicles like bicycles and tractors, and also of legged creatures like ants and humans. In these cases, the motion path can be used to define the basic motion of the models, and the rest of the motion can be added later. A legged creature animated with just a motion path would probably look stiff and unrealistic. The additional motion of the wheels in traction vehicles and the limbs in legged creatures can be created in both cases with simple interactive placement of keyframes or with advanced animation techniques like inverse kinematics or motion dynamics.

Motion path animation is defined in several steps, and it starts with a curve being drawn in three-dimensional space, usually with a curve modeling tool. Then the model to be animated is selected and **linked to the path**. The timing parameters of the path are then defined. This is usually done by typing the values of the frames in which the motion path animation is to start and end. When a motion path animation is first defined, a linear interpolation with constant speed is often applied as a default value in most software programs. But the speed and acceleration in the motion path can be refined after previewing the results by editing its timing parameters with an interpolation graph.

The alignment of a three-dimensional model to the path as the model moves through the path is an important detail in motion path animation. Most software programs will keep the object linked to the motion path so that the front of the animated object is always facing in the direction of the path (Fig. 11.2.5). This is also called keeping the direction of the object tangential to the path. In order to do this, most computer animation programs need to know which is the **front of the object** at the time when the object is linked to the motion path. In most cases, objects will be animated down the path in the position in which they were linked to the path, but some programs will only animate objects along the path in the position in which they were originally created.

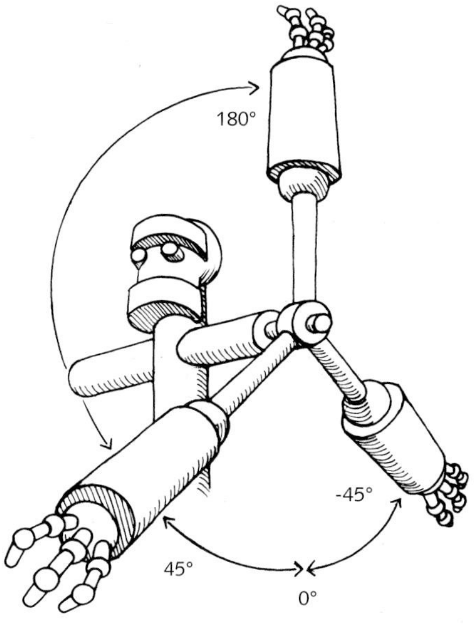

11.2.1 In forward kinematics motion is created by specifying the angle of a joint. In this case a total range of motion of 225 degrees (45, -45, and 180) is shown.

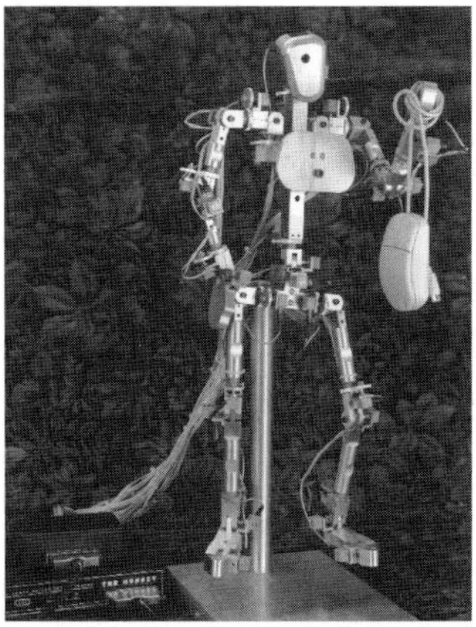

11.2.2 This articulated model can be used to input and visualize joint angles to animations based on forward kinematics techniques. (The Monkey™ is courtesy of Digital Image Design.)

Free-Form Shape Animation

Simple shape animation can be created by interpolating the shape of two objects on a point-by-point basis. When this interpolation is done between two versions of the same three-dimensional model it is usually called free-form shape animation, and when it is done between two different models,it is called morphing. **Free-form shape animation** can be created first by placing two versions of a three-dimensional polygonal or spline-based model in each of two contiguous keyframes, and then modifying the shape of one of the two models by pulling the points in the planar or curved mesh that define it. The in-between frames that constitute the shape transformation will be interpolated by the computer program.

The free-form shape animation process starts by identifying the points—or control vertices—in the model that will be animated. This is usually done in the wireframe mode. A single point or a group of points are selected and dragged to a new position. Each

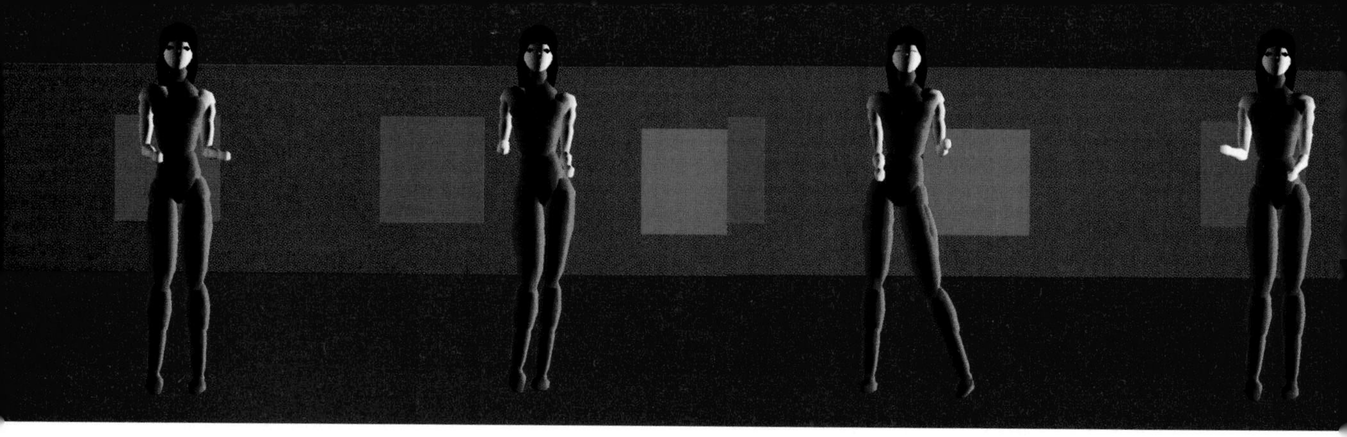

```
{
    {5 5 5}      {-5 -5 -5}    {n1 n2 n3} Nod
    {15 5 0}     {-15 -5 0}    {b a  }    Rchest
    {0 0 0}      {0 0 0}       {a a  }    Rshoulder
    {-90 0 0}    {-70 0 0}     {a a  }    Relbow
    {0 0 0}      {0 0 0}       {a a  }    Rpelvis
    {-25 5 -15}  {0 -10 0}     {a a a}    Rhip
    {50 0 0}     {0 0 0}       {a a  }    Rknee
    {0 0 0}      {0 0 0}       {a a  }    Rankle
    {0 10 0}     {0 -10 0}     {a a  }    Waist
    {-15 -5 0}   {15 5 0}      {b a  }    Lchest
    {0 0 0}      {0 0 0}       {a a  }    Lshoulder
    {-70 0 0}    {-90 0 0}     {a a  }    Lelbow
    {0 0 0}      {0 0 0}       {a a  }    Lpelvis
    {0 -20 0}    {-10 20 -25}  {a a a}    Lhip
    {0 0 0}      {20 0 0}      {a a  }    Lknee
    {0 0 0}      {0 0 0}       {a a  }    Lankle
} 'rhumba define_action
```

11.2.3 Still frames from *Danse Interactif*, a real-time procedurally animated interactive dance performance. These four images from the Rhumba Sequence represent the cycle the animated dancer goes through in completing the move. (Courtesy of Ken Perlin, New York University, Media Research Laboratory. © 1994 Ken Perlin.)

point in one model will be interpolated to only one point in the other model. Sometimes some or all of the points in a three-dimensional object may be locked so it is useful to check if the points in a model are locked before attempting to animate them with free-form shape animation techniques. Free-form shape animation can be very useful in the creation of squash and stretch effects. **Squashing** and **stretching** are commonly used in animation to emphasize the motion of objects in response to the forces of compression and expansion. Squash and stretch effects help characterize the mass and weight of moving objects as well as the material it is made of.

Three-Dimensional Morphing

Three-dimensional morphing is a very effective technique for creating shape animations that do not require as much time-consuming detail work as free-form shape interpolations. **Three-dimensional morphing** works by animating all the points of one object into the positions occupied by the points of another object (Fig. 11.2.6). The results of three-dimensional morphing animation are usually fascinating, but there are two important technical requirements that must be satisfied before this technique works to its fullest. First, the best results are obtained when each of the three-dimensional models has the same **number of points**. This fact implies that a fair amount of preplanning—especially during the modeling stage—is necessary for this technique to be practical. Many software programs will not even attempt three-dimensional morphing unless this condition is satisfied. Second, it is also necessary to specify the **order of correspondence** between the points in each of the three-dimensional models. Many software programs allow for the interactive linking of points between objects. This is helpful to make sure that the morphing results do not include morphing accidents—like objects that wrap inside out, overlapping surfaces or holes in the models—that may be distracting. In some cases, however, these results may be appropriate effects to tell a particular story.

Free-Form Lattices

Free-form shape animation can create striking results, but it requires a great deal of skill and time to manipulate large numbers of points one at a time. Using **external control structures** to regulate the shape animation of objects can be a better choice, especially in cases where a uniform shape deformation is desired. Two popular animation techniques that use external control structures are free-form lattices and wave functions.

A **free-form lattice** is a three-dimensional grid of points and lines that controls the points in a three-dimensional model. The control points in the freeform lattice are connected with imaginary springs to the points in the model. As the control points in the lattice are moved they push or pull the points in the object (Fig. 4.5.3). The ability to create shape animations by moving one or several points in a freeform lattice is directly related to the resolution of the lattice. A lattice with only a small number of points yields rough shape animations, while lattices with larger numbers of control points can be used to apply more subtle local distortions on the model controlled by the lattice.

11.2.4 The motion paths of two skaters are made visible here.

Wave Functions

A great variety of mathematical functions can be applied to a three-dimensional model with the purpose of changing its shape. Animating with functions can be an economical way to create animations because little work is required once it has been determined how to apply the function to the object (Fig. 11.2.7). For most animations that involve traditional storytelling, animating with functions provides an effective way to create the foundation of a motion that can be complemented with other techniques. Functions are also very effective for animating secondary motion or objects in a scene. This is easily accomplished by applying the function to just one branch of the hierarchical structure. However, most functions tend to be of limited use and are rarely used as the primary technique in a computer animation project. This is because the motion generated with functions—while interesting and exciting from a mathematical point of view—is usually too simple or monotonous to be used by itself, and also because developing new functions requires—for most productions—a significant amount of time, skill, and energy.

Many computer animation programs allow animators to define two-dimensional function curves of almost any shape and use them as control structures to animate the shape of objects. These control curves are often called **wave functions** since their shapes resemble the outline of a wave. (A similar wave function for creating procedural textures is described in Chapter 9.) The distortions created by applying wave functions to three-dimensional models are sometimes unpredictable, and a trial-and-error approach is often required. Some

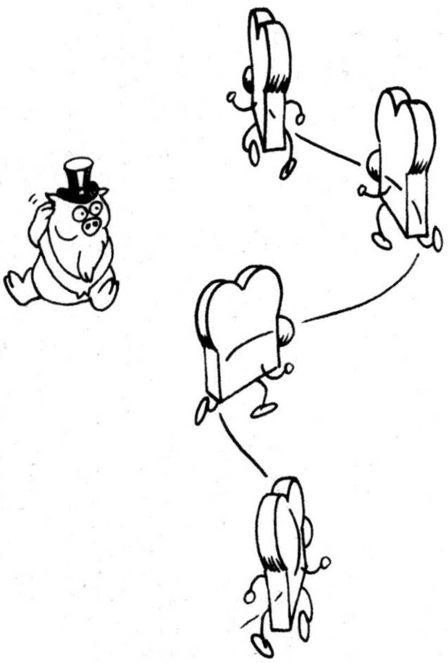

11.2.5 These cameras look down the motion path as they move. (*Medal of Honor* screen shots. © 1999 Electronic Arts Inc. All rights reserved.)

of the characteristics of this technique, however, are quite simple and easy to control (Fig. 11.2.8). The wave type variable determines the way in which the wave propagates from its center throughout the three-dimensional model. Functions can be easily looped and used to simulate the recurring motions, for example, of water waves. **Circular waves** are an excellent technique for recreating the motion of the water waves on the surface of a lake, and **planar waves** can recreate the effect of waves on the surface of the sea. **Spherical waves** can be used to recreate an explosion.

Animation of the Surface Characteristics

Several techniques used to render the surface characteristics that define the exterior appearance of objects and characters in still images are covered in Chapter 9. But these surface characteristics can also change throughout time. Changes in color, transparency, texture or reflectivity always indicate not only a change in the exterior appearance of objects or characters, but also a change in their inner emotions, chemical composition, or state of mind. Changes in the surface characteristics of objects or characters can be very useful elements of visual storytelling because they always happen as reactions to other actions or as responses to a variety of stimuli.

In our world, some of the changes in surface characteristics happen very rapidly—in a matter of seconds—while others require several months or even years to occur. Both the blushing of a face or the maturing of an apple, for example, involve changes in color and visual texture, but one happens in seconds while the other requires weeks. In both of these cases, the **timing of the transformations** of color and texture is crucial to the understanding of the action. If the reddening of an apple takes place throughout a long period of time we know that we are watching a **natural transformation**, but if it happens in a matter of seconds we assume that some **fantastic transformation** process is under way. Likewise, if an audience watches the blushing occur in a matter of seconds they will know that they are watching somebody express feelings of shame, excitement, or modesty. But if the reddening of the face takes place throughout several days then the audience would assume that transformation to be not the quick display of a sudden emotion but perhaps the reaction of the skin to an allergy or disease.

Animating the surface characteristics of objects or characters can create realistic or fantastic effects of material transformation and also communicate subtle or sudden changes of events in a story. The animation of surface characteristics is easily done with interpolation techniques. The process is simple but powerful. It starts by applying a set of surface characteristics to the objects in question in the keyframe at the beginning of a sequence. Then the same set of surface characteristics can be applied to the objects in the last keyframe of that sequence, and then modified with the parameter curves that represent each of the surface characteristics or by typing in new values.

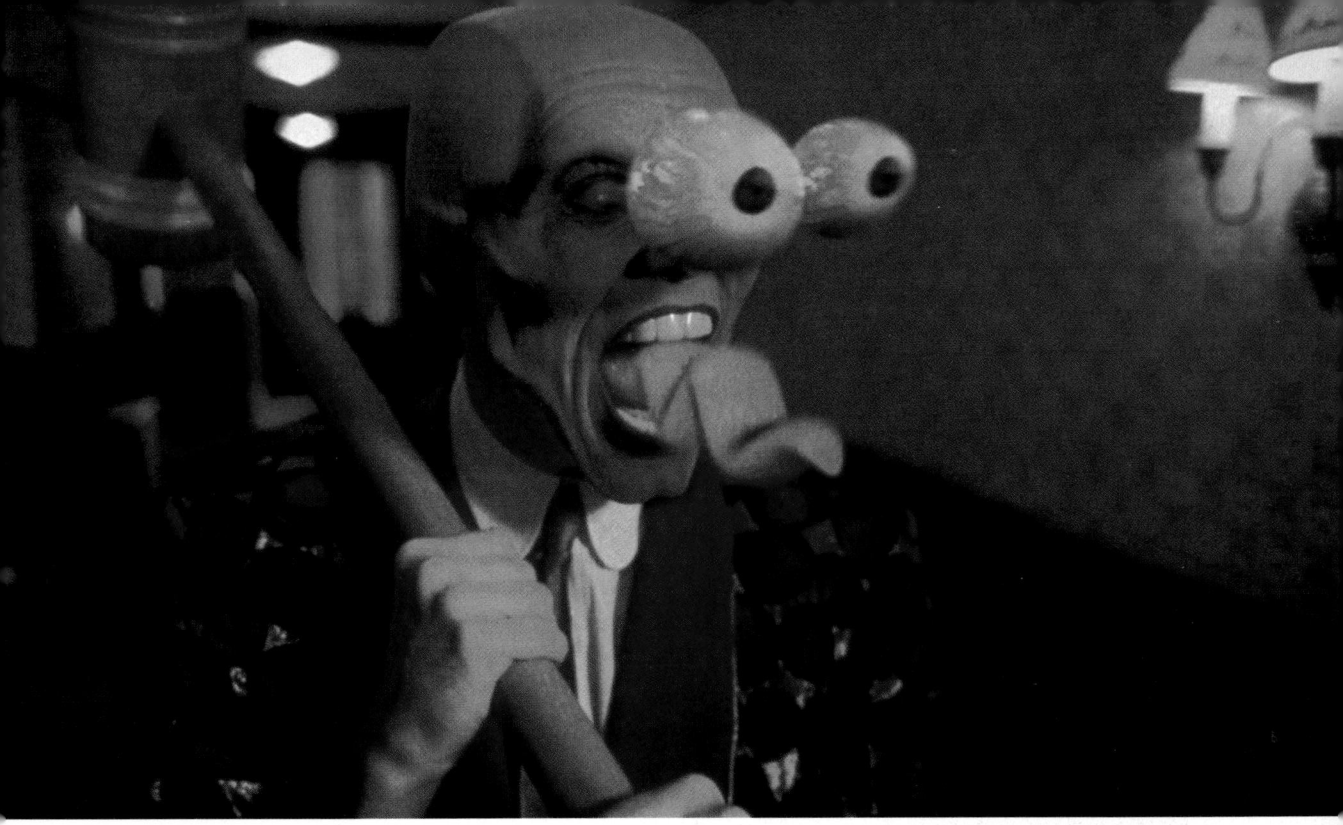

The parameter curves that represent color, transparency, reflectivity, and shading characteristics can be easily edited because those surface characteristics are usually controlled by a single numerical value or by a simple set of values, like RGB values, for example. The textures of a surface are usually controlled by as many as 20 variables and, consequently, as many parameter curves. Animating the two- and three-dimensional textures of surfaces usually requires increased setup time, additional rendering tests, and more trial and error than some of the simpler surface characteristics. Figures 11.2.9 and 11.2.10 illustrate the animation of a variety of surface characteristics. See Chapter 9 for more information about surface characteristics and their variables.

In addition to animating the standard shading attributes of a three-dimensional surface, it is also possible to create spectacular effects by mapping sequences of animated images on a three-dimensional surface and by animating the parameters of a three-dimensional procedural texture. **Mapping a sequence of images** is done by assigning two-dimensional picture files that are applied as maps to three-dimensional objects (Figs. 9.3.3, 9.5.1, and 9.6.2). The sequencing can be done on a one-on-one basis (one two-dimensional image per frame of three-dimensional computer animation) or by following a script where some two-dimensional images may be applied in different sequences and loops to frames in the three-dimensional animation.

11.2.6 This still frame from the film *The Mask* is an example of three-dimensional morphing. (© 1994 New Line Productions, Inc. All rights reserved. Courtesy of New Line Productions, Inc.)

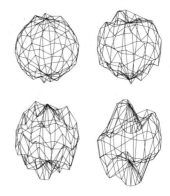

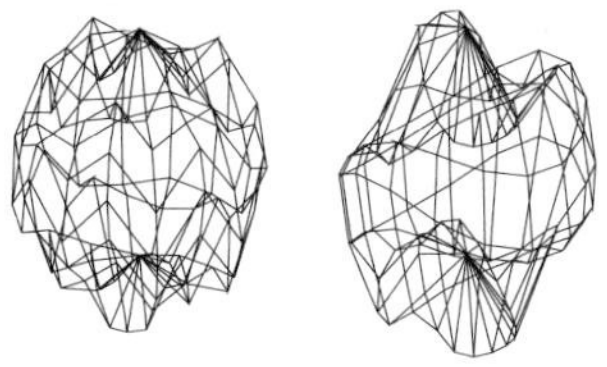

11.2.7 A circular sine function was used to distort a sphere.

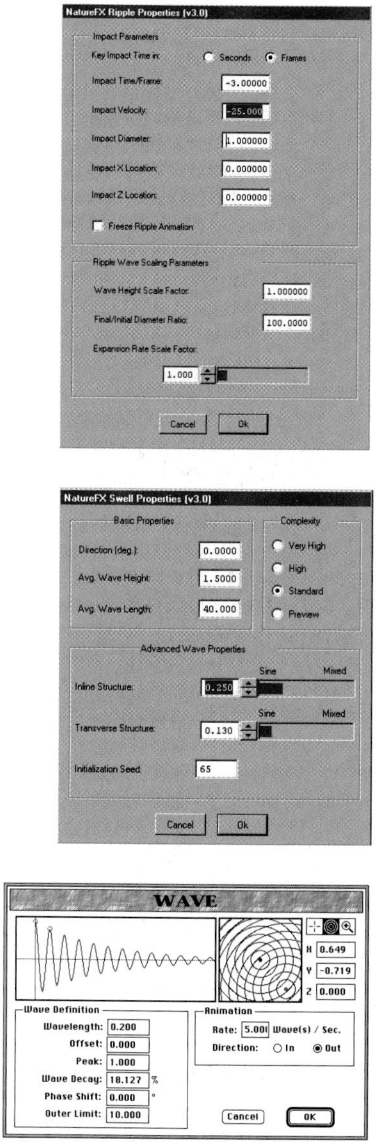

11.2.8 These dialog boxes show the implementation of a wave function in two different software programs. (Top: Ripple, and Swell dialog boxes from Nature FX, courtesy of Areté Entertainment, Inc. Bottom: Infini-D 3.0 dialog box. © 1991–1995 Specular International, Ltd.)

11.3 Camera Animation

The camera plays an important role in computer animation because its motion and the changes in some of its attributes can have a powerful storytelling effect. As explained in Chapter 7, the point of view of a camera and the type of camera shot are both defined by the position and orientation of the camera. All camera motions require a change in position and orientation of the camera. (The placement of cameras and their basic attributes are explained in Chapter 7.)

The motions of the virtual cameras used in computer animation are based on the camera moves defined in traditional cinematography. Most software programs use the same camera names used in traditional cinematography, but some use a slightly different nomenclature. All the possible camera moves can be expressed in terms of translations or rotations around one or several camera axes. In addition to changing the position and orientation of virtual cameras, their focal length and depth of field are some of the attributes that can be easily animated.

Position Camera Moves

The position of a camera can be easily defined by typing an **absolute position** value specified in XYZ world coordinates in the field or dialog box that controls the camera position. This technique can be useful for defining keyframes where the camera must be in a precise location. A more intuitive way to define the position of a camera consists of using one or several camera moves that are usually available as pull-down menu items in most computer animation programs.

The camera moves that are based on a change of the **position of the camera** include a dolly, a truck, and a boom. A **dolly** is a translation of the camera along the horizontal axis. A tracking or **traveling shot** occurs when a dolly moves along with the subject and follows it. A **truck** move is a translation of the camera along the depth axis, and it usually goes in or out of the scene. A **boom** is a translation of the camera along its the vertical axis. A **crane shot** can be implemented with a combination of boom, truck, and dolly camera moves (Fig. 11.3.1). Crane shots with computer-simulated cameras are not bound by many of the physical obstacles—walls, cliffs, trees, fire—of a standard real camera.

Orientation Camera Moves

The orientation of a camera can also be easily defined by typing an absolute position value specified in XYZ world coordinates in the field or dialog box that controls the camera orientation. This technique can be useful for defining keyframes where the camera must be looking in a precise direction or at a specific point in space. A more intuitive way to define the orientation of a camera consists of using one or several camera moves that can be saved as pull-down or pop-up menu items in many computer animation programs.

The camera moves that are based on the change of the **orientation of the camera** include a tilt, a roll, and a pan. A **tilt** is a rotation of the camera on its horizontal axis. A tilt is also called a pivot and is used to look up or down. A **roll** is created by rotating the camera around its Z axis. Roll camera moves are common when simulating fly-throughs. A **pan** is a move created by rotating the camera around its vertical axis (Fig. 11.3.2). Panning is very effective for scanning the scene from side to side while the camera remains stationary. Sometimes, especially when simulating flying cameras, a tilt move is called a pitch—as in airplanes pitching—and a pan move is called a yaw. (A zoom is a camera move that is achieved not by moving the position or orientation of the camera but by animating its focal length.)

Camera Motion Parallax

The **motion parallax** of a camera describes the visual effect that happens when two objects, one far and one near the camera, move in across the field of vision at the same constant speed. The object nearest to the camera will seem to be moving faster than the object that is far away, even though they are moving at the same speed and traveling the same distance. The reason for this visual illusion is that the object near the camera travels across a smaller area of the field of vision than the distant object has to travel. The object near the camera travels a larger percentage of the field of vision than the object that is further away (Fig. 11.3.3).

Camera Motion Paths

The technique of motion paths is especially useful for laying out complex camera moves—crane shots, underwater shots, and flying cameras in particular—consisting of several individual moves. As explained earlier, the motion path technique works by animating an object—the camera in this case—along a path defined in three-dimensional space. The paths are drawn with a simple curve modeling tool and edited just as any other object in three-dimensional space would be edited. Motion paths can be created with any type of curve but it is recommended to use b-spline or Bézier curves since both offer superior control for shaping curvature.

Once a camera is linked to the motion path and once the timing parameters of the path are defined, then it is possible to refine the motion of the camera. The speed and acceleration of a camera moving down a motion path can be fine-tuned with a timing interpolation graph. The constant speed that is commonly used as a default value in motion path animations can be enhanced with variable speeds, ease ins and ease outs (Fig. 11.1.7).

The position and orientation of a camera that is animated along a motion path can also be fine-tuned by adding standard camera moves, by adjusting the camera's point of interest, or by controlling

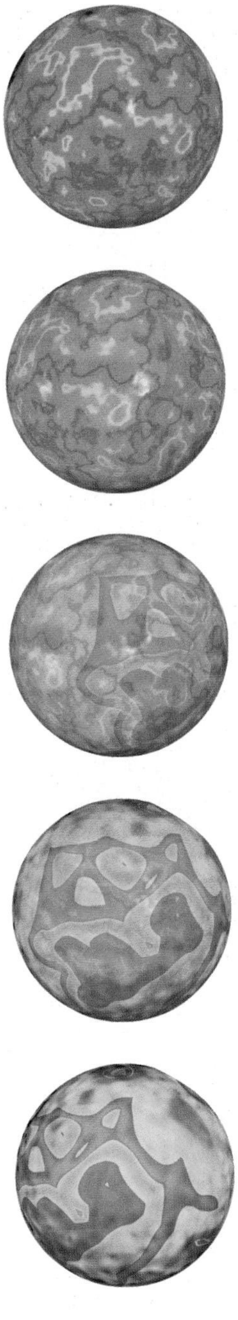

11.2.9 A sequence of animated surface textures where a shiny semi-precious stone turns into carved wood.

11.2.10 A lot of attitude in this character, Carl, with realistic fur! The NURBS surfaces were modeled with Maya software, and the fur created with a proprietary tool. Many fur characteristics, such as density, color and clumping, were controlled with image maps painted on the geometry surface. The color along the hairs changes from a dark root to a lighter tip, and the skin color underneath the fur can also be seen. The body and face animation was keyframed inverse kinematics, and the fur was driven by particle animation and dynamics. (© 2002 Blockbuster Entertainment/ Tippett Studio.)

the banking of the camera with an external object. A convenient feature of motion paths in many computer animation programs is that they can be converted to explicit transformations. This means that a motion that was originally defined by a path in three-dimensional space with just a timing interpolation graph can be converted to motions defined by the standard interpolation graphs for each of the geometric transformations along every axis. This conversion can help refine the motion by editing the interpolation parameter curves. Adjusting the point of interest of a camera as it moves along the motion path can be used to simulate the **sideways scanning** done by most live creatures as they move down a path (Fig. 11.3.4). The **banking motion** of flying or underwater cameras as they take the curves in a motion path can sometimes be easily set by linking the camera to an invisible object below or behind it. The purpose of this invisible object is to simulate weight or drag, and its animation can complement the motion of the camera.

Focal Length and Zoom Camera Moves

The focal length of a camera controls the way in which three-dimensional objects are seen by the camera. The **focal length** in a virtual camera is defined by the relation between the near clipping plane and the far clipping plane. This relation defines the way in which the objects in a three-dimensional environment are projected onto the projection plane of a virtual camera—or the surface of the film in a real camera. The focal length in a photographic camera is determined by the curvature and shape of the lens. For that reason, the unit to measure focal length even in virtual cameras is millimeters (mm). Standard camera lenses have a fixed focal length, but **zoom lenses** are capable of variable focal lengths by changing the distance between the point of view and the focal plane (Figs. 7.4.3 and 7.4.5). Some computer animation programs allow for the focal length to be animated independently or in conjunction with the near and the far clipping planes. This provides great flexibility when trying to clip—or remove—an object in the field of vision by placing it ahead of the near clipping plane or beyond the far clipping plane while maintaining a constant focal length.

A **zoom** is also a special type of camera move where the camera remains still but the framing of the image changes by gradually and continuously modifying the camera's focal length. In a zoom camera move, both the position and orientation of the camera remain untouched. With a zoom move it is common to migrate from one type of camera shot to another, for example, from an extreme close-up to a waist shot, or from a long shot that shows the scenery to a wide shot that focuses on a group of characters.

Depth of Field

The focusing properties of a lens are determined by its **depth of field**. The **focus** of a lens defines the plane that is perpendicular to the camera and that will be resolved into a sharp image. Only one plane in three-dimensional space can be in perfect focus when seen through any lens—our eyes included. But the areas that are slightly ahead and slightly behind the **focal plane** are also in focus, not perfect focus, but close enough so that almost nobody can tell the difference. The depth of field is bound by the near and the far focal planes, both of which are close enough to the focal plane to still be in focus (Figs. 7.2.1, 7.2.3 and 8.1.8).

In a real camera, a specific depth of field is determined by the combination of the focal length of the lens used, the **lens aperture** measured in f/stop units, and the distance between the camera and the subject, also called **focal distance**. As a general rule the smaller the lens aperture—which is inversely proportional to the f/stop numerical value—the greater the depth of field. Unlike photographic cameras, virtual cameras are capable of imaging in perfect focus all the objects in a three-dimensional environment. This means that issues of focussing and depth of field is often an afterthought when creating an image with three-dimensional computer graphics. In fact, many software programs do not support depth of field. But using the depth of field when rendering an image can contribute to the realism of the results. Depth of field should not be confused with the depth-fading rendering technique covered in Chapter 9.

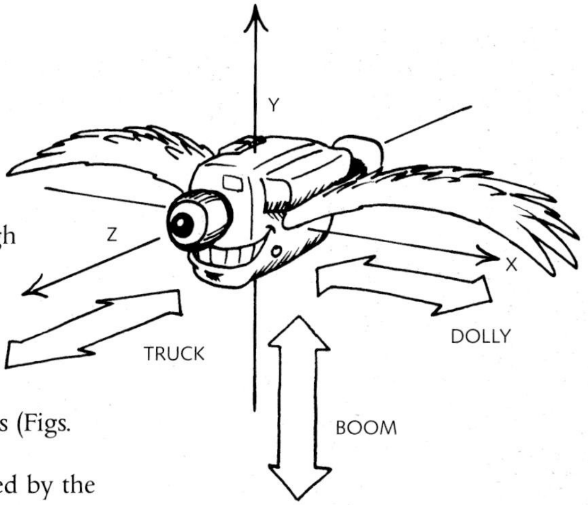

11.3.1 The three camera position moves: a dolly, a truck, and a boom. A crane shot can be made with a combination of any of these three moves and also any of the orientation moves illustrated in Figure 11.3.2.

11.4 Light Animation

The position and attributes of light sources in a computer animation project can be animated using keyframe interpolation techniques. The position and motion of light sources can be defined with the same interpolation techniques described earlier in the section on model animation. These techniques include the interactive specification of key poses, the editing of parameter curves, forward kinematics, and motion paths. A wide variety of lighting effects that affect the mood of a scene can be created by animating the intensity of a light source as well as its color, cone angle, and fall-off. These and other attributes of light sources are described throughout this section and also in Chapter 8.

Defining and scripting the animation of light sources can be a challenge to both art directors and computer animators. This is partly due to the lack of a standard system for scripting light animation. But writing down the description of light animations in a shot is often used as a preliminary step before the light animations are actually input into the software. These written descriptions are meant to

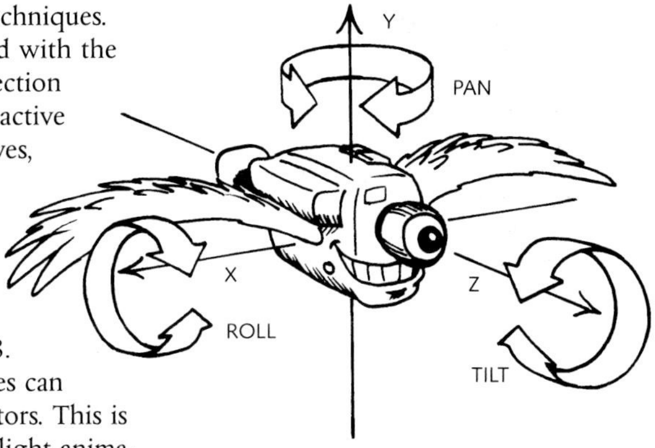

11.3.2 A tilt, a roll, and a pan camera moves.

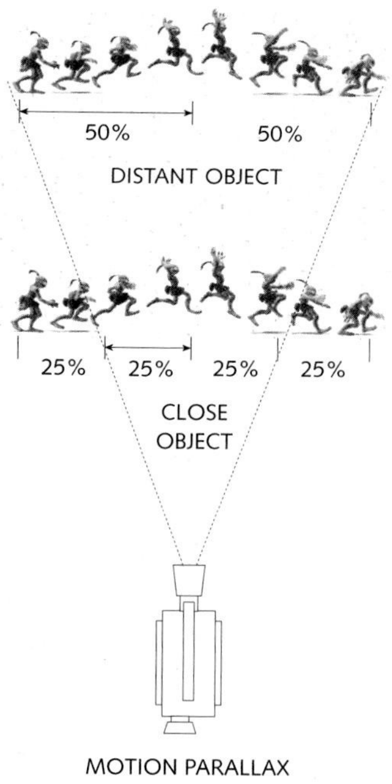

11.3.3 The motion parallax effect has to do with the fact that when a close and distant object move the same distance accross the camera, the object closest to the camera (bottom) moves only 25% of the field of view at that point while the distant object (top) moves 50% of the camera's field of view. (Jumping character © 1999 Oddworld Inhabitants, Inc. All rights reserved.)

give all those involved in the production a clear idea of what lighting effects are sought and what techniques may be required. Figure 11.4.1 has one such description.

A written description of the light animation is usually complemented—or followed—by a simple diagram that annotates the changes in the position or attributes of light in a way similar to a music score. This visual diagram can be a useful reference when scripting the animation of lights with the software program.

Moving lights in a three-dimensional environment should be exercised with great restraint because poorly animated light sources can be a great source of visual distraction in a shot. In principle, light sources should not be moved or animated unless we are trying to achieve a very specific change in the mood of a scene. Subtle emotional effects can be achieved, for example, by slowly increasing the intensity of a very narrow soft-edged spotlight that is focussed on the face of a character. An effect like this one can be especially effective when the **illumination level** in the scene is low. Spot lights that are dimmed or turned up are a very effective way of attracting the attention of the audience to a specific area or situation in a three-dimensional scene. Both point lights and spotlights can be turned on or off or gradually turned up or dimmed throughout an animated sequence. Turning lights on and off is easily achieved with linear interpolation, while dimming is done by easing in or out.

Light sources can also be animated when we are trying to achieve a specific lighting effect that is built on moving lights. Few light sources move in our world, and those that do have very specific characteristics. Animating the position and attributes of lights can simulate natural lighting effects, theatrical lighting effects based on artificial light sources, or both—natural lighting and artificial lighting often interact. **Natural lighting effects** are based on moving light sources like celestial bodies, the elements, natural phenomena, and a few animals.

Celestial Bodies

The light of **celestial bodies**—such as the sun or the moon—usually moves very slowly because those light sources are far from us. An exception to this rule is, of course, shooting stars and comets. The moving light of celestial bodies is usually perceived in the form of **moving shadows** because we can rarely tell that the sun or the moon are moving by just looking at them in real time. (Stop-motion animation can compress real time by recording still frames in a delayed fashion, for example, recording one still frame of the moving sun every minute.) Surreal lighting effects can be achieved by animating celestial bodies at speeds that do not correspond to their real speeds. The moving light created by a shooting star is a perfect example of a light animation that involves changes in both spatial position based on the speed and distance of the shooting star, and attributes such as the brightness and color determined by the moment when the asteroid enters the atmosphere of the Earth. The light of celestial bodies can be recreated with infinite light sources or with point light sources that have medium to high intensity and little or no fall-off. The color hue of the light of celestial bodies is constant but it may have, for example, a warm tint in the case of the sun or a slightly cold tint in the case of the moon. Short of procedural or parametric techniques the flickering effect of shooting stars can be implemented by creating an irregular pattern in the parameter curves that control the animation of the color or the fall-off of the light source.

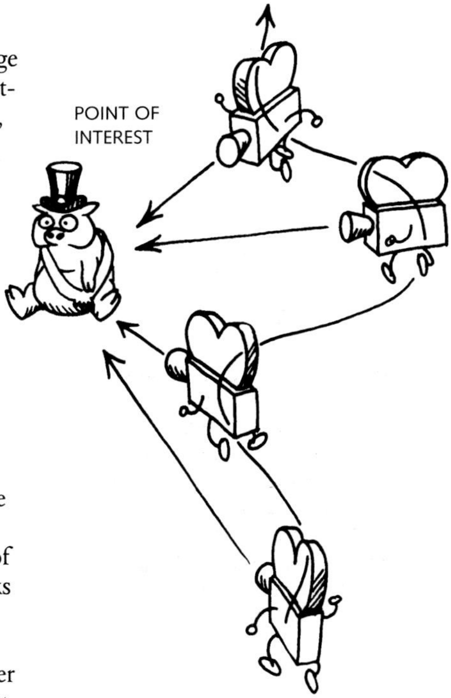

11.3.4 The point of interest is adjusted as the camera moves down the motion path or looks around the scene. (Top: Main character from *The ChubbChubbs.* © 2002 Sony Pictures Imageworks Inc. All Rights reserved.)

Natural Phenomena

The elements and various **natural phenomena** display a wide range of lighting behavior that involves motion. This type of natural lighting effect includes, for example, the light emitted by lightning, fire, or natural explosions such as an erupting volcano; the light reflected off the surface of moving water or refracted through moving water like a waterfall; and the light interrupted by the motion of objects that could be caused by wind in front of a light source (Fig. 11.4.2). The animation of these types of lighting effects can be done with a variety of techniques depending whether the light sources were defined with procedural techniques or as a collection of point lights and spot lights. In the former case, the animation of the light source would simply be done by animating the parameters that were used in the first place to define the procedural light (the characteristics of procedural lights are reviewed in Chapter 8). But in many situations, creating lighting effects with procedural techniques is not possible either because the software does not provide that option or because it would be computationally too expensive. In those instances, the lighting effects of moving natural phenomena can be simulated with a variety of tricks borrowed from traditional stage and movie special effects. Lighting tricks like these may seem crude when compared to the conceptual elegance of motion dynamics simulations, but they are often cheaper than simulations to produce and almost always as effective—at least from the point of view of the audience.

A trick that is quite common in stage lighting for simulating the light emitted by a small fire or a fireplace consists of using a couple of pulsating spot lights to project light through overlapping strips of colored gel that are constantly waved by a fan (Fig. 11.4.3). The irregular motion of the yellow, red, and orange stripes creates a pattern of transmitted light that can be very effective when projected on the subjects in the scene. This lighting trick, commonly used in both opera and theatre, can be easily simulated in computer animation with just a small group of spot lights and point lights and their parameter curves instead of using gel strips, a fan, and spot lights.

Computer animation can also be used to recreate the lighting effects created by light traveling through falling water, for example, the effect created in an interior space by moonlight, or street lights

> **Written Description of a Light Animation Sequence**
>
> - The length of the transformation scene is 10 seconds.
> - It takes place in an interior space with a round table with four chairs around it in the center of a room.
> - There is a window on the wall that is opposite to the wall with a closed door in the middle of it.
> - There is a wooden sculpture of a bird on the table.
> - The scene starts with the room lights turned off.
> - There is a fire outside. Its crackling sound can be heard, but the flames are barely visible through the closed window shades.
> - Suddenly a strong wind current throws the door open, and a whirling light flies into the room and glows more intensely as it circles over the table for 2 or 3 seconds.
> - The light hovers over the table, floating up and down for another couple of seconds.
> - The light sparkles, and as the sparks land on the table and the wooden sculpture, both glow gently for a couple of seconds and then, suddenly and unexpectedly, they vanish.

11.4.1 Written descriptions of a light animation can help to clarify what techniques may be required to produce the sequence.

traveling through rain. This trick may include arrays of small three-dimensional models that are animated off-screen between the simulated light source and the scene. In the case of rain, for example, the array of small three-dimensional models could include two or more layers of small cylindrical and translucent shapes that constantly move next to the light source. The two layers of translucent shape patterns can be built in the form of cylinders that rotate around the horizontal axis between the light source and the scene. The resulting top to bottom motions simulates falling water (Fig. 11.4.4). Two or more layers are necessary to avoid a simple pattern of light that is repeated at small intervals. The arrangement of the shapes in each of the layers should also be as irregular and different as possible in order to avoid a repeating motion pattern that is easy to identify. This lighting effect can be maximized by rotating the two cylindrical layers at different variable speeds. The density of the shapes on the rotating layers can yield a variety of effects that range from drizzle to a waterfall. There are alternate versions of this trick for instances when the extreme length of a scene may give audiences enough time to recognize the lighting pattern and get bored. One alternative to the rotating cylinders of shapes consists of a very long strip with a **translucent image map**—instead of translucent three-dimensional shapes—that is translated from top to bottom between the camera and the scene.

Another variation of the rotating cylinders can be used to simulate the **obstruction of light** caused by objects such as dry leaves being swept in front of the light source. This lighting effect can be achieved by animating groups of flat leaf-shaped models with a pseudo-random factor so that the effect is repeated each time with a slight variation. A primary motion may keep the leaves spiraling in front of the light source, and a secondary motion may keep them rotating around their center or flipping as they rotate. The rotation of several of these groups of leaves can be looped to provide a continuous effect. The effect of the leaves blocking the light can be enhanced by applying a transparency map that makes the leaves transparent on the edges.

The effect of light reflected off the surface of **moving water** can be recreated by placing spot lights shining up through a surface that represents water and that has an animate shape. The lighting effect created by a lightning storm can be recreated by inserting one or two white frames in the sequence just a couple of seconds before the sound of thunder is heard. After that a very strong light—placed in the area near where the lightning is supposed to have fallen—is suddenly turned up to a bright white color and then dimmed in a flickering way. The motion of artificial lights during an earthquake, for example, is an interesting convergence of artificial lighting and a natural phenomenon such as those described in Chapter 12.

Practical Lights

Many night or interior scenes have **practical lights** that move or change during the shot. Practical lights include flashlights, matches, torches, table lamps, and even fireflies. Many of us have been fascinated by the blinking patterns of light created by fireflies as they fly through the night. Other animals—such as the fluorescent fish that live in the depths of the oceans—are also light sources that move naturally. The light emitted by fireflies can be simulated with point lights or with spot lights that have a very wide cone angle and a narrow spread angle. Firefly light has a large amount of fall-off because it does not travel very far, and its color can be animated within a narrow range of fluorescent green hues. The blinking pattern of firefly light can be replicated by drawing parameter curves for color, fall-off, or cone angle so that they are interrupted with abrupt jumps. The parameter curve in Figure 11.4.5 represents the abrupt jumps in cone angle values that represent a blinking light. The small zig-zag variations along the vertical axis represent flickering, and the abrupt jumps and sharp 90-degree angle changes in direction represent blinking. The flat horizontal lines represent a constant darkness achieved by a cone angle value of zero.

11.4.2 An early example of natural phenomena lighting. (Courtesy of Rhythm & Hues Studios.)

Artificial Lights

Theatrical or **artificial lights** can be still or in motion and can be based on point lights or spot lights. Artificial still point lights include, for example, a bare light bulb. Man-made moving spot lights include, for example, the light reflectors used in stage or movie productions—and so commonly associated with Hollywood—the light projected in darkness by moving vehicles, or the light projected by flashlights or other appliances such as open refrigerators, copy machines, and televisions that are turned on in darkened environments.

Animating lights that resemble artificial moving lights should also be done with restraint, and only when a specific lighting effect is required. Animating spot lights in a dark scene can add a feeling of suspense or fear to the shot because the lighting effect may remind the audience of a search for something—or someone—that is hiding, or trying to hide from someone—or something—that is searching. Figure 11.4.6 shows why the evening lights in the urban landscape are so commonly used to set the mood in a scene.

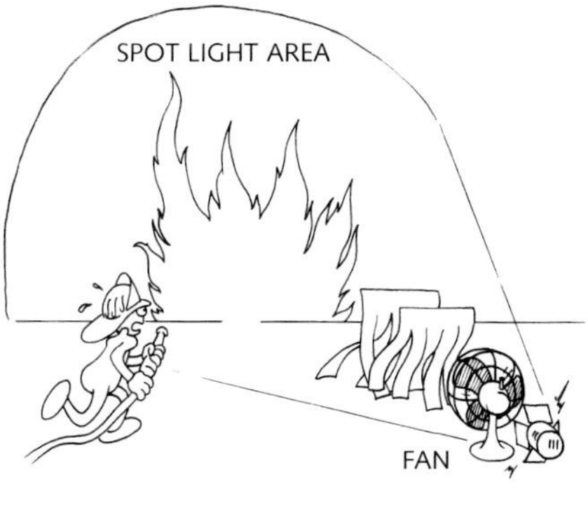

11.4.3 Fire effects can be simulated by projecting light through strips of colored gel moved by a fan.

11.5 Hierarchical Animation

Three-dimensional objects can be limitlessly grouped together in order to define the ways in which these objects relate to one another and behave when animated. Groupings of three-dimensional objects are called **hierarchical structures**, and within them some objects are always more dominant than others. (See Chapter 5 for additional features of hierarchical structures as applied to model rigging.)

Hierarchical diagrams are often represented as an inverted **tree structure** where the highest level of importance in the structure corresponds to the trunk of the tree. The main **branches** that come

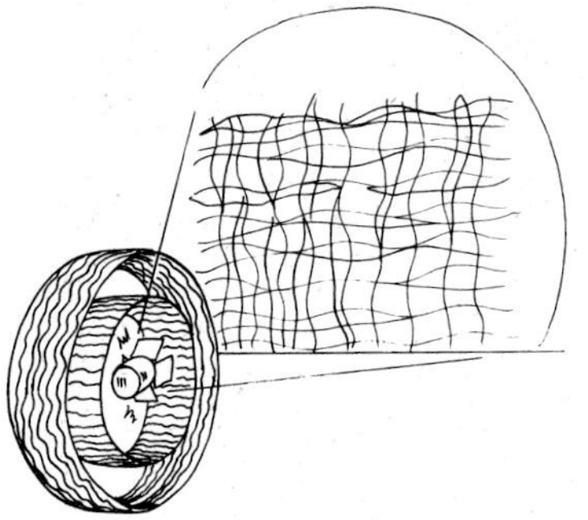

11.4.4 The effect of light being projected through rain or a waterfall can be achieved by rotating two cylindrical layers of translucent shapes at variable speeds between the light source and the scene.

directly out of the trunk represent the next level in the hierarchy; branches that come out of the main branches are at the next level and so on, until we get to the leaves, which represent the last level in the hierarchical structure. The objects within the hierarchy inherit attributes—including motion—from the dominant objects just as children inherit the attributes of their parents. It is also possible to animate just a selected branch in the structure without having to animate the entire structure. The relationships between objects—or parts of objects—in a hierarchical structure can be easily visualized with a schematic representation in the form of a line **hierarchy diagram**. These diagrams often consist of **boxes** that represent the items in the structure, and **lines** that represent the place of the items in the hierarchy and their relations with other items. In most cases, there is just one set of hierarchy diagrams per scene, and these diagrams control the animation of all the objects.

Levels of Precedence

Objects within hierarchical structures have well-defined **levels of precedence** or importance. The object or objects at the top of the hierarchy are called **parents**, and the objects below are called **children** and **grandchildren**. The most dominant object in a hierarchy is usually called the **root** of the hierarchy, and objects that are placed in the same branch of the hierarchy or at the same level in the hierarchy are often called **siblings**. A **null parent** is a node in the hierarchy that does not relate to any specific part in the model but that controls several child objects together. A null parent is used, for example, when two or more objects are grouped at the same level in the hierarchy. Nulls are usually represented as empty boxes in the structural diagrams. Figure 5.7.1 illustrates the use of a null node.

Hierarchical structures sometimes include objects that are assembled into an articulated figure. They may also include objects that are not physically connected to one another, and often they include both. **Articulated figures** are made of objects that are connected to others. Articulated figures with hierarchical groupings of objects are an essential tool for the creation of computer-based character animation. In most articulated figures, the connection between the objects is such that they touch each other so the connection happens in the form of a joint. There are many possible ways to group several objects in a hierarchical structure, but the hierarchy of parts in a model should always be driven by the motion requirements. Figures 11.5.1 and 11.5.2 show an articulated and a nonarticulated model each with their corresponding hierarchical diagrams. The hierarchy in both examples is quite simple since there is minimal branching.

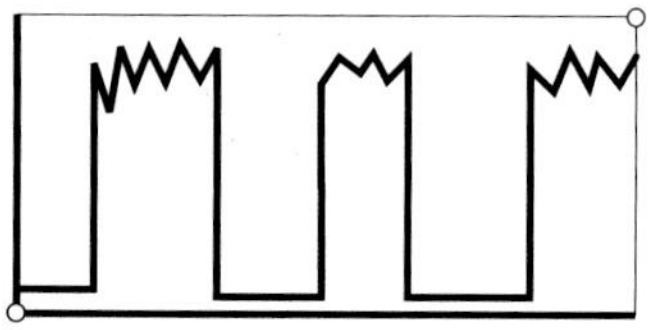

11.4.5 Parameter curve of the cone angle values of the light emitted by a firefly.

Joints and Degrees of Freedom

The type of **joints** used in computer animation are defined by the number of degrees of freedom that they have. **Degrees of freedom**

are used to express the ability of a joint to rotate around and/or to translate along one or several axes. One degree of freedom, for example, corresponds to the ability of a joint to rotate around one axis, while a joint with three degrees of freedom is capable of rotating around three axes. The knee, for example, is a joint with only one degree of freedom, whereas the shoulder has three degrees of freedom (go ahead, try it, you can rotate your arms around the X, Y, and Z axes). Joints can be catalogued according to their degrees of freedom from a simple one-dimensional **twist joint** or **bend joint** to a multidimensional **universal joint** that can rotate in all directions (Fig. 11.5.3). In addition to the number of degrees of freedom, joints are also defined by a **rotation range**, which restricts the rotation of

11.4.6 This nocturnal scene from the *Blade Runner* computer game displays a plethora of artificial lights traveling through the fog and casting shadows and interreflections. (© Westwood Studios. All rights reserved.)

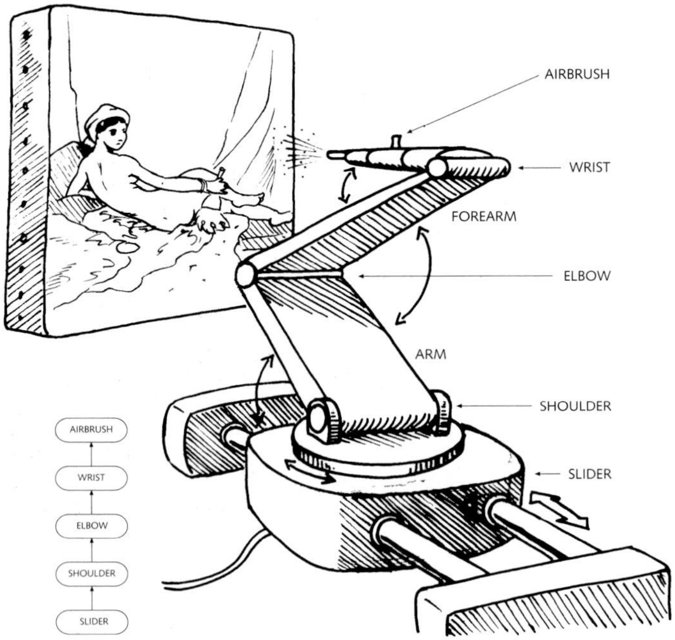

11.5.1 This spray-paint robot arm is an articulated figure with three joints. The shoulder has two degrees of freedom, and the elbow and wrist each have only one degree of freedom. The diagram on the left represents the root of the hierarchical structure.

the joint between a minimum and a maximum value (Fig. 11.5.4). A joint can have a different rotation range for each of its degrees of freedom. These **motion constrains** imposed by rotation ranges are especially useful when animating articulated figures with the inverse kinematics techniques described in Chapter 12.

The centers of objects—often called **centroids** or pivot points—play an important role in the hierarchical animation process because many operations are calculated based on their spatial position. These operations include all the geometric transformations as well as simulations of motion dynamics related to the center of gravity. By default most three-dimensional programs place the centroids in the geometric center of the objects. Most software programs also allow animators to interactively reposition the centroids of objects.

All computer animation that supports hierarchical structures offers some sort of hierarchy or **skeleton editor** for the purpose of creating links between objects and setting **joint information** such as stiffness and ranges of rotation. Skeleton editors are usually based on a graphical diagram and dialog boxes with information for each item in the diagram or a spreadsheet that lists all the items in the diagram. One of the most popular methods for establishing **links** between objects allows animators to build the links by clicking directly on the three-dimensional objects in any one of the camera views. Another method establishes hierarchical relationships by clicking on the boxes in the diagram that represents the links between the three-dimensional objects (Figs. 4.7.2 and 12.1.8). The programs that build the hierarchy from top to bottom require that the object that is to be the parent is clicked before the children in the hierarchy. The programs that build the hierarchy from bottom to top require users to select the children first and the parent last.

11.6 Two- and Three-Dimensional Integration

Combining and matching two-dimensional hand-drawn animation with three-dimensional computer renderings was pioneered in animated works like Disney's ***The Great Mouse Detective*** (1986) and ***Beauty and the Beast*** (1991), or ***Technological Threat*** by Bill Kroyer (1988, Fig. 1.3.10). At the time this technique represented a major challenge, but integrating elements from two-dimensional and three-dimensional elements in the same shot is a standard technique in the computer animation toolbox of today. Many animated movies and TV series that are primarily hand-drawn incorporate a fair amount of significant three-dimensional elements: the crowds in ***Prince of Egypt*** (Fig. 12.6.2), the octopus-tarantula monster in ***Princess Mononoke***, and the space vehicles in Matt Groening's ***Futurama*** and Disney's ***Atlantis*** and ***Lilo and Stitch***. "Tradigital" is the clever name that DreamWorks' Jeffrey Katzenberg has given to this melding of styles.

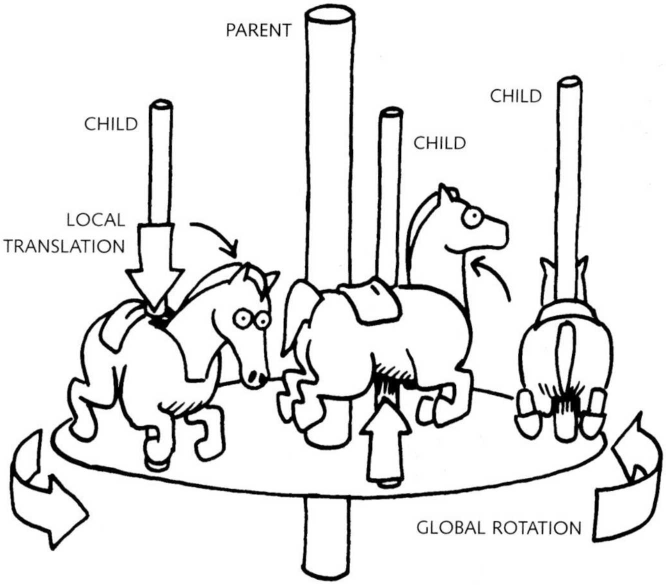

11.5.2 A merry-go-round is a good example of a hierarchical structure with multiple levels, where the motion of the objects in the parent levels determines the motion of those objects in the children levels. Everything rotates together, but each horse has a unique vertical motion and timing.

There are a few variations of the technique of **two- and three-dimensional integration**, each suited for different cases, including two-dimensional hand-drawn characters on three-dimensional computer-generated backgrounds, three-dimensional computer-generated characters and props on two-dimensional hand-drawn backgrounds, stop motion animation characters on three-dimensional computer-generated backgrounds, and combinations of the three. Each one of these variations requires a slightly different process.

The process for integrating two-dimensional hand-drawn characters on three-dimensional computer-generated backgrounds starts by laying out the shots on a three-dimensional system. This layout takes into account the action of the characters regardless of whether the shot involves camera moves. Printouts of each keyframe, usually in wireframe mode, can be used by the two-dimensional animators as templates for planning the character actions. Printouts and drawings are usually created at the same field size (Fig. 7.2.2). In shots with a moving three-dimensional camera, animators might need several continuous frames of the background to match their drawings to the speed and perspective of the camera. The progress of the two-dimensional animation can be checked or previsualized by quickly compositing the scanned pencil drawings with the three-dimensional backgrounds. This can be easily achieved by using the white background in the pencil test as a transparent alpha channel (see Chapter 14 for more information on matting and compositing with an alpha channel). Once the two-dimensional animation is completed and approved the drawings can be scanned in high resolution, inked and colored digitally, and composited in batch mode with the three-dimensional backgrounds. In cases with extreme camera moves, such as a long pan or a quick dolly, it may be necessary to use tracing or rotoscoping techniques (Fig. 13.3.1) to match the two-dimensional hand-drawn animated characters to the three-dimensional backgrounds or virtual sets.

11.5.3 (next page) A variety of joint types with different degrees of freedom: one degree, two, three, four, and six degrees.

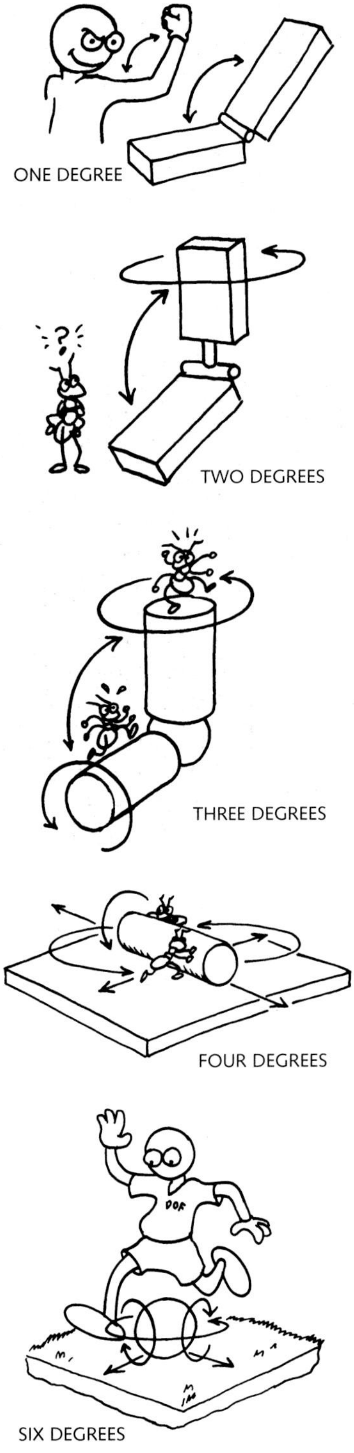

In the case of three-dimensional characters animated on two-dimensional backgrounds the integration process can be even simpler than matching two-dimensional characters to three-dimensional backgrounds. The two-dimensional background is scanned and used as a template to adjust the position and orientation of the three-dimensional camera (Fig. 12.6.2). This can be done by eyeballing the position of the camera or by using camera tracking software (Fig. 13.2.1) to aid matching the perspective of the three-dimensional camera to the perspective of the two-dimensional background. It is also possible to model both environments and models in three dimensions, use the three-dimensional environment as a template to paint two-dimensional backgrounds, and composite the painted backgrounds with the three-dimensional characters.

Combining characters created with stop motion animation techniques and three-dimensional computer-generated backgrounds provides another opportunity for two- and three-dimensional integration. In this case the integration process is fairly similar to the process of camera tracking for live action footage described in Chapter 13. The position of the virtual camera can be calculated with camera tracking software by providing the position and orientation of the camera used to record the stop motion as well as tracking markers used on the stop motion set (Fig. 11.6.1).

11.7 Getting Ready

Choose Appropriate Motion

Audiences learn a lot about the emotions and intentions of animated characters by the way they move. Make sure that the motion applied to the models matches the purpose of the scene. Motion should also match the level of rendering realism in the scene. For example, realistic renderings might make more sense if realistic motion is applied to the models, while sketchy motion may be more appropriate for simple renderings.

Avoid Still First Frames

One or several still frames at the beginning of an animated sequence usually look like a mistake, for example, when the camera starts rolling before the actors are ready. Unless the sequence calls for several frames of a motion hold, avoid starting your animations with still models. Instead, you can improve the sense of motion flow and continuity between scenes and shots by starting them with objects that are in motion, regardless of how subtle that motion may be.

Preview the Motion

Virtually all computer animation programs allow for the creation of motion flipbooks that can be played back directly onto the computer

screen. A **digital flipbook** consists of a sequence of image files displayed in an area of the screen, ranging from a small window to the full screen. Digital flipbooks can be played back at their final output speed, for example, 24 or 30 frames per second, or at slower speeds to analyze the animation in more detail. Before digital flipbooks were available, the motion tests were previewed by recording them onto a videotape, and playing them back on a videotape player.

11.5.4 These titanic characters from the *Command and Conquer 2* computer game have different types of joints and degrees of freedom. Can you figure out what they are? (© Westwood Studios. All rights reserved.)

Preview with Multiple Camera Views

It is helpful to use multiple active camera views when setting the keyframes in a three-dimensional animation. The camera perspective view is useful for previewing the motion from a specific point of view. But the other camera views, including the front view, side view, and top view, are useful for checking details, such as overlapping objects.

Unlock Objects before Animating

Remember to unlock the objects in the scene that were previously

11.6.1 A finished frame from *Das Rad* composed of a three-dimensional computer-generated background and a stop-motion foreground. The later can also be seen below against a blue screen, with a white marker to facilitate camera tracking. (© 2001 Filmakademie Baden-Wuerttemberg/ Gruber/Stenner/ Wittlinger.)

11.6.2 (opposite page) User-controlled dynamic cameras allow players to navigate through a computer game. (Images courtesy of Naughty Dog, Inc. "Naughty Dog" and the Naughty Dog Logo are registered trademarks of Naughty Dog, Inc., a wholly owned subsidiary of Sony Computer Entertainment America, Inc. *Jak & Daxter* is a trademark of Sony Computer Entertainment America, Inc. Created and developed by Naughty Dog, Inc. © 2001 Sony Computer Entertainment America, Inc. *Jak & Daxter* was developed for the Playstation 2 computer entertainment System.)

locked in a specific position, orientation, size, or spatial range, during the modeling process. In most software programs, locked objects will not be animated according to the animation score and/or parameter curves.

Follow the Storyboard

It is important to stick to the storyboard because other individuals may be working at the same time on the same sequence as you are. If you decide to interpret the storyboard liberally you may create animated sequences that will not match the previous shot or the one that follows, or even other aspects of the production, such as the soundtrack. Consult the production coordinator when you have an idea for improving the portion of the storyboard that you are working on. Maybe your idea can be carried out but only after other team members have been consulted.

Chapter 11

Key Terms

Absolute position
Acceleration
Articulated figures
Artificial lights
Attributes
Banking motion
Bend joint
Boom
Boxes
Branches
Celestial bodies
Centroids
Children
Circular waves
Constant speed
Crane shot
Curved interpolation
Degrees of freedom
Depth of field
Digital flipbook
Dolly
Ease functions
Ease in
Ease out
External control structures
Fantastic transformation
Focal distance
Focal length
Focal plane
Focus
Forward kinematics
Free-form lattice
Free-form shape animation
Front of the object
Function curve
Grandchildren
Hierarchical structures
Hierarchy diagram
Illumination level
In-between frames
Interactive specification of key poses
Interpolation ease
Joint information
Joints
Keyframe
Keyframe interpolation
Lens aperture
Levels of precedence
Linear interpolation
Lines
Linked to the path
Links
Mapping a sequence of images
Motion constrains
Motion parallax
Motion paths
Moving shadows
Moving water
Natural lighting effects
Natural phenomena
Natural transformation
Null parent
Number of points
Obstruction of light
Order of correspondence
Orientation of the camera
Pan
Parameter curve
Parents
Planar waves
Position of the camera
Practical lights
Rate of change
Roll
Root
Rotation range
Shape animation
Siblings
Sideways scanning
Skeleton editor
Slope
Spatial animation
Speed
Spherical waves
Squashing
Stretching
Three-dimensional morphing
Tilt
Timing of transformations
Transformation matrix
Translucent image map
Traveling shot
Tree structure
Two- and three-dimensional integration
Truck
Twist joint
Universal joint
Wave functions
Zoom
Zoom lenses

CHAPTER 12

Advanced Computer Animation Techniques

Summary

MOST OF THE ADVANCED ANIMATION TECHNIQUES covered in this chapter are quite different from those techniques based on the traditional keyframe approach. These techniques are used to simulate complex or realistic motion of objects and characters. Many of these techniques, in fact, start by capturing the motion of real actors and applying it to animated characters. This chapter also presents the **hybrid environment** in which some of the latest advanced animation techniques are almost always used in combination with others. The concept of working in layers or channels of motion is stressed throughout the chapter. One of the main reasons for using hybrid animation techniques is the fact that natural motion is too complex to be recreated with just one technique. For example, the motion of three-dimensional models can be controlled in detail if we provide their positions and angles to an inverse kinematics program, but their motions may not be physically correct. Likewise the motion of models will be realistic if their motion dynamics are simulated based on the forces applied to them, but it will be difficult to obtain a specific motion especially as the models become more complex.

QUICK INDEX

12.1 Inverse Kinematics

Inverse kinematics techniques are useful for animating complex models and motion rigs with a large number of joints. Unlike their counterpart, forward kinematics, **inverse kinematics** techniques determine the motion of entire skeletons based on the final angles of some of the key joints that define the motion. As explained in Chapter 11, forward kinematics techniques calculate the motion and final position of a model by first specifying the angles of its joints. That is, in essence, the inverse approach to inverse kinematics.

The inverse kinematics animation techniques require that the three-dimensional models to be animated are built as hierarchical structures. Inverse kinematics techniques are most commonly applied

12.1.1 (opposite page) Woody and Buzz Lightyear, the unforgettable characters from *Toy Story*, the first animated feature film produced entirely with three-dimensional computer animation techniques. (Images courtesy of The Walt Disney Company. © Disney Enterprises, Inc. All rights reserved.)

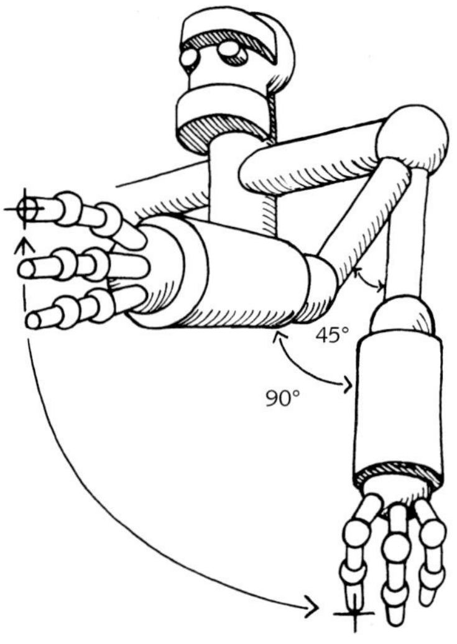

12.1.2 The end effector of an articulated chain representing an arm is usually the hand or a fingertip.

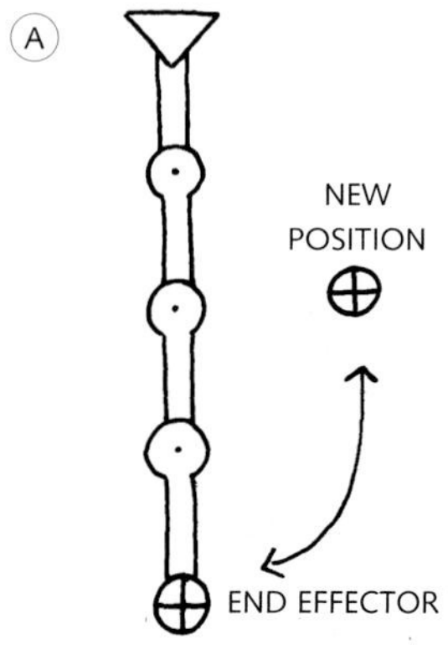

12.1.3 An inverse kinematics sequence that starts (A) without motion or position constrains may result in endless motion variations when the end effector is repositioned (B, opposite page).

to articulated figures that are defined as hierarchical skeletons constructed with links that are connected by joints, each with different motion constrains. Hierarchical skeletons are composed of many articulated chains that are grouped together in a hierarchy. Skeletons are also related to the skin surface surrounding them and the models attached to them. This hierarchical relation varies between programs, but in most cases, the root chain or different parts of the chain are the parents of the skin or models attached to them (read Chapter 5 for more details on skin).

Inverse kinematics techniques can greatly simplify the animation of models with multiple joints that have to move in a complex and somewhat realistic way. Trying to animate a running tiger, for example, with interactive specification of keyframes could turn into a long and tedious process of trial and error, especially if the tiger was running on an uneven terrain that had obstacles scattered along the way. But the same process could be simplified using inverse kinematics because this animation technique uses the position of the limbs or joints in an articulated figure to animate the entire figure into the desired configuration. The components of the inverse kinematics process include a hierarchical structure or chain, joints, motion constrains, and effectors. Articulated figures with hierarchical structures allow simultaneous movement of all its parts but always following the specified hierarchy. The hierarchy in an articulated figure prevents all of its parts from scattering in all directions when a transformation is applied to the figure. Hierarchical structures and motion rigging are covered in more detail in Chapter 11.

An articulated chain is composed of a chain root, a certain number of joints, and an effector. The **chain root** is usually the first joint in the first segment of an articulated chain. The chain root is often the parent of all the segments and joints in the articulated chain. The **effector**—also called **end effector**—in a hierarchical chain is the joint in an articulated figure that is used to determine the positions of a moving chain with inverse kinematics. When the effector in a chain is moved then the inverse kinematics are invoked and the rotations of the joints are automatically calculated. In the case of an arm reaching to push a button, for example, the end effector of the motion would be located in the hand or an extended fingertip (Fig. 12.1.2). The end effector of most arm motions is, in fact, usually placed in the hand or the fingertips.

A **joint** is defined by the articulation point where two segments of the articulated chain meet. Some inverse kinematics programs allow the joints in the chain to be rotated in any direction unless motion constrains have been placed on any specific joint. This means that the joints in the hierarchical chain can rotate in any direction during the calculation of new positions with inverse kinematics. This brings us to the fact that a hierarchical chain can follow the motion of an end effector in many different ways whenever motion constrains are not set (Fig. 12.1.3). Other programs, however, define the articulated chains as

12.1.4 Throwing a ball with inverse kinematics. Only the starting and ending positions need to be specified.

planar and will only allow the joints in a chain to rotate around one axis (usually the Z axis when looking at the chain sideways).

One of the big advantages of animating complex articulated figures with inverse kinematics is that if the figure has the proper joint motion constrains the motion of a single end effector can be used to determine how all the joints in the figure must rotate. The entire figure follows the motion of the end effector. But inverse kinematics techniques can save work during the animation process only as long as the joint **motion constrains** have been placed in a way that makes sense and leads to the desired motions. In most situations, animating a complex articulated figure with inverse kinematic techniques is often more efficient than using forward kinematics (Fig. 12.1.4). In some cases though, forward kinematics offers more direct and immediate control of the joint positions at any point during the animation process (Fig. 12.1.5).

Assigning motion constrains to each joint is necessary to contain the motion of a hierarchical chain so that only one configuration results when the end effector of the chain is dragged to a specific point. Figure 12.1.3 illustrates the results of animating a hierarchical chain with different rotation and position motion constrains but the same end effector. Motion constrains are often expressed in terms of degrees of freedom and rotation angles. They are covered in more detail in Chapter 11.

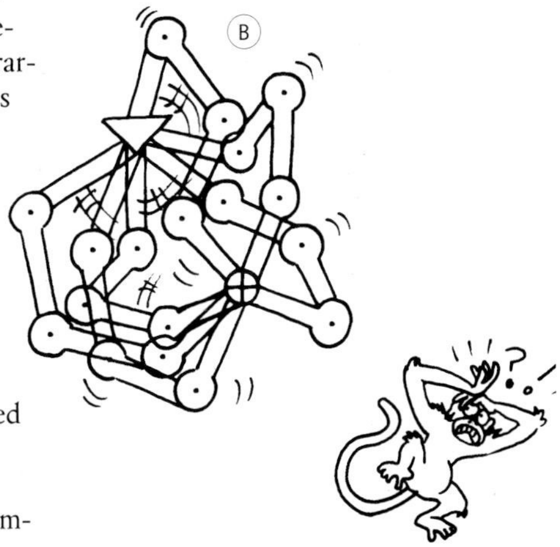

The hierarchy of skeletons that represent a complex articulated figure can be broken to facilitate the animation of a figure with a part or limb that should not follow the motion of the chain root. That would be the case, for example, of a character whose feet must remain on the ground or whose hands must remain attached to an object even as the chain root—usually located somewhere in the torso or hips—moves. In a **broken hierarchy,** some or all of the limbs do not descend from the chain root but instead have their own root. In a broken hierarchy, a hand, for example, is not directly controlled by the torso through the shoulder. In cases like this, it is necessary to somehow keep the split articulated chains together during the motion, and stretch the surface skin at the point where the two chains meet. This facilitates independent motions of each chain as well as a continuous skin surface (Fig. 12.1.7).

Inverse kinematics is a powerful technique for building secondary motions on top of primary motions. When animating a hierarchical model like a human body (Fig. 12.1.8) it is best to animate down the hierarchy before dealing with the details. This means that primary motions such as those of the torso would be specified before secondary motions such as those of the head or arms. Inverse kinematics can be an effective technique for laying out actions by specifying key poses at each keyframe. This approach can be complemented with the techniques presented in the next section of this chapter.

12.1.5 Throwing a ball with forward kinematics. All joint angles need to be specified.

12.2 Performance Animation and Motion Capture

Real-time **motion capture** is an advanced animation technique that allows animators to capture live motion with the aid of a machine and then apply it to computer animated characters. Motion capture is different from traditional keyframe animation because it captures all the motions of live actors as they move. Motion capture can also be used to create the **basic tracks of motion** that can later be enriched with other animation techniques. Much of the **secondary motion** in an animation based on motion capture techniques—such as the detailed animation of hands, fingers, and facial expressions—is usually added on top of the basic tracks of primary motion (Fig. 12.2.1).

Motion data that is captured and saved as XYZ joint positions can be manipulated directly and also applied, for example, to an inverse kinematics skeleton. Some motion capture methods are better suited for **live control** of animated characters, while others are more adequate for situations that require complex motion sequences with **multiple layers of motion**. Except for when the motion capture data is used to control live motion, the data collected with motion capture systems is subjected to different amounts of clean up and refinement in the computer animation system. This is because the **raw motion** captured often contains too much noise that has to be cleaned out or because it is not sufficient to generate by itself the motion required in the animation sequence.

A major attraction of motion capture techniques is that they may be used to produce animation in a cost-effective way, but only after all the initial setup has been worked out. Depending on the nature of the project, motion capture techniques make it possible to automate large portions of the character motion, and they can also eliminate some of the keyframe-based manual work.

Motion capture techniques began to be practical in the early 1980s when researchers experimented with potentiometers attached to human bodies for measuring the angles of joints. Light emitting diodes (LEDs) and mechanical armatures were also used early on to measure both the position and orientation of joints. Most of the early applications of motion control were limited to animating live simple cartoon characters or heads and faces, but not full body animation. These live animations would often be composited with live action. In many cases, a variety of helmets and armatures have been used to capture the motion of the face and body of an actor. Today, even though motion capture animation techniques are still being refined, there is an increasing variety of character animation based on motion capture techniques. Many off-the-shelf computer animation packages offer hookups for a range of motion capture gear that can bring motion data directly into the animation system. The prejudice about motion control being a technique that is used only by those who do not know how to animate the "old-fashioned way"—entirely by hand—is also slowly giving way to more progressive points of view.

Motion capture implies one or several real actors that generate motions for one or several animated characters (Fig. 12.2.2). Preparing both the **real actors** and the animated characters—or **virtual actors**—for the process of motion capture involves two somewhat independent series of steps: setting up the capture points on the human actor and setting up the hierarchical structures that will control the virtual actor. The exact positioning of the sampling points depends on the type of motion desired. But in all cases, it is necessary to establish a correspondence between the **sampling points** in real actors and the joints in the animated characters. Illogical correspondences between sampling points and joints in the animated characters can lead to unexpected and amusing results. Imagine the motion of an animated character whose neck joints are animated by the motion collected by the sampling points in its tail!

Motion capture is often used to capture primary motion, so sampling points are often distributed throughout the head, torso, and limbs. Secondary motions such as facial expressions and hand gestures are often added with other animation techniques to the captured primary motions. It is also important to make sure that the hierarchical structures of both real and virtual actors are structured so that the

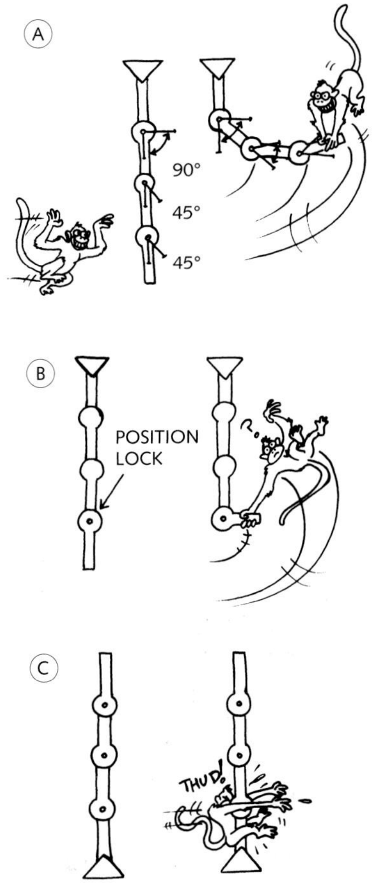

12.1.6 Three inverse kinematics sequences of a simple hierarchical chain. They all follow the same end effector but each has different motion constrains including a single rotation constrain (A), a single position constrain (B), and multiple position constrains (C).

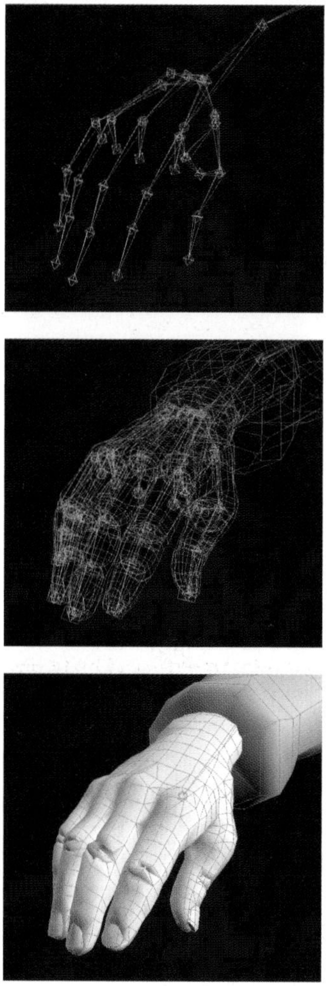

12.1.7 The pivot points in the skeleton that controls a hand animation are shown as diamonds (top). The yellow diamonds and webbing between the thumb and the index are flexible links that behave like springs. The red sphere on the palm is a pivot point that connects the hierarchical root of the skin to the skeleton. The wrinkles in the knuckles are modeled on the mesh (middle), and a material ID number has been applied to the fingernail mesh that is different from the skin material. (© 1999 Mondo Media, San Francisco, California.)

captured motion will result in the desired effects. Computer animation projects have a wide range of requirements in terms of the minimum number of both sampling points and joints in the figure. It is not necessary that the hierarchical structures be identical, but when the hierarchies of real and virtual actors are structured in different ways, the resulting motion will not be a direct translation of the captured motion. In these cases, the resulting motions will be **filtered** and modified. (The special modeling requirements of computer animation that is based on motion capture techniques—including continuous skin-like surfaces and clothing—are described in Chapter 5.)

A few high-end motion capture systems can be purchased with all the components integrated, functioning, and ready to be used. This includes, for example, the computer having enough external ports to accept data input from many motion sensors. It also includes having a transmission rate that is fast and wide enough to be able to process data input from many motion sensors sampling at rates that are adequate. But when assembling low-cost motion control systems from parts that are purchased separately it is often necessary to keep several issues in mind in order to have a functional system. These issues are related to the placement of the motion sensors on the actors, the stage used to capture the motion, and the type of motion capture technology.

The **number of motion sensors** used in a full-body motion capture gear—a body suit—varies from 70 in a very high-performance custom system to a dozen sensors in lower-cost units. The exact **placement of the sensors** depends on many factors, such as the number of sensors available, the type of motion sensor technology being used, the type of motion that is being captured, the type of data—rotation angles or XYZ position—being sent to the computer animation program, and the type of motion constrains implemented in the computer animation software. Regardless of their number, motion sensors are attached to the body of the actor with adhesive or elastic materials, or a combination or both. Motion capture for facial animation is covered later in this chapter.

Figure 12.2.3 illustrates a minimum configuration with eleven sensors for motion capture. Two sensors are placed in the upper body: one on the forehead just below the hairline, and one in the center of the chest right on the sternum. The sensors in the limbs are placed one on the back of each forearm below the elbow or close to the wrist, one on the back of each hand, one in the front of each shin just above the ankles, and one on the top of each foot. A sensor in the lower back or pelvis just below the waist is used to determine the position and direction of the body with respect to the floor. In this configuration, several important joints are not covered so their motion has to be derived with inverse kinematics techniques. Much of the subtle motion of the torso and the neck is also lost due to the small number of sensors placed on the body of the actor.

Figure 12.2.4 illustrates the implementation of a motion capture

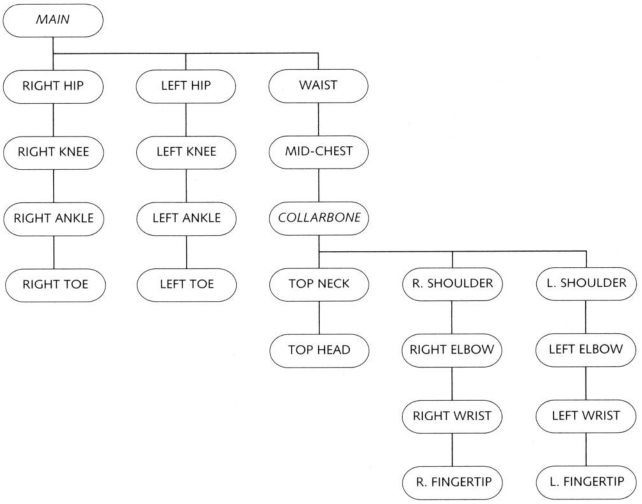

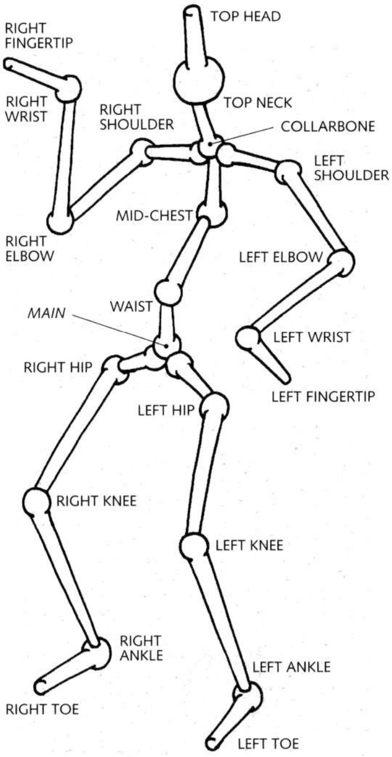

12.1.8 A simple articulated model and its corresponding hierarchical diagram.

system with 20 sensors. Compared to the previous configuration illustrated in 12.2.3, this one is able to capture a larger number of joint motions and also a greater degree of detail in the motion of the torso and the head. A motion capture configuration like this one assumes that much of the secondary motion will be added later on top of the initial motion capture. This configuration of motion sensors includes one sensor on the forehead, one on the chin, one on the back of the neck, one on the sides of each shoulder, one on the back of each forearm close to the elbow, one on the back of each hand, one on each side of the back, one on the sides of each hip, one in the lower back or pelvis, one on each knee, one in the front of each shin, and one on the top of each foot.

Real-Time Motion Capture Technologies

Several technologies are used for capturing motion in real time. Each of these technologies has advantages and disadvantages that make each more suitable for different applications of motion capture. Some of the factors that distinguish each technology from one another include their data accuracy, sampling rate, the freedom of motion they allow the live actors, the number of sampling points, the number of actors whose motions can be captured simultaneously. The number of sampling points were covered in the previous section. Useful sampling rates start at 30 samples per second or higher. When simple motions are being captured a small capture area can be adequate, but larger areas are preferred for capturing two or more actors interacting with each other. That way the motions do not have to be interrupted and the editing of motion is minimized. The basic technologies for motion capture include: prosthetic, acoustic, magnetic, and optical.

Prosthetic motion capture technologies provide accurate

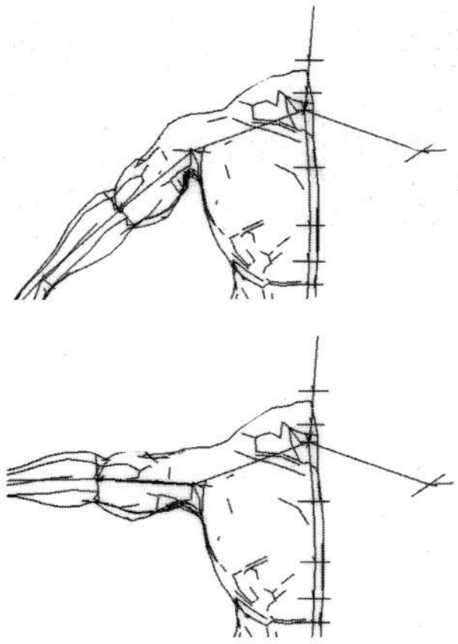

12.2.1 Two stages of the primary motion of an an arm, and the secondary motion of a shoulder. (Courtesy of Acclaim Entertainment, Inc., Advanced Technologies Group.)

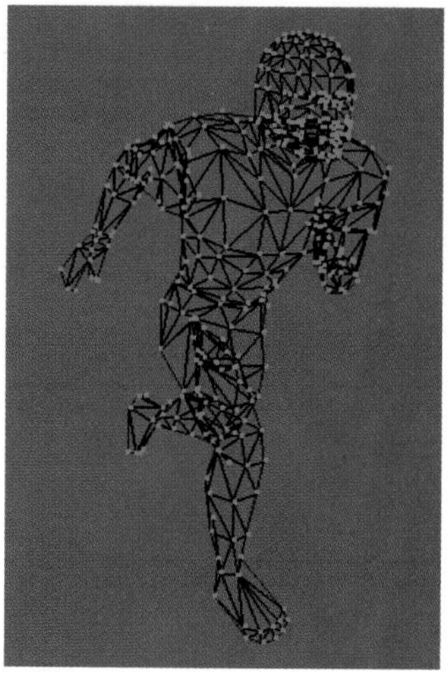

12.2.2 Characters from *Duel* animated with motion capture (top). Below is the polygonal mesh driven by the motion capture data in *Quarterback Club Team*™. (Courtesy of Acclaim Entertainment, Inc. All rights reserved.)

angular rotation data and are based on **potentiometers**, which are devices capable of measuring electromotive force based on the amount of energy that passes through the device as a result of the motion of a joint. However, a problem with prosthetic motion capture is that potentiometers are usually bulky and restrict the type of motion that can be performed by the individuals wearing them. Prosthetic motion capture technologies have been around for a long time and are still widely used in medical applications that measure or simulate the motion of patients with limited motion range.

Acoustic motion capture technologies are based on **transponders** that determine their position in space by sending radio signals from each sample point. **Magnetic motion capture** techniques are based on **receivers** that detect magnetic fields. Both acoustic and magnetic motion capture technologies require stages that do not create noise that may interfere with the data capture in any significant way. This may include, in the former case, hard polished surfaces around the stage that may generate an inordinate amount of echo. In the latter case, this may include metallic structures in the vicinity of the stage—including metal studs inside of walls and ceilings—that may create or bend magnetic fields. In the case of some motion capture systems based on magnetic technology, it is also necessary to construct a harness above the stage to hold the wires connecting the motion sensors to the computer system and to keep them out of the way of the motion of the actors.

Optical motion capture technologies use lights, cameras, and reflective dots to determine the position of the joints in three-dimensional space. Optical capture of motion is convenient because the actors are virtually free to perform any motion that they are capable of. Optical technologies have also excelled at the simultaneous motion capture of more than a single actor. Figure 12.2.5 illustrates a high performance optical system that employs between 50 and 70 sensors and several cameras. It is capable of capturing the motion of two actors simultaneously. An obvious problem with optical technologies for motion capture is the fact that some of the sampling points may be hidden intermittently by the motions of the actors, especially when two or more actors are being sampled at the same time. A common solution to this occlusion problem is to increase the number of cameras used to look at the sample points. This solution can provide detailed motion, but it also increases the complexity of the motion capture process.

Rotoscoping

Rotoscoping can be considered a form of time-delayed motion capture. Originally developed in the early days of cel animation to align hand-drawn cartoon characters to live action background plates, rotoscoping is still used today in visual effects and character animation. This technique can be used to capture motion that originated in reality by tracing, manually or automatically, still frames of a live action scene. The schematic information that results from this tracing is used to guide the placement and motion of three-dimensional animated figures (Fig. 13.3.1). In addition to its live action applications, rotoscoping is also used today for combining two-dimensional hand-drawn animated characters with three-dimensional backgrounds and sets (see Chapter 11 for more information on integration of 2D with 3D).

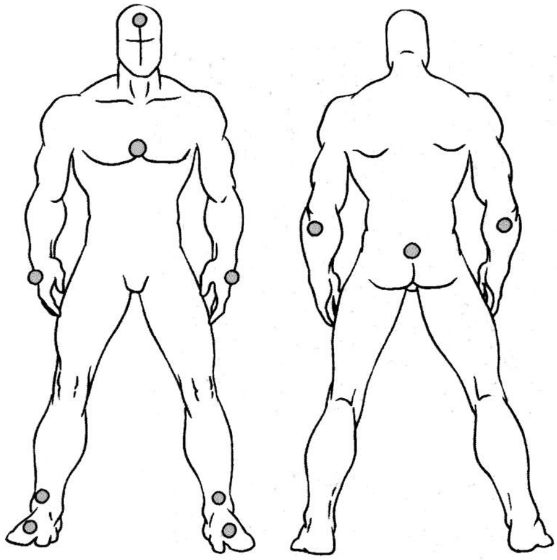

12.2.3 Motion capture system with eleven motion sensors.

Live Motion Control

In some applications related to live entertainment, the motion of live actors is both captured and applied to the animated characters in real time. In these cases, the motion is captured live, and the characters are animated and matted into live video in real time. In many of these instances, the animated characters are cartoons (Fig. 1.3.11). For that reason, the goal of the motion capture process is not to capture detailed and realistic motion but, instead, to capture theatrical motion that can bring a cartoon character alive (Figs. 12.2.6–12.2.8). In these cases, motion that looks too natural and not exaggerated is inappropriate because it often makes the cartoon character look stiff and spiritless. The motion that works best for most live cartoon characters is exaggerated and spirited. For this reason, it is common to have experienced puppeteers, actors, and dancers manipulate the input devices that generate the motion to be applied to the character. These professional performers are able to transmit emotion and expression through motions captured by a cold input peripheral. In situations where a sophisticated sensing system is lacking, it is common to have one or more individuals manipulating one or several input peripherals for controlling the motion of the character. These peripherals may include one for the lips, one for the XYZ displacement, one for joint rotations, and one for the camera position.

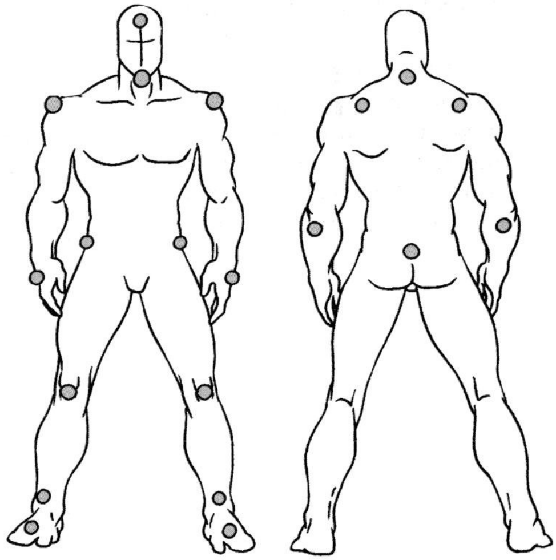

12.2.4 Motion capture system with twenty motion sensors.

Editing the Captured Motion

The result of the motion capture process is several tracks of motion that control different aspects of the animation. Each track is assigned to a channel, and usually each channel controls the motion of an object in the three-dimensional scene). The motion data in the channels are usually displayed by most computer animation software in the form of function curves (Fig. 12.2.9). Once all the data sets of captured motion are ported into their respective channels then the data can be attached to different joints. At that point it is possible to apply an inverse kinematics system to the skeleton.

But before the motion capture data can be used, all the anima-

12.2.5 Two actors wearing optical sensors for motion capture, engaged in a simultaneous two-person capture. (Courtesy of Acclaim Entertainment, Inc., Advanced Technologies Group.)

tion trees have to be clearly structured so that the motion subtleties in the form of multiple XYZ rotations will not be applied to the wrong joint. Blending several channels of motion requires using high-end tools so that the existing information is not wiped out. Several channels of motion are used to layer motions such as lip-syncing, hand motions, and rule-based facial expressions.

Channel Animation

Channel animation allows the collection or capture of all kinds of information in real time through a variety of input peripherals that are attached to a computer. The motion capture animation techniques covered earlier in this chapter are some of the most popular forms of channel animation. The data contained in the channels can also be used to control other aspects of the animation, such as the intensity of a light source, the density of a texture, the force of gravity, or the speed of a motion. The sets of data brought into the system are assigned to one or several **channels** in the **animation score** and used to drive the aspects of the animation controlled by those channels. For ease of work, the captured data is displayed in the form of **function curves**. The result of the live motion capture process, for example, is presented by most computer animation software in the form of function curves that control different aspects of the animation (Fig. 12.2.9).

In principle, all kinds of input peripherals can be used to input time-based information to the animation software. This includes **peripheral input devices** such as a joystick, a microphone, a music keyboard, a trackball, or a variety of motion capture gear. In all cases, a **device driver** is necessary for the animation software to be able to communicate with the peripherals.

12.2.6 Two performers do a live animation of *Moxy*, the animated character shown in Fig. 1.4.5. One of them is in charge of creating the voice of the character, and the other creates the motion of the head and hands with a simple motion capture system. (Produced by Colossal Pictures in association with the Cartoon Network. © 1993 Cartoon Network, Inc. All rights reserved. Courtesy of Colossal Pictures.)

The basic process of channel animation starts by identifying the active input devices and assigning each of them to one or several channels based on the number of degrees of freedom that they have. The degrees of freedom of input peripherals are defined by the rotations and translation that the device is capable of. A joystick with one button, for example, has three degrees of freedom because it can move along two axes and the button can be clicked. Motion capture gear can generate dozens of channels depending on the number of position points—each with XYZ degrees of freedom—that the gear is built with, which usually ranges between 10 and 70. Once each degree of freedom in the device is assigned to a channel, the second stage of the channel animation process consists of assigning each channel to the motion of an object. Figure 12.2.11 shows a few dialog boxes to control the process of assigning and blending channels.

During the data capture process some computer animation systems allow animators to preview the effect of the captured data and the links between the channels and the elements on the animation. But if the number of live channels is too large then the display of the ani-

12.2.7 The Gollum character was animated with a combination of keyframe animation techniques and motion capture. (*The Lord of the Rings: The Two Towers* © MMII, New Line Productions, Inc.™ The Saul Zaentz Company d/b/a Tolkien Enterprises under license to New Line Productions, Inc. All rights reserved. Photo appears courtesy of New Line Productions, Inc.)

mation can overburden the computer and slow down the sampling rate of the capture process. For that reason, it is often more practical to capture the data in a blind mode, and to preview the resulting animation only after the live data capture is complete. Afterwards any changes can be made to the resulting motion by editing the function curves of each channel.

12.3 Motion Dynamics

Motion dynamics animation techniques generate realistic motion of objects by simulating their physical properties and the natural laws of physical motion. Motion dynamics techniques take into account the characteristics of an object, such as weight, mass, inertia, and flexibility, as well as external forces such as friction or gravity, and even collisions with other objects. Just like the other techniques covered throughout this chapter, motion dynamics can be combined with other advanced animation techniques such as inverse kinematics and simple keyframe animation.

A **dynamic simulation** calculates the motion of objects through time by providing the software with some of the physical properties of an object—mainly its mass—as well as some information about the forces applied to the object (Fig. 12.3.1). The **mass** of an object is

12.2.8 Motion capture data generated by dancers from American Ballet Theatre was applied to characters in *Barbie and the Nutckracker*. (BARBIE and associated trademarks and trade dress are owned by, and used with permission from, Mattel, Inc. © 2003 Mattel, Inc. All rights reserved.)

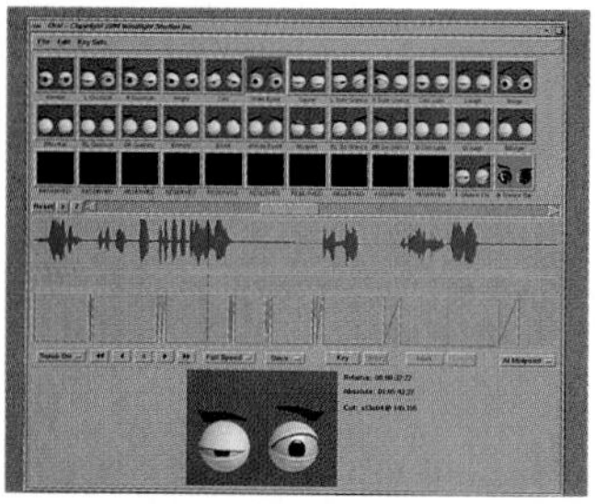

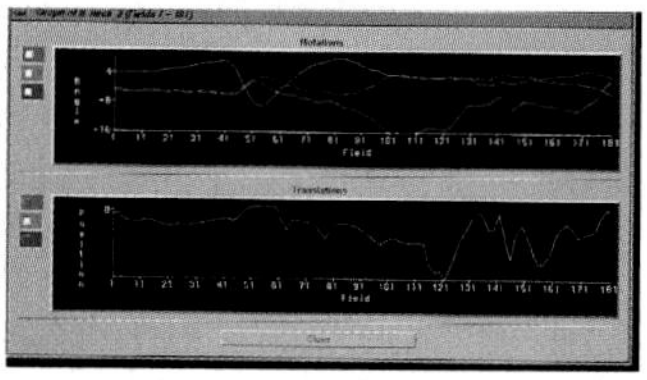

12.2.9 Eye-Sync and Soundwave software (top) were used to align the eye animation of a character in *Weldon Pond*, a pilot television program, to the voice soundtrack and waveform. This software allows animators to choose eye configurations from a library of key positions, assemble a motion sequence (red and blue lines), and playback a motion test in real time in synch with the soundtrack (green lines). A motion editor program (bottom) showing the rotation and translation data channels for one bone in an articulated skeleton. (Top: Courtesy of Acclaim Entertainment, Inc., Advanced Technologies Group. Bottom: Courtesy of CBS, Inc. and Windlight Studios.)

established by the product of the **volume** of the object and its **density** (mass = density × volume). Forces have a specific **strength** or **intensity**, and a **direction**. In simple terms, a dynamic simulation calculates the **acceleration** experienced by an object with a certain mass when a **force** is applied to it (force = mass × acceleration). The motion of objects is calculated by using the effects of acceleration on the object over distance and time to define the **velocity** and positions of the object through time.

Dynamic simulations are calculated based on a particular length of real time and then sampled at a specific rate of frames per second. Ideally, when the computer animation is recorded onto videotape, the dynamic simulation should be sampled at a minimum of 30 frames per second. Dynamic simulations are run by default on all of the elements that are present in the three-dimensional environment. Cameras and lights have to be turned off in the simulation so that they are not affected by it. Otherwise, the cameras can be moved by the simulated forces, and the moving lights can influence the final simulation.

Physical Properties of Objects

Mass is the physical property of an object that most influences a dynamic simulation. As mentioned earlier the mass of an object can be easily determined based on the volume and density of an object. The volume of three-dimensional objects can be automatically calculated

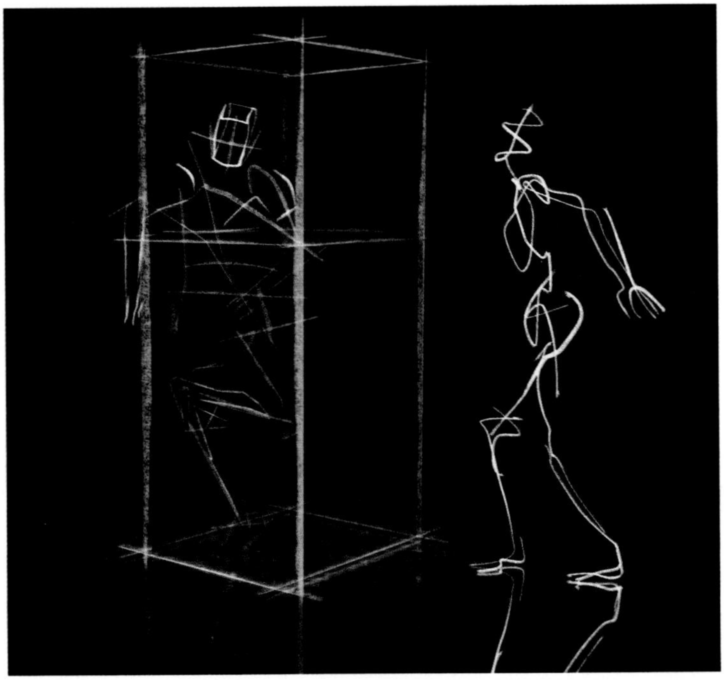

12.2.10 Still frame from a multimedia art installation in which motion captured human dancers represented as hand-drawn figures move in three-dimensional space. Short motions, or phrases, were performed, captured, and later augmented and placed within the virtual choreography as a whole. The positions of light-sensitive sensors attached to key points on the performer's body are recorded with optical cameras that record these points as coordinates in a three-dimensional data set. The motion capture data was manipulated with Character Studio, using its patented footstep-driven keyframe approach. (*Ghostcatching* © 1999 Bill T. Jones, Paul Kaiser, and Shelley Eshkar.)

by most computer animation programs, so the density of an object is often the only value that animators are required to provide in order for the software to calculate the mass of the object. Other characteristics of the object can also contribute to the realism of its motion. **Elasticity** and **stiffness**, for example, can be used to define the rigidity or flexibility of an object especially at the times of collisions (Fig. 12.3.2). **Rigid objects** do not bounce far from a collision, and their surfaces do not move much—if at all—after the collision. A solid ball made out of steel is an example of a rigid object that is extremely stiff and, as a result, does not deform when it hits most surfaces. But the steel ball bounces off the surface because it is somewhat elastic. **Flexible objects**, on the other hand, may bounce far away from the collision point. The surfaces of flexible objects also deform as a result of the collision and may keep moving moments after the collision took place. Objects made of hard rubber and gelatin, for example, well illustrate the range of flexibility based on characteristics of elasticity or stiffness. A solid ball made of **hard rubber**, for example, is a flexible object that is very elastic. As a result it bounces hard when it hits a surface, but it does not deform much because it is quite stiff. A solid sphere made out of **gelatin**, on the other hand, is not elastic at all. As a result it bounces little—or not at all—when it hits a surface, and it deforms greatly because it is not stiff at all.

The ability of flexible objects to absorb the impact of a collision by deforming their shape is usually controlled in dynamic simulations

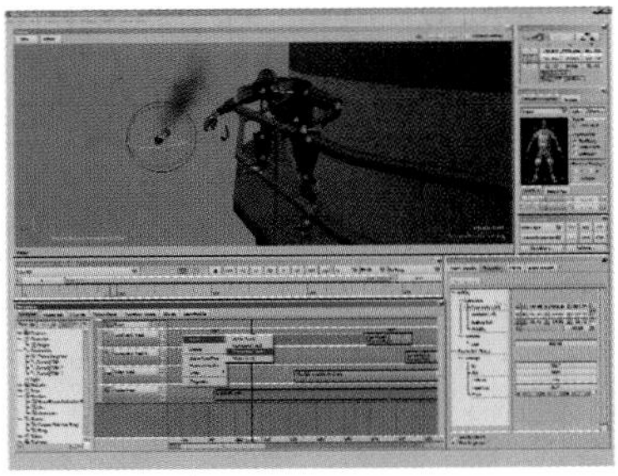

12.2.11a Animation can be derived from tracks containing constraints and commands. Two overlapping constraints that control the same character, for example, can be blended into new motion. (Motion Builder dialog box courtesy of Kaydara Inc.)

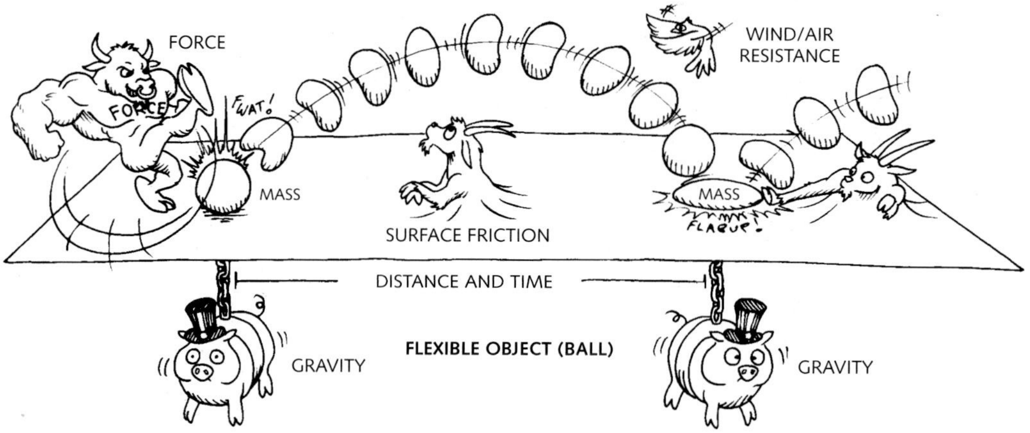

12.3.1 The dynamics simulation of flexible (ball, above) and rigid objects (anvil, opposite page) takes into account the mass of the objects and the forces that propel them, as well as the forces of gravity and friction, and the distance and time traveled by the object.

by applying the forces to a **flexible lattice** that controls the vertices in the object. With this technique the bending and deformation of the surface of an object is filtered by the way in which the lattice points control the vertices of the object. Some computer animation systems simulate stiffness with functions that simulate the effect of having **springs** between the vertices on the surface of the object. Springs have a natural rest position that they always return to after being stretched. Springs will move back and forth between the **stretched position** and the **rest position** until the initial balance is restored.

In some cases, the stiffness of rigid objects and the force of a collision are such that the real object is incapable of absorbing the force of impact and breaks or shatters. A dynamic simulation of an object breaking is much more complex than the simulation of objects that do not break because, in essence, the results of the collision would have to be applied to thousands of fragments instead of to just one object. In addition, issues of structural composition, brittleness, randomness, and chaos theory would have to be calculated to make the dynamics simulation as realistic as possible. In most productions—except those of a scientific nature—it would make more sense to fake the shattering of an object instead of simulating the motion dynamics of the event. One way to approximate the shattering of an object as a result of a collision consists of applying several forces to an object and approximate its values by trial and error until the resulting motion looks like it was the result of a dynamic simulation. This method, however, requires at least two models of the same object. One of the models is whole and is used until the collision takes place. The second model is shattered prior to the collision but all its parts are kept together, and it is used only after the collision. For example, an object can be thrown into a collision course with a specific linear force. But when the object reaches the collision point then the initial force is cancelled, the initial model is replaced with the shattered model, and one or several new point forces are applied to the second model in order to throw it away from the surface.

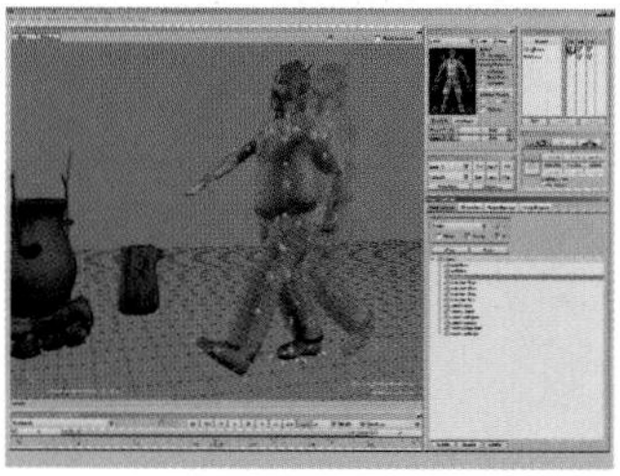

12.2.11b Motion-editing software like Motion Builder can be used to create a catalog of character poses by copying-and-pasting and matching poses from any track in the control rig. Poses are character independent and can be retargeted to any character. (Dialog box courtesy of Kaydara Inc.)

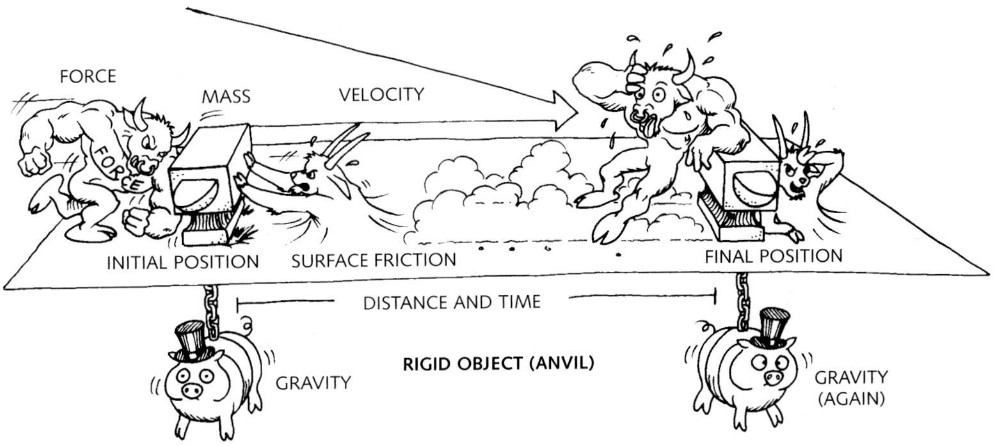

Types of Forces

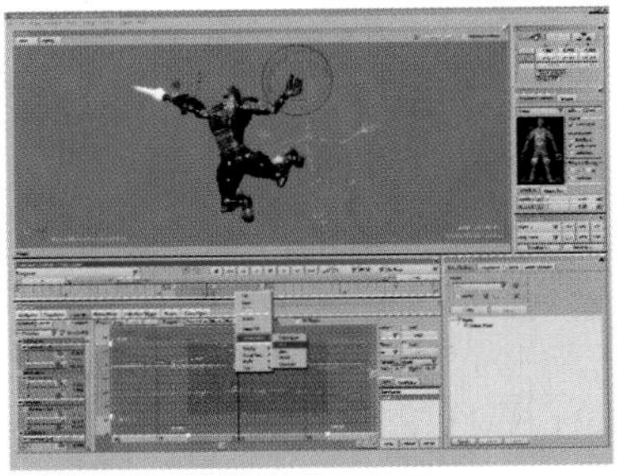

12.2.11c Some inverse kinematic controls allow to retarget motion from any source to any character. With control rigs one can animate over a motion source without altering the original animation, This provides animators with great control over the animation with minimal editing. (Motion Builder dialog box courtesy of Kaydara Inc.)

Many types of forces can be simulated with motion dynamics techniques. The basic forces include linear forces, point forces, and conical forces. These basic forces can be used in combination with one another to create more complex forces. A **linear force** is unidirectional; it has one intensity value, and is traditionally represented with a vector. Linear forces include the forces of wind and gravity, punching, or throwing. A **point force** or **radial force** travels like rays in all directions and is best illustrated with the forces released by a bomb that explodes in all directions. A **conical force** resembles a collection of linear forces that spreads out of a single point resembling the shape of a cone. When these forces impact a surface, they are strongest at the center of the impact area and weaker at the edges. The forces created by a fan, for example, are conical forces.

Simple forces can be combined with each other to produce variations of complex forces. Figure 1.2.8 illustrates the complex turbulent forces that are behind severe storms. In this case, the evolution of small clouds into giant storms was simulated with the aid of computer animation techniques. The simulation of the storm development can be a useful tool for understanding their behavior, and even to predict when a severe storm may appear based on the conditions that usually lead to the development of similar storms. The equations that are used to simulate storms or other time-dependent events can be solved first by specifying the initial values of wind velocity and direction, temperature, pressure, and moisture at selected locations within a specified three-dimensional rectangular region of the atmosphere. This region is often called the **simulation domain**. The changes in these values are then computed every few seconds over a time span of several hours. Due to the extremely large amount of data that is necessary to achieve a realistic simulation of this kind, it is not uncommon to perform the computations on a powerful computer system such as a supercomputer or a parallel processor.

12.3.2 (next page) During a collision flexible objects are elastic, but rigid objects do not bend much.

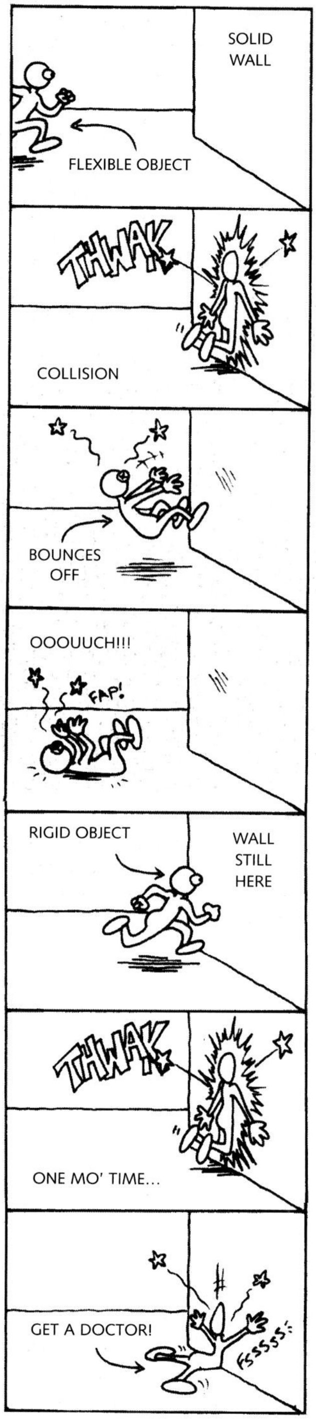

Performing the same type and number of calculations on one of today's microcomputers—or even a low-end super-microcomputer—could take several weeks and would be very impractical.

Forces can be applied locally or globally. **Local forces** affect only one object or one joint, while **global forces** affect all the objects in the three-dimensional environment. The force of the Earth's **gravity** is a good example of a global linear force. The force of one ball pushing just another ball on a billiard table is an example of a local force. Forces can also impact, attract, or resist objects. **Impacting forces** push objects away from the source of the force, like wind does. **Attracting forces** pull the objects in like magnets. **Resisting forces** offer resistance or opposition to objects moving through the three-dimensional environment. Examples of resisting forces that can slow motion down include friction and viscosity. **Friction** happens when one surface rubs against another. All spaces, unless they are a vacuum, have some amount of **viscosity** or **environmental density** that facilitates or impedes the motion of objects. In underwater scenes, for example, moving objects encounter more resistance from the density of water than they do from the density of air (Figs. 12.3.3 and 12.3.4).

The image shown in Figure 12.3.5 is a good example of a motion dynamics simulation created for a TV commercial. The animation of the car was created with a combination of techniques including the deformation of a flexible lattice that controls the vertices in the surface by applying wind forces to it. Each of the points on the lattice had a specific value of mass assigned to it, and they were all connected with simulated springs (Fig. 12.3.6).

The wind forces applied to the lattice were timed so that they would start at different points in time, and were focused on different areas of the lattice so that the motion would look as if driven by natural wind forces. The forces were applied in a variety of ways including linear, conical, and turbulent forces, all of which had intensity and directional parameters that were animated throughout the sequence. The forces had variable intensities so that they were strongest at the center and weaker at the edges.

The project pictured in Figures 12.3.5 and 12.3.6 is also a good example of a motion dynamics simulation that included **shortcuts in the simulation** to fit both the production deadlines and a limited budget. Early in the production process of this animation it was determined that it would not be possible to use collision detection techniques to keep the flying surface from colliding with the body of the car or from penetrating its space. This was due to both the number of points on the lattice and the number of forces applied to it. These conditions could translate into a situation that would exceed both the deadlines and budget allocated to the project. Instead, the simulated layer was kept away from the car by applying radial forces to it from below as if it were blowing in an upward direction. But the shortcuts used in this simulation were balanced by performing the

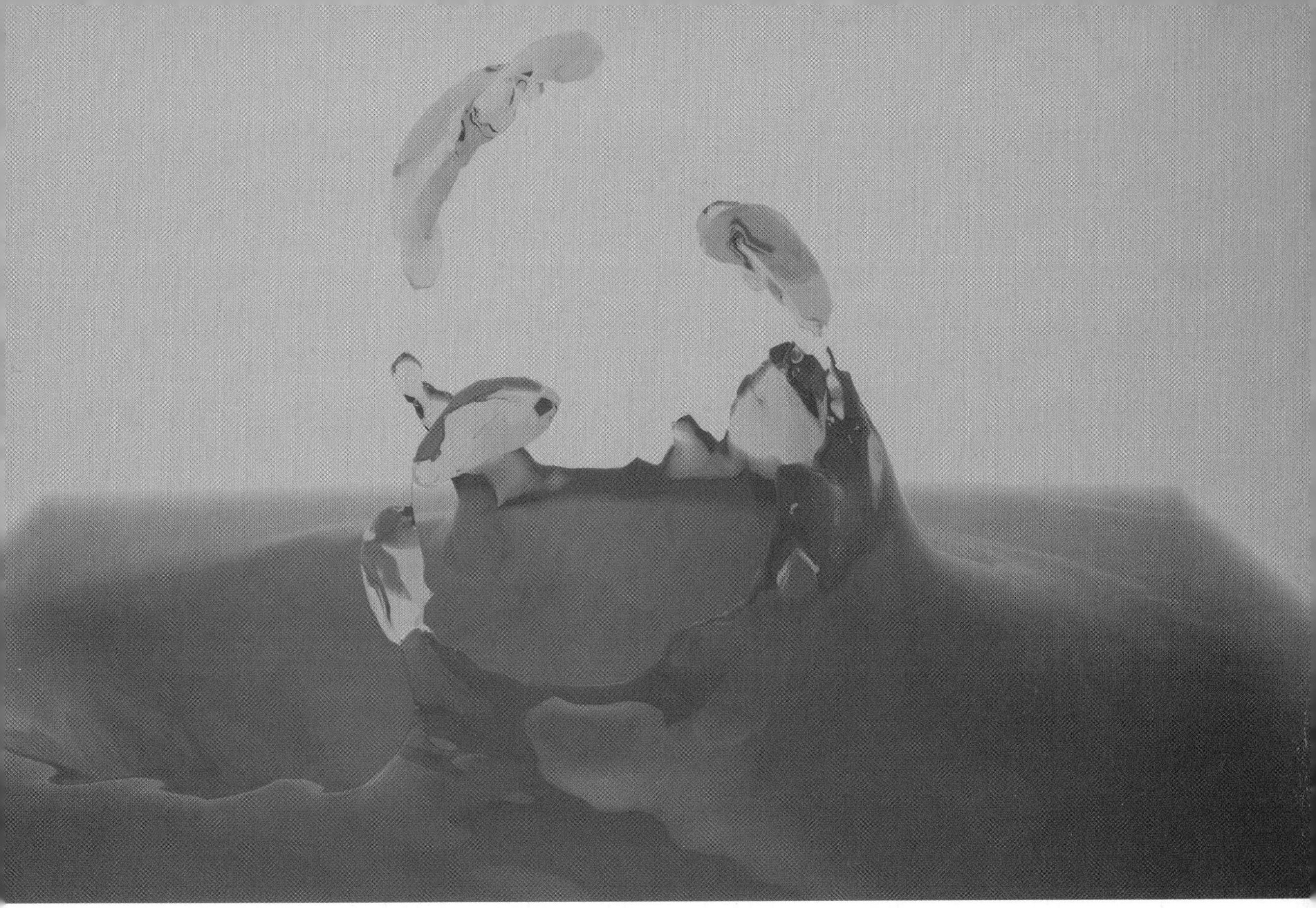

computation of the wind forces at intervals shorter than one frame. This was necessary due to the fact that in one cycle of this dynamics simulation the spring forces attached to each vertex on the mesh only affect the immediate neighboring vertices. For the forces to spread to several vertices and—as a result—for the cloth to ripple with detail it was necessary to simulate several cycles between frames so that the rendered images contained rippling that propagated throughout several vertices in the mesh. See Figures 1.2.9 and 5.5.11 for additional examples of cloth simulation with collision detection.

12.3.3 The water surface was modeled by simulating how a thrown object disturbs its shape. (Images courtesy of Areté Entertainment, Inc.)

Collision and Collision Detection

The motion that results from a collision can be calculated in a variety of ways. The simplest approach consists of aiming the collision forces at the center of the object, and assuming that the mass is distributed evenly throughout the object. Other approaches can be used to simulate richer and more realistic motion, but they are also much more time-consuming to calculate. One of these approaches starts by determining the accurate position of the **center of mass** of the object, as opposed to using the geometric center of the object as the

12.3.2 (opposite page) During a collision flexible objects are elastic, but rigid objects do not bend much.

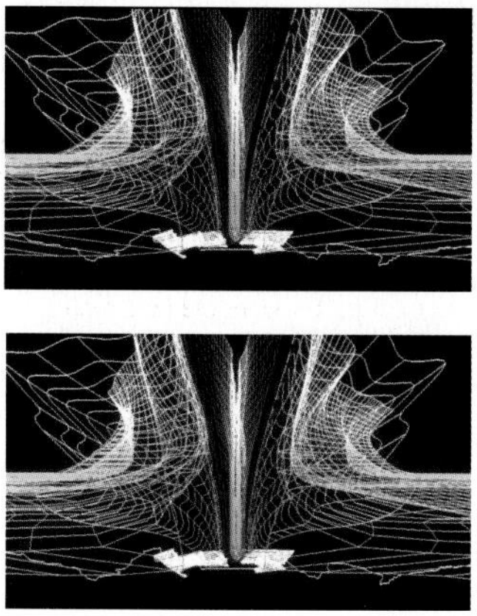

12.3.4 The walls of water were created with dynamics simulations and particle systems. (Photographs from the motion picture *Prince of Egypt*™ © 1998 DreamWorks L.L.C., reprinted with permission by DreamWorks Animation.)

center of mass. The **distribution of mass** is also calculated. Symmetric objects usually have a balanced distribution of mass, but irregular objects with an uneven distribution of mass such as meteorites tend to have unpredictable motion. When forces are applied to objects on parts other than the center of gravity they tend to produce motion that is not linear. These forces are call **torques** because the motion they produce is in the form of rotations or torsions with varying amounts of **rotational velocity** and acceleration, and changing orientations (Fig. 2.3.8).

One of the most interesting and useful applications of motion dynamics animation techniques consists of detecting collisions between the objects that are being animated. Real objects react naturally to a collision by deforming and changing the direction and speed of their motion, and even breaking. Simulated three-dimensional models, however, will naturally ignore other objects that penetrate their space unless collision detection techniques are used. Using **collision detection** techniques can add a lot of processing time and expense to a scene because they must constantly check the position and dynamic properties of objects in order to avoid overlapping objects. A simple, inexpensive alternative to collision detection for small animation projects that do not involve motion dynamics techniques consists of previewing the animation—in the form of a motion test, for example—and detecting the collisions visually. The correct positions of the overlapping objects can then be approximated manually, and the sequence can be previewed again with

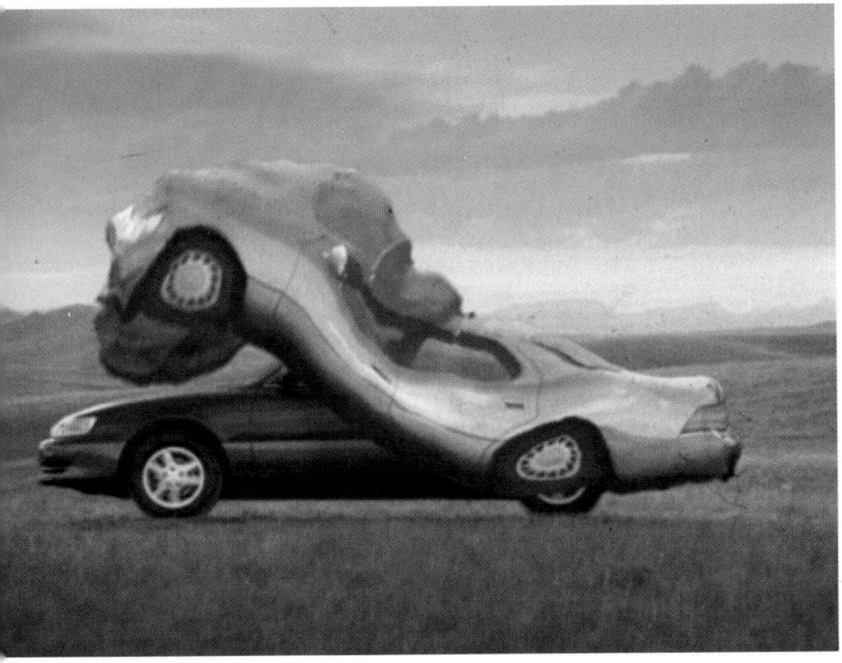

12.3.5 The main visual effect in this commercial project included the creation of a computer-generated surface that looks like a cloth covering the photographic image of a Lexus car. This surface is animated so that it ripples and flies away as if pushed by the wind. The image of an old car model was texture-mapped on the three-dimensional surface. The new car model is revealed after the computer-generated surface is lifted and flies away. (Animated by Mark Henne. Courtesy of Rhythm & Hues Studios.)

simple keyframe animation techniques. Some of the problems posed by visual detection of object collision include that it may require a lot of time in scenes with a multitude of objects.

Automatic collision detection is convenient because it frees the animator to do other tasks that are more important than detecting collisions visually. Automatic collision detection is also usually faster and more accurate than visual collision detection. There are many techniques for automatic collision detection, and a number of them are provided by turnkey commercial software. A common method for doing a first pass collision detection test consists of using rectangular or spherical **bounding volumes** or surfaces (Fig. 4.6.6). This method can save thousands of calculations by simply determining whether the boxes intersect at any point. If the bounding boxes intersect then a second stage collision detection test can be performed with the objects themselves to determine whether they intersect. A third stage collision detection test usually consists of checking the polygons of one of the intersecting objects against the polygons, or even edges, of the other intersecting object. In cases when the collision detection test is positive, then a response to the collision can be animated with motion dynamics techniques.

The approach for collision detection that relies on brute computing force consists of testing all the objects in the environment against each other. In an average computer animation production, this approach only makes sense when the motion in the scene is such that most of the objects are expected to bounce into each other.

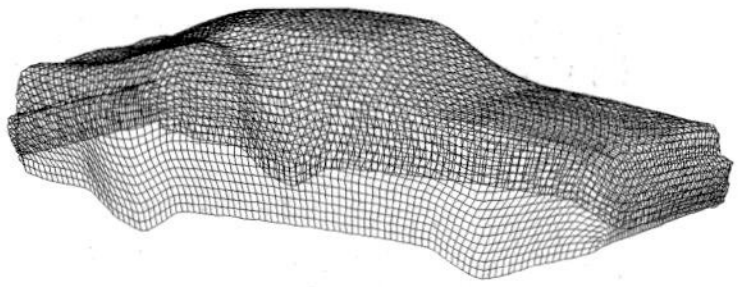

12.3.6 The resolution of the dynamic mesh used to model the Lexus car cover was a total of 6,000 points arranged in a grid of 60 columns by 100 rows. This high resolution was necessary to represent the detailed mapping of the surface required by the project. (Animated by Mark Henne. Courtesy of Rhythm & Hues Studios.)

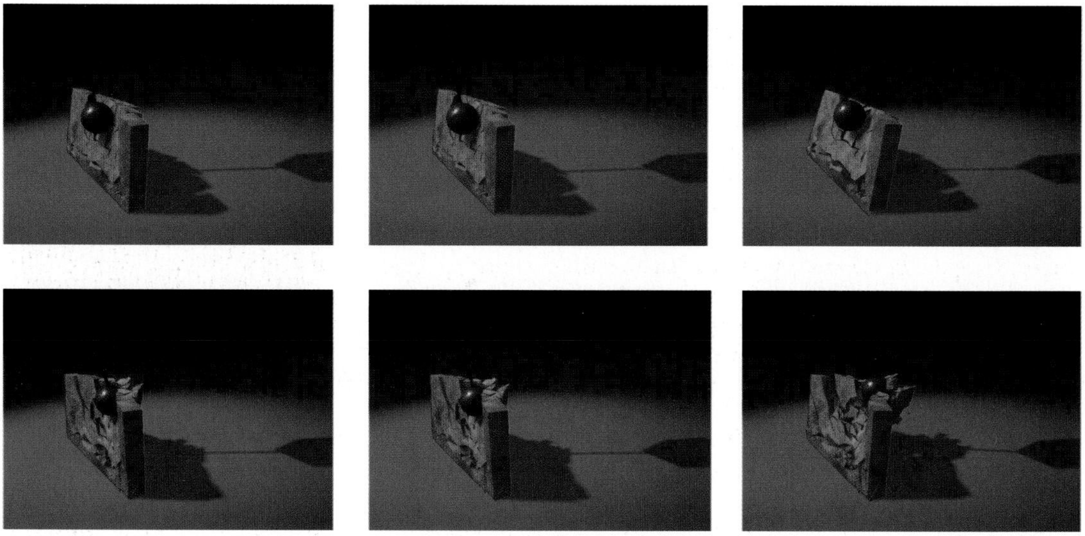

12.3.7 The animation of these adobe walls struck by wrecking balls is simulated with linear elastic fracture mechanics. The simulation determines where the cracks should start and in which direction they should propagate after analyzing the stress tensors that are computed over a finite element model. As the animation develops, the software remeshes the geometry to create the dynamic fractures. The wrecking ball in the bottom row has 50 times the mass of the ball on the top row. (Images courtesy of James F. O'Brien, W. Wooten, and J. Hodgins. © 1999, Georgia Institute of Technology.)

But a simpler and more economical method for collision detection can be implemented by identifying the **obstacles** that the moving object is likely to encounter along the **collision path**. Figure 12.3.7 shows colliding objects that break into smaller pieces based on a finite element analysis simulation.

12.4 Procedural Animation

Procedural or **rule-based motion** techniques animate the elements in the scene based on a set of procedures and rules that control motion. Rule-based animation has a wide range of applications that include the animation of natural phenomena, flying birds, growing plants, fantastic life forms, and humans dancing or gesturing. (See Chapter 5 for more information on modeling plants with procedural techniques.)

Particle Systems

One of the most popular forms of procedural animation is exemplified by the animation of particle systems. Animation with **particle systems** recreates the motion of particles that follow some generally defined motion. In the majority of computer animation programs, the particles themselves do not have a specific shape, but they can be used to control other objects or attributes. When particles are used to recreate the light of fireworks, for example, they represent a point of light with a variety of attributes such as intensity, flickering, and tail-tracking values (Fig. 5.5.6 and 12.4.1–12.4.2).

Particle systems are used to represent dynamic objects that have irregular and complex shapes, each with its own behavior. Particles have a life span during which they are created, behave a certain way, age, and die. Particles can also be used to control the motion of three-dimensional models—such as snow, water, or even a flock of birds—and to animate the growth process of plants by encoding their characteristics in a series of rules that can be used as the basis for a simulation (these methods are described in Chapter 5).

Flock Animation

There are many different strategies to generate flock animation. In most cases, the behavior of the birds in the flock is contained in a series of rules that constitute the computer model that simulates the flock animation. These rules control all the variables involved in the behavior of the flock. These rules include, for example, whether the flock has multiple leaders or a single leader and, if so, in which patterns does the rest of the flock follow the leader. Some of the basic variables provided by most computer software to control the motion of flock animation include the way in which the members of the flock move towards a target, how they avoid obstacles, and how they relate to other members in the flock as the flight conditions change throughout time.

Animating a flock of birds with rule-based techniques is a more practical alternative than using keyframe animation. Flocks can be simulated with particle systems so that each particle in the system represents a bird. Each bird in the flock moves according to the laws behind the physical simulation, its own perception of the environment formalized by the rules of the system, and by a series of parameters defined by the animator. The overall motion of a flock can be represented as the result of the behavior of each individual bird and the interactions between them. A common strategy to recreate the flying behavior of each bird is based on rules that simulate some of its perception and the action of flying. Once the model is expressed in terms of rules then several birds can be simulated and allowed to interact with each other.

A significant difference between particle systems and flock animation based on particle systems is that in flock animation the particles are replaced by three-dimensional models; they have orientation, and they also have more complex types of behavior.

The behavior of flocks is determined by the internal conditions of each bird in the flock, and also by the external conditions that affect the flight of each individual bird and the flock as a whole. Birds in the flock present many forms of behavior and goals. Common behaviors and goals of flocks include, for example, avoiding collisions with other birds in the flock or objects in the environment, matching the speed of nearby birds, and staying together. Each of these behaviors requires a specific acceleration and direction.

When the goals of dozens of birds are in play it is necessary to arbitrate all the individual requests. The flocking model used to create Figure 1.4.1 employs a variety of techniques to arbitrate indepen-

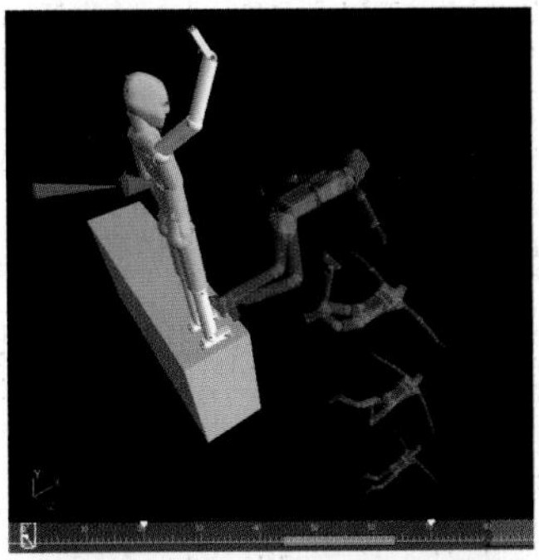

12.3.8 Complex human behaviors built in real time with endorphin physical simulation software. Animations can be imported into a variety of animation systems. Character stands waiting for his first interaction. A force represented by arrow is applied and secondary behaviors can also be specified, arms extended for example (top). After a quick punch to the head the character (bottom) recoils backwards, clutches at his back, impacts the ground as small secondary movements ripple through the body as the arm impacts on the ground, and finally relaxes into a "dead" behavior. (© 2003 Natural Motion.)

12.4.1 (next page) Simulation of a fireball for an effects escape sequence, also showing previsualization with proxy models and simplified rendering (Shrek™ and © 2001 DreamWorks L.L.C.)

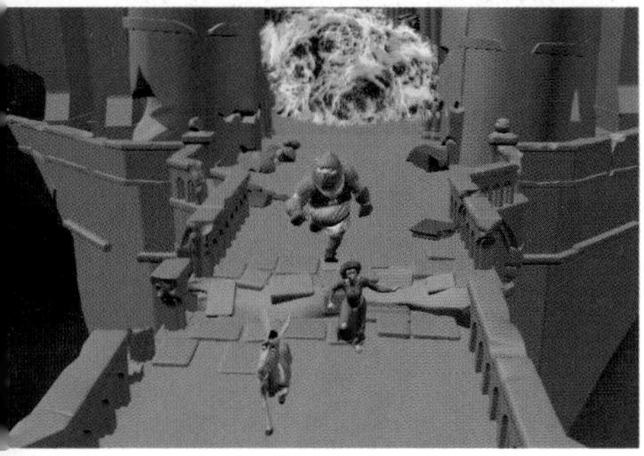

dent behaviors. These techniques are based on a prioritization of all the component behaviors and their acceleration requests. Depending on the situation different requests get a higher priority. For example, maintaining all the birds in the flock together can receive a low priority if the flock is about to collide with a large obstacle.

Computer animations of flocks can also be created with a combination of particle animation and keyframe animation. This is especially useful in cases when the computer animation software does not provide a full-fledged rule-based system. The flock animation in Fig. 1.4.1 was controlled mostly with simple parameters that are adjusted at the keyframes, but the relation between flock members cannot be specified in the form of rules. In that case the process started by creating a set number of particles that will represent the members of the flock as they move from a **source mesh** for particles to a **destination mesh**. The precise path of the motion can be controlled by the magnitude and direction of a simulated force of gravity, and also by the way in which the particles select the points (or vertices) on the source mesh to leave from and the points on the destination mesh to arrive to. The distribution of the particles on both meshes can be easily controlled by the shape of the meshes and by whether the source and destination meshes have the same shape and number of vertices. The distribution of particles can also be controlled with numerical values that randomize the mesh or by concentrating most flock members on a small group of vertices. The behavior of the flock as it moves from one point to another can be controlled in this example by numerical values that specify the amount of back-and-forth change, or jittering, in each of the geometric transformations, and the shape of the models being controlled by the particles. The shape of the three-dimensional model that is controlled by the moving particles can be specified in the form of one or several key shapes. Other approaches to flock animation are illustrated in Figures 12.4.3 and 12.6.1.

12.4.2 This detail of a still frame from *The Holy Bird* is based on the traditional dances of Okinawa as interpreted by artist Ryoichiro Debuchi. (Assistant designer: Atsuko Katakura. Hardware: IBM RISC/6000. Software: DDS, Feather, and Wavefront. Production: Digital Studio, Inc. Courtesy of Ryoichiro Debuchi.)

Goal-Oriented Animation

Some computer animation systems are capable of automatically choreographing the motion of an animated character based on a specific goal that has to be achieved. The animated characters in goal-oriented systems range from a simple robot arm or a fantastic creature to a more complex human-looking character. The goal for the character can be as simple as turning its head towards the light, or as complex as grabbing an object with the left hand, passing it to the right hand, and running out of the room while avoiding all the obstacles along the way. **Goal-oriented** computer animation is also often called **intention-based** or **automated** animation. Goal-oriented animation has its roots in the fields of robotics and expert systems, where computer systems are designed so that they can be as autonomous as possible, including the ability to plan different strategies to achieve a goal, evaluate the results, and continue to develop the strategies that were succesful while avoiding the strategies that lead to failure.

Goal-oriented animation techniques still belong by and large in research laboratories. Nevertheless their usefulness is slowly turning them into commercial products. The most important component of a goal-oriented animation system is the set of rules and procedures that allows a character to analyze and evaluate its environment and to determine the best way to achieve a goal, usually by reacting with motion, gestures, and manipulations of objects in the environment. Many goal-oriented animation systems also include an inverse kinematics module to deal with the position of jointed figures, and/or a motion dynamics module that deals with basic issues, including weights, forces, and collision detection.

Goal-based computer animation systems include the **codified procedures** that are necessary to analyze a goal, break it into tasks, evaluate the environment, predict and try to avoid potential obstacles, recover from mistakes, develop new strategies as a result of those experiences, and ultimately achieve the goal. Most existing goal-oriented computer animation systems specialize in a specific type of goal or a specific type of motion; otherwise their tasks would be too complex to implement. (When the complexity of goal-oriented animation approaches the complexity of human motion it is often more practical to record human motion itself directly on video or film.) Some goal-oriented systems, for example, specialize in simulating

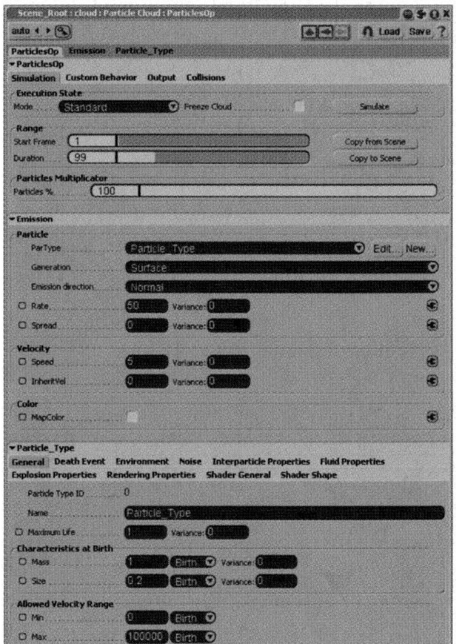

12.4.3 Parameters to control a flock animation. (Dialog box courtesy of Softimage Co.

12.4.4 These still frames from a goal-oriented animation (top left to bottom right) illustrate how the software can generate the motion paths necessary for a character to manipulate a pair of glasses with both hands. The motion of the arms is achieved with both inverse kinematics and a sensorimotor model based on neurophysiological studies. (Images from "Planning Motions with Intentions" by Yoshihito Koga, et al., SIGGRAPH '94 Conference Proceedings. Courtesy of Yoshihito Koga, Stanford University.)

human gaits and other forms of multilegged locomotion. Others can animate hands grasping and manipulating objects, or even body gestures and facial expressions.

One of the main tasks of goal-oriented animation system consists of determining what sequences and paths of motions are necessary to achieve a certain goal. Finding an optimal motion path that will allow the goal to be completed involves testing for collision detection, angles of motion, and grasp ability of limbs. Establishing a **sequence of motions** involves determining how many steps are necessary to complete a motion and what is the optimal order of execution. Simple goals that involve motion usually translate into simple motion paths and simple motion sequences. But as the goal increases in complexity so do the paths and sequences of motions necessary to complete the goal.

One of the biggest challenges of goal-oriented computer animation is to deal effectively with complex sequences of motions, both in terms of being able to complete the tasks and achieve the goal, and also in terms of producing natural motion when human figures are animated. For this reason, most are based on some sort of **motion planner**. The systems that animate characters that grasp and manipulate objects use a **manipulation planner**. In addition, goal-oriented systems include kinematics or dynamics techniques for calculating motion. The manipulation planner used to create the sequence of images in Figure 12.4.4, for example, defines paths in terms of transit paths and transfer paths. In this case, the goal for the animated figure consisted of reaching for the glasses and wearing them. The task of the animator is limited to selecting the object that has to be moved and the location where the object has to be repositioned. The motion planner of this goal-based animation system determines that the character has to use both hands in order to complete the action. Not too many individuals can grab a pair of lenses and put them on with just one hand. The **transit paths** define the motions of the character without the objects being manipulated, for example, getting the arm to a position from which it can reach the object. The **transfer paths** define arm motions that also move the object. Transfer tasks are generated by analyzing and planning the motion of the object from its initial position through the completion of the goal. During the calculation of the path the manipulation planner identifies all the possible ways of grasping the object and the configurations of the object requiring a grasp or regrasp.

The majority of motion planners have a simplified set of rules that specify how motion takes place in general, and which motions are allowed in particular. The animation system illustrated in Figure 12.4.4, for example, allows only the arms of the animated character to touch the objects in the environment that are to be grasped. Objects in the environment that are obstacles can only be touched for the purpose of achieving static stability. In the interest of efficiency, most goal-oriented systems limit the number of possible motions and grasps, or types of static and dynamic obstacles that are considered, or the number of possible solutions to situations when collisions occur.

A few goal-oriented animation systems attempt to automate the animation of human figures based on instructions given in plain English—or other human natural languages—as opposed to special-purpose animation languages. One example of such an approach is illustrated in Fiure 12.4.5. This animation system is able to automatically generate and animate conversations between human-looking figures. The conversations include motions such as facial expressions and arm gestures. The facial expressions are associated with motions of the head, eyes, and lips. The arm gestures include coordinated motions of the arms, wrists, and hands. The rules underlying this system are based on the relation between verbal and nonverbal communication. The combined meaning of speech, body language, and facial expressions can result in animated characters that are consistent, believable, and somewhat autonomous.

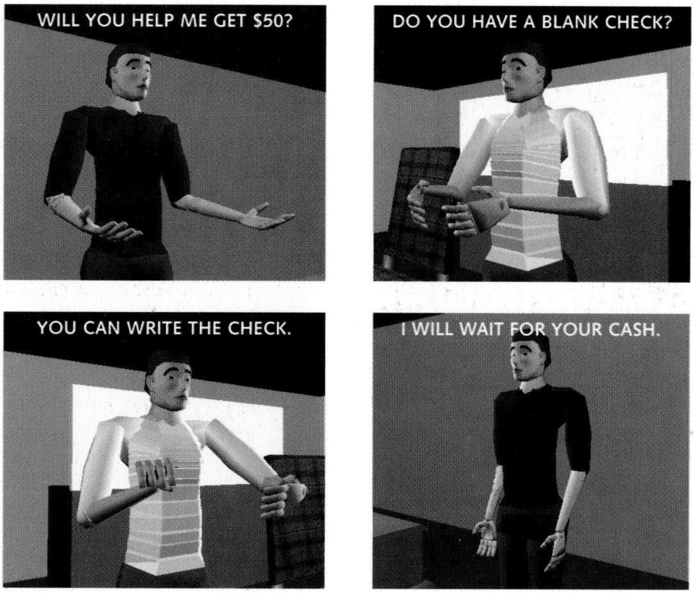

12.4.5 These four gestures were automatically generated by a goal-based animation system that creates a sequence of simple actions in response to a statement. First, a gesture requesting help accompanies the verbal request for money. Then an iconic gesture representing a rectangular check is generated from the words *blank check*. Later, a gesture representing writing on a piece of paper is generated from the mention of the action of writing a check. Finally, a motion of the hands up and down emphasizes the notion of waiting. (From "Animated Conversation: Rule-Based Generation of Facial Expression..." by J. Cassell et al., SIGGRAPH '94 Conference Proceedings. Courtesy of Dr. Justine Cassell.)

One of the most unique features of this rule-based animation system is that it is capable of accepting the text of the dialog within the context of a database that contains facts, goals, and beliefs of the animated characters about the world and about one another. The text of the dialog is preprocessed so that the linguistic and semantic aspects of a conversation can be interpreted by computer programs in charge of the speech synthesis, semantic analysis, and generation of gestures and facial expressions.

The rules of the program used to create the images in Figure 12.4.5 are based on a topology, or classification, of facial expressions and hand gestures that assign a meaning to a selection of gestures and expressions. It also establishes a semiotic relationship and a temporal synchronization between speech, gestures, and expressions. Much of the sequencing and coordination of actions is created with a computer model that activates transitions between actions based on conditions being met, or on rules of probability.

Within the computer animation program that was used to generate Figure 12.4.5 the **gesture motion** is specified with information about the location, type, timing, and handshape of individual gestures. The hand, wrist, and arm positions can be controlled independently. An interesting feature of this system allows users to control

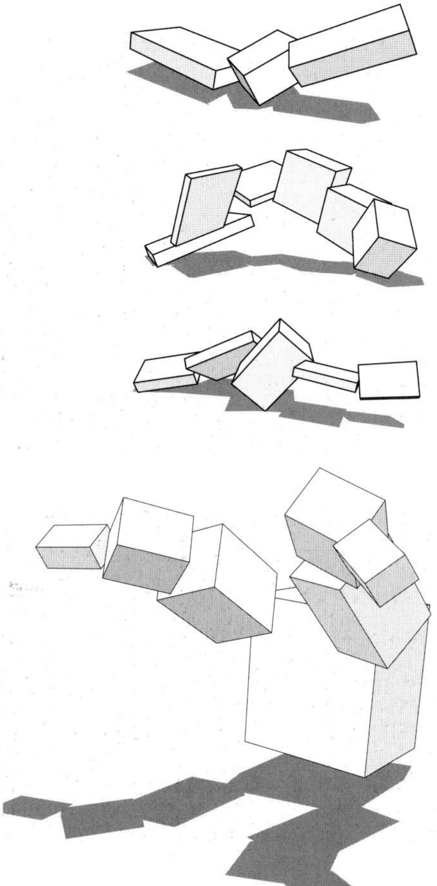

12.4.6 These simulated creatures were optimized over 100 generations for locomotion on land. Their motion techniques include shuffling, lumping, crawling, rocking, and hopping. (Images from "Evolving Virtual Creatures" by Karl Sims. Courtesy of Karl Sims, Thinking Machines Corporation.)

12.4.7 (above right) The virtual musical instruments in *Pipe Dream* were animated with procedural data generated in the MIDI format. (© 2002 ANIMUSIC.)

the expressiveness of the gesturing of a character by modifying the size of its **gesture space**, which is usually dependent on the virtual age group and culture of the animated characters. The facial expressions are generated both automatically when based on the intonation and phoneme—or spoken sounds—and by hand when they add meaning to the spoken discourse. Gazing, one action involved in facial expression, is controlled automatically based on the purpose of looking, for example, whether to look away to gain concentration or look at the other character to reinforce a point in the conversation.

In addition to simulating human-looking characters, it is also possible to simulate and animate artificial types of life with goal-oriented computer animation techniques. The three-dimensional creatures illustrated in Figures 12.4.6 and on page 370 (Key Terms) were created with a computer program that uses genetic algorithms to define the shape of the creatures and the processes by which their motion is controlled. These creatures are the result of a genetic evolution simulation that seeks to optimize a specific goal: their locomotion on water or land. This is achieved by running survival tests throughout 100 generations of approximately 300 members each. The survival tests consisted of a physical simulation where the creatures are tested for fitness based mostly on their speed and ability to control their speed and direction of motion. The fittest creatures within a generation are selected by the program for survival and reproduction.

The creatures in this example are able to sense contact with their own selves and with the environment, and can avoid obstacles. These creatures have a morphology that evolves from a simple control system that senses the environment, evaluates the situation, and reacts to it. The evolutionary process starts with a random generation of sets of nodes (body, limbs, and head) and the connections between them. A clear set of rules and procedures governs all the stages of this simulated world, including the initial assembly of the creatures, their behavior, their fitness evaluation, and their reproduction and optimization.

MIDI Output

Using music as the source for motion is another effective method for creating procedurally-driven animation. Unlike the digital recording of a specific sound or music, the **Musical Instrument Digital Interface** protocol, generally known as **MIDI**, contains information about how to play or interpret specific musical notes. MIDI contains information about the actual musical notes and keys, the length, the pressure, the instrument, and other parameters associated with musical interpretation. MIDI is commonly used to feed music synthetizers that execute the MIDI instructions in real time to create sound. Figure 12.4.7 shows an example of MIDI data used to procedurally drive the animation. In this case the MIDI data is processed with a proprietary software to generating sequences of motion for the given music. This software uses standard MIDI parameters like note, volume, pitch-bend, modulation, and sustain-pedal, to output position, rotation, scale, and light intensity information. The most interesting motions are obtained by using combinations of several algorithms to map the MIDI date to three-dimensional data. In the case of MIDImotion software, for example, the process is straightforward. Low notes can be mapped to large, slower-moving objects, while higher notes can be mapped to smaller, faster-moving objects. Drumstick motion can be derived by using a technique reminiscent of robotic motion planning. Additional motion such as ball trajectory and object impact can be calculated using basic physics. If the music is changed, the motion is automatically regenerated. Finally the generated parameter channels are used by commercial animation software via plug-in technology.

12.5 Facial Animation

The controls for facial animation have become very sophisticated because of an increased need for realistic animation. There are many techniques for animating **facial expressions**, including morphing between libraries of key poses, blend shapes, motion capture, motion dynamics simulations, and goal-oriented techniques. Facial animation is often generated with hybrid combinations of these techniques, and the relationship between the inner structure and the outer surface remains a key component in the success of the final result (Fig. 12.5.1). Facial animation is usually applied to the character after the body primary motion has been blocked out (Figs. 2.4.14 and 2.4.16).

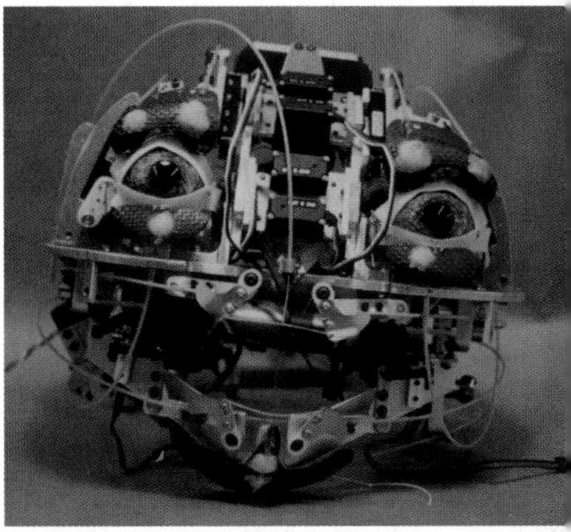

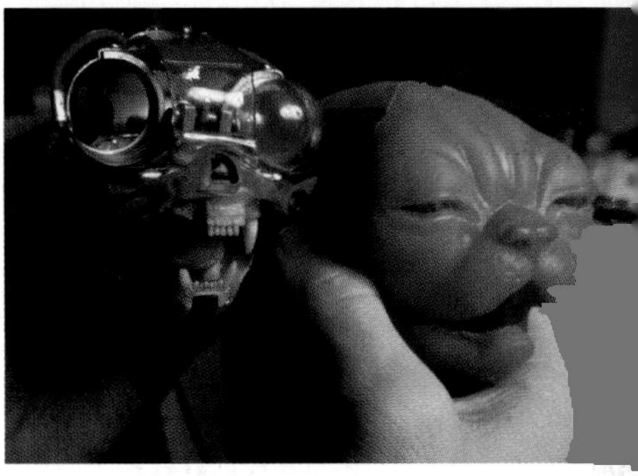

12.5.1 These two images illustrate the importance of animating the facial skin through the use of simulated bones, joints, and ligaments. On top, the mechanism of an animatronic cat's head built for a feature film appears alongside the skin that will eventually cover it. Below is a complex animatronic underskull for a feature film fantasy character. (Courtesy of Jim Henson's Creature Shop.)

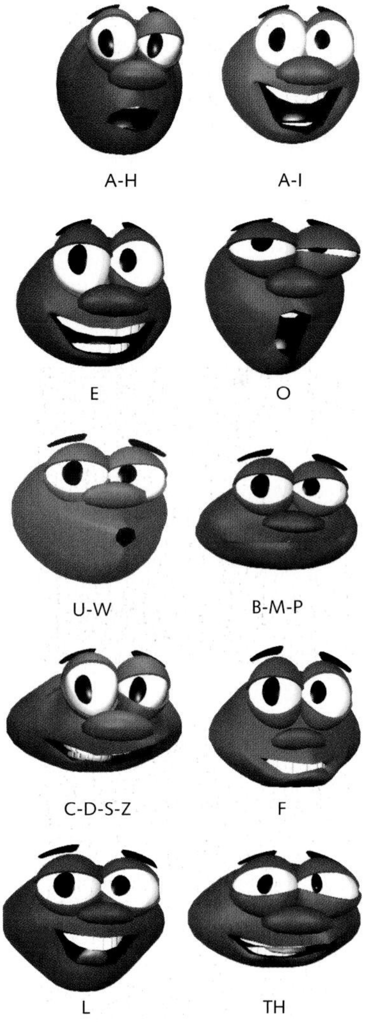

12.5.2 Basic phonems that can be used as target keyframes. (Sequence by Kevin Reagh, Horizons Animation (HA!). Image courtesy of the Horizons Companies.)

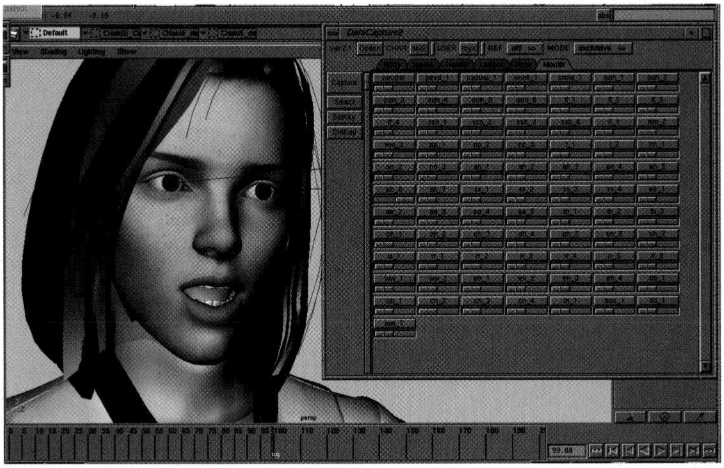

12.5.3 (top right) Lip configurations from a library of key positions can be synchronized to a graph representing the voice soundtrack of the main character in the animated movie *Final Fantasy: The Spirits Within.* (© 2001 FFFP.)

Facial Animation Tips

The facial animation of a character ends up being a big part of what audiences see on the screen. That is both because the dialogue lines that we hear are coming out of the character's mouth, and also because there is a wide range of non-verbal communication that can be achieved with facial expressions. When blocking out the animation of a face it is useful to start by animating the eyes because audiences usually look at the eyes first. A single null point usually controls the point of interest and direction in which the eyes look. It is also important to keep different timings for each of the different major components of a face, such as the eyebrows, lips, and nose; this approach often results in more engaging gestures and overlapping secondary motion. Controlling the jiggle of skin motion, especially in characters or creatures with skin that hangs, is also an effective way to convey secondary motion and a sense of mass. When synching the lips to the dialogue it is best to focus on animating the important intonations, which usually yields better results than overanimating the lip positions. The open mouth or the closed mouth positions are the most important shapes because they are the extremes that show emotion.

Morphing Targets and Phonems

Using targets and **morph interpolation** to keyframe specific emotions and using phonem shapes to do lip synch is a common way to do facial animation. One common side effect of using morph interpolation and blend shapes is that the resulting in-betweens become unpredictable. A **library of key expressions** is a simple and convenient way to store and retrieve many facial expressions. Libraries of key expressions are based on keyframing techniques and, therefore,

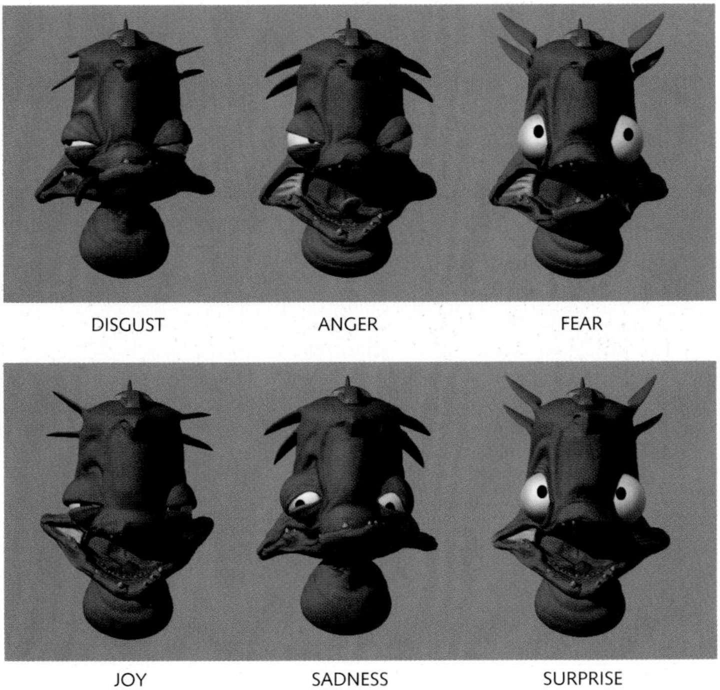

12.5.4 This character modeled with NURBS patches achieves his facial expressions with blend shapes.

require a fair amount of interactive work for placing the required expressions along the time line. Figure 12.5.2 shows a set of simplified **phonems** that can be used as morph targets. Figure 12.5.3 illustrates a library of lip key positions and an interface that allows animators to place those keyframes in the animation while viewing a graphic representation of the soundtrack. The **motion transitions** between facial expressions have to be checked for details in the interpolation that may look unnatural and, therefore, be distracting.

Blend Shapes

Blend shapes are used to create different expressions, or shapes, in a variety of ways. **Blend shapes** can be of sculpted by pulling vertices in the geometry, by using bones (Fig. 12.5.5), or by using **simulated muscles** that control both the way in which the skin moves and the facial expression (Fig. 12.5.6). In the latter implementation expression is achieved by tensing or relaxing the virtual muscles that control the skin position and then blend from one shape to another; the muscle forces are simulated with small virtual muscles that contract or relax (Fig. 12.5.4). This change is transmitted to a flexible lattice that represents facial skin. In order to simulate a realistic propagation of dynamic forces throughout the simulated skin, some animation systems employ a multilayer flexible lattice that permits an increased interaction of the spring forces (Figs. 12.5.6 and 12.5.7).

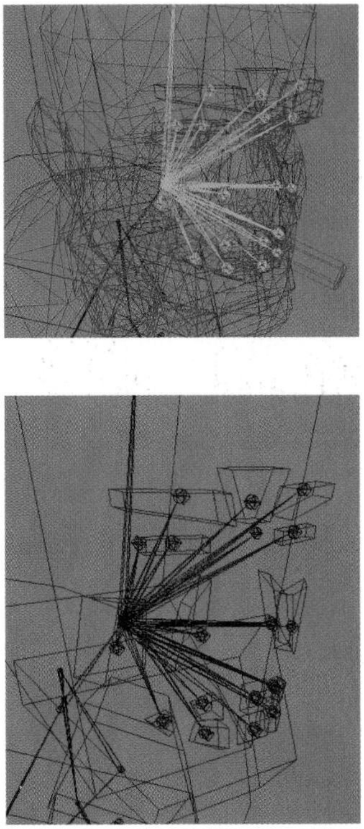

12.5.5 An example of bone-driven blend shapes. This facial animation rig for the *Medal of Honor* gunnery sergeant (with and without the polygonal skin) includes 21 bones: 8 for lips, 2 for nose, 4 for cheeks, 3 for eyebrows, and 4 for the eyes.

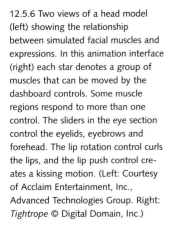

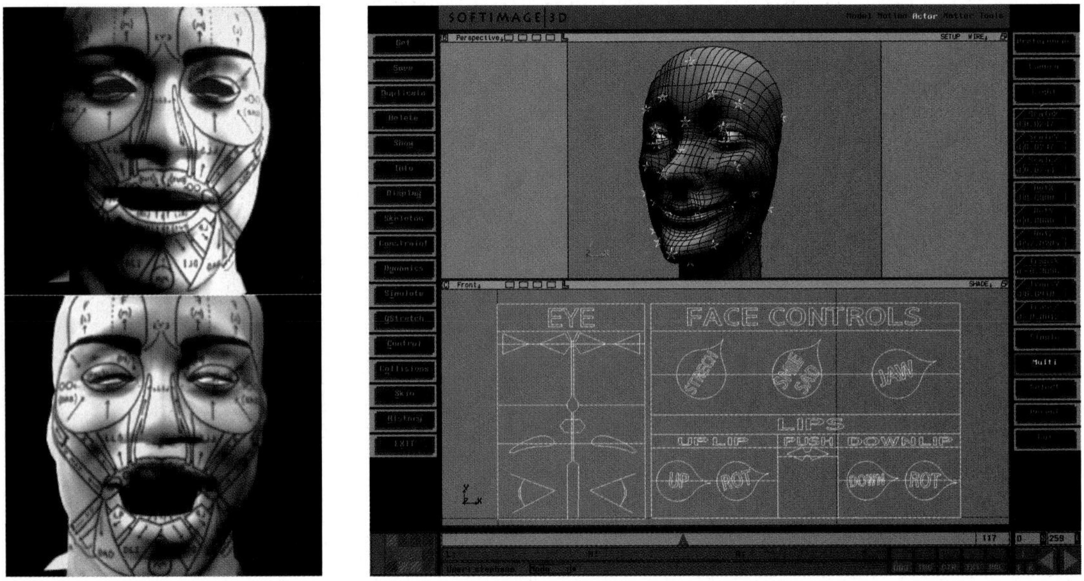

12.5.6 Two views of a head model (left) showing the relationship between simulated facial muscles and expressions. In this animation interface (right) each star denotes a group of muscles that can be moved by the dashboard controls. Some muscle regions respond to more than one control. The sliders in the eye section control the eyelids, eyebrows and forehead. The lip rotation control curls the lips, and the lip push control creates a kissing motion. (Left: Courtesy of Acclaim Entertainment, Inc., Advanced Technologies Group. Right: *Tightrope* © Digital Domain, Inc.)

Motion Capture and Dynamics Simulations

Facial motion capture data is usually obtained with a face tracker and markers on the face. The number and placement of sensors and markers in a **face tracker** varies from system to system. The model pictured in Fig. 9.3.3, for example, was captured with 80 markers and 45 control points in the Vicon system. Special contact lenses can be placed on the eyes to capture eyeball motion. It is very common to combine motion capture data with other facial animation techniques because often times the motion capture data is not sufficient to generate well defined expressions. Usually additional animation detail is built on top of the motion capture data. Figures 12.5.8–12.5.12 show different approaches to facial animation including motion capture and blend shapes (Fig. 12.5.8), and motion capture and biomecanical simulation techniques (Fig. 12.5.9).

The image shown in Figure 12.5.10 was created with a multitrack facial animation system that combines simulated muscles and key expressions—called snapshots in this system—that correspond to phonemes and emotions. The snapshots for phonemes consist of the lip positions that correspond to the emission of a particular sound. Both the emotion and the phoneme snapshots can be specified with intensity parameters that control the motion of different virtual muscles. For example, a specific facial expression could be defined as: raise_sup_lip 30%, lower_inf_lip 20%, open_jaw 15%.

The emotions can also be specified in a parametric fashion by defining the change, intensity, and duration of facial expressions over time. Some parameters of emotion that can be used to control virtual

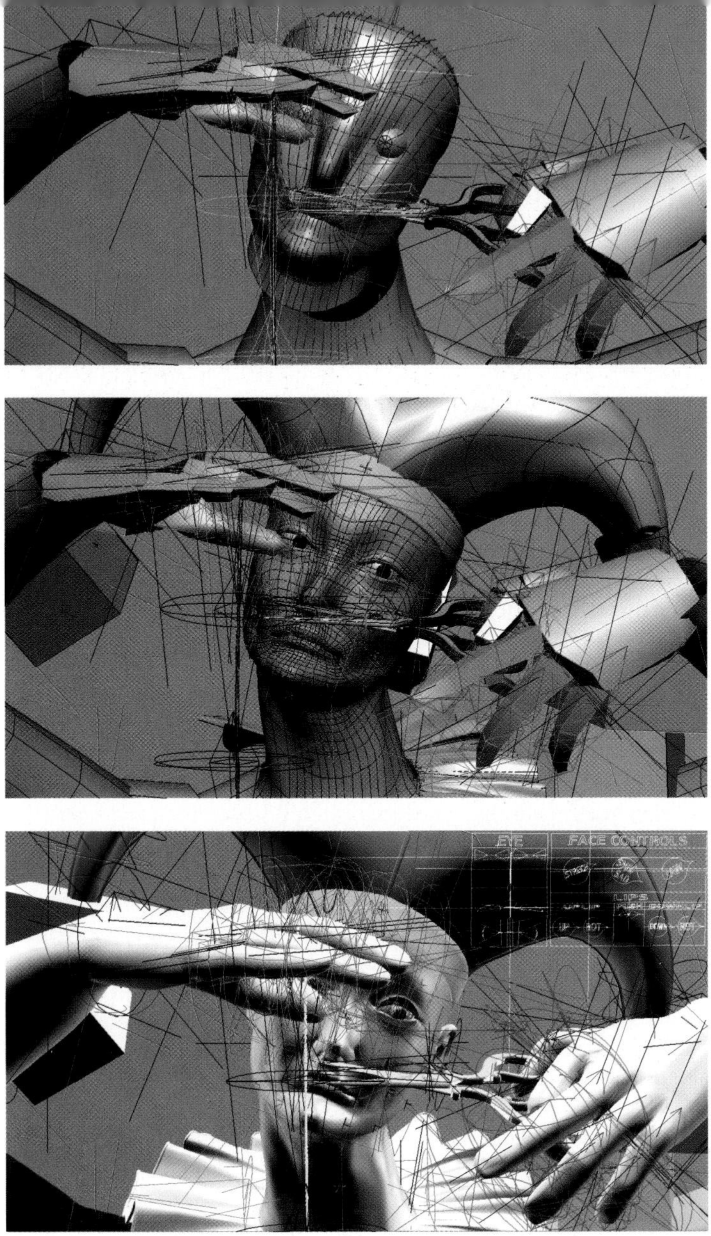

12.5.7 The blocking of the motion is done with proxy models, and it is rendered with hardware in real-time. This stage of the process is used solely to judge the performance of the character. The cyan wireframe diamond at the tip of the scissors represents the point of interest of the character. Each finger has null controls and effectors (top). After the body motion is in place, facial animation is done with the full geometry and the rest of the primary motion is fine tuned still with a more detailed proxy, then the secondary motion is added (middle). Using fast hardware rendering techniques the geometry is checked and the timing is refined (bottom). A detail of the final rendering is on page 269. (Director: Daniel Robichaud, Animation Supervisor: Stéphane Couture, Art Director: Michelle Deniaud. *Tightrope*, © Digital Domain, Inc.)

muscles include the length of time that it takes for the expression to start and to decay, its overall duration, and its transition to a relaxed state. Facial animation based on goal-oriented techniques is illustrated in Figure 12.4.5.

12.6 Crowd Animation

Crowds are like a large organism and, in that sense, virtual extras are not just moving props but living characters with personalities.

12.5.8 Two expressions of smiling and wonder created with a combination of motion capture and blend shapes. (Courtesy of Giant Studios.)

Crowds are also, in a way, like a single actor and, in that sense, they need to be directable. Ideally crowd animation systems combine several layers that give animators control over the actions of the entire crowd, groups within the crowd, and individual characters in the crowd. Some of the crowd animation techniques that are becoming standard tools include the ability to control the flow of moving crowds, do collision detection and avoidance, mix and match animation cycles from a library and blend between them, allow the crowd to interact with the main characters, define the eye lines, and be able to add keyframe animation to select characters on top of the library cycles. Some members of the crowd are seen only for a few seconds while others may be in the shot for several minutes—take, for example, the bar scene in *ANTZ*. For this reason the motions of the latter must be rich and interesting.

The techniques for animating computer-animated three-dimensional crowds were greatly refined during the late 1990s, starting with feature films like ***The Lion King*** and ***The Hunchback of Notre Dame,*** and continuing with films like ***Prince of Egypt***; ***A Bug's Life***, *ANTZ* and ***The Phantom Menace***. In *ANTZ*, for example, much of the action is defined by the crowds. There were about 720 crowd shots with average simulations of 2,000 ants, and the largest crowd at 80,000 ants. In many of the scenes the main two characters interact with the crowd. The two were keyframed by hand, and the rest of the ants were animated with the crowd simulation system (Figs. 2.4.14 and 2.4.16). In ***A Bug's Life*** there were over 430 crowd shots with about 600 distinct crowd characters, and about 2,300 snipets of actions in the animation library. Each of the crowd characters was named with a personality trait (shy, funny, aggressive). In ***Prince of Egypt*** there were four basic models for crowd characters plus several creations created with three-dimensional morphing. The groups animated with the crowd system included the slaves, the soldiers, and the locusts. Some shots had as few as 20 and others had several hundreds of thousands of characters (Fig. 12.6.3). All crowds in this animated film were rendered with a toon shader (short for non-realistic rendering).

In ***The Phantom Menace*** the battle scene between the droids and the Gungan army was created by assembling animation cycles from a library. Some of these cycles were created with motion capture and others with hand-drawn keyframe animation. The path for each creature was dictated by a particle simulator that animated a single particle for each type of creature, and then loaded the geometry and the appropriate animation cycles. Finally the software applied some generic rules, especially for the multiple physical interactions between creatures, and some customized roles. When each of the particles died so did the character that was controlled by it. The avoidance of the cavalry by the infantry was done with a collision detection system. The first episode of ***Star Wars*** had 110 shots with crowds, and an average of 95 frames per shot. There were about 140 animation cycles in the library, with most cycles being slightly under

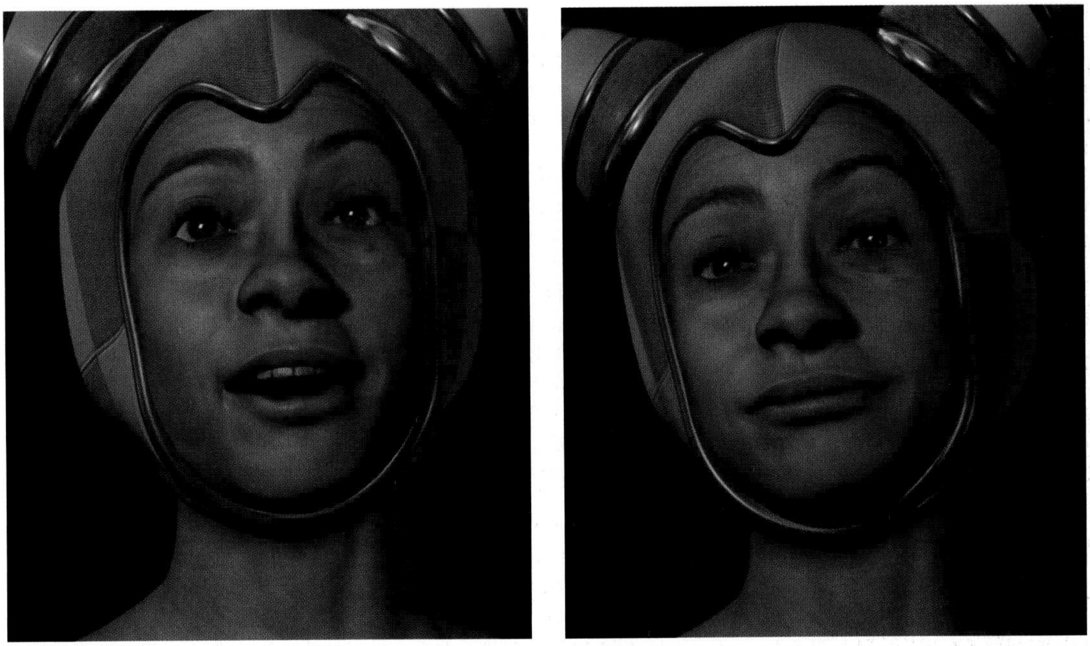

12.5.9 The facial expressions of this virtual actress were created with a combination of facial motion capture and biomedical simulations of muscles and tissue. (Images courtesy of Mark Sagar, Pacific Title Mirage, 1999.)

200 frames long. Figures 12.6.1 and 12.6.2 show two different approaches to crowd simulation software.

12.7 Location-Based and Interactive Entertainment

The entertainment industry has recently applied many computer animation techniques to areas that go beyond the confines of a traditional movie theater or a television set. Both motion rides and interactive games have unique creative and technical requirements that differentiate them from other applications of animation. **Location-based entertainment** is another name given to both motion rides and large—usually multiplayer—videogames that are bound to a specific location due to their size and equipment requirements (Figs. 12.7.1–12.7.3). The name of **virtual reality** is sometimes given to entertainment applications that are based on computer animations that try to simulate reality.

Motion Rides

Motion rides are a kind of movie rollercoaster where computer animations are shown in a theater constructed on a motion simulator. **Motion simulators** are platforms or bases that move—usually with pneumatic mechanisms—in response to a script of programmed motion. The motion of the platform is choreographed in conjunction with the motion of the camera in the computer animation. The size

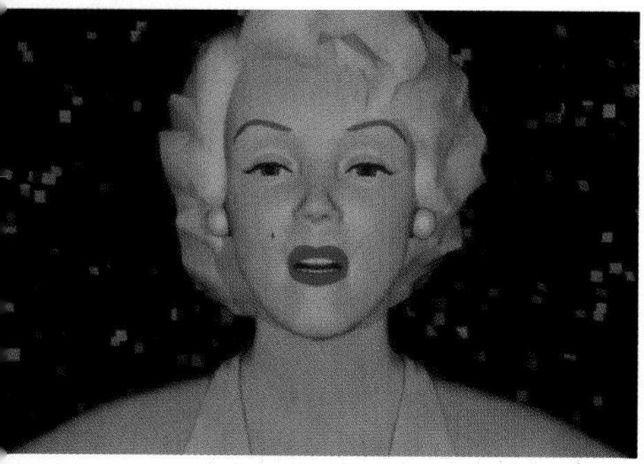

12.5.10 The facial animation of this surprised virtual Marilyn Monroe was generated using the SMILE system, which is a multilayer animation system with muscle deformation at the lower level and a high-level language to specify the emotions, the speech, and the eye motions. (© 1991 Nadia Magnenat Thalmann, MIRALab, University of Geneva, and Daniel Thalmann, Computer Graphics Lab, EPFL, Lausanne.)

12.5.11 Eve Solal, a virtual character animated with motion capture. (© 2002 Attitude Studio.)

of motion simulators varies, but on average they hold between ten and thirty seats. Motion rides can simulate the motion of the observer through space, or the motion of the environment around the observer, or both. Entertainment rides plunge viewers into fantasy worlds and they almost always take place in scenic theatrical environments. Rides usually explore realistic looking environments, but sometimes the environments are fantastic and have their own laws of physics. Typically the observer (the audience) rides a vehicle that can move at high speeds. This generates one of the most typical characteristics of motion rides—sudden changes of speed and direction.

The **entertainment value** of most motion rides is based on the story they tell, the synchronization of the motions of the simulated camera and environment, with those of the motion simulator, and the consistency of the motions and environments presented. Unlike computer animations that are meant to be ***watched***, motion rides are meant to be ***experienced***. Much of the effect of motion rides is based on the physical experience derived from fooling the sense of balance and orientation of the audience. This is done by simulating not only the moving images that the audience would see if they were moving, but also some of the physical sensations that they would feel if they were moving. For these reasons, the **synchronization of motions** between the motion simulator and the computer animation is essential for the success of a motion ride.

From the production point of view the synchronization of the motions is a process that requires a lot of trial and error, including the display or projection of wireframe motion tests of the computer animation while the motion of the base is fine tuned. The **field of view** and the **lines of sight** have to be carefully orchestrated so that the simulated and real motions are synchronized. An important issue to consider is the fact that the motion of the platform should be affected by both the motion of the simulated camera and some of the actions that take place in the simulated three-dimensional environment. The motion of the platform is mostly determined by camera-related issues like orientation and speed, but also by other motions, for example, an explosion or a giant monster trying to blow us away. The action in the three-dimensional environment is sometimes articulated in a simple way to the actions of the participants through the actions in the story line. For example, if the simulated spaceship that carries the audience shoots at a monster in the scene, the motion platform would move based on the recoiling motion of the ship as well as the turbulent forces generated by the monster as it tried to escape.

Another factor that is essential to the success of a motion ride is the **consistency of the motion** in the environments simulated on the motion platform. Consistency of motion implies that the platform will always move in a consistent and similar way in anticipation, or in reaction to the actions shown in the animation. In cases when the motion ride is based on the simulation of real motion, it is crucial that this realism of motion is always consistent. One inaccurate motion is

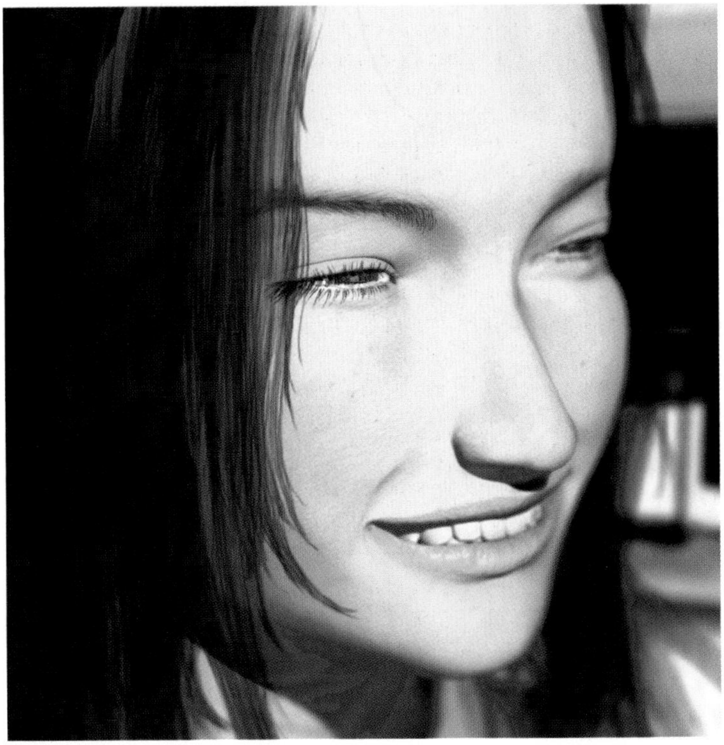

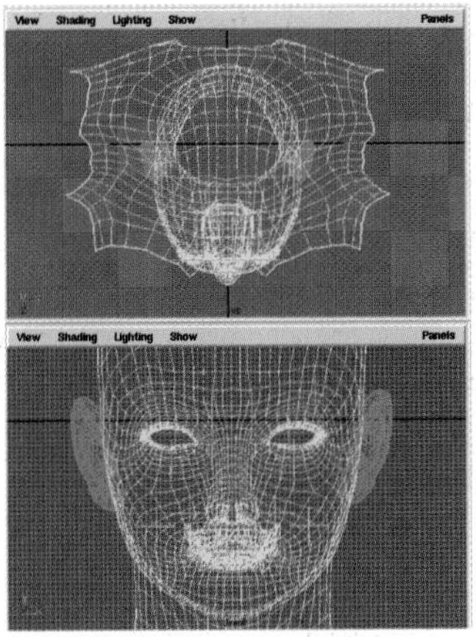

12.5.12 A single facial model may use facial motion capture data as a guide for deformation. Captured point data is converted to animation point data and mapped to the corresponding markers on the geometry.

enough to destroy the illusion of realism sought by so many motion rides. But consistent motion does not necessarily imply that the motion style will try to simulate real motion. A fantastic motion ride could have its own particular laws of physics or gravity forces for example, that are different from the natural laws of our reality. The audience can quickly adapt to any motion as long as it is consistent.

During the stage of preproduction it is important to design the animation based on the types of motions and effects that the motion simulator is capable of. It is useless to design a computer animation for a motion ride without taking into consideration the weaknesses and strengths of the motion base. The integration of computer animation and motion simulation technologies has to be seamless for motion rides to be effective. From this point of view the computer animations for motion rides are somewhat stylistically enslaved to the capabilities of motion simulation technology. Even platforms with six degrees of freedom (rotations and translations on XYZ) have motion limitations. A debate between creators of motion rides focuses on whether the images in a ride should be stylized versions of fantastic worlds or photorealistic simulations of our world. Most agree on one issue: Regardless of what the imagery looks like, the motion should be outstanding. This is especially important in cases when the renderings are simple.

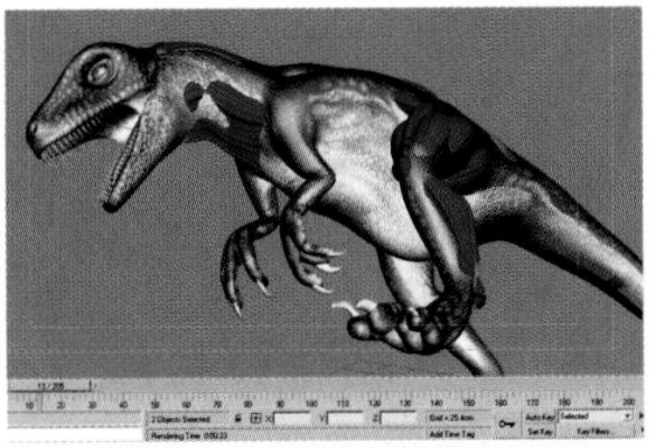

12.5.13 Ordinarily the skin of this dinosaur is displaced by the muscles underneath, but in this example the link between the muscles and the skin has been broken to show how the muscles flex and bulge while the skin remains undeformed. (Courtesy of Snoswell Design.)

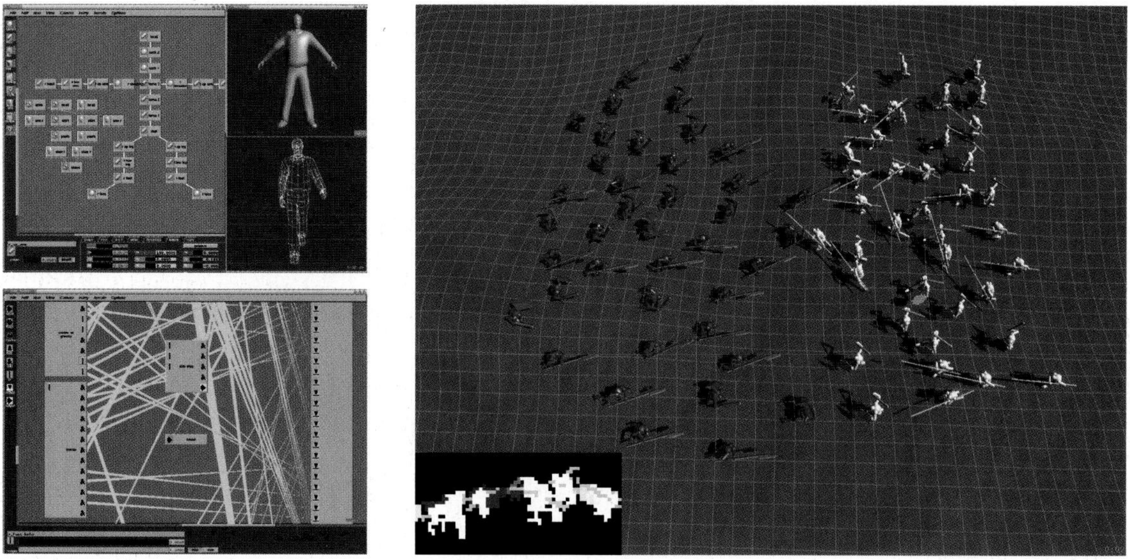

12.6.1 The Massive crowd animation software (above) used for *Lord of The Rings* uses agents with programmable physical attributes that rely on fuzzy logic to respond to the environment around them. The logic nodes used to power the simulation are interconnected with the graphical interface pictured above. A library of motion capture sequences are mapped to the agents' skeletons and invoked by the software as needed. Once the agents and their variations are finalized the crowd simulation begins on a battlefield (top right). (© 2002 Stephen Regelous.)

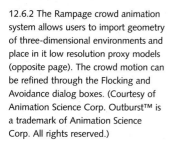

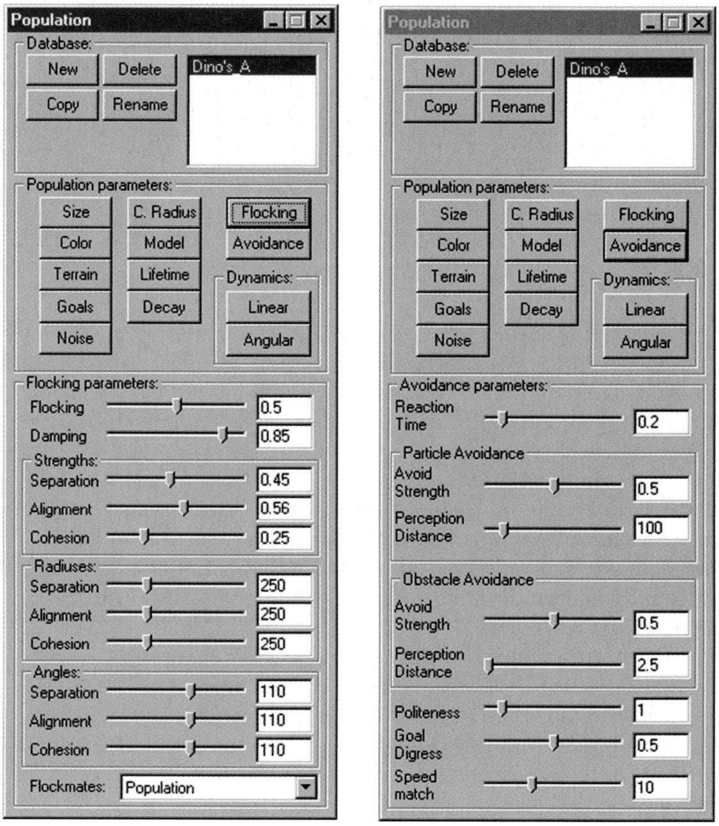

12.6.2 The Rampage crowd animation system allows users to import geometry of three-dimensional environments and place in it low resolution proxy models (opposite page). The crowd motion can be refined through the Flocking and Avoidance dialog boxes. (Courtesy of Animation Science Corp. Outburst™ is a trademark of Animation Science Corp. All rights reserved.)

12.6.3 This crowd scene was created from four basic character geometry models, plus several variations created with three-dimensional morphing. (Image from the motion picture *Prince of Egypt*™ © 1998 DreamWorks L.L.C., reprinted with permission by DreamWorks Animation.)

Production schedules for motion rides are usually longer than those of a computer animation intended for a traditional delivery format due to the additional task of synchronizing the motion of the animation to the motion of the platform and vice versa. This usually requires an animation design that takes into account what the motion base can do, and also the extended production times required to fine tune the motion of the platform to the animation motion tests back and forth until the desired effects are achieved.

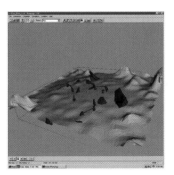

The film formats usually employed to record computer animations for motion rides require larger sizes and higher resolutions than other delivery formats. These formats include 70 mm film with five, eight, and fifteen perforations (also called 5, 8, and 15 perf). Both the size and resolution of the images have an impact on the computing and production times required to create animation for motion rides. Even though motion rides typically involve a fair amount of action most of them are, in essence, passive forms of entertainment from the point of view of **audience participation**. Most forms of location-based entertainment that include interactivity are in the form of games where the audience interacts with computer animations. But this interaction does not usually take place on motion simulators.

12.7.1 *Cosmic Pinball* is a four-minute motion simulator ride film that places the audience inside the game from the point of view of the pinball. (Produced for Showscan by Ben Stassen of Talent Factory, and animated by Jos Claesen and Toon Roebben of TRIX, both in Brussels, Belgium. Courtesy of Wavefront Technologies, Inc.)

12.7.2 In the *Loch Ness Expedition* game, eight vehicles—each carrying six participants—are connected to a computer that generates three-dimensional computer graphics in real time. (Game developed by Iwerks Entertainment and Evans & Sutherland. Courtesy of Evans & Sutherland Computer Corporation.)

12.7.3 (top right) *Osmose*, a real-time immersive virtual environment. (Copyright Char Davies/Softimage 1995–1999.)

Interactive Games

The functionality and image quality of today's interactive games continue to improve along with thechnological innovations. Popular technologies like the CD-ROM and the 24-bit color standard have redefined the meaning of state-of-the-art in the latest generation of interactive games, especially as it applies to three-dimensional computer animation. Interactive games are, in fact, so bound by technology that before dealing with creative issues it is imperative to understand the ways in which technology defines the creative boundaries in an interactive game. Early designs for an interactive game that do not consider the technical limitations of the delivery system result in wasted creative energy and costly production delays.

One of the critical aspects of many interactive games—especially action games—is the **response speed** of the game to the commands, actions, and requests of the user. This speed is determined by the processing speed of the hardware on which the game is played on, and it defines strategies for saving and displaying the three-dimensional computer animation that may be part of the game. Most **action-based games** for arcade use are delivered in self-contained kiosks with specialized hardware that is typically capable of very fast response speeds. The versions of arcade action games for home use are delivered in media that plugs into game platform systems or personal computers.

The interactive games that incorporate three-dimensional computer animation are generally based on one of two display strategies: playback of prerendered two-dimensional images, or real-time navigation and rendering of a three-dimensional scene. Playing back a sequence of prerendered two-dimensional images is common, for example, when the processing power of the system is limited, or

when exceptional savings in storage are derived from saving compressed two-dimensional files instead of a full-fledged three-dimensional database (Fig. 12.7.4). The latter can be rendered in real time as the player moves through the environment including realistic effects that approach cinematic quality, especially when a fast CPU and graphics processor are available.

As said earlier, when designing computer animation for interactive games it is of paramount importance to consider the playback limitations of the computer or game system. Action sequences that can be effective in the movie theatre environment invariably require a major amount of creative and technical work to be adapted to the medium and format of interactive games. Two of the issues that always come up in these adaptations include the modeling complexity of the three-dimensional scene and the color and image resolution of the rendered images. It is often the task of creative game designers and artists to find the best compromise between playing fun, aesthetic qualities, technological capabilities, response time, modeling complexity, and image resolution—a challenging task.

12.7.4 Cinematic sequence for the *Onimusha* game, awarded Best of Show at SIGGRAPH 2000. (© 2001 CAPCOM Co., Ltd. All rights reserved. Guest creator: Takeshi Kaneshiro. CGI by Links Digiworks. Composition © Mamoru Samuragoch. Character Samanosuke Akechi © Amuse/Fu Long Production.)

CHAPTER 12

Key Terms

Acceleration
Acoustic motion capture
Action-based games
Animation score
Attracting forces
Audience participation
Automated
Automatic collision detection
Basic tracks of motion
Blend shapes
Bounding volumes
Broken hierarchy
Center of mass
Chain root
Channel
Codified procedures
Collision detection
Collision path
Conical force
Consistency of the motion
Density
Destination mesh
Device driver
Dialog-based games
Direction
Distribution of mass
Dynamic simulation
Effector
End effector
Elasticity
Entertainment value
Environmental density
Face tracker
Facial expressions
Field of view
Filtered
Flexible lattice
Flexible objects
Force
Friction
Function curves
Gelatin
Gesture motion
Gesture space
Global forces
Goal-oriented
Gravity
Hard rubber
Hybrid environment
Impacting forces
Intensity
Intention-based
Inverse kinematics
Joint
Library of key expressions
Linear force
Lines of sight
Live control
Local forces
Location-based entertainment
Magnetic motion capture
Manipulation planner
Mass
MIDI
Morph interpolation
Motion capture
Motion constrains
Motion dynamics
Motion planner
Motion simulators
Motion transitions
Multiple layers of motion
Musical Instrument Digital Interface
Number of motion sensors
Obstacles
Optical motion capture
Particle systems
Peripheral input devices
Phonems
Placement of the sensors
Point force
Potentiometers
Procedural-based motion
Prosthetic motion capture
Radial force
Raw motion
Real actors
Receivers
Resisting forces
Response speed
Rest position
Rigid objects
Rotational velocity
Rotoscoping
Rule-based motion
Sampling points
Secondary motion
Sequence of motions
Shortcuts in the simulation
Simulated muscles
Simulation domain
Source mesh
Springs
Stiffness
Strength
Stretched position
Synchronization of motions
Torques
Transfer paths
Transit paths
Transponders
Velocity
Virtual actors
Virtual reality
Viscosity
Volume

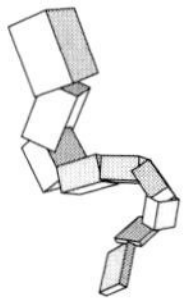

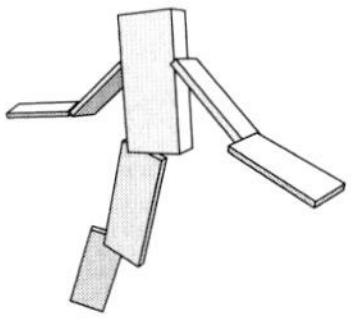

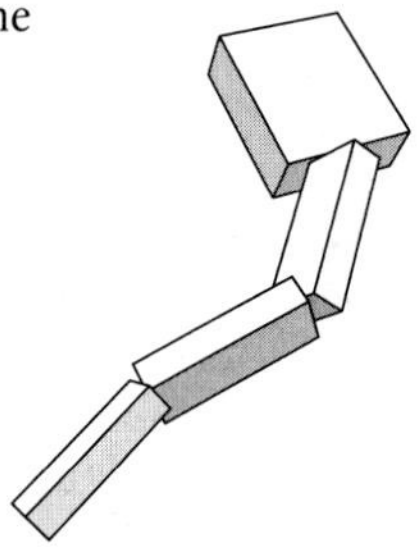

(Evolving virtual creatures by Karl Sims. Courtesy of Karl Sims, Thinking Machines Corporation.)

CHAPTER 13

13

Visual Effects Techniques

Summary

MOST VISUAL EFFECTS TODAY ARE CREATED with a combination of digital and traditional techniques. Often times the creative and production approach to creating visual effects for a live-action project is slightly different from a computer-generated character animation project, and some of those differences are discussed in this chapter. Most complex visual effects shots require the compositing techniques explained in Chapter 14 to integrate the multiple layers created with different effects techniques. Fortunately most of the digital and animation techniques required to create high-quality visual effects work can be implemented today with desktop computer systems.

QUICK INDEX

13.1 Basic Concepts of Digital Visual Effects

The process of creating visual effects for a movie, TV commercial, or music video starts well before the production of the final images. As mentioned in Chapter 2, preproduction and planning are essential in any project that involves computer animation, but this is particularly true in the production of visual effects for live-action projects. The increased need for planning is partly due to the increased number of processes and people involved in live-action: lighting the set, travelling to remote locations, changing weather, camera crews and live actors, to name a few. None of these factors affect the average character computer animation project. Visual effects preproduction must start early in the planning process. Because of the changing nature of the techniques and technologies used to create visual effects and the inherent requirement for constant innovation, two visual effects shows–including movies, TV programs, commercials, and music videos–are rarely alike (Fig. 13.1.1).

Generally speaking all visual effects fall into one of four major families of effects, but some specific techniques have crossover characteristics. Some effects are about *matching* the live-action source, for example, the camera matching technique. Others are about *combining*

13.1.1 How many visual effects techniques can you recognize in this shot from *Spy Kids?* (© 2002 Hybride. Images courtesy of Dimension Films.)

elements from multiple sources (compositing), *adding* or *deleting* elements, or *transforming* the source image (morphing).

The Core Visual Effects Team

13.1.2 The live-action footage shot in a blue screen stage (top) is used to previsualize the animation and layout of the shot, and to do a preliminary composite (opposite page). (Images courtesy of Framestore CFC and Bartle Bogle Hegarty.)

Depending on the complexity of the shots, the budget and the delivery schedule, the visual effects crew may range from half a dozen individuals to over one hundred. But there are a few key roles that, no matter how large or small the project might be, are always present in any visual effects team. The exact job titles for each one in the **visual effects core team** are sometimes different between companies but the roles performed are the same. The tasks in a big-budget production are divided among several individuals, while a single individual in a low-budget production might play a few of those roles. A visual effects, or **VFX**, artist or animator in a low-budget production might have limited resources available to get the job done. The same artist might also have flexibility to cross-over between different areas of expertise and participate in different aspects of the project. An artist in a big-budget show typically has more resources but also must focus on a single specialized task for the duration of the project. Often we fantasize about how wonderful it would be having the best of both worlds: the flexibility of a low-budget project with the plentiful resources of a big budget show.

Some of the key members in the core VFX team include a producer, a supervisor, and a few specialists. The **visual effects supervisor** is assigned with planning the overall production of visual effects and is also responsible for the final quality of each and every shot. This individual usually attends most of the preproduction meetings that involve visual effects. He or she supervises the group heads in the team, and interacts directly with the director and the

13.1.3 This still frame from aptly titled *Avenging Fist* illustrates a trend of low-cost and high-quality visual effects, and is also an example of the character extension technique. (© StarEast/Bob. Images courtesy of Menfond.)

cinematographer. In projects that involve multiple visual effects production companies a senior VFX supervisor makes the rounds reviewing work and providing feedback and direction. The **visual effects producer** is responsible for making sure that the crew has the necessary resources to get the job done within budget and that the team delivers the expected effects shots within the budget and deadline. This individual is also responsible for dealing with most of the legal and talent issues such as contracts, hiring negotiations, performance reviews, and space assignments. The VFX producer must constantly balance expenses and resources with complexity and quality, and frequently deals with rescheduling due to script revisions, production delays, and securing rendering resources. The **sequence supervisor**, the **computer animation supervisor**, the **compositing supervisor**, and other department supervisors are responsible for directly overseeing the work of the members in their respective areas. See Chapter 2 for additional descriptions of roles within small and large computer animation projects.

The Visual Effects Pipeline

Planning and creating visual effects follows a **production pipeline** with multiple steps, most of which are described in Chapter 2. Concepts and stories are developed during preproduction, usually with the aid of storyboards, animatics, and previsualization (Fig. 13.1.2). The final, or almost final, script is read by the VFX producer and supervisor who determine together the type of visual effects required. The shots with visual effects are "broken down," or analyzed into the specific techniques that should yield the desired result. Once the effects shots have been broken down the work is split into practical, or physical, and digital effects, and assigned to one or several production companies. Media delivery requirements are also locked down at this stage in the process.

PRELIMINARY COMPOSITE

13.2.1 Two-dimensional motion tracks created with boujou tracking software after analyzing several frames of live action moving clouds.(© 2002 2d3 Ltd.)

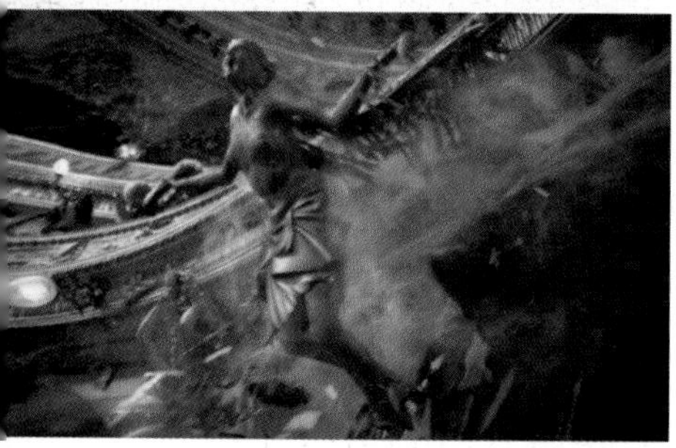

13.2.2a Inexplicable things happen during this *Nintendo's Game Boy Advance* commercial: one of the Caryatides sculptures that decorates the theater comes alive and the chandelier transforms itself into a dragon. The dragon chandelier was over a million polygons, and was modeled with scripts to generate 45,000 crystal pearls on NURBS surfaces that were deformed and animated around the main dragon skeleton.

Previsualization, or **previz**, and three-dimensional animatics are a crucial component of the VFX production process because they allow the director, cinematographer and VFX supervisor to conceptualize and refine a shot, and also to plan the actual shooting (Fig. 13.1.2). Most visual effects shots are the result of multiple VFX techniques used in combination. Consider, for example, the following effects **shot breakdown**: a live-action shot that involves a motorcycle stunt and pyrotechnic explosions shot in real time with a moving HD video camera against a blue screen. After converting the video into RGB image files the wires holding the stuntman are removed from the images. The digital frames are also tracked so that additional smoke trails can be added with computer-generated particles, and so that the set extensions can be matched to the live-action movie. This type of **effects salad** approach is common in effects movies, and is also increasingly used in well-organized low-budget productions that require sophisticated visual effects (Fig. 13.1.3).

With the exception of a few specialized visual effects techniques, such as camera tracking for example, the production of three-dimensional computer animation for visual effects is quite similar to the process followed for creating an all-computer animated movie. This process, described in detail in Chapter 2, includes the major stages of preproduction, modeling, rigging, animation, texturing, and rendering (Fig. 2.4.1). The need to **match reality**, and the dependence and key interaction with the live-action crew are two of the main differences between a character animated movie and a VFX movie. A top priority in a VFX movie is that the visual effects look real at all levels. A character animated movie may require exaggerated performances, squash and stretch for example, non-photorealistic rendering, and anatomically impossible poses (Fig. 10.5.11). But visual effects shots must fool the eye of moviegoers and make them believe that what they are seeing is real and not a manufactured moment. Other than that radical difference in creative philosophy and its practical implications the production pipelines of an all-animated movie and a movie with digital visual effects have some similarities. Nowhere is the interaction with the live-action material more evident than during the compositing process. While compositing is something of a convenience in an all-computer animated movie, it functions as a fundamental condition in the production of a VFX live-action movie. Compositing is used throughout the process: first to deliver temporary animatics or placeholder effects, called **temps**, later to incorporate changes and revisions, and finally to deliver the completed shot. As explained in Chapter 2, workflows are constantly fine-tuned and adapted to the needs of the project. Reviews of completed work and making revisions and changes are integral aspects of the VFX pipeline.

On the Set

Visual effects supervisors spend a considerable amount of time on the set, in the film laboratory, and at the postproduction facility.

Much of what ends up in a VFX shot starts on the set where the **cinematographer** and his/her team record the live-action material. They light the scene, measure the light and establish the recording parameters. The main task of the visual effects supervisor on the live set consists of making sure that the capture of data, images included, is done taking into account the needs of the VFX production process. Large movie productions may have multiple units of photography and one of them, usually the **second unit of photography**, is in charge or recording the live-action **background plates** (full frames) and the **VFX elements** (elements to be cut and pasted) that will become the sources for the visual effects work.

Deciding whether to use film or video to record the action is usually the decision of the director and cinematographer, also called DP or director of photography. Traditionally film negative was the only alternative for recording high-quality movie material, but high definition (HD) video is also used. ***Star Wars - Episode II*** and ***Spy Kids 2*** (Figs. 13.1.1 and 8.6.4) were two of the first high-profile movies with massive amounts of visual effects that employed HD video as the recording medium. Both of these productions used the blue/green screen technique throughout the show, and that process usually involves the participation of a VFX supervisor. Another key responsibility of the VFX team on the set is to make sure that sequences that might involve any kind of removal are shot twice: once with actors and once without. The latter is called a **clean background plate**.

In addition to the visual information recorded on film or video, other types of captured data include position markers to aid the camera tracking process, motion capture information, camera reports, survey data, and still images that can be used for texture maps. The **tracking markers** are essential to aiding the camera tracking process. These markers are made of different materials including reflective tape or small plastic spheres, including tennis and ping pong balls, and they must be placed within the field of vision in areas that might be easy to retouch later on in order to remove the markers. A locked-off camera does not require any tracking markers, a simple camera moves might require a small amount of markers, and a multi-rotation move might require several. **Lighting markers** are used to record the intensity and color of light, and the position of light sources. These markers are usually spheres, between one and two feet in diameter, each mounted on a rod so that they can be positioned anywhere on the set. The spheres are recorded at the beginning of a sequence as cameras roll and record the slate. One type of spherical lighting markers is reflective and is mostly used to capture environment reflections. Another is matte white and used to measure light color temperature, position of light sources, and rate of decay of spotlights. The third type of lighting marker is painted with a 17.5 percent gray color to use as a neutral average reflectance reference.

Camera and survey reports are helpful to recreate digitally the camera and environment. **Camera reports** include the lens focal length (in millimeters) and aperture (f/stop), as well as positional

13.2.2b The dragon was ray-traced to refract the environment through the crystals, and the multiple layers with the dragon renderings and mattes were composited into the live action. The gorgon creature was modeled with polygons, smoothed with subdivision surfaces, and keyframe animated. Much of the geometry and image maps were extracted from photographs using 3dEqualizer camera tracking software. Animation was done with Softimage XSI, and compositing with Discreet Inferno. (*Symphony* images courtesy of La Maison. © 2002 Leo Burnett - Quad - B. Aveillan. All digital visual effects done by La Maison.)

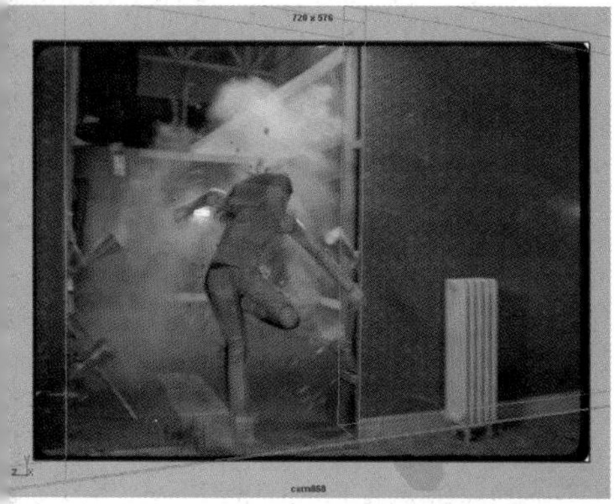

3D ROTOSCOPING

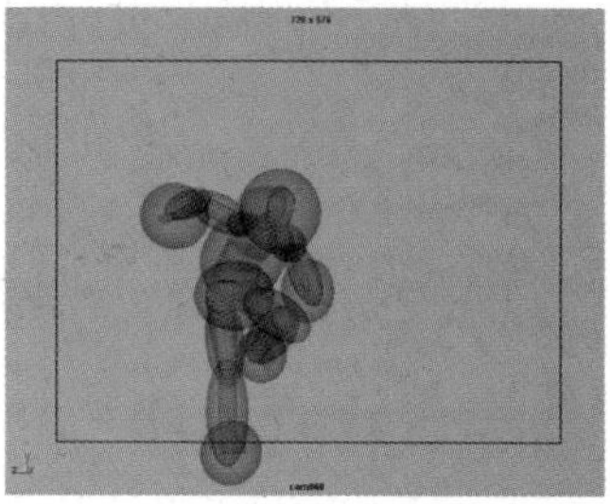

COLLISION VOLUMES

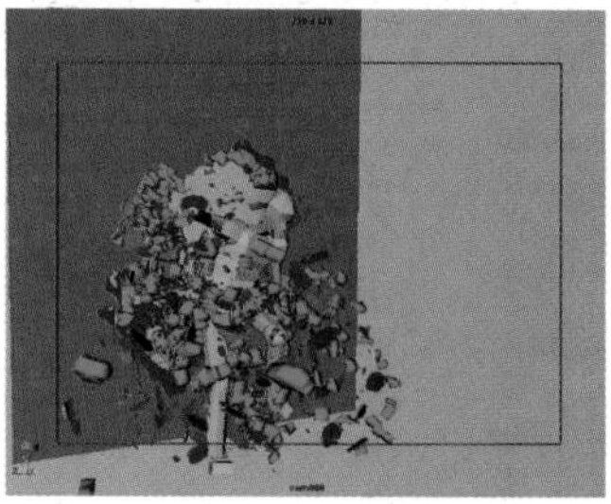

ANIMATION

13.3.1 Three-dimensional rotoscoping was used to create the *Odyssey* Levi's commercial. The video image of the actress is rotoscoped with a simplified three-dimensional reference model (top). The proxy model is used to establish collision fields (middle) that are used to drive the particle animation of wall debris and dust shown in Fig. 13.7.2. (Images courtesy of Framestore CFC and Bartle Bogle Hegarty.)

and rotational information (distance to subject, height, and tilt, pan, and roll angles). Some digital cameras and some motion control systems are able to capture this and other types of **metadata** automatically and record it onto videotape or other type of magnetic media. **Survey data** include ambient and incident light readings, and the position of markers and their distance and angle from the camera. When required survey laser systems can be used to calculate distances and angles or to scan portions of the set and convert it to XYZ modeling information (Fig. 5.6.13).

The capture of still images that can be used for mapping can be done with a 35 mm still camera or with a **digital still camera** of 4 **megapixels** (about 2,500 × 1,600 pixels of resolution) or, ideally, 8 megapixels (about 4,000 × 2,000 pixels). It is important to capture these image maps with as much color depth as possible, ideally 10-bits per RGB channel or above, although 8-bit color is more common in consumer still digital cameras. These image maps can also be used for high dynamic range rendering. (Read Chapter 6 for more information on HDR rendering, and Chapter 15 for color depth.)

Scanning Film and Delivery

After the background plates are recorded onto film or video they are brought to the digital environment so that effects can be added. For standard feature movie work film is usually scanned, or digitized, at 2K pixel resolution and 10-bit color. 4K **film scanning** is also used but is not yet practical for all productions due to the huge file sizes and increased cost of processing. A **2K file** can be defined in a variety of ways, but it includes 1920 × 1080, and 2048 × 1152 pixels. For low-budget or TV delivery 1K scans (about 1,280 × 720) usually provide sufficient quality since the resolution of standard television is around 525 horizontal lines. (Read Chapter 15 for additional details on pixel and color resolution, and aspect ratios.) High definition video is routinely converted to RGB files of 1920 × 1080 pixel resolution and color resolution ranging from 8-bit to 10-bit depth, and 3:1:1 to 4:4:4 sampling. As a general rule in VFX production, more image resolution is better than less. This means that the greater pixel count and color depth the better results we are likely to get after the image has been retouched, composited and color graded a few times. See Figures 14.1.2, 14.1.4, and 15.2.1 for examples of image quality loss due to insufficient resolution.

When the VFX shots are completed and approved they can be output to film and video, following some of the resolution considerations just mentioned. (A detailed description of the output issues can be found in Chapter 15). The VFX shots are then delivered and cut into the movie, which at this point is ready to go through the color grading process. During this stage the director of photography supervises color adjustments in specific scenes or throughout the entire movie. This is usually done in a few consecutive days right before the final mastering and release to audiences in movie theaters, television, or DVD. Color grading in itself is not a visual effects technique, but it deserves mention here because it is so commonly used to fine-tune and twist the mood and the look of the finished images (Fig. 14.5.1). Sometimes background plates are color graded *before* they are given to the VFX team. While not very common, this is usually done when the original plates require very drastic color shifts that might impact the final image quality if applied after the VFX are added. This can also be done to save time later in the process.

13.2 Camera Tracking

Matching live-action with computer animation is easy as long as there is a **locked off camera**, one that does not move. But as soon as the live-action camera moves we need a way to keep track of that motion. That way we can match our virtual camera with the real camera and give the illusion that the live-action plate and the computer-generated elements exist all in the same time and space. There are two basic ways to match the motion of a real and a virtual camera and the elements in the scene: camera tracking and motion control, explained later in the chapter.

Camera tracking has become one of today's key visual effects techniques because it allows to match a computer-generated object or camera with the motion, speed, and acceleration of a real camera *after* the live-action has been recorded. The **camera tracking** technique in itself does not produce finished images but numerical information that is used to match the movement of computer animated props, characters or camera with the live-action camera (Fig. 13.2.1). Camera tracking, or **match move** as it is also called, is done by placing several markers on a few significant still frames of the live-action so that the software can automatically identify the new position of the markers on all frames of the shot. After all the frames have been tracked a **motion path** is generated and used to match the computer-animated camera and objects to the live-action footage (Fig. 13.2.2).

Camera stabilization

Camera stabilization is a technique often used in conjunction with camera tracking. By comparing the positions of the same reference point in contiguous frames this technique can determine the amount of camera jitter and smooth out, or stabilize, the motion differences above a certain threshold between frames.

13.3 Rotoscoping

The technique of **rotoscoping** is a versatile way of matching animated elements to live-action footage. Originally developed by the Fleischer Brothers in the 1915, this technique was used by animators to match their work to live-action. They would manually trace live-action frames to find points of reference for the animated cartoons.

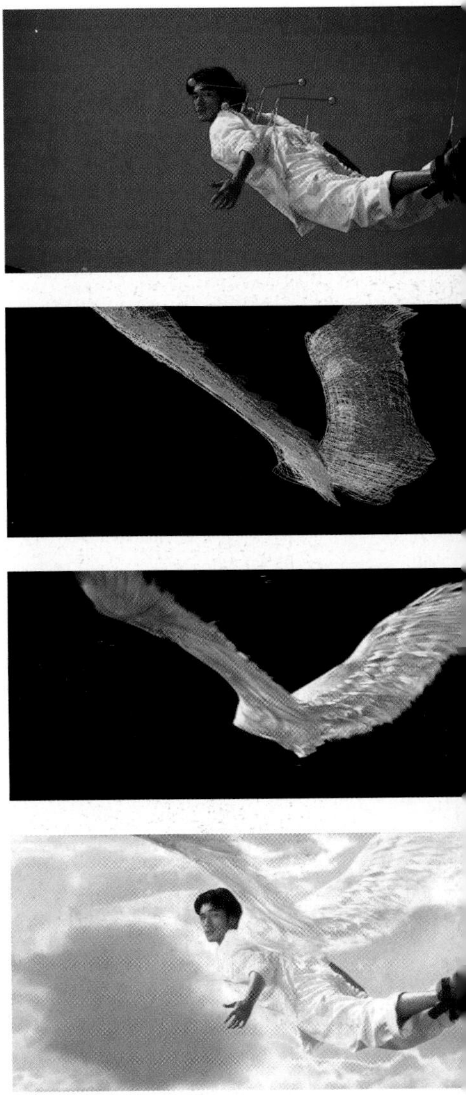

13.4.1 The performance of the actor is recorded against a green screen. The orange markers on his back are used to match the computer-animated wing extensions to the position and movement of the character. Translucency of wings is indicated with different colors before the final rendering and compositing. (Courtesy of Menfond. © GH Pictures China Ltd.)

A few decades later, in the years of optical compositing and hand-made matte paintings, rotoscoping was used to create moving or traveling mattes by tracing the moving elements of still frames one frame at a time. Those tracings can be used as masks with which three-dimensional objects can be laid over a live-action sequence. The basis of this technique is still the same today even though some of the rotoscoping processes can now be automated and the composting environment is almost exclusively digital. A newer form of rotoscoping is used to approximate the position and motion of three-dimensional computer animated models to live-action. This form of **three-dimensional rotoscoping** uses the live-action frames as a guideline to adjust the position of three-dimensional models in the desired way. The example in Figure 13.3.1 uses the spatial and motion information extracted through three-dimensional rotoscoping to simulate the collision between the running live-action actor and a wall. The particle animation driven by the rotoscoping information and a few finished composited frames are shown in Figure 13.7.2.

13.4.2 The movie *L'Anglaise et le Duc* by director Eric Rohmer was constructed from matte paintings and replications of crowds shot in green screen stages. (Visual effects by Buff. © Pathé, CER.)

13.4 Blue and Green Screens, and Chroma Key

Both blue and green colored screens are used to extract traveling mattes for live-action shots. The technical name for this technique is **chroma key** since any color can be used to achieve the effect of inserting, or keying, a foreground image over a flat color background. Historically the **blue screen** was more common in film production while green screens were used in television production, but today they both yield comparable results. However when shooting on film stock with high ASA ratings blue screens can be problematic since the blue emulsion layer in fast film is the one with the most visible grain. Another key factor in choosing either a blue or a green screen has to do with the colors of the foreground elements in the shot. Blue is a convenient color for matting because the flesh tones of most actors do not have any blue. Blonde hair, for example, has a fair amount of green. If the actors were wearing blue clothing though, **green screen** would be a better choice to pull mattes off the flat background.

With blue or green screens the actor or model to be matted over a background is positioned in between the camera and the screen. Since the background is of a uniform color, it is easy to isolate it from the rest of the colors in the scene and eliminate it from the negative (Figs. 13.4.1, 13.4.2, and 14.3.7). The color background, blue or green, can also be made black by using color filtering and color correction techniques. Blue screen shots yield a monochromatic matte composed of a flat background and the flat silhouettes of foreground objects or actors. Lighting blue or green screen shots is always done to avoid **color spill**, which is light reflecting blue or green off the screen and onto the actors. The final matte is used to composite, or combine, the color image of the background and the color image of the foreground. Read Chapter 14 for additional technical details on the compositing process.

13.5.1 The number of crates in this outdoor storage facility was increased using set extension techniques. The scene was recorded with the Cinemascope, 2.35:1, aspect ratio. (*Gorgeous* images courtesy of Menfond. © GH Pictures China Ltd.)

13.5.2 The cars in *Legend of Speed* are computer-generated props rendered with motion blur and volumetric lights. (Images courtesy of Menfond. © China Star Entertainment Ltd. / Win's Entertainment Ltd.)

Background Replacement and Wire Removal

Background replacement and wire removal are two techniques that go hand-in-hand with chroma key and blue/green screen techniques. **Background replacement** is achieved by compositing a new background into the flat color area, these can be computer-generated or matte paintings painted by hand with traditional or digital tools (Fig. 13.4.2). For shots that do not use blue or green screen and that have moving cameras, it is necessary to use either camera tracking or motion control for creating the traveling matte to insert the new background. **Wire removal** is a simple technique that starts by identifying in the background plates the wires and rigs that hold actors and props or the markers used for camera tracking. After areas have been identified that can be removed by using sections from a clean background plate or by hand-painting over them. Figure 13.4.1 shows markers removed, and Figure 1.4.13 shows still frames from a martial arts movie after the wires have been removed.

13.5 Set and Character Extensions

Often it is easier, faster and sometimes cheaper to build a set or a portion of it with three-dimensional computer-generation techniques than with real materials. **Set extensions** are usually built from measurements taken on location or by extracting the dimensions and camera points of view from the background plates. Many techniques can be used to build virtual set extensions including photogrammetry, covered later in this chapter. But the most common approach to computer-generated set extensions is modeling the three-dimensional geometry using the background plates as reference (Fig. 13.5.1). **Character extensions** can be built in a similar way, but because characters tend to move more than sets it is fairly common to use rotoscoping for tracking the extension to the motion of the character (Figs. 11.2.6, 13.1.3 and 13.4.1). **Computer-generated props** are also popular these days and they fall somewhere in between set and character extensions. Static props are similar to set extensions while props that live actors interact with are closer to character extensions (Fig. 13.5.2).

13.6.1 The army from the movie *The Emperor and the Assassin* was created with two-dimensional crowd replication techniques. The three source images above were included in the finished frame on the opposite page (top). (Images courtesy of Centro Digital Pictures Ltd.)

13.7.1 (opposite page, bottom) Stills from the dynamic simulation of a crash. The colors in the wireframe version represent the transition of particles from fire to smoke. The rendered frame includes the dust clusters created as debris from the crash (not rendered in this pass) hits the ground. See the final rendering with model, debris and particles on pages 150-151. (© CA Scanline / creaTV / Pro7.)

13.6 Crowd Replication

Crowds can be simulated with two- or three-dimensional techniques; the latter are described in Chapter 12. The crowds in both live-action movies ***Star Wars: Episode II*** and ***The Lord of the Rings: The Two Towers***, for example, were created with computer-animated three-dimensional models (Fig. 12.6.1). Animated feature movies ***ANTZ*** and ***The Prince of Egypt***, for example, also include three-dimensional crowds rendered in a non-photorealistic style (Figs. 2.4.16 and 12.6.2). The later combines three-dimensional crowds with two-dimensional hand-drawn characters and hand-painted backgrounds. **Two-dimensional crowd replication** is a popular technique that starts with a few live-action elements, groups of actors or animals for example, and usually requires less production steps than its three-dimensional equivalent. The essence of two-dimensional crowd replication is to define a few "seed" elements of the crowd and then to duplicate them within the frame, making sure that their scale, motion, and depth matches the perspective projection of the overall scene. Figure 13.6.1 shows an implementation of the crowd replication technique that uses a few rows of extras as a point of departure for the effect, while Figure 13.4.2 uses small clusters of actors moving toward the camera.

13.7 Computer-Generated Particles

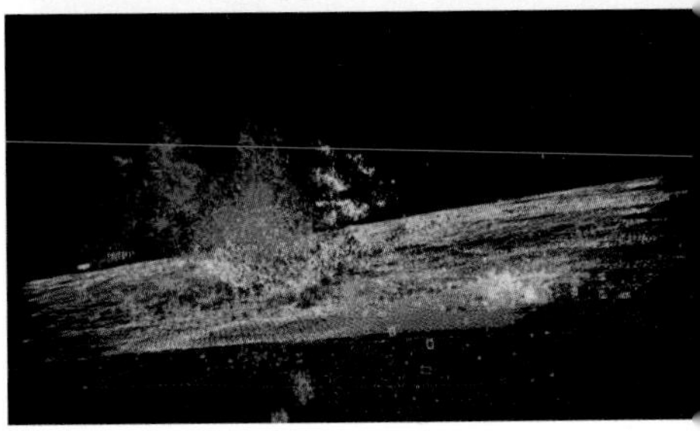

Computer-generated particles is a versatile technique that has become a staple in visual effects production, and it is also the bread-and-butter of many effects production houses. This technique essentially simulates the motion of particles that are subject to a variety of forces. By rendering thousands or millions of these particles in a variety of ways it is possible to simulate different materials such as fire, smoke, liquids, soil, and even hair. Read Chapter 12 for more information on motion dynamics and procedural techniques used to animate particles (Figs. 12.3.4 and 12.4.1). Figure 6.1.1 shows a realistic rendering created with particle systems to simulate an airplane crash, the simulation is calculated in several passes: first the debris alone, then the debris, fire, and smoke (Fig. 13.7.1). The images in Fig. 13.12.1 show a stylized effect including particles and other techniques.

13.8 Three-Dimensional Morphing

Three-dimensional morphing is achieved by applying interpolation techniques to the geometry of three-dimensional models. Three-dimensional morphing techniques blend the shape of objects by interpolating the positions of their vertices in space. The rate of morphing can be controlled with functions such as time, speed, or proximity to a source. The most predictable three-dimensional morphing results are obtained when both objects being morphed have the same number of vertices. (Fig. 11.2.6). Read Chapter 11 for more information on model and shape animation.

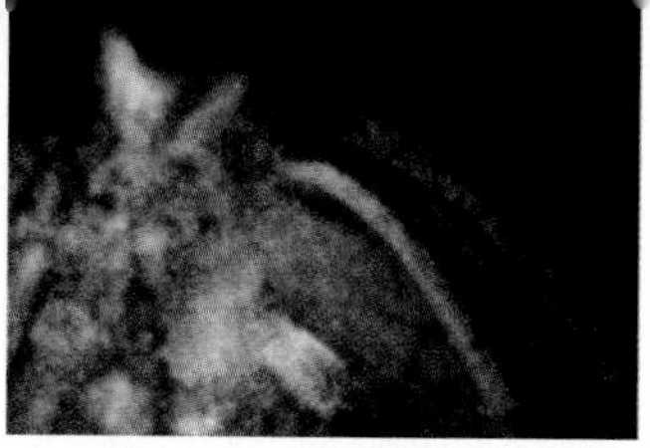

DUST PARTICLES

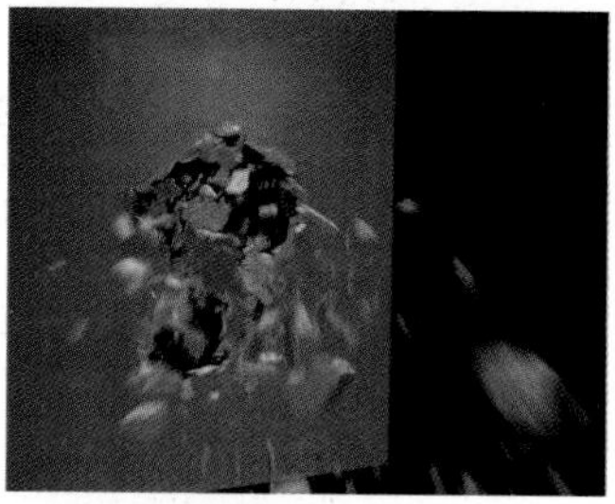

WALL DEBRIS

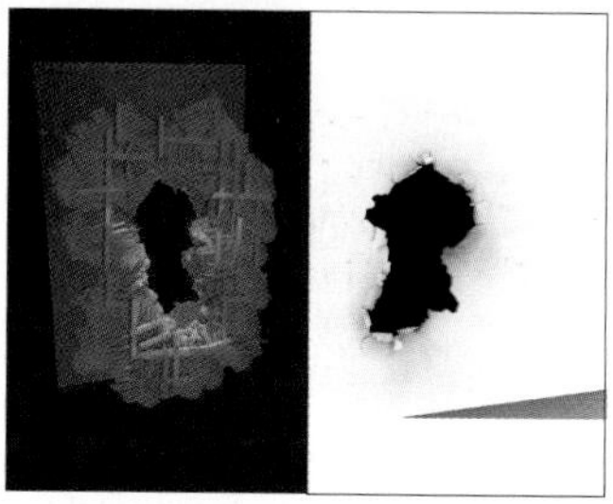

WALL INTERIOR, SHADOW PASS

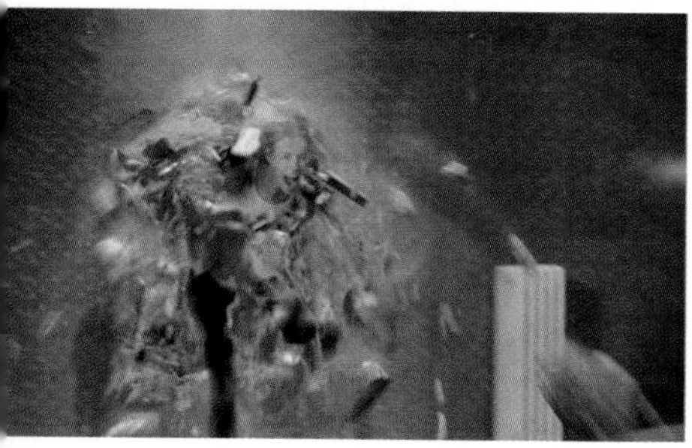

FINAL COMPOSITE

13.7.2 The particle animation of wall debris and dust was driven by a rotoscoped proxy model and the collision fields shown in Fig. 13.3.1. (Images courtesy of Framestore CFC and Bartle Bogle Hegarty.)

13.9 Motion Control

Before camera tracking techniques became feasible in the mid-1990s using a motion control system was the only sure way to match a computer-generated animation with the movement of a live-action camera. A **motion control** system is a precise motorized crane that moves a camera along a specific path in response to a well-defined numerical input. A motion control system is also capable of repeating the same translations, rotations and speeds over and over again. During the 1970s and 1980s, before computer animation and digital compositing became as prevalent as they are today, motion control systems offered the only solution for accurately repeating a specific move multiple times. Movies like ***Star Wars*** (1977) and ***The Empire Strikes Back*** (1980), for example, made extensive use of early motion control systems to film multiple scale models each on a separate pass. Since the same motion path was followed each recording pass, the different elements were aligned and synchronized. Those early motion control systems were mostly used to shoot in **stop motion** mode, or a single frame at a time. Modern motion control systems can be used to shoot that way and also continuous motion without any loss of accuracy.

Motion control systems today can be used to feed the numerical information that describes their path to a computer animation system, but a three-dimensional path can also be laid out with a computer animation system and then fed to a motion control system for execution. This way the same motion path can be used to animate either the virtual camera or the real camera regardless of which one records first. An identical motion path will result in perfectly matching acceleration, speed and direction of both the real and the virtual camera. The camera tracking techniques described earlier in the chapter are nowadays more commonly used for matching real and virtual motion than motion control systems.

13.10 Motion Capture and Virtual Characters

Motion capture is covered in Chapter 12, but it is mentioned again here because it is a technique commonly used in the production of visual effects and animation of virtual characters. In addition to the capture, editing and blending of the captured motion, one of the key issues in achieving high-quality results has to do with the performance of the actor whose motion is being captured. In the early days of motion capture little attention was paid to this aspect, which is now recognized as the key driver of believable virtual characters. The character Gollum (Fig. 12.2.7) from the movie ***Lord of the Rings: The Two Towers*** was so vivid and had such powerful prescence in great part because the actor who "played" the part acted his motions taking into account the personality pf the character and the limitation of motion capture. Pantomime techniques can be used to emphasize intention and to clearly delineate actions and movements. In the Barbie animated movies the movement of professional ballet dancers was captured and applied to three-dimensional characters (Fig. 12.2.8).

13.11 Photogrammetry

Photogrammetry is a technique that can extract three-dimensional models from two or more still images of a subject. In their most general implementation photogrammetry uses the still images of a subject to extract a depth map. That is converted to a polygonal model which can be textured map with some of the original images used to create the model in the first place (Fig. 5.6.2). Image-based rendering which is often used in conjunction with photogrammetry is described in Chapter 5.

Time Freeze

The technique of **time freeze**, also known as time slice or **bullet-time**, is a variation of the photogrammetry technique. Time freeze achieves an effect of frozen time or very slow motion time by collecting multiple images of the same action from different points of view. More specifically, time freeze starts by placing an array of still cameras around or along a subject. ***The Matrix***, for example, used 120 cameras arranged in a circle and hidden behind a green screen wall with holes for the 120 lenses to see the action (Fig. 13.11.2). Triggering the cameras is computer-controlled so that it can be accurately timed. When all the cameras record the same instant from 100 different points of view, for example, each still frame can be edited in sequence and viewed in motion. In this scenario the still from camera 1 would become frame 1 in the sequence, camera 2 would be frame 2, and so on. When viewed in motion this sequence of frames looks like a camera moving around a subject that is frozen in time. The cameras can also be triggered with a small delay, fractions of a second, between each one. When the still images are viewed in sequence the effect is of a moving camera around a subject frozen in time or one that moves in extreme slow motion, as the actor Keanu Reeves was when trying to avoid the bullets in *The Matrix*.

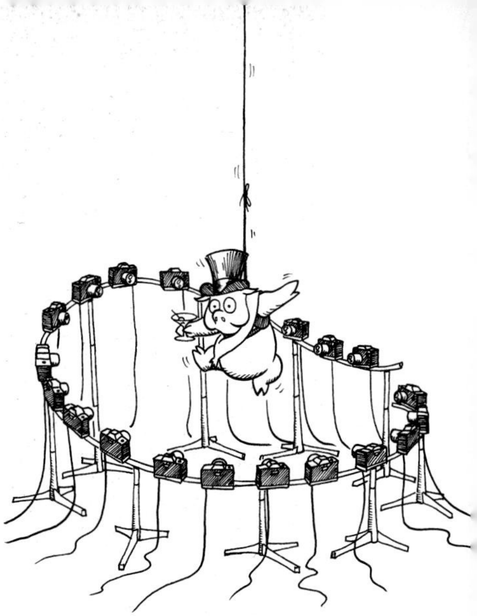

13.11.2 Multiple still photography cameras are used to create the time freeze effect by recording the same instant from different points of view.

13.12 Practical Effects

Practical effects are made in reality, not in the computer. Practical effects are created on locations, a sound stage or a miniature set. Practical effects, also called **special effects**, include real explosions (Fig. 14.2.1), stunts with or without wires (Fig. 1.4.13), models or miniatures, animatronics, facial and body make-up and prosthetics among others. Today's practical effects are usually another component of the visual effect shot, and after being recorded on film or video they can be enhanced further with digital tools, or combined with digital effects.

13.12.1 (next page) An actor filmed on blue screen is composited with layers of practical fire, particle systems, a live stadium, and a few distortion filters to simulate the heat and force wave running through his arms, face, and torso. (Images courtesy of Centro Digital Pictures Ltd.)

(Next page: A computer-generated human with skeleton and muscle simulation driven by Absolute Character software. (Courtesy of Snoswell Design.)

Chapter 13

Key Terms

2K file
Background plates
Background replacement
Blue screen
Bullet time
Camera reports
Camera tracking
Camera stabilization
Character extensions
Chroma key
Cinematographer
Clean background plate
Color spill
Computer-generated props
Compositing supervisor
Computer animation supervisor
Digital still camera
Film scanning
Green screen
Lighting markers
Match move
Match reality
Megapixels
Metadata
Motion control
Motion path
Practical effects
Previz
Production pipeline
Rotoscoping
Salad of effects
Second unit of photography
Set extensions
Sequence supervisor
Shot breakdown
Special effects
Survey reports
Temps
Three-dimensional rotoscoping
Time freeze
Tracking markers
Two-dimensional crowd replication
VFX
VFX elements
Visual effects core team
Visual effects producer
Visual effects supervisor
Visual look
Wire removal

SECTION V

Compositing and Output

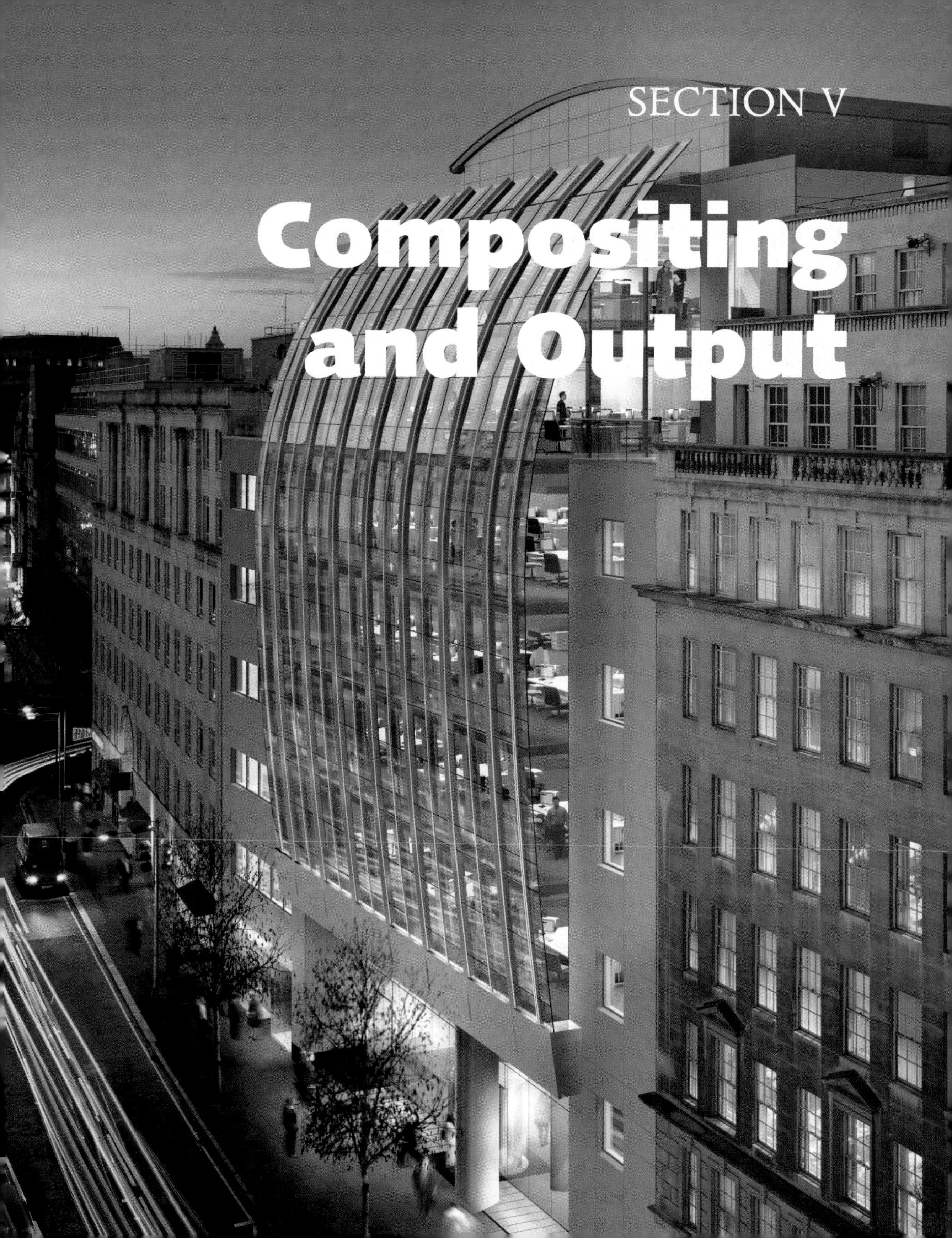

(Previous page) This birdseye view of an architectural project is a composite of computer-generated visualizations of buildings with a photograph of the actual location. (90 High Holborn. © Hayes Davidson.)

14.1.1 Computer animation and live action backgrounds were composited in this shot where the character surprises us with unexpected poses and action. The camera point of view accentuates the comedy of the moment. (© 2002 Blockbuster Entertainment/Tippett Studio.)

CHAPTER 14

14

Retouching, Compositing, and Color Grading

Summary

Once the three-dimensional scenes have been rendered, the resulting two-dimensional images can be enhanced with further digital processing. Image retouching and compositing are two of the most popular postprocessing techniques, along with color balance and correction and image sequencing.

QUICK INDEX

14.1 Basic Concepts of Image Manipulation

There are myriad techniques for enhancing and combining different live action elements, different two-dimensional renderings of three-dimensional environments, and combinations of live and computer-generated imagery. **Postprocessing** has its roots in traditional retouching just as three-dimensional computer modeling can be compared to the work of a sculptor working with traditional materials, and the rendering process can be compared to the work of lighting designers, make-up artists, photographers, and painters. Postprocessing can be compared to the work that photographers do in the darkroom, once the images have been recorded on film but before the final prints are made. **Image manipulation** techniques are used to modify the color, contrast, and brightness of images, as well as their content. These techniques can increase the overall brightness of an image or lower the contrast between light and dark tones. Techniques like retouching and compositing can also be used to remove mistakes or to combine areas of different sources into a single image (Fig. 14.1.1). Some of the basic concepts of image manipulation techniques include pixel and color resampling, editing with parameter curves and histograms, and compositing with alpha channels and transition effects.

Resampling the Pixel Resolution

One of the key techniques of image manipulation consists of changing the spatial resolution of an image. This is called **resampling an** image and is often used when the dimensions or the spatial resolution of an image need to be increased or decreased. It is necessary to resample an image, for example, when a scene has been rendered at a resolution of 72 **pixels per inch** (ppi) but the final output requires 300 dots per inch (dpi), or when a scene was rendered at a size of 1,000 × 1,000 pixels, but the client needs it at 500 × 500 pixels.

The continuous values of a live scene or a photograph are sampled when the live scene is digitized with a digitizing camera, or when a continuous tone photograph is scanned with a scanner. In both cases, the frequency of the sampling determines the resolution of the digital image. Many samples, or point measurements, of color result in many pixels. A few samples yield few pixels and a low resolution. When images are resampled the information contained in a digital file can change subtly or dramatically. When images are sampled down, the software averages the values of several pixels and discards some of the original information. When images are sampled up, the software averages the values of several pixels and creates new information. In either case, this averaging of pixel values is based on one of many **interpolation techniques** that create new pixel values by averaging the existing pixel values in different ways.

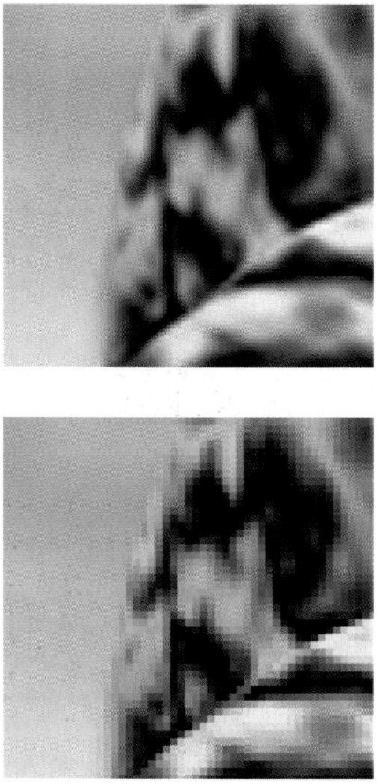

14.1.2 Details of an image originally rendered at 72 ppi and resampled to 300 ppi with weighted pixel interpolation (top) and with linear interpolation (bottom). The transitions and blending of resampled pixel color values are smoother when weighted pixel interpolation is used.

Simple interpolations, such as **neighbor pixel interpolation**, determine the value of a new pixel by averaging the values of only two pixels. When an image is resampled to double its original size, for example, the number of pixels that has to be created is twice the number of original pixels. With a simple interpolation technique each new pixel is created between two existing pixels, and its value is determined by averaging the value of just those two pixels. Resampling based on simple or linear interpolation techniques usually creates images with small defects like banding, aliased edges, or loss of detail.

There are more sophisticated resampling techniques on the other end of the interpolation spectrum. Some determine the value of a new pixel by averaging the values of many pixels and by assigning each of them a priority or weight based on their proximity to the new pixel being calculated. An example of a **weighted interpolation** technique is illustrated in Figure 14.1.2 where the values of several pixels are averaged to create a new single pixel. When an image is sampled down, some of its original information is lost, and the resampled image will look quite different from the original if it is resampled up again after having been resampled down.

Regardless of the pixel interpolation method used, when resampling an image it is important to determine whether maintaining the **file size** (the amount of space it takes to store it) is important. If maintaining the file size constant is an issue the physical **image dimensions** (height and width) of the file will surely change. Inversely, if the file size may change as a result of the resampling, then the dimensions remain constant. For example, a 46 KB image that measures 2 × 1.5 in. at 72 ppi can be resampled at 300 ppi and keep its file size of 46 KB constant but the dimensions change to .48 × .36 in. (Fig. 14.1.3). If the file size must remain constant, the absolute number of pixels also remains constant, but the image dimensions change because at the higher resolution more pixels are required to create an inch. If the file size can grow, so does the resolution and the number of pixels, while the dimensions remain unchanged. But if the 72 ppi image would be resampled to the dimension of 2 × 1.5 in. at the increased resolution of 300 ppi, its file size would increase to 792 KB.

15,552 PIXELS AT 72 PPI

15,552 PIXELS AT 300 PPI

269,400 PIXELS AT 300 PPI

14.1.3 An image with a resolution of 72 ppi and a total of 15,552 pixels, compared with two 300 ppi files each with a total of 15,552 pixels, and 269,400 pixels. Larger pixels result in a larger area as illustrated by the difference in image size between the first and second examples. The area in the third example is identical to the first example, but it is made up smaller pixels and, therefore, has more detail.

Resampling the Color Resolution

Another useful technique for manipulating images of three-dimensional rendered scenes consists of changing, or resampling, their color resolution. Satisfactory results when **resampling the color resolution** of a rendered image are obtained only when it is necessary to lower the color resolution but not when it is necessary to increase it. Increasing the color resolution of an image can be achieved with good results only by rerendering the three-dimensional scene at a higher color resolution. Color resampling is useful—and even necessary—when the image has been rendered at high color resolutions but needs to be displayed at a low resolution. This would be the case, for example, of renderings created at a resolution of 32-bit color for the purpose of feature film presentations that are adapted to the home videogame format and that had to be resampled down to 16-bit color to be displayed efficiently. Resampling the color resolution of entire projects is common now that many works and intellectual properties previously developed for high-resolution formats are now being released in home entertainment systems at lower color resolutions.

Most three-dimensional computer rendering systems create 24-bit or 32-bit color images. When color resampling is needed the process is very straightforward and is usually implemented in the form of choices listed in a dialog box or a pull-down menu. The most common resolutions for color images include 32-, 24-, 16-, 8-, and 4-bit color (Fig. 14.1.4). But the loss in color detail due to color resampling can be severe, for example, when going from the sixteen million colors of 24-bit color to the 256 colors available in 8-bit color. For this reason, the techniques of color dithering and color look-up tables are often used to minimize the artifacts and loss of detail created by color resampling. Both of these techniques are especially effective when 8-bit color is utilized.

Color dithering simulates shades of color with dot patterns of several colors. Dithering preserves some of the color detail that tends to be lost when 24-bit color images are sampled down to 4-bit or 8-bit color. But at the same time dithering lowers the apparent spatial resolution of an image because the dot patterns used to simulate shades of color often look like enlarged pixels (Fig. 14.1.4).

Color look-up tables, also called **indexed color**, are a popular technique in interactive projects where three-dimensional animated sequences are rendered in real-time in response to the users playing

3 BITS PER PIXEL: 6 COLORS | 4 BITS PER PIXEL: 16 COLORS | 4 BITS PER PIXEL WITH DITHERING

8 BITS PER PIXEL: 256 COLORS | 8 BITS PER CHANNEL | 16 BITS PER CHANNEL

14.1.4 This sequence shows the same image rendered at different color resolutions. In each case the values of each of the bitplanes are added to determine the final value of the pixels. A pixel in a 3-level bitmap displays one of six shades of color. A 4-level bitmap can display 16 colors, and the color accuracy is often improved with dithering techniques. At 8 bits per pixel the image contains 256 colors in a color look-up table. The full-color 8- and 16-bit color versions of the image contain millions of colors. (Photo by Ulf Wallin.)

the game. A **color look-up table** is a limited palette of colors that represents quite faithfully a much larger selection of colors. Color look-up tables contain a tight selection of colors (256 in the 8-bit color mode) that gives the impression of a much larger palette. The main purpose of color look-up tables is to optimize color accuracy in a low color resolution environment. When a full-color RGB image or sequence is converted to indexed color, there are different methods for choosing the colors that go in the look-up table. These methods include using a generic color look-up table or customizing the color manually or automatically.

It is convenient to use a generic color look-up table, often called a **system palette**, because it is a standard feature of most image manipulation software programs. A generic color look-up table produces acceptable results with images that have a balanced distribution of color. But generic palettes usually produce poor results when the colors in the sequence are biased toward a single hue—for example, a scene at dusk with mostly dark colors. In such cases, generic palettes usually lack the variety of color that is required to represent the subtle variations of color within a narrow chromatic range. One of the advantages of using a generic color look-up table is that it reduces memory requirements and increases performance because the generic color look-up table can be used with a variety of different images. In an indexed color environment, a generic look-up table only has to be loaded once for all images, as opposed to customized palettes which have to be loaded every time the image is used.

Custom color look-up tables can be built for a specific image or sequence by *manually* selecting the colors that best convey the variety of colors contained in the original full color version. Color look-up tables that are built especially for a series of sequences in a project should contain the most commonly used colors throughout the project (Fig. 14.1.5). Custom color look-up tables can also be built *automatically* by letting the software decide which limited color palette would best represent the thousands of subtle colors contained in a scene.

14.1.5 A full 8-bit color image (top) that is converted to indexed color (bottom) can retain a fair amount of color fidelity and crispness when a custom color look-up table is used. Most of the color detail was retained in this conversion, except for a slight increase in contrast and a compression or flattening of the darkest tones in some hues. (Screen shot from *Myst* CD-ROM computer game. Game and screen shot are © 1993 by Cyan, Inc. All rights reserved.)

Parameter Curves

The parameter or function curves are graphs that represent and control different attributes of an image, such as brightness or color. These attributes can be easily modified by manipulating the function curves without having to alter the image directly with a retouching tool. Making image manipulations that involve all of the image or large portions of it are best performed with function curves. The parameter curves used for image manipulation are similar to those used for controlling animation interpolations (read Chapter 11 for more information on animation interpolation).

Parameter curves for image manipulation are usually represented by a line that starts at the lower left corner of a square and ends at the upper right corner. The **straight diagonal line** (in a parameter curve) represents one or several untouched attributes of the original image. Any changes made to the line will result in changes to the image. Generally, if the line is pulled above the straight diagonal path the attribute increases, and if the line is moved below the diagonal path the the attribute being controlled by the line decreases (Fig. 14.1.6). The manner in which the parameter curve is redrawn also influences the way in which the attribute is controlled. If the parameter curve is redrawn with a series of **soft curves**, the attributes of the image change gradually as in a curved interpolation. If the parameter curve is redrawn with a series of **angular straight lines**, the attributes change abruptly as they sometimes do at the junction of two linear interpolations (Fig. 14.1.7).

Linear Color Space and Nonlinear Color Space

In simple terms, the concepts of linear and nonlinear color space are often used when it is necessary to convert images to a smaller file size while preserving as much image resolution as possible. A **linear color space** is used for direct and simple conversion, for example a mapping of 16 levels of gray that yields 8 levels that are numerically equally spaced (Fig. 14.1.6). A **nonlinear color space**, also called **log space**, is used for conversions that seek to preserve certain areas or levels of the image, for example a mapping of 16 levels of gray that yields 8 levels that are perceptually equally spaced (Fig. 14.1.7).

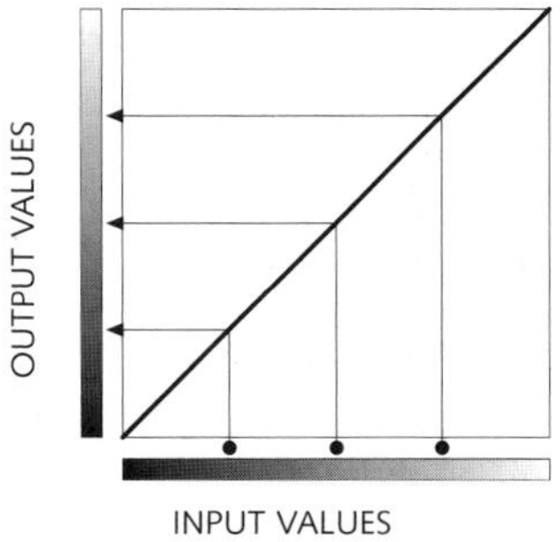

14.1.6 The unretouched image displays its brightness function curve as a straight diagonal line. When this curve is moved up the output values will be higher than the input values. If the histogram controls brightness, for example, the output values will be brighter than the input values.

Nonlinear color spaces are commonly used in visual effects production to store subtle information scanned from film negative or interpositive.

The Histogram

One of the principles of traditional painting and classic photography recommends the creation of images with a rich tonal range. In a monochromatic image, that means using a sample of gray values that is evenly and continuously distributed across the grayscale. In a color image, a rich tonal range includes color values as well as brightness and contrast. An image, a black-and-white photograph for example, that contains small amounts of pure black and pure white plus a continuous and even distribution of gray values usually has a wider expressive range than a mannerist image that dwells exclusively on the dark or light tones of the scale.

Looking at the histogram of an image is an effective way to analyze the distribution of values in each of the channels of the image. A **histogram** consists of a graphical representation of the distribution throughout the grayscale of the pixels that constitute an image. In a monochromatic image, the horizontal line in a histogram represents the range of gray values between pure black, usually represented with a value of 0 on the left side, and pure white, represented with a value of 255 in an 8-bit color scale. In a full-color image, RGB for example, each component color has a histogram. The combined component colors can also be controlled with a single histogram. The number of pixels that have intensity values between black and white are represented with a vertical line or bar. The larger the number of pixels on a single value the taller the line. These lines are located throughout the horizontal line in accordance with the pixel values contained in the image. An image with pixels that are evenly distributed throughout the grayscale has vertical lines all across the histogram, while an image with only dark and light values—but no midtones, for example—has vertical lines on the extremes of the histogram but not in its center. The histogram of an image with many dark values has lines mostly on its left side (Fig. 14.1.8).

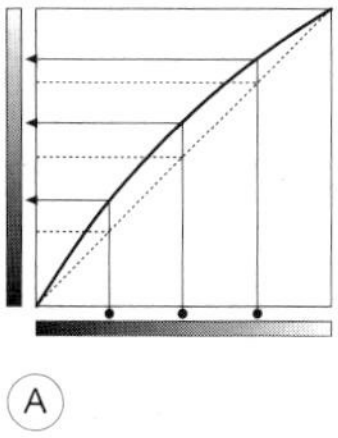

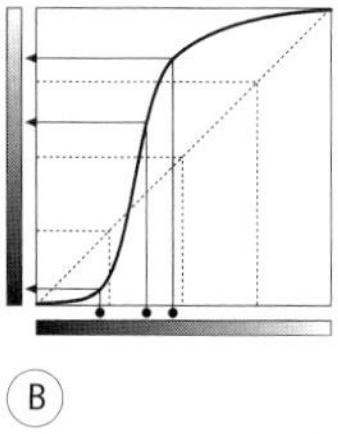

14.1.7 The brightness of the image increases in the midtones when the function curve is pulled up (A), the smooth curve results in a gradual change of the brightness values. Abrupt changes in the curve result in abrupt changes in the brightness values (B)—in this case, flattening the lightest and darkest values and compressing the midtones.

Image Layers

The numerical values and some of the components that define a two-dimensional rendered image can be organized in layers.

Working with multiple **image layers** or **channels** is similar to the process of painting on transparent acetate overlays that is still used in traditional cel animation. In this case, different components of the image are painted each on a cel, and the finished image can only be seen when all the layers are assembled in sequence. But when each layer or cel is viewed separately, only a part of the image is visible. The principle of using image layers is also the basis of four-color separation and a staple process in the graphic arts (Fig. 6.2.1).

Image layers are used for a variety of image manipulation purposes. As previously mentioned, image layers are used to display separately each of the component or primary colors of an image in several color modes including RGB, CMYK, and HSL. It is possible to work on a single layer separately from the other layers—for example, increase the brightness or apply a filter to a single layer and then merge the layers again and view the combined results.

The Alpha Channel and Masks

Image layers can also be used to composite and blend the contents of several layers and place the resulting image in a separate set of image layers. This process is called image compositing or blending, depending on the specific techniques used to combine the contents of the image layers. An **alpha channel** is commonly used to aid in the compositing of multiple layers, because it may contain a black-and-white image that masks or protects select parts of one or several of the layers being composited. One or several alpha channels may be used in the compositing process. The **mask** contained in the alpha channel is like the **stencils** traditionally used to label wooden cargo containers or to aid in the creation of images with the delicate techniques of airbrushing or silkscreen. In either case, the stencil is perforated with a design or with letterforms and placed on a surface. The solid areas of the stencil protect the surface underneath and the perforated areas allow the paint to reach the wooden plank in the case of the cargo container, or the paper surface being airbrushed or silkscreened. Compositing with a mask in the alpha channel allows select portions of images to be composited as **foreground elements** in front of a **background**. Figure 14.1.9 illustrates the compositing of a foreground image with a background. The compositing is done using all the possible combinations of masks derived from the simple shapes in the foreground (inside and outside) and the background (top and bottom).

14.2 Image Retouching

Digital image manipulation techniques can provide the best that both the **darkroom** of a photographer and the **studio** of a painter have to offer. For example, with image manipulation software, we can fine-tune the tonal range of rendered images, adjust their contrast and brightness, and apply digital filters to create special effects.

Postprocessing programs facilitate the blending of computer-gen-

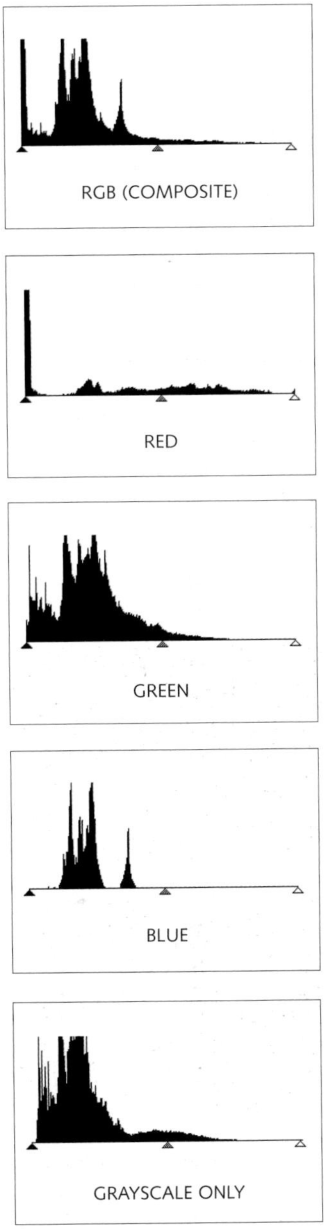

14.1.8 These histograms (for the color image in Figure 14.1.6) represent the distribution of pixels in the image throughout the tonal range. The continuity of the vertical lines in the graph reflect the continuity or discontinuity of levels in the image.

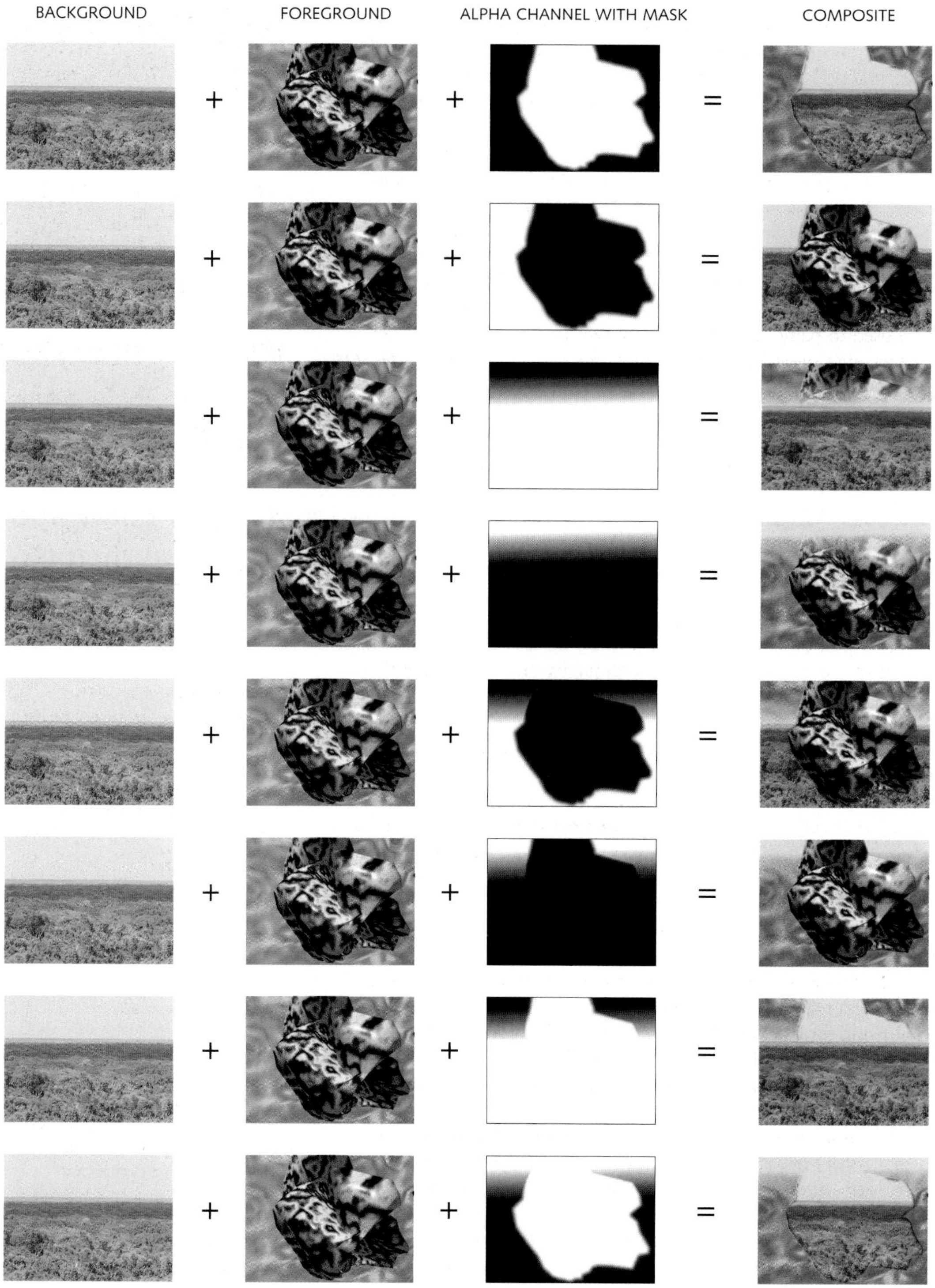
BACKGROUND
FOREGROUND
ALPHA CHANNEL WITH MASK
COMPOSITE

erated images with photographic or painted images. The final result can be output onto a variety of media only after the two types of images are combined with integrated tools and techniques. These capabilities are opening new creative avenues that were not possible with traditional tools.

Before computers came along, it was impractical to combine painting with photography because each occurred in very different, almost incompatible, media. Bringing the photographic image onto the canvas was cumbersome, and painting on photographic paper was limiting. The narrow focus of the traditional tools did not help either. Brushes and paint did not work well on photographic images, and many of photography's essential tools such as lenses and filters could not be used to paint. The closest these two media ever got before computers was retouching photographs for commercial advertisements or artistic collages. In the former case, the process of blending the painted image with the photograph was painstaking, limited, and extremely expensive. In the latter case, the painted image and the photographic image usually remained quite independent from each other.

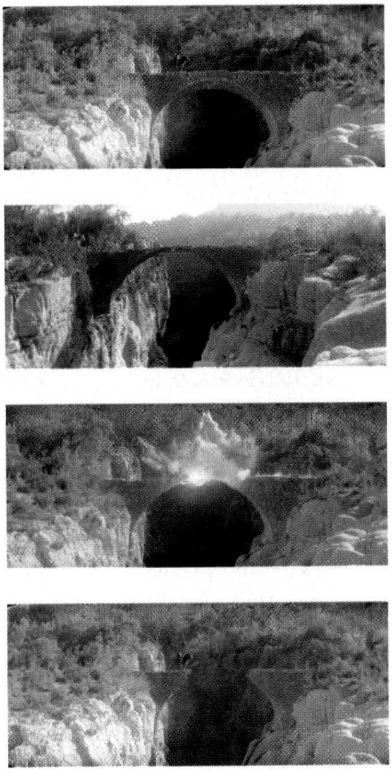

14.2.1 These frames show (from top to bottom) the original shot with the full bridge, the retouched bridge to make it seem more dangerous, the composite with an explosion, and the retouched bridge again after the explosion. (*Le Bossu*, a film by Philippe de Broca. Production: ALICÉLÉO. Visual Effects: Ex Machina Paris. Images courtesy of Ex Machina.)

Retouching Tools

A wide variety of tools is available for **retouching** rendered and live action images. Some of these digital tools are inspired by the tools of painters and illustrators, and others are based on the tools used by photographers. Retouching tools are typically used to touch up small mistakes in the rendered file or to add details that are missing (Fig. 14.2.1). As a general rule, when mistakes are made in the modeling or rendering process, it is best to model and render the scene again. But in a few cases, the production schedule or budget does not permit fixing of minor mistakes by remodeling or rendering again. This is especially true when the time it would take to render is beyond the production scope of the project, or when the computer-generated animation, for example, has already been composited with live action.

Some of the digital retouching tools that are inspired by **traditional painting tools** include brushes, pencils, and rubber stamps. These painting tools are used to paint over selected areas of the rendered image, and their simulated attributes, such as width or pressure, can be customized. In addition, the way in which these paint tools "deposit" the paint can also be customized in many different ways. The digital paint, for example, can have different degrees of transparency or can affect only a certain range of pixels with a certain color or brightness value. A variety of simulated paper textures can also be applied to the surface of the rendered image.

The retouching tools based on **photographic procedures** include a tool for lightening or darkening selective parts of the image interactively, just as dodging and burning are performed on photographs as the image on the film negative is projected onto photosensitive paper. The histogram editor itself and all the parameter curves are also retouching tools that are rooted in the photo-

14.1.9 (opposite page) Two original images were composited using eight different masks in the alpha channel. The background is a photograph of the tropical rain forest, and the foreground is a synthetic rock. In this masking setup the black areas in the mask block or cover the green background, and the white areas let it show through.

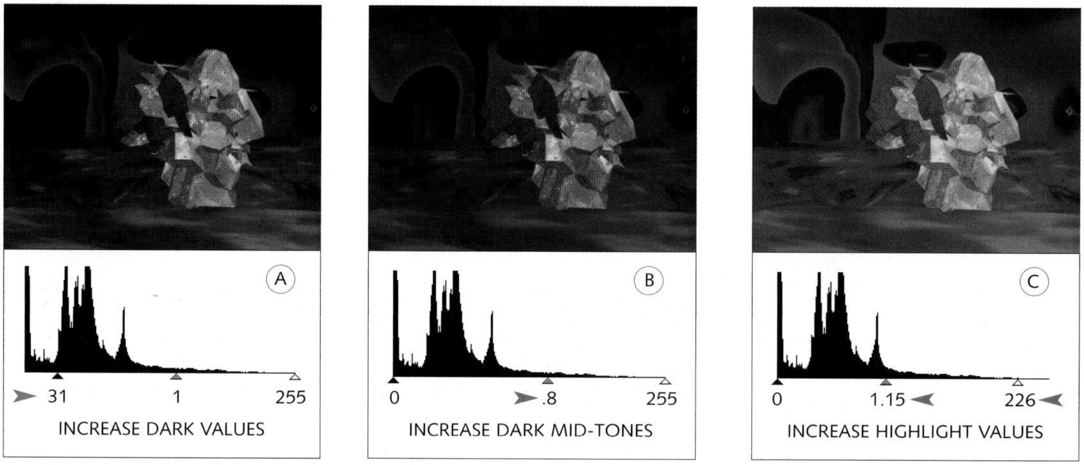

14.2.2 A histogram editor can be used to redistribute the color values in an image. The shadow editor can be used to increase the dark values in the image. The midtone editor can also be used to increase the dark values in a different tonal range. Both the highlight and mid-tone editor are used in this example to increase the overall highlight values in the image.

graphic tradition because they help define an image by adjusting the settings in which the imaging process occurs.

The **digital retouching tools** that are truly unique to computers are those for selecting different parts of the image. These tools provide techniques for selecting the pixels or areas of the rendered image that need to be retouched. The most common selection tools provided by retouching software are those that let the user enclose the selected area with a tool like a marquee or a free-form lasso. The more sophisticated selection tools allow the selection of image areas based on their pixel values. This method of selection works on contiguous pixels as well as pixels scattered throughout the image. All the pixels in an image within a specific color range can be easily manipulated or replaced with this selection method.

Editing the Tonal Range

One of the most useful tools provided by many image manipulation programs is the histogram. The histogram is a graph that shows the distribution of light, middle, and dark values in an image. Using a **histogram editor** makes it possible to modify with extreme accuracy the tonal range of an image, which defines many of the characteristics that give images their distinctive character. **Tonal range** includes the distribution of values throughout the grayscale and the relation between the highlights, midtones, and the shadows, the brightness and contrast levels, and the color balance of images.

The histograms in Figure 14.1.8 show an uneven distribution of pixel values across the tonal range represented by the width of the horizontal line. Each of the vertical lines represents the number of pixels in the image at each of the tonal values between black and white. The higher lines represent the most number of pixels at that tone of gray or particular color. The three triangles below the tonal range represent (from left to right) the shadow editor, the midtone editor, and the highlight editor. Their normal values are 0, 1, and 255, respectively. These markers are used to redistribute the pixel values across the tonal range. By sliding any or all of the editors to the right, for example, the darker values are given more prominence in the tonal range. Moving just the **shadow** editor to the right relocates the position of the pure black to a higher position in the tonal range (from 0 to 31), therefore increasing the proportion of dark values in the image (Fig. 14.2.2a). Moving the **midtone** editor to the right expands the presence of the dark values within the tonal range (Fig. 14.2.2b). Moving both the **highlight** editor and the midtone editor to the left, for example, increases the range of the light values in the image (Fig. 14.2.2c).

Using a histogram to effectively edit the tonal range of an image requires practice. A more straightforward method for editing the tonal range of an image is based on using simpler controls for **brightness** and **contrast**. These controls are often in the form of sliders, parametric curves, or fields that accept numerical values typed directly on the keyboard.

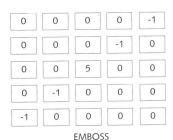

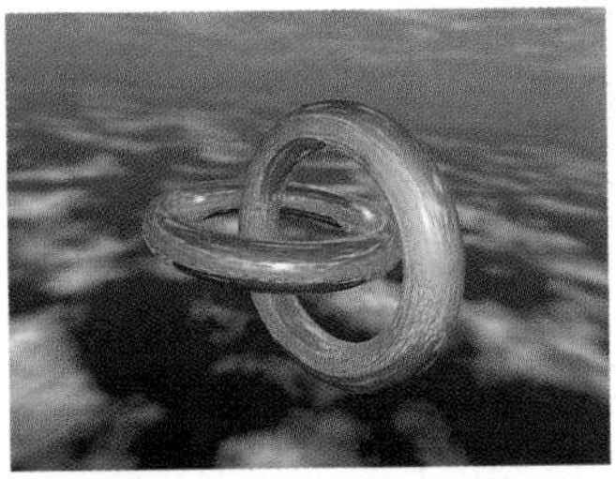

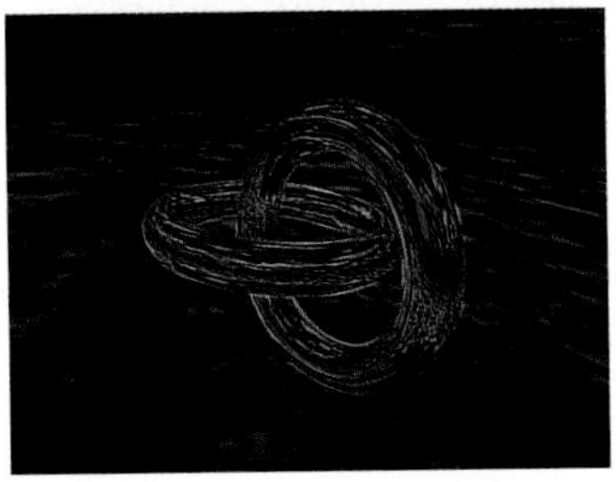

0	0	0	0	0
0	0	-1	0	0
0	-1	5	-1	0
0	0	-1	0	0
0	0	0	0	0

SHARPEN

0	0	0	0	-1
0	0	0	-1	0
0	0	5	0	0
0	-1	0	0	0
-1	0	0	0	0

EMBOSS

-1	0	0	0	-1
0	0	0	-1	0
0	0	5	0	0
0	-1	0	0	0
-1	0	0	0	0

EDGE DETECTION

14.2.3 In this example of custom filters applied to the image in Figure 6.11.1, the cel in the center of the 5 × 5 matrix contains the value that is to be used in the mathematical operation applied to the brightness of the pixel being evaluated. The cels adjacent to the center cel represent the pixels immediately surrounding the pixel being evaluated. The outer cels represent a second group of pixels that are a pixel away from the pixel being evaluated. The values used in each of the filtering variations are shown next to each image. The results include sharpening, embossing, and edge detection.

Digital Filters

Digital 2D filters are rarely applied during the actual 3D rendering process. These filters are usually applied to the two-dimensional images of three-dimensional scenes after the scenes have been rendered. Like their photographic relatives, digital filters modify the appearance of an image, but are able to change many more attributes and with much more precision than it is possible to change with photographic filters. Digital filters can be applied selectively to all of the image or only some areas. This capability turns digital filters into extraordinary retouching tools. Digital filters cover a wide range of special effects ranging from a simple blurring filter to a compound filter that adds lens flare and motion blur.

Digital filters work by submitting single pixels in the image or groups of them to a series of mathematical operations. Each type of filter is based on a unique combination of mathematical operations

14.2.4 A sharpening filter applied to an image.

14.2.5 A blurring filter applied to an image.

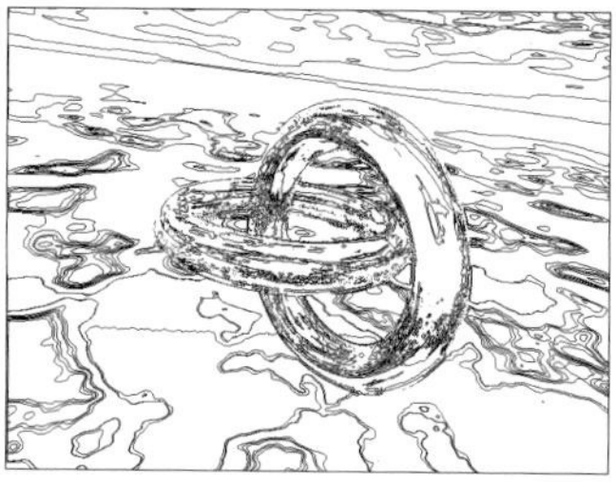

14.2.6 The edges of a rendered image were traced with an edge tracing filter to extract a two-dimensional contour.

that process the numerical values of pixels, both independently and in relation to the neighboring pixels. The matrix and values of a **custom filter** that convolutes, or twists, the brightness of the pixels in the image are shown in Figure 14.2.3.

Sharpening filters are commonly used to increase the contrast of adjacent pixels in areas of an image that may be blurred, for example, due to the lack of lighting during the rendering process. Sharpening filters can also be used to bring out more detail in surfaces that have been texture mapped or in images that have been resampled to a higher resolution. These filters use a variety of sharpening techniques that increase contrast based, for example, on differences of color or brightness, or only where edges of shapes are found. Even though sharpening filters are applied to every pixel of the selected image area, in some cases a **filter radius** is specified to determine the size of the filter as it looks for edges and determines how much sharpening should be applied (Fig. 14.2.4).

Blurring filters can be used to soften the areas of rendered images where too much contrast between adjacent pixels create jagged edges or **texture noise**. Blurring usually works by bringing the intensity or color values of adjacent pixels closer to one another (Fig. 14.2.5). On occasion, blurring filters are used as an antialiasing retouching tool. Blurring filters can also soften the sharp edges of polygonal renderings, and the edges of masks. This technique is very effective for eliminating the jagged edges and color aliasing that happen during compositing when the mask is too sharp and displays jagged edges.

A few additional filters that can be quite functional include edge detection filters, NTSC (National Television Standards Commission), and field deinterlacing filters. **Edge detection filters** identify the edges of a shape, isolate them, and even trace a contour around them. When combined with selection tools, both of these techniques are useful for creating the masks used in the compositing of images. Edge detection filters create tight masks quickly and avoid the repetitive manual work that is otherwise required to create masks (Fig. 14.2.6). An **NTSC color filter** clips the colors in an RGB image that are beyond the chromatic range of the NTSC video signal. NTSC color filters are extremely useful in maintaining the quality of color, and in making sure that colors are not too "hot" for the video standard (Fig. 14.2.7). **Deinterlacing filters** can be used in conjunction with NTSC filters to improve the quality of video images displayed on RGB monitors (Fig. 14.2.8). (For more details on NTSC read Chapter 15.)

In addition to the basic digital filters, dozens of striking visual effects can be achieved by filtering an image. A select group of these filters helps to fine-tune and refine renderings of three-dimensional scenes. But the majority of filters have such an overwhelming effect on the image that they are better suited to aid in the creation of special effects that visibly alter the original renderings or to prepare the two-dimensional images that are used as image maps. When used appropriately, even the filters that distort the image can create startling effects like bold changes in color, sensuous undulations and ripplings, delicate embossing and contouring, tingling textures, and faceted brushstrokes (Fig. 14.2.9).

14.3 Image Compositing and Blending

Image compositing consists of combining two or more different images into one in such a way that an illusion of time and space is created: It seems that all the images happened at the same time and place and were recorded together. When created with traditional tools—such as scissors, glue, and paper—image compositing results in a **collage**, which is an assembly or composition of image fragments or materials from different sources. In the film industry image compositing is also known as **matting** because of the masks, or **mattes**, used in the compositing process.

One of the main purposes of image compositing is usually to save expensive production costs or to simulate something that is physically impossible to create in our reality—for example, a family and their pets having a picnic on the surface of Saturn while their chauffeur drives their spaceship through the rings around the planet.

The process of compositing images from different sources into a single visually coherent image can be performed on both still and moving images. Still composites are often called collages, while moving composites result in dynamic composites or transition effects. Combining several shots from different sources into a single still or sequence is at the heart of all special visual effects, and also of many avant-garde artistic movements—such as Surrealism—that seek to subvert our notions of reality. Images are usually composited with masks (described earlier in this chapter), but when images are composited without masks the process is called image blending.

Traditional Matting Techniques

Before computers became popular production tools, painting and photographic techniques were used for matting and compositing. Most mattes were created by painting them directly on glass or on film, and compositing was done primarily done with the **optical printer**, a camera that photographs film projected onto the camera by a projector mounted in front of it. The optical printer was developed in the early 1940s, and it transformed the way special effects in movies were created for decades. The optical printer can duplicate an entire film onto a new roll, and it can also be used for compositing, slowing, or reversing the motion, reshooting through anamorphic lenses, balancing the contrast and the color values, zooming, panning, and creating transition effects. Today the optical printer is still used in conjunction with digital and high-resolution video technology, but it has been largely replaced by digital compositing, now the primary form of dynamic compositing.

The technique of **matte painting** was developed in the 1920s

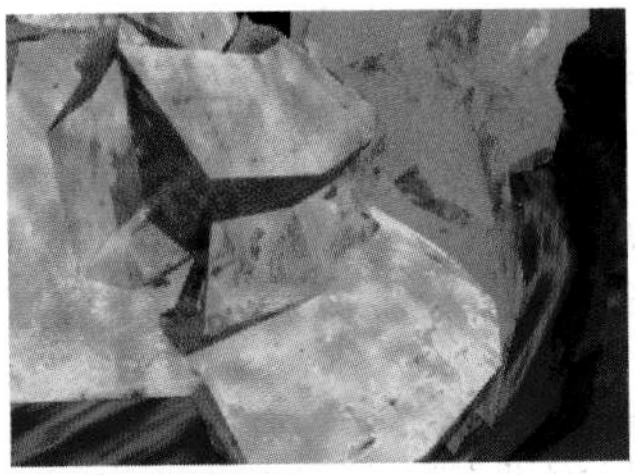

BEFORE NTSC FILTER

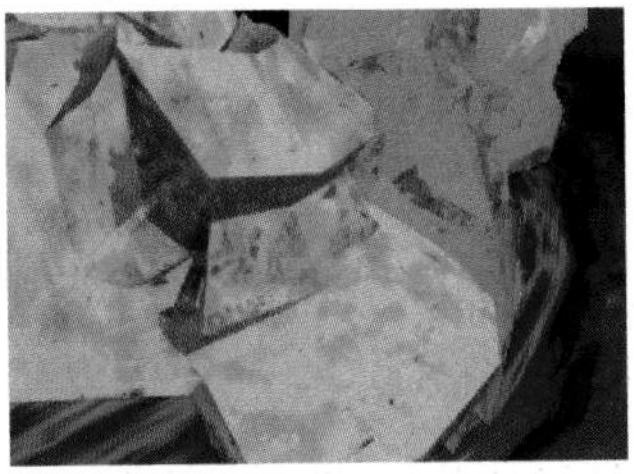

AFTER NTSC FILTER

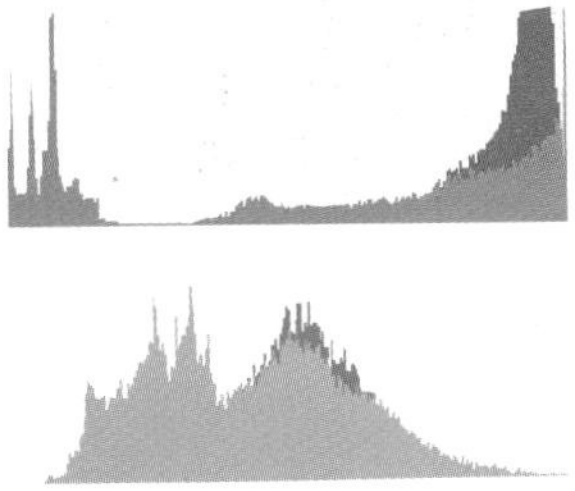

CLIPPED RED AND GREEN COLORS

14.2.7 Before and after an NTSC filter was applied to the image to remove the RGB colors that are beyond the chromatic range of NTSC video. The histograms for the colors red and green show (in the darker colors) the hues that were clipped by the filter.

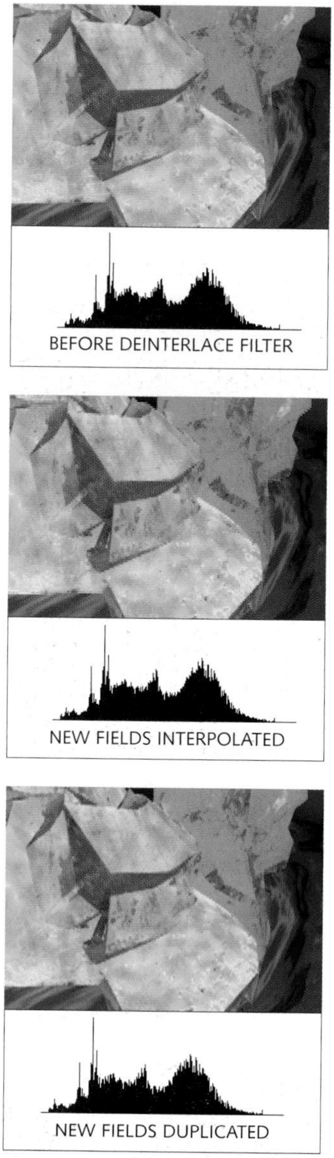

14.2.8 The histogram detail of the original image (top) can be compared with the histograms of images processed with a deinterlace filter. The middle histogram shows the result of new fields created—to replace those that were removed—by interpolation. The histogram on the bottom shows the result of new fields created by duplication.

by making detailed paintings on glass but leaving some areas empty so that the live action can be matted, or inserted, there. This is the simplest kind of matting and it is called a **stationary matte.** Initially the partially painted glass was placed in front of the camera, far enough away that both the painting and the live action could be seen through the unpainted areas in the glass, and then they were recorded together. As this technique developed, the clear areas through which the camera photographed the background action were painted black instead of being left transparent. This way it became possible to add the live action later by rewinding the film and making a double exposure. This innovation made possible the matting of figures in the foreground of the scene.

A **traveling matte** is a dynamic matte that was developed to composite moving elements in the scene. In this case, the blocked areas change every frame in exact synchronization with the foreground image action. The technique of traveling mattes has been perfected over the years, and today it has become a staple in the digital production of visual effects. Several methods and techniques are in use today for producing a traveling matte, including blue and green screen, rotoscoping, and camera tracking (read Chapter 13 for more information on all these techniques). A **garbage matte**, which can be stationary or traveling, is used to isolate and remove elements that are not a part of the shot, such as scaffoldings, lighting reflectors, and wires.

Rear and front projection, as well as in-camera compositing, are compositing techniques that do not involve the creation of a mask or matte because the actors or foreground objects act themselves as masks. While very popular during the earlier days of special effects, these three matting techniques are rarely used today since their digital counterparts offer greater control and are usually more efficient. In both rear and front projection, the matting is achieved by recording the actors or objects to be matted over live projections of the background. In **rear projection**, a translucent screen behind the actor or model is used to project previously shot material. While the actor acts or the model is moved the scene is photographed by a camera situated in front of the action. This simple trick was devised in the early 1930s, and it is a common technique still used in the filming of dialogues between actors inside mock-up cars. Street scenes are rear-projected, while the fake car is moved to simulate the vibration produced by motion. When color photography became the standard of the motion picture industry, rear projection posed many technical problems. This was because the large amounts of light that were needed to illuminate the scene brightly enough for the slow color film of the time also washed out the images projected on the rear translucent screen behind the live action. So front projection was developed, and in 1968 it was used with excellent results in the milestone film ***2001: A Space Odyssey*** to composite the image of a human actor in an ape costume with images of real apes shot elsewhere.

Front projection is based on a projector that is aligned at a 90-degree angle with the camera and a half-silvered mirror aligned at a 45-degree angle in relation to the camera and the projector. A front projection screen made of a highly reflective material is placed in front of the camera, and the actor or model is positioned in between the screen and the camera. The image is projected on the half-silvered mirror positioned at a 45-degree angle, which sends it to the screen. Ninety-five percent of the image bounces back from the reflective screen, passes through the two-way mirror, and goes directly to the camera.

In addition to the optical printer, simpler compositing was also created inside of the camera with a variety of techniques like exposing the same strip of film twice; this was called **in-camera compositing**. The idea of compositing foreground elements over a background is also a staple concept in traditional keyframe animation: Motion is simulated with two-dimensional foreground shapes that move over a background. The image compositing in this instance can be done by placing the foreground elements on a cel over the background, or with multiple exposures (sometimes with masks and sometimes without) on the same strip of film.

Compositing with Masks and Operators

A mask used in the compositing process consists of a monochromatic image that protects portions of another image being composited. As described earlier in this chapter, a mask is like a stencil: its solid areas protect the surface being masked, and its perforated areas expose the surface being masked. In many instances the mask or masks used in the compositing process are kept in a separate alpha channel, which is independent from each of the red, green, and blue channels in an RGB color image (Fig. 6.2.4). Image compositing with masks allows us to isolate and consolidate seamlessly multiple images; this is useful when reassembling complex three-dimensional scenes that were rendered in separate parts or layers. Large or complex three-dimensional environments can be rendered in parts, and the resulting images can be assembled back together in two dimensions with image compositing (Figs. 14.3.1–14.3.4).

In addition to compositing with several masks, **operators** or functions can also be used to composite multiple elements. Operators allow users to apply different functions to select parts of the image. Several compositing programs allow users to fine-tune the parameters and to customize their own functions. Figures 14.3.5 and 14.3.6 show two examples that have composited with a variety of operators. On the left side of the screen shots we see the large composite image, and the source images or images in process. On the right side we see the node tree or visual flowchart that is used to structure the operators and the sequence in which they will be applied to the images. Below the node tree we can see the variables and parameters of the active node in the tree.

Figure 14.3.5 shows an image with transparencies (glass and smoke) shot on blue screen and composited against a desktop. Figure

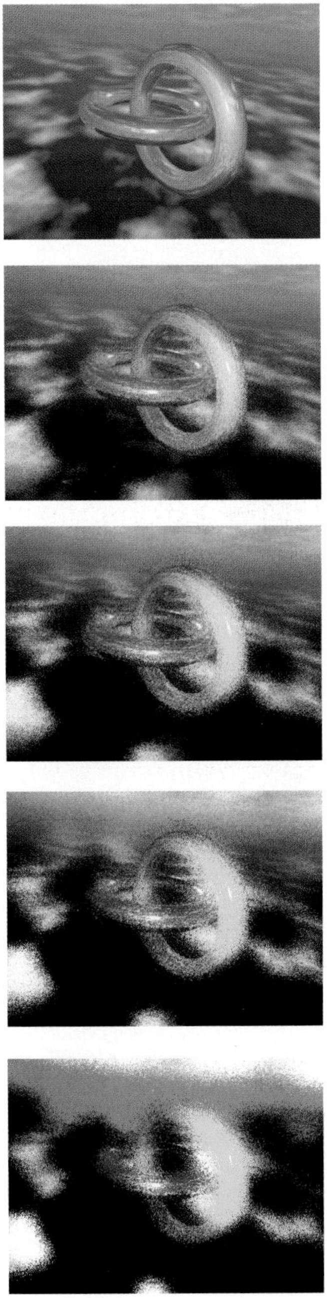

14.2.9 This sequence of images was created by applying the same filter to the initial image and to each of the subsequent images.

14.3.1 A live action image of the singer composited with renderings of a virtual environment. (From the music video *Agolo* by Angelique Kidjo. Courtesy of Telecreateurs, Medialab Paris, Phonogram, Michel Meyer, and ZAPDAN.)

FOREGROUND ELEMENTS

14.3.2 The sequence on the opposite page shows the final composited image (largest size), and some of the layers with image elements and masks. On top is the background pass of the garage and below a greyscale representation of the geometry depth of the scene, used to create a depth of field effect in the finished image. Next is a pass of the elements visible through the garage window, used to bring back detail lost to the volumetric light effect used in the background pass. The shadow pass is at the bottom. On this page is the rendering, or beauty pass, of the two characters. (Images courtesy of Wyse Advertising and Will Vinton Studios. Sal DeMarco and Michael Chaney, Producers. © 1999 Krylon Products Group.)

14.3.6 shows an image manipulation and compositing process that inserts a truck into the original background containing just one car. The node tree shows how the white truck is inserted and placed, colorized, and finally duplicated, scaled, and blurred. Figure 14.3.7 shows an additional example of matting with a blue screen, a convenient color for matting because the fleshtones of actors do not have a blue component (read Chapter 13 for more information on blue and green screen details).

Compositing without Masks

It is also possible to digitally composite images from multiple sources without using masks; in such cases the image compositing process is usually referred to as **image blending**. With this process multiple images can simply be blended, and the result looks like a collection of transluscent, or ghosted, images. Blending can also be controlled with many combinations of operators such as addition, difference, and multiplication (Fig. 14.3.8).

Two-Dimensional Morphing

Morphing is based on two-dimensional interpolation techniques that can be applied to renderings of three-dimensional scenes. Two-dimensional morphing is different from the three-dimensional interpolation techniques—sometimes also called morphing techniques—that blend the three-dimensional shape of objects in a simulated scene. **Two-dimensional morphing** is a special type of image blending that interpolates the values of pixels. This interpolation is based not only on the color value of pixels but also controlled by a grid that helps to match and interpolate the shapes of the two images or sequences being morphed (Fig. 14.3.9). The control grid is placed on the two images to be morphed or on two keyframes of the sequence to be morphed. The grid is adjusted in each of the images so that the points on the grid correspond to the areas that have to be morphed. The grid points control the color interpolation of the pixels as well as the spatial interpolation that is necessary for a pixel in the first image to be moved to the XY location of the corresponding pixel in the second image.

14.4 Image Sequencing

A great deal of a story narrated with images is actually told by the order and timing in which sequences of images are presented to the audience. The arrangement and composition of moving images is called **image sequencing** or **image editing**. The stage of image sequencing in any computer animation project is an important moment in the production process for two reasons. It is when ideas presented in the original storyboard can be finalized in a faithful and flawless way. Image sequencing is also the moment in the creative process when ideas can be fine-tuned to make the project more expressive or to conform to unexpected changes, such as a shorter or a longer running time.

In most computer animation productions, the image sequencing process is usually not done by the individual or production team that produced the computer animation in the first place. The final sequencing of images—and their subsequent output onto film, video, or photographic media—involves specialized techniques and skills. This is especially true when the image sequencing is done with nondigital film or video production techniques. But increasingly, as more of the final image sequencing process migrates to the digital realm, it is common for those involved in producing the computer animation to also be involved in some or all of the image sequencing.

The most common reason for computer animators to get involved with image sequencing is to create an animatic or a rough cut of the project. An **animatic** is a preliminary version of a computer animation and is used to visualize how the final project may look (read Chapter 2 for more information on animatics). Unlike an animatic, a **rough cut** of a computer animation usually contains the finished renderings and final motion. However, the final arrangement of the sequences presented in a rough cut is yet to be locked, and the transitions between sequences are not implemented. Rough cuts are used to preview the rhythm and timing of the sequences already arranged in the order specified in the storyboard. Rough cuts often result in modifications to the original plan in terms of the duration or length of a particular shot, scene, or sequence, or in terms of the order in which a series of shots, scenes, or sequences are presented.

Building a Sequence of Images

Most image sequencing software provides at least one pair of channels or **video tracks** for placing the different shots that are being edited as well as the transition effects that link them. The idea of using tracks to build a sequence of dynamic information comes from the predigital worlds of video and sound editing. Since its early days sound editing used multiple tracks of sound to composite simultaneous sounds—such as dialogue, background music, and sound effects—from a variety of sources. This layering of sound was possible because predigital sound editing systems had multiple tracks. The standard editing technique in predigital film and video, the **A/B roll editing** technique, is based on building a sequence by combining images arranged linearly in two different sources. Most image sequencing software today permits the user to sequence and combine images from two or more tracks, and in any order. This is commonly called **nonlinear editing**, and it makes reference to the fact that digital editing systems do not have to scan a linear medium (such as film or videotape) in order to find the source images.

Editing the different shots of a computer animation with digital sequencing software is usually done through a visual interface that

BACKGROUND

DEPTH MASK

FINAL COMPOSITE

WINDOW ELEMENTS ONLY

SHADOWS

14.3.3 The different components and props of the main character in the feature film *Stuart Little* were rendered in separate passes. Shown here are a wireframe version of the model, and a simple shading composited onto the background plate to check for scale and perspective, and the fur elements in a single pass. The final composite can be seen in Figure 14.3.4. (Images courtesy of Sony Pictures Imageworks.)

allows the editor to arrange animated segments by manipulating icons. This is done by dragging the icons that represent the source images into the proper position on the track and dropping them into place. Their location and duration can be further adjusted by sliding them on the video track or time line. This common method of image sequencing is called **copy-and-paste editing** because images are copied from the source files and then pasted in the sequence being built. In addition to the tracks that hold the animation clips, there are tracks for the transition effects between shots placed on different video tracks, and tracks for sound information.

Visual Rhythm and Tempo

Two of the key principles of dynamic image composition include rhythm and tempo (a thorough examination of *all* the principles of dynamic image composition is beyond the scope of this book). In practical terms, the visual rhythm sets the pace of a computer animation, and tempo sets the speed. In the context of image sequencing, the **visual rhythm** of a sequence or an animated project is the visual pattern created by the frequency of transitions between shots. The rhythm of image sequences can be, for example, predictable or surprising, regular and soothing, syncopated and lively, or irregular and chaotic. The tempo of image sequences ranges from slow to very fast. **Visual tempo**, or visual pace, is set primarily by the length of the individual shots in the sequence. The pace is fast when shots in a sequence stay only a couple of seconds on the screen; the pace is slow when shots are longer in length. When used in conjunction with the action contained in the animated images, rhythm and pace are effective ways of reinforcing the emotional content of a scene.

Transitions Between Shots

The techniques used to blend and composite moving images are called **transition effects**. Transitions between shots, as they are also called, can be simple or complex, ranging, for example, from a straight cut to a cross-dissolve combined with a wipe. Image layers, alpha channels, and masks are commonly used to combine sequences of computer animation just as they are used to combine still images.

Transition effects are useful from the visual point of view because they add visual interest and variation to a sequence. Transition effects can add funkiness and ornamentation. In addition to their immediate embellishment functions, transition effects are also an effective way to communicate the passage of time and to anticipate or play down the upcoming action. Transition effects, for example, break the continuity of one sequence or announce the beginning of a new one.

In addition to the information provided by the storyline and the action shown by the camera, transition effects help to define the **temporal** and **spatial relation** between shots or scenes. A quick

and simple transition effect, such as a straight cut, for example, reinforces the fact that the action shown in the second shot of a sequence occurs right after the final shot and also in the same physical location. A long cross-dissolve, on the other hand, hints that two consecutive shots happen in different places and also that a fair amount of time takes place between them. Some of the most commonly used transition effects include the cut, fades, cross-dissolves, wipes, and morphs. (Two-dimensional morphing is covered earlier in the chapter and illustrated in Fig. 14.3.9.)

14.3.4 Several layers of computer animation and live action were composited and retouched into this shot of the feature film *Stuart Little*. (Images courtesy of Sony Pictures Imageworks. © 1999 Global Entertainment Productions GmbH & Co. Medien KG. All rights reserved.)

A **cut** is a plain and immediate change from one shot to another. A cut is the simplest transition and also the most common. Cuts are made by placing the last frame of a sequence, or tail, right next to the first frame, or head, of another sequence (Fig. 14.4.1). A cut gets its name from the fact that when editing film a transition of this type is achieved by actually cutting two strips of film and then splicing them together with transparent glue or tape. A **soft cut** is a combination of a cross-dissolve and a cut. This effect provides a cut that is slightly expanded in time, and softened, by the effect of the two shots quickly fading into each other.

In a **fade-out**, the end of a shot vanishes gradually and reveals a still frame of solid color. When a shot fades into a black still frame, the effect is called **fade to black**. Fade-out transitions can also be made between shots so that the end of the first shot gradually vanishes into the early frames of the consecutive shot which suddenly pops into the sequence (Fig. 14.4.1). In a **fade-in** transition—which is the inverse of a fade-out—the first shot usually consists of a still black frame so that the second half of the transition seems to emerge from

14.3.5 The node tree on the right contains the operators that are applied to the two small source images. Three operators are concatenated in the upper right to make the spotlight effect on the ashtray. (RGrad1) is applied to the background to control the color correction, (Mult1) makes the background yellow, and (ColorMatch1) modifies the color. The mask for the (Blur1) operator is made with some ramps combined with the mask coming from (Rotoscope2), and is used to keep the smoke in focus and the front of the ashtray out of focus. (Photo courtesy of Photron. Shake dialog box courtesy of Apple Computer.)

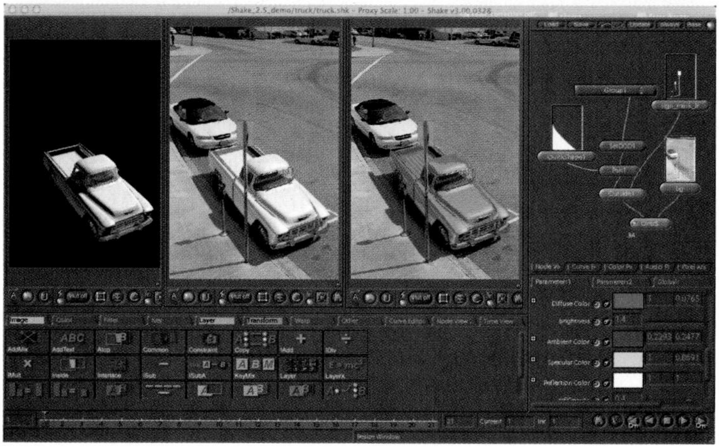

14.3.6 The visual flowchart (right) shows how a red truck has been added to the original background (thumbnail window, far right). The computer-generated white truck is first inserted, a shadow mask is created, and the truck is colorized. (Photo by Peter Warner. Truck modeled by Caleb Owens. Shake dialog box courtesy of Apple Computer.)

black. Sometimes a fade-in also starts with a first sequence of frames that is suddenly cut when the second sequence has fully appeared. Fades are defined by their length and by their intensity. Most fades are just a couple of seconds long, but a slow fade can last 10 seconds or more, and a quick fade lasts less than a dozen frames. The intensity of a fade is expressed in percentages. Fades usually go from 0 percent to 100 percent or vice versa, so that when the images are fully faded they are either fully invisible or fully visible. But in some situations partial fades can create interesting effects—for example, a sequence of shots that start their fade-in with a 20 percent fade-in value and are cut when they reach 80 percent.

A **cross-dissolve** is a transition effect where two shots fade into each other; as the first shot fades out, the second shot fades in (Fig. 14.4.1). Cross-dissolves are an effective way to give the audience a moment to pause and think about what they have just seen or what they are about to see. Cross-dissolves are effective links between two shots and can be used as adverbs in the visual grammar of computer animation. A cross-dissolve can say, for example, "and then," or "in the meantime," or "years later." Cross-dissolve transitions are effective ways to connect actions that happen in the distant past or in the future, or to present actions that occur only in the imagination of a protagonist in parallel with the real action.

There are many variations of cross-dissolve transitions. The most common form of a cross-dissolve consists of a gradual and delicate simultaneous transition from one shot to another. The length and intensity of cross-dissolves is expressed—as it is expressed in fades—in terms of frames and percentages. A very short cross-dissolve is often called a soft cut and is barely perceptible, but it adds an accent of slowness or acceleration to the transition between two shots. Slow cross-dissolves create a ghostly effect where the objects and characters in the scene seem to be transparent. Blending and **layering moving images** is best achieved with cross-dissolves. A dream sequence, for example, where images overlap with one another and objects suddenly materialize or vanish is a classic example of using cross-dissolve transitions for layering images. A **dither cross-dissolve** uses a coarse pattern to fade the two shots into one another.

Wipes are transition effects where the basic idea is that the second shot displaces the first shot by sliding into the frame, dropping or spreading over it. There are myriad variations of wipes, and one is illustrated in Figure 14.4.1. In the most common form of a wipe, called plainly a **wipe** or a side wipe, the second shot slides across the frame over the first shot. Wipes can also slide diagonally, along the vertical axis, radially, or using any geometric shape or edge as a template. Elaborate wipes include screen splits, spin wipes, interlaced wipes like venetian blinds, and page turns.

14.3.7 These two actors are in a green screen stage. The lighting of the shot is done carefully so that the light does not bounce off the screen and onto the actors. A landscape background is composited after the shot is completed and traveling mattes are extracted off the blue screen. (Images courtesy of Menfond. © StarEast/Bob.)

14.5 Color Grading

As mentioned in Chapter 13, the color of the images in one or several sequences can be adjusted at different points during the production or the postproduction stages. This color adjustment is called **color grading**, and it is also referred to as color timing, color balance, and color correction. The individuals most involved with color timing in a live-action movie are usually the cinematographer and the visual effects supervisor. The color supervisor or the art director would perform the same task in an animated movie.

Traditionally, color grading of film was done through photochemical processes and it was mostly used to correct mistakes of exposure, lighting, or film stock. **Color timing** derives its name from the fact that film could be left in different chemical solutions for different amounts of time and at different temperatures to achieve different results. Photochemical color timing was, and continues to be, a process that is sometimes difficult to control and where predictability and efficiency run at the expense of experimentation. Digital color grading is fully interactive, offers greater flexibility, and has a greater set of tools than photochemical timing. In spite of its

14.3.8 Two images (from Fig. 14.1.9) are composited without masks and with the following functions: Darker, Lighter, Difference, and Hard Light.

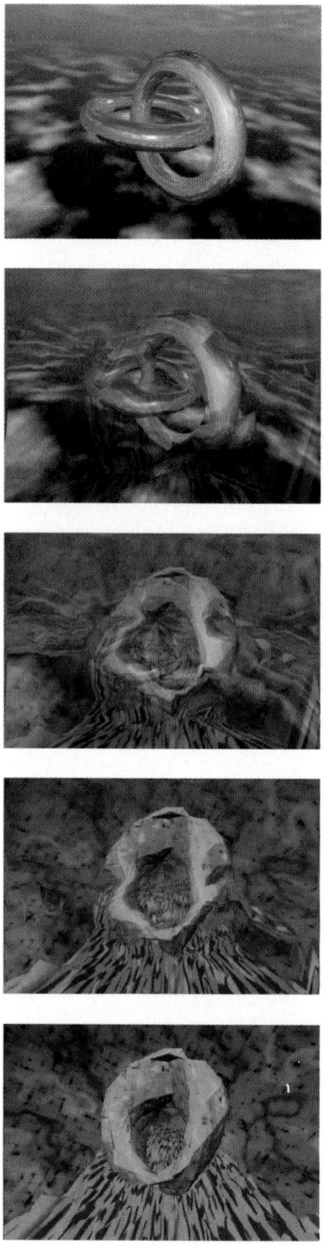

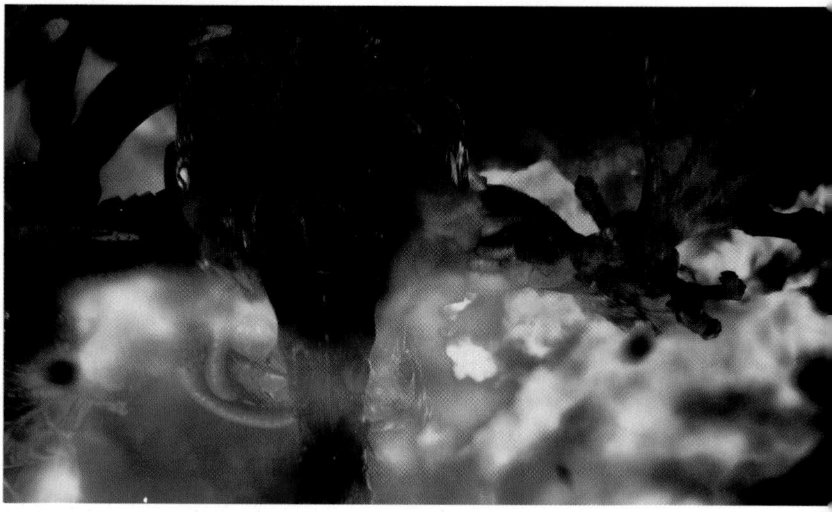

14.3.9 Two-dimensional morphing is a technique that blends still images into one another. The blending of the pixel color values is controlled by a grid that tags areas of the image to be blended with one another.

relative newness, digital color grading is widely available and is replacing photochemical grading as the premiere grading method.

At its simplest color grading is essentially the manipulation of the color and brightness values in a scene. Color corrections can be applied in layers or in sets: a **primary color correction** may take care of most of the desired result while a secondary color correction can be used to fine tune details. At its most complex color timing is a collection of filters and functions that control every aspect of the image, and that can be used to transform the overall **visual look** of a scene or an entire movie. The 2000 movie ***O Brother Where Art Thou?*** by the Coen Brothers or the 2001 movie ***Le fabuleux destin d'Amélie Poulain*** directed by Jean-Pierre Jeunet, for example, are two of the earliest examples of digital color grading used to drastically transform the overall look of the original live action and visual effects footage.

Many of the tools described earlier in this chapter are available in digital color grading systems: parameter curves, histograms, and selection or masking tools. The most sophisticated selection tools are called **power windows** because of their wide range of functionality. Power windows may select multiple areas at a time and offer a wide range of functionality, including ramps, selected areas and effects that change through time. Temporal control allows color graders to re-time the color of visal elements throughout an entire sequence in a semi-automated way. The hard edge shadows cast by a walking character, for example, could be first selected throughout the entire sequence, made lighter and slightly warmer in color, and given softer edges. One of the most dramatic uses of color grading is the **night-for-day** effect in which typically a scene shot in daylight is manipulated to the point of transforming the entire color palette and simulating the color and lighting conditions of a night scene (Fig 14.5.1).

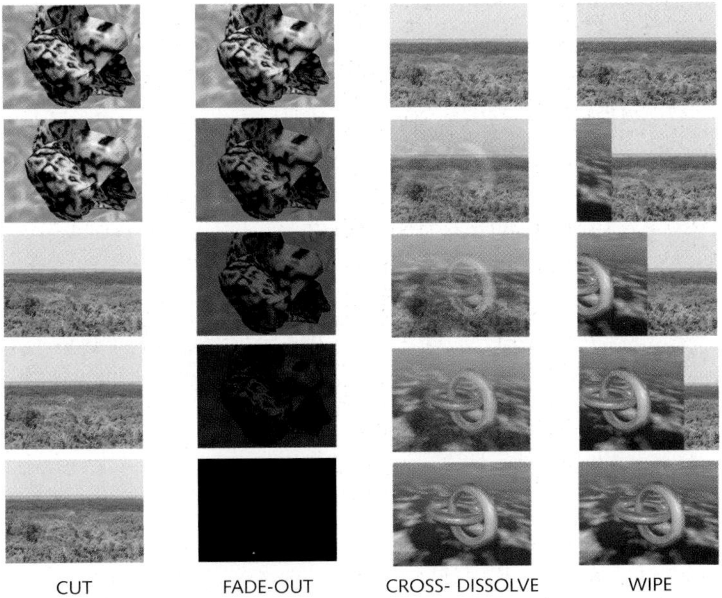

14.4.1 A cut between two animated sequences (far left), and three popular transitions: a fade-out, a cross-dissolve, and a wipe.

14.5.1 The night-for-day is achieved by drastically changing the overall color grading of a live action. (Images courtesy of da Vinci Systems.)

14.3.10 (opposite page, right) The compositing in *Final Fantasy* averaged 16 three-dimensional layers per shot; the highest count was 498 in a single shot. Explosions were created with a combination of techniques ranging from Renderman shaders to libraries of practical effects (dust, smoke, and fire) for compositing. (© 2001 FFFP.)

(Two characters spending time at home. © A.Film A/S.)

CHAPTER 14

Key Terms

A/B roll editing
Alpha channel
Angular straight lines
Animatic
Background
Blurring filters
Brightness
Channels
Collage
Color dithering
Color grading
Color look-up table
Color timing
Contrast
Copy-and-paste editing
Cross-dissolve
Custom filter
Cut
Darkroom
Deinterlacing filters
Digital filters
Digital retouching
Dither cross-dissolve
Edge detection filters
Fade to black
Fade-in
Fade-out
File size
Filter radius
Foreground elements
Front projection
Garbage matte
Highlight
Histogram
Histogram editor
Image blending
Image dimensions
Image editing
Image layers
Image manipulation
Image sequencing
In-camera compositing
Indexed color
Interpolation techniques
Layering moving images
Linear color space
Log color space
Mask
Matte
Matte painting
Matting
Midtone
Neighbor pixel interpolation
Night-for-day
Nonlinear editing
Nonlinear color space
NTSC color filter
Operators
Optical printer
Parameter curves
Photographic procedures
Pixels per inch
Postprocessing
Power windows
Primary color correction
Rear projection
Resampling an image, the color resolution
Retouching
Rough cut
Shadow
Sharpening filters
Soft curves
Soft cut
Spatial relation
Stationary matte
Stencils
Straight diagonal line
Studio
System palette
Temporal relation
Texture noise
Tonal range
Traditional painting tools
Transition effects
Traveling matte
Two-dimensional morphing
Video tracks
Visual rhythm
Visual tempo
Weighted interpolation
Wipe

CHAPTER 15

15

Image Resolution and Output

Summary

THE BASIC CONCEPTS REQUIRED TO OUTPUT computer-generated images in a variety of media are the focus of this chapter. The three types of image resolution—color, spatial, and temporal—are examined in detail. File formats are reviewed, as are the most popular delivery media, including video, film, paper, and CD-ROM, and their aspect ratios.

QUICK INDEX

15.1 Basic Concepts of Digital Output

Each of the professions and industries in which three-dimensional computer imaging is used today has different output requirements. This is due to the differences in the final product and the different forms of final delivery and distribution of products in each of these areas. The output of three-dimensional imagery in many of the art and design areas that deal with two-dimensional creation, for example, occurs primarily in the form of paper printouts and film slides, or transparencies. These areas include, for example, illustration, photography, and graphic arts. The new areas of interactive art, entertainment and virtual reality that include interactive videogames and on-line information services, for example, require that images be delivered in a variety of digital file formats. This delivery often happens through computer networks, or on magnetic or optical media. In some of the three-dimensional areas, including product design, sculpture, and architecture, the digital output includes both printouts for presentation purposes and digital files for computer-aided design and computer-aided manufacturing (CAD/CAM). In four-dimensional, or time-based, activities—including computer animation, gaming, and location-based entertainment—delivery usually takes place in the form of video, film, or digital files (Figs. 12.7.1–12.7.3).

The digital output process starts when rendered images are taken out of the computer system with the **output peripherals**. These include an array of devices such as printers, pen plotters, film or video recorders, and three-dimensional milling or casting machines (Fig. 15.1.1). Output peripherals are used for fixing the images created on the monitor onto other media that may include paper, film, video, and CD-ROM. This capture process is not automatic. It is based on a **translation of data**. This translation is made by software and electronic components of output peripherals called **digital-to-analog** converters or **DTAs**. The DTAs convert the digital information created with software back into continuous information. This process is just the inverse of scanning an image on paper that is to be used as a texture map or a background in a three-dimensional scene. In this case, the sensors in the input peripherals—called analog-to-digital converters—convert the continuous information contained in the image into digital information that can be manipulated by the program. DTAs convert the binary numbers that describe an image back into analog voltages that are subsequently converted into light, heat, or pressure by the imaging components of the output peripherals. The quality and sophistication of the digital-to-analog converters—their precision, definition and speed—often defines the quality of the final output as well as the cost of the output peripheral. High-quality DTAs provide digital output with low noise, high image resolution, and a wide chromatic range.

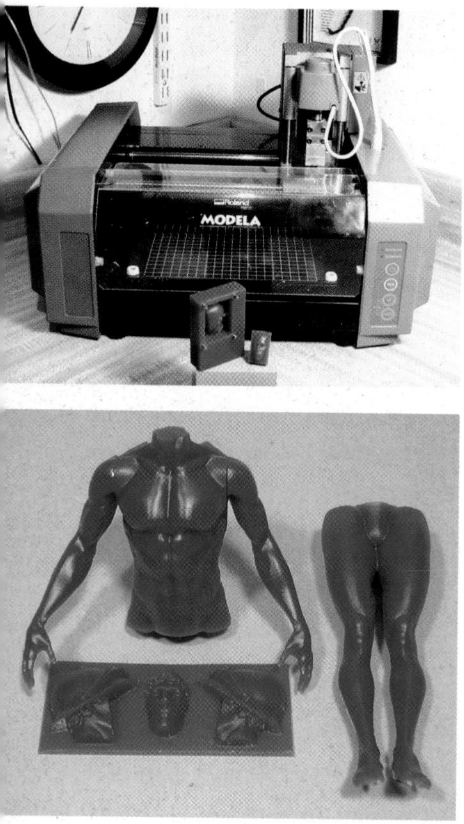

15.1.1 The body parts for the *Medicus* project were machined from a block of dark blue jewelers wax using the Roland MDX-20 milling machine. Due to the limitations of a three-axis output device, the model is created in several sections to have access undercuts. See Figure 15.8.2 for a later step in the fabrication process. (© 2002 Dan Platt, Solid Image Arts, LLC.)

15.2 Image Resolution

Image resolution can be defined as the amount of detail contained in an image or sequence of images. The resolution of an image is also called **image definition**, and it is related to many factors such as the quality of the input and output peripherals, the color depth of the computer system, the capabilities of the software that was used to create the image, and the quality of the output media. Having a good understanding of the basic issues of image resolution is fundamental in order to use three-dimensional computer imaging techniques to their fullest. There are four aspects of image resolution that are relevant to visual creators: spatial resolution, chromatic resolution, temporal resolution, and image compression.

Spatial Resolution

Computer-generated images are made of **pixels,** or picture elements, which are the little dots that we see when we get very close to the computer screen. **Spatial resolution** describes the amount of image detail and definition in digital images. Spatial resolution, also known as **pixel resolution**, has to do with the total number of pixels in an image, and is defined by the relation between the dimensions of an image and the number of pixels in the image. Spatial resolution can be expressed in terms of pixels, dots, or lines per inch.

The number of pixels that exist in an **image file** is measured in **pixels per inch** or **ppi**. When rendering a three-dimensional scene, for example, it is necessary to indicate the pixel resolution at which the image is to be rendered. The most general way to specify the absolute spatial resolution of a file is by using pixels per inch, regardless of the resolution of the output peripheral used to print or display the image. The spatial resolution of image files ranges from a low of 100 ppi to a high of 4,000 ppi.

The spatial resolution of a specific input or output **peripheral device** can be measured in **dots per inch** or **dpi**. This unit of resolution is often related to the number of sensors in an input peripheral, or the number of imaging heads in an output peripheral. A medium resolution ranges from 300 to 600 dpi, and high resolution ranges from 1,000 dpi and up.

Lines per inch or **lpi** is another unit for measuring spatial resolutions. lpi is used almost exclusively in digital prepress or in desktop publishing for measuring the number of lines—or rows of dots—in **halftone screens**. These screens are used for printing an image with traditional graphic arts mechanical reproduction techniques. Halftone screens of 65 lpi, for example, are commonly used for newspaper image quality while 150 lpi halftone screens yield great image definition on high-quality coated paper. A simple formula that can help determine the pixel (ppi) resolution needed when preparing files for **halftone output** specifies that the ppi resolution should not exceed 2.5 times the target lpi resolution (2.5:1 ratio). For example, a resolution of 300 ppi would be adequate when using halftone screens of 150 lpi (2:1 ratio) but probably overkill if 65 lpi screens (4.6:1 ratio) were used (Fig. 15.2.1).

When the **dot resolution** of the output peripheral matches exactly the pixel resolution of an image file, we can see the contents of the file displayed in optimal fashion, but these cases are rare. Most often we work with files whose ppi resolution does not match the dpi resolution of an output peripheral. In those cases, we can use specialized software to **resample** the pixel resolution of the file and match it to the dot resolution of the output peripheral. We can also let the internal software of the peripheral do the resampling for us. However, the results are generally better and more predictable when we do it.

Using pixels per inch as the unit to convey spatial resolution is convenient because often the resolution of the rendered images is different from the resolution of the peripherals used to output them. Images may be rendered at one resolution and displayed at another. For example, when an image is rendered in high resolution and then displayed in high or in low resolution, the high resolution image loses detail when displayed on a low resolution display, but it shows its true resolution when shown on a display with a higher resolution (Fig. 15.2.2). The fact that an image may look low resolution on a specific printout or monitor does not necessarily mean that the image is low resolution.

For example, a three-dimensional scene rendered at a resolution of 300 dpi, and horizontal and vertical dimensions of 3 × 2 in. has an absolute pixel size of 900 × 600 pixels. On a monitor with a resolution of 300 dpi, for example, there would be a 1:1 match so that each pixel in the file corresponds to a dot on the monitor. On a monitor

600 PPI RESOLUTION

300 PPI

150 PPI

50 PPI

15.2.1 Four different spatial resolutions (ranging from 50 to 600 ppi) reproduced here at the same 150 lpi halftone screen resolution. The top image is the original rendering. (© 2001 Dygra Films.)

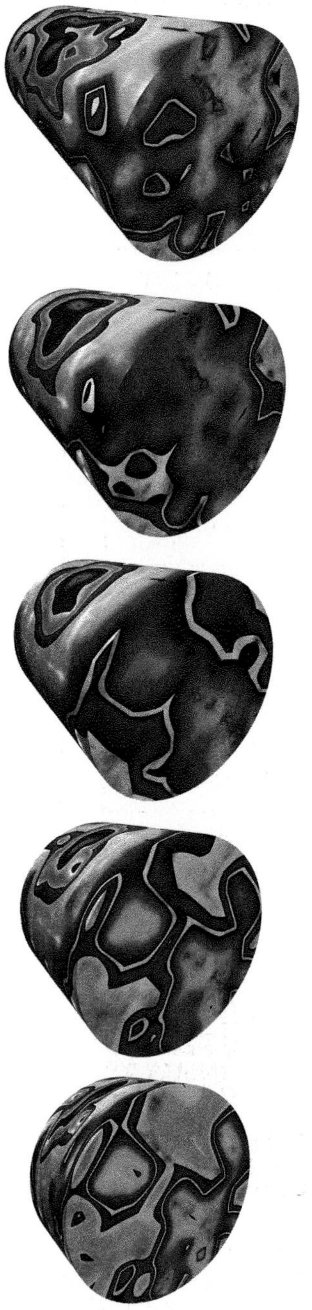

15.2.2 This sequence shows the 300 dpi images from Figure 9.6.8 output at the lower resolution of 72 dpi.

with a resolution of 100 dpi the results would be different due to the 3:1 ratio, 3 pixels for every dot. In cases such as this one, the discrepancy can be solved without resampling the file by keeping either the resolution or the dimensions constant. If the resolution is kept constant, each pixel in the image file is assigned to one dot in the output peripheral. In this case, the resolution is untouched, but the physical dimensions change. In the example of the 300 dpi 3 × 2 in. file the new dimensions at 100 dpi would be 9 × 6 in. If the dimensions are kept constant, every three pixels in the image file are assigned to one dot in the output peripheral. This leads to a significant loss of spatial resolution, but the dimensions remained untouched. The 300 dpi 3 × 2 in. file remains at the same size but with a lower resolution.

Spatial resolution is also used to define the amount of detail in video (not RGB) images. The number of horizontal lines of resolution is used to measure the spatial resolution of video. Some of the most common resolutions are 525 lines for the NTSC format, 625 for both the PAL and SECAM formats, and 720p and 1080i for the still evolving HD formats (720 lines for the progressive version and 1,080 for the interlaced version). As video technology and computer technology get closer together we might end up using pixels as the single unit for defining spatial resolution. (The section in this chapter on temporal resolution contains more detail about video formats.)

Color Resolution

The **color resolution** of an image is related to the amount of colors and shades of grey that may be contained in an image. Color, or chromatic, resolution is determined by the number of bitplanes used to create and display that image. A **bitplane** can be described as a grid where each cell in the bitplane stores a one-digit number. Since each cell on the grid is assigned to a **pixel**, or picture element, on the computer screen, the numerical value is translated into the color that is displayed on the pixel controlled by that cell. Multiple bitplanes can be thought of as layers in the **graphics memory** or **bitmap**. It is the number of layers in a bitmap that determines the number of colors that each pixel on the screen may have. Because of this, color resolution, or **color depth** as it is also called, is easily defined by the number of bits used to define each channel of an RGB color, for example, 8-bit, 10-bit, 12-bit, or 16-bit color.

A pixel in a bitmap with just one plane, for example, is capable of displaying only one of two colors: black or white. This is because each cell in a one-level bitmap grid can only store a one-digit number, in this case a zero or a one. When a bitmap has more than one plane then the numbers in the corresponding cells of each plane are added—using the conventions of the binary numerical system—to make a longer value. A bitmap with two planes is capable of displaying one of four possible colors—or values of gray—in each pixel (Fig. 13.1.4). This is because when we add the ones or zeros in the corresponding cells of each plane we end up with four possibilities:

00, 01, 10, and 11. In the binary numerical system, 00 equals our decimal 0. Binary 01 equals decimal 1, 10 equals 2, and 11 equals 3.

A bitmap with three planes is capable of displaying one of eight colors per pixel (Fig. 15.2.3). When we add the binary values (1 or 0) in the corresponding cells of each bitplane we end up with eight possible values expressed here, first in binary and then in decimal form.

000 = 0	011 = 3	110 = 6	001 = 1
100 = 4	111 = 7	010 = 2	101 = 5

In the **binary system**, numerical values are read from right to left. The digits in the first (rightmost) column represent the units, and their decimal value can be found by multiplying them times the number one, which is the result of two to the power of zero (2^0). The digits in the second column are multiplied times two, which is the result of 2^1. The digits in the third column are multiplied times 2^2.

BINARY	$2^2 = 4$	$2^1 = 2$	$2^0 = 1$	
DECIMAL	$\times 1$	$\times 1$	$\times 0$	
	4	**+ 2**	**+ 0**	**= 6**

The rule is very simple: the more bitplanes in a bitmap, the more color may be displayed in an image. The maximum number of colors that may exist in a computer-generated image can be calculated by elevating the number two—the base number in the binary system—to the power of the number of bitplanes. Standard configurations of color resolution include 8-bit color with 256 colors, 16-bit color with 65,000 plus colors, and 24-bit color with 16 million plus colors. Figure 15.2.4 shows a list of several possible configurations. This simple rule can be summarized in the following formula:

$$2^{(bitplanes)} = \textit{possible colors.}$$

In addition to the color resolution of an output peripheral, it is also important to consider its chromatic range, and the color conversion techniques used to convert color values from one color space to another. The **chromatic range** of any device defines the range of colors in the visible spectrum that the device is capable of reproducing. Not all media and techniques for creating color are capable of creating exactly the same colors. The CIE chromaticity diagram (Fig. 6.2.3) is a useful tool for visualizing the chromatic ranges of different media. This diagram can be used to bridge the different ranges or gamuts of color that are obtained when different color systems are used. It can also be used to narrow the amount of color that gets lost when an image file is output. Knowing which colors overlap across different media helps to work around the physical limitations of color reproduction.

The fact that many of the colors created with RGB computer monitors are too bright and saturated for display on standard televi-

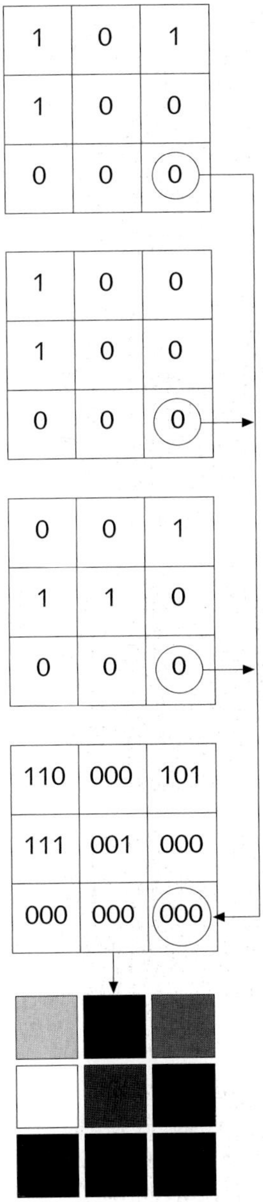

15.2.3 A three-level bitmap can display up to eight colors. The values of each of the bitplanes are added to determine the final value of the pixels.

sion sets is an example that illustrates a limitation created by the different chromatic ranges of different media. Many of these RGB colors have to be clipped before the image is transferred to videotape; otherwise, these saturated colors would fall outside the chromatic range of video. Clipping the colors that fall outside a chromatic range does not mean that the colors are removed altogether. Instead they are replaced with a color that is within the chromatic range and that resembles it the most. **Color clipping** is useful for avoiding distortions such as color bleeding in the final video recording. **Color bleeding** is the streaking and overflowing of colors that occurs on a television set when the colors in the video signal are too saturated. (To create color bleeding, turn the saturation controls on your television set all the way up.)

It is often necessary to **convert colors** from one color space to another, for example from the RGB color space to CMYK, as we convert an image rendered and retouched in the RGB color space into a **CMYK four-color separation** suitable for reproduction in a magazine. Each of the colors in an image is separated into its CMYK components because the printing presses used in mechanical reproduction reproduce color images by printing each of the CMYK layers with a different plate and ink (Figs. 6.2.1 and 6.2.5). In most cases, this color conversion and separation is done automatically by the computer software, and the quality of this conversion varies from program to program. In general, this conversion takes into account many production details—such as type of paper, ink, and printing press characteristics—related to the final printing of an image with a CMYK medium. The color conversion software will use default values if those details are unknown at the time of conversion.

Total Number of Colors per Number of Bitplanes
$2^{(\text{bitplanes})}$ = possible colors
2^1 = 2 colors
2^2 = 4 colors
2^3 = 8 colors
2^4 = 16 colors
2^5 = 32 colors
2^6 = 64 colors
2^7 = 128 colors
2^8 = 256 colors
2^{10} = 1,024 colors
2^{16} = 65,536 colors
2^{20} = 1,048,576 colors
2^{24} = 16,777,216 colors
2^{32} = 4,214,967,296 colors

15.2.4 The total number of colors that a computer can display is based on the number of bitplanes available in graphics memory. The number 2 raised to the power of the number of bitplanes results in the maximum number of colors that may be displayed by the system.

The color depth of a device becomes important when digitizing analog images, as is the case when a digital video camera records a live scene or when a datacine film scanner digitizes 35 mm film. When the analog video signal is digitized, for example, each pixel is captured as a numerical value that defines a specific level of color or grayscale. This analog-to-digital conversion process is called **quantization**. As mentioned earlier in this section, the shades of color are more precise when more bits or digits are used to represent a color in the form of a numerical value.

The **color sampling rate** is another aspect of color resolution that is relevant only when working with component digital video. The color sampling rate determines the frequency at which the analog video information is encoded into its luminance and chrominance components. In a fully digital world this sampling occurs at the full-color rate of 1:1:1, also known as **4:4:4 color**. This means that for every 4 samples of the luminance (Y) component there are also 4 samples each of chrominance (Pr and Pb). Unfortunately, sampling at a 4:4:4 rate requires more bandwidth that is available in most digital video equipment, so compromises are often made to achieve the highest possible color sampling rate at a reasonable cost. The color sampling rate used for NTSC mini-DV, for example, is

4:1:1, for DVD it is 4:2:0. The rate commonly available in 24p HD systems is 4:2:2, although that signal can also be output as low as 3:1:1 when recorded onto HDCAM videotape, or as high as 4:4:4 when recorded directly onto a hard disk RAID array.

For optimum color results it is important to make sure that the RGB monitor connected to the computer system being used is properly calibrated so that the colors displayed on the screen are as close as possible to the color values contained in the image file. For optimum **color calibration** it is always best to use specialized software and to enlist the help of a color expert. One small but important factor that always has a great impact on the proper calibration of an RGB monitor is the **gamma factor**. This factor is a number used to scale the brightness of the image according to the characteristics of the final output media. When the gamma factor has a value of one, for example, the numerical values of RGB color sent by the computer are used as they are to determine the voltages used by the RGB color guns located inside the monitor to create color. When the gamma factor has a value higher than one, the RGB numerical values are scaled by that number before they are applied to the voltages that control the colors emitted by the monitor (Fig. 15.2.5). A typical value used for video output, for example, is 2.2.

1.0 GAMMA

1.4 GAMMA

1.8 GAMMA

2.2 GAMMA

15.2.5 Four different gamma values applied to a frame from the river scene in *El Bosque Animado*. Gamma factors are used to calibrate different devices to optimize the display of images. (© 2001 Dygra Films.)

Temporal Resolution

Temporal resolution is related to the number of still images contained in a sequence of images displayed over time. Temporal resolution is almost always measured in terms of the number of images displayed within a specific amount of time, usually a second. Images in a sequence are often called **frames** because of the still frames contained in a strip of photographic film. A common unit for measuring temporal resolution is called **frames per second** or **fps**.

Each output media has a typical temporal resolution. Image sequences displayed on 35 mm film for example have a rate of 24 fps (early silent films ran at 16 and 20 fps). Temporal resolution in multimedia projects can range from 8 fps to 60 fps depending on the nature of the sequence, and on the playback power of the computer system. On **NTSC** video the rate is 30 fps (29.97 to be exact). NTSC is the acronym for the **National Television Systems Committee**, and is the standard used in the U.S.A., Japan, and most of Latin America. RGB purists jokingly refer to NTSC as *Never The Same Color*. The **PAL** and **SECAM** video formats are both displayed at the temporal resolution rate of 25 fps. PAL (**Phase Alternation by Line**) is used in Great Britain, Australia, parts of Europe, Asia, and Africa. SECAM is used in France and some European and African countries.

The conversion of temporal resolutions between film and NTSC video takes place through a standard process called a **3 to 2 pull-down**. This process is based on the fact that each frame of NTSC video is made of two **interlaced fields**. One field contains all the even scan lines in the frame, and the other field contains the odd

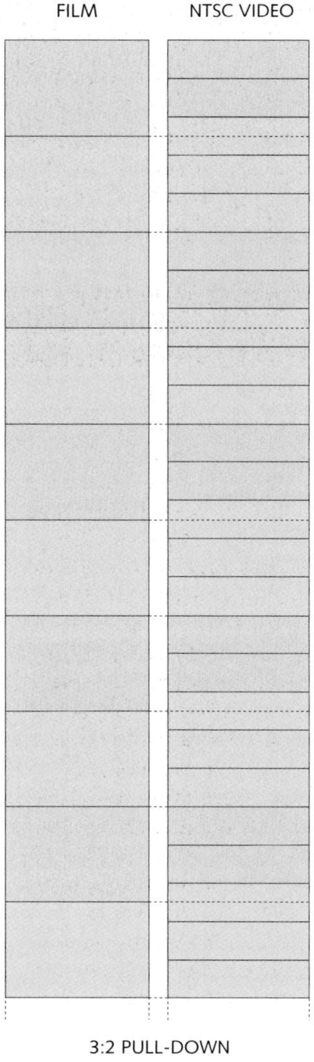

15.2.6 The 3:2 pull-down process used to transfer film to video or video to film converts the odd frames of film into two video fields and the even frames of film into three video fields.

scan lines. The 3:2 pull-down process converts the odd frames of film into two video fields and all the even film frames into three video fields (Fig. 15.2.6). The video-to-film conversion works by applying the inverse formula.

Image Compression

High-definition full color images contain so much information that it is often impractical to store, transmit or playback all the bits that represent their spatial, chromatic and temporal resolutions. **Image compression** techniques are used to minimize the size of image files while preserving as much quality as possible. Image compression is especially important today because of the large volume of files transmitted via public computer networks like the World Wide Web, high-bandwith private networks, or private intranets.

There are many types of compression techniques and each one of them yields different levels of efficiency and visual accuracy. The programs used to perform the compression and decompression of image files are called **codecs** (compression decompression software). Many of them are integral parts of some of the most popular file formats for moving images like JPEG, MPEG-2, MPEG-4, and QuickTime, and some can compress and decompress the information on the fly. Compression is about reducing the size of the file so that the transmission time is shorter and the storage requirements are smaller. Decompression is about bringing back the data to a format that can be viewed with standard software.

In terms of fidelity to the original file, compression techniques are separated in lossy and lossless. **Lossy compression** techniques discard image information as they compresses the file. When a lossy-compressed file, JPEG for example, is decompressed the result differs from the original; the amount of difference will depend on the various user-controlled settings and filters employed in the compression. **Lossless compression** techniques, on the other hand, retain the original information as they compress a file. But in spite of their fidelity, some lossless techniques can yield expanded files that may be slightly different from the original file. This is because different graphics software, computers and graphics cards might calculate the floating point decompression in slightly different ways.

15.3 Image File Formats and Aspect Ratios

Files that contain images are called **picture files** or image files. Computer imaging programs can save and retrieve images in a variety of **file formats**. Some of these formats are native to a specific program. This means that the files can only be retrieved by the program that was used to create them, and not by any other program. One solution to the lack of compatibility between **native file formats** consists of saving the visual information in **universal** or **portable image file formats**. Some of these portable file formats include

PICT, TIFF, and QuickTime, and are described next. In those few cases when the images cannot be saved in a portable format, it is possible to convert one native file format into the native file format of another program. This alternative solution to the file incompatibility problem is called **file format conversion**, and it is a standard feature in many computer imaging programs in the form of **import** and **export tools**. These tools translate image data files from and into other native or universal file formats. The results obtained with different file conversion utilities vary widely. Some file conversions are almost flawless, while others rarely produce desirable results. There is no easy way to know if a file conversion program will work or not; each has to be tried and evaluated. All file format conversions are directed by so-called **import** and **export filters**, which are tables that instruct the conversion utility how to translate each and all of the elements encountered in the original file.

There are several file formats for both still and moving images. Each of these has been designed with a specific goal in mind and, therefore, is better suited for a particular task. There are always trade-offs between the characteristics of a file; for example, a file format that preserves the fine detail in the image may also take up a lot of storage space (Fig. 15.3.1). It is common in everyday productions to integrate images in different file formats into one single document. It is also quite common to save an image in a variety of file formats as the image is created with different programs, or transferred between different computer platforms through a network (Fig. 6.11.1).

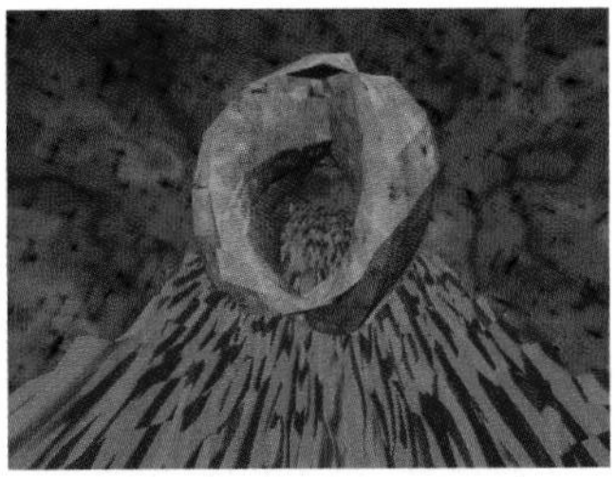

File Formats and Storage Requirements

EPS	2,460 KB (ASCII format, no preview)
TIFF	1,857 KB (16-bit/channel)
EPS	1,240 KB (binary format, with color preview)
CIN	1,228 KB (10-bit/channel)
EPS	1,220 KB (binary format, no preview)
TGA	1,220 KB (32-bit/pixel)
BMP	966 KB (8-bit/channel)
TGA	920 KB (24-bit/pixel)
TIFF	920 KB (8-bit/channel)
PICT	560 KB (32-bit/pixel)
JPEG	560 KB (no compression)
TIFF	440 KB (8-bit/channel, LZW compression)
PICT	380 KB (16-bit/pixel)
JPEG	150 KB (best quality)
GIF	115 KB (8-bit/pixel)
JPEG	110 KB (high quality)
JPEG	60 KB (medium quality)
JPEG	40 KB (low quality)

15.3.1 This chart compares the amount of storage required by the same still image (640 × 480 pixels) in a variety of file formats with different color resolutions and compression ratios. The compactness of the file format increases as the list moves down.

Still Images

Some of the most popular portable file formats for saving two-dimensional visual information in digital form include: PICT, TIFF, EPS, TGA, Cineon, JPEG, BMP, and GIF. There are many other portable file formats for saving still images, but an exhaustive listing is beyond the scope of this book. In addition to the dozens of universal file formats, there are also many native file formats that can only be read by the software that created them. In addition to being able to save single still images these file formats can also save **series of still images**. The majority of computer animations that are eventually recorded on film or videotape are rendered as series of still frames because each frame has to be recorded, one at a time, on film or videotape. Series of numbered still files are commonly used to save the still frames in a computer animation sequence. The numbering of sequential files is usually done automatically by the animation program that creates them. One convention for numbering files in a sequence consists of adding an extension to the filename, for example, Dance.0001 for the first frame, Dance.0010 for the tenth frame, and so on.

Some of the issues that distinguish one file format from another includes their popularity, their compression schemes, their ability to store alpha or Z-depth channels, and their color depth. Today most still image file formats offer a variety of color depth flavors that range

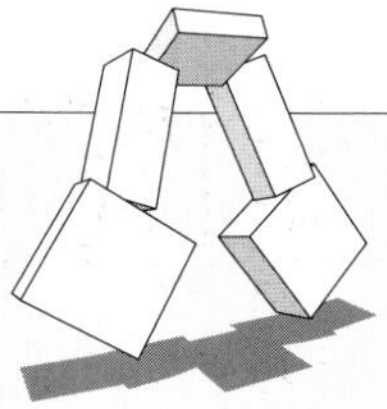

```
%!PS-Adobe-3.0 EPSF-3.0
%%Title: Sims-1.eps
%%BoundingBox: 0 0 200 200
%%EndComments

200 200 scale
.001 setlinewidth
1.5 setmiterlimit
/quad { setgray newpath moveto lineto
lineto lineto closepath
  gsave fill grestore .0 setgray stroke } def

0.4531 0.1716 0.4111 0.0544 0.6423
0.1391 0.6648 0.2546 1 quad
0.6648 0.2546 0.6423 0.1391 0.6456
0.1343 0.6677 0.2502 0.865 quad
0.6997 0.5376 0.7810 0.5643 0.8535
0.9500 0.7641 0.8703 1 quad
0.7073 0.5358 0.7898 0.5622 0.7810
0.5643 0.6997 0.5376 1 quad
0.6456 0.1343 0.6423 0.1391 0.4111
0.0544 0.4145 0.0500 1 quad
0.7392 0.3909 0.6664 0.4162 0.6398
0.2082 0.7161 0.1902 0.975 quad
0.5966 0.2084 0.6724 0.1909 0.7161
0.1902 0.6398 0.2082 1 quad
0.5966 0.2084 0.6398 0.2082 0.6664
0.4162 0.6240 0.4105 1 quad
0.6061 0.4571 0.6747 0.3831 0.6606
0.4622 0.5828 0.5444 1 quad
0.6747 0.3831 0.7774 0.4697 0.7777
0.5593 0.6606 0.4622 0.887 quad
0.7810 0.5643 0.7898 0.5622 0.8620
0.9474 0.8535 0.9500 1 quad
0.6985 0.6377 0.5828 0.5444 0.6606
0.4622 0.7777 0.5593 1 quad
0.6347 0.5379 0.5792 0.5772 0.3892
0.6422 0.4382 0.6031 0.956 quad
0.4382 0.6031 0.4076 0.5317 0.6053
0.4730 0.6347 0.5379 1 quad
0.4382 0.6031 0.3892 0.6422 0.3608
0.5746 0.4076 0.5317 1 quad
0.1447 0.3282 0.2239 0.2544 0.4006
0.5145 0.3501 0.6173 0.831 quad
0.1447 0.3282 0.1380 0.3320 0.2179
0.2579 0.2239 0.2544 1 quad
0.3501 0.6173 0.3436 0.6204 0.1380
0.3320 0.1447 0.3282 1 quad
showpage

%%EndDocument
```

15.3.2 Listing of the EPS program that generated the line drawing of the creature above (described in more detail in Chapter 12).

from 8-bit to 16-bit per each (RGB) color channel, or 24-bit to 48-bit for the entire file. Originally most of these portable file formats could only save color with a resolution of 8 bits of color for each RGB channel. Two notable early exceptions to this standard include TIFF, which can save color information in 8-bit or 16-bit linear modes, and Cineon which saves color in 10-bit logarithmic mode. The more recent OpenEXR format offers 16-bit logarithmic color depth.

The **TIFF** file format, from **Tagged Image File Format**, is popular in a variety of production environments ranging from prepress to animation, and is especially useful when the rendered image has to be reproduced in a printed publication. The TIFF format has 8-bit and 16-bit color per channel versions, and it preserves detailed grayscale information that is fundamental for generating the high-quality halftones (grids of dots of varying size) used in the graphic arts. TIFF files tend to be large and several applications usually provide compression options. **LZW**, short for Lempel-Ziv-Welsh, is a popular compression technique developed in 1984 that is commonly applied to images in the TIFF and GIF formats.

The **EPS** file format, or **Encapsulated PostScript**, is also popular in prepress applications, and can be quite useful and effective when high-quality line wireframe drawings are needed. Information saved in the EPS file format is always imaged at the best resolution possible in EPS-compatible output peripherals because EPS is a **device-independent file format**. EPS files usually require significant amounts of memory for storage and transfer. EPS files are almost identical to PostScript files except for the **header information** that is found at the beginning of EPS files. This header information is inserted automatically by the application that generates the EPS file, and it includes data that is needed in order to import the file into another application program and output it properly (Fig. 15.3.2).

The **Cineon** uncompressed file format is commonly used in the motion pictures and visual effects industries to store images that have been scanned from film. This format was developed by the Kodak Eastman Company to capture the subtlety and dynamic range of images originally captured on motion picture film, and it typically allocates 10 bits of color depth for each RGB channel. The Cineon format also offers a unique color space that excels at reproducig the subtle changes in density that exist on the original negative film that is the preferred scanning source. The **DPX** file format is a generic version of Cineon with the additional ability to store metadata information within its file header.

The **JPEG** file format, from **Joint Photographic Experts Group**, is one of the most popular 8-bit per color channel file formats that offers image compression. This is useful when large amounts of data have to be archived or transmitted over computer networks. JPEG works by removing on a frame by frame basis data that is redundant or data whose removal is almost imperceptible to the human eye. One of the main strengths of the JPEG format lies in the fact that it provides great compression and decompression speed as well as huge savings in file size (Fig. 15.3.3). The JPEG file format uses a lossy compression technique because it discards image information as it compresses the file. For this reason, the settings of the JPEG compression should be chosen with care, keeping in mind that increasing the compression decreases the image quality and vice versa. A copy of the original uncompressed file should always be archived in case the compression settings applied to the file were too extreme and the image becomes illegible. **JPEG 2000** is a newer version of this standard that uses **wavelet compression** techniques instead of discrete cosine transforms (**DCT**). A few of the improvements offered by JPEG 2000 include the lack of 8 × 8 pixel block artifacts, and a motion version.

The **GIF** file format, from **Graphics Interchange Format**, is popular for compressing and storing images that are distributed on the Web—in fact, GIF was originally developed by the Compuserve on-line service. This file format is also compact enough to facilitate the uploading and downloading of still images over e-mail, Internet-based bulletin boards, and on-line services. The GIF format is based on an indexed color standard that ranges from 1-bit to 8-bit color depth for the three combined RGB channels and allows for a total maximum of 256 colors. These colors may be chosen from a customized color look-up table, but in some cases the colors of the system's color palette are automatically applied to GIF files. GIF also employs a lossless compression technique that requires a decompression utility before the file can be displayed on the receiving end.

The **PICT** file format, from the word picture, is a versatile format used by drawing and photo-retouching programs. PICT offers fair image quality with a relatively small file size. The PICT file format is used because of its compact size and compatibility across computer platforms. The **BMP** file format is another generic 8-bit per color channel bitmap format that is used in the Windows environment. The **PICS** file format derives its name from the word pictures, and is convenient when a series of images is required for animation purposes. A PICS file consists of several PICT files stored together.

The **TGA** file format is popular with video-oriented software because it saves the files in an 8-bit per color channel format that is convenient for transferring the digital data into the video environment. TGA is short for **TARGA**, the name of the family of graphics boards products developed in the early 1980s that pioneered video input and output with micro-computers. The TGA file format is not as prevalent as it used to be, but it is still widely used.

The **OpenEXR** file format was initially developed as a proprietary format at Industrial Light & Magic but released as an open source format in 2003. OpenEXR was designed to better simulate the response of film negative to changes in exposure, and provides a higher dynamic range and color precision than existing 8-bit and 10-bit file formats. OpenEXR is based on a 16-bit floating point log color space, and can be used uncompressed or with several lossless image compression options that can deliver a 2:1 lossless compression ratio on images with film grain.

NO JPEG COMPRESSION, 556 KB

MAXIMUM QUALITY, 149 KB

HIGH QUALITY, 105 KB

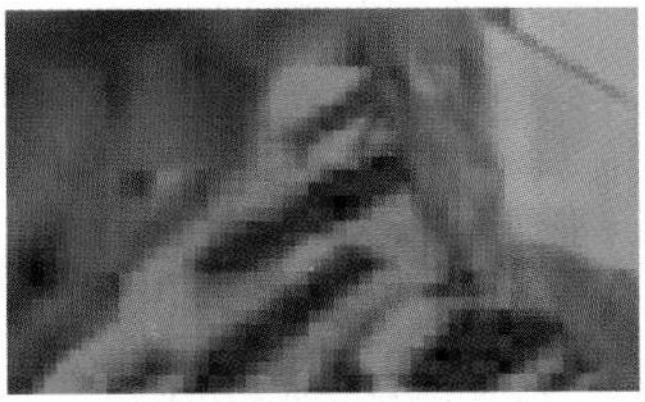

MEDIUM QUALITY, 61 KB

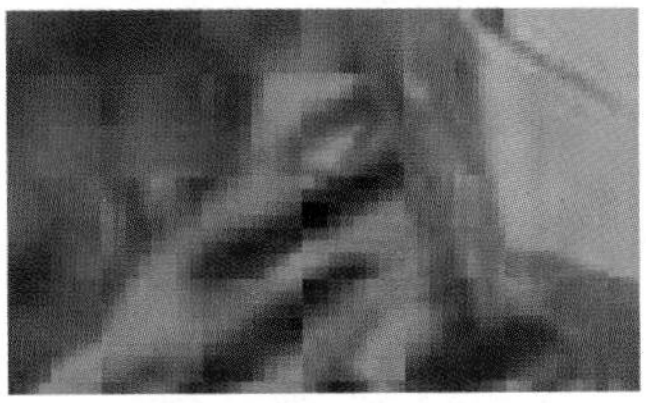

LOW QUALITY, 39 KB

15.3.3 The JPEG compression options yield very different file sizes. Low compression results in higher image quality. The image degradation and blocking that results from maximum compression can be clearly appreciated in the enlarged detail at the bottom.

15.3.4 Computer animations saved in the QuickTime format have a playback controller at the bottom of the window.

Sequences of Moving Images

Some of the most popular file formats for saving sequences of two-dimensional images in a **self-contained format** include: QuickTime, QuickTime VR, MPEG, AVI, Windows Media, OMF, and AAF. These file formats are commonly used when the animated sequence is played back directly from a fast peripheral storage of the computer—as is the case with many interactive projects—or through computer networks. But sequences of images that are not played directly on the computer monitor, especially those destined to be recorded on film or videotape, are commonly saved in some of the same file formats used to save still images—mostly TIFF and TGA. In these cases, each individual sequential frame is assigned a number that reflects its place in the sequence.

The **QuickTime** file format stores both visual data and audio in one or several tracks. In most cases, a QuickTime file is displayed within a window that has a **playback controller,** such as those available in videotape players (Fig. 15.3.4). QuickTime is a versatile format that facilitates saving computer animation files at different spatial resolutions, and at different window sizes, for example, ranging from a small 160×120 pixels to a full-screen 640×480 pixels. QuickTime also plays the files back at different temporal resolutions, for example, 10 frames per second (fps) or 30 fps.

The QuickTime file format provides a variety of **compression options** for video or animated images. As with other compressed file formats, the quality and effectiveness of a QuickTime file is based on the relation between the compression ratio, the playback speed, and the image fidelity. The QuickTime file format provides several compression options. One of them is especially designed to compress computer animation; another one is designed to compress photographic images and is based on the motion JPEG compression method. Some of the differences between each of these compression techniques are related to the time that it takes to compress and decompress an image. With some options the compression speed is high so that users do not have to wait long as the file is compressed but the compression ratio is low. With other options the compression ratio is good and that results in great space savings, but the compression time is slow. QuickTime is capable of online video streams and supports the **FireWire** (IEEE 1394) digital video serial interface, popular for video input/output from a computer system. QuickTime also provides sound sampling at different rates ranging from 8 to 48 kHz, and it is compatible with the popular MIDI format.

The **QuickTime VR** file format, also known as **QTVR**, creates panoramic views of real or virtual environments. This is done by assembling several still images that have been taken around the same point of rotation out toward the surrounding environment. The still images are stitched into a single panoramic image that represents a cylindrical view from the point of rotation. Once the QTVR file is assembled, the viewer can look in any direction and zoom in and out.

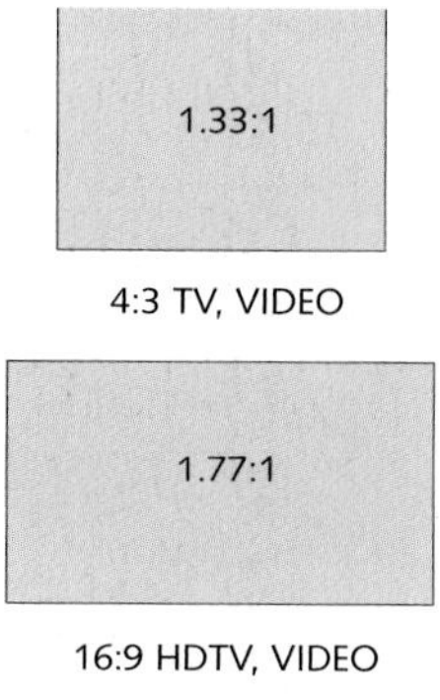

15.3.5 Aspect ratios (width and height) of common formats in video (above) and film (opposite page), represented here with a fixed height of 1 for comparison purposes. Relative dimensions are not represented here.

The **MPEG** file format is another popular format for compressed moving images including video and animation. This file format was developed by the **Motion Pictures Experts Group**, which is affiliated with the International Standards Organization (**ISO**). The data compression in MPEG is based on the removal of data that is identical or similar not only within a frame but also between one frame to another. This lossy compression technique can realize impressive savings in file size while keeping a reasonable quality for most applications. MPEG files can only be displayed with utility programs called **MPEG viewers**, that usually provide a variety of dithering techniques for improving the final image quality. **MPEG-1** was initially developed to store moving images on Video-CD and for other types of low-bandwidth video compression. It provides a resolution of 352 × 240 pixels at 30 fps, which is roughly equivalent to the quality of VHS videotape. Incidentally, the **MP3** file format used to record music is an audio-only subset of MPEG-1; MP3 is the shortened name for MPEG-1 Layer III. **MPEG-2** is a higher-quality standard for high-bandwidth audio and video compression introduced in 1995. It offers a resolution of 704 × 480 at 30 fps, about twice the resolution of videotape. MPEG-2 requires dedicated hardware for playback, and it has become the compression standard for DVDs. **MPEG-4** is a newer standard issued in 2000 that offers added functionality. In addition to improved video and audio features, MPEG-4 has extensions for coding 3D polygonal meshes, and for defining and animating synthetic faces and bodies.

The **AVI** file format (**Audio Video Interleaved**) was introduced by Microsoft in 1992 as a generic digital format for moving images. Unlike the QuickTime format AVI is not a cross-platform format, but AVI files can usually be converted and played by the QuickTime player. **Windows Media** is a more recent format developed by Microsoft that uses efficient compression for streaming material with high pixel resolutions.

The **Flash**, or SWF, file format was developed by Macromedia and it handles graphics and animation. Flash files are usually more compact than GIF and JPEG because they can vector information instead of bitmaps. Flash also offers interactive capability and is popular with online applications such as the Web.

Two standards commonly used in postproduction for exchanging media between applications and platforms are OMF and AAF. The **OMF** file format, from Open Media Framework, offers 8-bit color per channel and different levels of lossy compression. It supports video, imbedded audio, effects, and edit decision lists (EDLs). OMF is used almost exclusively in nonlinear editing workflows based on Avid systems. The open source **Advanced Authoring Format**, or **AAF**, was designed to facilitate the authoring and postproduction processes. AAF is able to embed different types of content and authoring metadata information in the same *wrapper* while referencing back to the source files including video, animation, audio, and MIDI files among others. One of the strongest features of

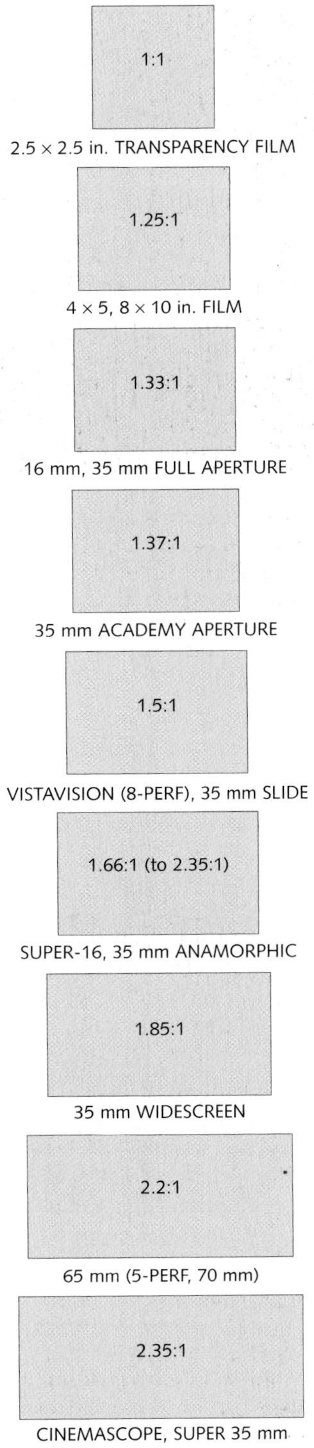

AAF is its ability to describe the process by which media in this format was created from the original source files. **MXF** is a related file format used to transport AAF content between systems.

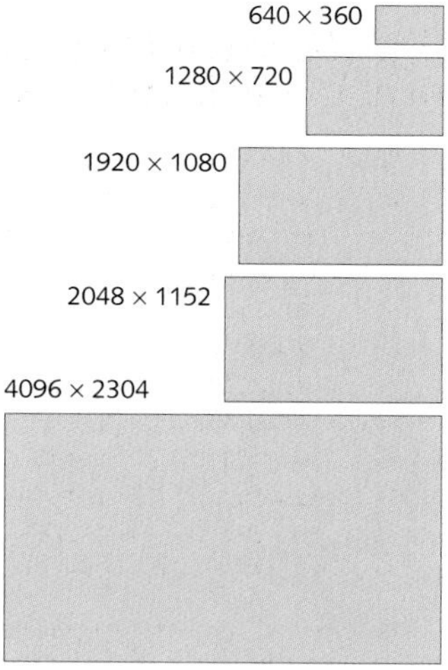

15.3.6 The same aspect ratio, 16:9, showing relative size of different pixel resolutions ranging from Standard Definition video to a 4K digital file.

Aspect Ratios

Aspect ratios are not a component of file formats but both are part of the output process and, for that reason, they are closely related. **Aspect ratios** define the proportion between width and height in the image active area of a specific medium. Standard definition TV screens, for example, have a fixed aspect ration of 4:3 (4 wide by 3 high), while high definition video has a 16:9 aspect ratio. Film cameras offer a wide variety of recording aspect ratios to choose from, including 1.618:1, based on the classic golden section {1+sqrt(5)}/2, and 1.66.1, which is used to shoot the anamorphic version of 2.35:1. The numerical value of aspect ratios can be expressed in a variety of ways. TV screens, as mentioned before, have an aspect ratio of 4:3 that can also be expressed as 1.33:1. In the later format the number 1 represents a fixed unit for the height while the width is a variable number; this format makes it easy to compare aspect ratios of different media. The 4:3 format is used because some people find it easy to remember due to its lack of decimal numbers. To make matters a bit more confusing, the 1.33:1 format is often expressed as 1:1.33, but in this context both arrangements usually mean exactly the same thing. Figure 15.3.5 shows the aspect ratios (with a fixed height of 1) for some of the most popular film and video output formats.

Image aspect ratios are not to be confused with **pixel aspect ratios**. Most pixels are round, or square, but some are not. **Nonsquare pixels**, tall ovals actually, are common in NTSC digital video and their ratio is 10:11. Most software programs automatically compensate for nonsquare pixels, but if uncorrected this discrepancy may impact the image aspect ratio.

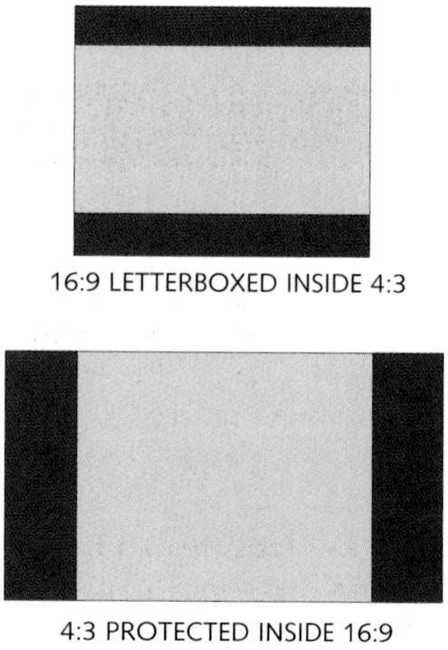

15.3.7 The 16:9 aspect ratio is sometimes letterboxed into a 4:3 screen to broadcast feature movies on standard definition TV (top). A show might be recorded on 16:9 aspect ratio but "protecting" the 4:3 aspect ratio for a potential standard definition release.

An aspect ratio can be output in a variety of sizes, the same way a 35 mm photographic negative can be used to create different sizes of prints on photographic paper. When rendering an image for a specific output media we can choose a variety of pixel resolutions for the aspect ratio depending on a variety of issues like desired visual quality, planned distribution medium, deadline and budget available. Rendering final images in the 16:9 aspect ratio (1.77:1), for example, could be done at 4096 × 2304 pixels, 2048 × 1152, 1920 × 1080, 1280 × 720, or 640 × 360 (Fig. 15.3.6). Keep in mind that there are always minor aspect ratio and pixel count differences between software programs, regions of the world, input and output devices. The aspect ratio of the image captured by a standard definition NTSC video camera, for example, is not identical to the aspect ratio of the image displayed on the TV screen: a few pixels are not displayed. This fact accounts for the small difference in aspect ratios assigned to NTSC video: 1.333:1 and 1.327:1. This disparity between the captured and the displayed or projected aspect ratio is common in all output media, film included.

When a format conversion between media is necessary usually the aspect ratio is impacted. When a production is recorded at 16:9, for example, there are usually two ways to show it in a 4:3 delivery medium such as a standard definition TV 16:9 is the native aspect ratio of HD cameras). The first method consists of cropping the extremes of the 16:9 image to accomodate the narrower aspect ratio of 4:3, assuming the recording was "protected" for a 4:3 release (most of the action happening in the center of the frame). The second method, called letterbox, consists of fitting the width of the 16:9 material to the width of the 4:3 delivery medium. The later solution results in a smaller image and two empty black areas above and below the image area, but has the advantage of preserving the original composition and showing camera moves in their original form (Fig. 15.3.7).

15.4 Output on Paper

There is a great variety of printing technologies used for creating digital prints on paper. These include electrostatic, dye sublimation, ink jet, and pen plotters. Each of these printing technologies has strengths and weaknesses in the areas of resolution, paper size (Fig. 15.4.1), chromatic range, dye stability, and cost. The software required to control a specific type of printer is called a **printer driver**. The "preparation" for printing of an image sent from a computer to a printer is often called **ripping**, from raster image processing. Printers often are as good (or as bad) as their RIP engines.

Metric ISO A Paper Sizes

Size	*Millimeters*	*Inches*
AO	841 × 1,189	(33.11 × 46.81)
A1	594 × 841	(23.39 × 33.11)
A2	420 × 594	(16.54 × 23.39)
A3	297 × 420	(11.69 × 16.54)
A4	210 × 297	(8.27 × 11.69)
A5	148 × 210	(5.83 × 8.27)
A6	105 × 148	(4.13 × 5.83)
A7	74 × 105	(2.91 × 4.13)
A8	52 × 74	(2.05 × 2.91)
A9	37 × 52	(1.46 × 2.05)
A10	26 × 37	(1.02 × 1.46)

American ANSI Paper Sizes

Size	*Millimeters*	*Inches*
A	8.5 × 11	(215.9 × 279.4)
B	11 × 17	(279.4 × 431.8)
C	17 × 22	(431.8 × 558.8)
D	24 × 36	(609.6 × 914.4)
E	36 × 48	(914.4 × 1219.2)

Architectural Sizes

Size	*Millimeters*	*Inches*
A	9 × 12	(228.6 × 304.8)
B	12 × 18	(304.8 × 457.2)
C	18 × 24	(457.2 × 609.6)
D	24 × 36	(609.6 × 914.4)
E	36 × 48	(914.4 × 1219.2)

15.4.1 International standard paper sizes used to specify the size of computer output on paper.

Electrostatic Printing

Electrostatic output technology is the most popular method for creating medium resolution black and white prints, but is also used to create color prints. **Electrostatic** technology is commonly known as **laser printing**, and it is capable of resolutions that range from 300 to 1,000 dpi and higher. The output process with this technology typically consists of a laser beam that draws the image with electrical charges on a rotating metal drum, which in turn transfers charges onto the sheet of paper. Then the electrostatic energy on the paper attracts fine powder, or **toner**, to create an image directly on the surface of the paper. Finally, the toner is melted with heat on the paper. Many laser printers are able to print PostScript files and this further enhances the quality of their output, especially of line drawings. Electrostatic printing offers an affordable way of creating proofs on paper and heat-resistant acetate with sizes that range from letter size (8.5 × 11 in.) to tabloid size (11 × 17 in.).

Ink Jet Printing

Ink jet printers work like miniature airbrushes that spray microscopic drops of color ink on a sheet or a roll of paper. The nozzles through

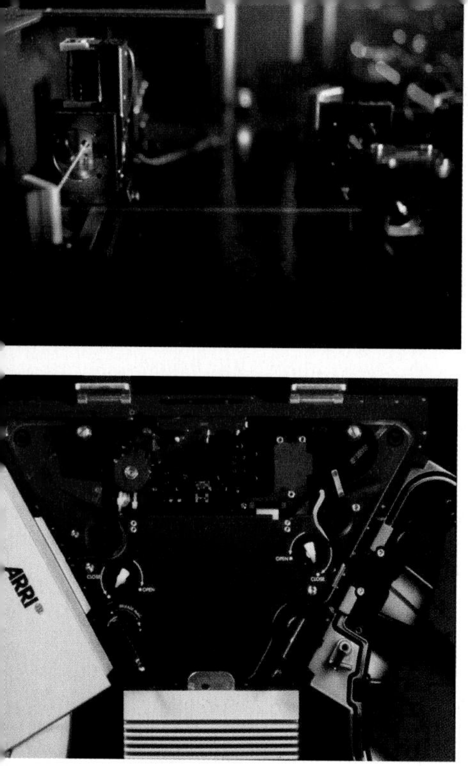

15.5.1 Detailed views of an ARRI laser film recorder. (© Arnold + Richter.)

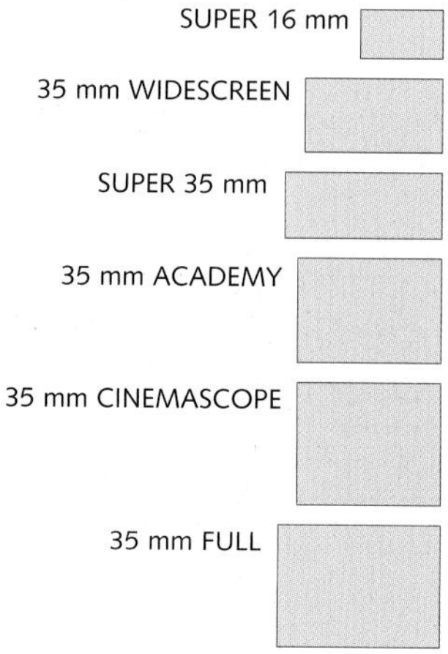

15.5.2 Relative sizes of the major film aspect ratios (above and opposite page).

which the ink is sprayed are so thin that most of the ink dyes used in ink jet printers are based on vegetable dyes that have very small molecules. The small molecular size of the dyes allows the ink to pass through the narrow nozzles of the ink jet printers. However, another characteristic of vegetable dyes—as opposed to mineral dyes—is that the large majority are **fugitive dyes**, which means that they fade rapidly when exposed to the ultraviolet radiation of sunlight. This makes the ink jet printouts unstable unless they are coated with a transparent substance that acts as a filter of ultraviolet radiation, this is called **UV coating**. Using permanent dyes on acid-free paper with UV coating is the best way to create **archival-quality digital prints**. The strengths of ink jet printing include the excellent color and image fidelity, and the great availability of paper sizes and types. Ink jet printing also requires that RGB files are converted into the CMYK color format before they can be printed. In fact, most ink jet printers spray CMYK or CMY ink simultaneously on the paper, each color through a different nozzle. Of all the technologies for printing on paper that do not involve photographic processes, ink jet and dye sublimation are unique because of their good image and color fidelity.

Dye Sublimation Printing

Dye sublimation is a color printing technology that uses extreme heat to sublimate the dyes contained on a roll of acetate onto a sheet of paper. Sublimation happens to materials with such physical properties that when heated they are transformed from a solid state directly into a gaseous state, without passing through the liquid state. The sublimated dyes reach the paper in a gaseous state, and the pattern that they create on the paper is irregular but delicate. This pattern resembles the shape and pattern of the grains in photographic emulsions. For this reason, and also because of the pearl finish of the paper used in dye sublimation, prints created with this technology resemble traditional photographic prints on paper. The irregular pattern created by the sublimated dyes that reach the paper in a gaseous state also softens the regularity of the grid of pins (dpi) that apply heat to form the image. This softening helps to increase the apparent resolution of dye sublimation printers, which is usually around 300 dpi but looks more detailed. Dye sublimation prints also offer great dye stability and excellent color range, but their cost is still higher than other techniques, and the maximum paper size rarely exceeds 11 × 14 in. This printing technology usually requires that RGB files be converted into the CMYK color format before they can be printed.

Pen Plotters

Pen plotters have long been the preferred output technology for creating line drawings that do not require shading. **Pen plotters** create line drawings on paper with one or several pens. Unlike other peripherals that also output onto paper, pen plotters do not create images with dots. Instead, pen plotters create drawings with continuous lines. As a result the image definition of line drawings created with pen plotters is excellent. The image definition of continuous tone images created with pen plotters, however, is quite limited because shading can only be simulated with cross-hatching patterns. Pen plotters are still quite popular in applications such as industrial design or architecture where drawings in very large formats, 36 × 48 in. for example, are necessary. High resolution electrostatic printers are an alternative to pen plotters when smaller size output is required.

Digital Video Recording Formats	Color Sampling	Color Quantization	Compression Ratio	Recording Rates (bps)	Tape Width
High-Definition					
D6	4:2:2	10/8-bit	Uncompressed	995 Mbps	19 mm
HDCAM-SR	4:2:2	10-bit	2.7:1, MPEG-4	440 Mbps	1/2 in.
HD-D5	4:2:2	10-bit	4:1, DCT	235 Mbps	1/2 in.
HDCAM	3:1:1	8-bit	4:1, DCT	142 Mbps	1/2 in.
DVCPRO 100/D-7	4:1:1~2:2	8-bit	6.7:1	100 Mbps	1/4 in.
Standard-Definition					
D1	4:2:2	8-bit	Uncompressed	180 Mbps	19 mm
Digital Betacam	4:2:2	10-bit	2:1, DCT-based	90 Mbps	1/2 in.
IMX	4:2:2	8-bit	3.3:1, MPEG-1	50 Mbps	1/2 in.
D9	4:2:2	8-bit	3.3:1, DV	50 Mbps	1/2 in.
DV (NTSC)/DVCAM	4:1:1	8-bit	5:1, DV	25 Mbps	1/4 in.
D-VHS	4:2:0	8-bit	MPEG-2	25 Mbps	1/2 in.
Betacam SX	4:2:2	8-bit	7:1, MPEG-2	18 Mbps	1/2 in.
DVD	4:2:0	8-bit	MPEG-2	3.5~9 Mbps	N.A.

15.6.1 Some of the most popular component (not composite) video recording formats used in HD and standard definition production. A few notes: Recording rates are for video only, no audio. D6 records 1080i at 995 Mbps and 1080/24P at 796 Mbps. HDCAM pre-filters the 1920 lines down to 1440 to minimize high-frequency noise, without prefiltering the compression ratio would be closer to 7:1. D9 was initially called Digital S. The color sampling rate for DV PAL is 4:2:0.

15.5 Output on Photographic Media

In spite of the technological advances and innovations in the area of image output, photographic media are still the medium of choice when superb image quality and flexible size are required. The imaging devices that output on photographic media have a wide range of applications. Some are used to record stills on transparency film or photographic paper, or to record high-quality animation for projection in public theatres. Others are used to create and assemble images on high-contrast film for use in graphic arts mechanical reproduction.

Film Recorders

Film recorders are used to record computer images on both photographic film and paper. First-generation film recorders typically used a black-and-white monitor with filters for imaging on the film, but newer recorders use a laser beam to write directly on the film (Fig. 15.5.1). The high-end film recorders provide excellent resolution, chromatic range, and image permanence. Output on photographic film almost always requires that the images are sent to the recorder in the RGB color format. Film recorders for still images provide a convenient way to generate still images on transparency or negative film, and most accept the major film formats including 35 mm, 4 × 5 in., and 8 × 10 in. The film recorders used for motion picture film accept a variety of film formats, ranging from 16 mm to 35 mm.

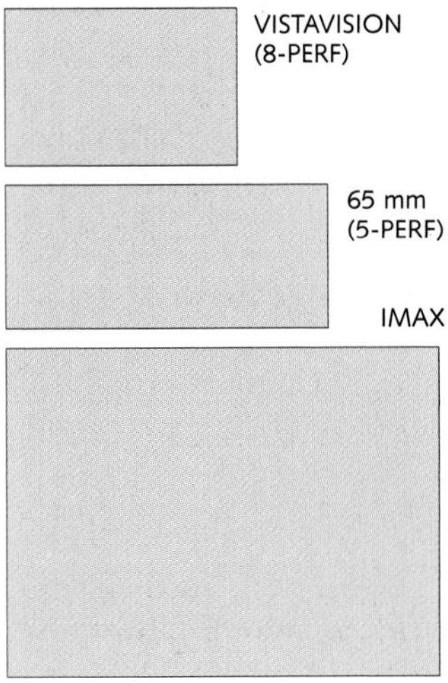

Imagesetters

Imagesetters are high-resolution output peripherals that create black-and-white images. They are the preferred peripheral for outputting the

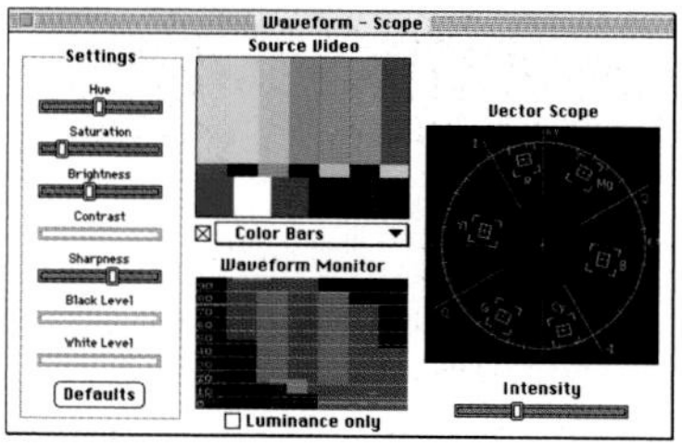

15.6.2 A computer-simulated waveform monitor and vectorscope display with properly adjusted split field vertical color bars). (Adobe Premiere™ dialog box is reprinted with express permission by Adobe Systems Inc. Adobe and Adobe Premiere are trademarks of Adobe Systems Inc. or its subsidiaries and are registered in certain jurisdictions.)

films that contain the CMYK or spot color separations required for mechanical reproduction. (All the reproductions of three-dimensional imagery contained in this book, for example, were color separated, and output with digital imagesetters.) **Imagesetters** get their name from the photographic typesetters that were used to set type before digital technology transformed the typesetting industry. Imagesetters are capable of spatial resolutions in excess of 2,500 dpi both for line art and for shaded images with halftone screens. Typically, a laser beam is used to draw the image directly on photosensitive film or paper, which is then developed and fixed with chemical solutions. The paper used in most imagesetters comes in rolls of different dimensions that accomodate the main paper sizes listed in Figure 15.4.1.

15.6 Output on Video

Videotape is the medium of choice for recording sequences of moving images intended for display on television sets, but video is sometimes also used to record still images. Output on video is commonly done on a wide variety of video formats, each one with its own peculiar advantages and limitations. This variety can sometimes complicate a task that in principle seems simple. A few of the video formats used are still analog, but the trend is towards digital video formats. Some of the former include Hi-8 mm; VHS, Betacam and D3 ½ in.; U-matic ¾ in.; and D2 19 mm. The formats favored today for professional production are mostly digital component formats, and each one has a unique way of sampling, quantizing and compressing the video information, as well as different recording rates (bits per second) and tape requirements. Figure 15.6.1 summarizes the main features of digital video recording formats.

Two of the most popular standards for encoding **Standard Definition (SD)** video signals include NTSC and PAL. The NTSC signal is used in the U.S.A., Japan, and most of Latin America. The PAL signal is used in most of the world, including most countries in Europe. The NTSC video standards were developed in the early 1950s, while PAL was developed almost 10 years later. NTSC has a resolution of 525 lines of information, but displays only 487 lines at the rate of 30 frames per second. The aspect ration of NTSC is 4:3 (or 1.33:1). The PAL video standard displays 625 lines of information, but displays only 576 lines at the rate of 25 frames per second. PAL also has a unique automatic color correction system. Both NTSC and PAL use interlaced display of fields, but PAL does it at 50 Hz, while NTSC does it at almost 60 Hz.

NTSC is a **composite video** signal that combines different types of information, including **luminance**, **chrominance** (color saturation and hue), and **timing sync information** (horizontal line synchronizing pulses, both horizontal and vertical blanking intervals, color reference burst, and reference black level). In **component video** the luminance and chrominance (or chroma) information remain as separate components usually referred to as Y, R-Y and B-

File Formats for Moving Images

.aaf	Advanced Authoring Format
.avi	Audio Video Interleaved
.mpg	Motion Pictures Experts Group
.omf	Open Media Framework
.qt	QuickTime
.qtvr	QuickTime VR
.rm	Real Media
.swf	Flash

15.7.1 Some of the most popular file formats and their name extensions for moving images are listed here.

Y; or Y (luminance), Pr and Pb (digitized color difference signal). An RGB video signal is also considered component video.

One of the **digital video** formats that is popular for independent productions or students' demo reels is **mini-DV**, almost identical to its cousin **DVCAM**. This component format uses 1/4 in. wide tape for recording standard definition video for both professional and consumer markets at a variety of rates including: 60i, 50i, 30p and 24p. DV is compressed to about 5:1, using a proprietary variant of DCT-based intrafield compression. The DV video recording rate is around 25 megabits per second. A few flavors of pseudo-high definition DV are emerging.

The **High Definition** (**HD**) digital video format is larger and wider than standard definition NTSC or PAL. The native aspect ratio of HD is 16:9, and at 1920 × 1080 active pixels the resolution is about twice of standard television. A few additional rows of pixels are masked and inactive, and used to set the black level. There are a few major flavors of HD recording, each with different resolutions and frame rates: 1080/24p (which stands for 1080 active lines of progressive, non-interlaced, video at 24 fps, same rate as film); 1080/60i (1080 active lines of interlaced video at 60 fps); and 720p (720 lines of progressive video). Most 24p HD cameras capture color depth at 12-bit, output it at 10-bit, and sometimes record it at 8-bit (Fig. 15.6.1). To make things a bit more complicated these HD formats used for recording images can be broadcast at slightly different resolutions depending on the country and TV network. MPEG-2 image compression is commonly used when the signal is transmitted to homes.

The quality of the final video output is largely determined by the video format, the quality of the videotape, and the video recording equipment. The quality of video output is also influenced by the proper balance and correction of RGB colors before they are recorded onto video, and by the calibration of the gamma factor. As mentioned earlier, the chromatic range of the RGB color model exceeds the range of video media, and often images in the RGB format contain colors that are outside the chromatic range of video and that create severe color distortions when displayed on video. For that reason, it is necessary to prepare images that were created in the RGB format before they are output to video. This is achieved through a **color correction** process that clips—or removes—the RGB colors that exceed the chromatic range of video, and replaces them with the closest equivalent color within the chromatic range of video.

Another technical detail that has major consequences when outputting computer images onto video is the calibration of the **gamma factor**. The gamma factor—also known as gamma—makes the video image look as close as possible to the original RGB information by compensating for the loss of information between the voltages sent by the computer to the monitor, and the amount of light output by the monitor (Fig. 15.2.5). Other tools that are also useful in monitoring the quality of the video signal include the **vectorscope** and the

Theoretical Speeds of Network Standards

56K Modem	56 Kbps
ISDN (Integrated Services Digital Network)	128 Kbps
BRI (Basic Rate Interface)	384 Kbps
A-DSL (Asynchronous Digital Signal Level)	384 Kbps to 1.544 Mbps
T1	1.544 Mbps
10-Base Ethernet	10 Mbps
100-Base Ethernet	100 Mbps
ATM OC-3 (Asynchronous Transfer Mode)	155 Mbps
ATM OC-5	622 Mbps
HiPPI (High Performance Parallel Interface)	Up to 100 Mbps
FDDI (Fiber Data Distribution Interface)	100 Mbps
Gigabit Ethernet	1,000 Mbps (1 Gbps)
Fiber Channel	1 Gbps

15.7.2 Theoretical speeds in bits per second (bps) of different computer network standards, some still in the experimental stage. Often the overhead of managing the data brings the actual throughput 5 to 10 times less than the theoretical bit rate. BRI is popular for video conferencing. HiPPI and fiber channel are used for short distances between computers and storage devices. T1's signal is not distance-sensitive, while DSL suffers from data attenuation—its speed depends on the distance between the server and the computer. FDDI's popularity is fading.

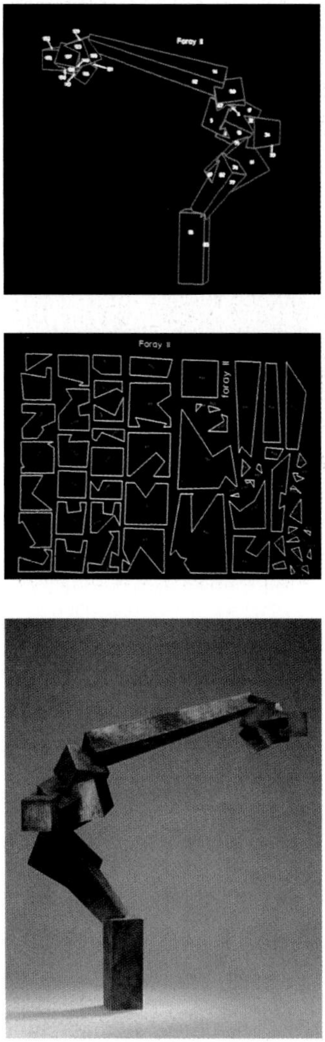

15.8.1 *Foray* is a bronze sculpture created by Bruce Beasley, who uses computers to both compose and fabricate his sculptures. On top is the wireframe visualization, in the middle are the flat patterns to be cut in metal, and the finished piece is at the bottom. (Photograph by Lee Fatherree. Courtesy of Bruce Beasley.)

waveform monitor. Both of these devices—whether real or simulated with software—display a graphical representation of the video signal. These graphs help to make sure, for example, that the colors fall within "legal" limits or that they are distributed evenly throughout the color spectrum, or that the transitions between color gradations are smooth and constant (Fig. 15.6.2).

Flickering is another common problem that occurs when computer-generated images are recorded onto NTSC video. **Flickering** happens for a variety of reasons but mostly due to that fact that each frame of NTSC video is displayed as two interlaced fields. One field contains all the even scan lines in the frame, and the other field contains the odd scan lines. RGB monitors are usually **noninterlaced**, so flickering occurs when a computer-generated image contains visual data such as horizontal lines or textures that are only one pixel high. This happens because that information appears only on one of the video fields and not on the other one (using antialiasing techniques can greatly reduce this problem). Flickering also happens when regular video cameras are used to record from an RGB monitor. This happens because the **refresh rate**, also called the scanning rate, of most NTSC video equipment is 60 Hz, while most RGB monitors usually have a faster rate. This type of flickering results in a diagonal line that rolls continuously from the top to the bottom of the video screen.

The aspect ration of video has to be taken into consideration when recording computer-generated images onto videotape. Not only is the aspect ratio of video different from the aspect ratio of several RGB monitors, but also up to 20 percent of the image is cut off when computer-animation is displayed on television video monitors. (This has to do with the fact that the video signal uses some of the scan lines at the bottom of the screen to carry sync information.) An easy way to avoid having computer animations cut off is to preview them on a TV monitor and to use the field guides that specify the video **action safe areas** (Fig. 7.2.2).

15.7 Output on Digital Media

A considerable amount of three-dimensional computer renderings are delivered today in formats that can be readily used in digital media such as videogames or multimedia presentations. Professionals from a wide variety of visual disciplines are increasingly working with three-dimensional computer graphics in a **digital creative environment.** The traditional fields of graphic arts, broadcasting, and film each uses three-dimensional creations in a specialized way, but they are all able to share their imagery in the form of **digital information**.

Three-dimensional images are output on digital media when they need to be played directly on the RGB monitor directly from the computer. This is the case, for example, when an animator wants to preview a motion test in the form of a sequence of low resolution files, or flipbook, stored in the hard disk. Other examples include the distribution of three-dimensional imagery and animation on CD-ROMs or through networks of computers.

One of the main concerns with images delivered in digital media is that they are compact enough to load fast, but image detail is also important. To find the right balance between speed and detail it is necessary to perform tests that compare the amount of image detail against the loading speed and storage efficiency. Multiplayer online games, for example, cannot afford using images with 16-bit color per RGB channel images for this reason. The image quality would be superb, better than the standard 8-bit, but the loading speed would be too slow. The balance between speed and detail keeps changing as graphics hardware continues to become more powerful and sophisticated and less expensive.

CD-ROM and DVD

CD-ROMs and DVDs are popular media for storing interactive content like games, educational materials, and feature films. Many of the file formats described earlier in the chapter are used in these media, with the preferred formats being the most compact ones.

Technically speaking, the **compact disk-read only memory**, commonly known as **CD-ROM**, is a type of peripheral memory, but it can also be defined as output media because of its popularity for distributing visual projects. This medium is extremely convenient because it uses optical technology to store large amounts of information per disk, about 660 MB, in a format that is as permanent and stable as can be. Furthermore, the **read-time**—or time that it takes for the computer to find and read information from the CD-ROM—is minimal due to the laser beam technology used for this purpose.

CD-ROMs can contain all types of information. One CD-ROM, for example, may be filled up with over 60 minutes of very high-quality audio sampled at 44 KHz and in 16-bit stereo format, or with 450 images in 24-bit color RGB format at 640 × 480 pixel resolution. The same CD-ROM could also be filled up with over 20 hours of low resolution audio sampled at 11 KHz and in 8-bit stereo format, or with 26,500 monochromatic images at 512 × 342 pixel resolution. About 70 minutes of encoded MPEG-1 video fill up one CD-ROM.

The optical **DVD**, or **digital versatile disk**, is the same size as a CD-ROM but has a storage capacity larger than CD-ROM. There are a few versions of the popular **red laser DVD**. For example a single-sided and single-layered DVD, called **DVD-5**, can hold up to 4.7 gigabytes of information. The single-sided and double-layered version, called **DVD-9**, can hold up to 8.5 GB of information. A **Video-DVD** is a variant of the DVD also popular for distributing high-quality video information like live action and animated feature films. DVDs use **variable bit rate** (VBR) MPEG-2 compression, multi-channel audio, and subtitling capabilities. Some of the formats proposed for the emerging **blue laser DVD** include high definition

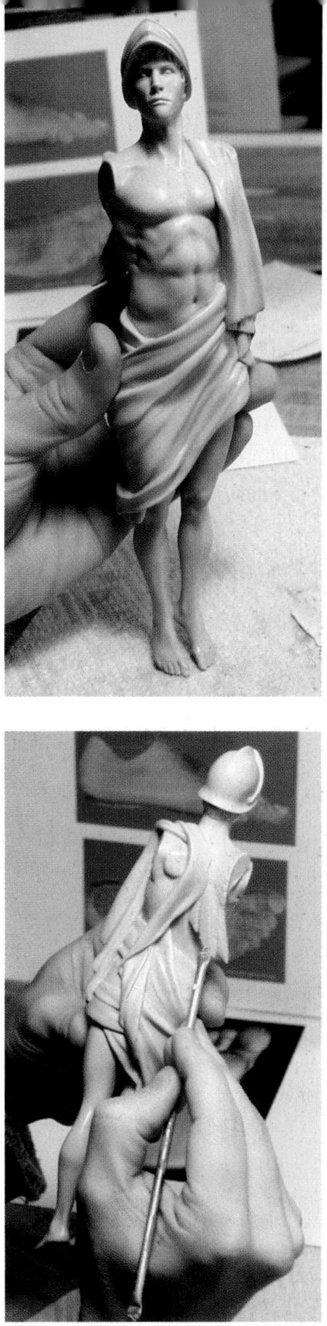

15.8.2 The finished model is cast in a fast-curing urethane tooling resin from the master pattern, detailed and painted. See Figure 15.1.1 for an earlier step in the fabrication process. (© 2002 Dan Platt, Solid Image Arts, LLC.)

15.8.3 The stereo lithography process hardens liquid polymer with two computer-controlled laser beams.

15.8.4 (opposite page) The first image shows a stereo lithographic model 4 in. in diameter fabricated with a cornstarch-and-water material, which was then infiltrated with cyanoacrylate resin to add strength. The second image shows the bronze casting that was made directly from the stereo lithography part using a slightly modified version of the traditional lost wax process: the stereo lithography material and wax both break down at about the same temperature. The small stubs will become air vents, and the main gate through which the metal entered the casting can be seen in the lower left corner of the image. The finished bronze casting is at the bottom. (© 1999 Bathsheba Grossman.)

capability and storage capacities that exceed 25 GB of data on a single-sided single-layer DVD.

Network Downloading and Streaming

During the early days of the Internet it would have been adventurous trying to play computer animations in real time through a computer network. But advances in network technology today are contributing to make the distribution of computer-generated images and animations commonplace. The distribution of computer-generated images through a network serves different needs, and the system requirements in each case can have significant differences. A simple application of network distribution consists of playing back a sequence of animated images—sometimes called a **digital flipbook**—from one computer on the network directly on the monitor of another computer connected to the network and typically in the same room. There are two different strategies for sending animated sequences through a network: downloading and streaming.

Downloading involves copying a file through the network from the server onto another computer before it is played. The main advantage of dowloanding is superior playback quality because the file is being played locally. Another advantage is that the file can be saved for future use. However, downloading large files through narrow-bandwith networks is time-consuming and often tedious. **Streaming** involves an almost instant playback of the file. Streaming files are played virtually as soon as they reach the local computer through the network. The great advantage of streaming is the ability to view files immediately, without having to wait until the entire file is dowloaded. Disadvantages include the uneven playback quality due to factors like network bandwith and traffic, and the fact that streamed files cannot be saved in the local computer for future use. Standards for streaming three-dimensional data across networks is still evolving, and there are currently many competing standards.

In many computer animation production companies, digital files constantly travel through the **local area network**, or **LAN**. A computer that is dedicated to serving the requests of the network users is called a **server**, and many networks use multiple or **mirror servers** to increase efficiency. Animation files can be accessed by a **single user**, or simultaneously by **multiple users**. The latter would be the case if several individuals in different locations—a client in the meeting room and the production team in their studios, for example—needed to play back the same digital file as they spoke over the phone. A situation such as this one would benefit from a network with a wide bandwidth and/or the digital files having some form of data compression. There already are several networks in use that allow multiple simultaneous users to access a file with a minute loss in speed or resolution. Some of these solutions, however, require multiple servers and deep pockets.

The speed at which images are transmitted though networks of computers is an issue that influences the performance of playing back files remotely. The speeds at which files can travel through networks is related primarily to the bandwidth of the communication paths that files travel through between computers as well as inside a single computer. These paths can be divided into three types: paths in a digital network, phone lines and modems, and paths inside the computer itself. The **bandwidth**, or transmission capacity, of these different media is measured with different units that express the amount of information that travels through the path per second. The bandwidth of digital networks is generally measured in **megabits per second** (Mbps). The bandwidth or speeds of modems operating on phone lines is measured in bits or **kilobits per second** (Kbps). The bandwidth of computer internal data channels is measured in **megabytes per second** (MBps). This seemingly arbitrary variety of bandwidth units is rooted in very different magnitudes of transmission capacity and in different traditions that date back to the early days of telephone transmission and computer engineering.

Planning the live playback of digital files through a network requires a wide variety of strategies depending on the purpose of the playback. Using internal networks, or **intranets**, can be different from using open-ended networks that go into the outside world. In the case of an intranet, a controlled network environment, it is possible to use specialized hardware for compression and decompression that increase the playback speed of an animation file through any network. In controlled network environments, each node can also be set up with specialized hardware and high bandwidth lines. In cases such as this, it makes sense to design the playback of the file by making extensive use of real-time file compression and decompression and high bandwidths. But in situations when the file is played in a wide variety of environments and throughout different bandwidths it is usually wiser to choose the lowest common denominator so that the file can be played by the largest number of viewers. In any case, the number of products for software-based compression and decompression is increasing, as well as the resulting quality and performance.

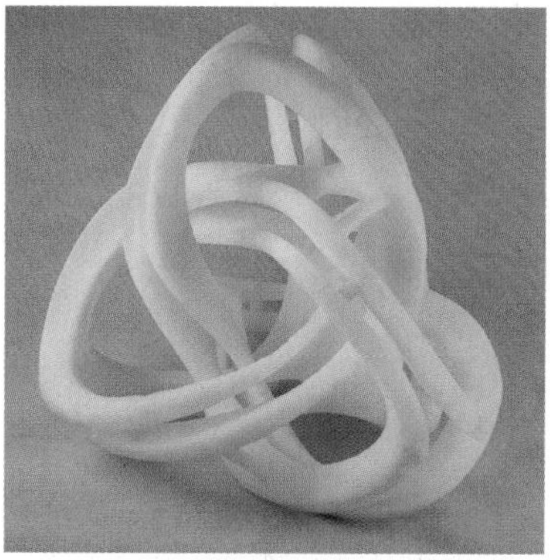

The speed of digital networks is based on many factors, including the type of material that the network lines are made of (optical fiber or copper, for example), and the type of communications standards and protocol. As illustrated in Figure 15.7.2, the speed of modems and computer networks spreads a broad range. It is difficult to say that there is a standard network communications speed or bandwidth because this type of technology is still changing dramatically every couple of years. In the meantime, there are two key ideas to keep in mind. First, there is a significant difference in speed

15.8.5 The finished *Medicus* physical sculpture. See Figure 5.2.3 for the initial three-dimensional computer model. (© 2002 Dan Platt, Solid Image Arts, LLC.)

between the theoretical and the actual speeds of computer networks. This is due, in part, to the overhead of creating and managing the data packets that travel through the network; this can bring the actual throughput 5 to 10 times less than the theoretical bit rate! Second, data still travels inside the computer—and between the hard disks, RAM, and the computer—faster than it travels through computer networks.

The speed of internal data channels of specialized computers for visual creation is in the range of 5 to 80 megabytes per second. As a point of reference, a low rate of 10 megabytes per second travelling through the computer internal bus, for example, would be equivalent to a high rate of 80 megabits per second ($10 \times 1{,}000{,}000 \times 8 = 80{,}000{,}000$) traveling through a computer network. Compare that to the average range of telephone-based modem bandwidth: between 28,000 bits per second (28 Kbps) and 56,000 bps.

The total bandwidth and performance of file transmission over networks takes into account a multitude of factors, and cannot be determined by just one of the three data paths. In many instances, the performance of network distribution and playback of digital files is fast inside the computer, slow as the files are sent through the modem, and then fast again or very fast as the files travel through a network. For example, a file would travel fast inside a computer with an internal bus bandwidth of 40 megabytes (320 megabits) per second, it would then slow down as it goes through a 14,400 bits per second modem, zip through a high-speed optical fiber network at 135 megabits per second, slow down again through an standard Ethernet connection at 10 megabits per second, and play back even slower at a very slow computer with a bus bandwidth of only 2 megabytes (16 megabits) per second.

15.8 Output on Three-Dimensional Media

The data used to describe three-dimensional models in virtual environments can also be used in a variety of ways to actually build the object with real material. The details of the techniques used to translate digital three-dimensional data into real three-dimensional objects are beyond the scope of this book. But some of the basic techniques are implemented with cutting machines, milling machines, and stereo lithography machines.

Computer-controlled **cutting machines** are able to cut two-dimensional shapes usually with a laser beam. These shapes are parts in structure that can be assembled by hand or under robot control. The shape of these parts is described as a series of XY coordinates or complex curves that are followed by the cutting tool. The work illustrated in Figure 15.8.1 was assembled from two-dimensional shapes created by unfolding a three-dimensional model with software designed for that purpose. This example was composed directly on the computer by previewing a large combination of shapes. All the planes in the scuplture were numbered and dimensioned on the computer screen. Once the model was fully resolved, the three-dimensional shapes were unfolded into two-dimensional patterns, plotted directly on foamcore, and a model was constructed. This model was sent to the foundry, and was burned out for a traditional lost wax casting. (If a sculpture is going to be fabricated rather than cast, the patterns are plotted on pattern paper for transfer to bronze plate.)

Milling machines, also known as subtractive rapid prototyping, are able to shape blocks of material such as plastic, wood, or stone by placing a rotating cutter on their surface, and moving across from top to bottom. The continuous motion of the cutting head along the three axes results in the modeling of a three-dimensional object. A wide variety of shapes can be created by using different cutting paths and by attaching different cutting tools to the milling machine (Fig. 15.8.6). The finished piece shown in Figure 15.8.5 was created by injecting hot toy wax formula into a flexible silicone mold previously created around parts machined on blue jewelers wax (Fig. 15.1.1). After cooling the wax reproduction is carefully removed and retooled by hand to remove imperfections and enhance delicate features. The cleaned-up pink figure becomes the master pattern that is molded again in silicone, recast in a fast-curing urethane tooling resin, finished, and painted (Fig. 15.8.2).

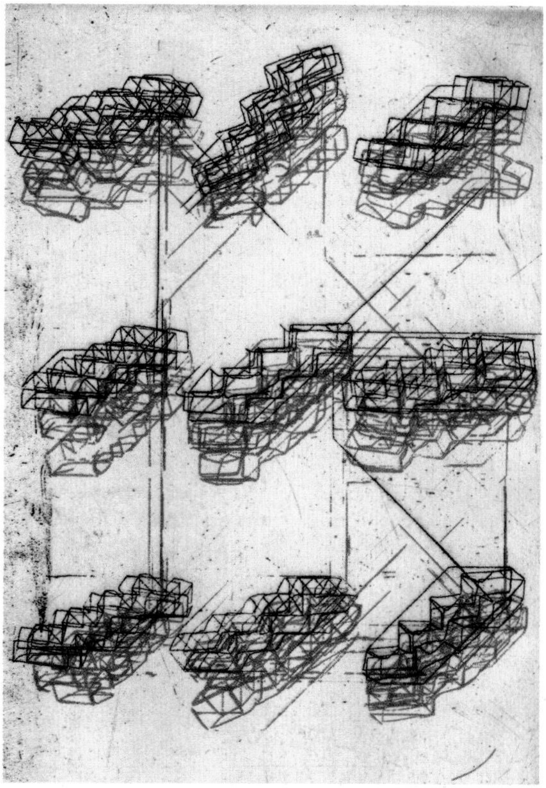

15.8.6 Detail of *Freedom and Imprisonment*, a traditional printmaking work partially created with computer-controlled engraving. The 4-color three-dimensional paths were engraved with a needle directly on the copper plates used to make the print. (© Isaac V. Kerlow.)

Stereo Lithography

Stereo lithography is a process by which a liquid plastic or resin is shaped and solidified by two computer-controlled laser beams. The beams are perpendicular to each other and they move according to the XYZ positions on the surface of an object that has been modeled with software but is yet to be built in the physical world. One laser beam is focused at the transparent container from the front, and the other beam is focused from the side. The liquid plastic solidifies where the two laser beams intersect in the liquid inside the container (Fig. 15.8.3). With stereo lithography, shell surfaces or solid objects can be built by using the data contained in the digital model file to direct the motion of the two laser beams. Figure 15.8.4 shows three steps in the process of converting the model rendered in Figure 3.6.5 into a real bronze sculpture.

Chapter 15

Key Terms

3 to 2 (3:2) pull-down
4:4:4 color
Action safe areas
Advanced Authoring Format, AAF
Archival-quality digital prints
Aspect ratios
Audio Video Interleaved
AVI
Bandwidth
Binary system
Bitmap
Bitplane
Blue laser DVD
BMP
CD-ROM
Chromatic range
Chrominance
Cineon
CMYK four-color separation
Codecs
Color bleeding
Color calibration
Color clipping
Color correction
Color depth
Color resolution
Color sampling rate
Compact disk-read only memory
Component video
Composite video
Compression options
Convert colors
Cutting machines
DCT
Device-independent file format
Digital creative environment
Digital flipbook
Digital information
Digital-to-analog
Digital versatile disk
Digital video, DV
Dot resolution
Dots per inch, dpi
Downloading
DPX
DTAs
DVCAM
DVD
DVD-5, DVD-9
Dye sublimation
Electrostatic
Encapsulated PostScript
EPS
Export filters
Export tools
File format conversion
File formats
Film recorders
FireWire
Flickering
Frames
Frames per second (fps)
Fugitive dyes
Gamma factor
GIF
Graphics Interchange Format
Graphics memory
Halftone output
Halftone screens
Header information
High Definition, HD
Image compression
Image definition
Image file
Image resolution
Imagesetters
Import filters
Import tools
Ink jet printers
Interlaced fields
Intranets
ISO
Joint Photographic Experts Group
JPEG, JPEG 2000
Kilobits per second
LAN
Laser printing
Lines per inch, lpi
Local area network
Lossless compression
Lossy compression
Luminance
LZW
Megabits per second
Megabytes per second
Milling machines
Mini-DV
Mirror servers
MPEG, MPEG-1, MPEG-2, MPEG-4
MPEG viewers
Motion Pictures Experts Group
Multiple users
MXF
Native file formats
Noninterlaced fields
Nonsquare pixels
NTSC
National Television Systems Committee
OpenEXR
Output peripherals
PAL
Pen plotters
Peripheral device
Phase Alternation by Line
PICT
Picture files
Pixel
Pixel aspect ratios
Pixel resolution
Pixels per inch
Playback controller
Portable image file formats
ppi
Printer driver
Quantization
QuickTime
QuickTime VR, QTVR
Read-time
Red laser DVD
Refresh rate
Resample
Ripping
SECAM
Self-contained format
Series of still images
Servers
SGI
Single user
Spatial resolution
Standard Definition, SD
Stereo lithography
Streaming
Tagged Image File Format
TARGA
Temporal resolution
TGA
TIFF
Timing sync information
Toner
Translation of data
Universal image file formats
UV coating
Variable bit rate
VBR
Vectorscope
Video-DVD
Waveform monitor
Wavelet compression
Windows Media

www.artof3d.com

Visit *www.artof3d.com* to find an up-to-date listing of useful resources including:

1. Links to websites of software and hardware manufacturers.
2. Links to websites of computer animation news and users' groups.
3. Links to websites of three-dimensional computer animation software and hardware manufacturers.
4. Links to websites of computer animation and visual effects production companies.
5. List of suggested readings.
6. Additional information about the history of three-dimensional computer animation and visual effects.

(Above: © 2002 Harald Siepermann. Next page: Cus-Cús from *El bosque animado.* © 2001 Dygra Films.)

Index

• D •

(Still frame from a commercial featuring *Ray*. © 2002 Blockbuster Entertainment/Tippett Studio.)

Book is set in 10 on 11 Columbus Monotype, with headings and captions in Syntax, and guest appearances by Hoefler St. Agustin Civilité, and Zapf Dingbats.

www.artof3d.com

The End